To God Be the Glory Daily Devotional

By Garry Glaub

Copyright © 2011 by Garry Glaub

To God Be the Glory Daily Devotional
by Garry Glaub

Printed in the United States of America

ISBN 978-0-615-54927-9 soft cover
ISBN 978-0-984-75330-7 hard cover

All rights reserved solely by the author. The author guarantees all contents are original and do not infringe upon the legal rights of any other person or work. No part of this work may be reproduced in any form without the permission of the author. The views expressed in this book are not necessarily those of the publisher.

Unless otherwise indicated, Bible quotations are taken from the New King James Version of the Bible. Copyright © 1982 by Thomas Nelson, Inc. Used by permission.

Table of Contents

While a Table of Contents may not seem necessary in a daily devotional, there are special days in our yearly calendar. The days in the following chart have applicable devotionals, which includes many American holidays in addition to the Jewish Feasts of Moses, spoken of in Leviticus 23.

Page #	Holiday	2012	2013	2014
13	New Year's Day	Jan. 1	Jan. 1	Jan. 1
108	Valentine's Day	Feb. 14	Feb. 14	Feb. 14
193	Palm Sunday	April 1	March 24	April 13
209	Passover (Pesach)	April 7	March 26	April 15
214	Easter Sunday	April 8	March 31	April 20
245	Israel's Independence Day	April 26	April 16	May 6
275	Mother's Day	May 13	May 12	May 11
297	Pentecost (Shavuot)	May 27	May 19	June 8
300	Memorial Day	May 28	May 27	May 26

Page #	Holiday	2012.	2013	2014
341	Father's Day	June 17	June 16	June 15
380	Independence Day	July 4	July 4	July 4
508	Labor Day	Sept. 3	Sept. 2	Sept. 1
562	Day of Atonement *(Yom Kippur)*	Sept. 26	Sept. 13	Oct. 3
577	Tabernacles *(Sukkot)*	Oct. 1	Sept. 18	Oct. 8
697	Thanksgiving Day	Nov. 22	Nov. 28	Nov. 27
699	Black Friday	Nov. 23	Nov. 29	Nov. 28
781	Christmas Day	Dec. 25	Dec. 25	Dec. 25

Dedication

And there are also many other things that Jesus did, which if they were written one by one, I suppose that even the world itself could not contain the books that would be written. Amen.
John 21:25 (NKJV)

This is another of those books written because of what Jesus did! Though He accomplishes so much in the lives of His followers, the greatest accomplishment occurred almost 2,000 years ago on a hill outside Jerusalem. This book is dedicated to Jesus Christ, because my life never will be the same!

To God be the glory!

Preface

This book began after watching the movie "Julie and Julia," a story of a woman who wrote a blog as she cooked every dish in Julia Child's cookbook, "Mastering the Art of French Cooking." That inspired me to write a daily blog about the subject that was most important in my life. That subject is God: the Father, the Son and the Holy Spirit.

The blog consisted of daily discourses of how God appeared in my life. There were days of spiritual dryness, but the Lord helped me to honor my commitment to Him and write on a daily basis. When the year had been completed, I prayed about assembling the devotionals in book form. Some had to be re-written, as they were just too personal to apply to the lives of others. Through the process, God performed many miracles, and made me continuously aware of His presence.

After the last devotional, Dave and Barbara Rann hosted a potluck dinner at their house to celebrate the year's completion. Jeff and Kathy Kirst; Blake, Lola and Starla Goetz; Peter, Lisa, Larsen, Lela and Logan McCarroll; Tommy and Jodie Vasquez; and Paul Hansen all attended. David Harms could not make it from Oklahoma City, but sent a check to buy steaks for everyone! My Dad helped, too. The bottom line is this could not have been accomplished without so many others, who God brought into my life to raise my arms and keep them lifted up. Whenever I was weak, they kept me encouraged with His strength. Thanks to all for your love and assistance!

January 1: Resolutions

On New Year's Eve, many people across the world make resolutions, attempting to change some aspect of themselves. Typically, those changes have to do with what is on the outside, rather than what is on the inside. Losing weight, quitting smoking, quitting drinking, getting out of debt, becoming more organized and spending more time with family are some of the items that top the list of most common resolutions.

The word "resolution" comes from the same Old English root word as resolve, which points to making a decision or deciding upon a course of action. To be resolute is to be firm or unwavering. Yet the deeper truth of resolutions is that showers often can last longer! Comedian Joey Adams said, "May all your troubles last as long as your New Years' resolutions." Noted American author and humorist Mark Twain had this to say: "Now is the accepted time to make your regular, annual good resolutions. Next week you can begin paving hell with them as usual."

Of course, we all are aware that the road to hell is paved with good intentions. Fortunately, for Christians, God's intentions in our lives supersede our own intentions, as He will complete His work in us! Resolutions can remind Christians of the great gifts God has given to each of us:

**[22] *Through* the LORD's mercies we are not consumed,
Because His compassions fail not.
[23] *They are* new every morning;
Great *is* Your faithfulness.
Lamentations 3:22-23 (NKJV)**

With our Lord's forgiveness of us on a daily basis, we can walk in freedom! God grants us the ability to change, yet without His presence in our lives, those changes are amazingly short-lived. Yet instead of focusing on the outer manifestations of those resolutions, God desires for us to focus on the motives within.

Motives have to do with the heart, and when those motives change, actions can follow suit.

> ³ **Who may ascend into the hill of the LORD?**
> **Or who may stand in His holy place?**
> ⁴ **He who has clean hands and a pure heart,**
> **Who has not lifted up his soul to an idol,**
> **Nor sworn deceitfully.**
> **Psalm 24:3-4 (NKJV)**

Our Lord desires for actions to change, as what others see should reflect the changes that He has made on the inside of each of us. But never lose sight that the inner changes must occur first. So as we say goodbye to one year and greet another, what changes would God like to see in our lives? At the top of the list, He always desires for us to draw closer to Him. If that is our desire, then He certainly will grant us the desires of our heart, as He desires more closeness in His relationship with us! Have we read the entire Bible? If God was giving a speech tomorrow, would we be there to hear it? He has given us His Word. By not reading the Bible, it seems as if we do not care what He has to say. Prayer is also vastly important, especially the gift He has given us to pray for others. If we often make bad decisions, we should pray for godly wisdom and let that be our resolution.

If we are focusing on God, and deepening that relationship, He will help with all those other issues that seem to grab the spotlight in the hopes and dreams of unbelievers. Each year, we are one year closer to seeing His face. Each day, we are one day closer to sitting at His feet. Each moment, we are one moment closer to the Lord calling us home! On the Jewish New Year, Yom Kippur, God's chosen people made atonement for their sins. This is a great time to reflect on our sins of the past year, ask for His forgiveness and pray for His help in following the straight and narrow path that leads to life with Him, in Him and through Him! Happy New Year!

⁵ **If any of you lacks wisdom, let him ask of God, who gives to all liberally and without reproach, and it will be given to**

him. ⁶ **But let him ask in faith, with no doubting, for he who doubts is like a wave of the sea driven and tossed by the wind.** ⁷ **For let not that man suppose that he will receive anything from the Lord;** ⁸ **he is a double-minded man, unstable in all his ways.**
James 1:5-8 (NKJV)

January 2: Denial

Most people think that denial is duh river in duh country of Egypt. Yet denial is a powerful aspect of life. One way or another, each decision is a denial of sorts. Either we are denying the flesh or denying the Spirit; there is no middle ground.

Today, we live in a culture with a pervasive denial of responsibility, yet that attribute did not begin in modern times. By comparing the reigns in Israel of King Saul and King David, one of the most significant differences occurs not in their propensity to make mistakes but in the manner the kings handled those mistakes. While David asked for the Lord's forgiveness, Saul typically walked in a more prideful way, blaming each error-plagued situation on extraneous people or circumstances. That behavior is paramount in politics, yet it reaches every level of humanity. A man who owns his mistakes is bigger than he who plays the blame game. God is ready, willing and able to forgive us for all mistakes if we are humble enough to ask Him, but without ownership, that is impossible. By blaming others for causing our sin, we are making excuses for behavior that has no excuse. Our minds are capable of rationalizing any behavior, yet when we want forgiveness, God desires to hear our broken hearts.

Peter demonstrated the most serious aspect of denial when he denied the Lord on the night before the crucifixion. Moments after bragging to Jesus that he loved the Lord more than all others, Peter displayed the typical result that occurs when we brag and rely on ourselves. Reliance on self leads to failure. Sadly, some Christians feel that there are sins that would cause God to turn His back upon us, but He did not turn His back on

Peter after the triple threat of denial. Truly, each sin that we commit is a denial of Jesus, for as Christians, God has cut the chains. We are no longer bound by sin, but instead, sin becomes a choice. Often, we do not remember making that conscious choice to fall into sin as believers, but usually can remember a time when our focus upon the Lord began to waver. Satan continues to lead his demonic host in spiritual battles against God's people, and he performs that job well, having had many years to perfect those abilities. For example, a well-placed advertisement can cause a man to stumble into lust, without considering that potential mistake when opening the magazine. That simple stumble can lead to more problems and more sins, if not kept in check. In the same manner that a sailor can find himself far from his planned arrival when his two-week journey is one-degree off course, a Christian can get lost quickly if his spiritual compass is not pointed to true north.

Another important message concerning denial in the Bible comes from the words of Jesus:

[24] Then Jesus said to His disciples, "If anyone desires to come after Me, let him deny himself, and take up his cross, and follow Me. [25] For whoever desires to save his life will lose it, but whoever loses his life for My sake will find it. [26] For what profit is it to a man if he gains the whole world, and loses his own soul? Or what will a man give in exchange for his soul? Matthew 16:24-26 (NKJV)

Denying self involves ignoring the desires of the flesh. Taking up the cross is an additional step allowing Christians to become a part of the crucifixion of our Lord. For Jesus, the cross was not a burden, but a gift. He gave His life so that we might live, and we know that the greatest love is to lay down one's life for a friend. Romans 6:3 reminds us that we are baptized into Christ's death, and to take up the cross is to be willing for our old sinful selves to die, as our Lord gives us new lives in Him! That is the willingness to give all of our lives to God, not just parts of them. Are we willing to give Him our spouse, our children and our career? Are we willing to give Him our past, our present and our future? He requires all of us! While the world reminds us to, "Deny, deny, deny," Christians should follow God's plan to deny self, while confessing Jesus as Lord and Savior! His power is so great it cannot be denied!

[32] "Therefore whoever confesses Me before men, him I will also confess before My Father who is in heaven. [33] But whoever denies Me before men, him I will also deny before My Father who is in heaven.
Matthew 10:32-33 (NKJV)

January 3: Be strong and of good courage

Herman Melville said, "Familiarity with danger makes a brave man braver, but less daring." Many aspects of life can change our perspective when familiarity increases. Certainly, a battle-tested veteran reacts much differently than a novice in his initial battle, and often can forget when confronted with that novice that they, too, once were in the same position.

When Moses passed the baton to Joshua to lead the Jews into the Promised Land, he repeated the words, "Be strong and of good courage," in Deuteronomy 31:6, Deuteronomy 31:7 and Deuteronomy 31:23. We can get an inkling of where Moses had heard those words, as soon after, when God speaks to Joshua, our Lord also repeats those words in Joshua 1:6, Joshua 1:9 and Joshua 1:18.

[5] No man shall *be able to* stand before you all the days of your life; as I was with Moses, *so* I will be with you. I will not leave you nor forsake you. [6] Be strong and of good courage, for to this people you shall divide as an inheritance the land which I swore to their fathers to give them. [7] Only be strong and very courageous, that you may observe to do according to all the law which Moses My servant commanded you; do not turn from it to the right hand or to the left, that you may prosper wherever you go.
Joshua 1:5-7 (NKJV)

Strength and courage came easier to Joshua than to most before entering the Promised Land. Other than Joshua and Caleb, all of the adults who departed Egypt led by God died in the wilderness, due to their disobedience of the Lord. That lengthy list included Moses and Aaron. In those 40 years, the Jews had seen many hardships that had become nothing more than dust in their pasts, thanks to the protective hand of God. Yet when Moses sent 12 spies into the Promised Land, all but Joshua and Caleb returned greatly disgruntled at the presence of powerful giants. While all others demonstrated cowardice and weakness, we see the opposite in the words of both Caleb and Joshua:

Then Caleb quieted the people before Moses, and said, "Let us go up at once and take possession, for we are well able to overcome it."
Numbers 13:30 (NKJV)

[7]"The land we passed through to spy out *is* an exceedingly good land. [8] If the LORD delights in us, then He will bring us into this land and give it to us, 'a land which flows with milk and honey.' [9] Only do not rebel against the LORD, nor fear the people of the land, for they *are* our bread; their protection has departed from them, and the LORD *is* with us. Do not fear them."
Numbers 14:7-9 (NKJV)

Life experiences in the lives of Christians should lead us to the same conclusion. Strength is not muscular power. Neither is it physical presence. Instead, it is the unwavering path that leads us to God. It is the strength of conviction that what He tells us in His Word is truth! At the same time, courage is not reliance upon self, but instead, is reliance upon our Lord, who has promised to never leave or forsake us. Though the giants surpassed the Jews in size, strength and numbers, those giants paled in comparison to God. When we feel overmatched and defeated, we have lost sight of the fact that we are soldiers in the army of the Lord!

Strength and courage cannot exist without God, yet our ability to rely on those attributes increases along with our faith, based on God's continued presence in our lives. After Job had endured a great trial, it is difficult to imagine that he ever questioned the Lord again! In that manner, God uses trials in our lives to draw us closer to Him, and additionally, increases our strength and courage. Battle-tested Christians often can endure stronger attacks from the enemy, as what really increases is the ability to rely on God! Instead of praying for trials to end, pray for strength and courage to increase. We should desire to fight valiantly for the Lord! In any battle, we should fear God, not man, for He alone is worthy.

[3] **"Great and marvelous *are* Your works,**
Lord God Almighty!
Just and true *are* Your ways,
O King of the saints!
[4] **Who shall not fear You, O Lord, and glorify Your name?**
For *You* alone *are* holy.
For all nations shall come and worship before You,
For Your judgments have been manifested."
Revelation 15:3-4 (NKJV)

January 4: A calming influence

One of the oddities of farm life is what occurs immediately after a chicken has lost its head on the chopping block. Without eyes to see or a brain to think, that dead chicken frantically runs for a few moments before dropping dead. There is something unsettling when watching this headless dash! Yet all of us know what it feels like to make a mad dash without sight or a plan before crashing to a halt.

As Christians, that unplanned sprint is synonymous with the flesh, or reliance upon self. When relying upon God in the midst of turmoil, it does not matter what we see in front of us. God is not limited by what we can see! In fact, He is not limited by anything, including time!

³⁵ On the same day, when evening had come, He said to them, "Let us cross over to the other side." ³⁶ Now when they had left the multitude, they took Him along in the boat as He was. And other little boats were also with Him. ³⁷ And a great windstorm arose, and the waves beat into the boat, so that it was already filling. ³⁸ But He was in the stern, asleep on a pillow. And they awoke Him and said to Him, "Teacher, do You not care that we are perishing?"
³⁹ Then He arose and rebuked the wind, and said to the sea, "Peace, be still!" And the wind ceased and there was a great calm. ⁴⁰ But He said to them, "Why are you so fearful? How *is it* that you have no faith?" ⁴¹ And they feared exceedingly, and said to one another, "Who can this be, that even the wind and the sea obey Him!"
Mark 4:35-41 (NKJV)

If God is not panicking in a situation, there is no reason for us to panic. To simplify that statement, understand that God never panics! On that day described in Mark, in the midst of what others perceived as turmoil, Jesus was sleeping restfully. While God does allow trials in each of our lives, any turmoil is perceived rather than actual, for He holds our hands throughout each difficulty. If we had to face those trials alone, turmoil would be more than perceived, but there is nothing too difficult for us to face with God in our lives.

Sometimes, God places people in our lives that need godly advice in the midst of trial. Often, we can see their inability to trust the Lord, and the same trial seems to repeat itself. Yet a great place to begin is a reflection upon our own lives, remembering first that God demonstrated enormous patience with us, and expects us to exhibit that same gift of the Spirit when dealing with others. When our storehouse of patience is running low, we can have the tendency to scream, "Shut up and sit down!" Yet that is not what Jesus had to say. He said, "Peace, be still!" Certainly, Jesus was speaking to the waves, but the same words pertained to the people! Fear reveals a lack of trust in God.

For we walk by faith, not by sight."
2 Corinthians 5:7 (NKJV)

Like the headless chicken, when our eyes no longer can see in the darkness around us, we still should have spiritual sight through our faith in a God who never will leave our sides. That promise does not change when the waves get larger, when we fear for our very lives. Even in the midst of the noisiest storm, we can have the ability to "be still and know that He is God!" Crashing waves may sprinkle a mist upon us, but with God on our side, we always will remain above water! We should keep our eyes on Jesus and our trust in the Almighty God!

[31] And immediately Jesus stretched out *His* hand and caught him, and said to him, "O you of little faith, why did you doubt?" [32] And when they got into the boat, the wind ceased.
Matthew 14:31-32 (NKJV)

January 5: The rod of God

Regardless of the size of a factory, all workers have a common purpose, to put out the best product. It has little to do with the position of the worker, as they might be on the assembly line, in management or an engineer involved in design. Collectively, they work together to achieve a finished product. Whether a skilled laborer, someone who brings previous knowledge and experience to the position, or an unskilled laborer, someone who learns all necessary components while on the current job, all involved are integral parts of the finished product.

As Christians, we are all unskilled laborers, though God continues to give us on-the-job training. Every talent and ability that we have comes from Him! Though the human tendency is to look at Billy Graham and see him differently than the man steadfastly teaching Sunday school to the second-graders, the difference between those two men is not in natural talent, but in God-given calling. If size of ministry was a measuring factor in godliness, righteousness or significance, then how would we measure Jesus? Truly, how many people were following Him at the time of His crucifixion? Though one week before that pivotal event, Jesus rode from the Mount of Olives on a donkey and the mob hailed Him as King of the Jews. Within the week, the mob asked Pontius Pilate to release Barabbas, not the innocent Jesus. Other than John, His disciples all went into hiding, confused how it was possible that man could kill God! Certainly, they doubted. Yet including His closest friends and disciples, and the women brave enough to remain with Jesus at the cross, there were less than 20 followers. Does that make Joel Osteen, Rick Warren or Benny Hinn more important than Jesus?

[16]Most assuredly, I say to you, a servant is not greater than his master; nor is he who is sent greater than he who sent him. [17] If you know these things, blessed are you if you do them.
John 13:16-17 (NKJV)

As Christians, God calls all of us to be laborers in the harvest. Some plant seeds, others water the seeds and others reap the crop, but none of those jobs is greater in importance. Though God called Moses to lead the children of Israel, it had nothing to do with the power of Moses. According to Exodus 3-4, Moses had no confidence. He gave God seven excuses why he should not be the one in that position, including a problem with stuttering. Yet God chose Moses specifically. Our Lord also placed a support team beside Moses:

[8] Now Amalek came and fought with Israel in Rephidim. [9] And Moses said to Joshua, "Choose us some men and go out, fight with Amalek. Tomorrow I will stand on the top of the hill with the rod of God in my hand." [10] So Joshua did as Moses said to him, and fought with Amalek. And Moses, Aaron, and Hur went up to the top of the hill. [11] And so it was, when Moses held up his hand, that Israel prevailed; and when he let down his hand, Amalek prevailed. [12] But Moses' hands *became* heavy; so they took a stone and put *it* under him, and he sat on it. And Aaron and Hur supported his hands, one on one side, and the other on the other side; and his hands were steady until the going down of the sun. [13] So

Joshua defeated Amalek and his people with the edge of the sword.
Exodus 17:8-13 (NKJV)

God could have won this battle without Moses, and did not need Aaron, Hur or Joshua either. In fact, God did not need the army to lift a hand. Yet God involves us in His processes. That involvement increases our faith! When Jesus walked on this earth, He did not do the baptizing, but called His disciples to perform that task (John 4:2)! It does not matter if the rod of God is in our hands, nor does it matter if we help others to raise it. Some cannot even see those holding up the rod, as they are involved on the front lines of the battle. Wherever God has called us to be is the perfect place, but He does not call us to sit on the couch, believing that we have no talents or abilities that He can use. Step out in faith and get involved in serving Him! Ministry to family comes first, but no matter how busy we are in our careers, God desires for us to be involved in His harvest!

Then He said to them, "The harvest truly *is* great, but the laborers *are* few; therefore pray the Lord of the harvest to send out laborers into His harvest.
Luke 10:2 (NKJV)

January 6: Declaration of faith

A wise man once said, "Faith isn't faith until it is all you are holding onto." While many walking this earth believe that religion is nothing more than a crutch to give hope to the hopeless, their belief takes more faith than a belief in God. Yet belief in God is nothing without acting upon that belief. James, the brother of Jesus, wrote:

You believe that there is one God. You do well. Even the demons believe—and tremble!
James 2:19 (NKJV)

When God created man, He placed inside each individual the knowledge of Him, and then when He created the heavens and the earth, He surrounded us with evidence that pointed to Himself. Life, for each of us, becomes that search to not only find God, but to know Him. Once we know Him, the desire grows to know Him more deeply. Yet it all comes back to that faith. All of us know what occurs when we rely upon others. People eventually will let us down, regardless of their desire to please. In the same manner, we let others down, and we also let ourselves down. Our decisions without God lead us down destructive paths, and when we get to a breaking point in that journey is when God enters the picture. When life is going smoothly, what percentage of people offer praises to the Lord? Certainly, the hotline to God starts ringing more frequently when our marriages fail, when our family members have serious illnesses and when we lose our jobs and cannot pay the bills. But God desires to be our confidante in every situation, not just the difficult ones!

Abraham gave us an example of faith in action. At the age of 75, God promised him that he would have a son, and through that son, God would multiply Abraham's descendants exceedingly. Yet Abraham hit a speed bump in the road when he began to wonder how God could provide a child through the loins of a senior citizen. Though Abraham's wife Sarah was 10 years younger, how could she become pregnant, after remaining barren throughout her youth? At Sarah's suggestion, Abraham slept with her Egyptian nurse, Hagar. With Abraham well-advanced in years, likely in his mid eighties, he fathered Ishmael.

Yet this was not the child to continue the line of the Jews, as God had promised. Instead, God also multiplied Ishmael's descendants exceedingly. In fact, the Arabs that have come from Ishmael, and Abraham, greatly outnumber the Jews, and to this day, seek to kill the Jews. God's plan remained in place, though it conflicted man's understanding of what was possible with the Lord's miraculous hand. At the age of 100, Abraham fathered Isaac, with his 90-year-old, barren wife, Sarah. Years later, God asked Abraham to sacrifice that son upon an altar!

That was the moment when Abraham understood that he was holding onto God and only God. When works go hand-in-hand with faith, that faith springs to life. Abraham trusted God's request, without knowing God's reason or asking why God would request this act of obedience. Because God never had let Abraham down, he trusted that God was going to perform another miracle. Of course, He did! At the last moment, God provided a substitute sacrifice in the place of Isaac, an unblemished, male ram, and just as promised, God blessed the descendants of Isaac exceedingly. By faith, Abraham exhibited his trust in God.

⁵ Therefore He who supplies the Spirit to you and works miracles among you, *does He do it* **by the works of the law, or by the hearing of faith? ⁶ just as Abraham** *"believed God, and it was accounted to him for righteousness."* **⁷ Therefore know that** *only* **those who are of faith are sons of Abraham. ⁸ And the Scripture, foreseeing that God would justify the Gentiles by faith, preached the gospel to Abraham beforehand,** *saying, "In you all the nations shall be blessed."* **⁹ So then those who** *are* **of faith are blessed with believing Abraham. Galatians 3:5-9 (NKJV)**

While Abraham's blood may not run through our veins, we are in the same family of God. Just like Abraham, without reaching the end of ourselves, we cannot find the beginning of God. Our God is the only god, not limited by man-made laws or people. He can perform the greatest miracles without straining. Remember, He breathed the world into existence. There is nothing so great that He cannot accomplish it or so small that He does not notice it. We should let our faith in God affect every aspect of our lives, and let that faith speak loudly to a deaf world, which is crying out in its pain for help.

⁴ And behold, the word of the LORD *came* **to him, saying, "This one shall not be your heir, but one who will come from your own body shall be your heir." ⁵ Then He brought him outside and said, "Look now toward heaven, and count the**

stars if you are able to number them." And He said to him, "So shall your descendants be."
⁶ And he believed in the LORD, and He accounted it to him for righteousness.
Genesis 15:4-6 (NKJV)

January 7: Life's rollercoaster ride

Everyone blessed with the gift of life finds themselves riding on an intense rollercoaster, complete with loops, sharp turns, precipitous highs and unfathomable lows. Emotions seem to mark each aspect of that journey with joy and sorrow carrying us through one hill; pleasure and pain rounding us through a curve; and celebration and grief joining us at the journey's end.

Often, we focus on others, who seem to be experiencing more highs than lows on their rollercoaster rides. Comparing ourselves to others tends to cloud our judgment, as we only see those people when they are soaring above the crowd. Somehow, we miss those comparisons when our friends and foes are taking a subterranean plunge. As Christians, God directs our journeys through life. By focusing on others, we lose sight of the fact that His plans have a purpose, individually, in each of our lives. Without difficult times, how special would joyful times be?

In the same way that God created the seasons of spring, summer winter and fall, our lives have those same seasons. Christian lives also contain distinct differences as we draw closer to God. Looking back, there is nothing like that initial season, the honeymoon with God. Becoming a Christian and feeling the enormous burden of sin removed brings us joy, relief, hope, love and many other feelings and emotions. Typically, the trials begin soon after, as we head into a new season. The first trial in the life of a Christian teaches us that God never will walk away. From that point on, the trials get more difficult, but our abilities to rely on His power continue to grow stronger still. Most Christians would not reflect upon this season as the easiest, but it might be thought of as the most special.

Additionally, we have seasons that contain mountaintop experiences. There is nothing like that closeness to the Lord. When we are sitting with God on the peak, we can look down and around, seeing the past problems that He carried us through, seeing the difficult paths that brought us to the mountaintop, and seeing the valleys that lie ahead. It is the calm before and after the storm, with rest for the weary and refreshment for the soul. The Bread of Life gives us food, the Living Water gives us drink and Jesus gives us rest in Him:

^{28} Come to Me, all *you* who labor and are heavy laden, and I will give you rest. ^{29} Take My yoke upon you and learn from Me, for I am gentle and lowly in heart, and you will find rest for your souls. ^{30} For My yoke *is* easy and My burden is light."
Matthew 11:28-30 (NKJV)

Another season occurs when Christians come to the end of their journeys. Friends and families grieve, as we will not be able to create new memories together on this earth. But for Christians, a different journey begins. When we leave this earth, God grants us righteousness in Him. Sin no longer will darken our days, as that nature will be gone forever. Pain and tears also will disappear with God's miraculous provision. Illness, disease and injury will be gone, too. There will be no more brokenness, despair, anger, depression, blame or imperfection. When watching an older Christian approach death, we can see God grant them increasing serenity as that day approaches. And in addition to being with our Savior for all of eternity, we get to share that with our fellow believers!

Enjoy the ride! Each day is a gift, and it does not matter if we are presently on a path that involves the lowest low, the life that has been given to us is precious. Every aspect of the journey is a new lesson, created by God to draw us closer to Him. There is no better place to be than exactly where God wants us! Embrace where He has us today!

being confident of this very thing, that He who has begun a good work in you will complete *it* until the day of Jesus Christ;
Philippians 1:6 (NKJV)

January 8: Doers, not hearers

We are surrounded by broken people in a broken world. Watching the nightly news reminds most of us that we somehow have remained unscathed throughout another day of murders, rapes, robberies and disasters. Though not being directly involved in the various tragedies, "unscathed" is the wrong word. As Christians, if we are not somehow touched by the magnitude of events in the lives of our fellow humans, we cannot be walking with God's love.

Jesus was confronted by a lawyer interested in eternal life. That lawyer appears to be involved in the interpretation of Mosaic law, rather than a man involved in the judicial system. The lawyer asked the Lord how to gain eternal life. As He often did, Jesus answered a question with a question, getting him to look inside for the answer. Certainly, there is much deeper comprehension when issues are applied in a personal manner, as most of us have great difficulty learning from someone else's mistakes. When questioned, the man answered rightly; at least they were the right words. He said that if we love the Lord with all our heart, soul, strength and mind, and in addition, love our neighbors as ourselves, we will be saved, paraphrasing Deuteronomy 6:5 and Leviticus 19:18.

That seems to suggest that we can be saved by following the law, rather than by accepting Jesus into our hearts as our Savior. Salvation can be obtained by following the law, but one infraction is failure. While it is a path to salvation, it is not a path that sinners can take, and we all are sinners:

knowing that a man is not justified by the works of the law but by faith in Jesus Christ, even we have believed in Christ Jesus, that we might be justified by faith in Christ and not by

the works of the law; for by the works of the law no flesh shall be justified.
Galatians 2:16 (NKJV)

Instead, Jesus demonstrated His position as the ablest teacher by pointing the man's thoughts to a more accurate interpretation of those verses. Jesus shared with him the story of the "Good Samaritan."

[30] **Then Jesus answered and said: "A certain *man* went down from Jerusalem to Jericho, and fell among thieves, who stripped him of his clothing, wounded *him*, and departed, leaving *him* half dead.** [31] **Now by chance a certain priest came down that road. And when he saw him, he passed by on the other side.** [32] **Likewise a Levite, when he arrived at the place, came and looked, and passed by on the other side.** [33] **But a certain Samaritan, as he journeyed, came where he was. And when he saw him, he had compassion.** [34] **So he went to *him* and bandaged his wounds, pouring on oil and wine; and he set him on his own animal, brought him to an inn, and took care of him.** [35] **On the next day, when he departed, he took out two denarii, gave *them* to the innkeeper, and said to him, 'Take care of him; and whatever more you spend, when I come again, I will repay you.'** [36] **So which of these three do you think was neighbor to him who fell among the thieves?"** [37] **And he said, "He who showed mercy on him." Then Jesus said to him, "Go and do likewise."**
Luke 10:30-37 (NKJV)

First, we notice that the ones unwilling to help a brother in need were religious men, well-educated in the Old Testament law, just as the man who originally asked Jesus the question. Instead, the man willing to come to the man's aid, through much personal sacrifice, was looked upon as an untouchable, a Samaritan. There was a long history of animosity between Jews and Samaritans. Remember, when Jesus offended the Jews, they could come up with no more offensive insult than calling Him a Samaritan (John 8:48). Samaritans did not feel any more warmly for the Jews. This enmity had existed for centuries.

When the Jews were taken into Babylonian captivity, the Babylonian king did not desire for the land to become fallow, so he sent people from Babylon to live in the land. (2 Kings 17:26) These were non-Jewish colonists in a land that had been given to the Jews by God.

When the Jews returned, both co-existed, but not peacefully. In fact, when Alexander the Great came through Israel and treated the Jews favorably, the Samaritans also claimed to be of Hebrew descent. Yet soon after, the Samaritans assassinated a governor appointed by Alexander, leading the well-known conqueror to take Samaria. The city of Samaria, the capital of the northern section of Israel, remained the center for the worship of false idols. Most of those in Jerusalem not interested in following God's laws found their ways to that idolatrous city, which was very similar to most of our cities today. Samaria's religion was of an a la carte variety, mixing parts of God's law with other beliefs. Yet God tells us who He is in His Word. We cannot change Him by picking and choosing which aspects we like! That makes the tale of the "Good Samaritan" much more meaningful.

As Christians, we are not called to come to the aid of our fellow believers any more readily than we are called to help all brothers in need. It does not matter how dirty they appear, or whether or not we share the same social status. God created every single human and by His hand, each one is "fearfully and wonderfully made." (Psalm 139:14) Would Jesus walk past a broken man, lying on the ground? Sadly, with the Lord living inside of us, there are frequent occurrences when we carry Jesus right past those who are hurting. Just as in the parable shared by Jesus, we should not let our religion give us a sanctimonious stance in relation to those who do not know Him. Is there a more amplified message than love? We are not responsible for how those broken people receive our hand of compassion, but through the Holy Spirit, those deeds are seeds to plant of the love of God. It is nothing to be a hearer of the Word of God and everything to be a doer of that same Word! Share the love of God with others, just as He shared it with us! Above all, have compassion, feeling the pain of others. Never lose sight of the fact that God could choose to place us in that same position, as we have not earned any better treatment. Instead, God has shared His compassion with us! "Go and do likewise!"

[20] "And he arose and came to his father. But when he was still a great way off, his father saw him and had compassion, and ran and fell on his neck and kissed him. [21] And the son said to him, 'Father, I have sinned against heaven and in your sight, and am no longer worthy to be called your son.'
Luke 15:20-21 (NKJV)

January 9: Temptation before ministry

When Jesus taught in the Temple during Passover, both Mary and Joseph thought He was with their large party returning to Nazareth, after traveling to Jerusalem for the feast. At the age of 12, Jesus still was a boy by earthly standards and Jewish standards, as well. In the Middle Ages, rabbis set the age standard of 13 for a boy's bar-mitzvah, but boys younger than 13 who were advanced in their religious training and knowledge were allowed to take part in religious ceremonies. Certainly, Jesus had that ability at a very early age.

[46] Now so it was *that* after three days they found Him in the temple, sitting in the midst of the teachers, both listening to them and asking them questions. [47] And all who heard Him were astonished at His understanding and answers. [48] So when they saw Him, they were amazed; and His mother said to Him, "Son, why have You done this to us? Look, Your father and I have sought You anxiously."
[49] And He said to them, "Why did you seek Me? Did you not know that I must be about My Father's business?" [50] But they did not understand the statement which He spoke to them.
Luke 2:46-50 (NKJV)

Interestingly, though Jesus' knowledge of the Scriptures amazed the best-educated rabbis, He was not to begin His ministry for 18 more years! Instead, Jesus continued to grow in every way and was still subject to His earthly parents.

[51] Then He went down with them and came to Nazareth, and was subject to them, but His mother kept all these things in her heart. [52] And Jesus increased in wisdom and stature, and in favor with God and men.
Luke 2:51-52 (NKJV)

The beginning of His ministry had nothing to do with Jesus being ready, but everything to do with God preparing the other pieces of the puzzle. Of course, all of those occurred in God's perfect timing and He could have had it all ready when Jesus was 12. But by the age of 30, Jesus had demonstrated His work ethic. He was not lazy, depending upon the provision of earthly parents, but instead, certainly helped support the household as a carpenter. He grew physically and intellectually, and was respected by others for His integrity and honor. Additionally, His actions pleased God the Father.

Still, before beginning His ministry, two important events needed to occur. First, Jesus came to John the Baptist to be baptized. John was sent to "prepare the way of the Lord," and obviously, John realized that Jesus should have baptized John. Yet this was an act of obedience and submission. John's baptism was a baptism of repentance, and with Jesus being without sin, He did not need to repent. Some believe that circumcision is synonymous with baptism for the Jews, yet Jesus also had been circumcised like all Jewish boys on the eighth day of life. Instead, by His baptism, Jesus identified Himself with sinners. Remember, on the cross Jesus not only bore our sin, but "became sin for us," according to 2 Corinthians 5:21. Additionally, the baptism of Jesus brought Him into the priestly order of Melchizedek, who was a king and a priest, unlike all of the Levites, who were only priests. We can see the Levitical rites of becoming a priest in Exodus 29, which also included "baptism:"

"And Aaron and his sons you shall bring to the door of the tabernacle of meeting, and you shall wash them with water.

Exodus 29:4 (NKJV)

After His baptism, attended by the Father, Son and Holy Spirit, Jesus immediately departed into the wilderness to endure 40 days of temptation, directed by the "deceiver of the brethren." Many misunderstand that trial, thinking that because Jesus is God that it was simple to endure and deny the wiles of Satan. Yet He was tempted in every way imaginable, tempted in all of the ways we are tempted. Relying on the power of the Holy Spirit, Jesus was able to endure, just as we are. For we have the same Holy Spirit dwelling inside of each of us as believers. Interestingly, God the Father did not deem Jesus ready and prepared for ministry until these events had taken place. Jesus did not begin His ministry until the age of 30, yet in our culture, we often place people into ministry when they are much younger.

Can those younger than 30 relate to the older congregation, based on the difficulties of life endured by all of us? Have those who are younger grown in stature and knowledge, and grown in favor with men and God? Enduring all temptations prepares a path for ministry, and just as the Prodigal Son felt the need to sow his wild oats as a young man, most people are much different at 20 than they are at 40. Regardless of age, an important factor in any ministry is that ability to endure. Certainly, temptations and trials grow stronger for those who lead the battle charge. Satan hates anyone who works for the kingdom of God. The more love we have for the Lord, the more hate Satan carries for us!

This is not reserved for pastors, teachers and worship leaders. Every person who has come to the Lord is a minister of the gospel to those God places in our path. That ministry truly will begin upon similar steps taken by our Lord: growth in knowledge of God's Word; growth in morals and ethics to gain favor with others; maturity, both spiritually and emotionally; a public profession of faith and repentance through baptism; and a period of test or trial.

Christians all will have those periods of trial. Moses had three different periods of 40 years in his life: 40 years in Pharaoh's court, 40 years in Midian and then 40 years leading the Jews in the wilderness. His "desert time" prepared Moses for ministry, just as the 40 days of Jesus in the wilderness prepared our Savior. If we desire to be used by God in ministry, we should be ready for our time in the desert, for we cannot pass a trial without learning to rely on God, rather than self, to endure.

**[1] Then the LORD spoke to Moses and Aaron, saying: [2] "Take a census of the sons of Kohath from among the children of Levi, by their families, by their fathers' house, [3] from thirty years old and above, even to fifty years old, all who enter the service to do the work in the tabernacle of meeting.
Numbers 4:1-3 (NKJV)**

January 10: Practice what you preach!

Most people are disgusted by hypocrisy, which makes perfect sense, as all of us take our turns as hypocrites. Pointing at hypocrites exposes our own hypocrisy! We comment about the idiot driving in front of us, who forgot to use his turn signal, and then moments later, we also fail to signal when turning! Typically, the traits in others that bother us the most are ones we see in ourselves. The word hypocrite in Greek (*hupokrites*), referred to a stage actor, and in the same manner, hypocrisy reflects an act that does not coincide with our claims.

Most anti-Christians are turned off by the hypocrisy of those espousing Christian beliefs. Part of that has to do with their misinterpretation of Christianity. Christians are not better than non-Christians! There will be some people in heaven who have committed many more sins than some of the people in hell. Instead, the difference is the forgiveness of Christians by the hand of Jesus, as we must ask for His forgiveness. Certainly, churches are filled with sinners. That being said, our testimonies could be much more powerful if we were able to practice what we preach. Another way of saying that is to let our walk reflect our talk.

In Greek, the word for walk is *"peripateo."* In 335 B.C., the philosopher Aristotle founded the Peripatetic School in ancient Greece, where people were heavily into philosophy. People of that time frequently discussed the meaning of "ultimate reality." The school's name refers to the act of walking, and as an adjective, "*peripatetic*" is often used to mean wandering or walking about. Aristotle said philosophy had no meaning unless it affected the way we live.

What a great application this is to our Christian beliefs. If the Bible does not affect our lives, either we truly do not believe what we claim to believe or we are unwilling to follow God. Often, it comes down to sheer laziness. We continue in our sins when we try to fight that battle under our own power, alone. Following the teachings of the Bible is not a water faucet that we can turn on or off in a moment's notice, as God does not perfect us instantly. Yet He does promise that He will complete His work in us. The path to God is a slow, progressive journey. That is why it is called a walk! Sometimes, it is easier to understand the meaning of a word by looking at the antonyms and synonyms. For instance, a walk is not a run. Nor is it a crawl, a ride or soaring above others.

> Don't walk in front of me; I may not follow. Don't walk behind me; I may not lead. Just walk beside me and be my friend."
> –Albert Camus

Certainly, Jesus desires to lead us beside still waters and in the paths of righteousness, but He walks beside us. The Christian walk is an act of friendship by our Savior, who carries on a conversation with us every step of the way, if we are willing to both talk and listen. Talking to God involves prayer, while listening to God comes from the reading of His Word! If we choose to pray without ceasing and continuously study the Bible, we will grow closer to Him!

For we are His workmanship, created in Christ Jesus for good works, which God prepared beforehand that we should walk in them.
Ephesians 2:10 (NKJV)

Christianity should not be words, but works, as God calls us to practice what we preach. Let our actions speak to an unbelieving world! He has a calling on each of our lives. Are we walking in a way that honors Him?

I, therefore, the prisoner of the Lord, beseech you to walk worthy of the calling with which you were called,
Ephesians 4:1 (NKJV)

God calls us to follow Him, not just to hear Him! Jesus gave us the best example, as God came to earth as a man, demonstrating how to act, live and walk. If we emulate His behavior, hypocrisy will fade from our lives. Practice reveals repetitive, learned behavior. If we continue to follow God's laws, we will get better at following Him. Then, we can practice what we preach!

And walk in love, as Christ also has loved us and given Himself for us, an offering and a sacrifice to God for a sweet-smelling aroma.
Ephesians 5:2 (NKJV)

January 11: To owe or not to owe

We all struggle when measuring our own actions against the actions of others. Yet instead of measuring ourselves against others, we should measure our lives against the real benchmark, the life of Jesus. He never sinned. Additionally, He never acted in a way to glorify Himself, but instead, those actions always pointed to His Father.

On *Yom Kippur*, the Day of Atonement, Jews attend services at a temple, fasting and praying in reflection upon the previous year. On that day in Old Testament times, the high priest performed sacrifices to cover the sins of the people. Today, without a temple to perform sacrifices to cover those sins, each Jew assesses whether or not they are a good person or bad person based upon the deeds of the year. Basically, the wealth of labor dictates the final result, at least by their own measurements. By performing more good deeds than bad, they believe they are good people. That is the same system most people in the world desire, but it is not the system that God has constructed.

God's measurement is not a balance sheet, filled with our assets and our liabilities. Instead, He has told us in His Word:

[23] for all have sinned and fall short of the glory of God, [24] being justified freely by His grace through the redemption that is in Christ Jesus, [25] whom God set forth *as* a propitiation by His blood, through faith, to demonstrate His righteousness, because in His forbearance God had passed over the sins that were previously committed, [26] to demonstrate at the present time His righteousness, that He might be just and the justifier of the one who has faith in Jesus.
Romans 6:23-26 (NKJV)

The word for sin in the Greek is *hamartia*, and the term comes from archery. When a shot did not hit the bull's-eye, it was called a sin. It did not have to be far from the target, but even the narrowest of misses was still considered sin. That is the same in our lives, where we can have the best intent, and still miss by the narrowest of margins. In God's eyes, that is still sin. A great example would be a white lie, even with the intent of not hurting someone's feelings.

God knew that we could not live perfect lives, so He put a plan in place to remove that sin from our lives. In order to remove the sin, we need a scapegoat. Yet before we see the need for a scapegoat, we have to recognize the spiritual condition we are in without God. We are spiritually destitute! When faced with a righteous God, we have absolutely nothing to offer! All of the people who found themselves in the presence of God in the Bible felt so unworthy, they put their faces in the dirt! We are able to have a relationship with God only because He allows that relationship. Why would the Creator of all want to have a relationship with us? It is a kind of love we never have been faced with.

⁴ Now to him who works, the wages are not counted as grace but as debt ⁵ But to him who does not work but believes on Him who justifies the ungodly, his faith is accounted for righteousness,
Romans 4:4-5 (NKJV)

Which system works better for us? If judged on works, we certainly will be found to owe, and the penalty will be far worse than debtor's prison! Instead of a system of works, those who believe in Jesus Christ as Lord and Savior are under the system of grace. He paid the price for each of our sins through His death. When He died, He said, "It is finished," letting us know that He already has accomplished the payment for us. Walk with joy in the miracle of the grace of Jesus!

And He said to me, "My grace is sufficient for you, for My strength is made perfect in weakness."
2 Corinthians 12:9 (NKJV)

January 12: Why do we continue to fail?

One of the most memorable openings of any television show was the horrendous crash of the skier in ABC's Wide World of Sports, paired with the line, "The thrill of victory and the agony of defeat." Each of us knows the emotions associated with both scenarios. When defeat is temporary, rather than permanent, we are pressed to turn the tides, for "when the going gets tough, the tough get going." Why does God put us in positions where we will fail?

We tend to complain when the skies open and the rain starts to fall upon us, desiring sunny skies all of the time. Yet we somehow forget that if the skies are always sunny, it is called drought! Those failures teach us patience. Patience is the ability to take a large quantity of punishment without getting angry, or without taking vengeance. Lest we forget, patience is a gift of the Holy Spirit. Interestingly, in Greek, the opposite of revenge is meekness. The Bible speaks much of meekness, and its meaning is not weakness, but power under control. Jesus told us in the Sermon on the Mount in Matthew 5:5, **"Blessed are the meek, for they shall inherit the earth."** Colossians reminds us what attributes we should have as believers:

[12] **Therefore, as *the* elect of God, holy and beloved, put on tender mercies, kindness, humility, meekness, longsuffering;** [13] **bearing with one another, and forgiving one another, if anyone has a complaint against another; even as Christ forgave you, so you also *must do*.** [14] **But above all these things put on love, which is the bond of perfection.**
Colossians 3:12-14 (NKJV)

We know these are attributes of God and attributes of His Son, who walked on this earth. Jesus said,

[28] **Come to Me, all *you* who labor and are heavy laden, and I will give you rest.** [29] **Take My yoke upon you and learn from Me, for I am meek and lowly in heart, and you will find rest for your souls.** [30] **For My yoke *is* easy and My burden is light."**
Matthew 11:28-30 (NKJV)

Many people defend their angry actions, saying they acted in "righteous anger," and then point to Jesus turning over the tables of vendors in the Temple. Notice that Jesus was not offended by what the vendors had done to Him, but by what they had done to His Father's temple. We also should remember John 8:7 stating, **"Let he who is without sin cast the first stone."** Jesus was sinless, and we are far from His standard. Instead of fighting against the people we believe have wronged us, we should leave that to the Lord. After all, Paul reminds us,

Beloved, do not avenge yourselves, but *rather* give place to wrath; for it is written, *"Vengeance is Mine, I will repay,"* says the Lord.
Romans 12:19 (NKJV)

Each time we fail, we should look back and see how we handled that defeat. Was it with patience or with anger? Often, our failures remind us of how far we have to go for God to complete His work in us. That should give us less judgmental hearts when dealing with others, also struggling with their own failures. Never forget that God has a purpose in each situation, whether the thrill of victory or the agony of defeat.

Not a word failed of any good thing which the LORD had spoken to the house of Israel. All came to pass.
Joshua 21:45 (NKJV)

January 13: There is nothing to fear!

Franklin Delano Roosevelt, the 32nd President of the United States, is well known for his saying, "There is nothing to fear but fear itself." Fear can be one of the most debilitating feelings, pervasive to the very core of our beings. When fear sets in, every action becomes paralyzed, with the question "what if" resonating throughout the soul through worry. Every decision involves a balance point between success and failure. Knowing this, many people hesitate to make decisions, though lack of a decision is still a decision! Fear does not come from the Lord.

For God has not given us a spirit of fear, but of power and of love and of a sound mind.
2 Timothy 1:7 (NKJV)

Timothy was Paul's spiritual son, as Paul shared the gospel with Timothy when just a boy. Additionally, Paul's influence upon Timothy did not stop there, including further encouragement of Timothy in ministry in the first epistle. The second epistle written by Paul to Timothy found Paul imprisoned, yet still concerned for his protégé. Timothy was no longer a boy, but in the 15 or so years since Timothy's salvation, he was preaching to people with many more life experiences. Still, God had called Timothy to this position. If Timothy felt overwhelmed and began to fear, Paul reminded him that fear was of the devil, not of the Lord. Yet three attributes to offset that fear did come from the Lord – power, love and a sound mind.

Power is the Greek work *dynameos*, where we get our word dynamite. The TNT in this situation would be Timothy Not Timid! This power could be physical or moral, residing within a person, but the best description is "power in action." Each action would involve a decision, and rather than worrying that the wrong decision had been made, a powerful man would trust in the Lord. Often, that involves stepping out in faith based on our decisions.

Love is the second attribute that can alleviate fear. In this verse, that love is *agape*, which points to the same kind of love that God exhibits to us. One of the greatest reminders of the power of love comes from Proverbs:

Hatred stirs up strife,
But love covers all sins.
Proverbs 10:12 (NKJV)

Even when we make mistakes, those we have had repeated contact with should be able to see our unmistaken motive, love. According to the "love chapter:"

[4] **Love suffers long *and* is kind; love does not envy; love does not parade itself, is not puffed up;** [5] **does not behave rudely, does not seek its own, is not provoked, thinks no evil;** [6] **does not rejoice in iniquity, but rejoices in the truth;** [7] **bears all things, believes all things, hopes all things, endures all things.** [8] **Love never fails.**
1 Corinthians 13:4-8 (NKJV)

Love enables us to make the most difficult decisions, and to endure the ensuing battles.

Lastly, God also gives us a sound mind. That sound mind helps us to make those hard choices, to weigh the potential situations with logic and wisdom, though there are times when God seems to answer our prayers in what seems to be an illogical way.

[8] "For My thoughts *are* not your thoughts,
Nor *are* your ways My ways," says the LORD.
[9] "For *as* the heavens are higher than the earth,
So are My ways higher than your ways,
And My thoughts than your thoughts.
Isaiah 55:8-9 (NKJV)

God does not place us into the easiest of situations, as He wants us to grow. That growth is reliance upon Him, rather than reliance upon self. Can a plant grow without water or sunshine? In the same manner, we cannot grow without Living Water or the Son of God! God stretches us with those difficult decisions, and if we rely upon Him, He will give us power, love and a sound mind. When we fear, instead of trusting in the Lord, we question each decision, worrying about all aspects that might go wrong. FDR was correct in his assessment that we should be afraid of fear, yet our only true fear should be the fear of the Lord, which is the beginning of wisdom!

**Fear not, for I *am* with you;
Be not dismayed, for I *am* your God.
I will strengthen you,
Yes, I will help you,
I will uphold you with My righteous right hand.'
Isaiah 41:10 (NKJV)**

January 14: The amazing race

One of the greatest gifts that God has given to believers is the church. In the church, hearing the Word of God can be the most special aspect; we also get the opportunity to worship the Lord in spirit and in truth; fellowship with other like-minded individuals is another incredible blessing. Churches should be hospitals rather than battlefields, but any time opinionated humans gather together, there will be disagreements. With the human condition, if there are two people, there are three opinions. With so many different interpretations and philosophies, choosing the correct church is instrumental in the growth of a Christian. All Christians need food and it does not matter if we are little lambs or fat sheep, God desires to give us daily bread. Fat sheep still can die from starvation, though they might be able to stay healthy longer than the skinny sheep when there is a shortage of food.

God desires to feed His children. Sadly, there are not enough Christians willing to open the Bible and put in time studying alone. Because God has promised that He will teach us all things, we all should spend time in His Word. Would we rather have a pastor tell us what is in God's Word, or would we rather hear from the One who wrote it? That does not mean that pastors cannot help us learn. Yet that never should be the only spiritual food that we eat, as all men make mistakes; all pastors misinterpret occasionally, based on their own life experiences, weaknesses and stumbling blocks; all of us have blind spots!

Certainly, one of the greatest points of emphasis to every believer is not to major in the minors. By choosing our battles wisely, a difference in opinion on a verse's interpretation does not have to be discussed at length, especially with a person who does not like to be questioned. Does it really matter if we believe in a pre-tribulation rapture, a mid-tribulation rapture or a post-tribulation rapture? Will that belief affect our salvation? As Christians, we all believe that Jesus is coming back for us. Whenever that occurs will be in His perfect timing. God's decision should be sufficient for all of us. When we finally get to heaven, surely each of us will find a doctrine we did not understand correctly.

[10] Now I plead with you, brethren, by the name of our Lord Jesus Christ, that you all speak the same thing, and *that* there be no divisions among you, but *that* you be perfectly joined together in the same mind and in the same judgment.
[11] For it has been declared to me concerning you, my

brethren, by those of Chloe's *household*, that there are contentions among you. [12] **Now I say this, that each of you says, "I am of Paul," or "I am of Apollos," or "I am of Cephas," or "I am of Christ."** [13] **Is Christ divided? Was Paul crucified for you? Or were you baptized in the name of Paul? 1 Corinthians 1:10-13 (NKJV)**

Through the unity of the Holy Spirit, we will become like-minded. Yet because each of us has a different path, we can see things very diversely. What if a group of individuals all were traveling to Chicago, Illinois, from different locations? One person might begin the journey to Chicago from the top of Mt. Everest; another, from Paris, France; another from Antarctica; and still another from St. Louis, Missouri. All four would have dissimilar ideas of what that journey entailed. In fact, each aspect of that journey would be different until arriving at the final destination.

Our Christian walks are much like that scenario, as the Holy Spirit speaks to us individually. He pulls us out of incredibly diverse walks of life and starts us on the path that leads to God. Our different life experiences, ministries, relationships and churches become a part of that diversity, but God already has promised to complete His work in us. If He will complete the work, then we must be incomplete! The unity in the body of Christ comes from the similar love that God has given us, in the midst of diverse people. An ex-Mormon who became a Christian wrote this in one of her books:

> "It is useless to pour water into a cup that's already full. In the same way, it is useless to teach a person another perspective when they are absolutely sure that they are right and don't want to learn anything else. One way that Satan can deceive us is to make us so positive we have to be right that our minds become closed and we are no longer teachable.
> -- Ex-Mormon Carma Naylor

One of the greatest attributes of those seeking knowledge and understanding is an open mind. Along with that, each of us needs a humble heart, esteeming others above self. Both of those will help us to walk with love for those whose paths intersect ours on the journey that leads to God. Yes, those people will let us down and we will let those people down, too. Yet our trust should remain steadfast in the Lord. When we approach any battle, we should attempt to be a part of the solution, rather than a part of the problem. Would we rather be right or be happy? Appreciate the differences in others and hand any issue over to the Lord in prayer. There is nothing too big for Him to handle.

My soul, wait silently for God alone,
For my expectation *is* from Him.
Psalm 62:5 (NKJV)

January 15: For such a time as this!

What is the most frequent complaint? For many of us, it is, "I'm tired." Why is it that we have this unexpressed expectation for life to go smoothly? When God instructed us in the 10 Commandments to not covet, He was telling us to accept the situation He puts us into, knowing that God selected that situation specifically for each of us. Can we trust that God knows what He is doing?

[1] Now as *Jesus* passed by, He saw a man who was blind from birth. [2] And His disciples asked Him, saying, "Rabbi, who sinned, this man or his parents, that he was born blind?"
[3] Jesus answered, "Neither this man nor his parents sinned, but that the works of God should be revealed in him.
John 9:1-3 (NKJV)

First of all, how can we tell if a man has been blind since birth or became blind later in life, simply by walking past him? It is likely that this man was known to Jesus and His disciples. The question asked by the disciples is an interesting one. Who sinned? The answer that Jesus tells us is that sin can cause hardship, trial or sickness, but in this case, the man had done nothing wrong. In fact, Jesus reminded them that neither had the man's parents. So what was the purpose of his blindness?

Though they were near other waters, Jesus made clay from His own spit and the dirt of the ground and sent the blind man to the Pools of Siloam to wash the clay from his eye. He walked in faith, as any blind man has to do. Imagine walking without vision! When the blind man journeyed the distance to the pool, walking in faith, he was given the gift of sight. The purpose of his blindness was so that the Lord could heal him, and in so doing, God would be glorified. Others certainly witnessed the miracle, and had their spiritual eyes opened to believe in Jesus as Messiah, too.

Are we willing to suffer severe hardship for the Lord? He might not heal us, but even could demonstrate to others the peace we continue to have in the midst of a trial. After coming to the Lord, the next decision each of us needs to make is whether or not we can trust Him. He has proven Himself trustworthy. We need to let Him involve us in His miraculous plans!

January 16: What is your cross to bear?

When we take a close look at this world, it is difficult to fathom how strongly each of us is tied to it. Everywhere we turn, there is brokenness all around us, from homelessness to substance-abuse issues to poverty, hunger, famine and war. Natural disasters seem to be increasing, with massive death and destruction occurring from earthquakes, tsunamis, fires and even oil spills. Because this life is all we know, we often let our earthly circumstances overwhelm us, forgetting the hope of glory that will come.

[23] **Then He said to *them* all, "If anyone desires to come after Me, let him deny himself, and take up his cross daily, and follow Me.** [24] **For whoever desires to save his life will lose it, but whoever loses his life for My sake will save it.** [25] **For what**

profit is it to a man if he gains the whole world, and is himself destroyed or lost?
Luke 9:23-25 (NKJV)

What was the perspective of the disciples when Jesus spoke the above verse to them? It is doubtful they made the connection between the cross and crucifixion until after His death. Though crucifixion began in the 6th century B.C., it was perfected by the Romans as the most brutal form of torture. Jesus teaches us to join Him in suffering, but the burden that we carry is a light affliction, as Paul termed his sufferings on this earth in 2 Corinthians:

^{17} For our light affliction, which is but for a moment, is working for us a far more exceeding *and* eternal weight of glory, ^{18} while we do not look at the things which are seen, but at the things which are not seen. For the things which are seen *are* temporary, but the things which are not seen *are* eternal.
2 Corinthians 4:17-18 (NKJV)

Do we look at the sufferings of this age as light? Paul was beaten, imprisoned and shipwrecked numerous times. He had constant aches, pains and a distracting disorder of the eyes making it difficult to even read the Hebrew scrolls. Yet Paul was able to understand that the burden Jesus carried on His cross was far weightier than the comparatively feather-light weight that each of us must shoulder as believers. Additionally, we know that most of us build the crosses that we are to carry! Though the Lord forgives our sins, the ramifications of those sins remain with us, and frequently, are a part of our cross bearing.

Why is it that God does not make our lives simple when we come to Him? He could make every Christian a millionaire, with fame and abundance. Sadly, we spend so much more time in prayer asking for God's help than in praising Him for the blessings. If we were as thankful as God deserves, we could praise Him every moment of every day and it still would not be enough! Instead, we selfishly pray, "What are You going to do for me now, God?" Though we do not deserve it, He continues to bless us, yet He keeps us in places where we will look to Him for guidance, assistance and love.

We should carry our crosses with joy, knowing that the burden of our sin already has been carried by the only One with wide enough shoulders to sustain that weight. If that is all He ever would accomplish on our behalves, it was enough, yet He continues to bless us on a daily basis. Jesus carried His own cross through the streets of Jerusalem to a hilltop outside the city walls. Beaten, bloodied and bruised, He sustained the weight of the cross as well as the hatred of the mob. We were all a part of that angry mob, cheering Him derisively to His death. If we want to join Him in life, we have to be willing to join Him in His death! Pick up the cross today and follow Him. Where He leads, we will follow!

He leads me in the paths of righteousness
For His name's sake.
 Psalm 23:3 (NKJV)

January 17: Relationships

Life is all about relationships, as family, friends and co-workers either can enhance each experience or can make each one much more stressful. Before pointing fingers, we need to realize that we carry that same tenuous arrangement in the lives of others. Occasionally, at the very least, we will make the lives of others stressful. Without having the relationship with God as the focus of our lives, we have no chance in our other relationships. Even with that relationship with our Creator intact, there will be failures in our interpersonal relationships. God knows our weaknesses and consequently, much of the Bible instructs us in how to get along with others. The last half of the 10 Commandments gives us laws concerning others. When we fail, how should we handle that?

[29] **Let no corrupt word proceed out of your mouth, but what is good for necessary edification, that it may impart grace to the hearers.** [30] **And do not grieve the Holy Spirit of God, by whom you were sealed for the day of redemption.** [31] **Let all bitterness, wrath, anger, clamor, and evil speaking be put away from you, with all malice.** [32] **And be kind to one another, tenderhearted, forgiving one another, even as God in Christ forgave you.**
Ephesians 4:29-32 (NKJV)

Bitterness is a wonderful description, for it is when something leaves a bad taste in our mouths. When a person does something that bothers us, if we dwell on that issue, a weed is planted. The more we think about the situation, bitterness takes root and begins to make all of our life taste in that same foul way. That root can take us over if we give it enough time or energy. Instead, forgiveness takes that bitterness and cuts it away. Instead of a bitter taste, only a pleasant taste remains. Part of that forgiveness is the knowledge of what God forgave in each of our lives. When we do not resolve conflicts, we grieve the Holy Spirit.

Grieve is a deep word here. Commonly when we feel grief, it is overbearing sadness for a loss, as in the death of a close relative. When the verse tells us "do not grieve the Holy Spirit," it reminds us that first of all, it is possible for us to do that! In itself, that teaches us much about God, as we can see how the smallest of our actions can affect Him! Since it is possible through our sin, and because we all sin, we all will grieve the Holy Spirit. Since the tri-unity of God is one, in the same manner, we grieve the Father and the Son through our sin. The Holy Spirit protects us for the day of redemption, though we obviously continue to sin.

Remember, the devil is looking for a foothold in our lives. He will use situations where others let us down as well as situations where we let others down to cause huge issues in our lives. Once again, that foothold will not happen unless the situation is not resolved. Let it go! In the grand scheme of it all, is it really that big of a deal? Forgive, as we have been forgiven.

[1] **Therefore, laying aside all malice, all deceit, hypocrisy, envy, and all evil speaking,** [2] **as newborn babes, desire the pure milk of the word, that you may grow thereby,** [3] **if indeed you have tasted that the Lord** *is* **gracious.**
1 Peter 2:1-3 (NKJV)

January 18: Where is your confidence?

Pride is the ugliest attribute in others, but when looking in the mirror, we often forget how that same pride looks on us. In our society, we seem to draw the line between pride and self-confidence, though after drawing the line, we forget where we placed it. How many times do we lose friends or relationships because of that useless pride? Certainly, the "love chapter" of the Bible teaches us about pride's opposite and by negating each statement, we can place pride (or our own names) in the place of "love."

Pride never suffers long and is never kind; pride envies; pride parades itself and is puffed up; pride behaves rudely, seeks its own, is provoked, thinks evil; pride rejoices in iniquity, but never rejoices in truth; pride cannot bear anything, never believes, never hopes and never endures. Pride fails.

Pride *goes* **before destruction,**
And a haughty spirit before a fall.
Proverbs 16:18 (NKJV)

Everyone walking this earth begins with an addiction to sin, and typically, even when trying to conquer sin, our failures occur when pride gets in the way. Just as Peter bragged to Jesus, "I love you more than the rest; I am willing to die for you," on the same night that he denied Jesus three times, we get in trouble by using sweeping generalizations like never and always. Modern-day culture seems to honor self-confidence, without understanding how often that self-confidence passes to pride.

Interestingly, in all 14 times the word "confident" is used in the Bible, it is a positive attribute when relying upon God and is a negative attribute when relying upon self.

being confident of this very thing, that He who has begun a good work in you will complete *it* until the day of Jesus Christ;
Philippians 1:6 (NKJV)

How can we be confident that we will conquer that sin addiction? Because God is going to complete His work in us! That has nothing to do with our own actions, as we are merely the recipients of His gift! Without our eyes focused upon our Gift-Giver, we are destined for failure.

> "A proud man is always looking down on things and people; and, of course, as long as you're looking down, you can't see something that's above you." -- C.S. Lewis

When a man brags about his accomplishments, there always is exaggeration, if not hyperbole. By looking at any job seeker's resume, this prideful exaggeration is apparent. Instead of having absolute confidence in our past, we should have confidence in God's future in us. Confidence in self is fleeting, yet confidence in God is perfect knowledge, irrefutable because of His promises!

I can do all things through Christ who strengthens me.
Philippians 4:12 (NKJV)

"I am the vine, you *are* the branches. He who abides in Me, and I in him, bears much fruit; for without Me you can do nothing.
John 15:5 (NKJV)

Are we walking confidently in our battles against sin? If we have given our lives to the Lord, the bondage of sin has been removed, as have our old sins. Yet we sometimes continue to choose sin. If struggling, walk in confidence that God can conquer that sin. If we are confident in our own strength, only failure will knock upon our doors. Instead, brag of the mighty power of God, for He will enable us to walk in victory! Have confidence in God!

[1] **The LORD *is* my light and my salvation;
Whom shall I fear?
The LORD *is* the strength of my life;
Of whom shall I be afraid?
[2] When the wicked came against me
To eat up my flesh,
My enemies and foes,
They stumbled and fell.
[3] Though an army may encamp against me,
My heart shall not fear;
Though war may rise against me,
In this I *will be* confident.
Psalm 27:1-3 (NKJV)**

January 19: Who is your neighbor?

Daily, Mr. Rogers serenaded the television audience with his personally-written theme song, "Won't you be my neighbor?" Though Fred Rogers was a Presbyterian minister, he likely would not have been the neighbor of choice for many of us. Yet we rarely get the opportunity to place our best friends on that list. Having endured neighbors who have loudly partied until the middle of the night, we often are surrounded with people who test our patience. Yet God's instructions to us as believers are simple to interpret:

**So he answered and said, "'*You shall love the LORD your God with all your heart, with all your soul, with all your strength, and with all your mind,*' and '*your neighbor as yourself.*'"
Luke 10:27 (NKJV)**

These are the two commandments that Jesus highlighted in summation of the Old Testament Law. In Exodus, the first five commandments instruct us concerning a righteous relationship with God, while the last five commandments instruct us concerning that correct relationship with others. Notice that this love of God begins in the heart and ends in the mind, completing the circuit of who we are. Each part of us needs to love the Lord, not a small part of us! The sequential order of these instructions is not accidental, as until we have the right relationship with God, we cannot correctly restore relationships with others. Yet there are believers who put all of the emphasis on their relationship with the Lord, forgetting about the remainder of His commandments.

If God did not desire for us to demonstrate His love to the sinners on this earth, He would remove us as soon as we turned to Him! Yet that is not what occurs. Instead, He desires for us to love others in the same manner that He loves us. Interestingly, the verse in Luke does not tell us to love our neighbors if they deserve it, or if they are really sweet Christians. Instead, Jesus reminds us to love our neighbors in the same manner that we love ourselves!

With man's most common sin being pride, love of self is not a rarity in our world. God wants us to have a sacrificial love for our neighbors. Would we put ourselves in harm's way to save our neighbor? It is natural to love those who love us, but the greater calling is to love those who do not love us! This applies inside the church as easily as it does outside of the church! Certainly, there are people who have personalities that push our buttons. As difficult as it may be to like them, we are called to love them! Once again, it is a matter of trust. If God chose them for His family, who are we to question His motive? Sometimes, we lose perspective by thinking they do not deserve our love. Yet we do not deserve God's love, though He graciously chose to give it to us!

Our challenge is to love those who despise us. Who is the greatest example of this behavior? Jesus! Reflect on that sinless Man, who endured the most humiliating and painful of deaths in punishment for the sins of man. Mocked and ridiculed, He remained lovingly concerned for them even unto death. "Father, forgive them. They know not what they do!" When a person is a slave to sin, he serves Satan blindly. Sin is not a choice, but a way of life to the unsaved. If our neighbor is a captive of the great deceiver, we should shower them with the abundant love of a Savior, who is the only One to save them from that bondage! That journey might begin with our sacrificial love!

[43] "**You have heard that it was said, *'You shall love your neighbor* and hate your enemy.'** [44] **But I say to you, love your enemies, bless those who curse you, do good to those who hate you, and pray for those who spitefully use you and persecute you,** [45] **that you may be sons of your Father in heaven; for He makes His sun rise on the evil and on the good, and sends rain on the just and on the unjust.**
Matthew 5:43-45 (NKJV)

January 20: G.P.S.

One of the most convenient advancements in technology is the Global Positioning System (GPS). Many cars today include a GPS system factory-installed, while others use a portable device to bring an interactive map directly to the driver. Any time there is an unobstructed line of sight to four or more of the GPS satellites, the map displays an extremely accurate position that includes each potential street and avenue in the vicinity. For men, who have proven the inability to ask anyone for directions and would rather drive around for hours to find their way, GPS is a perfect compromise. Most systems even offer a choice of gender of voice, in addition to different languages.

God has given us a more important GPS (God's Prodding System). When Christians sin, the Holy Spirit reminds us how to return to the path God has laid out before us. Sometimes, even Christians find themselves far off course, but God is certainly capable to correct that misguided course and return us to the straight and narrow path. Upon missing a turn when using a GPS in the car, the system begins recalculating the quickest correction to find the destination. God does not have to recalculate, for He already knows each choice that we will make!

Additionally, the user can select different options, utilizing the most direct path or even the one with the most freeways. Yet in our Christian walks, the most direct paths are rarely the ones that God desires for us. While God's plan may not seem logical to our limited minds, we must remember that His ways are not our ways!

As Christians, we all find ourselves on roads that were not along the planned route. When differentiation from the path comes from our own mistaken decision, God's admonishment is not one of panic, but still, He instructs us how to get back to where He intends for us to go. The first step is repentance!

For godly sorrow produces repentance *leading* to salvation, not to be regretted; but the sorrow of the world produces death.
2 Corinthians 7:10 (NKJV)

God has given us free will to make our own choices, and to plan our own routes. Some of those routes are in His perfect will, when we follow His plan in our lives. Others involve His permissive will, as often, God allows us to make the wrong choices. Yet He takes those wrong choices as teaching tools in each of our lives. Most of the time, we can look back and see the intersections when we chose to go the wrong way. Along with that, we can see the difficulties that occurred because of those wrong choices, hopefully, giving us the insight to make a different choice if we ever approach a similar intersection in the future.

And we know that all things work together for good to those who love God, to those who are the called according to *His* purpose.
Romans 8:28 (NKJV)

Sometimes, we ignore the GPS so drastically that the blue line of the planned route is no longer on the screen. Listen! God never asks for us to make turns that will not be beneficial to us, to others and to Him! But if we get lost, we should not hesitate to stop and ask Him for directions.

"So I will restore to you the years that the swarming locust has eaten,
The crawling locust,
The consuming locust,
And the chewing locust,
My great army which I sent among you.
Joel 2:25 (NKJV)

January 21: The just shall live by faith!

An actor delivering his lines can change the meaning of the sentence by choosing which word to emphasize. Sometimes, when he does not grasp the personality of the role he is playing, that emphasis can greatly alter the portrait that the director is attempting to paint. Often, that occurs when he takes one line out of context, as a deeper reading will offer a deeper understanding. Many times, directors instruct the actors how to deliver the line correctly, at least in their own interpretation of what they would like to see on the stage or screen.

In the Bible, there are many verses that are either quoted or repeated. Since the entire Bible is God-breathed, those repetitive verses are reminders to us that we should spend enough time reading to comprehend the meaning of those verses. When God speaks to us, if we do not listen, He tells us again. How many times do parents have to remind their children? Just because a child does not choose to acknowledge the parent's instruction does not mean that the parent simply surrenders by ceasing that instruction. Instead, most parents become more demonstrative with their words, as they pass the point from encouragement to demand.

One of those repetitive verses comes from a minor prophet in the Old Testament book of Habakkuk. The difference between Major Prophets and Minor Prophets has nothing to do with power. Instead, the Major Prophets are called that because their books are longer. Yet the Minor Prophets spoke with the same power, but packed that power into fewer words. Most of us should be familiar with the phrase in the fourth verse:

² **Then the L**ORD **answered me and said:**
"Write the vision
And make *it* **plain on tablets,**
That he may run who reads it.
³**For the vision** *is* **yet for an appointed time;**
But at the end it will speak, and it will not lie.
Though it tarries, wait for it;
Because it will surely come,
It will not tarry.
⁴**"Behold the proud,**
His soul is not upright in him;
But the just shall live by his faith.
Habakkuk 2:2-4 (NKJV)

Three more times in the New Testament, this verse is quoted, yet each of those quotations seem to emphasize a different word.

¹⁶ **For I am not ashamed of the gospel of Christ, for it is the power of God to salvation for everyone who believes, for the Jew first and also for the Greek.** ¹⁷ **For in it the righteousness of God is revealed from faith to faith; as it is written,** *"The just shall live by faith."*
Romans 1:16-17 (NKJV)

In Romans, when quoting Habakkuk, Paul describes the process of how a sinner can come into the presence of a righteous God. It occurs through justification, which is the opposite of condemnation. In justification, God pardons those who believe in the work of Jesus Christ on the cross. To be justified is to walk in the knowledge that it was "just if I'd" never sinned! So in this passage, Paul emphasizes the word, "just," as in "the *just* shall live by faith!" This verse is quoted again in Hebrews:

³² **But recall the former days in which, after you were illuminated, you endured a great struggle with sufferings:** ³³

partly while you were made a spectacle both by reproaches and tribulations, and partly while you became companions of those who were so treated; [34] for you had compassion on me in my chains, and joyfully accepted the plundering of your goods, knowing that you have a better and an enduring possession for yourselves in heaven. [35] Therefore do not cast away your confidence, which has great reward. [36] For you have need of endurance, so that after you have done the will of God, you may receive the promise:
[37] *"For yet a little while,*
And He who is coming will come and will not tarry.
[38] *Now the just shall live by faith;*
But if anyone draws back,
My soul has no pleasure in him."
Hebrews 10:32-38 (NKJV)

In the passage above, Paul discusses the importance of endurance in our lives. Though God illuminates our lives with His presence, we continue to endure earthly difficulties and sufferings. He reminds us to confidently stay the course, regardless of those trials. Upon quoting Habakkuk, this time, emphasis is on the word, "live," as "the just shall *live* by faith!" Certainly, it is no surprise where Paul is going next:

[10] **For as many as are of the works of the law are under the curse; for it is written,** *"Cursed is everyone who does not continue in all things which are written in the book of the law, to do them."* [11] **But that no one is justified by the law in the sight of God** *is* **evident, for** *"the just shall live by faith."* [12] **Yet the law is not of faith, but** *"the man who does them shall live by them."*
[13] **Christ has redeemed us from the curse of the law, having become a curse for us (for it is written,** *"Cursed is everyone who hangs on a tree"*), [14] **that the blessing of Abraham might come upon the Gentiles in Christ Jesus, that we might receive the promise of the Spirit through faith.**
Galatians 3:10-14 (NKJV)

Lastly, in Galatians, Paul emphasizes "faith," as in "the just shall live by *faith*!" Faith is the hope of things not seen. As Christians, we understand that "believing is seeing," rather than the more often accepted statement that "seeing is believing." If we understand the power and principles of electricity, it is not blind faith to expect a light to go on when we turn the switch! Though we cannot see electricity, we have faith that the process will work.

This is a wonderful example of the amazing depth that God offers each of us through His Word. This is such a simple phrase of only six words, "the just shall live by faith." With three of those words being emphasized in different New Testament passages, the statement changes meaning completely! Are we just, not by our own actions but by the saving grace of Jesus Christ? Are we willing to endure a life of trials for our Lord, with His promise of a heavenly life when this one is over? Are we willing to trust in Him with faith, standing on His promises regardless of the difficulties? The depth of this phrase should inspire us to read the Bible in a deeper way! Lord, give us our daily bread, for man cannot live by bread alone, but by every word that proceeds from the mouth of God!

One witness shall not rise against a man concerning any iniquity or any sin that he commits; by the mouth of two or three witnesses the matter shall be established.
Deuteronomy 19:15 (NKJV)

January 22: Measurements

Years keep flying by, once again proving the analogy that once a vehicle reaches the top of the hill, gravity greatly increases the downhill speed. The farther over-the-hill we are, the faster that time seems to pass. Measuring that speed can be difficult, at best, but measurements depend most upon the one doing the measuring. Often in the Bible, God tells us about the integrity He requires when His children are measuring:

You shall have honest scales, honest weights, an honest ephah, and an honest hin: I *am* the LORD your God, who brought you out of the land of Egypt.
Leviticus 19:36 (NKJV)

One of the least rewarding jobs on farms 50 years ago was picking cotton. Paid by the pound, it took painstaking time and effort to fill a sack with cotton, only to find out how little weight the sack contained. Placing a few rocks in the sack could increase the pay quickly, but would not be an honest representation of the weight of the sack. In the same manner, dishonest businessmen in biblical times weighed the scales in their favor. The problem was so pervasive that buyers had great difficulty finding a vendor with an honest scale.

As Christians, God holds us to a different set of rules, and a different grading scale, as well. Non-believers measure their lives in mostly monetary ways. "More" seems to be the operative word, with more pay, more vacation, more possessions and more size in regard to housing. It is a slippery slope when as believers, we find ourselves drawn to the same trappings of the world that entice non-believers. God reminds us in 1 Timothy 6:10 that the love of money is the root of all evil. On the other hand, Paul reminds us how we are to view our lives before we came to know the Lord.

[8] Yet indeed I also count all things loss for the excellence of the knowledge of Christ Jesus my Lord, for whom I have suffered the loss of all things, and count them as rubbish, that I may gain Christ [9] and be found in Him, not having my own righteousness, which *is* from the law, but that which *is* through faith in Christ, the righteousness which is from God by faith; [10] that I may know Him and the power of His resurrection, and the fellowship of His sufferings, being conformed to His death, [11] if, by any means, I may attain to the resurrection from the dead.
Philippians 3:8-11 (NKJV)

How important should those possessions be to us? Count them all loss! Our desire still should be for more, but rather than more possessions, Christians should desire more knowledge of God. That should be heart knowledge! Our faith, hope and love should all increase as we continue to draw closer to the Lord. There is no greater thing than knowing Him, and nothing apart from God can satisfy our thirsty souls!

O God, You *are* my God;
Early will I seek You;
My soul thirsts for You;
My flesh longs for You
In a dry and thirsty land
Where there is no water.
Psalm 63:1 (NKJV)

As Christians, our perspectives should change in regard to how we measure ourselves. Instead of trying to "keep up with the Joneses," we should measure ourselves against God's Word. To demonstrate our love for God, we should focus on obeying His commandments. We know that while we are on this earth we will continue to sin. That is not an excuse for us not trying to follow each and every one of God's commandments. Yet the greatest gift is in how God measures us! Certainly, there will be people in hell who have committed fewer sins than some of the Christians in heaven. Being a Christian has nothing to do with our actions, but instead, depends on God's act. By following Jesus, we have accepted His gift, grace, which is the forgiveness of our sins. We are measured by the life of Jesus, just as He was measured by our sinful lives when He took the punishment for our sins at Calvary.

Each year, thousands of people take the Scholastic Aptitude Test (SAT). If the outcome of the SAT had to do with eternity, instead of college, Christians would have a huge advantage. While unbelievers would be sweating bullets, knowing that their entire futures ride on the outcome of this test, Christians would get to sit and watch while the One who wrote the test was taking the exam for us! Of course, He made a perfect score for us, solidifying our future. That is the only grading scale that we can measure up to! Though our old lives should be counted loss, we gain Christ Jesus!

⁶ Now godliness with contentment is great gain. ⁷ For we brought nothing into *this* world, *and it is* certain we can carry nothing out. ⁸ And having food and clothing, with these we shall be content. ⁹ But those who desire to be rich fall into temptation and a snare, and *into* many foolish and harmful lusts which drown men in destruction and perdition. ¹⁰ For the love of money is a root of all *kinds of* evil, for which some have strayed from the faith in their greediness, and pierced themselves through with many sorrows.
1 Timothy 6:6-10 (NKJV)

January 23: When life needs a do-over

In the 1991 movie "City Slickers," a touching comedy about some old friends in mid-life crisis on a cattle drive, one of the characters had made some horrendous, life-changing decisions. In the discussion about those decisions, his friends reminded him that in some cases it was like playing backyard baseball as a kid, when the ball got stuck in the tree. The rule in that case was for a "do-over," and in the same sense, they reminded him that his life could be a do-over!

Each of us has felt that same way. We all make mistakes and find ourselves in positions we never envisioned. Only hindsight involves perfect vision. Yet a partial do-over seems to be a better choice than a complete one. None of us would desire to endure adolescence again. Additionally, final exams or working as the French-fry cook at a fast food restaurant are equally unappealing. To start over as a baby only would be worthwhile if we could retain the experiential knowledge obtained from all of our mistakes. Basically, this would allow us to lose the pain, but keep the knowledge. In the Gospel of John, Jesus tells Nicodemus of a similar situation:

[1] There was a man of the Pharisees named Nicodemus, a ruler of the Jews. [2] This man came to Jesus by night and said to Him, "Rabbi, we know that You are a teacher come from God; for no one can do these signs that You do unless God is with him." [3] Jesus answered and said to him, "Most assuredly, I say to you, unless one is born again, he cannot see the kingdom of God." [4] Nicodemus said to Him, "How can a man be born when he is old? Can he enter a second time into his mother's womb and be born?" [5] Jesus answered, "Most assuredly, I say to you, unless one is born of water and the Spirit, he cannot enter the kingdom of God. [6] "That which is born of the flesh is flesh, and that which is born of the Spirit is spirit. [7] "Do not marvel that I said to you, 'You must be born again.' [8] "The wind blows where it wishes, and you hear the sound of it, but cannot tell where it comes from and where it goes. So is everyone who is born of the Spirit."
John 3:1-8 (NKJV)

Being born again is a do-over. When we decide to live for Jesus, instead of living for ourselves, God wipes the slate clean and we get to start freshly! All of our sins are gone, and we no longer have to pay the price of punishment for those sins. The punishment is death, according to Romans 6:23. After we acknowledge the role Jesus played as the Lamb of God, who takes away the sins of the world, we are not punished with death because He received that punished for our sins. Similar to the law of double jeopardy in the American court system, God will not punish the same sin twice.

But a residual effect of the sin in our lives remains, as sin has ramifications. After committing murder, by asking God for forgiveness, He will forgive the sin. Yet, there still might be that prison sentence to contend with. Additionally, the more difficult ramifications of that sin occur in our minds. We continue to remember our sins, though God does not. Satan has a way of reminding us of the pleasures associated with sin, while the Holy Spirit gives us the bigger picture including the accompanying brokenness. If there was not some pleasure associated with sin, it would not have such a strong attraction to us.

¹ I beseech you therefore, brethren, by the mercies of God, that you present your bodies a living sacrifice, holy, acceptable to God, which is your reasonable service. ² And do not be conformed to this world, but be transformed by the renewing of your mind, that you may prove what is that good and acceptable and perfect will of God.
Romans 12:1-2 (NKJV)

God changes our hearts, but we are responsible for the renewing of our minds. That is a much longer process of filling our minds with the things of God, rather than filling our minds with the things of the world. In order to do that, we must present our bodies as living sacrifices. That is a great picture, for in the Old Testament sacrificial system, animals were killed on the altar. God gave us the sacrificial system as a precursor to what Jesus would accomplish on our behalves, as there cannot be forgiveness of sin without the spilling of innocent blood. A living sacrifice keeps trying to get up off the altar and crawl away, which explains the daily process involved.

The benefit to each of us is transformation! In Greek, the word for transformation is *metamorpho*, from the same root word for metamorphosis. Think of a caterpillar that turns into a butterfly! Many feel like they need a do-over in their lives, wanting to stop creeping along, with everyone stepping on them and squishing them as a caterpillar! If we want to fly like beautiful butterflies then we need to be born again!

Whoever has been born of God does not sin, for His seed remains in him; and he cannot sin, because he has been born of God.
1 John 3:9 (NKJV)

January 24: God's tears on a soggy world!

Thunderstorms are beautiful, and are especially noticeable in regions where they occur infrequently. Rain is an amazing gift, watering plants in a wide variety of locations, yet often, we selfishly complain about the inconvenience that rain brings to our busy lives. All plants need water to survive and through rain, God has mercy upon plants never seen, having promised to His people that if we follow Him, He will bring rain in season. Droughts can have an instantaneous effect upon our food supply, causing famine. The Bible tells us about God's first rainstorm:

[1] **Then the LORD said to Noah, "Come into the ark, you and all your household, because I have seen that you are righteous before Me in this generation.** [2] **"You shall take with you seven each of every clean animal, a male and his female; two each of animals that are unclean, a male and his female;** [3] **"also seven each of birds of the air, male and female, to keep the species alive on the face of all the earth.** [4] **"For after seven more days I will cause it to rain on the earth forty days and forty nights, and I will destroy from the face of the earth all living things that I have made."** [5] **And Noah did according to all that the LORD commanded him.** [6] **Noah was six hundred years old when the floodwaters were on the earth.** [7] **So Noah, with his sons, his wife, and his sons' wives, went into the ark because of the waters of the flood.** [8] **Of clean animals, of animals that are unclean, of birds, and of everything that creeps on the earth,** [9] **two by two they went into the ark to Noah, male and female, as God had commanded Noah.** [10] **And it came to pass after seven days that the waters of the flood were on the earth.** [11] **In the six hundredth year of Noah's life, in the second month, the seventeenth day of the month, on that day all the fountains of the great deep were broken up, and the windows of heaven were opened.** [12] **And the rain was on the earth forty days and forty nights.**
Genesis 7:1-12 (NKJV)

Up until that time, there was no rain! Certainly, Noah needed more of an explanation when God told him it was going to rain for 40 days and 40 nights. "Rain? What is that?" Another verse in Genesis explains the way that God watered the plants without rain on the pre-Flood earth:

**[4] This is the history of the heavens and the earth when they were created, in the day that the LORD God made the earth and the heavens, [5] before any plant of the field was in the earth and before any herb of the field had grown. For the LORD God had not caused it to rain on the earth, and there was no man to till the ground; [6] but a mist went up from the earth and watered the whole face of the ground.
Genesis 2:4-6 (NKJV)**

Imagine the panic that people must have felt when the skies opened! Certainly, the people on that first, rainy day had no idea what was happening, or whether or not it ever would stop. In fact, it likely took time before they realized it was only water. Their worst fears were imagined, as God flooded the earth and destroyed His creation, apart from eight people and a representation of each animal.

We should look upon rain in a different light, especially as Christians. Imagine each raindrop as a tear from God. Imagine the sadness He felt to destroy His own creation! The book of Revelation tells us about God's coming judgment on a sinful earth. Though God promised that He never would destroy the earth by flood again, He will destroy the earth in another way, fire. Throughout Revelation, we read about His judgments, but what is most apparent is that even in the midst of judgment, God has grace! His goal is for all to believe, and knowing that what takes most of us to find Him is to be flat on our backs looking up, He often puts us exactly in that position. When we are willing to ask for the Lord's forgiveness, He washes us white as snow.

His grace falls like rain and washes us clean. We are washed daily in His Word. Each one of those raindrops represents the pain we placed on the heart of God with our sinful lives. After the rainstorm, make a fresh start with Him by confessing sins and asking for His forgiveness. God mercifully rains on land no one sees, and mercifully, grants us forgiveness even though we do not deserve it! There is no fresher smell than right after a storm and anyone can have that same, fresh start!

[25] "**Who has divided a channel for the overflowing** *water,*
Or a path for the thunderbolt,
[26] **To cause it to rain on a land** *where there is* **no one,**
A wilderness in which *there is* **no man;**
[27] **To satisfy the desolate waste,**
And cause to spring forth the growth of tender grass?
Job 38:25-27 (NKJV)

January 25: God will stretch His children!

During basic training in the military, one of the team-building exercises is the confidence course. On the course are a series of obstacles designed to stretch the limits of each soldier, both individually and collectively. One of those obstacles is a balance beam, 50 feet in the air, with only a sawdust pit for protection. Another is a tower without walls. To ascend, the soldier must pull his feet above his head in a backward somersault, each level until reaching the top. Descending involves even more courage, peering many feet down while somersaulting forward, gripping the floor of the structure, one floor at a time. Other soldiers assist team members to ensure safety, but reliance upon self and others extends the limits of each participant.

The point of this exercise is to remind each soldier in no uncertain terms that the limits we place upon ourselves are arbitrary. By visualizing a loss of life or limb, most of those limits are fear-based. Upon completing the course, each soldier begins to set new goals, based on confidence rather than fear. Even with fellow soldiers joining in the process, there are some exercises that not every soldier accomplishes, yet part of the lesson is in the attempt. Even after falling, by wiping off the sawdust, placing a band-aid on the scrape and "getting back on the horse," the soldier receives encouragement to try again.

Often in our lives, we feel that the situations facing us are hopeless. Physical vision may reveal exactly that. Yet God has reminded us to walk by faith, not by sight. He also has given us many promises, and as God is incapable of breaking even one of those promises, we can take those to the bank. His Word is His word! Here is one that we should focus on when facing adversity:

[12] Therefore let him who thinks he stands take heed lest he fall. [13] No temptation has overtaken you except such as is common to man; but God is faithful, who will not allow you to be tempted beyond what you are able, but with the temptation will also make the way of escape, that you may be able to bear it.
1 Corinthians 10:12-13 (NKJV)

God does not put us into situations to make us fail, though we often fail. He puts us into situations where we can learn to rely on His power, rather than our own power. Alone, we continuously will fail, but with God, all things are possible! He never will give us more than we can handle. If faced with a great difficulty, take it as a compliment. God only places us in great difficulties when He has given us great spiritual strength to rely upon Him! It might appear to be scary or difficult, but when we walk through the valley of the shadow of death, He is with us!

His desire is to stretch us and to mold us as a potter molds clay, so that He can use us for His purposes. Are we willing? Our willingness really has no effect upon God, who will stretch us regardless. For as a runner stretches his muscles before a race, God desires for our spiritual muscles to be loosened up and ready to work properly. Willingness and obedience are two wonderful attributes in a Christian's relationship with the Lord, for both reveal a strong desire to serve Him. Have confidence in

Him, for that stretching is spiritual conditioning, rather than stretching us to the point of failure.

[29] For whom He foreknew, He also predestined *to be* conformed to the image of His Son, that He might be the firstborn among many brethren. [30] Moreover whom He predestined, these He also called; whom He called, these He also justified; and whom He justified, these He also glorified. Romans 8:29-30 (NKJV)

[1] Now concerning the ministering to the saints, it is superfluous for me to write to you; [2] for I know your willingness, about which I boast of you to the Macedonians, that Achaia was ready a year ago; and your zeal has stirred up the majority.
2 Corinthians 9:1-2 (NKJV)

January 26: Need a drink?

When thirsty, we have so many beverages to choose from. Athletes seem to rely on electrolyte replacement drinks, like Gatorade. Invented by scientists at the University of Florida in 1965, Gatorade is available in a wide variety of flavors. Many choose sugared beverages, like soft drinks or lemonade. But when we are really thirsty, nothing satisfies that yearning like water. With two-thirds of the human body consisting of water, when that balance in hydration becomes unstable, lethargy takes over.

When the Jews wandered in the wilderness for 40 years, one of their greatest needs was water. Tiring of their complaints, Moses miraculously supplied those needs through God's hand by striking a rock, as water flowed freely for the Jews to drink. Moses answered their cries in a similar manner another time, though God had instructed Moses to speak to the rock the second time, rather than strike it. Regardless of his disobedience, the water again flowed freely. The Lord punished that disobedience by disallowing Moses entrance into the Promised Land.

Behold, I will stand before you there on the rock in Horeb; and you shall strike the rock, and water will come out of it, that the people may drink."
Exodus 17:6 (NKJV)

Visiting the Holy Land today reminds us of that same need for water in the stark, desert topography, particularly in the south. A week in Israel has been described as the equivalent of a year in Bible college, as seeing where Jesus walked blesses visual learners by making the Bible a picture book, with images that never will fade. One of the stops on most Holy Land tours is an aqueduct, located on the outskirts of Caesarea, on the Mediterranean Sea. Though not biblical in nature, the ancient structure used for water transportation offers much spiritual significance.

In eight miles, the aqueduct lowered only by inches, to enable water's constant flow. Romans understood the necessity of fresh water and its relationship to survival. Though we can do without food for six weeks and still survive, going without water for even one day decreases proper body functions through dehydration. But all water is not the same. Just a few feet from the aqueduct is the Mediterranean Sea, and its far-reaching, salty waters could not supply any of our needs for thirst.

Jesus is our Living Water. He can supply every need, if we only let Him. That involves faith, trusting that He will take care of us. By turning to the world to supply those needs, it is like drinking from the salty sea, instead of from the Fountain of Life. Though both fresh and salt water might look the same to our eyes, that is only appearance. Drinking salt water would leave us thirstier, and eventually, would destroy us! By avoiding the false sustenance that Satan has to offer and drinking from God's well, we never will thirst again! As Moses learned, we should not be results-oriented. God still honored the disobedience of Moses by allowing the Jews to receive water to abate their thirst, yet that disobedience greatly affected the life of Moses. Obey God, and He will supply every need by giving Living Water to His children.

[13] Jesus answered and said to her, "Whoever drinks of this water will thirst again, [14] "but whoever drinks of the water that I shall give him will never thirst. But the water that I shall give him will become in him a fountain of water springing up into everlasting life."
John 4:13-14 (NKJV)

January 27: Whose battle is it?

God's creation is so amazingly different. We can go from the cool, moist breeze and warm, fine sand of an ocean; to the dry, oven-like air of the desert; to the crisp, clean pine smell of the mountains. In California, all of those topographies are within reach in the same day. God's diversity in creation demonstrates His artistry, and amazingly, each of those places tugs at our hearts differently. Because God created unique personalities, some desire the ocean, while others are more content in the desert. Others desire that mountaintop experience.

Certainly, part of the desire to be in mountains is the solitude, as with each step becoming increasingly difficult, there just are not many people willing to do the work to get to the summit. There are no hot dog stands along the path, either. In fact, a mountaintop is one of the few places where we can see what God made, instead of what man made. Storms in the mountains have their own personality, too. Lightning and thunder seem to be only feet away, and the raindrops do not have far to fall. It seems like the height of the mountains holds the clouds back and the storms just hover there.

All that being said, mountain views are breathtaking, seemingly changing with each step. Depending on the difficulty of the hike or climb, hikers do not always take the time to turn around. That is part of the human condition as rarely do each of us take the time to reflect on accomplishments in our lives. But on a mountain, each step is another accomplishment. Sometimes, we get lost in our pursuits of the summit, or another lofty goal, and forget to pursue the enjoyment of each step of the journey. But when lungs start to ache, and rest must occur, a simple about-face reveals the previously-taken path, including length of journey. All those items in the past seem so small when looked at from above, as perspective changes drastically with a bird's eye view!

This journey called life is a lot like that. Think of David in the Valley of Elah, approaching the 9'9" Goliath without fear, for he knew that it was not his battle, but the Lord's. Battles are fought in valleys, the low places of our lives. When faced with an enemy, and that enemy is upon us, everything seems so big. But when the battle is over, we return home to the mountains. Looking down upon the valley, what seemed so large, now appears to be very small and inconsequential.

**[44] And the Philistine said to David, "Come to me, and I will give your flesh to the birds of the air and the beasts of the field!" [45] Then David said to the Philistine, "You come to me with a sword, with a spear, and with a javelin. But I come to you in the name of the LORD of hosts, the God of the armies of Israel, whom you have defied. [46] "This day the LORD will deliver you into my hand, and I will strike you and take your head from you. And this day I will give the carcasses of the camp of the Philistines to the birds of the air and the wild beasts of the earth, that all the earth may know that there is a God in Israel. [47] "Then all this assembly shall know that the LORD does not save with sword and spear; for the battle is the LORD's, and He will give you into our hands."
1 Samuel 17:44-47 (NKJV)**

If we are the Lord's, then our battles are His. David picked up five, smooth stones for his sling. With the first one, he killed Goliath. The small size of the stones revealed the power of God, rather than the power of man. David did not pick up five stones because he planned to miss, but because David knew the giant had four brothers, and likely, he would be a target of their vengeance. God has promised that He never will leave us or forsake us. Anything in our paths, He has allowed to be there. If our enemies or trials are large, we should not forget that our God is larger still! After the battle, get out of the valley and climb the mountain. With each step, we can see where we came from. Notice that we cannot see where we are going, but we know that it is going to be beautiful when we get there. It is okay to look back on the past, but do not dwell on it. That perspective often brings a memory of God's hand in getting us through the difficulties, even to the point that sometimes, it is hard to believe we ever were on the valley floor!

A man owned a sweet dog, never allowed into the house. That dog would sit outside and sniff at the door, waiting for his master to open it. More than anything, the dog wanted to go inside. It had nothing to do with what was there, but it had everything to do with who was there. Heaven is the same for us! We do not know what it will be like when we get there, but we know Who will be there! We cannot see the mountaintop, but we know the view will be great and that it will have been well worth the journey when we arrive…and when we dwell in the house of the Lord forever!

Surely goodness and mercy shall follow me
All the days of my life;
And I will dwell in the house of the LORD
Forever.
Psalm 23:6 (NKJV)

Then all this assembly shall know that the LORD does not save with sword and spear; for the battle *is* the LORD's, and He will give you into our hands."
1 Samuel 17:47 (NKJV)

January 28: God, where are You?

Reflections in lakes that are surrounded by wildlife, trees and other vegetation are simply majestic. Sometimes, the colors in the water are even more vibrant than the ones being reflected. Yet when the wind ripples the water, that reflection disappears. It has nothing to do with the depth of the water, as only the surface is affected by the wind. An old adage says, "Still waters run deep," describing that there is much more beneath the surface of a quiet exterior. Some people quietly and introspectively go through life, while pretentious people point to themselves in every action, desiring the attention of others in order to make themselves feel important. That behavior points to pride, and according to the Bible,

[18] **Pride goes before destruction,**
And a haughty spirit before a fall.
[19] **Better to be of a humble spirit with the lowly,**
Than to divide the spoil with the proud.
Proverbs 16:18-19 (NKJV)

Pride was the reason for the fall of Satan, and is certainly the downfall of every man. In Greek mythology, Narcissus fell in love with a reflection in a pool, not knowing that it was his own image. Unable to walk away from that beauty, he perished there. Instead of trying to see our own faces in the reflection, we should look for the face of God, our Creator, who cannot take His eyes away from His children!

[1] **The LORD is my shepherd;**
I shall not want.
[2] **He makes me to lie down in green pastures;**
He leads me beside the still waters.
Psalms 23:1-2 (NKJV)

Those still waters are places of sustenance and peace. When hot and tired, there is nothing that tastes better than a cool drink of water. When Elijah ran from Jezebel and found himself exhausted and depleted far from home in a cave, the Lord came to him, nourished him and restored him. What water could be as satisfying as Living Water? All around Elijah was tumult: an earthquake, fire and a powerful wind.

[11] **Then He said, "Go out, and stand on the mountain before the LORD. 'And behold, the LORD passed by, and a great and strong wind tore into the mountains and broke the rocks in pieces before the LORD, but the LORD was not in the**

wind; and after the wind an earthquake, but the LORD was not in the earthquake; [12] and after the earthquake a fire, but the LORD was not in the fire; and after the fire a still small voice.
1 Kings 19:11-12 (NKJV)

When the tumult subsided, Elijah heard the still, small voice. It is in those times beside the still waters that we see the Lord, feel His presence and hear His voice. That is difficult to do in our bustling world, where we struggle to exist without a television blaring, an iPod playing or a computer eating the hours away. If we want to hear God's voice, we should read His Word. Listening to Earth, Wind and Fire cannot compare to the voice of the Lord. Do not forget what He said,

Be still, and know that I am God;
Psalms 46:10 (NKJV)

Sometimes, it takes that stillness to see His reflection, and know He never has left our sides. Even with the ripples, He was there, whether or not we could see Him!

[16] **that the waters which came down from upstream stood** *still, and* **rose in a heap very far away at Adam, the city that** *is* **beside Zaretan. So the waters that went down into the Sea of the Arabah, the Salt Sea, failed,** *and* **were cut off; and the people crossed over opposite Jericho.** [17] **Then the priests who bore the ark of the covenant of the LORD stood firm on dry ground in the midst of the Jordan; and all Israel crossed over on dry ground, until all the people had crossed completely over the Jordan.**
Joshua 3:16-17 (NKJV)

January 29: Do you hear His voice?

A sweet and godly woman in her 80's lived in a nursing home. One night while in bed, she felt a strong prodding from the Lord to go across the hall and speak with another woman, who had moved into the facility that day. Because it was late, the sweet woman told the Lord she would visit in the morning, but again, she felt Him urging her to go at that moment. The prodding continued several more times until she put on her robe and ventured across the hall. Even at the late hour, the new resident was awake, and the two women sat and talked. Of course, the discussion quickly turned to the subject of Jesus Christ, and after a while, the new resident invited Jesus into her heart as Lord and Savior. The joyful and dutiful woman returned to her own room for a restful sleep and slept later than normal, having been up most of the night. She awoke to much activity and asked what was going on. "The woman across the hall, who only moved in yesterday, passed away last night, poor dear," said the attendant.

God speaks to us all in different ways. Some people are much more sensitive to the still, small voice within. Additionally, some people feel God speaking the loudest when they are reading the Bible. Others seem to be more aware of their dreams. Some need God to repeat what He is saying numerous times. Often, a particular verse will keep popping up. However we hear the Lord, if we are His, we hear His voice:

[25] Jesus answered them, "I told you, and you do not believe. The works that I do in My Father's name, they bear witness of Me. [26] "But you do not believe, because you are not of My sheep, as I said to you. [27] "My sheep hear My voice, and I know them, and they follow Me. [28] "And I give them eternal life, and they shall never perish; neither shall anyone snatch them out of My hand.
John 10:25-28 (NKJV)

One of the greatest gifts to Christians is prayer, and we all should pray for unsaved friends and family. Yet God does not always give us insight into the miracles He performs in the stillness of the night, without sight or sound. Some may not know that God answered their prayers until arriving in heaven and seeing those they prayed for. Intercessory prayers are the sweetest, devoid of selfish motives.

Both Paul and Moses were willing to give up their own salvation if God would not save their people! Do we have that same heart for evangelism? All of us have those special people in our lives that we would love to bring to the Lord, as we know the joy and peace it would add to their lives, and we want to share eternity with them. Sometimes, God will use us in those lives. Yet sometimes, He will not.

Now it came to pass, when Jesus finished commanding His twelve disciples, that He departed from there to teach and to preach in their cities.
Matthew 11:1 (NKJV)

Jesus commanded His disciples to go out and spread the gospel. While they were busy in the Lord's work, He was teaching and preaching to their families and friends! Sometimes, we lose sight of the master plan of our omnipotent God. He is so much bigger than we imagine. He loves us, and knows the hearts that He gave us. If those hearts are grieving for our lost family and friends, He will go to them. What makes us think that He has to use us?

[53] Now it came to pass, when Jesus had finished these parables, that He departed from there. [54] And when He had come to His own country, He taught them in their synagogue, so that they were astonished and said, "Where did this Man get this wisdom and these mighty works? [55] "Is this not the carpenter's son? Is not His mother called Mary? And His brothers James, Joses, Simon, and Judas? [56] "And His sisters, are they not all with us? Where then did this Man get all these things?" [57] So they were offended at Him. But Jesus said to them, "A prophet is not without honor except in his own country and in his own house." [58] Now He did not do many mighty works there because of their unbelief.
Matthew 13:53-58 (NKJV)

Did the people who knew Jesus as a boy see God in Him? It is difficult for the people from our past to see anything more in us than the person they used to know. That speaks more of the blindness of the world than the lack of transformation in our lives. Yet we can pray for them! When the Lord puts it on our hearts to share His love with our unsaved friends and family, we need to be obedient. But if we feel closed doors, it is time for knee mail! Spend time in prayer for them, and stay busy in what He has called. Leave it to Him. He never lets us down!

January 30: His sheep hear His voice!

A frequent statement in Christian conversations is, "The Lord told me to do this." While there certainly are people throughout the Bible and throughout history who heard God's voice audibly, most of us are not in that small group. Though it might seem like an easier way to hear from God verbally, that certainly would depend upon the situation. It also might scare us to death. In Job 38-40, we see God questioning Job, and it does not seem to be pleasant for Job in any way! Certainly, Job would prefer to hide, but we all know that we cannot hide from God. God speaks to Christians in a variety of ways, through His Word, through others and even through dreams and visions.

[28] "And it shall come to pass afterward
That I will pour out My Spirit on all flesh;
Your sons and your daughters shall prophesy,
Your old men shall dream dreams,
Your young men shall see visions.
[29] And also on My menservants and on My maidservants
I will pour out My Spirit in those days.
Joel 2:28-29 (NKJV)

With most people desiring youth, if God speaks through dreams (images in the sleeping hours) instead of through visions (images during the day), that person has transcended from young to old! Most of the time, God speaks through His Word. Upon reading a verse, Christians will feel their minds racing toward how that verse needs to be applied to the current situation. It also is amazing how we can open the Bible and the one verse that catches our eyes will be a perfect answer to the situation we have been praying about. That is one verse of the 54,387 that are in the Bible, with a direct application to the present! God uses people, places, and a variety of other sources to speak to us. How many times have we been in church when the pastor seemed to be speaking directly to us? Sometimes, the pastor's description of a scenario is so picturesque that it seems too personal to match another's life. Does the pastor know that his words are falling on needing ears? Probably not, but that is often how God works.

When the same verse keeps popping up, it surely is time to study that verse and find out more about its meaning in context. That is a key to studying the Bible, for taking verses out of context rarely reveals the true meaning. Upon understanding the verse in context, the next step is to apply that verse personally to our lives. If the verse continues to pop up, it is possible that we are applying it erroneously. Sometimes, we have a tendency of applying the verse with our brains rather than applying it with our hearts. God continues to remind us until we heed His words. Jesus told His disciples that reminding us is exactly what the Holy Spirit will do:

[25] "These things I have spoken to you while being present with you. [26] "But the Helper, the Holy Spirit, whom the Father will send in My name, He will teach you all things, and bring to your remembrance all things that I said to you. John 14:25-26 (NKJV)

We cannot remember something that we never have experienced. A memory involves fishing something out of the past, rather than experiencing something anew. In order to remember a lesson, or even a verse, we need to have experienced it first. In the case of a verse, the key is to read the Bible!

Often, people claim to feel a strong prodding from God, yet differentiating between God and our own wicked hearts is another matter entirely. Balance that prodding against the Word of God. If it conflicts what God says in His Word, it is not His voice! Additionally, the more difficult task for us is to balance that prodding against our own hearts. Often, we feel that God wants us to do something because we want it very badly. For example, what if God said to go out and buy a Lamborghini? Does that sound like the kind of thing that God would tell us to do in His Word? He does tell us that we should be of one Accord but He is not referring to a Japanese automobile! There certainly are ways to spend that money more wisely than to buy a $280,000 car. Yet, there could be situations that God has told someone to do exactly that. What if He wanted the buyer to speak about Him to the salesman? The more common answer here, though, is that this person is probably hearing the voice of their own heart, rather than the voice of God. The Lord tells us about our own hearts:

^{9} **"The heart is deceitful above all things,
And desperately wicked;
Who can know it?
^{10} I, the LORD, search the heart,
I test the mind,
Even to give every man according to his ways,
According to the fruit of his doings.
Jeremiah 17:9-10 (NKJV)**

Lesson number one in hearing God is to find a quiet place and read His Word. If we want to hear God's voice, read His Word out loud! He loves us and desires a close relationship with us. How can we have a close relationship without communication? Prayer is an awesome gift, as it enables us to speak to the Creator of the universe any time we want. Yet what is more important, us speaking to God or God speaking to us? He has many more important words for us! Listen!

**"Listen to Me, My people;
And give ear to Me, O My nation:
For law will proceed from Me,
And I will make My justice rest
As a light of the peoples.
Isaiah 51:4 (NKJV)**

"Listen to this, O Job;
Stand still and consider
the wondrous works
of God."
Job 37:14 (NKJV)

January 31: Twelve

Just as God breathed the world into existence during creation, He also breathed the Bible into existence.

[16] All Scripture *is* given by inspiration of God, and *is* profitable for doctrine, for reproof, for correction, for instruction in righteousness, [17] that the man of God may be complete, thoroughly equipped for every good work.
2 Timothy 3:16-17 (NKJV)

The Greek word for "inspiration" is *theopneustos*, a combination of the root words for God (*theo*) and breathe (*pneo*). If each word was specifically chosen by God, then each word carries weight and significance. Some people are mathematically-minded, while others seem to see numbers and begin a brain freeze. Yet the numbers in the Bible carry power. Simply looking at individual numbers can give us great insight into their meaning. Never forget, it was not man who invented math, but God, the great mathematician!

Twelve is an interesting number in the Bible, which we also can see in many aspects of our lives. There are 12 months in a year (Daniel 4:29). Additionally, historians give us an accurate representation of the Hebrew calendar consisting of 12 months of 30 days, which is based upon the lunar cycle. Also, God mentions many of those months in the Old Testament.

In Genesis, God gives us one of the most significant 12's in the Bible with the number of Jacob's sons. Reuben, Simeon, Levi, Judah, Issachar, Zebulun, Dan, Joseph, Benjamin, Naphtali, Gad and Asher each became the leader of a tribe of Israel. Occasionally in biblical lists of the tribes, one or more fall into disfavor, being replaced by the sons of Joseph (Manasseh and Ephraim), but there always are 12 tribes. With that representation comes many other aspects. For instance, there are 12 spies who enter the Promised Land, one from each tribe. When the children of Israel officially enter that land, they are instructed to each place a memorial stone at the Jordan River. Consequently, there are 12 stones. There also are 12 precious stones on the ephod of the high priest. Those tribes remain in the future, as a remnant of Jews preaches to the world under judgment. That remnant includes 12,000 in each tribe for a total of 144,000. On the other side of the coin, Ishmael also had 12 sons, which down the road, became the Arab nation that continues to attempt to eradicate the Jews from the earth.

Interestingly, 12 men are specifically mentioned as anointed by God. They are Aaron (Exodus 29:7), Nadab (Exodus 29:7), Abihu (Exodus 29:7), Eleazar (Exodus 29:7), Ithamar (Exodus 29:7), Saul (1 Samuel 10:1), David (1 Samuel 16:13), Absalom (2 Samuel 19:10), Solomon (1 Kings 1:39), Jehu (2 Kings 9:6), Joash (2 Kings 11:12) and Jehoahaz (2 Kings 23:30). Even their places in order are significant, with Saul in the sixth spot and David in the seventh. Six is the number of man and seven the number of completeness.

Jesus chose 12 apostles, and after Judas killed himself, the others cast lots to replace him with Matthias, rather than just existing with 11. In Revelation, we see that the New Jerusalem will have many 12's:

[14] Now the wall of the city had <u>twelve foundations</u>, and on them were the <u>names of the twelve apostles</u> of the Lamb. [15] And he who talked with me had a gold reed to measure the city, its gates, and its wall. [16] The city is laid out as a square; its length is as great as its breadth. And he measured the city with the reed: <u>twelve thousand furlongs</u>. Its length, breadth, and height are equal. [17] Then he measured its wall: one hundred *and* forty-four cubits, *according* to the measure of a man, that is, of an angel. [18] The construction of its wall was *of* jasper; and the city *was* pure gold, like clear glass. [19] The

foundations of the wall of the city *were* adorned with all kinds of precious stones: the first foundation *was* jasper, the second sapphire, the third chalcedony, the fourth emerald, [20] the fifth sardonyx, the sixth sardius, the seventh chrysolite, the eighth beryl, the ninth topaz, the tenth chrysoprase, the eleventh jacinth, and the twelfth amethyst. [21] The <u>twelve gates</u> *were* <u>twelve pearls</u>: each individual gate was of one pearl. And the street of the city *was* pure gold, like transparent glass.
Revelation 21:14-21 (NKJV)

Even the foundations of the wall have 12 different precious stones! Jesus first spoke publicly when He was 12, and a Jewish boy becomes a man after completing 12 years! So what is the significance of 12? It is a perfect number pointing to governmental rule. Though we might be more familiar with purchasing a dozen eggs or a dozen doughnuts, God's representation of this number has to do with rulers. Though there are 12 inches on a ruler, that is not the kind of ruler to understand here. When reading the Bible, understand that every word is meaningful, pointing to the power of an omnipotent and omniscient God! He does not do anything haphazardly or accidentally. When reading His Word, go deeper! There is much more below the surface, like an iceberg!

[6] **For unto us a Child is born,**
Unto us a Son is given;
And the government will be upon His shoulder.
And His name will be called
Wonderful, Counselor, Mighty God,
Everlasting Father, Prince of Peace.
[7] **Of the increase of** *His* **government and peace**
There will be **no end,**
Upon the throne of David and over His kingdom,
To order it and establish it with judgment and justice
From that time forward, even forever.
The zeal of the Lord of hosts will perform this.
Isaiah 9:6-7 (NKJV)

February 1: Perfect plan for imperfect people!

Why did God create us with free will? Since He is perfect, why would He create a people who cannot be perfect? Often, it feels like the best we can accomplish still will disappoint God, breaking His heart each time we sin.

Certainly, God did not desire robots. He could have created us to do anything He wanted, but God was not lonely, in need of elaborate toys. He created us in order to share His enormous love with us. As little as we know about love, we do understand that it is only a gift when freely given. Think of a violent dictator, who only will accept complete obedience and adoration from his people, with the threat of death for any act of disobedience. His subjects do not worship the dictator in love, but in fear. The perceived love that the dictator might feel is not a gift, but a requirement. God does not desire that, or expect it. He wants us to love Him for what He did for us.

[18] There is no fear in love; but perfect love casts out fear, because fear involves torment. But he who fears has not been made perfect in love. [19] We love Him because He first loved us.
1 John 4:18-19 (NKJV)

God's Word reminds us to fear the Lord, but fear in that context speaks of the awe and reverence we should have for Him, rather than us quaking in our boots! He knows that we are not perfect. Though we are not perfect, God's love can perfect us! It will not occur on this earth, but if we receive the gift He has given us, the gift of His Son, He will complete us. He will make us whole. He will make us holy!

One of the biggest hurdles we have to cross when we ruminate on these deep subjects is that God is not a bigger and better one of us. Many people erroneously refer to Him as the Man Upstairs. Though He created us in His image, we are not able to grasp the concept of His perfection and how strongly it contrasts with our imperfection. It is as difficult as picturing the difference between a very large number and infinity. God is limitless, never was born and never will die, ALL powerful, ALL knowing, ALL loving...

²² And He put all *things* under His feet, and gave Him *to be* head over all *things* to the church, ²³ which is His body, the fullness of Him who fills all in all.
Ephesians 1:22-23 (NKJV)

He is everything, and fills everything. He is our all in all! Nothing we can do will surprise God, or break His heart. For as Christians, when He looks at us, God does not see His creation that continues to fail. Instead, He sees the end result, the completed work He will accomplish in us!

being confident of this very thing, that He who has begun a good work in you will complete *it* until the day of Jesus Christ;
Philippians 1:6 (NKJV)

When we are struggling with sin, we need to know that sin separates us from God, but that sin did not surprise our Lord. He has a plan that will bring us closer to Him, and that plan is forgiveness!

February 2: Freedom in forgiveness

As Christians, we often notice the multitude of people not following God, who appear to be extremely prosperous. Similarly, we also notice the number of Christians who appear to be heavily burdened. King David surely felt this way. Many of the Psalms written by David, described as "a man after God's own heart," concerned this subject.

¹Do not fret because of evildoers,
Nor be envious of the workers of iniquity.
²For they shall soon be cut down like the grass,
And wither as the green herb.

Psalm 37:1-2 (NKJV)

Sin would not be such a strong draw to us if there was not pleasure involved, yet a deeper understanding of its attraction reveals that we are slaves to sin.

When Adam sinned, man's nature became one of sin, and as all of us are Adam's ancestors, we have become the sons of disobedience. That sin nature is apparent when watching the behavior of a small child. Do they feel a strong desire to always tell the truth? Quite the contrary! That is sin nature and it remains with every man, until a special event occurs. That event is the acceptance of Jesus as Lord and Savior. When that occurs, the chains are gone, instantly! Chris Tomlin wrote a chorus to an updated version of John Newton's hymn "Amazing Grace," that says, "My chains are gone. I've been set free. My God, my Savior, has ransomed me. And like a flood, His mercy reigns, unending love, amazing grace!"

[17] But God be thanked that *though* you were slaves of sin, yet you obeyed from the heart that form of doctrine to which you were delivered. [18] And having been set free from sin, you became slaves of righteousness.
Romans 6:17-18 (NKJV)

One of the stumbling blocks many have as believers is the difficulty in differentiating between earthly prosperity and heavenly prosperity. God's promises remind us that He will take care of our needs, but that differs greatly from our desires, until those desires become to walk in God's will. He will feed us, clothe us and fill us with His presence. What more could we ask? Yet when faced with our neighbor's beautiful house and car, and photos of their expensive vacation, it is easy to question why we do not have those benefits when following the Lord. We wonder why God is blessing our neighbor, who does not believe God exists!

A better question would be who would be willing to trade places with that neighbor for eternity? Would we rather have his earthly gains and his eternal damnation than our earthly provision and heavenly home? Even that action is sin, as God instructs us not to covet in His 10th Commandment. Be content in everything, for He is incapable of giving bad gifts. He already gave us the greatest gift in His Son, who received the death we earned when He carried our sins on Calvary! The ball and chain have been removed and we now can walk in freedom of that heavy burden!

February 3: Grace, the greatest gift

Once we understand our spiritual condition, that without God we are nothing, then we can appreciate the need for a Savior. We often lose sight of the abject poverty of our souls without Jesus, by taking credit in some way for our salvation. Why did God choose us? Did it have anything to do with the gifts He gave us, how He wanted us to use those gifts, or the people we would be able to share the Gospel with? No, as He does not need us. He chose us! Just as easily, He could have used anyone else to accomplish what He chose for us to accomplish. He chose us for His pleasure and His purpose! Why would He choose a wretched sinner? Because that speaks of His nature, rather than ours. We have trouble understanding that kind of love, for we do not see it anywhere else. What is the greatest love?

Greater love has no one than this, than to lay down one's life for his friends.
John 15:13 (NKJV)

Jesus did more than just lay down His life. The Bible reminds us that He loved us that much while we were still sinners. When a woman falls in love with a prisoner, in jail for a violent crime, what could she possibly see in Him? Potential? Jesus does not see potential in us, what He might accomplish in us; He sees the work that He will complete in us.

What can wash away our sins? Nothing but the blood of Jesus! In the Garden of Eden when Adam sinned, God killed an innocent animal and clothed the naked couple. He "covered their sin" by the spilling of innocent blood. That is exactly what happened with the Old Testament sacrificial system, as God gave the Jews a remedy for sin in His Law. Once again, by the spilling of innocent blood, there was forgiveness.

And according to the law almost all things are purified with blood, and without shedding of blood there is no remission. Hebrews 9:22 (NKJV)

When Jesus endured the cross, and suffered death, the ultimate sacrifice occurred. Jesus was the only one who could live on this earth and be sin-free. Thus, He was the only one who could be innocent in the eyes of His Father.

His death did not occur for the just, but the unjust. In Romans, Paul reminds us that there is not one righteous man. We often forget that each talent and ability that we have is but a gift of God. Through His gifts, He enables us to touch others. But that need for grace is the most telling reminder, for we never should lose sight of the fact that we are far away from God without it. Grace has been described as getting what we do not deserve, unmerited favor, or with the acronym "God's Riches At Christ's Expense." Yet it is more than that. Grace is the greatest gift given to the most unworthy recipients. We could spend the rest of eternity in contemplation and thankfulness for His gift of grace. All of our hope, faith and love hinge on what He accomplished on our behalves.

Though Jesus loved the whole world and came to save everyone, His gift is not received by all. We have to open the gift! How we do that is to receive Him as our Lord and Savior, acknowledging what He did for us on the cross and acknowledging that He is God. Additionally, we need to confess our sins.

⁸ If we say that we have no sin, we deceive ourselves, and the truth is not in us. ⁹ If we confess our sins, He is faithful and just to forgive us our sins and to cleanse us from all unrighteousness.
1 John 1:8-9 (NKJV)

To receive the greatest gift, we must make the smallest sacrifice. We must humble ourselves to acknowledge our sins to Him, for without that acceptance, we cannot know His love! One of the hurdles in that process is the acknowledgment of our worthlessness without God. Before the foundations of the world, He chose His children, to demonstrate His love and grace for us. None of us deserve His love, as we never could do enough to earn the greatest gift. Try to walk today in focus of His gift. To God be the glory!

For I say, through the grace given to me, to everyone who is among you, not to think *of himself* more highly than he ought to think, but to think soberly, as God has dealt to each one a measure of faith.
Romans 12:3 (NKJV)

February 4: We have the Holy Spirit, but does He have us?

In human relationships, there often are times when one person falls in love, yet the other is in the relationship for different reasons. For example, without love or attraction, one person may remain for financial stability. Additionally, relationships are dynamic, enduring periods of great change, even in regard to love. Some find that love grows as they remain together, enduring obstacles arm-in-arm, while others see their love wither and die in the midst of hardship, or after time.

God's love for His children is the tie that binds. His love for us never increases, for He loves us completely from the onset. Nor does His love for us wane. Our love for Him is what is in question.

When God has set us free from the bondage of sin, why do we continue to sin? Our sin nature remains, but we have a different calling. That calling is to serve a risen Savior. In that moment that we become His, He gives us a new heart and gives the awareness of sin in our lives. That does not mean that all the sinful habits disappear instantaneously. In our walks with the Lord, He continues to change behaviors as we draw nearer to Him. Additionally, He reveals sin we were not even aware of!

John the Baptist put it very eloquently when he said, **"He must increase, but I *must* decrease."** While he was speaking of the difference between his own ministry and that of Jesus, the verse in John 3 also speaks of the presence of the Lord in each of our lives. Each day, we should be dying to self, which means that parts of our old natures will pass away as they are replaced with the nature of Jesus. The longer we walk with Him, the more we should reflect who He is, much in the same way that Jesus reflected the image of the Father!

If we are forgiven, why should we worry about sin? Some professing to be Christians seem to wallow in the same sins they committed before, as if they have a license to sin.

[15] What then? Shall we sin because we are not under law but under grace? Certainly not! [16] Do you not know that to whom you present yourselves slaves to obey, you are that one's slaves whom you obey, whether of sin *leading* to death, or of obedience *leading* to righteousness?
Romans 6:15-16 (NKJV)

Rather than allowing the Holy Spirit to change them, instead, they wrongly believe that their sins cannot be conquered. That is a weak excuse when God tells us in His Word:

I can do all things through Christ who strengthens me.
Philippians 4:13 (NKJV)

Just because we have the Holy Spirit does not mean that the Holy Spirit has us! If we love Him, we should desire to please

Him. That comes from obedience to God's laws, in addition to repentance when we fail to reach His mark of perfection. After the bonds are gone, if we sin, it is by choice. Yet if all a sinner knows is sin, how can he choose anything else? The sinner has only one choice, but as Christians, we have the ability to choose either.

[12] **If we endure,**
We shall also reign with *Him*.
If we deny *Him*,
He also will deny us.
[13] **If we are faithless,**
He remains faithful;
He cannot deny Himself.
1 Timothy 2:12-13 (NKJV)

It is about His faithfulness, not ours. If we are His, He promises to get us back on His path. It is hard to fathom how the Creator of all cares so deeply for each of us, but He does. Think of the degree He went to in order to demonstrate that. Jesus departed heaven, became a man, came to earth and died a brutal death at the hands of those He came to save. And still, He loves us. He will retain the scars of this world for all of eternity. In fact, someone said those scars will be the only man-made things in heaven. Someday, we will see those nail-scarred hands!

"And I will pour on the house of David and on the inhabitants of Jerusalem the Spirit of grace and supplication; then they will look on Me whom they pierced. Yes, they will mourn for Him as one mourns for *his* only *son*, and grieve for Him as one grieves for a firstborn.
Zechariah 12:10 (NKJV)

February 5: Who is in charge?

Starting in the 1920s and culminating with a larger focus on the last 15 years, archaeologists have uncovered much of the city of Beit She'an, Israel, where the bodies of King Saul and Jonathan were brought after dying in battle. Often, death comes at an unforeseen time as we tend to forget that life is but a vapor. It has nothing to do with wealth or power. With civilizations built upon civilizations, only God knows when one will end and another will begin. God told of five world empires before they occurred through Daniel. That was when powerful King Nebuchadnezzar became the best known "oxy-moron!" Filled with foolish pride from his power and wealth, Nebuchadnezzar grazed like an oxen for seven years, as God punished the king. Yet after seven years, Nebuchadnezzar was able to acknowledge the power of God and humbled himself. At that time, God restored him as king.

Sometimes, we lose sight of who is really in charge when a political candidate we support fails to win. There is no reason to fear, as God's plan will come to fruition.

[20] **Daniel answered and said:**
"Blessed be the name of God forever and ever,
For wisdom and might are His.
[21]**And He changes the times and the seasons;**
He removes kings and raises up kings;
He gives wisdom to the wise
And knowledge to those who have understanding.
Daniel 2:20-21 (NKJV)

God calls us to pray for our leaders. That might be easier when the candidate of our choice seems to be representing our beliefs and decisions.

[1]**Therefore I exhort first of all that supplications, prayers, intercessions,** *and* **giving of thanks be made for all men,** [2] **for kings and all who are in authority, that we may lead a quiet and peaceable life in all godliness and reverence.** [3] **For this** *is* **good and acceptable in the sight of God our Savior,** [4] **who desires all men to be saved and to come to the knowledge of the truth.**
1 Timothy 2:1-4 (NKJV)

It might not be the easiest task, but none of God's promises for this world seem to have anything to do with ease! Trust Him. He is in charge and He has a purpose and a plan. What seems to mankind to be chaotic and unsettling is nothing more than a blink of the eye to our God, who continues to work the events of the sinful earth into His master plan. Our Lord sits patiently, completing the intricately-woven jigsaw puzzle. Just because we cannot solve it does not make it unsolvable!

[1] Let every soul be subject to the governing authorities. For there is no authority except from God, and the authorities that exist are appointed by God. [2] Therefore whoever resists the authority resists the ordinance of God, and those who resist will bring judgment on themselves. [3] For rulers are not a terror to good works, but to evil. Do you want to be unafraid of the authority? Do what is good, and you will have praise from the same. [4] For he is God's minister to you for good. But if you do evil, be afraid; for he does not bear the sword in vain; for he is God's minister, an avenger to *execute* wrath on him who practices evil. [5] Therefore *you* must be subject, not only because of wrath but also for conscience' sake. [6] For because of this you also pay taxes, for they are God's ministers attending continually to this very thing. [7] Render therefore to all their due: taxes to whom taxes *are due,* customs to whom customs, fear to whom fear, honor to whom honor.
Romans 13:1-7 (NKJV)

February 6: Can we trust our walks?

If we notice a flat tire on the car, the first option is typically to put some air in the tire and see if it remains full. Rubbing water on the pumped tire might reveal air bubbles, showing us where the tire is leaking. Once isolating the leak, we can assess how serious of a problem exists. That process might reveal an embedded nail. Another option is to replace the flat tire with the spare, but if we choose to drive, we either will have to trust a potentially leaky tire or will be forced to drive without a back-up if the spare also should fail. A slow leak can sometimes be more problematic than a complete blowout, as by trusting an unworthy tire, serious consequences may arise. The expense of the car does not matter. Extras and accessories are not going to help a car make it down the road. Leather seats, GPS and Bluetooth, wireless telephone capabilities may ease the passage, but will not get us from one place to another. That is truly where the rubber meets the road.

In a spiritual sense, instead of tires, the Lord gives us those same sentiments in application to our walks. In biblical times, the majority of the population walked everywhere in their sandals. Roads were not asphalt, but dirt and dust. Feet were typically the dirtiest parts of their bodies. Interestingly, that was the body part on His disciples that Jesus chose to wash the night before He was crucified!

[2] And supper being ended, the devil having already put it into the heart of Judas Iscariot, Simon's *son,* to betray Him, [3] Jesus, knowing that the Father had given all things into His hands, and that He had come from God and was going to God, [4] rose from supper and laid aside His garments, took a towel and girded Himself. [5] After that, He poured water into a basin and began to wash the disciples' feet, and to wipe *them* with the towel with which He was girded. [6] Then He came to Simon Peter. And *Peter* said to Him, "Lord, are You washing my feet?"
[7] Jesus answered and said to him, "What I am doing you do not understand now, but you will know after this."
[8] Peter said to Him, "You shall never wash my feet!" Jesus answered him, "If I do not wash you, you have no part with Me."
[9] Simon Peter said to Him, "Lord, not my feet only, but also *my* hands and *my* head!" [10] Jesus said to him, "He who is bathed needs only to wash *his* feet, but is completely clean; and you are clean, but not all of you." [11] For He knew who would betray Him; therefore He said, "You are not all clean."
John 13:2-11 (NKJV)

Our walks carry us to our destinations. Many of those destinations have been incredibly dirty, but when we come to the Lord, He cleans our feet, cleans our past through His forgiveness and starts us on a new path to a new destination. He made our feet, but our shoes are the man-made parts that continue to carry the dust and dirt.

⁴ So when the LORD saw that he turned aside to look, God called to him from the midst of the bush and said, "Moses, Moses!"
And he said, "Here I am."
⁵ Then He said, "Do not draw near this place. Take your sandals off your feet, for the place where you stand *is* holy ground." Moreover He said, "I *am* the God of your father— the God of Abraham, the God of Isaac, and the God of Jacob." And Moses hid his face, for he was afraid to look upon God.
Exodus 3:4-5 (NKJV)

Our walks are in Jesus; our walks are with Jesus; our walks are because of Jesus; our walks are to Jesus! He will lead us to holy ground. If we are trusting in the Lord, He will make sure that our tires do not go flat. When there is a slow leak in our lives, we should question, can we trust our walk?

Behold, God *is* my salvation,
I will trust and not be afraid;
'For YAH, the LORD, *is* my
strength and song;
He also has become my
salvation."
Isaiah 12:2 (NKJV)

For to this *end* we both labor and suffer reproach, because we trust in the living God, who is *the* Savior of all men, especially of those who believe.
1 Timothy 4:10 (NKJV)

February 7: Another one bites the dust!

Ever ridden in the back of a pickup truck down an unpaved, country road? Dust flies everywhere, but that dust is magnified greatly when passing another vehicle, moving in the opposite direction. It is even worse when there is a slow-moving vehicle just ahead, going in the same direction. That dust is so pervasive that it finds its way into closed mouths! Each time a car passes, it is "Another One Bites the Dust."

There sure was a lot of dust around in biblical times. Think of God's promise to Israel that if they followed Him and stayed away from idols, He would water their crops and land. We know that the Israelites were just like us, and often strayed from the Lord. Consequently, their land had much drought. Without that water washing the land clean, dust was prevalent.

In the Bible, and in Hebrew tradition, there are many references to dust. On the night before Jesus died, He washed the dust from the feet of the disciples. Dust is emblematic of death or the grave, as we are reminded in the phrase, "ashes to ashes and dust to dust." Though that is not a direct quote from the Bible, it does reflect the thoughts of Genesis 2:7 and Genesis 3:19. God formed man from death, giving him life and man will return to death, though that refers to the mortal body, rather than the spiritual one. Only Jesus can wash that death from our walks! Jews mourned by putting on sackcloth and covering themselves in ashes. An extreme showing of affliction or humiliation occurred when sitting in the dust:

"Come down and sit in the dust,
O virgin daughter of Babylon;
Sit on the ground without a throne,
O daughter of the Chaldeans!
For you shall no more be called
Tender and delicate."
Isaiah 47:1 (NKJV)

We live in a world that is authored by God, but controlled by Satan. Dust is everywhere and that dust is the death that Satan wants to give us. He is the prince of the power of the air according to Ephesians 2, and because of him, there is dust in the wind. Let Jesus wash that dust from our dirty feet and give us eternal life with Him! What can wash away our sins? Nothing but the blood of Jesus!

He raises the poor from the dust
***And* lifts the beggar from the ash heap,**
To set *them* among princes
And make them inherit the throne of glory.
"For the pillars of the earth *are* the LORD's,
And He has set the world upon them.
1 Samuel 2:8 (NKJV)

My soul clings to the dust;
Revive me according
to Your word.
Psalm 119:25 (NKJV)

February 8: Who is eternity's Top Chef?

Are we hungry? If so, what are we hungry for? Food can be one of the most enjoyable aspects of life. Some chefs have a real talent for creating tasty morsels with a variety of ingredients and flavors. Yet even tasteless food can give energy, strength and endurance. Junk food does not fall into that category, though. Usually loaded in fat or sugar, those foods only give false energy. They can fill our bellies, fooling us into thinking that we have enough energy to proceed, but soon after starting, a crash occurs.

God reminds us that **"Man shall not live by bread alone, but by every word that proceeds from the mouth of the Lord,"** in Deuteronomy 8:3, and that verse also is quoted in Matthew 4:4. The Gospel of John begins by telling us that Jesus is in title, the Word of God. He is God and existed always. He is the Word and gave us the Word, and He walked on this earth as a man.

Sometimes, we lose sight of how important the Bible is to our daily survival and walk with the Lord. Which food will supply our needs better: a meal prepared by a top chef or reading a chapter of God's Holy Bible? Since we exist in the flesh, we have the tendency to fill the needs of the flesh.

[16] I say then: Walk in the Spirit, and you shall not fulfill the lust of the flesh. [17] For the flesh lusts against the Spirit, and the Spirit against the flesh; and these are contrary to one another, so that you do not do the things that you wish. Galatians 5:16-17 (NKJV)

Bob Dylan wrote a song in 1979 called, "Gotta Serve Somebody." The truth is, we are all looking for an answer to the question of who to serve. In a way, that answer is blowing in the wind, for the Holy Spirit in Greek is *pneuma*, the same word used for wind! We are either serving the God who made us, or we are serving Satan, the former angel that God gave earthly dominion to for the time being. Satan is a talented liar, who understands that the best lies contain at least a morsel of truth. That is the same formula for rat poison, which is 97% food and 3% poison. The truth will lure us, but the lie will kill us! Many messages lead people down the wrong path, with that bastardized formula of truth mixed with lies. Sadly, some of these lies come from pulpits. Look at the controversy in the Episcopal Church and the split that is occurring over the open sexuality of clergy and we can get a taste of this. Yet it is much more pervasive than one issue.

God desires to feed us; He desires to nurture us. Through His Word, we draw nearer to Him. If our walks are not leading us closer to the Lord, we should check our food. If it says, "Hostess Twinkies" on the package, we might want to shop somewhere else! That false energy only can make us trip and fall. But remember, God does not need a pastor, preacher, teacher or friend to share His Word with us. If we open His Book, the Holy Spirit will teach us all things, and will fill us with the food that will help us to soar like eagles!

But the Helper, the Holy Spirit, whom the Father will send in My name, He will teach you all things, and bring to your remembrance all things that I said to you.
John 14:26 (NKJV)

But you have an anointing
from the Holy One, and
you know all things.
1 John 2:20 (NKJV)

February 9: What do you want to see?

In the spring, when flowers start to bloom, the sweet aromas of many of those flowers put a spring into our steps, especially following a cold and snowy winter. That is also a perfect time for spring cleaning, airing out the musty smells of the closed house with open windows. One of the most fulfilling tasks is to wash the screens on the windows. It is amazing to see how much dirt collects on those screens. Afterwards, those windows need a good cleaning, too. Everything appears so much brighter through clean windows!

In our lives, we have the choice of looking ahead to the big picture through that freshly cleaned window or looking back through the small window covered in dirt, obstructing an otherwise clear view. Through the small window is the view of our past sins, but through the big window is the view of our future, the hope of our glory in Jesus Christ. Why do we wallow in the past, remembering our sins, when our Savior already has forgotten them?

As far as the east is from the west,
So far has He removed our transgressions from us.
Psalms 103:12 (NKJV)

He will again have compassion on us,
And will subdue our iniquities.
You will cast all our sins
Into the depths of the sea.

Micah 7:19 (NKJV)

Indeed *it was* for *my own* peace
***That* I had great bitterness;**
But You have lovingly *delivered* my soul from the pit of corruption,
For You have cast all my sins behind Your back.
Isaiah 38:17 (NKJV)

Our sins are on the ocean floor, covered in mud. How often do we dredge up those sins in our memories, though our Savior has promised us that He does not do that? The phrase "forgive and forget" gives us a great example. Truthfully, we are limited in our powers of forgiveness. We are capable of forgiving others, but mostly are incapable in regards to forgetting. It is difficult for us to comprehend how God knows everything, but does not remember our sin. He <u>chooses</u> not to remember our sin, which is a true gift. Once our sin has been dealt with, it is gone. It was dealt with when Jesus received the punishment we both earned and deserved on the cross, and it becomes His responsibility when we ask for His forgiveness.

When we feel like our sin is weighing us down, maybe we are focusing too much upon it! It does not matter how much sin is in our pasts, for God does not see the dead man, the person we used to be. He does not even see the person we are now. He sees the finished product, which He will make us into! Let go and let God! The big picture is Christ in us!

[8] For by grace you have been saved through faith, and that not of yourselves; *it is* the gift of God, [9] not of works, lest anyone should boast.
Ephesians 2:8-9 (NKJV)

And He said to me, "My grace is sufficient for you, for My strength is made perfect in weakness."

2 Corinthians 12:9 (NKJV)

February 10: Memories!

Advice is a form of nostalgia, according to a song called "Sunscreen." "Dispensing it is a way of fishing the past from the disposal, wiping it off, painting over the ugly parts and recycling it for more than it's worth." If we have the ability to learn from the past, we certainly can improve our present and future. Age should bring wisdom as its companion, and as those years roll silently by, we find ourselves looking at an enormously different world than the one we remember. For most of us, it is easy to reflect on a time when the internet was not a daily part of life or when the new technology was an 8-track tape player! In college, it could take three trips just to move in the music collection while now, 10 times that amount of music fits in the palm of our hands on an iPod! Additionally, as we age, our memories do not seem to work as well as they used to and in some ways, that can be a huge blessing!

The difficulty of adolescence is a great memory to forget, as are the pains of broken relationships and the sadness of the death of friends and family members. We always will remember those pains, but not with the same intensity that overwhelmed us initially. If God forgets our sins, why does He not give us the ability to forget in the same manner?

It is not for the pain that sin still can cause that God allows us to keep those memories. It is for the benefits. What benefits could there possibly be from remembering our sins, our failures and our biggest defeats? Through those sins, we should acquire an enormous amount of thankfulness for God's grace and mercy.

[41] "There was a certain creditor who had two debtors. One owed five hundred denarii, and the other fifty. [42] And when they had nothing with which to repay, he freely forgave them both. Tell Me, therefore, which of them will love him more?" [43] Simon answered and said, "I suppose the *one* whom he forgave more."

And He said to him, "You have rightly judged."
Luke 7:41-43 (NKJV)

Paul saw himself as the chief sinner on the earth (1 Timothy 1:15). Many of us feel like we have replaced Paul in that role. That is the Lord's way of letting us understand how much He loves us! At the age of 20, most of us do not fully grasp that Christ died for our sins. That does not mean that 20-year-olds cannot grasp the depth of that forgiveness, but after many years of walking in sin, we can go from the poorest creature to the wealthiest, all with God's gift of forgiveness. What does He want in exchange?

God has a way of bringing people, who are wallowing in the same sins that engulfed us, into our lives. That is because through our own stumbling, the Lord has given us an amazing gift of hindsight, and through that hindsight, a wealth of compassion. A great definition of compassion is feeling someone else's pain, and that certainly is love. Love is what heals us, and we know from 1 John 4 that God is love! The key is to forget the pain of our sinful failures and remember the gift of that burden being removed from our shoulders!

[7] Beloved, let us love one another, for love is of God; and everyone who loves is born of God and knows God. [8] He who does not love does not know God, for God is love. [9] In this the love of God was manifested toward us, that God has sent His only begotten Son into the world, that we might live through Him. [10] In this is love, not that we loved God, but that He loved us and sent His Son *to be* the propitiation for our sins. [11] Beloved, if God so loved us, we also ought to love one another.
1 John 4:7-11 (NKJV)

February 11: The yoke's on you!

Everywhere we look there are people in pain. Unemployment is rising, along with credit card debt, foreclosures, homelessness and even suicide. Though we have a tendency to see this through an egocentric, American perspective, our economy adversely has affected the world's economy. Back in the 1930s when the collapse of the stock market led to the Great Depression, the economy of the United States was not tied as deeply into the economy of the world, but now, our bank failures, bailouts and bad decisions have caused a chain reaction. Those difficulties are not just for unbelievers, as God also placed His children in difficult situations, though we often respond with, "What are You doing, God?"

That question has a good and bad side. Obviously, the bad side is what right do we have to question God, who has promised that He never will leave us or forsake us? He feeds the birds of the air and clothes the flowers more ornately than King Solomon (Matthew 6:26), and loves us more! The good side of that question, though, is if we are asking God what He is doing, then we are acknowledging that He is doing something! What is He doing?

Do we ever learn lessons when life is easy? Most of us do not! Bill Gates said, "It's fine to celebrate success but it is more important to heed the lessons of failure." When the seas are calm and the wind is blowing, we cruise around the ocean gleefully. But sailing in a storm, we remember each mistake. Those lessons are as apparent in life as they are in the physical world. Take metallurgy, for example. When gold is heated, it becomes stronger through purification.

[28] Come to Me, all *you* who labor and are heavy laden, and I will give you rest. [29] Take My yoke upon you and learn from Me, for I am gentle and lowly in heart, and you will find rest for your souls. [30] For My yoke *is* easy and My burden is light."
Matthew 11:28-30 (NKJV)

If we are the Lord's then we should not feel heavily burdened. If we are sailing under our own power, we might feel the weight of the world on our shoulders. Yet the shoulders of Jesus already carried the burden of the world, when He suffered and died for us at the cross. Give Him the burden! Trust that He can handle it. It can be so difficult to hand off that difficulty to Him. It is like a relay race where we are running the anchor leg. Though in last place, far behind the other competitors, when we hand the baton to Jesus, He runs for us, past all of the other obstacles, to arrive in first place at the finish line. Amazingly, though, He holds onto us as He also carries the baton of burden. He is the wind in our sails. He is the author and finisher of our faith. Let Him finish for us.

February 12: Whole lotta shakin' goin' on!

At 4:53 p.m. on January 12, 2010, a 7.0 earthquake struck with an epicenter 16 miles from Port-au-Prince, the capital city of Haiti. At that moment and in the ensuing days, over 200,000 people lost their lives in Haiti, with estimates of over 300,000 injured and over 1 million people instantly homeless. That latter number is over 10% of the population of Haiti, the poorest country in the Western Hemisphere. In events of that magnitude of sadness, many question the presence of the Lord. Pat Robertson blamed the event on Haiti's "pact with the devil," and the comment outraged the masses.

Yet throughout the Bible, particularly in the Old Testament, God used weather and natural disasters to speak to His people. Elijah was taken to heaven in a whirlwind. The moment that Jesus died on the cross, an earthquake tore the temple veil from top to bottom (Matthew 27:51-53). There are multiple examples of similar events. In Isaiah, God said,

**I form the light and create darkness,
I make peace and create calamity;
I, the LORD, do all these *things.*'
Isaiah 45:7 (NKJV)**

For those who think that God once acted in that regard, but no longer speaks through those kinds of events, the Lord told us that He is the same yesterday, today and forever. One thing God is incapable of is change! God has given dominion of the earth to Satan, for a time, though we must remember, Satan is not the sovereign ruler. Anything that occurs is God's will, for His purposes. (Read Job for clarification). That becomes increasingly difficult in the minds of many believers, who cannot fathom how a loving God can allow devastation of that magnitude. Before we question God, we need to remind ourselves of the difference between His knowledge and ours. He is omniscient, and it should occur to us that God never has said, "It occurred to Me." He has known everything for all of eternity! Because the Father sent His Son to save the world, and in that act demonstrated the greatest love, either those who died were believers and are with Him in heaven, or they never would have made that decision, regardless of the length of their lives. God has gone to the farthest degree imaginable to draw us to Him. We know that the earthquake in Haiti, the earthquake in Japan, the one causing the Indian tsunami, Hurricane Katrina in New Orleans and similar events are signs of the times. Just before He was crucified, Jesus told His disciples,

[4] And Jesus answered and said to them: "Take heed that no one deceives you. [5] For many will come in My name, saying, 'I am the Christ,' and will deceive many. [6] And you will hear of wars and rumors of wars. See that you are not troubled; for all *these things* must come to pass, but the end is not yet. [7] For nation will rise against nation, and kingdom against kingdom. And there will be famines, pestilences, and earthquakes in various places. [8] All these *are* the beginning of sorrows.
[9] "Then they will deliver you up to tribulation and kill you, and you will be hated by all nations for My name's sake. [10] And then many will be offended, will betray one another, and will hate one another. [11] Then many false prophets will rise up and deceive many. [12] And because lawlessness will abound, the love of many will grow cold. [13] But he who endures to the end shall be saved. [14] And this gospel of the kingdom will be preached in all the world as a witness to all the nations, and then the end will come.
Matthew 24:4-14 (NKJV)

We are told that these events will be like labor pains. To remind those who have not given birth, labor pains increase in frequency and intensity before the birth occurs. Revelation instructs us that these judgments grow more severe as that period continues. Why would a loving God put His creation under such duress and destruction?

We learn our lessons when under duress. When God judges a sinful earth, He still has redemption on His mind. Even in wrath, God is 100% loving. In that time, many will fall to their knees and ask Jesus to become the Savior of their lives. Others will turn their hearts coldly away from Him. As much emphasis as we put on this life, we are here for one purpose. That purpose is to make a decision of who we will serve.

So in the aftermath of natural disasters, know that we serve a loving God, and even earthquakes are an example of His love. God is love and He cannot contradict His own character. Pray for the families, come alongside the survivors and thank God for His mighty plan that we are not always meant to understand.

"No one can serve two masters; for either he will hate the one and love the other, or else he will be loyal to the one and despise the other. You cannot serve God and mammon. Matthew 6:24 (NKJV)

February 13: Are we willing to be prisoners?

Prison is a rough place, and thankfully, most of us do not know that from personal experience. Certainly, the greatest difficulty of prison life can have more to do with the treatment by fellow inmates than with the loss of liberty that goes with the prison sentence. It is most difficult for those with less than life sentences, for their thoughts, hopes and plans force them to think ahead to life past imprisonment. But the inmates who know that they will certainly die in prison seem to adjust to the life they are faced with.

A quadriplegic came into a doctor's office, and even in the wheelchair, was one of the most upbeat people the physician ever had come in contact with. The physician asked him how long he had been a quadriplegic and what had caused it. When the man had been a teenager, he and his sister were riding in the backseat of the car, with their mother driving. He and his sister were arguing, and his mother kept yelling at them to stop. When they did not, the mother pulled over the car, pulled out a gun and shot them! His sister died, his mother went to prison and he became a quadriplegic! Most erroneously expect that the end of the story would be that the mother was distracted and it caused a car accident. Yet regardless of what caused the incredible changes in three lives, the young man endured that amazing obstacle and found happiness. One of the lessons of this story is that we all have a balance point, a place of stasis. Happy people will find that happiness again, while depressed people will find the depression they seek. As Christians, our joy should come from the Lord!

We seem to put judgments on situations. Would it always be rough to be a quadriplegic? Would a person born with blindness be able to grasp what they were missing, or would they be content in the life they always had known? Would being a prisoner always be a negative?

for you had compassion on me in my chains, and joyfully accepted the plundering of your goods, knowing that you have a better and an enduring possession for yourselves in heaven.
Hebrews 10:34 (NKJV)

[8] Therefore, though I might be very bold in Christ to command you what is fitting, [9] yet for love's sake I rather appeal *to you*—**being such a one as Paul, the aged, and now also a prisoner of Jesus Christ—**
Philemon 8-9 (NKJV)

Paul tells us that he is a prisoner of Jesus Christ, and he is not alone in that capacity. It was an easy description for Paul, as he was literally a prisoner in his life, as well. The word for prisoner in Greek denotes the binding, or the prisoner who is bound. Paul also tells us that he is a "bondservant" of Jesus Christ, and that word is the same for "slave." Our society gives us negative connotations of all three of those words, prisoner, slave and servant. Regardless of how our society sees the words, those stations are gifts of God. How many prisoners worry about where their next meal will come from or if they will be able to put a roof over their heads?

While we as believes are bound to Christ Jesus, it is not the weighty connection of a ball and chain that tethers us. Instead, we are bound to Him with a lifeline of support. He is the parachute we wear with our plane going down, but instead of descending to the broken world below, He puts the wind in our sails and lifts us up to new lives in Him. We should walk in the joy that He captured our hearts and desires to be with us! Our needs are all supplied by *Jehovah-jireh*!

[13] so that it has become evident to the whole palace guard, and to all the rest, that my chains are in Christ; [14] and most of the brethren in the Lord, having become confident by my chains, are much more bold to speak the word without fear. Philippians 1:13-14 (NKJV)

February 14: The greatest love

Saint Valentine's Day commemorates the death and burial of an early Christian martyr, though modern-day culture associates the day with the affection of intimate companions. Pope Gelasius I established the day in A.D. 496, and early church tradition speaks of the martyrdom of numerous individuals named Valentine, who lost their lives for their unwavering beliefs in Jesus Christ as their Lord and Savior. Though most of the records associated with these early believers have been lost, church tradition still speaks of two men, both buried on the *Via Flaminia*, a Roman road that leads from Rome to Riminia, a region of Italy on the Adriatic Sea.

Valentine of Rome, a priest in Rome, was martyred around A.D. 269. His relics are in Rome and Dublin. Additionally, Valentine of Terni, who was the bishop of Interamna, was martyred around A.D. 197. His relics are in modern-day Terni. A third Valentine was martyred in Africa, supposedly on February 14, though nothing else is known of him.

So how does death become associated with love, for all future generations?

Greater love has no one than this, than to lay down one's life for his friends.
John 15:13 (NKJV)

Sacrificial love is much different than romantic love. Somehow, Saint Valentine's Day has taken on a different flavor with the addition of chocolate to the equation. It has become more of a *quid pro quo* situation, which in Latin means "this for that." Jesus did not die on the cross with the feeling of "if you scratch My back, I'll scratch yours." Instead, He died so that we might live. His death is the gift that keeps on giving.

Some people have difficulty understanding the concept. How could the death of a man 2,000 years ago have anything to do with our lives today? We have to comprehend that we are all sinners, and God must punish sin. If a murderer went before a judge and promised that he never would kill again, would the judge simply let the murderer off the hook? A righteous judge could not do that. In the same manner, God simply cannot ignore sin. That is why Jesus departed heaven as God and became a man, as He was the only one who could live a life without sin. When He died, He took our sins upon His shoulders and received the punishment that we were due to receive.

We do not think of that gift often enough. Many of us would be hard-pressed to find anyone in our lives we would be willing to die for. Yet most mothers certainly know this feeling. Having carried that life in them for nine months, there is a special connection. Many fathers also have that same feeling.

Additionally, many of us have friends that we deeply care about. Though what makes the life and death of Jesus so amazing is that He sacrificed His life for those who hated Him! Would any of us be willing to die in place of the idiotic driver who just cut us off? Would we be willing to die for the neighbor who keeps us up on Saturday nights with parties until the wee hours? Would we be willing to die for the co-worker who lied about us in order to receive a promotion we had earned?

And walk in love, as Christ also has loved us and given Himself for us, an offering and a sacrifice to God for a sweet-smelling aroma.
Ephesians 5:2 (NKJV)

Though the world celebrates this day with chocolate and flowers, do not forget the true significance of the greatest love. It has nothing in common with fleeting affection, and if we have Jesus Christ as our Lord and Savior, He will shower us with His love for eternity! Whether or not Christians have earthly spouses, God desires an intimate relationship with each of His children, which supersedes any other intimacy. Celebrate His love each and every day! Additionally, share His love with others, especially those who do not know Him. That unwarranted love could speak to their souls, just as it did to ours! Happy Valentine's Day!

[7] Beloved, let us love one another, for love is of God; and everyone who loves is born of God and knows God. [8] He who does not love does not know God, for God is love. [9] In this the love of God was manifested toward us, that God has sent His only begotten Son into the world, that we might live through Him. [10] In this is love, not that we loved God, but that He loved us and sent His Son *to be* **the propitiation for our sins. [11] Beloved, if God so loved us, we also ought to love one another.**
1 John 4:7-11 (NKJV)

By this we know love, because He laid down His life for us. And we also ought to lay down our lives for the brethren.

1 John 3:16 (NKJV)
February 15: Sin nature

When dealing with children, it is imperative not to give them any ideas of how to misbehave. For instance, when seeing a child drinking from a glass, simply by saying, "No matter what, do not throw that glass on the ground," will cause an idea to sprout in the mind of that child. "Throwing a glass must be fun," will think the child, "or he would not have told me not to do it." Without the well-intended advice from the adult, the child never would have dreamed of throwing the glass, but with the request, the child becomes incapable of "just saying no."

What is it in us that rarely evokes a different response? As adults, we are no better than children. What is our typical response if we go to a restaurant and the waiter says, "Don't touch the plate. It's very hot?" As soon as the waiter puts down the plate and leaves the table, we have to touch it and see exactly how hot it is. Is it curiosity? We frequently get burned by our behavior. Do we all want to be "A Rebel Without a Cause," who suddenly finds a cause? God certainly saw the same behavior in the Garden of Eden.

After creating the world and placing Adam and Eve in the Garden, God instructed them that they were allowed to eat anything they wanted EXCEPT one particular fruit:

**[15] Then the LORD God took the man and put him in the garden of Eden to tend and keep it. [16] And the LORD God commanded the man, saying, "Of every tree of the garden you may freely eat; [17] but of the tree of the knowledge of good and evil you shall not eat, for in the day that you eat of it you shall surely die.
Genesis 2:15-17 (NKJV)**

Did Adam understand what God meant? Adam certainly understood that God did not want him to eat the fruit of that tree, but he might not have understood what death was. Up to that time, there had not been any death, and though God surely had explained the concept to Adam, Adam's understanding certainly was not experiential. It was not Adam that tasted the fruit first. It was Eve, at the insistence of the slimy serpent tricking her into that taste. When Eve tasted the fruit, she then gave it to her husband and he ate of it, too. From that moment, both Adam and Eve were destined for physical death. Hal Lindsay said, "If you are born once, you will die twice, but if you are born twice, you will only die once!" Those who are born again will only taste of physical death, as they have been promised eternal, spiritual life in Jesus Christ. Yet unbelievers will go from death to death.

The first sin caused all of mankind to change, as we are all relatives of Adam, the "sons of disobedience." Now, as in every generation after Adam, we are born into sin. The little boy who threw the glass had no other choice, based on the nature inside of him. Can we choose not to sin? Yes, but without the presence of Jesus living inside of us, we do not have the power to control that urge. As Christians, we will continue to sin, and in the same sense will continue to give into the powers of trickery used by the slimy one. Yet, when we have Jesus living inside of us, the Holy Spirit gives us His power to choose another option. Just as Adam had the ability to walk away from sin, based on the walking/talking relationship he had with the Lord, we have the ability to turn away. Choose Jesus, instead of sin, and rely on His power to turn away from the slimy, crafty one!

The decision to choose Jesus occurs in one moment, yet the decision to sin or not to sin occurs moment-by-moment and day-by-day.

Say to them: '*As* I live,' says the Lord GOD, 'I have no pleasure in the death of the wicked, but that the wicked turn from his way and live. Turn, turn from your evil ways! For why should you die, O house of Israel?'
Ezekiel 33:11 (NKJV)

February 16: A sprinkle a day helps keep the odor away!

A weekly cleaning day may include a trip to the Laundromat and the assorted tasks at home of dusting, vacuuming and window cleaning, along with the dreaded cleaning of the bathroom. Based on other time requirements, the weekly tasks are sometimes put off for an additional week. When that happens, though, cleaning always takes twice as long. There just are not any shortcuts. It is amazing how quickly dust returns and how dirty the clothes become by week's end. Regardless of what gets those clothes dirty, they must be cleaned again and again.

This world is a dirty place! We can come directly from a bath and find ourselves covered in muck and mire in moments! When God created the world, it was not designed that way. When Adam and Eve lived in the pre-sin Garden of Eden, there was probably no such thing as a dust mite. But when sin entered the picture, all of creation changed:

[22] For we know that the whole creation groans and labors with birth pangs together until now. [23] Not only *that*, but we also who have the firstfruits of the Spirit, even we ourselves groan within ourselves, eagerly waiting for the adoption, the redemption of our body.
Romans 8:22-23 (NKJV)

Each of us yearns to be redeemed, and according to Romans, that includes every aspect of creation: the dirt, ocean, animals and even dust mites! Jesus redeems us, as He bought us at a price. Salvation is a free gift, but never forget that the price was not a cheap one! He bought us with His life, with His blood.

In the same manner that our possessions need cleaning, we need spiritual cleansing even more often. That cleansing comes from God's forgiveness of our sins. When Jesus comes to dwell in our hearts, He forgives us for all past, present and future sins.

Yet we still have the responsibility of coming to Him and asking for that forgiveness.

If we confess our sins, He is faithful and just to forgive us *our* sins and to cleanse us from all unrighteousness.
1 John 1:9 (NKJV)

Next time we are busy house cleaning, we should not leave out the most important part of that regular cleansing. We should ask the Lord for His forgiveness of our sins, and remember that only His blood can make us white as snow!

I acknowledged my sin to You,
And my iniquity I have not hidden.
I said, "I will confess my transgressions to the LORD,"
And You forgave the iniquity of my sin.
Psalm 32:5 (NKJV)

February 17: Do you want to win the lottery?

For those who ever have purchased a lottery ticket, the odds are stacked. If the lottery involves picking six numbers between 1 and 99, the odds of winning are 1 in 1,120,529,256. Even knowing the near certainty of losing, many people continue to play. Studies show that poor people play more often, with the hopelessness of poverty pushing people to attempt to improve their condition. In that manner, it is a legal tax on the poor. The saddest aspect of the lottery, though, is that most people who win the mega-millions find that it changes their lives negatively.

When we play the lottery, we have no control over the luck or fate that will have the correct numbers pop up in our favor. But each of us has the ability to win a more important lottery and we have plenty of control in that lottery. Have all of us considered the value of eternal life in heaven?

[4] But God, who is rich in mercy, because of His great love with which He loved us, [5] even when we were dead in trespasses, made us alive together with Christ (by grace you

have been saved), [6] and raised *us* up together, and made *us* sit together in the heavenly *places* in Christ Jesus, [7] that in the ages to come He might show the exceeding riches of His grace in His kindness toward us in Christ Jesus.
Ephesians 2:4-7 (NKJV)

Our frail, human minds have great difficulty grasping eternity. Even our lives on this earth seem like they last a long time, though when an 85-year-old is preparing for death, he often thinks about the brevity of the time he spent here. After 1 million of those 85-year time periods in heaven, we will be no closer to the end, as there is no end! Some people have a faulty concept of heaven, often depicted as sitting around on clouds playing harps. They erroneously think that we will get bored after a time. Yet Paul reminded us how incredible heaven will be! **"In the ages to come, He might show the exceeding riches of His grace in His kindness toward us in Christ Jesus."**

Most Christians understand that Jesus has been incredibly kind to us on this earth. He chose us to serve Him, though all we deserved was death. "Why us," is a constant question, and the answer has nothing to do with our redeeming qualities. Without Him, we are unredeemable; we are clanging cymbals; we are nothing! So instead of the riches of the world, we have obtained the riches of His mercy and grace.

For anyone who truly wants to win the lottery, they can accept Jesus into their life as Lord and Savior. He does not promise abundance while on the earth, but we certainly will have abundant life with Him for all of eternity! Check out all the superlatives in the following verse: exceedingly, abundantly, above all, above all we ask, above all we think, and then, build that promise exponentially!

[20] Now unto him that is able to do exceeding abundantly above all that we ask or think, according to the power that worketh in us, [21] Unto him *be* glory in the church by Christ Jesus throughout all ages, world without end. Amen.

Ephesians 3:20-21 (KJV)

February 18: Talk is cheap!

Most people have days filled with words, with business meetings, conversations and gossip around the water cooler. Some young mothers complain that there are not multi-syllabic words in the day and they feel isolated, but that is the anomaly in our society. Many extroverts derive energy from being around people, while introverts derive energy from being alone. That does not mean that extroverts cannot exist alone or that introverts cannot attend a party, but it is more about which actions provide energy and which actions sap that energy.

In the play "My Fair Lady," Eliza Doolittle sang a song called, "Show Me:"

> "Words, words, words, I'm so sick of words. I get words all day through, first from him now from you, is that all you blighters can do? Don't talk of stars burning above, if you're in love, show me!"

That song seems to reflect what God must feel with our prayers and promises. It is hard to believe that He does not tire of our words and desires for our actions to be more in line with those words. According to the Bible, we are to take our oaths to Him very seriously, but most of us have made promises to God and broken them. Most of those broken promises concern sins that we promised never to commit again. God teaches us that it is better not to make a promise than to break one. Prayers can be just as empty, as too many have to do with our own selfish desires. God has promised to supply our needs, but His idea of what we need is starkly different from what we think we need. In every facet of Christian life, our deeds should match our words.

In the South, outward friendliness to acquaintances goes hand-in-hand with people making friendly comments to strangers. On the other hand, in New York City, people tend to turn their faces away from strangers, hesitant to share "their" space. Can we tell what a person is really like from their words or do we have to study their actions? The Lord told us:

**[34] Brood of vipers! How can you, being evil, speak good things? For out of the abundance of the heart the mouth speaks. [35] A good man out of the good treasure of his heart brings forth good things, and an evil man out of the evil treasure brings forth evil things. [36] But I say to you that for every idle word men may speak, they will give account of it in the day of judgment. [37] For by your words you will be justified, and by your words you will be condemned."
Matthew 12:34-37 (NKJV)**

We are to choose our words carefully! Maybe our prayers should be more in line with one from King David:

**Let the words of my mouth and the meditation of my heart
Be acceptable in Your sight,
O LORD, my strength and my Redeemer.
Psalm 19:14 (NKJV)**

We know that our hearts are wicked and deceitful, but the Lord gives us new hearts. When our words come from that new heart, they are aligned with Him, but the old heart of flesh is still capable of idle words. Though the childhood rhyme reminds us that, "sticks and stones can break my bones, but words can never hurt me," we know that words can leave deeper bruises than stones. Choose them wisely!

February 19: Slip sliding away!

One of the most interesting sporting events is the Olympics, with national patriotism more of a draw than monetary gain. Though success in the worldwide competition can be a springboard to financial success in the lives of some athletes, many others achieve gold medals and return to lives of relative anonymity. Sometimes, politics get in the way of this competition. In 1980, United States President Jimmy Carter decided to boycott the

Olympics in a stance against the Soviet Union's war with Afghanistan. The United States tried a different approach when Adolf Hitler's Germany hosted the 1936 Olympics in Berlin. The crowning moment saw Jesse Owens and his four gold medals, defeating the blonde-haired, blue-eyed athletes of Hitler's perceived superior race! Occasionally, death comes to the Olympics, with the worst occasion being the politically-based murder of 11 Israeli athletes at the 1972 Olympics.

Sadly, on the first day of competition in the 2010 Winter Olympics, a luge competitor from Georgia named Nodar Kumaritashvili died on a training run. Luge takes more guts than almost any other sport. Sliders reach speeds approaching 100 M.P.H. lying on their backs with their feet leading the way down the icy track. They control the small metal sleds with their calves, and in that tucked position, have to be at least partially blind.

Spiritually, we all find ourselves on an even more slippery slope in our lives. Habitual sin controls at least a part of each of our lives. Illegal drugs are a perfect example. Taking drugs rarely is a one-time event in the life of a user. In the desire to recreate that high, or that removal from the drudgery of daily life, the user increases usage or turns to a stronger drug. He continues down the slippery slope, with his body in jeopardy, as well as every relationship. Even knowing that the behavior is wrong, each time becomes easier. The next fix becomes the focal point of life, as everything else pales in comparison. That slope leads to death, though most people sliding down that icy hill have all the best hopes of an easy landing and another ride. Yet, it does not have to be drug use to create that effect in our lives. All sin leads to the same place, and that place is judgment from the Lord.

Vengeance is Mine, and recompense;
Their foot shall slip in *due* time;
For the day of their calamity *is* at hand,
And the things to come hasten upon them.
Deuteronomy 32:35 (NKJV)

God knows our motives better than we do and understands the attraction that sin has in our lives. All the way down that slippery slope, He is there, offering a hand of support and another path. That path leads to Him and is on solid ground.

You enlarged my path under me;
So my feet did not slip.
  Samuel 22:37 (NKJV)

On Christ the Solid Rock we stand. All other ground is sinking sand, or an icy slope. When we are standing on the Cornerstone, our foundation will be solid, not slippery!

February 20: A simple story of love!

Just an hour and a half southeast of Palm Springs, California, is a one-of-a-kind, desolate town on the edge of the Salton Sea called Niland. John Donne did not have anything on this place as, "No man is in Niland!" There is not a man in Niland; but there is a saint. Leonard Knight, at the ripe old age of 78, has offered his tireless energy for the last 30 years creating a piece of folk art that he uses to share his love for Jesus.

Born and raised in Vermont, Leonard left high school after his sophomore year. He served in the army during the Korean War and ventured west. While visiting his sister in San Diego, he asked Jesus into his heart, and his life changed on the spot. He struggled with people who tried to make the relationship with God complicated, as many told him God could not be known without deeply understanding every aspect of the Bible. Leonard was a simple man; he found God in a simple way; he loved the Lord with his simple heart. Back in Vermont after his father's death, Leonard decided that his way to share the Lord's love was by putting the message "God is love" on a hot-air balloon and flying it above the curious people. Not being a simple task, the project grew too big for him as the years it took to assemble the balloon caused the weathered fabric to rip when inflated. He had relocated to Slab City, outside of Niland, CA, with his old van carrying the decaying, balloon fabric and a homemade inflating device. When the balloon would not hold air, another idea inflated in Leonard's mind and Salvation Mountain was born.

With years of labor, Leonard has created a place as colorful as Oz. He could have filled an Olympic-sized swimming pool with the gallons of paint he has used. There are enough bales of hay in the construction to feed a thousand horses for a year. He has created his own adobe and painted the Lord's love across the world's most interesting billboard. And for all those years, Leonard has lived simply inside the caves of his creation in a location that reaches as high as 120 degrees in the summer. His weathered face reveals his time in the sun. His thin frame reveals that he has enough food to survive, but not an abundance of it.

Why? What would cause a man to spend his life creating this? It was the calling the Lord put on Leonard's life. It might appear strange to the masses of people who visit, but like it or not, one cannot help but be impacted by this simple man and his simple message, always accompanied by a welcoming smile and the offer of a tour. What must have seemed crazy to many has become world renowned, and even was featured in the movie, "Into the Wild." God calls some to be preachers, others to be teachers. Some He gives the gift of hospitality or encouragement. God gave Leonard the ability to live alone simply and create a slice of heaven in an isolated section of desert. Though isolated, God did not ask Leonard to travel to others, but instead, brought the people to Leonard.

[12] **For as the body is one and has many members, but all the members of that one body, being many, are one body, so also** *is* **Christ.** [13] **For by one Spirit we were all baptized into one body— whether Jews or Greeks, whether slaves or free—and have all been made to drink into one Spirit.** [14] **For in fact the body is not one member but many.**
[15] **If the foot should say, "Because I am not a hand, I am not of the body," is it therefore not of the body?** [16] **And if the ear should say, "Because I am not an eye, I am not of the body,"**

is it therefore not of the body? [17] If the whole body *were* an eye, where *would be* the hearing? If the whole *were* hearing, where *would be* the smelling? [18] But now God has set the members, each one of them, in the body just as He pleased. [19] And if they *were* all one member, where *would* the body *be?* [20] But now indeed *there are* many members, yet one body.
1 Corinthians 12:12-20 (NKJV)

All of the gifts the Lord gives are to glorify Him, not us! If we are walking in His Spirit, He will use us to further His kingdom in amazing ways. Though it never may be in the way we imagine or desire, the result will be spectacular. Remember, there is nothing about the Lord that is ordinary, and what He designs for us will far surpass what we have in mind. The key is to find that place in the body where God desires us to be. Though no man is an island, many men come to Niland to see a saint who loves the Lord! God puts people everywhere to share His love. That love is simple and it is bigger than any love we ever can know. We should be the unique person He created us to be in Him, today! Never underestimate the power of God's love to make the simplest task something special. There is nothing mundane about our God, who deals in miracles!

[4] **For as we have many members in one body, but all the members do not have the same function,** [5] **so we,** *being* **many, are one body in Christ, and individually members of one another.**
Romans 12:4-5 (NKJV)

February 21: Fill your lamps with oil!

Part of life on this earth is to know the pain of being in what appears to be a hopeless situation. Even Jesus found Himself in a situation that seemed to offer no way of escape. When Jesus felt the weight of the world dropping onto His shoulders, He went to His Father in prayer, and often, the place of that prayer was the Garden of Gethsemane, located in Jerusalem at the base of the Mount of Olives.

Jesus and His disciples spent much time in that garden, and were there the night before His crucifixion. In fact, it is where Judas brought the guards when he betrayed Jesus with a kiss. It is where Jesus reminded His disciples to join Him in prayer, saying, "Rise and pray, lest you enter into temptation." Jesus prayed three separate times that if it was the Father's will, to let this cup pass from Him. Anticipating the events to come, our Lord sweated blood.

In the Bible, olive oil is emblematic of the Holy Spirit. We are to keep oil in our lamps to keep those lamps lit (Matthew 25). Even the process of making olive oil points to our Lord, as when the olive is crushed, the oil remains. When Jesus was crushed, beaten and bruised, He left the Holy Spirit in His place. We never should lose sight of what our Savior endured for us, accepting His Father's will to suffer in our places by becoming a man, for God cannot suffer. Though the physical pain was great, it was the separation from His Father that pained Jesus the most. He did not just carry our sins, He became sin for us.

For He made Him who knew no sin *to be* sin for us, that we might become the righteousness of God in Him.
2 Corinthians 5:21 (NKJV)

Part of the issue we are facing in those times of trial is faith. Do we truly believe what God has told us in His Word? If we do, then we will realize that every trial that He allows in our lives, He already has handled by making two promises. We **can** handle the trial and there **is** a way of escape. Jesus prayed for a way of escape before He went to the cross. The fact that the Father did not offer a way of escape reminded Jesus, and should remind us, that there was no other way for us to have a relationship with the Father apart from the events of the cross. The Father loved Jesus so much, yet Isaiah 53 reminds us, **"Yet it pleased the Lord to bruise Him."** It pleased the Father, for through that bruising, He opened the door for us to know His love.

When we find ourselves in troublesome situations and feel alone, know Jesus will join us in our Garden of Gethsemane. He never will leave us, or forsake us. How much oil is in your lamp?

February 22: Standing on the promises of God!

When we look at the world today, we can see so much brokenness. In the midst of recession, most of the political pundits have announced that the recession is over. With 10% of the population unemployed in the United States, there are many who might disagree with that statement. In addition to that 10% are the people on total commission, the under-employed or the self-employed, who may have jobs but are enduring the effect of shrinking pay checks. Anyone struggling can assess they are not alone.

What would the Lord have us do in the midst of this trial? Faith is not tested when everything is coming up roses. God never makes mistakes, so any situation that we find ourselves in has been designed specifically for us. With so many people hurting, we should focus upon standing on the promises of God. R. Kelso Carter, who lived from 1849-1926, wrote the words and music to the great hymn, and those words surely spoke loudly to the folks enduring the Great Depression only a few years later.

"Standing on the promises of Christ my King, through eternal ages let his praises ring;
glory in the highest, I will shout and sing, standing on the promises of God.
Standing on the promises that cannot fail, when the howling storms of doubt and fear assail, by the living Word of God I shall prevail, standing on the promises of God.
Standing on the promises of Christ the Lord, bound to Him eternally by love's strong cord, overcoming daily with the Spirit's sword, standing on the promises of God.
Standing on the promises I cannot fall, listening every moment to the Spirit's call, resting in my Savior as my all in all, standing on the promises of God.

Standing, standing, standing on the promises of Christ my Savior;
standing, standing, I'm standing on the promises of God."

What a great reminder! God's Word is filled with promises to us, and He has not broken a promise. That is the beauty of His Word, as we can see time and time again, how steadfast He is to follow through on every promise. Sometimes, when we are going through tough times, it is better to remind ourselves of these promises, rather than to struggle in the trial.

February 23: Confess to a good God!

We cannot help but pick up some dirt in our daily walks, no matter how much we focus on God and the teachings of God. What can begin with the best attempt can turn into the worst in a matter of moments. Tell a child to "be good" and we have set him up for failure, as with sin nature, we cannot be good! "Act good, for a while," is much more manageable! We are children of God and in the same manner that a child cannot be good, we cannot either. We have moments of following the Lord, but God has reminded us that we are sinners, saved by His grace. But God is good, and He is faithful to forgive us when we come to Him.

[8] If we say that we have no sin, we deceive ourselves, and the truth is not in us. [9] If we confess our sins, He is faithful and just to forgive us *our* sins and to cleanse us from all unrighteousness. [10] If we say that we have not sinned, we make Him a liar, and His word is not in us.
1 John 1:8-10 (NKJV)

Can we really make God a liar? No! He is incapable of telling a lie. What the passage is saying is that if we were telling the truth by saying that we have not sinned, God would be wrong. But we cannot get through even a day without sinning. Simply by saying we are not sinners, we have sinned by lying! We are all sinners, and will continue to be sinners until we are united with our Savior.

For those of us who have accepted Jesus into our hearts as Lord and Savior, He forgave every sin that we ever committed when we came to Him. He also forgave every sin that we ever will commit. This is not a license to sin, but God understands our nature of sin. The prophet, Jeremiah, reminds us that:

"The heart *is* deceitful above all *things*,
And desperately wicked;
Who can know it?"
Jeremiah 17:9 (NKJV)

When we come to the Lord, He replaces that heart of stone with a heart of flesh. As much as we love the Lord, we continue to sin, and it feels horrible to blow it over and over again, as if we are letting God down, but for Him to feel disappointment would mean that He had other expectations. Every sin that we commit, God knew we would commit! And still He saved us!

God reminds us that we are to confess our sins. If we do, He promises to forgive our sins and cleanse us from **all unrighteousness.** We have an awareness of some sins, but in regard to others, we walk in unawareness. If we confess the sins that we are aware of, He also will forgive and cleanse us from the sins we are unaware of!

What does this have to do with struggling in a recession? It gives us the perspective of what this world and this struggle are all about. What if we lose our jobs? What if we miss some meals? Does it really matter in the grand scheme of it all? In that grand scheme, believers in the Lord will spend all of eternity with Jesus, our Savior! Take that first step upon the Word of God and stand on promise #1!

February 24: Pathways and gates

We often can feel conflicted, not knowing which direction to turn. GPS can help when driving, but there are times when even that technological advancement gets it entirely wrong. The Bible is our spiritual GPS, giving us the answers to many age-old questions. Yet some of those daily decisions do not seem to have a biblical answer. If we are being offered a job in New York City and another one in Tokyo, Japan, there is probably not a Bible verse that is going to tell us specifically which job to take! In cases like that, we are instructed to wait on the Lord, to pray, and to seek Him. When we do that, He often will open one door and close another. In biblical times, they cast lots, which would be the modern-day equivalent of rolling dice. God already knows which decision we will make! That brings us to the most important promise in the Bible for believers, while still on the earth:

And we know that all things work together for good to those who love God, to those who are the called according to *His* purpose.
Romans 8:28 (NKJV)

What an amazing promise! It does not say that all things that we do correctly work out for our good, but **all things**. Every bad decision, God still can turn around for our good! What an amazing God! Just to make sure that we fall into this category, who are those who love God and are the called according to His purpose? Anyone who has asked Him into their hearts! When we are going through difficult times upon this earth, we sometimes forget how brief those difficulties will last. Even if the duration of the trial was to be our entire lives upon this earth, it would pale in comparison to the amount of time we are going to spend with Him for eternity.

One way of grasping this is to understand the difference between God's perfect will and His permissive will. Think of a detour sign. While it may take less time to travel directly from point A to point B, when we choose a waypoint that sends us on a wild-goose chase, God faithfully brings us back to the path He has designed for us! Do we see the Lord in each of those detours? No, but He certainly is there, guiding our paths.

Your word *is* a lamp to my feet

And a light to my path.
Psalms 119:105 (NKJV)

Robert Frost wrote, "Two roads diverged in a wood, and I--I took the one less traveled by, and that has made all the difference." God's path is the one with all the blessings. That road more traveled by is the one with all the potholes, which cause us to trip and fall! If following the world, we are on the path to destruction.

[13] "Enter by the narrow gate; for wide *is* the gate and broad *is* the way that leads to destruction, and there are many who go in by it. [14] Because narrow *is* the gate and difficult *is* the way which leads to life, and there are few who find it.
  Matthew 7:13-14 (NKJV)

Yet there is a difference between the path and the gate. As Christians, we occasionally can find ourselves on the wrong path, but God will make sure He gets us to the right gate! So take another step and stand on promise #2.

February 25: Who conducts your symphony?

Does God plan the sin in our lives? No, but He knows every sin that we are going to choose to commit, and uses our faulty choices to draw us closer to Him.

And we know that all things work together for good to those who love God, to those who are the called according to *His* purpose.
Romans 8:28 (NKJV)

For those who ever have heard a symphony orchestra, when arriving early, a familiar sound is the musicians tuning their instruments. It is such a cacophony of discordant sound, with some instruments severely out of tune, and each musician playing at their own pace and with their own cadence. That sound is as irritating as fingernails on a chalkboard. Yet after some time, the conductor marches to the podium. He directs each and every musician to play a unique piece on their own instrument, according to the conductor's rhythm. When they are all playing together, the sound is melodic and harmonious.

Now look at this analogy as it pertains to our Christian walks. God is the Conductor, as He directs each of us, though we choose whether or not to follow His lead. What would happen if all of a sudden we heard a flute piping the wrong high note in the midst of the symphony? In the Romans 8:28 philosophy, God would cover it. He could have all the other instruments play in that new key. He could have a bass drum play at exactly the same moment, overpowering the sound of the flute. He could let the flutist's wrong note teach the musician a very important lesson about following the music on the sheet in front of him. Yet, however God would choose to handle the situation, by His promise, the symphony would continue to glorify Him and even be for the good of the flutist.

Those sounds that conflict the harmony of the symphony are representative of sin in this analogy, and our own sin should bother us more than fingernails on a chalkboard. God's perfect will has our lives making beautiful music unto Him. Yet He understands our propensity to sin. Rather than allowing sin to weigh us down, He has given us the gift of His Holy Spirit to convict us of our sins. That word "convict" refers to convincing, rather than finding us guilty in a court of law. Through the act of convicting us, the Holy Spirit teaches us to do it God's way. He is certainly as important as the Conductor in the orchestra! If we are members of God's orchestra, know that He will not fire us for making mistakes! That should give us confidence in Him, rather than confidence in our own behavior. It also should take the pressure off. God does not want us walking as rigid robots. He wants us to be the unique creations He made, while loving His law and Word. Yet do not forget that God is the Conductor! He leads the orchestra! Follow Him!

[8] And when He has come, He will convict the world of sin, and of righteousness, and of judgment: [9] of sin, because they do not believe in Me; [10] of righteousness, because I go to My

Father and you see Me no more; [11] of judgment, because the ruler of this world is judged.
John 16:8-11 (NKJV)

If anyone serves Me, let him follow Me; and where I am, there My servant will be also. If anyone serves Me, him *My* Father will honor.
John 12:26 (NKJV)

February 26: Praise Him!

Many pastors today are spreading a prosperity message. One of the fallacies of this teaching states that Jesus grew up wealthier than those who surrounded Him, based on the gifts of gold, frankincense and myrrh brought by the Magi. It is easy to see why this message of earthly prosperity is prevalent, as it seems like an easier path. "Name it and claim it" goes hand-in-hand with "blab it and grab it!" Yet having discussed some promises that give a believer power, we need to notice a promise that is noticeably absent. God has not promised that our Christian lives will be easy. Every one of the disciples of Jesus died as martyrs, except for John, and John was placed in a cauldron of burning oil! If God offered riches to everyone who turned to Him, would not everyone come for that reason alone?

Instead, Jesus told us:

[18] "If the world hates you, you know that it hated Me before *it hated* you. [19] If you were of the world, the world would love its own. Yet because you are not of the world, but I chose you out of the world, therefore the world hates you. [20] Remember the word that I said to you, 'A servant is not greater than his master.' If they persecuted Me, they will also persecute you.
John 15:18-20 (NKJV)

Jesus also told us:

> These things I have spoken to you, that in Me you may have peace. In the world you will have tribulation; but be of good cheer, I have overcome the world."
> John 16:33 (NKJV)

So, do not be surprised when life is difficult! When it is difficult, stand on the promises we already have discussed, and follow the advice in this Bible verse:

> [16] **Rejoice always,** [17] **pray without ceasing,** [18] **in everything give thanks; for this is the will of God in Christ Jesus for you.**
> 1 Thessalonians 5:16-18 (NKJV)

It does not say to give thanks for all the seemingly wonderful things in our lives. It says to give thanks **for everything**. It is difficult to imagine a parent thanking God after the death of their child, but Job did exactly that. In fact, he thanked God for not just the death of one child, but for the death of all 10 of his children. God deserves our praise and our thanks. This relies heavily on the other promises God has made to believers. If we have accepted Him into our lives, and He has forgiven our sins, we do not need anything else! If we truly believe that all things will work together for our good, then even the death of a child, the loss of a job or the brokenness of our lives will be for our good. We just need to thank Him for it.

When looking around, it may seem as if we are in the darkest hole imaginable. Yet how dark can it be with Jesus Christ as our Lord and Savior? He is the Light of the world, and light cannot exist with darkness. That place might seem dark, but all we have to do is open our spiritual eyes and see the Light!

February 27: A perfect 10!

Athletes always strive for perfection, though in many ways, perfection is a fleeting goal. In man's eyes, perfection always is changing. By watching the figure skating at the Olympics, we can see that to some people, a triple axel is perfection. An axel is a jump with a forward takeoff invented in 1882 by Norwegian skater Axel Paulsen. Dick Button was the first to land a double axel in competition, at the 1948 Winter Olympics. Thirty years later, Vern Taylor landed the first triple axel in competition. Now skaters are working on the quadruple axel, though as yet, no one has landed it in competition. Bigger and better continues to drive us. In God's eyes, though, perfection does not change. A perfect life is one without sin, and only Jesus could manage that. So do we have any chance at perfection?

[3] I thank my God upon every remembrance of you, [4] always in every prayer of mine making request for you all with joy, [5] for your fellowship in the gospel from the first day until now, [6] being confident of this very thing, that He who has begun a good work in you will complete *it* until the day of Jesus Christ;
Philippians 1:3-6 (NKJV)

We fail, but God never fails. He is the one responsible for us becoming more like Him. He will put us in situations where we will grow closer to Him. God is going to complete His work in us. So what is our part in this formula? This is very important. God is going to keep teaching us lessons, through the various trials of life. Before qualifying for the Olympics, the athletes have to prove themselves in the Olympic Trials. In the same manner, we endure trials to become more like the Lord.

[2] My brethren, count it all joy when you fall into various trials, [3] knowing that the testing of your faith produces patience. [4] But let patience have *its* perfect work, that you may be perfect and complete, lacking nothing.
James 1:2-4 (NKJV)

Lessons are not always easy. Sometimes, we have to get gently prodded in one direction. When we fail to listen, sometimes we have to get hit in the head! The shepherd's staff worked in both ways. The crook at the end could gently bring the straying sheep back. If the sheep went astray too many times, the shepherd might choose to pop the sheep in the butt with the staff to get the sheep's attention.

If we learn the first time, we are more apt to get the gentle correction rather than the attention getter. We should learn our lessons well.

If God is going to perfect us, why did He not make us perfect the first time? Why did He allow us to live in these sinful bodies on this sinful earth? Paul certainly understood that feeling:

> [15] For what I am doing, I do not understand. For what I will to do, that I do not practice; but what I hate, that I do. [16] If, then, I do what I will not to do, I agree with the law that *it is* good. [17] But now, *it is* no longer I who do it, but sin that dwells in me.
> **Romans 7:15-17 (NKJV)**

What we hate we continue to do! Sin still is a part of our lives. The key to it all is the desire of our hearts. As Christians, though we continue to sin, we should desire to do it God's way. When self dies to the point where we desire His will in our lives, He will work out the rest of the details. Think of David, who was a man after God's own heart. If we delight in the Lord, the Word tells us that God will give us the desires of our hearts. If the desire of our hearts is to do it His way, then it is easy to see how God will give us that desire. He will accomplish that by perfecting us, by putting us in glorified bodies that never will have to worry or sorrow about sin ever again. Praise God!

February 28: Eleven

Eleven is a significant number in the Bible. Though certainly not as prevalent as either 10 or 12, "11" seems to be related to both. While 12 is a perfect number in government, 10 appears to be perfection in Divine order (an example would be the 10 Commandments). With that in mind, "11" seems to be missing the mark on both of those. Either it is one more than the perfect number of Divine order or one less than the perfect number of government.

Once again, as God has chosen every word in the Bible, we know He is a God of order. There is no such thing as a coincidence with Him, and walking with Him reminds us of His powerful hand in each of our lives.

While 10 and 12 seem to be complete numbers, 11 is incomplete! It is a number which points to disorder, disorganization, imperfection, and disintegration. In the family of Joseph, the 11 that comes to mind is the number of brothers remaining after selling Joseph into slavery. Certainly, without Joseph, those brothers were incomplete, even though they suffered with jealousy when he was with them.

Then he dreamed still another dream and told it to his brothers, and said, "Look, I have dreamed another dream. And this time, the sun, the moon, and the eleven stars bowed down to me."
Genesis 37:9 (NKJV)

Another 11 appears in the life of Joseph, but not so overtly. He was sold into slavery at the age of 17 and appeared before Pharaoh at the age of 30. Additionally, he spent two years in prison. By subtracting two and 17 from 30, we find that Joseph spent 11 years in Potiphar's house. It certainly was not a perfect place for Joseph, with Potiphar's wife lusting for him. Yet God's perfect plan was fulfilled when Joseph became second in command in all of Egypt. What a great reminder the life of Joseph is to every believer who does not feel they are exactly where God wants them to be! Trials are a part of the preparation.

The most significant occurrence of 11 seems to be the number of apostles of Jesus after Judas committed suicide. Jesus handpicked the 12, and as soon as one was gone, they cast lots to select the 12th. Many biblical scholars believe that the apostles acted before praying, thinking that God had intended Saul of Tarsus to convert to Christianity and become the 12th apostle. Though Paul was an apostle, Matthias was not a mistake. God does not make mistakes. In Acts 2:14, Matthias stood up with the other 11 as an apostle, one set apart by God as the foundation of the church. The group was incomplete with only 11

When the Jews departed from Egypt, they wandered in the wilderness for 40 years. Yet we also know that the journey only should have taken 11 days. If they were following the Lord in heart, soul, mind and strength, what would have occurred on that 12th day? The children of Israel would have entered the Promised Land and received complete administration of the laws God had given them!

Interestingly, Jehoiakim reigned 11 years when Nebuchadnezzar came up and began his disintegrating work on Jerusalem (2 Kings 23:36, 2 Kings 34:1):

^{5} Jehoiakim *was* twenty-five years old when he became king, and he reigned eleven years in Jerusalem. And he did evil in the sight of the L<small>ORD</small> his God. ^{6} Nebuchadnezzar king of Babylon came up against him, and bound him in bronze *fetters* to carry him off to Babylon.
2 Chronicles 36:5-6 (NKJV)

Additionally, Zedekiah reigned 11 years before Nebuchadnezzar completed the task, putting a temporary end to Jerusalem's rule in Israel (2 Chronicles 36:11, Jeremiah 39:2 and Jeremiah 52:1). Another interesting usage of 11 in the Bible occurs in the parable of the laborers, where the workers hired in the 11th hour receive the same blessings as those hired earlier:

^{1} "For the kingdom of heaven is like a landowner who went out early in the morning to hire laborers for his vineyard. ^{2} Now when he had agreed with the laborers for a denarius a day, he sent them into his vineyard. ^{3} And he went out about the third hour and saw others standing idle in the marketplace, ^{4} and said to them, 'You also go into the vineyard, and whatever is right I will give you.' So they went. ^{5} Again he went out about the sixth and the ninth hour, and did likewise. ^{6} And about the eleventh hour he went out and found others standing idle, and said to them, 'Why have you

been standing here idle all day?' ⁷ **They said to him, 'Because no one hired us.' He said to them, 'You also go into the vineyard, and whatever is right you will receive.'**
Matthew 20:1-7 (NKJV)

With the Hebrew day beginning at 6 a.m., this refers to 5 p.m., typically the end of our work days! Are we in the 11th hour on this earth? Only God knows. When Israel became a nation again in 1948 and the Jews re-inhabited Jerusalem in 1967, all the events leading to the Lord's return have taken place. That being said, God does not desire for us to wait for His arrival, but to go into the fields and help with the harvest. Just as the number 11, we are incomplete without God! Our hearts should be distraught for those who do not know Him. On this day filled with 11's, we should let God use us to bring others into His kingdom!

Then He said to them, "The harvest truly *is* great, but the laborers *are* few; therefore pray the Lord of the harvest to send out laborers into His harvest.
Luke 10:2 (NKJV)

March 1: "All My Trials" by the Temptations

A common nightmare for adults returns us to high school or college for a final exam we have not prepared for. According to those who study dreams, that reflects a situation in our lives where we feel "under the gun." That interpretation of a "dreamologist" may carry a hint of logic, but is merely guesswork. Without God's help, Daniel would have failed miserably in dream interpretation, along with the "experts" in King Nebuchadnezzar's court. Dreams can be places where God speaks to us, though they also can be places of temptation. Yet this seemingly common dream does remind us of the pressures of final exams, when the measurement of success and failure occurred in the moment of turning in that paper.

More important than any final exam in school are the day-by-day tests that God allows in each of our lives. The word for trial in

Greek is *peirasmo,* which is the state of being tested, often by suffering. Interestingly, it is the same word for temptation, which is a trial with a beneficial purpose. Even Jesus had to endure those trials and temptations when He walked as a man on this earth. Immediately after being baptized, Jesus fasted for 40 days and nights and then battled Satan's frontal assaults. Described by Matthew, Mark and Luke, we see that Satan offered Jesus the world. Jesus did not question Satan's ability to give the world to Jesus, as He knew that Satan had dominion over the earth. Yet Jesus remained sin-free and thwarted Satan with His knowledge of the Word of God. Satan misquoted or misinterpreted God's Word in all of his arguments to Jesus. This should remind us that while Satan is powerful, he is not ALL POWERFUL! He has spent thousands of years practicing his art of deceit. While he can pack quite a punch in his dealings with us as believers, he cannot battle the power of God. The power of God is available to us through the Bible, with God dwelling inside of every believer! How can we battle Satan without knowing what the Word says? This brings us to another powerful promise from our Lord:

No temptation has overtaken you except such as is common to man; but God *is* faithful, who will not allow you to be tempted beyond what you are able, but with the temptation will also make the way of escape, that you may be able to bear *it.*
1 Corinthians 10:13 (NKJV)

Breaking this verse down, the first part is that we all stumble in the same ways. Secondly, we see that though we are not faithful, God is! Thirdly, He only allows hurdles in our paths that we are able to jump over. When we find ourselves behind an approaching hurdle, God has a message for us. As difficult as the upcoming task may be, God is telling us that with His power, we have the strength that will sustain us. Jesus is the door and the way of escape. When we turn to Him, we are powered by God rather than powered by self. Remember, Satan brings the battle, but God allows that to happen for a purpose. Satan despises those who are working for the kingdom of God;

certainly, the more we love the Lord, the bigger target will be on our heads from Satan. It may be difficult, but we should remember who is in charge of our lives! Through every trial, God is testing us, and just as silver is purified and made stronger under intense heat, God is drawing us closer.

I will bring the *one*-third through the fire,
Will refine them as silver is refined,
And test them as gold is tested.
They will call on My name,
And I will answer them.
I will say, 'This *is* My people';
And each one will say, 'The LORD *is* my God.' "
Zechariah 13:9 (NKJV)

March 2: Perfect or forgiven?

With endless stories of Christian pastors who stumble into sinful places, many unbelievers stand on the outside pointing fingers of blame. The common feeling is, "How can you be a Christian with a mess like that in your life?" Another common feeling is, "Practice what you preach!" Ted Haggard, the pastor of the 14,000 member New Life Church in Colorado Springs, Colorado, was one of the most influential members of the evangelical movement until the world watched him fall. Haggard was caught in an affair with a homosexual hustler, who charges that Haggard also asked him to buy crystal methamphetamine to accentuate the experience. Haggard was not alone. Jimmy Swaggart went through his own struggles, too. In 1988, two years after exposing a rival pastor for having numerous affairs, photographs surfaced of Swaggart with a prostitute. Three years later, he was arrested in Indio, California, for soliciting a prostitute. Because Swaggart and Haggard have staggered, does it mean they are destined for hell?

As Christians, we are forgiven, not perfect. That perfection will not occur until we are face to face with our Savior. The stumbles continue, though if we are drawing closer to Jesus daily, we should see more of Him and less of ourselves when we look into a mirror. Satan, called both the great deceiver and the accuser of the brethren, continues his lying ways. All of us have sinned and have felt the reminder from Satan that we are not the Lord's, yet that is a lie straight from the pit of hell. Before we became Christians, we were slaves to sin. Sin did not bother us. Some of those sins were incredibly hurtful to those around us, but our selfish desires superseded their pain. As Christians, we still have that propensity to run toward sin, but the pleasure that sin once gave seems empty at best. If the Holy Spirit dwells inside of us, as He does in every believer, He will remind us of our sin. It is a constant battle, and as long as the battle goes on, we know that we are His. Logically, why would Satan ever belittle us for sin if we are fighting in his army?

[7] Nevertheless I tell you the truth. It is to your advantage that I go away; for if I do not go away, the Helper will not come to you; but if I depart, I will send Him to you. [8] And when He has come, He will convict the world of sin, and of righteousness, and of judgment: [9] of sin, because they do not believe in Me; [10] of righteousness, because I go to My Father and you see Me no more; [11] of judgment, because the ruler of this world is judged.
[12] "I still have many things to say to you, but you cannot bear *them* **now. [13] However, when He, the Spirit of truth, has come, He will guide you into all truth; for He will not speak on His own** *authority,* **but whatever He hears He will speak; and He will tell you things to come.**
John 16:7-13 (NKJV)

The Holy Spirit does His job perfectly. Be careful in casting stones at other believers who have stumbled. A saying originated by a martyr in the 1500's comes to mind, "There but for the grace of God go I!" God faithfully will complete His work in each of us!

March 3: Walk in the Spirit

We rely heavily on our automobiles to get us to school, work, church, shopping and the remainder of our leisure activities. In fact, in the United States, we put an average of 12,000 miles per year on our cars. Some people spend more time in an airplane than in a car, zipping around the world. Whether we travel by car or airplane, all of our lives seem to be more inclined to getting us there faster and allowing us to go farther. Except in large, metropolitan areas like New York City, walking seems to have been replaced by speedier methods of transportation.

Jesus walked a lot. He grew up in Nazareth, and as devout Jews were required to go to Jerusalem three times a year for the feasts of Passover (*Matzos*), Weeks (*Shavuot*) and Tabernacles (*Sukkot*), Jesus would have walked 240 miles roundtrip, three times a year. In 25 years, that adds up to 18,000 miles. During the three-year ministry of our Lord, He likely walked an average of 15-20 miles a day. Walking allows an individual to do a lot of reflecting on the situations at hand. Additionally, it is a great time to pray, or to talk with a good friend. Often, those walks are through beautiful countryside, unfettered by noise or tumult. Unlike running, walking does not leave us out of breath. It is slow but methodical progress.

[16] I say then: Walk in the Spirit, and you shall not fulfill the lust of the flesh. [17] For the flesh lusts against the Spirit, and the Spirit against the flesh; and these are contrary to one another, so that you do not do the things that you wish. [18] But if you are led by the Spirit, you are not under the law. Galatians 5:16-18 (NKJV)

This passage says nothing about running in the Spirit, driving in the Spirit or flying in the Spirit. It sounds like it is more of a slow, methodical progress than what Forrest Gump would attempt! It may be true that "Delta gets you there," but in this case, faster and farther is not the answer. When we walk with the Lord, we have moments when we are walking closely to Him, and other moments when we are not so close. When His desires are at the forefront, we are walking in the Spirit. Yet when our worldly desires get in the way, we find ourselves walking in the flesh.

> ⁶ For to be carnally minded *is* death, but to be spiritually minded *is* life and peace. ⁷ Because the carnal mind *is* enmity against God; for it is not subject to the law of God, nor indeed can be. ⁸ So then, those who are in the flesh cannot please God.
> **Romans 8:6-8 (NKJV)**

Verse 8 above sums it up. We cannot please God when we are walking in the flesh. Yet keep in mind that when the Lord looks at His chosen, He sees the righteousness of His Son in us, rather than the person who continues to stumble and fall. As much as we desire to run to God, He desires for us to walk with Him. In 1913, C. Austin Miles wrote the hymn, "In the Garden," that says, "He walks with me and He talks with me and tells me I am His own, and the joy we share as we tarry there, none other has ever known." Take a walk with Jesus!

> **Do you not know that friendship with the world is enmity with God? Whoever therefore wants to be a friend of the world makes himself an enemy of God.**
> **James 4:4 (NKJV)**

> **Therefore do not let sin reign**
> **in your mortal body, that you**
> **should obey it in its lusts.**
> **Romans 6:12 (NKJV)**

March 4: Carnal carnage

Churches today are filled with carnal Christians. While none of us are able to walk in the Spirit all the time, there is a difference between incidental sin and habitual or lifestyle sin. This is where the subject arises of "license to sin." We know that when we came to the Lord, He forgave all of our past, present and future sins. Some people acknowledge that they cannot stop sinning, and knowing that God will forgive whatever they do, they just continue in their sins. Rather than allowing the Lord to come into their lives and clean them, they are satisfied with dirt. Instead of a "license to sin," we have had the bonds of sin removed and have the freedom not to sin! Once the Lord has come into our hearts and lives, we can choose not to sin! Unfortunately, it is not a one-time decision, but a moment-by-moment one, and until we see Jesus face-to-face, sin will continue in our lives.

When we choose to follow Jesus, He does not remove all of the sinful habits from our lives immediately. Instead, He sends in the Holy Spirit Cleaning Crew. The Holy Spirit begins sweeping out the cracks and crevices of our lives and ridding us of sin. He might begin with sexual promiscuity, and proceed to drugs, alcohol, lying, pride and the like. Some legalistic Christians are quick to judge other believers, who are still struggling with major issues.

We often forget how many sins still controlled our lives soon after becoming Christians, especially when seeing others still involved in harmful practices. Yet it is God who will complete His work in the lives of believers. Additionally, it is His time frame to teach His followers how to draw nearer to Him. Lastly, He does not accomplish the work in the same order or manner in each of us! Rather than judging our fellow, stumbling believers, we should be encouraging them to "be strong and of good courage," when walking away from sinful behaviors.
Remember, the battle is the Lord's and He will win it, as He did on Calvary. A different situation occurs when that person's sin involves us in the process.

The Bible gives us a procedure of how to deal with fellow Christians who sin against us. First, we are to go to them individually. If they do not heed our words, then we are to go to them with an elder. If they still choose to ignore our words, the Lord says to cast them out of the church, that Satan might have his way with them. This seems harsh, but God's purpose is for the sin to break them into coming back into His arms. After 25 years of serving the Lord, a church elder left his wife and moved in with a girlfriend. The pastor of the church went to visit the elder at the new home. He knocked on the door, entered, sat on the couch and cried. No words were necessary. No condemnation was necessary, either. The next day, the elder returned to his wife! That was not man's heart, but God's heart. God does not condemn us. **"There is no condemnation in Christ Jesus."** Instead, His heart breaks with us and for us, as He knows the destruction of sin in our lives. Yet the sins of many carnal Christians are not sins against us, but against God. What should we do there?

Brethren, if a man is overtaken in any trespass, you who *are* **spiritual restore such a one in a spirit of gentleness, considering yourself lest you also be tempted.**
Galatians 6:1 (NKJV)

There is that world "gentleness" again! Rather than words of judgment, our words need to be covered in love. We all have sin in our lives, but who wants to live in a dirty house? We must seek the Lord and find the dirt He wants to sweep out of our hearts today!

And above all things have fervent love for one another, for *"love will cover a multitude of sins."*
1 Peter 4:8 (NKJV)

March 5: To Kill a Mockingbird

2010 was the 50th anniversary of the publishing of Harper Lee's book, "To Kill a Mockingbird." Set in Macomb, Alabama, and dealing with the topics of racial injustice and the loss of innocence, the book won the Pulitzer Prize in 1960, while the author won the Presidential Medal of Freedom in 2007. In the book and movie of the same name, Attorney Atticus Finch represents a black man, who has been accused of raping a white woman in a Southern town with severe class distinctions. After buying his son a gun, Finch instructs his son:

> "I'd rather you shoot at tin cans in the backyard, but I know you'll go after birds. Shoot all the blue jays you want, if you can hit 'em, but remember it's a sin to kill a mockingbird."

In the book, why is it a sin to kill a mockingbird? Mockingbirds spend their lives peacefully singing the songs of others. That word, "others," includes birds, insects and other animals. Recently, a woman tired of hearing her Labrador retriever bark incessantly in the backyard and sent the dog to training to silence the dog. One day she became completely disgruntled to hear the noise begin again, until she remembered that the dog was inside. Upon further inspection, she discovered the noise coming from a mockingbird. They mimic other animals, particularly birds, often in quick succession. For anyone who has had a mockingbird outside of their window, that desire to kill the mockingbird is based on both sleep deprivation and frustration. In the springtime in an attempt to lure a mate, mockingbirds often begin their litany of songs around 3 a.m. Unlike the mockingbird, God does not mimic the song of others:

[10] **But no one says, 'Where *is* God my Maker,**
Who gives songs in the night,
[11] **Who teaches us more than the beasts of the earth,**
And makes us wiser than the birds of heaven?'
[12] **There they cry out, but He does not answer,**
Because of the pride of evil men.
Job 35:10-12 (NKJV)

Jesus told us that He is the Bread of life, and we also know from the opening of the Gospel of John that one of the titles of Jesus is the Word. In the Old Testament, God fed the Jews in the wilderness with manna, the honey wafer that fell from heaven new and fresh each day. Meaning "what is it," *manna* is the name the Jews gave to God's provision, as they tired of its sameness. Yet the sustenance was enough to keep them alive and well. In the same manner, God has given us His Word. Even with repetitive reading of the Bible, the words remain the same, but the message can hit us right between the eyes depending on the places God has us in our lives. The Bible reminds us in both the Old and New Testaments that we do not live by just bread, but by the words that come from the Lord.

(Deuteronomy 8:3, Matthew 4:4 and Luke 4:4). Those words are new and fresh each day. Satan tries to copy God in many ways, but God's message is one that no one can mimic!

March 6: Gray areas

We live in a black and white world. In New York, there are black and white cookies. Some of the greatest movies are in black and white. Newspapers are printed in black and white. Even Michael Jackson, before his death, was black and white! Is God's law black and white? Is it a sin to drink or smoke? Where does divorce fit in this discussion? How about joining into the spirit of things au-natural at a nude beach? Is it okay to buy another Lamborghini, to go with the Rolls-Royce and Mercedes-Benz, when a friend cannot get to work because his 1969 Volkswagen Bug broke down again?

Many people will bring up the concept of moral relativism. That is the belief that if we think that something is wrong, it is wrong, but if we think something is right, it is right. Problematic in that logical discussion is the importance of us and our conviction. What is more important, our law or God's law?

[16] *"This is the covenant that I will make with them after those days, says the LORD: I will put My laws into their hearts, and in their minds I will write them,"* [17] **then He adds,** *"Their sins and their lawless deeds I will remember no more."*
Hebrews 10:16-17 (NKJV)

In the passage above, as well as in a very similar quotation of this passage in the Old Testament (see Jeremiah 31:31-34), God says that He will put His law on the minds and hearts of the Jews. Do all of us have the same understanding of God's law now? Men of faith and believers in the inerrancy of God's Word still can struggle with sin and even with the understanding of the definition of sin. However, whether or not we sin has nothing to do with our acceptance or understanding of the commission of that sin. For example, if a person never has read the Bible and has a sexual relationship with his neighbor's wife, it still is sin. We cannot rationalize our behavior. "He does not love her and their relationship virtually has been over for years!" "If it would not have been me, it would have been someone else." Regardless of what he said or felt, it would not change God's seventh commandment to not commit adultery, whether or not we ever had read those commandments.

While it is difficult to grasp this for some, God created us in His image. That does not mean that we have His nose, His eyes and His jawbone. Instead, He has imprinted us with the knowledge of Him. There is a God-shaped vessel inside each of us. We can choose to fill it with God as He is the only perfect fit. Instead, most try to cram in drugs, fame, money, or any host of things that simply cannot fill the void. Another common error occurs when we choose the parts of the Bible that we are willing to follow. When we do that, we create a god in our image, one we are willing to worship. That is exactly what idolatry is. God tells us exactly who He is. He tells us exactly what His laws are. What gives us the right to decide which law is good and which law is bad, when those laws were set by an omniscient God?

Yet there are gray areas. It does not say smoking is a sin in the Bible. It does not say that shooting up heroin is a sin, specifically, but we do know that the same root word we have for pharmacy is *pharmakei*, the Greek word for sorcery. In 1 Corinthians, Paul told us that we as Christians have freedom. One of the issues of Paul's day was in eating meat that had been offered to idols. It was not against God's law, but it caused weaker brothers to stumble. So Paul said:

[11] And because of your knowledge shall the weak brother perish, for whom Christ died? [12] But when you thus sin against the brethren, and wound their weak conscience, you sin against Christ.
1 Corinthians 8:11-12 (NKJV)

It is good neither to eat meat nor drink wine nor *do anything* by which your brother stumbles or is offended or is made weak.

Romans 14:21 (NKJV)

In that regard, God tells us to stay away from the gray areas. When our concerns extend to the spiritual welfare of our brethren, we start to understand God's love for us in a whole new way! In this black and white world, when we find ourselves in a gray area, we should desire to please God.

Who is weak, and I am not weak? Who is made to stumble, and I do not burn *with indignation*?
2 Corinthians 11:29 (NKJV)

March 7: Where are You, God?

Sometimes we feel alone and are desperate to feel God's presence again in our lives. Unfortunately, we often equate that aloneness with God's behavior and God's love rather than our own. Just because we do not see Him, hear Him or feel Him does not mean that He is not there. Most importantly, it does not mean that God is not in the midst of what we are enduring.

God loves us so much that He cannot take His eyes away from us. Though we sometimes may not feel His presence, that usually has more to do with the sin in our lives that separates us from Him. "Usually" is a key word in the previous sentence, for sin is not always the reason for God's seemingly deaf ear or distance from us. Job endured God's distance not because of sin, but because God wanted to draw him even closer! King David, a man after God's own heart, wrote a number of psalms with that feeling of being removed from the presence of God. In fact, Jesus felt that same distance! Though Jesus never sinned, the distance that He felt was a response to sin, just as it is so often in our own lives, yet it was a response to our sins that Jesus was carrying. David wrote these prophetic words from what he was feeling, though Jesus lived the words on the cross:

My God, My God, why have You forsaken Me?
***Why are You so* far from helping Me,**
***And from* the words of My groaning?**

Psalm 22:1 (NKJV)

When the sins of the world were heaped upon the mighty shoulders of our Savior, He felt the separation from His Father that sin causes. A righteous God cannot look upon sin. At that moment on the cross, Jesus felt a loss of relationship with His Father for the only time in all of eternity. Notice the words in the verse above. Jesus does not refer to "My Father," but to "My God." Jesus speaks of God twice, and we know that God is in three persons. Jesus is speaking to the Father and the Holy Spirit! So in that verse, Jesus not only felt the separation from the Father, but also from the Holy Spirit.

We as Christians have the Father, Son and Holy Spirit living inside of us. It should shame us to think of the places we have carried God and how we have involved Him in our sinful lives.

²³"Am I a God near at hand," says the Lord,
"And not a God afar off?
²⁴ Can anyone hide himself in secret places,
So I shall not see him?" says the Lord;
"Do I not fill heaven and earth?" says the Lord.
Jeremiah 23:23-24 (NKJV)

God is everywhere. He cannot be far off, though He may seem that way at times in our lives. If we do not sense His presence, we should begin by confessing our sins to Him! Once that has occurred, if we continue to feel separation, we should wait on the Lord. Sometimes, He uses those "dry periods" to draw us nearer.

⁸'These people draw near to Me with their mouth,
And honor Me with their lips,
But their heart is far from Me.
⁹ And in vain they worship Me,
Teaching as doctrines the commandments of men.' "
Matthew 15:8-9 (NKJV)

March 8: No veil makes God available!

When Jesus died on the cross, the temple veil was torn in two. At the time of Jesus, the temple was a very significant place, where the Jews performed all sacrifices to cover their sins, according to the Law of Moses. Yet notice that the blood of the sacrifice <u>covered</u> their sins; it did not take those sins away! Inside the temple, the veil separated the inner chamber known as the "Holy of Holies" from the outer chambers. The "Holy of Holies" was the earthly dwelling place of God's presence, and the only person allowed inside was the high priest. Yet even the high priest only could enter that chamber once a year, on *Yom Kippur*, the Day of Atonement.

Solomon's temple was 30 cubits high, according to 1 Kings 6:2, with a cubit being the average distance between the bend in the elbow and the tip of the middle finger, commonly about 18 inches. So the veil was at least 45 feet high. According to Exodus, the veil was made of blue, purple and scarlet material fashioned into linen and twisted together, and adorned with cherubim. Additionally, according to the writings of the Jewish historian Josephus, the veil was at least 4 inches thick and horses tied to each side could not pull the veil apart. That makes what occurred at the death of Jesus even more of a miracle:

**^{50} And Jesus cried out again with a loud voice, and yielded up His spirit. ^{51} Then, behold, the veil of the temple was torn in two from top to bottom; and the earth quaked, and the rocks were split, ^{52} and the graves were opened; and many bodies of the saints who had fallen asleep were raised; ^{53} and coming out of the graves after His resurrection, they went into the holy city and appeared to many.
Matthew 27:50-53 (NKJV)**

When the veil was torn from top to bottom, it gave us access into the "Holy of Holies!" Notice that the action started at the top, where man could not reach. God accomplished that feat. Jesus is our High Priest (according to Hebrews 3:1 and Hebrews 4:14), and He takes us into the throne room of God!

**⁵ For *there is* one God and one Mediator between God and men, *the* Man Christ Jesus, ⁶ who gave Himself a ransom for all, to be testified in due time, ⁷ for which I was appointed a preacher and an apostle—I am speaking the truth in Christ *and* not lying— a teacher of the Gentiles in faith and truth.
1 Timothy 2:5-7 (NKJV)**

That should give us a better concept of the gift of prayer. Now, at any time we like, we are invited into the throne room of the Creator and Ruler of all to have a private and personal conversation! This should not be once a year, as in the Day of Atonement. When we feel separated from God, we should come to Him in prayer

**¹ Behold, the LORD's hand is not shortened,
That it cannot save;
Nor His ear heavy,
That it cannot hear.
² But your iniquities have separated you from your God;
And your sins have hidden *His* face from you,
So that He will not hear.
Isaiah 59:1-2 (NKJV)**

He always hears the confession of our sins. The best part is that because of the work that Jesus did on the cross, God does not just cover our sins, He removes them! The Hebrew word for "removed" is הרחיק , pronounced hir-khiq, and comes from the root word of "far." Because our sin is far from God, we can be near to Him! Come to Him and let Him take away the burden that is creating that distance between us and Him! God did not place the distance there!

The next day John saw Jesus coming toward him, and said, "Behold! The Lamb of God who takes away the sin of the world!

John 1:29 (NKJV)

March 9: Sitting on the dock of the bay!

Trouble seems to come at us in waves, and an old adage says that trouble happens in threes. Instead of counting those calamities, and waiting for another to occur, we should stop counting! According to Paul, we are supposed to count all things of this world as loss. Instead of focusing on those losses, we should be counting our blessings! The gain is Christ, who remains in our lives. The problem lies in perspective. If we are living as if we are citizens of this world, rather than citizens of heaven, our minds become set on the things of this world. Most people worry most about the loss of money, and with money driving this Satan-dominated world, that should be no surprise.

**[7] But what things were gain to me, these I have counted loss for Christ. [8] Yet indeed I also count all things loss for the excellence of the knowledge of Christ Jesus my Lord, for whom I have suffered the loss of all things, and count them as rubbish, that I may gain Christ [9] and be found in Him, not having my own righteousness, which *is* from the law, but that which *is* through faith in Christ, the righteousness which is from God by faith; [10] that I may know Him and the power of His resurrection, and the fellowship of His sufferings, being conformed to His death, [11] if, by any means, I may attain to the resurrection from the dead.
Philippians 3:7-11 (NKJV)**

Those waves of trouble are analogous to a tsunami, and it often feels like that difficult storm has arrived in our lives. When the 9.0 earthquake hit coastal Japan on March 11, 2011, it caused a tsunami that also devastated the Japanese coast. Yet when the plates moved against each other at the ocean floor, they displaced so much water that the ensuing tsunami began to move across the ocean at a rate of 500 MPH. Amazingly, the residual of the tsunami hit the California coast, 5,600 miles away, so strongly that one man died, in addition to causing millions of dollars of damage.

God created this world and created the balance of every element on this earth. How can we not see His existence or hand in our daily lives? He controls every aspect, including the far-reaching capabilities of each wave from the mighty ocean. Listen in on this conversation God has with Job:

[8]"Or *who* shut in the sea with doors,
When it burst forth *and* issued from the womb;
[9]When I made the clouds its garment,
And thick darkness its swaddling band;
[10]When I fixed My limit for it,
And set bars and doors;
[11]When I said,
'This far you may come, but no farther,
And here your proud waves must stop!'
Job 38:8-11 (NKJV)

If He cares about the waves of the ocean, God also cares about the waves of trouble in our lives! Jesus certainly had bigger difficulties to face than we do, and we are in the fellowship of His suffering as believers. The simple fact that God allowed His Son to suffer should remind us what is in store for each believer. When we feel like there is a tsunami approaching, we either can give up, letting the waves take us under, or we can ride those waves. We can remain on top of any difficulty with God's help and in the process, He will show us things we never would have seen from below the water!

"Again, the kingdom of heaven is like treasure hidden in a field, which a man found and hid; and for joy over it he goes and sells all that he has and buys that field.
Matthew 13:44 (NKJV)

March 10: Temptations common to man!

Mark Twain said, "I deal with temptation by yielding to it." William Shakespeare gave us a different perspective when he said, "'Tis one thing to be tempted, another thing to fail." We know every man will face temptation, and at least part of the time, every man will yield to it. That is the battle called life. The Greek word for temptation is *peirasmos* (πειρασμός), and it is the same word for a test. Those temptations have not changed much over time as they are the identical ones that faced Adam and Eve.

**⁶ So when the woman saw that the tree *was* good for food, that it *was* pleasant to the eyes, and a tree desirable to make *one* wise, she took of its fruit and ate. She also gave to her husband with her, and he ate. ⁷ Then the eyes of both of them opened, and they knew that they *were* naked; and they sewed fig leaves together and made themselves coverings.
Genesis 3:6-7 (NKJV)**

A verse in the New Testament helps to put that Old Testament verse into perspective:

**¹⁶ For all that is in the world—the lust of the flesh, the lust of the eyes, and the pride of life—is not of the Father but is of the world. ¹⁷ And the world is passing away, and the lust of it; but he who does the will of God abides forever.
1 John 2:16-17 (NKJV)**

Eve was hungry for the fruit that God had forbidden both Adam and Eve to eat. In that hunger, she wanted to satisfy the "lust of the flesh." We are physical and spiritual beings. The spirit craves God while the flesh craves carnal sustenance, like food, drink and sex. Eve also noticed that the fruit was pleasant to the eyes, and demonstrated the "lust of the eyes" that Paul described. Satan told Eve that if she ate of the fruit that God had forbidden, she would be "like God, knowing good and evil." Wanting to have that knowledge, she demonstrated the "pride of life."

Eve failed the test in front of her that day, as did Adam, who followed his wife into that failure. As they did, they cast us all into our roles as the "sons of disobedience." Lest we blame Adam and Eve for our plight, each one of us would have failed in the same manner. What we need to remember is that our God is omniscient (all-knowing), omnipotent (all-powerful) and omnipresent (existing everywhere simultaneously). Satan, on the other hand, is none of those. Instead, he is cunningly deceitful and knows what deceptive practices will work best to cause us to stumble. He was masterful in his ploy against Eve, and has had years since to perfect his evil craft.

Remember that Satan's destructive forces involve one-third of the angels from heaven, who followed him in his folly to become God's equal. Knowing that there are more angels than the sands of the sea reminds us of the major, daily battle going on. Spiritual warfare is not imagined. Nor is it less damaging than physical warfare. We should open our spiritual eyes and realize that the Lord, our God, will fight our battles for us! He has surrounded us with His heavenly host! Whether Satan attacks with the lust of the flesh, the lust of the eyes, the pride of life, or a combination of those, God will help us in the midst of battle!

When Satan besieged Jesus in the wilderness, Jesus deflected that attack by using the Word of God correctly. According to Ephesians, the Bible is our only offensive weapon for use in spiritual battles. We are to be well-armed with the sword of the Spirit, yet lest we forget, that involves plenty of time in the study of God's Word!

[10] **Finally, my brethren, be strong in the Lord and in the power of His might.** [11] **Put on the whole armor of God, that you may be able to stand against the wiles of the devil.** [12] **For we do not wrestle against flesh and blood, but against principalities, against powers, against the rulers of the darkness of this age, against spiritual *hosts* of wickedness in the heavenly *places*.** [13] **Therefore take up the whole armor of God, that you may be able to withstand in the evil day, and having done all, to stand.** [14] **Stand therefore, having girded your waist with truth, having put on the breastplate of righteousness,** [15] **and having shod your feet with the preparation of the gospel of peace;** [16] **above all, taking the shield of faith with which you will be able to quench all the fiery darts of the wicked one.** [17] **And take the helmet of**

salvation, and the sword of the Spirit, which is the word of God; [18] praying always with all prayer and supplication in the Spirit, being watchful to this end with all perseverance and supplication for all the saints— [19] and for me, that utterance may be given to me, that I may open my mouth boldly to make known the mystery of the gospel, [20] for which I am an ambassador in chains; that in it I may speak boldly, as I ought to speak.
Ephesians 6:10-20 (NKJV)

March 11: Lust of the flesh

One of the greatest difficulties when dieting occurs in the brain. If the dieter gives up ice cream, for example, all that person can think about is ice cream. Yet it is interesting that when fasting for three days, after that initial period of hunger, the physical craving seems to pass. Without proper nourishment, the body ceases to function properly, and in that manner, food is vital for our survival. But when focusing upon feeding the flesh, we de-emphasize feeding the Spirit.

Just as God is in three persons, He created us in three parts: body, soul and spirit. We know the most about the body, and frankly, tend to focus on the body. Gym memberships are more pervasive than church memberships, as spiritual well-being gets lost in the shuffle. When bodies crave food, our stomachs growl! We also crave liquid to drink, and cannot exist without it. Sex is another craving that takes over the lives of many. Tiger Woods certainly could tell us about how strong that desire can be, though he is certainly not alone in that pursuit. Our souls, on the other hand, are tied more to our brains and who we are as humans. Lastly, the spirit is the part of us that connects with God. Satan tries to trip us with the lust of the flesh, the lust of the eyes and the pride of life, according to 1 John. Not surprisingly, that was the same strategy that Satan attempted on Jesus:

[1] **Then Jesus was led up by the Spirit into the wilderness to be tempted by the devil.** [2] **And when He had fasted forty days**

and forty nights, afterward He was hungry. ³ Now when the tempter came to Him, he said, "If You are the Son of God, command that these stones become bread." ⁴ But He answered and said, "It is written, *'Man shall not live by bread alone, but by every word that proceeds from the mouth of God.'"*
Matthew 4:1-4 (NKJV)

That first attempt by Satan to tempt our Messiah was through the lust of the flesh. Personally, it is sometimes difficult for us to grasp God being hungry, yet when Jesus departed heaven for earth, He not only became a man, but also, took on the frailties of the human body. One of those aspects was the need for physical sustenance, food and drink. As hungry and weak as Jesus had become in His 40-day fast, our Lord still did not give into the temptations of the wily one. Rather than satisfy an urge to keep His earthly body strong, Jesus made a decision to strengthen His spiritual connection with the Father. We can gratify the flesh, but we never can satisfy the desires of the flesh. Only God can satisfy, and though Satan attempts to fool us into believing that he can supply our needs, he can only supply our wants.

When I was a child, I spoke as a child, I understood as a child, I thought as a child; but when I became a man, I put away childish things.
1 Corinthians 13:11 (NKJV)

Flee also youthful lusts; but pursue righteousness, faith, love, peace with those who call on the Lord out of a pure heart.
2 Timothy 2:22 (NKJV)

As we age, most of us come to realize that our priorities change. What we often perceive as needs are actually desires. By allowing those desires to control us, we are feeding a beast that never can get enough. In the same manner that we find ourselves hungry again just hours after a meal at a Chinese restaurant, no meal can satisfy the flesh. Instead, we need to feed the Spirit!

[11] But you, O man of God, flee these things and pursue righteousness, godliness, faith, love, patience, gentleness. [12] Fight the good fight of faith, lay hold on eternal life, to which you were also called and have confessed the good confession in the presence of many witnesses.
1 Timothy 6:11-12 (NKJV)

But put on the Lord Jesus Christ, and make no provision for the flesh, to *fulfill its* lusts.
Romans 13:14 (NKJV)

March 12: See no evil?

One of the most interesting stops in the City of David, outside the walls of Jerusalem, is Hezekiah's Tunnel, discussed in 2 Kings 20. In the days of King Hezekiah, crews started on opposite ends, dug through solid granite and connected the 533-meter tunnel in the middle, to bring water into the city. Walking through the tunnel in modern times has not changed since the days it was built, apart from the flashlights carried by some tourists. Walking through the pitch darkness, waist-deep in cold water, the greatest challenge involves the varying heights of the ceiling, which is sometimes lower than the height of an average person. Without a flashlight, meandering through the tunnel is similar to the journey of a blind man:

[6] When He had said these things, He spat on the ground and made clay with the saliva; and He anointed the eyes of the blind man with the clay. [7] And He said to him, "Go, wash in the pool of Siloam" (which is translated, Sent). So he went and washed, and came back seeing.
John 9:6-7 (NKJV)

The blind man faithfully obeyed Jesus, and was healed, emerging with vision at the Pool of Siloam, exactly where Hezekiah's Tunnel emerges from that pitch blackness. What would it be like to be blind from birth? How did the man make the journey to the Pool of Siloam? Walking through that tunnel is a straight path without potential missed turns, but it does cause bumps on the head from a lower-than-expected ceiling. How does a blind man go anywhere? How powerful would the "lust of the eyes" be to a man who never had functioning eyes?

Jesus gave the man sight that day, and in that miracle, opened up an entirely new aspect of potential temptations from Satan, but that was certainly welcome in the life of the man who had lived in darkness for so many years. Of all our senses, sight is the one most people would struggle the most without. Though we place a priority on physical sight, spiritual sight is the greatest gift.

The LORD opens *the eyes of* **the blind;**
The LORD raises those who are bowed down;
The LORD loves the righteous.
Psalms 146:8 (NKJV)

He answered and said, "Whether He is a sinner *or not* **I do not know. One thing I know: that though I was blind, now I see."**
John 9:25 (NKJV)

God has gifted each believer with spiritual sight. It is only through those eyes that we can see the things of God. As believers, we have the ability to see God everywhere and in everything. As "Amazing Grace" reminds us, "I once was lost, but now am found, was blind, but now I see." Walk thankfully in the miracle He has given us of spiritual sight!

March 13: Lust of the eyes

An old adage says that the eyes are the windows to the soul, demonstrating the ability to look into a man's eyes and see either the good that drives him or the evil that poisons him. Jesus gave us the same impression when He said:

But I say to you that whoever looks at a woman to lust for her has already committed adultery with her in his heart.

Matthew 5:28

If a man has decided to sin in his heart, it will occur in action, as man has a tendency to run to sin. When the serpent tempted Eve in the Garden of Eden, she lusted with her eyes for the fruit on the tree in the midst of the garden. Knowing it was the only fruit God had instructed Adam and Eve not to eat did not dissuade her in this pursuit. The New King James Version says that the fruit was **"pleasant to the eyes,"** but the literal translation is it was a desirable thing. The Hebrew word for pleasant or desirable is תאוה "tah-av-**aw**," and other times the word is used in the Old Testament, it is translated "lust" or "greedily." This applies directly to the last of the 10 Commandments to not covet.

Satan also attempted a similar ploy with Jesus after our Lord's baptism, 40-day fast, and journey in the wilderness:

⁵ Then the devil, taking Him up on a high mountain, showed Him all the kingdoms of the world in a moment of time. ⁶ And the devil said to Him, "All this authority I will give You, and their glory; for *this* has been delivered to me, and I give it to whomever I wish. ⁷ Therefore, if You will worship before me, all will be Yours." ⁸ And Jesus answered and said to him, "Get behind Me, Satan! For it is written, *'You shall worship the LORD your God, and Him only you shall serve.'* "
Luke 4:5-8 (NKJV)

Though this verse just as easily can apply to the "pride of life," as Satan is appealing to man's lust for power, it also can reflect the "lust of the eyes," as Satan had Jesus look upon the seemingly desirable cities. When a man took his children to the foothills above a city, he pointed out the lights below. "Those," he said, indicating the distant city, "are the lights of the places dominated by Satan." Then he motioned to the stars in the sky and said, "Those are the lights controlled by God. Which do you desire the most?"

Sexual lust drives most men, though women stumble in the same manner. Interestingly, in this passage, Satan did not use that ploy in his temptations of Jesus. Maybe he knew that Jesus was faithful to His bride, and that bride includes each of us as believers. Men seem to be driven more by the desires for food and sex, and along with it, power and greed. In the same manner, pretty things seem to appeal more to women. So whether it is a pretty piece of fruit, a diamond necklace, or the city lights of what man created, Satan offers these to both men and women in an attempt to get their eyes away from God.

Why do we desire more than the Lord wants to give us? That is an interesting question, especially when we understand that when our hearts are aligned with the heart of God, He gives us the desires of our hearts. God blesses us more than we ask to be blessed, as He loves us so much that He cannot help but demonstrate that love for us.

In this battle with Satan, learn to accept what the Lord wills and what the Lord gives. Desire is a slippery slope that begins in childhood. One of the first words a baby utters is "Mine," and that selfish desire for more possessions never can be satisfied. The world's richest man of his day, John D. Rockefeller, responded when someone asked him how much was enough money. "Just a little more money than I have," was his notable response. Instead, God has called us to be content wherever He has us!

But those who desire to be rich fall into temptation and a snare, and *into* many foolish and harmful lusts which drown men in destruction and perdition.
1 Timothy 6:9 (NKJV)

March 14: Is it a lion's pride or our lyin' pride?

Lucifer was the most powerful angel in heaven at one time. He was **"full of wisdom and perfect in beauty,"** according to Ezekiel 28. Yet in all of his talents, abilities and attributes that God gifted him with at his creation, Lucifer started to believe that those abilities had more to do with him than they had to do with God. In that mental miscue, Lucifer's aspirations grew mightily:

[13] For you have said in your heart:
'I will ascend into heaven,
I will exalt my throne above the stars of God;
I will also sit on the mount of the congregation
On the farthest sides of the north;
[14] I will ascend above the heights of the clouds,
I will be like the Most High.'
Isaiah 14:13-14 (NKJV)

With the sin of pride causing the fall, Lucifer was cast from heaven and became Satan. From that point on, Satan used his intelligence deceptively to cause others to fall and to follow him. His lies continually remind us of our abilities and talents, and completely sidestep the acknowledgment of the God who gave us all we have and made us all we are.

A dear friend in the Lord once shared some words of wisdom, speaking of pride. "I work really hard at not letting pride rule my life, and becoming more humble. Then, I find myself becoming proud of how humble I have become and the whole cycle starts over again!" To think that we can get through this life without pride is prideful! Just as Lucifer's fall from heaven was prideful, and the subsequent sin of Adam and Eve was prideful, so is each and every sin in our lives.

We worship ourselves, rather than God. We put our own desires above God's. We use God's name in a flippant way, making Him lower than He should be in our eyes. We continue working, trying to improve our condition, rather than ending our week with a day of rest and worship. We fail to give respect to our parents, as God placed us in specific families for His reasons. We take another's life, either physically or verbally, uncaring of the effect that will have on others, or even the effect it will have on ourselves. We sleep with whomever we like, whether married or not, because that gratifies our selves rather than glorifying God. We take the possessions of others because we want them, putting our desires above God's or the desires of others. We fail to tell the truth, elevating our own status, covering our own mistakes and using our words to destroy. We see what others have and desire more for ourselves, discontentedly ignoring what God has in store for us.

Notice that each of the sentences in the previous paragraph deal with pride and how it relates to the 10 Commandments! Each of our sins has its basis in our own pride! C.S. Lewis said, "A proud man is always looking down on things and people; and, of course, as long as you're looking down, you can't see something that's above you."

We all should reflect upon the many gifts in our lives, and instead of taking credit for earning them, be thankful to Him who gave those gifts. As quickly as He gave them, He can take them away. The biggest step is to go from "I want" to the contentment of being where we are and the satisfaction of having what we have.

March 15: The pride of life

As we age, the tendency in each of our lives is to look back with pride at what we have accomplished. Often, that is a false sense of accomplishment, as we tend to remember the accolades, rather than the pitfalls. Most people approaching death reflect upon their lives, which went by much faster than imagined. We should not measure our impacts upon this world by the amount of money we earned, or whether we will be remembered for generations to come. Instead, our legacy should be measured by our priorities, for by serving God, we accomplish what God desired for us.

Mountain climbers set their goals based on pride. By ascending Mt. Everest, any mountaineer can boast in making it to the highest point on the earth, and that special accomplishment even may be mentioned on their gravestone when death arrives. Yet we should be more interested in living quiet, godly lives, slowly affecting those around us to love the Lord and follow Him. Sadly, most of us struggle with the desire to be much more important than we truly are. By reading a person's resume, we often get a glimpse into how highly that person esteems self!

When Satan tempted Eve in the Garden of Eden, she desired wisdom, to be like God. Lucifer also had the same desire, to be "like the Most High." Ironically, true wisdom is following the ways of God rather than rocking the boat and rebelling against Him. Paul tells us of people with worldly intelligence, who do not follow God:

Professing to be wise, they became fools...
Romans 1:22 (NKJV)

A part of that "pride of life" is taking credit for the gifts that only God can give. When Satan tempted Jesus in the wilderness, he attempted to ensnare Jesus with this strategy. That temptation is depicted by both Matthew and Luke, though the second and third temptations are in a different order in the two books.

[9] **Then he brought Him to Jerusalem, set Him on the pinnacle of the temple, and said to Him, "If You are the Son of God, throw Yourself down from here.** [10] **For it is written: 'He shall give His angels charge over you,** *To keep you,'* [11] **and, 'In their** *hands they shall bear you up,* **Lest you dash your foot against a stone.' "** [12] **And Jesus answered and said to him, "It has been said,** *'You shall not* **tempt the LORD your God.'**
Luke 4:9-12 (NKJV)

God gave Jesus the gift of life and to flaunt that gift would be to act in a prideful manner. We know that Jesus had every reason to be filled with pride, unlike us, yet still He was the most humble of men. Regardless of the status in our lives, God has placed us into those roles. We know that God appoints kings and countries. There are no accidents. He has gifted each of us with all of our skills and abilities. What part of that tells us that we should be proud of our accomplishments? When we get to heaven, any crown that we "earned," we will cast at the feet of

Jesus, for we finally will understand that all we "accomplished" was His accomplishment, His gift.

¹⁸**Pride *goes* before destruction,
And a haughty spirit before a fall.
¹⁹Better *to be* of a humble spirit with the lowly,
Than to divide the spoil with the proud.
Proverbs 16:18-19 (NKJV)**

March 16: The miracle book!

One of the most special aspects of having a relationship with the Lord is that He continues to be a God of miracles. Paul reminds us in Hebrews 13:8 that, **"Jesus Christ is the same yesterday, today and forever."** Certainly, the God of the Old Testament performed countless miracles, including large-scale ones like the Great Flood, which destroyed all of the earth apart from eight people and representatives of each animal the Lord had created. God often spoke to His people through those miracles. Think of Elijah closing the skies from raining for three and a half years, and then opening the skies with prayer to our God, who cannot change!

In the New Testament, our miraculous God came to dwell among us, as He sent His Son to be born of a virgin. Yet that was only one of many miracles performed by and through the life of Jesus, who made the blind to see, the deaf to hear, the lame to walk and the dead to return to life! He cast out demons and made lepers clean again, as well. While all of those miracles occurred in the physical realm, they also continue to give us examples of what occurs in the spiritual realm when we give our lives to Jesus.

When we have no eyes to see, He gives us spiritual sight. When we have no ears to hear, we miraculously hear His voice, as He calls to us just as a Shepherd calls to His sheep. Broken and withered legs leave us immobile in the dust, yet Jesus gives us legs to rise and follow Him. With all of us destined for spiritual death through our sin, Jesus restores that spiritual life in Him when we decide to walk with our Lord. Just as Jesus brought Lazarus back to life with the words, "Lazarus, come forth," He calls to each of us, who without Him are walking as zombies, like cast members of "Night of the Living Dead."

> Miracles are a retelling in small letters of the very same story which is written across the whole world in letters too large for some of us to see." -- C.S. Lewis

How many miracles did Jesus perform?

And there are also many other things that Jesus did, which if they were written one by one, I suppose that even the world itself could not contain the books that would be written. Amen.
John 21:25 (NKJV)

How many miracles does Jesus continue to perform? He works His miraculous hand in the lives of His children on a daily basis, yesterday, today and forever! When we sleep, His eyes remain upon us, as God loves us so much that He cannot take His eyes away from us! Sadly, while the Lord is guiding us, protecting us and blessing us with His miraculous touch, most of those miracles occur without us even giving thanks to Him! A miracle to one man is a mere coincidence to another. Yet there are times when we acknowledge His hand guarding us and guiding us all the way. That is the time for "The Miracle Book!"

One solution is to find a blank journal and begin to write down the miracles God has performed in our lives. Then, we spend time reflecting upon our pasts, when He revealed His love to us. Especially, do not forget the "little miracles." Remember, there is truly no such thing as a little miracle, for the smallest details reveal how deeply God is involved in our lives, demonstrating the depth of His intimacy and love for us. Each time a miracle occurs, add it to the journal. Unfortunately, our eyes and ears seem to focus on what is immediately in front of us, yet when we write down those special events, those memories are captured forever.

When life's difficulties cause faith to waver, pull out the "Miracle Book" for a reminder of God's love. He has promised to never leave us or forsake us, yet when under spiritual duress, we somehow change that verse in our minds and walk as if He will "sometimes" leave us or "often" forsake us! Constant reminders of His unwavering love can build our faith, helping us to endure the spiritual battles that lie before us.

For in it the righteousness of God is revealed from faith to faith; as it is written, *"The just shall live by faith."* **Romans 1:17 (NKJV)**

As we grow as Christians, our "Miracle Books" will be larger than the Encyclopedia Britannica! That reveals more about our God, who is both big and powerful enough to accomplish those miracles in each of our lives constantly! God gave us an example of His miracles in the writings of the prophets and apostles, yet He wants a personal relationship with each of us. His love for us includes those special miracles, enhancing the intimacy of our individual walks with God. Remember the love He has shown us!

So Jesus said to them, "Because of your unbelief; for assuredly, I say to you, if you have faith as a mustard seed, you will say to this mountain, 'Move from here to there,' and it will move; and nothing will be impossible for you. Matthew 17:20 (NKJV)

March 17: Be lifted up!

Construction gives us many analogies in regard to the Christian walk, as we know that Jesus Christ is the Chief Cornerstone, while the apostles and prophets are the foundation of the Church (Ephesians 2:20). We also know that the body of Christ is the temple of the Holy Spirit, His dwelling place (1 Corinthians 6:19). Certainly, we often apply that terminology to individual Christians, as God resides in each of us, yet a farther-reaching aspect is that God dwells collectively within His body of believers. We are the modern-day tabernacle, as "the Word became flesh and was 'tabernacled' among us," according to John in the Greek translation. Yet the construction analogies continue. Without a proper foundation, it is not worth erecting any building. When building a structure in the proper order – cornerstone, foundation, inner walls, outer walls and roof – soon we have a useful edifice!

Notice that we need many walls to support a roof. In the same manner, we are called to be the support in the lives of fellow believers. The Greek word for edification is *oikodomen,* which refers to "the things of building up." It can apply to part of the body or the entire body of Christ. Interestingly, this is not an Old Testament word, but is used exclusively in the New Testament, as the mystery revealed by Paul is the Church. In fact, Paul is the only one to use either "edify" or "edification," beginning in the following verse in Romans:

Therefore let us pursue the things *which make* for peace and the things by which one may edify another.
Romans 14:19 (NKJV)

Just as one beam does not support a roof, one person cannot stand alone. We need others to support us, and while God has the power to supply all of our needs, He uses other believers to walk beside us. Another aspect of construction is demolition. Sadly, the human condition makes it easier to destroy a shaky building and cast aside its broken pieces, rather than put in time, energy and love to shore up the unsteady walls of that historic structure. In our Christian walks, that edification can be accomplished in many different ways.

First, prayer is a priority. When God places us in the lives of others, at the very least, we should be lifting them up to the Lord in our prayers. Secondly, walking beside them as friends or mentors can make incredible impact. Walking is slow, forward progress, and as opposed to running, does not leave us out of breath, but able to discuss and encourage. Barnabas touched the lives of many with his gift of encouragement. In the same manner, we should lift up our fellow believers with our words. This does not mean we should fill them with false pride through our compliments. Instead, we need to help with problems or weaknesses. Jesus sent His disciples out in pairs. Just as a husband and wife often fill in the gaps with different strengths and weaknesses, fellow believers can fill in the gaps for one another. Discipleship is a key. Teach one another individually, as that closeness makes a deeper impact.

Even so you, since you are zealous for spiritual *gifts, let it be* for the edification of the church *that* you seek to excel.
1 Corinthians 14:12 (NKJV)

Lastly, ensure that pride is out of the picture. When we accomplish God's tasks for self gain or notoriety, it is wasted effort. Yet when we place "self" on the altar of God, allowing Him to open doors, close doors and lead us on the paths of righteousness for His sake, then we do not feel the need to grade our own effort. Whether we see success or failure, God sees His will being accomplished when we truly follow Him. Thankfulness to those walking the long and winding road beside us is a sweet acknowledgment, for none of us could accomplish one small task without the help of God's followers. Yet beside each member of the body of Christ is another. Sometimes invisible or un-thanked, God uses us to raise the lives of others, while using others to raise our lives just as sweetly! The primary accomplishment is that God will be high and lifted up, exalted above all. He is the name above every name and worthy of our praises!

Therefore I write these things being absent, lest being present I should use sharpness, according to the authority which the Lord has given me for edification and not for destruction.
2 Corinthians 13:10 (NKJV)

March 18: Praise Him in the storms!

With talks of global warming hitting a critical mass, this winter has been one of the coldest on record. Snowfall totals in the northeast have frustrated many living in that area. In the same manner, last year's Southern California summer also broke records for cold temperatures. Those ups and downs in weather patterns around the world should remind us of ourselves, as God also created us to be in periods of change.

That is no different in the lives of believers. Though we think that the extreme changes will not occur once we come to the Lord, the truth is, we tend to go through more hardship once we become Christians. The difference occurs, though, in how we handle those hardships.

Often, when all is well in our lives, we can be so busy riding the tide of happiness that we forget to take the time to thank the Lord. On the opposite side of the spectrum, we certainly fail to praise Him when life seems to be going badly. Our tendencies are to handle both of those in the wrong way, unfortunately. We forget to be thankful for the ease of passage and at the same time, we rarely praise Him when difficulties are in our pathways! Paul is one of the greatest examples of exemplary behavior in dire circumstances. He was shipwrecked, beaten and imprisoned, yet he never lost sight of God's plan. Here's an example from when he was falsely imprisoned in Philippi:

[25] **But at midnight Paul and Silas were praying and singing hymns to God, and the prisoners were listening to them.** [26] **Suddenly there was a great earthquake, so that the foundations of the prison were shaken; and immediately all the doors were opened and everyone's chains were loosed.** [27] **And the keeper of the prison, awaking from sleep and seeing the prison doors open, supposing the prisoners had fled, drew his sword and was about to kill himself.** [28] **But Paul called with a loud voice, saying, "Do yourself no harm, for we are all here."**

²⁹ Then he called for a light, ran in, and fell down trembling before Paul and Silas. ³⁰ And he brought them out and said, "Sirs, what must I do to be saved?"
³¹ So they said, "Believe on the Lord Jesus Christ, and you will be saved, you and your household." ³² Then they spoke the word of the Lord to him and to all who were in his house. ³³ And he took them the same hour of the night and washed *their* stripes. And immediately he and all his family were baptized. ³⁴ Now when he had brought them into his house, he set food before them; and he rejoiced, having believed in God with all his household.
Acts 16:25-34 (NKJV)

God's plan was to use Paul and Silas to bring other believers into that saving knowledge of Jesus Christ, and the Lord used Paul's joy in the midst of trouble to demonstrate that inner peace, the peace that passes understanding. If we fail to praise the Lord when our lives seem to be difficult, we are acting as if God has lied to us. He has told us that He will use all for our benefit and for His glory. When we fail to acknowledge His hand on the entirety of our lives, we certainly are not trusting in Him. Just as temperatures rise and fall, so do our lives. Yet we know that God's hand remains upon us, through the easiest of circumstances and through the most difficult. We should step out in faith today and praise Him for the most difficult aspect of our lives!

March 19: The hiding place

Looking around the world today, we can see that many Christians are in the midst of persecution for their beliefs. Certainly, those of us in the United States are living in a different time and age. It is not "politically correct" to be a Christian, with the only theme that seems not to be tolerated being intolerance! By embracing Christianity and acknowledging the sinfulness of sex outside of marriage and abortion, among other sins, the majority of the population expresses intense displeasure at the Christian's intolerance concerning the rights and decisions of others to live in a way pleasing unto themselves. Yet, the

Bible reminds us that God loved the world so much He sent His Son, not to condemn the world, but that in Him we might have eternal life. At the same time, God has given us His laws that He expects us to follow. He tells us, **"If you love Me, obey my commandments."**

Compared to the rest of the world, the persecutions that we face as believers in the United States are small potatoes. Many Christians, especially in nations practicing Islam, face death for their beliefs in Jesus Christ. Jesus told us of a time when persecution would be prevalent.

**⁹ "Then they will deliver you up to tribulation and kill you, and you will be hated by all nations for My name's sake. ¹⁰ And then many will be offended, will betray one another, and will hate one another. ¹¹ Then many false prophets will rise up and deceive many. ¹² And because lawlessness will abound, the love of many will grow cold. ¹³ But he who endures to the end shall be saved. ¹⁴ And this gospel of the kingdom will be preached in all the world as a witness to all the nations, and then the end will come.
Matthew 24:9-14 (NKJV)**

How would we handle such severe persecution in our Christian lives? Are we prepared for the battles that many in the world are enduring at this moment? God does not call us all to be martyrs. Yet He holds the hand of anyone He calls to endure martyrdom, just as He did with Stephen, the first Christian after Jesus to die for his beliefs. As believers, we should continue to focus on two aspects of persecution. First, we should be praying for our Christian brothers and sisters in harm's way because of their beliefs and secondly, we should be thankful for where God has us. That does not mean we should expect our lives to be that easy. Jesus reminded us that He was persecuted and a slave is not better than the Master. We also will be under duress. Corrie Ten Boom comes to mind. Her family protected many Jews in the Netherlands during World War II, and though they saved many lives, finally were imprisoned in concentration camps before the war ended. Corrie Ten Boom survived the holocaust and said this:

> "You will never feel that Jesus is everything you need until Jesus is everything you have."

If we are focusing on money, food, possessions and the like, we lose sight of God's sufficiency in our lives. Take away the money, the food and the possessions and give us His grace! As the Lord told Paul, when Paul asked that the thorn in his flesh be removed:

And He said to me, "My grace is sufficient for you, for My strength is made perfect in weakness."
1 Corinthians 12:9 (NKJV)

Another Ten Boom, Corrie's sister Betsie, who died in the Ravensbruck concentration camp, said:

> "There is no pit so deep that God's love is not deeper still."

If we are in a pit, know that God's love can find us there just as easily. In fact, God's love can find us there more easily, for it is in those pits that we know we cannot rely on ourselves and we are forced to acknowledge that He is the only one who can save us. There are no atheists in foxholes! Draw nearer to Him today, and pray for our Christian brothers and sisters around the world.

March 20: Dogs and diamonds!

Many of us have strong bonds with our pets, and the death of a pet can affect us just as deeply as the death of a close friend or relative. A dog is referred to as "man's best friend," which is a step up from the fact that "diamonds are a girl's best friend," regardless of the connection to Marilyn Monroe. With an estimated 400 million dogs in the world performing such tasks as hunting, herding, search and rescue, caring for the handicapped, protection, assisting police and more simply, companionship, dogs have become a focus of our culture. As God created animals, there is nothing wrong with loving a pet. God gave man dominion over the animals, but God still wants us to treat His creation well:

"You shall not muzzle an ox while it treads out *the grain.* **Deuteronomy 25:4 (NKJV)**

A righteous *man* **regards the life of his animal,**
But the tender mercies of the wicked *are* **cruel.**
Proverbs 12:10 (NKJV)

Yet, God does not want us choosing animals over people. PETA (People for the Ethical Treatment of Animals) has become prevalent in our society, and while the idea is great, the people involved take that philosophy to an extreme. Others, who grasp the upside-down nature of caring for an animal, but ignoring a person, have their own group called PETA (People Eating Tasty Animals)! The truth is, God wants us to love our neighbors as ourselves. With man's biggest hurdle being his own pride, man certainly does not have trouble loving himself. Yet when we begin to love our neighbors, and even our enemies, with that same love, lives can be changed.

People without children seem to emphasize their pets more strongly than others. Certainly, those pets are blessings from God and can help to abate loneliness. Yet while our pets have sweet souls and unique personalities, God has not endowed them with eternal spirits. While many Christians would love to see their pets beside them in heaven, we know that God will give us everything we need to be joyous for all of eternity. We do not know what we will need, but God does. In the meantime, He can teach us about unconditional love from our pets, which love us no matter what we do. That is one of the many benefits of man's best friend. We get to see a snippet of how God loves us! It is sad that we sometimes can experience that more readily from our pets than we can from our friends and families! At the same time, our friends and families can feel the same about their own pet's love compared to the love we are giving them.

Our lesson is to continue to focus our love in a godly way on the people the Lord puts in our pathways on a daily basis. We also can continue to love our pets, too, for God has given us enough love to go around! Do not forget:

And above all things have fervent love for one another, for *"love will cover a multitude of sins."*
1 Peter 4:8 (NKJV)

March 21: Why was Jesus a carpenter?

The Father could have chosen any profession for Jesus, so why was He a carpenter?

Is this not the carpenter, the Son of Mary, and brother of James, Joses, Judas, and Simon? And are not His sisters here with us?" So they were offended at Him.
Mark 6:3 (NKJV)

It followed the biblical principle of working with our hands.

Let him who stole steal no longer, but rather let him labor, working with *his* hands what is good, that he may have something to give him who has need
 Ephesians 4:28 (NKJV)

He earned a living by the sweat of His brow:

In the sweat of thy face shalt thou eat bread, till thou return unto the ground; for out of it wast thou taken: for dust thou *art*, and unto dust shalt thou return.
Genesis 3:19 (KJV)

God made the world from nothing. He breathed the world into existence. When Jesus came to earth as a man, He remained Creator, as His job was building up an object from wood.

Building up is the same word used as "edify," and that word in Greek is *oikodomeo* (οἰκοδομέω). It would not have been as prophetically significant if Jesus had been a demolition man! We are called to edify others.

Let no corrupt word proceed out of your mouth, but what is good for necessary edification, that it may impart grace to the hearers.
Ephesians 4:29 (NKJV)

He could have been a Rabbi, with His knowledge of the Tanakh (the Jewish Bible), but He was too young. His ministry began when He turned 30.

Now Jesus Himself began *His ministry at* about thirty years of age,
Luke 3:23 (NKJV)

Why do we have pastors in their twenties today? The Levites had to be from ages 30-50:

from thirty years old and above, even to fifty years old, all who enter the service to do the work in the tabernacle of meeting.
Numbers 4:3 (NKJV)

The verse in Numbers describes a Levite, though Jesus was not a Levite. Instead, He was from the tribe of Judah. Is a young man in his twenties old enough to understand the pitfalls of the congregation he is preaching to? If anyone would have been able to handle this, Jesus would have, but interestingly, the Father had Him wait until He was 30!

Another reason for Jesus to be working was that He needed food to survive in His earthly body:

For even when we were with you, we commanded you this: If anyone will not work, neither shall he eat.
2 Thessalonians 3:10 (NKJV)

It is significant that Jesus worked driving nails into wood, and died after those nails were driven through Him into a cross of wood. His first profession was "shaping" wood, and then His next profession was shaping people!

Should we all be carpenters? No, we should work diligently in the profession God has placed us into, being godly influences in the lives of those we come in contact with. Pray for them and edify them, just as the Lord would have done! We never know when our lives, the joy in our hearts and the peace in our walks will open the door to the heart in one of our co-workers. Remember, God has a purpose and a plan, and there are no accidents! That includes where we work and who we work with!

March 22: God is gracious!

God's grace is incredibly difficult to fathom. There are many people who do not feel the need for grace, for when looking introspectively, they have no awareness of the depravity of sin. Just because we have not murdered and dismembered a dozen victims does not mean that we have not sinned greatly. Part of our misunderstanding of sin has to do with the fact that we are surrounded by sin and sinners. Interestingly, prophets and apostles who have been in the presence of God do not feel so comfortable. The apostle John was known as the one who Jesus loved, but when called up to heaven to see the future events of Revelation, John heard the voice of Jesus, and then reacted:

[17] And when I saw Him, I fell at His feet as dead. But He laid His right hand on me, saying to me, "Do not be afraid; I am the First and the Last. [18] I *am* He who lives, and was dead, and behold, I am alive forevermore. Amen. And I have the keys of Hades and of Death. [19] Write the things which you have seen, and the things which are, and the things which will take place after this.
Revelation 1:17-19 (NKJV)

Though John walked beside Jesus for three years, he no longer felt worthy to be in His presence. That unworthiness testifies of a sinful man being in the presence of a sinless God. John felt much more comfortable with his face in the dirt than looking at his Savior and friend. Yet Jesus has bridged the gap of that separation with His accomplishment at the cross. Because He willingly received the just punishment for our sins, we receive the gift of grace for the life He lived. That gift is not deserved or earned, but afterwards, it should change every aspect of our lives.

How can we dare to carry a grudge against anyone after God has forgiven us? Grace to a Christian is not just a received gift, but a gift to pass on!

[37] "Judge not, and you shall not be judged. Condemn not, and you shall not be condemned. Forgive, and you will be forgiven. [38] Give, and it will be given to you: good measure, pressed down, shaken together, and running over will be put into your bosom. For with the same measure that you use, it will be measured back to you."
Luke 6:37-38 (NKJV)

God desires for us to speak loudly through our actions to a world that needs to hear His voice. When we exhibit grace in the lives of others, that testifies of God's gift. It is natural to hold others accountable for their failings, but it is godly to forgive them quickly, just as God has forgiven us. Let God's grace permeate our lives, hearts and actions!

March 23: Honor God with your work!

Our jobs take up the most time of any of our daily activities, though sleeping might be a close second. After those two activities have been completed, over two-thirds of the day is gone! With that much time being accounted for, we should examine our jobs through the eyes of the Lord. Other professions in the Bible can give us some perspective on how God views the work day.

God smiled upon the sacrifice of Abel (Genesis 4:4), who was a shepherd, but did not smile upon the sacrifice of Cain, who was a farmer. Before becoming the King of Israel, David was a shepherd and a harpist. Paul was a Pharisee, but earned his living as a tentmaker. Many of the disciples were fishermen. Luke was a doctor and Matthew was a tax collector. Boaz had a large farm, employing many farmhands.

While these are just a few of the professions mentioned in the Bible, most of those professions still exist today, though we now have many that did not exist in biblical times. The United States has become a nation where the typical man does not earn his living by the sweat of his brow, or by the work of his hands. We have outsourced most of our labor to other countries, so while most of the profits return to our country, the products are not made here and the labor is not even done by us. Instead of working, we make phone calls and write emails. Yet whatever living we make, it should be an honest living as our jobs must not violate God's commandments.

Let him who stole steal no longer, but rather let him labor, working with *his* hands what is good, that he may have something to give him who has need.
Ephesians 4:28 (NKJV)

Notice in the above verse that the reason for working is not to feed ourselves. Instead, it is so we can help others in need. The word for "labor" is *kopiao* (κοπιάω), which means "getting tired in toil." We are to get tired in the work, but not to get tired of the work. We should honor God in the way we handle the professions He has placed us into. We should not be watching the clock, waiting to go home. When compared to a non-Christian employee, a Christian should be exemplary in the eyes of the boss. Unfortunately, that can be the exception, rather than the rule. We can steal the time from our bosses just as easily as we can steal pencils, paper and tools. Diligence is the key. Do not ever forget that co-workers can see God in our lives when we exhibit godly behavior. Instead, we are quicker to witness with our words than with our actions. Those words mean so much more when our actions are just as truthful!

Make a new commitment to honoring God in whatever work He has given! Toil for Him, knowing that He placed each of us specifically into those roles. If God wants us somewhere else, He certainly has the ability to open that door. Honor Him, and that includes not working on the Sabbath! Instead of God bless America, how about America bless God?

March 24: Shattered

Coming to the Lord is so simple, and at the same time, so complicated. Simply, we have to be broken, yet the process of that brokenness is the complicated part that is different for each of us. Brokenness has been described as the acute and constant awareness of God's presence, alongside the devastation from the presence of our sin. Some become broken through a smaller trial, yet others really need to reach the pit of despair before they find the end of themselves, and the beginning of God.

Saul of Damascus persecuted the early Christians, and was one of those responsible for the death of Stephen, the first martyr of Christianity. Jesus spoke to Saul from heaven and blinded Saul on the Damascus Road. It is certain that Jesus prepared Saul's heart for years, but that was the moment when Saul became Paul, stopped persecuting Christians and began serving the Lord with his life. Nebuchadnezzar, the King of Babylon, is another telling example:

[28] All *this* came upon King Nebuchadnezzar. [29] At the end of the twelve months he was walking about the royal palace of Babylon. [30] The king spoke, saying, "Is not this great Babylon, that I have built for a royal dwelling by my mighty power and for the honor of my majesty?"
[31] While the word *was still* in the king's mouth, a voice fell from heaven: "King Nebuchadnezzar, to you it is spoken: the kingdom has departed from you! [32] And they shall drive you from men, and your dwelling *shall be* with the beasts of the

field. They shall make you eat grass like oxen; and seven times shall pass over you, until you know that the Most High rules in the kingdom of men, and gives it to whomever He chooses."
[33]That very hour the word was fulfilled concerning Nebuchadnezzar; he was driven from men and ate grass like oxen; his body was wet with the dew of heaven till his hair had grown like eagles' *feathers* and his nails like birds' *claws*.
Daniel 4:28-33 (NKJV)

Pride led Nebuchadnezzar down a painful path, which included a step worse than homelessness. Did you notice the "I's" and "my's" in the king's boastful statement, before God got Nebuchadnezzar's attention? When we are still unwilling to take responsibility for our own sins, we are not yet to the point of brokenness. An example of this would be a person with addictions, who believes he could give up those substances at any time. Truthfully, it is not until we can admit our own inability to control those impulses that we are willing to hand it all over to Jesus! The Lord already has demonstrated the length He will go to in order to get our attention. Nebuchadnezzar took seven years of eating grass before becoming humble. Amazingly, after that humbleness, the Lord restored him to his role as King of Babylon.

> "God will never plant the seed of His life upon the soil of a hard, unbroken spirit. He will only plant that seed where the conviction of His spirit has brought brokenness, where the soil has been watered with the tears of repentance as well as the tears of joy." --Alan Redpath

> Brokenness and freedom go together, in that order; first suffering, then comfort; first trouble, then joy; first felt unworthiness, then felt love; first death to the self, then resurrection of the soul. --Larry Crabb

The Greek word for broken is *sunthlao* (συνθλάω), from *sun* meaning "together" and *thlao*, meaning "to break in pieces or to shatter." We can either be broken in our pride when we come to Jesus, or broken because of our pride, when we refuse to come to Jesus, with the latter being permanent separation from God. Lest we forget, that choice is one each of us gets to make:

And whoever falls on this stone will be broken; but on whomever it falls, it will grind him to powder."
Matthew 21:44 (NKJV)

March 25: Take a load off!

Most of us have seen enough cartoons to picture a piano being dropped on the head of a person. Because it was an unrealistic cartoon, that monstrous piano caused damage, not death. Though the piano weighed a ton and dropped many floors, the recipient lived most of the time, flattened to the ground, with little birdies flying around their heads. Though it is doubtful that any of us have had a piano fall upon our heads, or any other musical instruments, we all know the feeling that something similar is about to happen. Life can be difficult, especially as Christians. Many people expect a life of ease when they decide to walk away from the world and walk with Jesus. Somehow, we forget that the devil is in control of this world!

If God never will let go of us, how can the devil possibly win in his battle against us? He cannot have us for eternity, but he certainly can ruin our testimonies! That is his greatest goal, once we come to the Lord. We should not forget that if we decided to follow Jesus, we left the devil's team! That angers the team captain, who cannot have us back, so he tries to make us fail. He certainly does not want us to be able to bat clean-up for God's team! We know that we are going to be attacked. How should we deal with those attacks?

> "It is not a question of God allowing or not allowing things to happen. It is part of living. Some things we do to ourselves, other things we do to each other. Our Father knows about every bird which falls to the ground, but He does not always prevent it from falling. What are

we to learn from this? That our response to what happens is more important than what happens. Here is a mystery: one man's experience drives him to curse God, while another man's identical experience drives him to bless God. Your response to what happens is more important than what happens." -- Chip Brogden

"We all know people who have been made much meaner and more irritable and more intolerable to live with by suffering: it is not right to say that all suffering perfects. It only perfects one type of person ... the one who accepts the call of God in Christ Jesus." -- Oswald Chambers

"Our problems are opportunities to discover God's solutions." -- Unknown

"God places the heaviest burden on those who can carry its weight!" -- Reggie White

"God whispers to us in our pleasures, speaks to us in our conscience, but shouts in our pains: It is His megaphone to rouse a deaf world." – C. S. Lewis

"We turn to God for help when our foundations are shaking, only to learn that it is God who is shaking them." -- Charles C. West

strengthening the souls of the disciples, exhorting *them* **to continue in the faith, and** *saying,* **"We must through many tribulations enter the kingdom of God."**
Acts 14:22 (NKJV)

Know that the trials are coming! Respond the way the Lord would have us respond! If we truly believe His promises, we can walk through the greatest difficulty with joy and peace.

March 26: The shoes of the Jews

A wise person once uttered the words, "You can eat an elephant one bite at a time," referring to enduring any hardship by taking small steps. Some of our obstacles are nothing more than hurdles, taking one step to cross and place in the memory banks. Yet other obstacles seem to go on for years. Even those lasting difficulties are conquerable, thanks to the Lord's guidance. We may not have endurance alone, but God supernaturally can sustain us through anything!

5 And I have led you forty years in the wilderness. Your clothes have not worn out on you, and your sandals have not worn out on your feet. 6 You have not eaten bread, nor have you drunk wine or *similar* drink, that you may know that I *am* the LORD your God.
Deuteronomy 29:5-6 (NKJV)

Doubtfully, none of us own shoes worn daily with soles that have lasted four decades! In the same manner that God can make shoes endure the elements and all that we can dish out against them, He can protect His children from wearing out! In the same manner that an old, godly farmer still manages to perform the physical tasks that were easy when he was a younger man, God can sustain us through any difficulty. Somehow, we look around and see what "normally" occurs in the world, forgetting that we are set apart by the God we serve. He performs miracles in our daily lives as all things are possible through Him. What happened to God's servant, Moses?

Moses *was* one hundred and twenty years old when he died. His eyes were not dim nor his natural vigor diminished.
Deuteronomy 34:7 (NKJV)

When the obstacles in front of us seem insurmountable, we know that they only seem that way! God puts us into those situations to see how we will respond! Our choices are to throw in the towel, or take a bite of elephant. For inspiration, remember the news of the shoes of the Jews!

March 27: Get out of the boat!

We often find ourselves in situations where we do not know what to do. We can pray for hours, days, weeks and years, look for an answer in God's Word, and still, the answer does not seem apparent. Sometimes, when we do not hear or see an answer from God we are to wait. **"Be still and know that I am God,"** comes directly to mind! We also know that God's three answers to prayer are, "Yes," "No," and "Not now!" Yet sometimes, we need to step out in faith!

Peter often acted rashly, before he thought. Many Bible scholars speak of Peter as, "open mouth, insert foot" or "he of the foot-shaped mouth." We all know exactly how that feels. Though Peter often erred in his actions, his heart was courageous. When the mob came to the Garden of Gethsemane to arrest Jesus, Peter pulled out a sword and sliced off the ear of Malchus, which potentially would have been punished by Peter's own death! Peter loved the Lord more than his own life, but Jesus healed the ear of Malchus, as God had more important tasks for Peter to complete. That included writing part of the New Testament! Peter was a courageous man. We also see that courage when Jesus walked on the Sea of Galilee. Only Peter had the faith to step out of the boat and walk toward the Lord. Yet Peter doubted and needed the Lord to rescue him.

There are two categories of people in this event, those who act without thought and those so busy considering what to do that they fail to act. Who had the greatest blessing that day? Was it Peter, who tried to walk on water like the Lord, and actually did for a few moments before failing? Or was it the other disciples, sitting on the sideline, just watching? When we keep our eyes upon Jesus and look full in His wonderful face, we will not fall. Yet any time we focus on the world and not on our precious Lord, the world will devour us! With our eyes on the Prize, we can do mighty things! Yet, never forget, that involves stepping out of the boat. If we remain in the boat, we are not stepping out in faith to see what the Lord will do in our lives.

God gives each of us at least one spiritual gift, and along with that, a ministry. We cannot use the gift or fulfill the ministry entrusted to us by sitting in the boat! It might feel like a safe place, but waves can capsize a boat just as easily! It takes a step from our comfort zone for the Lord to stretch us!

[29] And when Peter had come down out of the boat, he walked on the water to go to Jesus. [30] But when he saw that the wind *was* boisterous, he was afraid; and beginning to sink he cried out, saying, "Lord, save me!"
Matthew 14:29-30 (NKJV)

March 28: Peaks and Valleys

Hall of Fame boxer Muhammad Ali said, "It isn't the mountains ahead to climb that wear you out; it's the pebble in your shoe." Certainly, we can waste time worrying about those future mountains, but a minor inconvenience in the present is far more debilitating than a major hurdle yet to occur. Typically, we find that our greatest worries rarely come to fruition. With that in mind, worry becomes one of the greatest time wasters in life, especially in the life of a believer.

Jesus had more to worry about than anyone else. He knew that those He came to save did not believe. He knew the Jewish leadership wanted to kill Him, and also knew that desire would become reality very shortly. Jesus knew that His impending death would be painful, humiliating and would create separation between He and His Father. With the greatest right to worry, He still chose not to! He reminded us:

These things I have spoken to you, that in Me you may have peace. In the world you will have tribulation; but be of good cheer, I have overcome the world."
John 16:33 (NKJV)

Surely, we understand that a broken world filled with unbelievers will not be the most hospitable host to those choosing to follow God and God's Word. The greatest step is to take our eyes away from that world and focus them on our future hope. Even in the midst of adversity in our lives, God still reigns on His throne of glory. Just because we will face tribulation does not mean that we walk that path without God's help or His care! No pebble in our shoes is blind to a God who loves us immensely.

[4] **For whatever is born of God overcomes the world. And this is the victory that has overcome the world— our faith.** [5] **Who is he who overcomes the world, but he who believes that Jesus is the Son of God?**
1 John 5:4-5 (NKJV)

Sir Edmund Hillary, the first man to summit the world's highest peak, Mt. Everest, said, "It's not the mountain we conquer, but ourselves." Jesus conquered the world for us. If His death on the cross was the end of the story, we would be in deep trouble. But because Jesus conquered death, and has asked us to join Him in that resurrection, we do not have a mountain to conquer. The victory lies in trusting God, who never will let go of us!

Be anxious for nothing, but in everything by prayer and supplication, with thanksgiving, let your requests be made known to God;
Philippians 4:6 (NKJV)

March 29: Reflections

Walking around Yosemite National Park reveals numerous reflections of huge, rock structures in assorted lakes, creeks and streams. Those reflections are similar to the structures being reflected, but certainly not identical. In fact, the mirror images are not solid. One small pebble in the water can send ripples through the reflection until that image quickly disappears. Reflections on our lives can give similar results. Our limited brains do not always remind us accurately of the past. Some of us focus more on the negative (the glass is half empty), while some of us focus more on the positive (the glass is half full). Most situations have a degree of both. When our perspective changes in the present, the past always will seem slightly altered from the time when we faced the situation originally.

God wants us to reflect on at least two aspects of our lives. One of the most important reflections has to do with the Lord's miraculous hand in delivering us from trials. When the Israelites were fleeing from Pharaoh's army and came across an impassable obstacle called the Red Sea, God miraculously turned back the waters and created a path of dry land through the midst of the sea. Imagine walking on that ground, looking up at the huge waters overhead that could come crashing down at any moment! Once the Jews were safely on the other side, with Pharaoh's soldiers in hot pursuit, God allowed the waters to crash down, drowning each member of the Egyptian army. Though the Jews were able to see God's hand deliver them miraculously, they created a golden calf to worship days later! Most of us are dumbfounded how the Jews could have fallen so far away days after God's great miracle, yet all of us are exactly the same! Do we turn to Him first when faced with adversity? Or do we turn to Him when nothing else works?

Looking back at our sins is another healthy reflection, though we should not overdo this. To remember the changes our Lord has made in our lives is a blessing, but we should be careful not to let those memories defeat us! God has forgiven our sins, if we have repented, and along with that, God has forgotten our sins. His Word reminds us in His eyes, our sin is gone!

Indeed *it was* for *my own* peace
***That* I had great bitterness;**
But You have lovingly *delivered* my soul from the pit of corruption,
For You have cast all my sins behind Your back.
Isaiah 38:17 (NKJV)

As far as the east is from the west,

So far has He removed our
transgressions from us.
  Psalm 103:12 (NKJV)

He will again have compassion on us, And will subdue our iniquities. You will cast all our sins Into the depths of the sea.
Micah 7:19 (NKJV)

Paul looked back at his old, sinful life. He thought of himself as the worst of all whom God had saved. Most of us have felt that same way. That speaks of the power of God and the love of God, who even can save our wretched souls. To God be the glory! Thanks be to God for reflections of the past and the visions of the future: who we once were and who we will become based on God's saving grace!

[12] And I thank Christ Jesus our Lord who has enabled me, because He counted me faithful, putting *me* into the ministry, [13] although I was formerly a blasphemer, a persecutor, and an insolent man; but I obtained mercy because I did *it* ignorantly in unbelief. [14] And the grace of our Lord was exceedingly abundant, with faith and love which are in Christ Jesus. [15] This *is* a faithful saying and worthy of all acceptance, that Christ Jesus came into the world to save sinners, of whom I am chief. [16] However, for this reason I obtained mercy, that in me first Jesus Christ might show all longsuffering, as a pattern to those who are going to believe on Him for everlasting life. [17] Now to the King eternal, immortal, invisible, to God who alone is wise, *be* honor and glory forever and ever. Amen.
1 Timothy 1:12-17 (NKJV)

March 30: On death and dying

Death is not just an end to life, but a part of it, as well. Each of us has death in our future, but the key is whether that death is of a physical nature or a spiritual one. Nothing is sadder than the death of a friend or family member who does not have a relationship with Jesus. Often, we spend hours wondering if more prayers or words might have convinced that loved one of the importance of that decision. Jesus explained an event to help our limited understanding:

[19] "There was a certain rich man who was clothed in purple and fine linen and fared sumptuously every day. [20] But there was a certain beggar named Lazarus, full of sores, who was laid at his gate, [21] desiring to be fed with the crumbs which fell from the rich man's table. Moreover the dogs came and licked his sores. [22] So it was that the beggar died, and was carried by the angels to Abraham's bosom. The rich man also died and was buried. [23] And being in torments in Hades, he lifted up his eyes and saw Abraham afar off, and Lazarus in his bosom.
[24] "Then he cried and said, 'Father Abraham, have mercy on me, and send Lazarus that he may dip the tip of his finger in water and cool my tongue; for I am tormented in this flame.' [25] But Abraham said, 'Son, remember that in your lifetime you received your good things, and likewise Lazarus evil things; but now he is comforted and you are tormented. [26] And besides all this, between us and you there is a great gulf fixed, so that those who want to pass from here to you cannot, nor can those from there pass to us.'
[27] "Then he said, 'I beg you therefore, father, that you would send him to my father's house, [28] for I have five brothers, that he may testify to them, lest they also come to this place of torment.' [29] Abraham said to him, 'They have Moses and the prophets; let them hear them.' [30] And he said, 'No, father Abraham; but if one goes to them from the dead, they will repent.' [31] But he said to him, 'If they do not hear Moses and the prophets, neither will they be persuaded though one rise from the dead.' "
Luke 16:19-31 (NKJV)

In this explanation, we can see that nothing would have changed the rich man's mind, regardless of the power of the prophet. Remember, God Himself departed heaven and came to earth! Instead of convincing the world about the importance of a relationship with Him, the world killed Jesus. Think of the limited number following Jesus at the time of His death! Signs and wonders do not convince people of God's love. Instead, the Holy Spirit draws us!

God gives us all the opportunities to know Him personally. It is a blessing that He involves us in the process of sharing His kingdom with others, yet God does not need us. He can use us to share His words, He can speak through a burning bush, He can communicate by giving a donkey the power of language or He can write it in the sky if He so chooses! Our inabilities to listen cannot change God's will. When we get to heaven, we certainly will discover the multitude of ways that God tried to get our attention.

Yet the lesson of the day is to make every moment count. In our conversations, if the Holy Spirit opens the door ever so slightly, are we willing to step through that door and share about the miracles that God has performed in our lives? We are so adamant at not offending others, yet what is the greatest offense? How many people on Judgment Day will be looking at us, saying, "Why didn't you tell me?" If our friend was drowning, would we not at the very least throw him a rope? In addition to living in the moment, we should dwell in the thankfulness of what we have been given. Did we deserve salvation more than others who have not received it? No! Through our lives, actions and motives, all we deserved was death, yet the Lord in His infinite mercy and grace gave us eternal life in Him. Never forget that each person in our paths is one breath away from death, and one decision away from eternal life!

My flesh and my heart fail;
***But* God *is* the strength of my**
heart and my portion forever.
Psalm 73:26 (NKJV)

March 31: Ten

Ten is an amazing number that carries much weight in our daily lives. As our whole system of mathematics operates on a base of 10, we not only emphasize decades, but centuries and millennia. When a person reaches the age of 49, it is really no big deal, but "50" crosses that half-century line into oblivion! Ten begins the most important part of the countdown before a rocket launch and also is the number of perfection given by judges who are grading competitions in sports, like gymnastics and ice skating. In a similar manner, "Ten" is the name given to a popular movie in 1979, based on a rating of the beauty of its star, Bo Derek.

In biblical occurrences, 10 is a perfect number demonstrating a Divine order. Though there are frequent occurrences of that number, the most important reference would be to the commandments of God. When Moses went to the top of Mt. Sinai to receive them, God wrote the commandments on two tablets of stone. While the first four commandments highlight man's relationship with God, the final six commandments emphasize man's relationship with man. There is no law in all of human history that matches the righteous law of God.

And what great nation *is there* that has *such* statutes and righteous judgments as are in all this law which I set before you this day?
Deuteronomy 4:8 (NKJV)

The commandments, reflecting the perfect number of 10, are also perfect! If atheists followed the final six commandments dealing with man's relationship with other men, their lives would be easier, though they would miss entirely the blessing of that perfect life in God, with God and through God. The 10 Commandments do not need an assist!

You shall not add to the word which I command you, nor take from it, that you may keep the commandments of the LORD your God which I command you.

Deuteronomy 4:2 (NKJV)

Another interesting 10 that occurs in the Bible is the number of generations before the Great Flood, offering a countdown of sorts before God destroyed all but eight people. Those generations were Adam, Seth, Enosh, Cainan, Mahalalel, Jared, Enoch, Methuselah, Lamech and Noah. Some have pointed out that by looking at the meaning of each of those names, we get an amazing sentence: 'Man' 'Appointed' 'Mortal Sorrow.' 'The Blessed God' 'Shall Come Down' 'Teaching.' 'His Death Shall Bring' 'the Despairing' 'Rest or Comfort.' At the time of Noah, Satan attempted to pull a fast one on the Lord. Satan's demonic angels had taken earthly wives (Genesis 6:1-4), contaminating the bloodlines and creating a race of giants. God spared Noah and his family from destruction, as Noah's bloodline was secure, ensuring that the bloodline of Jesus also remained perfect:

This is the genealogy of Noah. Noah was a just man, perfect in his generations. Noah walked with God.
Genesis 6:9 (NKJV)

How interesting that the 10th generation was the final one before the Flood! Ten generations point to completeness of the whole existence of a nation or family in another verse, as well.

[3] "An Ammonite or Moabite shall not enter the assembly of the LORD; even to the tenth generation none of his *descendants* shall enter the assembly of the LORD forever, [4] because they did not meet you with bread and water on the road when you came out of Egypt, and because they hired against you Balaam the son of Beor from Pethor of Mesopotamia, to curse you.
Deuteronomy 23:3-4 (NKJV)

Additionally, fire came down from heaven 10 times in the Old Testament, with six of those occurring in judgment: In Genesis 19:24, fire falls on Sodom and Gomorrah; in Leviticus 9:24, fire falls on the first offerings; in Leviticus 10:2, fire falls on Nadab and Abihu; in Numbers 11:1, fire falls on the murmurers at

Taberah; in Numbers 16:35, fire falls on Korah and his company; in 1 Kings 18:38, fire falls on Elijah's offering at Mt. Carmel; in 2 Kings 1:10, fire falls on Elijah's enemies; in 2 Kings 1:12, fire falls again on Elijah's enemies; in 1 Chronicles 21:26, fire falls on David's sacrifice; and in 2 Chronicles 7:1, fire falls on Solomon's sacrifice.

In the New Testament, there are 10 kingdom parables in the Gospel according to Matthew, seven in Matthew 13 and three in Matthew 22 and 25. The tenth kingdom parable is about 10 virgins. Five of those virgins kept oil in their lamps and were prepared when a call went out that their bridegroom was ready for them. In the Bible, oil is emblematic of the Holy Spirit, and Jesus is the bridegroom, stressing to us all that we should walk in the Spirit, not in the flesh, if we want to be prepared for the return of our Savior! Also symbolic is the number of virgins ready for the Bridegroom: five, which is the number of grace!

While there are many more 10's in the Bible, we always should remember that it is one of God's perfect numbers. This is another great day of self-reflection. How do we rate on a scale of 1-10, where walking in the flesh is a 1 and walking in the Spirit is a 10? God is the perfect judge, unlike the Russian judge in the Olympics, who always rated the athletes from other countries much lower than deserved. God certainly rates us higher than deserved. If God gives us a 10, then we are like the five virgins, prepared for the return of Jesus! We should check our lamps for oil!

[6] **"And at midnight a cry was *heard:* 'Behold, the bridegroom is coming; go out to meet him!'** [7] **Then all those virgins arose and trimmed their lamps.** [8] **And the foolish said to the wise, 'Give us *some* of your oil, for our lamps are going out.'** [9] **But the wise answered, saying, *'No,* lest there should not be enough for us and you; but go rather to those who sell, and buy for yourselves.'** [10] **And while they went to buy, the bridegroom came, and those who were ready went in with him to the wedding; and the door was shut.**

Matthew 25:6-10 (NKJV)

April 1: Psalm 22

In the gospels are seven statements made by Jesus on the cross. Amazingly, those are all depicted in the prophetic Psalm 22. Remember, the number seven is significant in the Bible, as it stands for completeness. Look over those verses in Psalm 22 and see how they apply to the statements on the cross.

The first statement is identical, as the Holy Spirit wanted to ensure that we could see that significance:

My God, My God, why have You forsaken Me?
Why are You so far from helping Me,
And from the words of My groaning?
Psalms 22:1 (NKJV)

And at the ninth hour Jesus cried out with a loud voice, saying, "Eloi, Eloi, lama sabachthani?" which is translated, "My God, My God, why have You forsaken Me?"
Mark 15:34 (NKJV)

This verse is one of the most powerful in the entire Bible! When Jesus was on the cross, for the only time in His existence, He felt separation from His Father and from the Holy Spirit. Why? Because the sins of the world had been cast upon His shoulders and sin separates us from God. Jesus stated the phrase twice: "My God, My God." Why twice? Because Jesus is referring to God the Father and God the Holy Spirit. He did not need to talk to Himself, or there would have been a third "My God." The other important issue to notice is that for the only time, Jesus does not refer to God as "My Father." Because of our sins on His shoulders, the relationship was temporarily gone. That was anguish to Jesus, but He had to only endure it for a short period of time. The saddest part is that hell will be an eternity filled with the anguish of that separation. The Bible tells us in Philippians 2:9-11 that **"every knee shall bow and every tongue confess that Jesus Christ is Lord."** At the Judgment, every non-believer and every atheist will have to confront the Lord they chose to ignore. They will have to live eternally without Him and that separation will be horrible.

Here is the second statement:

⁷ All those who see Me ridicule Me;
They shoot out the lip, they shake the head, *saying***,**
⁸ "He trusted in the LORD, let Him rescue Him;
Let Him deliver Him, since He delights in Him!"
Psalms 22:7-8 (NKJV)

Then Jesus said, "Father, forgive them, for they do not know what they do." And they divided His garments and cast lots. Luke 23:34 (NKJV)

The Holy Spirit describes here in detail the scene at the cross. Jesus not only endured the physical pain of the cross, devised as the most painful death imaginable, but also the humiliation of ridicule from the same people He came to save. And still, in the Gospels it tells us that He asked the Father to forgive **"them"** for not knowing what they were doing. We were in that mob. He died for our sins, too, and we would have been the same as the rest, who gave Him an illegal trial, crucified an innocent man, threw rocks at Him, and spit at Him. Never forget our participation in His death! He could have stopped the process at any moment. He chose to endure this for us. In the Old Testament, God set aside six cities of refuge for anyone who had committed manslaughter. Basically, manslaughter is second-degree murder, not premeditated. The manslayer could remain in the city of refuge until the high priest died and then, they could go free. We are in that group, as our High Priest died on the cross. It shows that we are only second-degree murderers, as we did not know what we were doing. That makes us eligible from the Law of the Old Testament to flee to a City of Refuge.

Next is the third statement our Lord made on the cross:

⁹ **But You *are* He who took Me out of the womb;**
You made Me trust *while* on My mother's breasts.
¹⁰ **I was cast upon You from birth.**
From My mother's womb
You *have been* My God.
Psalms 22:9-10 (NKJV)

²⁶ **When Jesus therefore saw His mother, and the disciple whom He loved standing by, He said to His mother, "Woman, behold your son!"** ²⁷ **Then He said to the disciple, "Behold your mother!" And from that hour that disciple took her to his own *home*.**
John 19:26 -27 (NKJV)

There were people present at the cross who did not hate Him. One of those people was His mother, Mary. Remember, an angel of the Lord told her before she was pregnant that she was going to bear the Son of God. What a daunting task for a young girl, who could have been stoned to death under the Law for becoming pregnant out of marriage. At the wedding in Cana, she wanted Him to reveal Himself for who He was, but He told her, **"Woman, my time is not yet come."** Now, His time is come, and His mother looked on with a broken heart. We know the perspective of mothers, who would do anything to take away the pain of their children. The pain He experienced is worse than what anyone has endured. The most special part is that even when He is in agony, He is still thinking of others. The New Testament tells us that Jesus had brothers and sisters, but He assigned His disciple John to take care of His mother.

This verse in Psalm 22 encompasses the fourth statement:

My strength is dried up like a potsherd,
And My tongue clings to My jaws;
You have brought Me to the dust of death.
Psalms 22:15 (NKJV)

²⁸ **After this, Jesus, knowing that all things were now accomplished, that the Scripture might be fulfilled, said, "I**

<u>thirst!"</u> ²⁹ **Now a vessel full of sour wine was sitting there; and they filled a sponge with sour wine, put *it* on hyssop, and put *it* to His mouth.**
John 19:28-29 (NKJV)

A potsherd, is a broken piece of pottery, a shard. We know that without Jesus, we are all broken pieces of pottery, cast aside. Yet the Master Potter puts that pot back together and fills it with His Living Water! The verses following in the psalm tell us more of the agony of the cross. This reminds us that Jesus is fully God and fully man. The aspect of Him that is fully man was thirsty on the cross. Ever experienced severe pain? Our mouths dry up like at no other time. He knows our pain! In the Book of John, Jesus is described as the Living Water. Once we drink from that Water, we never will thirst again. It is hard to imagine the Living Water being thirsty. Once again, He died this death on the cross so that we do not have to. In the tribulation, God will pour out his wrath on a sinful earth, but here, God poured out His wrath on His Son, who was a scapegoat for our sins! Those of us who have asked Him into our hearts will be judged for the perfect life He lived as He was judged for the sinful lives that we have lived.

For He made Him who knew no sin *to be* sin for us, that we might become the righteousness of God in Him.
2 Corinthians 5:21 (NKJV)

Here is His fifth statement:

¹⁹ But You, O LORD, do not be far from Me;
O My Strength, hasten to help Me!
²⁰ Deliver Me from the sword,
My precious *life* from the power of the dog.
Psalms 22:19-20 (NKJV)

And when Jesus had cried out with a loud voice, He said, <u>"Father, 'into Your hands I commit My spirit.'</u> " Having said this, He breathed His last.
Luke 23:46 (NKJV)

Jesus felt the separation from His Father, but knew that was only temporary. He asks in this psalm that the Father not be far from Him. We have been looking at this from the perspective of Jesus, but do not miss the perspective of the Father. Imagine how difficult it must have been for God the Father to allow Jesus to endure this event! How hard it must have been to look away! Isaiah 53, the other incredible description of the cross in the Old Testament tells us:

Yet it pleased the LORD to bruise Him;
He has put *Him* to grief.
When You make His soul an offering for sin,
He shall see *His* seed, He shall prolong *His* days,
And the pleasure of the LORD shall prosper in His hand.
Isaiah 53:10 (NKJV)

Wow! It pleased God the Father to have His Son tortured in this manner. Why?! Because He knew what we would receive because of it! Without the spilling of innocent blood, there can be no forgiveness of sin. God created us so that we might know His love. Is there a better example of love for us than Jesus laying down His life for us? If we ever seem to be overwhelmed by the cares of this world, we should take them to the cross and remember what has been endured for us!

Here is His sixth statement:

²⁵ My praise *shall be* of You in the great assembly;
I will pay My vows before those who fear Him.
²⁶ The poor shall eat and be satisfied;
Those who seek Him will praise the LORD.
Let your heart live forever!
Psalms 22:25-26 (NKJV)

And Jesus said to him, "Assuredly, I say to you, today you will be with Me in Paradise."
Luke 23:43 (NKJV)

Jesus made a vow to the thief on the cross that **"Today, you will be with me in Paradise."** That statement reveals much as crucifixion could take many days to complete. Those being crucified would not bleed to death, but would basically suffocate as they could not sustain their own weight. One of the most difficult documents to read is a medical description of the death in a crucifixion, for it lets us know in graphic terms the suffering of our Savior. But Jesus knew, as He was 100% God, that He would die that day. The other aspect of this statement that is the most comforting is that Jesus does not require that we live godly lives. It does not matter what sins have been committed. He has the ability and the heart to forgive that sin, even in our last, dying breaths. That does not mean that we should put that decision off, though, for there are no guarantees that we will have the same opportunity as the thief on the cross. A severe heart attack could take our chance away to ask for forgiveness. More importantly, He died so we could live more abundantly. If we never had walked with the Lord as Christians, we would miss so much joy!

And finally, His seventh statement on the cross:

**They will come and declare His righteousness to a people who will be born,
That He has done *this*.
Psalms 22:31 (NKJV)**

**So when Jesus had received the sour wine, He said, "It is finished!" And bowing His head, He gave up His spirit.
John 19:30 (NKJV)**

This is summed up in the Gospels by Jesus' final statement, "It is finished!" He did what He came to do. He knew what He had to do. He knew the pain that He would feel, and the physical pain was nothing compared to the heartache of not feeling the presence of His Father. But His heart broke as the people He came to save would not receive Him or His love. Jesus said repetitively, **"If there is any other way, let this cup pass from**

Me." There was no other way, but we can tell from those statements how heavy the burden was on Him. This word in the Greek is *Tetelestai*! When a prisoner had served his sentence, he was given a piece of paper with this statement written on it to prove to people that he had paid his debt to society. Though we translate *tetelestai* to mean "it is finished," it specifically means "paid in full." We have an enormous sin debt that Jesus paid. For all who think that it is about us and our good works, Jesus summed it up by telling us that we do not need to do anything because He has done it all for us. Which part of "all" do we not understand? Never confuse this with a license to sin, as when He comes into our hearts, He cleans us up. But we have to catch the fish before we can clean it! As J. Vernon McGee said, "His righteousness will satisfy a Holy God." Our little good works would not get us a step forward without what Jesus did for us. Receive the gift. It is truly the gift that keeps on giving.

April 2: Time and the Gospels

When reading the different accounts in the gospels concerning the day our Lord was crucified, the timing of it all seems to be a bit off. Mark says,

[24] And when they crucified Him, they divided His garments, casting lots for them to determine what every man should take.
[25] Now it was the third hour, and they crucified Him. [26] And the inscription of His accusation was written above: THE KING OF THE JEWS.
Mark 15:24-26 (NKJV)

The third hour is 9 a.m. to the Jews. Yet John seems to give us a different story:

[13] When Pilate therefore heard that saying, he brought Jesus out and sat down in the judgment seat in a place that is called *The* Pavement, but in Hebrew, Gabbatha. [14] Now it was the Preparation Day of the Passover, and about the sixth hour. And he said to the Jews, "Behold your King!"

¹⁵ **But they cried out, "Away with *Him,* away with *Him!* Crucify Him!"**
Pilate said to them, "Shall I crucify your King?"
The chief priests answered, "We have no king but Caesar!"
¹⁶ **Then he delivered Him to them to be crucified. Then they took Jesus and led *Him* away.**
John 19:13-16 (NKJV)

According to John, three hours after Mark said that Jesus was on the cross, Jesus was in the judgment area of the Praetorium. There seems to be a contradiction here, yet that conflict is in our understanding, rather than in the Holy Spirit's perfect inspiration.

Though the Gospel of Mark is the only one to emphasize the third hour as being the time of the crucifixion of Jesus, Mark is in complete agreement with Matthew and Luke when it comes to darkness falling over the land for three hours (Matthew 27:45-56, Luke 23:44-49 and Mark 15:33-34). Based on the accounts of the gospels, we do not know what time the arrest of Jesus took place, but we do know that after that time, He was taken to Annas, the father-in-law of the high priest; He was taken to Caiaphas; He was taken to Pontius Pilate; He was taken to Herod; He was taken back to Pontius Pilate. At each of these locations, there was a trial of sorts. We do know that each of those locations was nearby. That seems like a large number of trials to occur early in the morning along with a march, carrying the cross to Calvary. Yet the Jews were incredibly angry at Jesus' claim to be the Son of God. They wanted to have Him killed immediately.

Some scholars have tried to explain the time difference as having to do with the Gospel of Mark using the common Jewish time, while stating that John was using the common Roman time. That is both possible and plausible, yet this is not the only explanation. Scholars believe that Mark was Peter's secretary, and hence, the Gospel of Mark describes Peter's observance or experience. Peter was a broken man after the events of the night before. He began by bragging that though everyone else might turn their backs on Jesus, he loved Jesus more than the rest. Jesus told Peter that he would deny the Lord three times before the cock crowed. The Gospel of Mark says that Peter would deny the Lord three times before the cock crowed twice, while the other gospels all stated that Peter would deny the Lord three times before the cock crowed once. The minority report is probably the most believable as Peter was the one in question. Being that the Gospel of Mark is Peter's eyewitness report, it is plausible that Peter never would forget the events of that evening.

Along with that, is it possible that after denying the Lord, Peter was no longer an eyewitness to the events? It is difficult to imagine Peter hanging around after he denied Jesus! His assessment of 9 a.m. could be a mere estimation from an absent Peter. He certainly was not in his right frame of mind when the crucifixion occurred. We know that John was an eyewitness, as Jesus spoke to him from the cross, telling John to take care of Mary and telling Mary to take care of John! Lastly, people of that time did not wear wristwatches, and time was an estimation based on the location of the sun in the sky. Peter is not mentioned as being present there. As Peter normally was filled with courage, Satan attacked him that night in his strength, rather than in his weakness.

That might seem strange to some, but it is more likely in each of our lives as believers. Why? When we are weak in an area and are aware of that weakness, we have more of a tendency to hand that weakness over to Jesus. Where we are weak, He is strong. Instead, when we are strong in an area, our pride tells us that we can handle it alone, and consequently, we leave ourselves open to attack by Satan and his demons! After the resurrection of Jesus, one of His first acts was to restore the broken Peter. He asked Peter three times, "Do you love me?" As Jesus continued to ask Peter that question, it is easy to imagine how sad it made Peter, while each time reminded him of an additional denial of the Lord.

We have no idea what time Jesus was crucified. Yet we know that He was! God's Word is perfect, and He has a perfect explanation. We just do not know what it is! In the meantime, the lesson for us is to trust God and to trust God's Word! The story of Peter is one of the saddest of that day. Some people feel like God cannot forgive the depth of sin in their lives. Is there anything worse than denying the Lord? Yet Jesus restored Peter to His flock almost immediately. That is just another example of how much the Lord loves each of us! As a wise man stated, "The nails did not hold Him to the cross. It was His love for you and me!" There is no greater love than what Jesus did for us!

April 3: God provides!

Provision is described by our good friend Daniel Webster as the process or act of providing, yet a secondary definition states it is also a measure taken beforehand to deal with a need or contingency. Robert L. Short had this to say:

> The childish idea that prayer is a handle by which we can take hold of God and obtain whatever we desire, leads to easy disillusionment with both what we had thought to be God and what we had thought to be prayer.

God's timing always is perfect, and the measures He has taken truly occurs beforehand. In fact, God decided His plan of action before the foundation of the world. We serve a God who answers our prayers, yet those answers certainly are more grandiose than our perceived, simple-minded requests. One of the names of God in the Old Testament is *Jehovah-jireh*, specifically mentioned when God supplies the ram of sacrifice instead of Isaac, with Abraham dutifully following God's request (Genesis 22:14). God is not our provider when it is convenient for Him. In fact, *Jehovah-jireh* is not only His name, but His nature! He cannot fail to supply the needs of His children, as it would conflict with His nature.

Sadly, many of us seem to fail miserably in our communication with God. We ignore Him unless we have a perceived need not in obvious supply. God loves to bless His children, but has a much larger perspective concerning what each of us truly needs. Instead of desiring things, we should desire Him! As the world economy continues to weaken, more people are concerned with making ends meet. Yet God desires for us to come to the end of ourselves where we will find the beginning of Him! Those are the ends that need to meet, as He always will meet our needs.

[27] **Consider the lilies, how they grow: they neither toil nor spin; and yet I say to you, even Solomon in all his glory was not arrayed like one of these.** [28] **If then God so clothes the grass, which today is in the field and tomorrow is thrown into the oven, how much more *will He clothe* you, O *you* of little faith?**
[29] **"And do not seek what you should eat or what you should drink, nor have an anxious mind.** [30] **For all these things the nations of the world seek after, and your Father knows that you need these things.** [31] **But seek the kingdom of God, and all these things shall be added to you.**
[32] **"Do not fear, little flock, for it is your Father's good pleasure to give you the kingdom.** [33] **Sell what you have and give alms; provide yourselves money bags which do not grow old, a treasure in the heavens that does not fail, where no thief approaches nor moth destroys.** [34] **For where your treasure is, there your heart will be also.**
Luke 12:27-34 (NKJV)

More than the air we breathe, we need a closer walk with our Lord. When walking closely at His side, it is much simpler to trust that nothing can harm us. Yet do not be disillusioned by the timing of His provision. It may seem late to our worried minds, yet we know that God already has made the decision of when the perfect time for our provision will be!

April 4: White as snow!

One of the most beautiful sights in all of God's creation is the pristine morning following a snowstorm. Before footprints or car tracks have changed the perfection, it is wonderful to be the first person up in the morning, to admire all of God's creation, covered in soft billows of white. Though cold and wet, it is amazing to see how snow falls from heaven and covers everything.

"Come now, and let us reason together,"
Says the LORD,
"Though your sins are like scarlet,
They shall be as white as snow;
Though they are red like crimson,
They shall be as wool.
Isaiah 1:18 (NKJV)

The whiteness of snow is almost blinding, and just a spot of blood would soil that color. Yet He removes that stain from our lives. Our lives have much more than a spot of blood soiling them. Most of our lives show signs of a massacre. Yet through God's hand, His miracle, the sin blemish has been removed! What a glorious day in the Lord's creation! Just as the white snow covers everything in our sight on a snowy, winter morning, God is willing and able to cover all of our sins. Yet we have to be willing for Him to accomplish that on our behalves.

Snow can be an inconvenience in our daily routines, making it difficult to drive to work. Yet let it be a reminder of God's covering on each of our lives!

The heavens declare the glory of
God; And the firmament shows His handiwork.
Psalm 19:1 (NKJV)

April 5: Creation of Creator?

Walking around Yosemite, there are two factions of people: there are those who are amazed at what the Creator has given us and there are those who are more enamored with the creation itself. New agers worship the earth, or the non-existent, mother goddess of the earth, both heresies. This is not a new twist in the development of mankind, as throughout time, polytheists have worshipped the sun god, the moon god, the wind god, etc. Those same people thought they had to please the multitude of gods to have their crops grow. What they were missing is that the only God is a jealous God who is pleased only by their decision to worship Him alone!

Though we cannot see God, we can see Him in his creation. If we see an amazing building, we do not have to meet the architect to know much about him, and in the same facet, we can see that God is the greatest mathematician, artist and architect. We can see His mercy, His sense of humor and His grandeur. Paul told us about this, too:

[18] For the wrath of God is revealed from heaven against all ungodliness and unrighteousness of men, who suppress the truth in unrighteousness, [19] because what may be known of God is manifest in them, for God has shown *it* to them. [20] For since the creation of the world His invisible *attributes* are clearly seen, being understood by the things that are made, *even* His eternal power and Godhead, so that they are without excuse, [21] because, although they knew God, they did not glorify *Him* as God, nor were thankful, but became futile in their thoughts, and their foolish hearts were darkened. [22] Professing to be wise, they became fools, [23] and changed the glory of the incorruptible God into an image made like corruptible man—and birds and four-footed animals and creeping things.
Romans 1:18-23 (NKJV)

Jesus told us some additional information about seeing the Father:

[7] "If you had known Me, you would have known My Father also; and from now on you know Him and have seen Him." [8] Philip said to Him, "Lord, show us the Father, and it is sufficient for us." [9] Jesus said to him, "Have I been with you so long, and yet you have not known Me, Philip? He who has seen Me has seen the Father; so how can you say, 'Show us the Father'? [10] Do you not believe that I am in the Father,

and the Father in Me? The words that I speak to you I do not speak on My own *authority;* but the Father who dwells in Me does the works. [11] Believe Me that I *am* in the Father and the Father in Me, or else believe Me for the sake of the works themselves.
[12] "Most assuredly, I say to you, he who believes in Me, the works that I do he will do also; and greater *works* than these he will do, because I go to My Father.
John 14:7-12 (NKJV)

God made this earth and each of us with that same artistry! Praise be to the only God! He is mighty!

[13] For You formed my inward parts;
You covered me in my mother's womb.
[14] I will praise You, for I am fearfully *and* wonderfully made;
Marvelous are Your works,
And *that* my soul knows very well.
Psalm 139:13-14 (NKJV)

April 6: He is risen, indeed!

The succinct way that the Bible fits together through the 66 books and 40 different authors is amazing! Even with the message spread out across thousands of years, the passages constantly agree. Yet in the description of Resurrection Day through four highly-respected authors, there is more disagreement than agreement!

In Matthew, when Mary Magdalene and the other Mary arrived at the tomb, shortly after daybreak, there was one angel sitting on top of the large stone sealing the tomb. After an earthquake in which he moved the stone, she was told that Jesus had risen. In Mark, the stone already had been moved when Mary Magdalene arrived, and she was accompanied by both the other Mary and Salome. They walked into the tomb and a young man (angel) was seated where Jesus should be. In Luke, the stone already had been removed when the women got there. These women were not specifically identified, but were the ones who had been following Jesus. In Luke's description, there were two angels in the tomb. John takes a different path as well. Only Mary Magdalene was at the tomb. She had arrived before sunrise to see the tomb open and empty. John also says there were two angels present. She ran to tell Peter and John, who were the next people to arrive at the empty tomb.

Notice that each of the four different writers described an event they did not personally witness. Certainly, they heard Mary Magdalene talk about the event. When faced with a traumatic event, do we always have perfect recollection of the order? If we asked people on Wall Street on September 11 the exact order of events, certainly there would be much disagreement. Sometimes, the person asking the questions in an interview can put his own bias into the situation and deduce a different fact.

On that resurrection day, there were many different descriptions of the events that transpired. Luke says that Jesus appeared to Peter before He appeared to the 11 remaining disciples. John says that Jesus appeared to 10 of the 11 remaining disciples as Thomas was not present. Thomas did not see Jesus for another eight days. Mark, writing through the eyes of Peter, did not describe Peter seeing Jesus before the time that He appeared to the 11 disciples. There is so much that does not seem to fit, and yet...

There is one aspect that all of them describe in exactly the same way...

Jesus has risen! They saw Him, spoke with Him, did not recognize Him at first in the different descriptions and even touched the nail holes in his hands and feet. He was not just badly injured at the cross, making a miraculous recovery. The centurion put a spear into His side and blood and water gushed outwards to ensure that He was dead. A body never was discovered. Have we seen Him?

³ For I delivered to you first of all that which I also received: that Christ died for our sins according to the Scriptures, ⁴ and that He was buried, and that He rose again the third day according to the Scriptures, ⁵ and that He was seen by Cephas, then by the twelve. ⁶ After that He was seen by over five hundred brethren at once, of whom the greater part remain to the present, but some have fallen asleep. ⁷ After that He was seen by James, then by all the apostles. ⁸ Then last of all He was seen by me also, as by one born out of due time.
1 Corinthians 15:3-8 (NKJV)

In a court case, the most irrefutable evidence is an eyewitness and in the case of the resurrection of Jesus, there were over 500 eyewitnesses! That is enough for all of us who know Jesus as our Lord and Savior. Yet in the martyrdom of all of the apostles except for John, we see the conviction of each of these men, who saw! Because they saw, they were willing to die rather than recant that description. When we have felt His existence in our day-to-day lives, it is easy to believe that on that morning almost 2,000 years ago, He who had been killed was alive again! The death of Jesus was an amazing event, as He carried our sins on His shoulders to shield us from the punishment we had earned in our own sinful lives. Yet without the resurrection, it all would have been for nothing. Because He lives, we too can live!

⁵ Let this mind be in you which was also in Christ Jesus, ⁶ who, being in the form of God, did not consider it robbery to be equal with God, ⁷ but made Himself of no reputation, taking the form of a bondservant, *and* coming in the likeness of men. ⁸ And being found in appearance as a man, He humbled Himself and became obedient to *the point of* death, even the death of the cross. ⁹ Therefore God also has highly exalted Him and given Him the name which is above every name, ¹⁰ that at the name of Jesus every knee should bow, of those in heaven, and of those on earth, and of those under the earth, ¹¹ and *that* every tongue should confess that Jesus Christ *is* Lord, to the glory of God the Father.
Philippians 2:5-11 (NKJV)

Jesus is risen, indeed! Walk in the joy and the celebration of His life, death and resurrection. "I serve a risen Savior, He's in the world today. I know that He is living whatever men may say; I see His hand of mercy; I hear His voice of cheer, and just the time I need Him, He's always near. He lives, He lives, Christ Jesus lives today! He walks with me and talks with me along life's narrow way. He lives, He lives, salvation to impart! You ask me how I know He lives, He lives within my heart!"

April 7: Passover

At sundown, the feast week of Passover begins. On the Jewish calendar, Monday is the 14th of *Nisan* in the year 5770, with sundown beginning a new day. The Passover feast, called the *Seder*, commemorates the end of the Jews' slavery to Egypt. Historians believe that occurred in the year 1441 B.C., over 3,450 years ago. Passover (*Pesach* in Hebrew) occurs along with the first full moon after the first day of spring. Before this day was mathematically determined, it was the first full moon after the barley harvest. Passover is one of three feasts of Moses in which the able-bodied Jewish men were required to make the trip to Jerusalem yearly. In the Book of Exodus, the Bible instructs the Jews how to keep the feast of Passover and that it is to be kept through all their generations. They are to acquire one, unblemished male lamb per each household on the tenth of *Nisan*. At sundown on the 15th of *Nisan*, they are to gather together and kill the ram, taking some of the blood and place that blood on the doorposts. After roasting the lamb in fire, they are to eat what they can and burn the remains before daylight.

On that night of the first *Seder*, the Angel of death killed each of the firstborn in any home not protected by the blood of the lamb. He "passed over" those marked homes, sparing the firstborn in those families. The next day, the Jews began their journey to the Promised Land. Years later, on another Passover evening, Jesus celebrated the Last Supper with His disciples on the night before His crucifixion.

All of the food items in the Seder, the Passover Feast, point to God's redemption:

- ***Maror***: These are the bitter herbs, sometimes horseradish and at other times varieties of lettuce, to symbolize the bitter years of slavery for the Jews in Egypt. When redeemed, God takes that bitterness and replaces it with joy!
- ***Charoset***: This is a mixture of apples, figs, dates, nuts, cinnamon and wine to symbolize the mortar or clay used to make bricks, as the Jews did in slavery. When redeemed, we are no longer slaves to sin, but have been purchased by the blood of the Lamb of God!
- ***Beitzah***: This is a hard-boiled egg to symbolize the renewal of life through fertility and the continuation of the Jews as a culture and people. God's Word told us of the restoration of Israel over 1,000 years before the event occurred in 1948. We also know that the 12 tribes will be around in the Great Tribulation and the Millennium. Just as eggs became a part of Easter due to the Pagans (with *Ishtar*, the goddess of fertility), this aspect of the *Seder* is most likely tied to the Babylonian gods during the Jews' captivity there.
- ***Karpas***: This is either celery or parsley, dipped into salt water, to symbolize the bitter taste of slavery and the tears of the Jewish people. We know that God keeps all of our tears in a bottle, according to Psalms. Again, He replaces our sadness with joy.
- ***Zeroah***: Most Jews still eat lamb at Passover, and even if they do not, there is a shank bone of a lamb on the table. The lamb is symbolic of the forgiveness of sins. The Torah teaches that there is no forgiveness of sins apart from the spilling of innocent blood, and the killing of the Paschal lamb points to the sacrificial system set up through the Law of Moses. This is significant, as there is no longer a temple to perform the sacrificial rituals. There has been no sacrifice since the last temple was destroyed by the Romans in A.D. 70. With the life, death and resurrection of Jesus, the Lamb of God, we

have forgiveness of sins without the sacrificial system of the temple. Jesus redeemed us! He purchased us with the spilling of His own innocent blood!
- **Wine**: The strong taste of wine is symbolic of the richness of the Jews' relationship when they were following God. At the Seder, four toasts of wine are performed at different times in the ceremony, pointing to four "I will" statements of God:

1. **I will take you out of Egypt (Cup of Sanctification).** Just as God chose the Jews as His people and promised to deliver them from Egypt to the Promised Land, He has fulfilled or will fulfill every promise He has made. This is a special time to reflect on the world of sin He has carried us out of, the promises He has fulfilled in our lives and the promises still to come! Along with that, He chose us, just as He chose the Jews!
2. **I will deliver you from slavery (Cup of Judgment).** Though the Jews were physically enslaved, we were all spiritually enslaved, as we lived in bondage to our sins. This is a wonderful time to reflect on the death our lives have earned, and the judgment that we would have received without the life, death and resurrection of Jesus. At this point in the *Seder*, we drip some of the wine onto our plates, so the cup is not full. This signifies the price of our redemption. To the Jews, this has to do with the plagues, but for Christians, the cost of our redemption is the death on the cross of our Messiah! As we drip the wine, we should think of our precious Messiah's blood dripping upon the ground. His blood was shed for each of us, personally!
3. **I will redeem you with the demonstration of my power (Cup of Redemption).** This is extremely significant to a Christian, as this is the last cup Jesus drank from at the *Seder* of the Last Supper. Here is how Jesus shared the third cup with His disciples that night:

[27] Then He took the cup, and gave thanks, and gave *it* to them, saying, "Drink from it, all of you. [28] For this is My

blood of the new covenant, which is shed for many for the remission of sins. ²⁹ But I say to you, I will not drink of this fruit of the vine from now on until that day when I drink it new with you in My Father's kingdom."
Matthew 26:27-29 (NKJV)

As Christians, we understand the significance of Christ's blood as the price of our redemption, but try to visualize the disciples that night, the night before Jesus died for our sins! He told them that His blood would be shed for them and that was the only way they would be forgiven. What a solemn occasion!

> 4. **I will acquire you as a nation (Cup of Celebration).** This cup is reserved for after the dinner. At the Last Supper, there was not a final cup, as Jesus told them He would not drink from the cup again until they and we were all together with Him. It was not time to celebrate until after His death and resurrection. This *Seder* will not finish until we gather together with our Lord at the Wedding Supper of the Lamb! We will join Him in the Cup of Celebration to complete this *Seder*. We have been baptized into His crucifixion and resurrection, and we will share the end of the Last Supper with Him!

A special glass is also poured for the prophet Elijah, and the door is opened for his arrival. In the second to last verse of the Old Testament, the Lord foretells that Elijah will return:

⁴"**Remember the Law of Moses, My servant,
Which I commanded him in Horeb for all Israel,
With the statutes and judgments.**
⁵**Behold, I will send you Elijah the prophet
Before the coming of the great and dreadful day of the LORD.
⁶And he will turn
The hearts of the fathers to the children,
And the hearts of the children to their fathers,
Lest I come and strike the earth with a curse.**
Malachi 4:4-6 (NKJV)

- *Matzos*: This is the unleavened bread eaten at the Passover. Notice that the matzos are striped, as "by His stripes we are healed," and each cracker is pierced with holes ("they pierced His hands and His feet.)" Leavening (*Chametz*) is removed from the house. This is the yeast for bread or fermentation. Yeast puffs bread up, and in the same sense, sin puffs up man, as we understand the connection between pride and sin. Throughout the week, for eight days, Jews do not eat leavened bread in the Passover meal or in the Feast of Unleavened Bread, pointing ahead to Jesus! God came to earth and lived as a sinless man, so that He would be punished for our sins. If He had sinned, Jesus would have had to receive His own punishment through death, as Romans tells us that **"the wages of sin is death."** Instead, as Paul tells us,

For He made Him who knew no sin *to be* sin for us, that we might become the righteousness of God in Him.
2 Corinthians 5:21(NKJV)

- *Aficoman* (meaning "what comes after" or dessert). Earlier in the *Seder* when the unleavened bread is eaten, part of the *matzos* is hidden, for the children to search for. Whoever finds the *matzos* is rewarded with money or a gift, and all of the children receive a reward. Once this last piece of *matzos* is eaten, nothing else should be, in order to keep the taste of *matzo* in their mouths. Rabbis have difficulty explaining the significance of this event, and typically, the reason is to keep the children from getting restless during the ceremony. As Christians, though, we realize that leaven is a symbol of sin, and in the usage of unleavened bread, it points to the sinless Bread of life, Jesus. Though He is hidden from their eyes, that will change when the fullness of the Gentiles has taken place. Jesus is the taste that will always remain, once they see Him!

Though we as Christians do not celebrate Passover, it is significant in our walks with the Lord. Without understanding the Jewish tradition of the feast, we cannot understand the deep meaning of the words of our Lord the night before His crucifixion. What an awesome day it is!

April 8: Why was Jesus crucified?

The answer would depend upon perspective. From the Jewish perspective, Jesus was crucified because He was a threat, yet it is the Jewish leadership in question more than the Jews as a whole. Each person makes his own choices and the Jewish people were fickle, at best. Certainly, there were many Jews in the mobs following Jesus, drawn to His miracles more than they were drawn to His heart, almost as if they were watching David Copperfield in Las Vegas. The same Jews who acknowledged Him as King a week before the crucifixion took their places in the mob calling for Pontius Pilate to release Barabbas instead of Jesus, calling for the death of Jesus! The Jewish leadership was quite another story. They were offended by the "ostentatious" miracles of Jesus, including bringing back Lazarus from dead to live, healing on the Sabbath and giving sight to the blind. How many times did Jesus perform miracles and ask the recipient not to announce it? With the Pharisees, pride was at the center of it all. Just as Herod elected to kill all the young male children of the region in an attempt to protect his own ability to rule and reign, the Jewish leadership did not want to hand over the keys of the kingdom to Jesus!

Additionally, Jesus had pointed out their sinful behavior. When confronted with our own sin, we have the choice of becoming the proverbial ostrich with its head in the sand or we have to acknowledge the truth. The Pharisees buried their heads deeply! They continued to tail Jesus, trying to catch Him in any wrongdoing. Additionally, they tried to trip Him up with their questions. Yet His questions further exposed their own sins. Think of the woman caught in adultery (John 8). Though we do not know exactly what Jesus wrote in the dirt that caused them to flee, it might have been the name of the man, also caught in the act of adultery, who was noticeably absent at the projected stoning. It certainly was a set-up, yet in a manner of moments, Jesus handled the situation wisely. Though it was Old Testament law to stone the woman and the man, Jesus said, **"Let him who is without sin cast the first stone."** Upon scrawling in the dirt, all the accusers fled. But it was the claims of Jesus to be God that caused them to crucify Him. They claimed that He was a heretic. Sadly, the Pharisees had the greatest opportunity to see Jesus as Messiah, as they were most familiar with the Old Testament. The large number of prophecies that applied to Jesus became overlooked when clouded with their own spiritual pride.

Another perspective would be that of the Romans. Certainly, Pontius Pilate did not desire to crucify Jesus. He had the distinct ability to make the decision, as Israel was under Roman rule. Yet neither he nor Herod found Jesus guilty. Pilate's wife warned him to be very careful, saying,

While he was sitting on the judgment seat, his wife sent to him, saying, "Have nothing to do with that just Man, for I have suffered many things today in a dream because of Him."
Matthew 27:19 (NKJV)

Pilate allowed the crucifixion trying not to anger his superiors. Being a feast day, Pilate desired to retain control over the city of Jerusalem, and with the Jewish leadership pushing an angry mob toward riot, Pilate desired for the situation to end as quickly as possible. He took the easy way out, rather than the way of honor and integrity, shortly after his conversation with Jesus concerning the meaning of truth.

Through the perspectives of Father, Son and Holy Spirit, Jesus was crucified because it was the only way that the plan of the Father could be accomplished. How do we know that? When Jesus was in the Garden of Gethsemane, He prayed three separate times, that if there was any other way to accomplish this, for the Father to let this cup pass from Him.

⁴¹ **And He was withdrawn from them about a stone's throw, and He knelt down and prayed,** ⁴² **saying, "Father, if it is Your will, take this cup away from Me; nevertheless not My will, but Yours, be done."** ⁴³ **Then an angel appeared to Him from heaven, strengthening Him.** ⁴⁴ **And being in agony, He prayed more earnestly. Then His sweat became like great drops of blood falling down to the ground.**
Luke 22:41-44 (NKJV)

The cup that Jesus was about to drink was the cross, which involved separation from the Father and Holy Spirit for the only time in the world's history. The Father's answer was to send Jesus to the cross, for as Isaiah 53 reminds us, **"Yet it pleased the Lord to bruise Him."** Because there can be no forgiveness of sin without the spilling of innocent blood (Hebrews 9:22), an innocent man had to die to cover our sins. As Paul reminds us in 2 Corinthians 5:21: **"For God made Him who knew no sin to become sin for us that we might become the righteousness of God in Him."** Jesus was not only punished for our sins; He became sin for us! Jesus had to be crucified so that we could have a relationship with God!

Personally, He was punished for OUR SINS! Jesus was given the death that we deserved and have earned with our lives, just as we will be given the life that He earned and deserved with His life! Each of us placed Him on the cross; we spat in His face; we beat Him with sticks; we laughed at Him and ridiculed Him; and we live because He died! In John 15:13, Jesus told us**, "Greater love has no one than this, than to lay down one's life for his friends."** He died for each of us while we hated Him. (Paul tells us in Romans that while we were still sinners, Christ died for us!) He willingly departed heaven to be crucified so that we might live. There never can be a greater example of love! "It was not the nails that held Him to the cross, it was His love for us!"

⁵ **Let this mind be in you which was also in Christ Jesus,** ⁶ **who, being in the form of God, did not consider it robbery to be equal with God,** ⁷ **but made Himself of no reputation,**

taking the form of a bondservant, *and* coming in the likeness of men. ⁸ And being found in appearance as a man, He humbled Himself and became obedient to *the point of* death, even the death of the cross. ⁹ Therefore God also has highly exalted Him and given Him the name which is above every name, ¹⁰ that at the name of Jesus every knee should bow, of those in heaven, and of those on earth, and of those under the earth, ¹¹ and *that* every tongue should confess that Jesus Christ *is* Lord, to the glory of God the Father.
Philippians 2:5-11 (NKJV)

Praise God for His love on this day of celebration of the resurrection of our Lord Jesus! But let us remember, every day is Easter. He is risen!

April 9: Together or separate?

While Passover occurs on the first full moon after spring begins, Easter occurs on the first Sunday of spring. After the resurrection and ascension of Jesus, the tradition of Passover continued with additional significance for the followers of the Son of God. Most of the first Christians were Jews, who understood the fulfillment of Passover in the death of Jesus. Sadly, this became a schism with "*quartodecimanism*," which comes from the Latin "*quarta decima*," meaning fourteen. Most of the Messianic Jews continued to celebrate the death and resurrection of Jesus beginning on the eve of the 14ᵗʰ of Nisan, while most of the Gentiles preferred celebrating the same event on the following Sunday. That continues to this day!

The saddest part is that God's intent of Jew and Gentile worshipping together began separating very early on in the life of the Church. Polycarp, Eusebius and many of the early Church fathers agreed with the Jews, but as time went on, the schism increased. It got to a point of complete separation. An analogy of the situation would be if a person invited us to a party of their friends, who we never had met. Upon arrival at the party, we had that friend thrown out and remained with his old friends and our new acquaintances. God's chosen people shared the Gospel with the Gentiles, and then the Gentiles cast the Jews aside and continued on their own!

How sad that the knowledge of Jesus as Messiah did not hold the two together, but instead, other interpretations pushed them apart. Paul tells us of the earliest separation of beliefs, as Peter was continuing in the custom that Jews were not to eat with Gentiles. This was not a law from the Torah, but certainly was the custom of the time. Paul called Peter out for this faulty conclusion in Galatians:

[11] Now when Peter had come to Antioch, I withstood him to his face, because he was to be blamed; [12] for before certain men came from James, he would eat with the Gentiles; but when they came, he withdrew and separated himself, fearing those who were of the circumcision. [13] And the rest of the Jews also played the hypocrite with him, so that even Barnabas was carried away with their hypocrisy.
[14] But when I saw that they were not straightforward about the truth of the gospel, I said to Peter before *them* all, "If you, being a Jew, live in the manner of Gentiles and not as the Jews, why do you compel Gentiles to live as Jews? [15] We *who are* Jews by nature, and not sinners of the Gentiles, [16] knowing that a man is not justified by the works of the law but by faith in Jesus Christ, even we have believed in Christ Jesus, that we might be justified by faith in Christ and not by the works of the law; for by the works of the law no flesh shall be justified.
Galatians 2:11-16 (NKJV)

Today, we do exactly the same. Each denomination has its own spin and interpretation of Scripture, and most believe they are the only ones who are guided by God! Constant disagreement seems to drive us more than the love of Jesus as our Savior. Are there going to be denominations in heaven? Interestingly, in reference to that time, the word Church is singular! While we all seem to have our own beliefs and interpretations of God's Word, we should not separate based on small, doctrinal disagreements!

Each one of us will find when we get to heaven that we had something wrong! What we cannot get wrong is the absolute knowledge that Jesus died for our sins. Without receiving Him and His forgiveness, we are lost! That is what Easter, and Passover, are all about. Let us celebrate what our Lord did for us!

April 10: Slow to anger

When we think about the attributes of God, we seem to focus on His goodness rather than His wrath. Many church pastors seem to avoid the subject of God's wrath entirely when preaching, as those are not the words that fill the seats. Yet we need to understand that God is perfectly good at the same time that He is perfectly wrathful. The two may seem like opposites, but they do not conflict. The best news for us is that God does not have a short fuse.

[8] The LORD *is* merciful and gracious,
Slow to anger, and abounding in mercy.
[9] He will not always strive *with us*,
Nor will He keep *His anger* forever.
[10] He has not dealt with us according to our sins,
Nor punished us according to our iniquities.
Psalm 103:8-10 (NKJV)

By our actions, we deserve God's wrath all of the time, yet through His mercy, He does not give us what we deserve. What is the difference between wrath and anger? Anger is the evoked emotion, while wrath is the action. Anger is the whistle on the boiling tea kettle, while wrath is the scalding steam. Though God demonstrates His wrath throughout the Bible, the culmination of that wrath is in the Book of Revelation, where God pours out His wrath upon a sinful earth. In the midst of that time, however, there will be more people who come to know Jesus as Lord and Savior than ever before. That demonstrates His abounding mercy and grace along with His wrath. Because God is love, He never can be anything other than love.

As we grow as Christians, we are to become more like God each day. Similar to looking in a mirror, our image should be a reflection of the image of God. When peering into a lake, the calmer the water, the more apparent the reflection, yet God's desire in the life of the believer is for His reflection to be most apparent in our lives even in the midst of tumult! The reflection never will become the image being reflected, and in the same way, we never will become God. Anger is one of our greatest difficulties, yet we need to understand that anger is not a sin. How could it be, as God demonstrates anger without sinning? Paul instructs us:

***"Be angry, and do not sin"*: do not let the sun go down on your wrath, [27] nor give place to the devil.**
Ephesians 4:26 (NKJV)

Righteous anger is not blowing up at a driver who cuts us off in traffic. Neither is it insulting someone who has insulted us. Anger should be directed at sin, not the sinner. It is the example of hating the sin and loving the sinner. Understand that just as God's anger does not conflict His love, our anger needs to be based in love. The Bible reminds us to love our enemies; to love our neighbors as ourselves; to lay down our lives for our friends to demonstrate the greatest love! As we step out into the world today, we should be reminded of the fine line that we walk when we venture into the element of anger!

***He who* slow to anger *is* better than the mighty,**
And he who rules his spirit than he who takes a city.
Proverbs 16:32 (NKJV)

April 11: Patience!

Driving requires much patience, especially in highly-populated urban areas. It is unsettling to be stuck behind someone creeping along below the speed limit in the fast lane, and we often look like caged animals, eyes darting for possible openings of escape. Especially on less-traveled mountain roads, the winding nature can remove the ability to pass. In those cases, one overly cautious driver can lead what appears to be a funeral procession down the serpentine road. Often there are more people following the leader than there are people dwelling in those remote locations. We always seem to be in a rush to get where we are going, though those few moments spared by passing dangerously are rarely utilized. Sometimes we forget that patience is one of the gifts of the Holy Spirit, and when overcome by impatience, we are not walking in the Spirit.

Patience is not what a successful doctor has! Instead, patience is abiding under difficult circumstances. It could be following inconsiderate drivers down a curvy, mountain road. It could be struggling to love and support a friend rolling in sin like a pig in mud. It could be waiting on the Lord to renew our strength. Regardless of the situation that the Lord puts us in, we know that He is inordinately patient with us!

Praying for patience might be a mistake to some Christians. King Solomon asked God for wisdom, and God gave it to him because it revealed Solomon's heart to have compassion for the people. Yet when praying for patience, in order to teach that patience, the Lord can place us into some extremely difficult circumstances! It is not much different than praying to be placed in prison! God certainly will teach us peace through the midst of the fire. Truly, we all need more patience, and we know that God will help us through the learning process. When we continue to have peace like a river flowing through us in the midst of dire circumstances, we know the meaning of patience.

Jesus told His disciples:

By your patience possess your souls.
Luke 21:19 (NKJV)

By taking the opposite approach, when we are exhibiting impatience, someone else controls us, the enemy of God. Paul highlighted patience as a necessary virtue in any ministry God places us into:

[3] We give no offense in anything, that our ministry may not be blamed. [4] But in all *things* we commend ourselves as ministers of God: in much patience, in tribulations, in needs, in distresses, [5] in stripes, in imprisonments, in tumults, in labors, in sleeplessness, in fastings; [6] by purity, by knowledge, by longsuffering, by kindness, by the Holy Spirit, by sincere love...
2 Corinthians 6:3-6 (NKJV)

Part of learning patience involves slowing down! When we are still, we know that He is God, and most importantly, we know that we are not. Impatience involves our prideful actions of trying to be the god of our own lives. Because God never makes mistakes, patience involves moving at the pace He has placed in our lives! When we are teenagers, we erroneously think that the 70 or so years of a man's life will pass slowly, but when asking a 70-year-old how quickly it passed, words cannot express the blazing speed. Soon, believers all will be with the Lord for eternity! And then, we all will realize how brief any of our trials on earth were!

[9] Let love be without hypocrisy. Abhor what is evil. Cling to what is good. [10] Be kindly affectionate to one another with brotherly love, in honor giving preference to one another; [11] not lagging in diligence, fervent in spirit, serving the Lord; [12] rejoicing in hope, patient in tribulation, continuing steadfastly in prayer; [13] distributing to the needs of the saints, given to hospitality.
Romans 12:9-13 (NKJV)

April 12: A salt and battery

People seldom quibble over the price of salt at the grocery store, for it is both plentiful and inexpensive. In fact, few cupboards worldwide are without salt. It greatly enhances flavor and at the same time, is a preservative. In the Sermon on the Mount, Jesus compared believers to salt:

You are the salt of the earth; but if the salt loses its flavor, how shall it be seasoned? It is then good for nothing but to be thrown out and trampled underfoot by men.
Matthew 5:13 (NKJV)

In snowy climates, salt also melts snow and ice, which demonstrates that it even can serve a purpose when being trampled underfoot! Yet God desires for us to make life more savory for those around us. How can we accomplish that calling? It is not by judging unbelievers that we will have impact on their lives. That impact comes through love. When we seem to have a short supply of love, God desires for us to go to Him for an increase, as He has more love than the world has salt! Mark Twain said,

> "Almost any man worthy of his salt would fight to defend his home, but no one ever heard of a man going to war for his boarding house."

Which home should we be most interested in fighting for, our earthly home or our heavenly one? Instead of battling and battering our neighbors, we should love them to the Kingdom of God. If we are rubbing salt in their wounds, that salt should not sting, but should remind each recipient of the love of our Creator. When we have lost our love and lost our flavor, we no longer can be a pillar of the community. Lot's wife certainly adds flavor to the story of Sodom and Gomorrah!

But his wife looked back behind him, and she became a pillar of salt.
Genesis 19:26 (NKJV)

Instead of loving those God placed in her path, she loved being a part of the world. Rather than flavoring those around her, Lot's wife was trampled underfoot.

[32] Remember Lot's wife. [33] Whoever seeks to save his life will lose it, and whoever loses his life will preserve it.

Luke 17:32-33 (NKJV)

April 13: The ego tree

Before a baby is born, the seed is planted. Let us call that seed, "sin nature." That baby wants food, a blanket or a diaper change, and he is not thinking that we need a little sleep first, before we take care of his needs. He wants it now! The ego tree begins to grow, and continues with one of an infant's first words, "Mine." That one word demonstrates selfishness, and the tree continues to grow. As that child grows, his needs take precedence over the needs of others in every way. Just wait to see all the gifts he wants for Christmas! Most of the time, thankfulness will be non-existent. Once a little sapling, our ego tree is going to become a California sequoia before too long. It is not a fatal flaw in some people; it is the fatal flaw of all people. Pride! It caused Lucifer to fall from heaven; it caused Adam and Eve to sin in the Garden of Eden; it causes each of us to be separated from God.

^{16}These six *things* the LORD hates,
Yes, seven *are* an abomination to Him:
^{17}A proud look,
A lying tongue,
Hands that shed innocent blood,
^{18}A heart that devises wicked plans,
Feet that are swift in running to evil,
^{19}A false witness *who* speaks lies,
And one who sows discord among brethren.
Proverbs 6:16-19 (NKJV)

We spend hours studying God's love, yet we also know that God is capable of hatred. In the simple verse above, we see seven actions that will cause hatred in the Lord. Is it surprising that each of those can be tied closely to pride? The first one is a no-brainer, as someone strutting with a proud look is merely demonstrating on the outside what is occurring on the inside. Lying is the second offense mentioned, and most lies are to make us look better. The third offense goes hand-in-hand with the seventh commandment to not kill. Murder is certainly putting one's own life ahead of the lives of others. To satisfy anger, a life is extinguished. Once again, it points to pride. Next, even one who plans evil causes hatred in God, and the one planning is certainly trying to elevate his own status in an unethical way. Next, are feet that run toward evil. Joseph ran away from evil, yet when we decide to sin, we do not just walk slowly to accomplish that feat. We sprint. All sin points to pride, of us putting our own desires ahead of God's desires in our lives. Next, is not just any lie, but the lie which condemns an innocent man. Two false witnesses lied about Jesus in His trial with Caiaphas. Lastly, the man who sows discord among brethren is mentioned. This can be done through lies or even spreading the truth. It brings up the old adage, "if you don't have anything nice to say, don't say anything at all." Gossip spreads like a forest fire in a dry, windy climate. Once again, the typical reason that we have negative comments about someone else is those comments make us feel bigger or more important.

Pride! We all have an ego tree growing in our backyard. What does the Lord do with trees? He prunes them.

[1] **"I am the true vine, and My Father is the vinedresser.** [2] **Every branch in Me that does not bear fruit He takes away; and every *branch* that bears fruit He prunes, that it may bear more fruit.** [3] **You are already clean because of the word which I have spoken to you.** [4] **Abide in Me, and I in you. As the branch cannot bear fruit of itself, unless it abides in the vine, neither can you, unless you abide in Me.**
    John 15:1-4 (NKJV)

What do we have to be proud of? The money we have in a bank account? With many situations beyond our control, that could be wiped out in moments. Are we proud of our looks, our intelligence, or our accomplishments? Which of those were not gifts of God? Without the Lord, we are lost, blind, deaf and dead! He purchased our lives with His blood. We can boast in the Lord, but we have nothing to boast about in ourselves. Every talent is what He gave, not what we earned!

A man's pride will bring him low,
But the humble in spirit will retain honor.
Proverbs 29:23 (NKJV)

April 14: On fire!

Remember what it was like soon after becoming a Christian? The world changed overnight. The greatest gift was in knowing that Jesus received the punishment for our sinful lives in the same way that we would be receiving the honor for His perfect life. Walking in that new freedom, it certainly felt like the weight of the world had been removed from our shoulders. After that day, most new believers carry their Bibles everywhere. Inside that book, God speaks to us. We are hungry to hear Him, and thirsty for His words that are all that can satisfy. After finding His forgiveness, we want everyone to know His love and forgiveness in the same sense. The honeymoon began.

Does the honeymoon have to end? While the everyday walk with the Lord never would be boring or monotonous, the newness wears away. We can try to keep the honeymoon alive in the same way that some married couples do, by putting a priority on the freshness of our walks with the Lord. We can do that by spending our free time learning God's Word, for no matter how many times we read it, we learn new lessons each time. It is so special to be on fire for Christ in a society where we are most concerned with burning out.

[1] Now Moses was tending the flock of Jethro his father-in-law, the priest of Midian. And he led the flock to the back of the desert, and came to Horeb, the mountain of God. [2] And the Angel of the LORD appeared to him in a flame of fire from the midst of a bush. So he looked, and behold, the bush was burning with fire, but the bush *was* not consumed. [3] Then Moses said, "I will now turn aside and see this great sight, why the bush does not burn."
Exodus 3:1-3 (NKJV)

In our Christian walks, we should be on fire for the Lord and He will not allow us to be consumed. Look at the life of the apostle Paul, who endured imprisonment, shipwreck, stoning, beating and ridicule, but kept His fire for the Lord burning brightly. Paul understood that his rest would come after the end of the race, but not before the race was run, and won, for the Lord! If we are tired, God will sustain us! Just like a runner who feels oxygen deprivation near race's end, we need to keep running through the pain! When we get to the end, God has the best retirement plan available!

April 15: Faith and overcoming obstacles

Happy Tax Day to all who have to pay Uncle Sam, and render unto Sam what is Sam's. This day it is easy to reflect on how much or little we have earned in the past year. Some of us have the tendency of looking at the lives of others to see what appears to be relative ease, while losing sight of the gifts God has given us. As Christians, we are not to look at others and covet what they have. God has given to each one what He has chosen to give. These gifts are not earned, nor are they luck. They are part of God's destiny in our lives. The Bible tells us that God has given each of us a measure of faith.

[3] For I say, through the grace given to me, to everyone who is among you, not to think *of himself* more highly than he ought to think, but to think soberly, as God has dealt to each one a measure of faith. [4] For as we have many members in one body, but all the members do not have the same function, [5] so we, *being* many, are one body in Christ, and individually members of one another. [6] Having then gifts differing according to the grace that is given to us, *let us use them:* if prophecy, *let us prophesy* in proportion to our faith; [7] or ministry, *let us use it* in *our* ministering; he who teaches, in teaching; [8] he who exhorts, in exhortation; he who gives, with liberality; he who leads, with diligence; he who shows mercy, with cheerfulness.
Romans 12:3-8 (NKJV)

What would we rather have as a gift from God, the faith that leads to eternal salvation or the finances to make our walks through this life easier? Even when enduring difficult times, God only will put us in situations He has given us the faith to conquer. If those situations are difficult, we can choose to approach them from at least two angles:

Either we can look with a "poor me" attitude, crying, complaining and knowing that the road is going to be hard.

OR

We can praise the Lord for giving us a large amount of faith, enough to endure the very difficult tasks in front of us.

**These things I have spoken to you, that in Me you may have peace. In the world you will have tribulation; but be of good cheer, I have overcome the world."
John 16:33 (NKJV)**

What is more important, having the financial ability to do whatever we want or having the exact amount that God wants us to have? God wants to stretch us to trust in Him rather than in self! Some may trust in horses (wealth); some may trust in chariots (power), but we will trust in the name of our Lord!

April 16: Changing times

Bob Dylan wrote a song in 1964 called, "The Times They Are a-Changin,'" and when looking at the world today, we should feel like holding tighter to the Word of God, as the times definitely have changed. Jesus warned us in Matthew 24 of famines and earthquakes that will occur in various places before the tribulation. Are we in that time? It sure does seem that way, but only time will tell. Worldwide recession is obvious. Earthquakes in Japan, Haiti, Chile, China and Mexico have caused much death and destruction. Seismologists who are not well-versed in biblical prophecy are saying that we had an average amount of earthquakes in the 7.0+ range in 2009, but they also say that if the earthquakes continue, it will be worth further study into what is going on.

If that was the only aspect of unfulfilled Bible prophecy splashing across the front of our daily newspapers, curiosity would not be so heightened. Yet the issues happening with the nation of Israel further reveal that we are entering interesting times.

According to reports, Iran is about to become a nuclear power, as their first reactor could open soon. Along with that, experts have estimated that Iran already has enriched enough uranium to construct two nuclear weapons. Up to this time, the nations with nuclear capabilities have used those weapons as a deterrent in warfare, rather than as an aggressive threat. Yet Iran's President Mahmoud Ahmadinejad has said that he will wipe Israel from the map. Nuclear weapons would certainly facilitate that act. Yet we also know that Israel has nuclear weapons. Is it possible that Ahmadinejad will accomplish his goal? Not according to God:

^{14}I will bring back the captives of My people Israel;
They shall build the waste cities and inhabit *them;*
They shall plant vineyards and drink wine from them;
They shall also make gardens and eat fruit from them.
^{15}I will plant them in their land,
And no longer shall they be pulled up
From the land I have given them,"
Says the LORD your God.
Amos 9:14-15 (NKJV)

What is even more concerning is the stance of the United States toward the nation of Israel. Since the formation of Israel as a nation on May 14, 1948, the United States has been Israel's biggest supporter. For the first time in that history, we have a president who does not support Israel. Though the polls demonstrated that most Israelis would have voted for Barack Obama had they been given the opportunity, now that feeling is quite different. The American president supports the

Palestinians above the Israelis, and tensions between the United States and Israel never have been stronger. Why is this a concern?

> [1] Now the LORD had said to Abram:
> "Get out of your country, From your family
> And from your father's house,
> To a land that I will show you.
> [2] I will make you a great nation;
> I will bless you
> And make your name great;
> And you shall be a blessing.
> [3] I will bless those who bless you,
> And I will curse him who curses you;
> And in you all the families of the earth shall be blessed."
> **Genesis 12:1-3 (NKJV)**

If we as a nation curse Israel, God will curse us as a nation! Individually, that is quite different. Personally, we can continue to bless Israel! As difficult as these times may seem to be, do not forget the blessing that goes hand in hand. What a great witnessing tool! God has told us years in advance what is going to happen. Does that not testify strongly of who He is? Do not be afraid! God is in charge!

April 17: Inlets and outlets

Israel is an amazing country, though very small. In the south, the city of Eilat borders the Red Sea. From that point, Jordan, Egypt and Saudi Arabia are all visible. In the north, from the old city of Dan, Lebanon and Syria are both visible. It is amazing to see the stark contrast between the desert landscape north of Eilat and only hours away, see the mountain topography of Dan. The focus of the entire world remains on this little country, relatively the same size as New Jersey. The bodies of water in Israel also are starkly different. The greatest contrast exists between the Sea of Galilee and the Dead Sea, and both have spiritual significance.

The Sea of Galilee is filled with fresh water. It has an outlet and an inlet. The inlet brings melted snow from 9,200-foot tall Mt. Hermon, thought by many to be the site of our Lord's transfiguration. The outlet is the Jordan River, where Jesus and many others have been baptized. The Jordan River is the inlet for the Dead Sea, yet there is no outlet for the Dead Sea. Consequently, there is a buildup of minerals (it is 33% salt) and it cannot sustain any life.

He who believes in Me, as the Scripture has said, out of his heart will flow rivers of living water."
John 7:38 (NKJV)

Spiritually, we are filled with rivers of Living Water. We need an inlet and an outlet to grow. Our inlets are the Holy Spirit, prayer, fellowship and Bible study. Our outlet is telling others of the amazing love that Jesus has given us. Without that outlet, we are like the Dead Sea, unable to support life. We should not float through our walks with the Lord! Instead, we should use our inlet and our outlet!

Let no corrupt word proceed out of your mouth, but what is good for necessary edification, that it may impart grace to the hearers.
Ephesians 4:29 (NKJV)

For out of the abundance of the heart the mouth speaks.
Matthew 12:34 (NKJV)

April 18: The whole is the sum of the parts; the hole is from some of the parts!

We know that as believers, the Holy Spirit dwells inside of us, but there are other verses that also say that the Father and Son are in there, as well. That should not surprise us as there is one God, though He is in three persons. Though it might be difficult for us to grasp, all of God lives inside each of us. God does not fracture Himself into microscopic particles and spread Himself out through the Body of believers. That makes complete sense, but it is a huge blessing that the God who created all, the omnipotent, omniscient, omnipresent God, is completely inside of each of us! In the worship song "Enough," Chris Tomlin writes,

"All of You is more than enough for all of me
For every thirst and every need
You satisfy me with Your love
And all I have in You is more than enough
You are my supply
My breath of life
Still more awesome than I know
You are my reward
worth living for
Still more awesome than I know
All of You is more than enough for all of me
For every thirst and every need
You satisfy me with Your love
And all I have in You is more than enough
You're my sacrifice
Of greatest price
Still more awesome than I know
You're the coming King
My everything
Still more awesome than I know
More than all I want
More than all I need
You are more than enough for me
More than all I know
More than all I can say
You are more than enough for me."

In the same sense that the Lord does not desire to give us only a part of Himself, neither does He desire for us to give Him only a part of ourselves! He wants all of us! If we already have given Him the alcohol, or drugs, or sexual immorality, He also desires the lying and the pride.

[22] "The lamp of the body is the eye. If therefore your eye is good, your whole body will be full of light. [23] But if your eye is bad, your whole body will be full of darkness. If therefore the light that is in you is darkness, how great *is* that darkness!
[24] "No one can serve two masters; for either he will hate the one and love the other, or else he will be loyal to the one and despise the other.
Matthew 6:22-24 (NKJV)

We cannot partially serve God and partially serve Satan. He wants our allegiance and loyalty. God wants to make us clean vessels. In Psalm 22, an Old Testament depiction of Jesus on the Christ, it says, **"My strength is dried up like a potsherd."** A potsherd is a shard of broken pottery, cast aside into the dirt. Job scraped his boils with a potsherd. When we were walking in the world without the Lord, we were potsherds. All of us without God certainly felt less than whole, unwanted and cast aside by the world. Yet the Master Potter put us back together and filled us with His Living Water. There are no more holes, once we are His. We are whole. Wholeness is holiness. Is there something we have been holding back, a secret part of our life we have not been willing to give the Lord? He desires for us to hand it to Him, and when we do, the blessing will be ours!

Does not the potter have power over the clay, from the same lump to make one vessel for honor and another for dishonor? Romans 9:21 (NKJV)

April 19: Walk circumspectly!

When Paul wrote his books that would become a large portion of the New Testament, the days were evil. Yet looking around in our society, the days have become more evil. An old adage tells us that history repeats itself, though with the addition of technology, many sins that used to be done in shame and secret have become easier. It used to be when a man purchased a pornographic magazine, he ducked into a shop, purchased the magazine and exited before friends or family would catch him.

Now, in the privacy of their own homes, men anonymously look at the same pornographic images plastered all over the internet. As Christians, we continue to battle our sin natures, yet God reminds us in His Word how we are supposed to live our lives:

^{15} **See then that you walk circumspectly, not as fools but as wise,** ^{16} **redeeming the time, because the days are evil.**
^{17} **Therefore do not be unwise, but understand what the will of the Lord** *is.* ^{18} **And do not be drunk with wine, in which is dissipation; but be filled with the Spirit,**
Ephesians 5:15-18 (NKJV)

What does it mean to walk circumspectly? Paul tells us in the phrase immediately following. It means to walk wisely, rather than as a fool. There is an entire book in the Bible teaching us wisdom, called Proverbs. That is a great place to start if we need to know how to walk with wisdom. Here are some gems from Proverbs: Whoever spreads slander is a fool (Proverbs 10:18). To do evil is like sport to a fool (Proverbs 10:23). The way of a fool is right in his own eyes (Proverbs 12:15). The companion of fools will be destroyed (Proverbs 13:20). Fools mock at sin (Proverbs 14:9). The father of a fool has no joy (Proverbs 17:21). There are more great verses dealing with fools in Proverbs, but a great summation is a verse from Psalms: A fool says in his heart that there is no God (Psalm 53:1).

All of us make mistakes. All of us continue to sin. That will continue until the day that the Lord completes His work in us, when He sees us face to face. The good news for us is that if the Holy Spirit dwells inside of us, then there will be a battle. Yet if there is no reminder either before the sin, during the sin or after the sin, then there is no battle. Without a battle, it is certain that God does not hold that person's allegiance, and the Holy Spirit does not reside in that person. It does not matter how many times that person has attended church or how many good deeds they have committed.

Though we are going to make bad decisions, the Bible gives us instructions on how to live our lives in a godly manner. Just as Joseph ran when tempted by Potiphar's wife, we are to run away from sin. Instead, how often do we run toward sin? Each day, we need to be more aware of the choices we make. In addition, we need to have that awareness heightened of what choices exist all around us. Let the Lord increase in our lives today! Be filled with the Spirit and walk wisely.

April 20: Renewal

One of the most important pieces of software that a user can purchase for the computer concerns virus protection. Whether that software is McAfee, Norton or Kaspersky, without it, we could be in for a world of hurt! Computers are expensive and a simple virus can wreak havoc in that system. For a pittance of the price of the computer, a user can insure that no virus makes its ways into the system.

In a similar manner, God protects His children from viruses, especially those that can destroy the operating system. Those viruses in a believer's life are sins, which certainly can destroy more than computer hardware. Sins are the cancers in the lives of men, and just like cancer, they can eat us alive from the inside out. In the same manner that a computer's virus software removes the virus, God removes the viruses from our lives.

**[9] Hide Your face from my sins,
And blot out all my iniquities.
[10] Create in me a clean heart, O God,
And renew a steadfast spirit within me.
[11] Do not cast me away from Your presence,
And do not take Your Holy Spirit from me.
[12] Restore to me the joy of Your salvation,
And uphold me *by Your* generous Spirit.
[13] *Then* I will teach transgressors Your ways,
And sinners shall be converted to You.
Psalm 51:9-13 (NKJV)**

A righteous God cannot even look upon sin. Yet throughout man's history, God has given remedies to that sin. In the Old Testament, believers had to adhere to the strict constraints of the sacrificial system, which demonstrated that all men were sinners, and slaves to that sin. Then God gave the greatest gift in the form of His Son, who died to pay for our sins. Believers are no longer slaves to sin, but sadly, we still choose sin when walking in the flesh. When we renew our relationship with God, and along with that, our virus protection software, He cleans our hearts by blotting out those iniquities. It is only then that we can restore the joy of salvation, which is apparent when walking in the Spirit. All believers remember that joy of having the burden of sin removed from their shoulders.

In David's psalm, he worried about the Lord removing the Holy Spirit. In the New Testament, the Holy Spirit is another Helper, promised to us by both the Father and Jesus. We need to understand the difference in Greek between two different words for "another:" *allos* (ἄλλος) and *heteros* (ἕτερος). *Allos* expresses a numerical difference and denotes "another of the same sort"; *heteros* expresses a qualitative difference and denotes "another of a different sort." When Jesus promised to send another Helper, He was referring to another one just like Himself. The Holy Spirit will abide with us forever, as a promise and a guarantee of God's purchase of us with the blood of Jesus.
Walking in that freedom of God's removal of both our sins and our punishment from those sins is a demonstration to unbelievers of our God of grace. Joy in the midst of difficulties speaks of His love with a megaphone. Just as many of us were drawn to the Lord because of His grace, when others see His grace in our lives, they learn of God's love! He gives us the best virus protection possible! If that joy is missing in our lives, walk obediently and ask for His forgiveness!

For we are His workmanship, created in Christ Jesus for good works, which God prepared beforehand that we should walk in them.
Ephesians 2:10 (NKJV)

**Now the Lord is the Spirit; and where the Spirit of the Lord *is*, there *is* liberty.
2 Corinthians 3:17 (NKJV)**

April 21: Filled with the Spirit!

It can be depressing to watch the nightly news or read about world events in the morning newspaper. With the world seemingly spinning out of control, we do not have a chance to get through it unscathed without the Spirit of God controlling us. While Satan has dominion over the earth, never forget that God gave him that dominion and it is only for a time. In the Book of Job, the earliest book written in the Bible, God removed the hedge of protection from Job (Job 1:9-12). That demonstrates that the only way Satan can attack us is if God allows that attack to occur. Additionally, God is not cruel or uncaring, so we know that if He allows an attack, He has a purpose. Typically, that purpose is for us to draw closer to Him. Being filled with the Spirit helps us to live in the moment and to remember that each moment is in God's plan.

When the Bible refers to a man "filled with the Spirit," does it mean <u>for that moment,</u> that the man was walking strongly with the Lord? If we are Spirit-filled Christians, does it mean that we <u>must be able</u> to speak in tongues, as the 120 in the upper room did on that first Day of Pentecost? Can we be <u>partially filled</u> with the Spirit?

The word "filled" in Greek is πίμπλημι, and it means "to fill completely." Yet interestingly, that verb is in the aorist tense, which describes an event that took place at one time in the past. So, being filled with the Spirit occurs at one moment. Think of a gas tank. If it is filled, it is not approaching fullness. Nor is it approaching emptiness, but it is filled to the brim. The Holy Spirit is fully in each Christian at the moment when we accept Jesus Christ as our Lord and Savior. He is not in limited supply, where we can run out of His power when we use Him too often! When Jesus came to this earth as a teacher, He was with His apostles for three years on a daily basis, though they were not together every moment. When Jesus returned to heaven, and gave us the gift of the Holy Spirit, He left us in good hands. The Holy Spirit is living inside of us, with us <u>every moment</u> of our Christian lives, whether we are awake or asleep,. He continues to teach us and according to the Bible, He accomplishes other feats in us, as well:

But you shall receive power when the Holy Spirit has come upon you; and you shall be witnesses to Me in Jerusalem, and in all Judea and Samaria, and to the end of the earth." Acts 1:8 (NKJV)

He gives us power, the power to say no to sin! There are times when all of us fall prey to the wiles of Satan and choose sin. The best news for the believer is that we serve a God who forgives, though each sin we choose still has ramifications. Those far-reaching tentacles still can destroy lives, including our own, as well as the lives of those we love. Our loved ones are often innocent bystanders splattered when the bombs of sin go off in our lives. Yet, if we have a personal relationship with Jesus, there will be a time when He removes even the ability to sin. That is a future time, when we look upon His face and see the scars He endured for us!

In the meantime, He has given us the power to be witnesses for Him to others. When we are walking in sin, those words are empty and hypocritical. The greatest task that each of us can accomplish for our Lord is to spread the Gospel to others, comfort the broken, give rest to the weary, give food to the hungry and offer arms of love to the lonely. Notice that most of those are actions, not words! Let Him use us for His purposes! But before doing so, we should clean up our acts!

[1] "Judge not, that you be not judged. [2] For with what judgment you judge, you will be judged; and with the measure you use, it will be measured back to you. [3] And why do you look at the speck in your brother's eye, but do not consider the plank in your own eye? [4] Or how can you say to

your brother, 'Let me remove the speck from your eye'; and look, a plank *is* in your own eye? ⁵ Hypocrite! First remove the plank from your own eye, and then you will see clearly to remove the speck from your brother's eye.
Matthew 7:1-5 (NKJV)

April 22: His eye is on the sparrow

So many people seem to be enduring difficult periods of discouragement lately. Though we realize that life is a series of peaks and valleys, it seems like there are a lot more valleys for a majority of the people alive today. Valleys are where the battles occur, as there is enough room for the opposing forces to mount up and face each other. In the earth's future, we know of a world-ending battle that will occur on the plains of Megiddo, northwest of Jerusalem. While standing in that valley that will see the Battle of Armageddon, Napoleon prophetically stated, "All the armies of the world could maneuver their forces on this vast plain."

Just as the final battle is no surprise to the Lord, either in occurrence or outcome, the many battles that each of us fight on a daily basis are in His perfect plan, as well. Yet, when we are discouraged, we lose sight of the miracles that God is accomplishing even in the midst of trial. Job, the most righteous man on the earth, certainly served as a great example for all of us in his self-pity. We all find ourselves in that position and we know that our struggles cannot hold a candle to what Job was called to endure. Yet God's plan was to draw Job even closer. Of course, His plan came to fruition, as Job came to know God in a much deeper way through the pain.

Most of us waste far too much time worrying about so much that is beyond our control. Yet what does God say about that?

⁶ Be anxious for nothing, but in everything by prayer and supplication, with thanksgiving, let your requests be made known to God; ⁷ and the peace of God, which surpasses all

understanding, will guard your hearts and minds through Christ Jesus.
Philippians 4:6-7 (NKJV)

God gives us a simple command, yet acting on that command becomes more complicated as we often walk by sight, not by faith. If we trust Him, then when we feel unsettled, we will hand that burden over to God, and then walk in peace, knowing that His will certainly will be done.

[25] "Therefore I say to you, do not worry about your life, what you will eat or what you will drink; nor about your body, what you will put on. Is not life more than food and the body more than clothing? [26] Look at the birds of the air, for they neither sow nor reap nor gather into barns; yet your heavenly Father feeds them. Are you not of more value than they? [27] Which of you by worrying can add one cubit to his stature?
Matthew 6:25-27 (NKJV)

God made the birds and the flowers, yet He loves us so much more. The Bible tells us that He mercifully waters the plants in areas man never sees! Why do we worry about our basic needs? Maybe part of that problem is that we desire more than He intends to give! He will give us enough! Trust Him and know that His eye is on the sparrow and we know He watches us!

April 23: Submission

French philosopher Simone Weil said, "Obvious and inexorable oppression that cannot be overcome does not give rise to revolt but to submission." Canadian historian Goldwin Smith said, "The Roman legions were formed in the first instance of citizen soldiers, who yet had been made to submit to a rigid discipline, and to feel that in that submission lay their strength."

Submission is a difficult subject in the world today. Sometimes, we feel as if we are being forced to submit to the ideas of others. For example, the modern-day acceptance of premarital sex for all couples, is rampant on almost every show on television. But are we truly being forced to watch? We can choose to turn off the television and read the Bible instead. Submission carries a negative connotation to most people. Webster defines it as the condition of being submissive, humble or compliant or in another context, the act of submitting to the authority or control of another. Leave it to Webster, who as a Christian, understood the word better than most today, using the most godly attribute, humbleness. Common thought has us believe that submission is weakness.

Ephesians 5 and 6 give us much insight into the meaning of submission:

[17] Therefore do not be unwise, but understand what the will of the Lord *is*. [18] And do not be drunk with wine, in which is dissipation; but be filled with the Spirit, [19] speaking to one another in psalms and hymns and spiritual songs, singing and making melody in your heart to the Lord, [20] giving thanks always for all things to God the Father in the name of our Lord Jesus Christ, [21] submitting to one another in the fear of God.
Ephesians 5:17-21 (NKJV)

Additionally, Paul writes that wives are to submit to husbands. Does this mean that women are less important to God? To answer that question, look at the life of Jesus! Does Jesus have less power or knowledge than God the Father or God the Holy Spirit? No! All of them are omnipotent and omniscient, equal. Yet they all have a place. Jesus does the will of the Father and the Holy Spirit always points to Jesus. Marriages are an instructional tool designed by God to teach us to submit one to another and additionally, to understand the intimacy that God desires in His relationship with us! Jesus willingly accepted His role of submission to the Father, just as a colonel submits to the general in the military.

This verse sums it all up:

[5] **Let this mind be in you which was also in Christ Jesus,** [6] **who, being in the form of God, did not consider it robbery to be equal with God,** [7] **but made Himself of no reputation, taking the form of a bondservant, *and* coming in the likeness of men.** [8] **And being found in appearance as a man, He humbled Himself and became obedient to *the point of* death, even the death of the cross.** [9] **Therefore God also has highly exalted Him and given Him the name which is above every name,** [10] **that at the name of Jesus every knee should bow, of those in heaven, and of those on earth, and of those under the earth,** [11] **and *that* every tongue should confess that Jesus Christ *is* Lord, to the glory of God the Father.**
Philippians 2:5-11 (NKJV)

Jesus submitted Himself more than any of us ever will submit ourselves! If He can consider Himself of no reputation, being God, how hard could it be for us to do the same, when all we are worthy of is death? Submit one to another as it is commanded by God!

April 24: Talking like a sailor

When we are trying to concentrate, extraneous noises like sirens or power tools can make that task extremely difficult. Yet as Christians, foul language is even more offensive, especially when the Lord's name is part of that curse. A few years ago, some interesting billboards lined the interstate near Palm Springs, California, after an advertising agency in Ft. Lauderdale came up with 17 non-denominational messages from God. One of them said,

> "Keep using My name in vain and I'll make rush hour longer." – God

Surprisingly, our society accepts the usage of those phrases more than others. The Federal Communications Commission disallowed seven words on television, but the Lord's name in vain was not on that list! Its acceptance by world standards boggles the mind. That gives us a reminder of who is in charge of this world. Satan, in his pride, hates God. Imagine a created being, who thinks he is equal with his Creator? As much intelligence as Satan has, he knows that he has no chance at beating God in any contest, yet his pride will not let Satan accept that fact. Remember his fall from grace:

**[12] "How you are fallen from heaven,
O Lucifer, son of the morning!**
How **you are cut down to the ground,
You who weakened the nations!
[13] For you have said in your heart:
'I will ascend into heaven,
I will exalt my throne above the stars of God;
I will also sit on the mount of the congregation
On the farthest sides of the north;
[14] I will ascend above the heights of the clouds,
I will be like the Most High.'
Isaiah 14:12-14 (NKJV)**

Desiring to be worshipped like the Most High, Satan has it in his plan to draw as many away from the Lord as he can. One of his many strategies includes running God's name through the mud. As Christians, it hurts when we hear people using the name in a curse that is the name above all names. At the name of Jesus, every knee shall bow and every tongue confess that Jesus Christ is Lord! If they do not worship Him now, they certainly will in the future. We know that, for God has promised us. In the meantime, we should not subject ourselves to hearing His name in that manner. We can choose not to attend those movies and not to associate with people who speak that way. They might only be words, but words come from the heart!

April 25: Pick it up!

Ever get tired of sinning? Before we had relationships with God, sinning was understandable, as we were slaves to sin, according to the Bible. Rather than having a battle raging within us between the Spirit and the flesh, we were simply, flesh driven. Yet after we become believers, there is a war that rages on day after day whether or not to sin. The Bible reminds us that after we are believers, sinning becomes a choice for us, and the saddest part is that sometimes we choose to sin. Even knowing how it saddens God does not factor into the equation. But we know what God's plan is for each one of us:

…being confident of this very thing, that He who has begun a good work in you will complete *it* until the day of Jesus Christ;
Philippians 1:6 (NKJV)

If God is going to perfect us, why did He not make us perfect the first time? Why did He allow us to live in these sinful bodies on this sinful earth? Romans 7 strikes home so deeply:

[14] For we know that the law is spiritual, but I am carnal, sold under sin. [15] For what I am doing, I do not understand. For what I will to do, that I do not practice; but what I hate, that I do.
Romans 7:14-15 (NKJV)

Though we hate sin, we continue to sin. Sin still is a big part of our lives. But the key to it all is the desires of our hearts. As Christians, though we continue to sin, we desire to do it God's way. When self dies to the point where we desire His will in our lives, He will work out the rest of the details. Think of David, who the Bible describes as a man after God's own heart. If we delight in the Lord, the Word tells us that God will give us the desires of our hearts. If the desire of our heart is to do it His way, then it is certain He will give us that desire. By perfecting us! By putting us in glorified bodies that never will have to worry or sorrow about sin ever again. Praise God!

Otherwise, there would have been disappearances all over the planet every time someone accepted the Lord. So they would not struggle with sin again, He could have chosen to take each new believer to heaven that very moment. But instead, God chose to have us continue in the struggle with sin, to pick up our crosses and follow Him. On that path, through our many struggles and sins, we realize how weak we are without Him and how strong He is! Additionally, with us still here, we are able to speak through our words, thoughts and actions to the people of a broken world, who desperately need Jesus as their Lord and Savior.

If we are tired of the struggle, do not lose sight of the fact that God still has us here for His purposes. Quit whining and look for the opportunities that He is placing into our paths on a daily basis. Lord, forgive us for the number of times we have complained, "I'm tired." Our rest is in Him and when He no longer wants us here, He will do something about that. In the meantime, we should pray that He uses us for His purposes!

April 26: Happy Anniversary! Yom Ha'atzmaut, the Day of Independence!

Each year, Israel celebrates an amazing anniversary. Over sixty years ago, Israel became a nation, (based on the Hebrew calendar on the fifth of *Ayar*)! Throughout the Bible, prophets told us of events that would occur to the Jews in Israel in the latter days. Yet when Israel disappeared from existence in A.D. 70 at the hands of the Romans, and the Jews were spread to the four corners of the earth, even Bible scholars lost sight of God's plan. Many of those "scholars" began to apply God's promises made to Israel to His church, instead. What they thought was, because Israel did not exist anymore, those prophecies could not really mean "Israel."

Fifty years before Israel became a nation, Theodore Herzl wrote a book entitled, *"Der Judenstaat,"* which means "the Jewish state." In that book, Herzl laid out the plan to bring the Jews back into the land they once had occupied. Fifty years later, Herzl's book and idea became a reality. With 6 million Jews murdered in the death camps of Nazi Germany, the Jews wanted to ensure that they never would be subject to an Adolf Hitler, or similar despot, again. On May 14, 1948, the United Nations announced that the resolution had passed and Israel was a nation! A well-known photo of that moment shows Israel's first Prime

Minister, David Ben-Gurion, making the announcement that the U.N. resolution had passed, beneath a photo of Herzl.

Imagine the excitement in each of the Jews in Israel at the time! Additionally, there was enormous excitement in many Jews around the world, who immediately began to make plans to relocate to a nation where they would be the majority, instead of the hated minority. Within days, the Arabs attacked. Though the Jews had inhabited the land almost 2,000 years before Islam began as a religion, the Muslims felt the land was theirs. Wars have continued to this day, and sadly, this nation the size of the state of New Jersey has continued to receive the animosity of the world, though with God's hand, Israel has flourished. This tiny nation has more medical doctors per capita than anywhere in the world; Israel has more people with PhD's per capita than anywhere else; the technology of Israel rivals the Silicon Valley! Fruits and vegetables flourish there, too; Israel has truly become a land flowing with milk and honey!

Where does this leave us? As Christians, Israel is the greatest reminder that God says what He means and means what He says, exactly! Additionally, though we know that the Jews are God's chosen people, we should keep in mind that Israel and the Jews are a great example of God's grace. That grace enabled God to forgive each of us for our many sins. He does not love the Jews any more, or less, than He loves each of us! Yet we are reminded by His Word that Israel is the apple of His eye, and that we should pray for the peace of Jerusalem. The world is coming against Israel in regard to the Palestinians. Yet we know from God's Word, what will occur:

[14] **I will bring back the captives of My people Israel;**
They shall build the waste cities and inhabit *them;*
They shall plant vineyards and drink wine from them;
They shall also make gardens and eat fruit from them.
[15] **I will plant them in their land,**
And no longer shall they be pulled up
From the land I have given them,"
Says the LORD your God.

Amos 9:14-15 (NKJV)

A day is coming when God will open the eyes of the Jews to see Jesus. Remember, Jesus was a descendant of David from both Mary's side of the family (blood) and Joseph's side of the family (legal), and David is the son or root of Jesse!

[10] "**And in that day there shall be a Root of Jesse,
Who shall stand as a banner to the people;
For the Gentiles shall seek Him,
And His resting place shall be glorious."
[11] It shall come to pass in that day
That the Lord shall set His hand again the second time
To recover the remnant of His people who are left,
From Assyria and Egypt,
From Pathros and Cush,
From Elam and Shinar,
From Hamath and the islands of the sea.
Isaiah 11:10-11 (NKJV)**

Many wrongly believe the above verses refer to the return from the Babylonian captivity, but notice that it says "a second time." Additionally, Shinar refers to Babylon, but the other places refer to many other locations. "Islands of the sea" is a Hebrew colloquialism for distant places. This refers to the four corners of the earth.

So today, let us honor the Jews, pray for the peace of Jerusalem, and praise God for being a God of grace! How can He continue to love us when we are dirty sinners? Be thankful for His forgiveness in our lives. Be thankful for His Word! It is perfect and He never will break a promise! That gives us so much to be excited about for if He loved the Jews enough to bring back Israel, He will fulfill His promises to us, too! We should read all those promises as they are amazing! For those who have not yet accomplished that feat, read the entire Bible!

April 27: Trouble comes in little packages!

Walking as a Christian certainly is not an easy path. At the moment we make the decision to follow Jesus, God gives us new hearts. Yet that is not the moment that He perfects us or completes His work in us. Instead, the daily lessons and changes begin! Walk away from one addiction, and another stares us in the face. The most difficult aspect to change deals with the smallest part…the tongue.

**[5] See how great a forest a little fire kindles! [6] And the tongue *is* a fire, a world of iniquity. The tongue is so set among our members that it defiles the whole body, and sets on fire the course of nature; and it is set on fire by hell. [7] For every kind of beast and bird, of reptile and creature of the sea, is tamed and has been tamed by mankind. [8] But no man can tame the tongue. *It is* an unruly evil, full of deadly poison. [9] With it we bless our God and Father, and with it we curse men, who have been made in the similitude of God. [10] Out of the same mouth proceed blessing and cursing. My brethren, these things ought not to be so. [11] Does a spring send forth fresh *water* and bitter from the same opening? [12] Can a fig tree, my brethren, bear olives, or a grapevine bear figs? Thus no spring yields both salt water and fresh.
James 3:5-12 (NKJV)**

As we grow in Christ, our mouths should shrink! Instead of being quick to speak, we should be quick to listen. A wise man pointed out that because God gave us two ears and only one mouth, at the least, we should listen twice as much as we talk! Yet instead, we speak of our rights, our wants, how other people are failing, how they let us down, etc. In libel suits, truth is a defense, yet God does not draw the line at speaking truth. If that truth proceeds to destroy a Christian brother's character, is it worth speaking? Here is an example. Say that a brother in the Lord shares with us in confidence that on a business trip, he strongly considered sleeping with a woman other than his wife. He told us so that we would pray for him and check in with him often, reminding him of God's love and Word. If we tell one person, the chances are strong that person will tell two others. Those two will tell four others. Those four share the story with eight others. Somewhere along the way, instead of our friend considering sleeping with another woman, the act actually occurred in the retelling of the story. Soon, our little spark has become a forest fire and has destroyed a man's character, and possibly, his marriage.

One way of ascertaining the words that proceed from our mouths is motive. Are the words being spoken to edify another and to glorify God? More likely, are the words being spoken to edify us? If we build ourselves up with our own words, God certainly will break us down, for he hates pride and exalts the humble.

[5] Likewise you younger people, submit yourselves to *your* elders. Yes, all of *you* be submissive to one another, and be clothed with humility, for
    "God resists the proud,
    But gives grace to the humble."
[6] Therefore humble yourselves under the mighty hand of God, that He may exalt you in due time, [7] casting all your care upon Him, for He cares for you.
1 Peter 5:5-7 (NKJV)

If this is a problem area, know that it is for everyone. Even if we spend the rest of our lives emphasizing this issue, James reminds us that no man can tame the tongue! But what we need to remember is that we can improve, even though we never can conquer our tiniest member. Let the Holy Spirit guide us, and remind us, when we speak in self-edification or destruction rather than the edification of others. For the rest of the day, make a point of thinking of the words that emanate from us and how they can or will affect others. Glorify God!

April 28: Are keys to open or to close?

Often, God stretches us, letting us know exactly how much we have been trusting and relying upon Him. Sadly, we rarely trust

Him the way we need to and unfortunately, this is not a lesson that we can learn once and for all! Look at the Jews in the wilderness, who somehow forgot the miracles of God after Moses went up the mountain to meet with God, and created a golden calf to worship in His place. God continuously reminds us of who He is and how much He loves us. We often ask for specific answers to prayer, and then finally give in to God, accepting that whatever He gives is better than anything we can ask for. It is yet another example from our Lord on the gift of prayer, as we know that prayer changes our hearts, rather than changing God! Why would perfection need to change? The only thing perfection could become if it changed would be imperfection and that is impossible for God!

We know who holds the key to each of our lives:

**[22] The key of the house of David
I will lay on his shoulder;
So he shall open, and no one shall shut;
And he shall shut, and no one shall open.
[23] I will fasten him *as* a peg in a secure place,
And he will become a glorious throne to his father's house.
Isaiah 22:22-23 (NKJV)**

This is the benefit of a walk with the Lord. A walk is slow progress in a forward direction. There is time to talk and reflect. Reflection is a look back on the past, and each time we do that, we remember all the gifts God has given and all the miracles He has performed in our lives. He is incapable of giving bad gifts to those He loves.

**[6] Therefore humble yourselves under the mighty hand of God, that He may exalt you in due time, [7] casting all your care upon Him, for He cares for you.
1 Peter 5:6-7 (NKJV)**

Jesus has the keys to every door. He can open the doors or lock them, and keep them closed. We should be so thankful that He opened the door of our hearts and came into our lives.

April 29: You're still here!

Watching a talented gymnast doing flips along a balance beam, teetering high enough above the ground that a missed step could cause severe injury, is a less than peaceful picture. Sometimes, the balance between our heavenly home and our earthly visit feels exactly like that. Those of us who have found salvation in Jesus Christ have been told that we, even at this moment, are **"seated in the heavenly places in Christ Jesus,"** according to Ephesians 2:6. God, being outside of time, sees His completed work in us! So though we struggle in our earthly tents, the temporary home that God has given us for a time, this is not the culmination of His work in us.

Even as Christians, we have the tendencies to focus more on this earth than we do on heaven, as earth is tangible. We can see it, feel it, smell it, touch it and even taste it if we choose. A mud pie should not get our taste buds salivating like our thoughts of the Wedding Supper of the Lamb, though. A desire to have children or grandchildren drives many Christians. Others seem to focus on seeing those near and dear coming to know the Lord. Others desire a bigger house, a better job or look forward to the freedom of retirement. Is the world supposed to be a friendly place for us?

[4] **Adulterers and adulteresses! Do you not know that friendship with the world is enmity with God? Whoever therefore wants to be a friend of the world makes himself an enemy of God.** [5] **Or do you think that the Scripture says in vain, "The Spirit who dwells in us yearns jealously"?**
[6] **But He gives more grace. Therefore He says:**
   "God resists the proud,
   But gives grace to the humble."
[7] **Therefore submit to God. Resist the devil and he will flee from you.** [8] **Draw near to God and He will draw near to you.**

Cleanse *your* **hands,** *you* **sinners; and purify** *your* **hearts,** *you* **double-minded.**
James 4:4-8 (NKJV)

The double-mindedness discussed by James has to do with our worldly desires that often get in the way of our heavenly desires. Once again, when our hearts become reflections of God's heart, **then** God gives us the desires of our hearts. Yet when our earthly desires get in the way, for God to grant us what we wish would cause us to stumble. God might do that just to demonstrate to us that He desires more for us than what we ever could imagine. Janis Joplin certainly missed the boat, and the car, with "Oh, Lord, won't You buy me a Mercedes-Benz!"

We should not lose sight of the fact that eternal life with the Lord began for us the moment we asked Jesus into our hearts. There might be a blink of the eye when we leave our bodies at the time of our physical deaths, but it is at that moment when we will be absent from the body and present with the Lord. We are called to be in the world, but not of the world (John 15:19 and John 17:13-17). Maneuver through this planet as if we are strangers in a strange land. Do not become a resident!

April 30: What dreams may come

One of the strangest parts of life occurs not in our waking moments, but while asleep. Dreams are such a different experience. They can be happy, sad, scary, stressful or beautiful. Though they are seemingly different for all of us, what is likely is that they are often triggered by an event that happens in real life. Some people spend their lives studying dreams and others spend their lives interpreting dreams. Many people still put much credibility into some of the dream interpretations given by Sigmund Freud, but the only dream interpreter worth his weight was Daniel (though Joseph showed talent, too).

When Nebuchadnezzar, the King of Babylon, was losing sleep due to a repeating dream, he asked his court of advisors to not only interpret the dream, but before he told them anything about it, they were also to tell him what he was dreaming. With God's help, Daniel gave the king both the dream and its interpretation. Even the description of the dream tells us that Nebuchadnezzar had the ability to see.

What occurs in the dream of a blind man? Scientists say that a person blind from birth has only auditory dreams. Someone who had lost their sight could dream of the people or places they remembered, but when someone appeared in the dream who they only had known after they had become blind, it would be nothing more than a hazy blur.

In His miraculous walk on this earth, Jesus made the blind to see.

So the multitude marveled when they saw *the* mute speaking, *the* maimed made whole, *the* lame walking, and *the* blind seeing; and they glorified the God of Israel.
Matthew 15:31 (NKJV)

In John 9, Jesus healed a man who had been blind since birth. That affected the man's waking hours and his sleeping ones miraculously, as even his dreams became a Technicolor change! Imagine dreaming in only sounds, with everything completely black.

Even though we know that God can speak in dreams, we also know that Satan also can find his way into our most susceptible states, when we are asleep. But every one of us was blind before we met Jesus as our Savior. He gave us legs to walk, ears to hear, a heart to feel and eyes to see. Without Him, we were dead, but just like Lazarus, He has raised us from the dead in the same manner that He gave us sight!

Through the sight Jesus has given us, He has given us hope of what dreams may come. We should dream to see His face and be by His side for all of eternity.

May 1: Do the evil really prosper?

Liars, cheaters and schemers seem to be more pervasive in our culture than those with integrity. Sometimes, it seems as though the underhanded are being rewarded handsomely for unethical behavior. We are reminded that "practice makes perfect," yet only perfect practice leads to perfection. Truly, all of us practice imperfectly, as without God, we have no chance at perfection. Yet, what we can see is intent. As Christians, we should do our best to represent the morals and ethics of our God. But when others seem to be getting ahead by cheating the system, one of the most difficult decisions is to accept the current status and remain steadfast.

We all have many situations in our lives where the wicked seem to prosper. It often seems like doing the right thing goes hand-in-hand with finishing last, as humility, meekness and godliness are not regarded by the world as winning attributes. King David waxed poetic in many psalms, feeling that same way, as he seemed to be watching his enemies gaining advantages. Then he wrote,

[1]**Do not fret because of evildoers,
Nor be envious of the workers of iniquity.
[2]Nor they shall soon be cut down like the grass,
And wither as the green herb.
[3]Trust in the LORD, and do good;
Dwell in the land, and feed on His faithfulness.
[4]Delight yourself also in the LORD,
And He shall give you the desires of your heart.
[5]Commit your way to the LORD,
Trust also in Him,
And He shall bring** *it* **to pass.
[6]He shall bring forth your righteousness as the light,
And your justice as the noonday.
[7]Rest in the LORD, and wait patiently for Him;
Do not fret because of him who prospers in his way,
Because of the man who brings wicked schemes to pass.**

⁸Cease from anger, and forsake wrath;
Do not fret—*it* only *causes* harm.
⁹For evildoers shall be cut off;
But those who wait on the LORD,
They shall inherit the earth.
¹⁰For yet a little while and the wicked *shall be* no *more;*
Indeed, you will look carefully for his place,
But it *shall be* no *more.*
¹¹But the meek shall inherit the earth,
And shall delight themselves in the abundance of peace.
Psalm 37:1-11 (NKJV)

Someday, we will live in a time when evil and evil people are gone! Until that time, we are to trust in the Lord, knowing that He continues to be in charge of our lives. Never forget that those not serving the Lord are captives of the evil one, just as each of us used to be before Jesus opened our eyes. Pray for them and do not fall into the trap the enemy sets for us to sink to their level of anger and hatred. How did Jesus handle it? **"He was led as a lamb to the slaughter, yet He opened not His mouth,"** according to Isaiah 53! We do not need to defend ourselves, for we serve a God who will represent us in His perfect timing.

May 2: Where do we lay our heads?

Homelessness seems to be increasing all across the world. Statistics estimate that there are currently at least 2.5 million homeless people in the United States alone, with that number increasing. There are many reasons for homelessness, and at the top of the list are those with substance abuse issues, along with the mentally ill. Yet there are also a number of people who have lost their jobs in a slowing economy, and simply, have no place to go. Homeless shelters are bursting at the seams.

Sadly, even Christians seem to make judgments concerning many who call the streets home. Often, we ascertain that any money donated will immediately be used to purchase drugs or alcohol. Without hearing a word about their pasts, we decide that they are lazy. King Solomon shared his wisdom with us concerning the poor:

He who gives to the poor will not lack,
But he who hides his eyes will have many curses.
Proverbs 28:27 (NKJV)

Our welfare system is certainly not the best answer, but if our hearts were where God desires for them to be, we would have great difficulty walking blindly past a beggar. Certainly, money is not the answer, but we always have the opportunity to purchase food for them. Remember, Jesus was homeless!

And Jesus said to him, "Foxes have holes and birds of the air *have* **nests, but the Son of Man has nowhere to lay** *His* **head."**
Matthew 8:20 (NKJV)

It is easy to make judgments when we see the walks of others, based on preconceived ideas, previous experiences and prejudices. While there are some scary people on the street, there are others in that position due to some unforeseen difficulties in life. Regardless of the reason they are there, it is not an easy existence. Working at a soup kitchen, rescue mission or homeless shelter is eye-opening. Yet the greatest gift is taking the time to share the gospel with those who are broken. One of the best reminders is that true wealth is the presence of Jesus Christ in our hearts, as salvation is worth more than all of the gold and silver on the earth! We lose sight of the wealth Jesus truly has given us by calling us to serve Him!

The law of Your mouth *is* **better to me**
Than thousands of *coins of* **gold and silver.**
Psalm 119:72 (NKJV)

Then Peter said, "Silver and gold I do not have, but what I do have I give you: In the name of Jesus Christ of Nazareth, rise up and walk."
Acts 3:6 (NKJV)

May 3: Whose side should we be on?

Rank	Country	# of Muslims	% Muslims
1	Indonesia	196,809,102	86.1
2	Pakistan	167,616,000	97
3	Bangladesh	144,376,690	89
4	Nigeria	77,139,500	50
5	Egypt	69,390,000	90
6	Turkey	71,374,066	99.8
7	Iran	69,085,877	98
8	Sudan	27,565,551	70
9	Algeria	33,431,977	99
10	Afghanistan	32,410,997	99
11	Morocco	33,386,187	99
12	Iraq	30,296,989	97
13	Malaysia	16,748,920	60.4
14	Saudi Arabia	27,601,038	100
15	Uzbekistan	24,087,360	88
16	Yemen	22,783,247	99
17	Syria	17,464,500	90
18	Kazakhstan	8,674,095	57
19	Niger	11,945,411	90
20	Burkina Faso	6,614,000	50
21	Mali	10,795,862	90
22	Senegal	10,958,520	94
23	Tunisia	10,175,917	97
24	Guinea	8,679,721	85
25	Somalia	9,549,107	99.9
26	Azerbaijan	8,103,384	99.4
27	Tajikistan	6,999,229	97
28	Sierra Leone	3,776,864	60
29	Libya	5,988,372	97
30	Jordan	5,290,137	95
31	United Arab Emirates	4,128,887	76
32	Kyrgyzstan	4,017,652	75
33	Turkmenistan	4,547,920	89

34	Chad	2,722,513	54
35	Lebanon	2,517,872	60
36	Kuwait	3,229,655	95
37	Albania	2,532,868	79.9
38	Mauritania	3,123,688	99.99
39	Oman	2,396,610	93
40	Kosovo	1,890,000	90
41	The Gambia	1,530,000	90
42	Bahrain	847,919	81
43	Comoros	782,040	98
44	Katar	576,622	77.5
45	Djibouti	466,592	94
46	Brunei	255,519	67
47	Maldives	350,000	100
	TOTAL	1.2 billion!	

Above are all the countries with a majority of Muslims, though there are another 500-700 million Muslims in the world. According to the CIA World Facts Book, one in every four persons on this earth practices Islam, and that number is growing at a rate of 2.9% each year. In the last 50 years, the population of Muslims on the earth has increased at an alarmingly high rate of 235%! Is this a surprise?

**[9] The Angel of the LORD said to her, "Return to your mistress, and submit yourself under her hand." [10] Then the Angel of the LORD said to her, "I will multiply your descendants exceedingly, so that they shall not be counted for multitude." [11] And the Angel of the LORD said to her: "Behold, you *are* with child, And you shall bear a son. You shall call his name Ishmael, Because the LORD has heard your affliction. [12] He shall be a wild man; His hand *shall be* against every man, And every man's hand against him. And he shall dwell in the presence of all his brethren."
Genesis 16:9-12 (NKJV)**

In Hebrew, verse 12 specifically says, "he will have a personality like a wild donkey." Just as promised, God increased the Arab nation. Ishmael's descendants became the Muslims of today. God's promise was true in regard to combative personalities. Take the Jews out of the mix and the Muslims continue to fight each other. An example would be the Iran-Iraq war. The Arabs are not content with the oil-rich land that God gave them. On the other hand, when looking at a map of the Middle East, we notice the tiniest little spit of land called Israel. Muslims want that land, too, and though they make transparent pleas to the bleeding hearts of the world concerning the plight of the Palestinians, in truth, all the Muslims care about is the eradication of Israel and the Jews. Yet God made promises to the Jews, too. After making a covenant with Abraham, he re-stated that covenant to Isaac:

² Then the LORD appeared to him and said: "Do not go down to Egypt; live in the land of which I shall tell you. ³ Dwell in this land, and I will be with you and bless you; for to you and your descendants I give all these lands, and I will perform the oath which I swore to Abraham your father. ⁴ And I will make your descendants multiply as the stars of heaven; I will give to your descendants all these lands; and in your seed all the nations of the earth shall be blessed; ⁵ because Abraham obeyed My voice and kept My charge, My commandments, My statutes, and My laws."
Genesis 26:2-5 (NKJV)

There are around 14 million Jews on the earth. Compare that to the 1.8 billion Muslims! With 47 Muslim nations, there is one Jewish nation, the nation of Israel with 5,743,349 Jews. The United States has a similar number of Jews, but for the first time, Israel has more. After 6 million Jews died in the death camps of Nazi Germany, is it possible that the "fullness of the Gentiles" referred to in Romans 11 will take place when the number of Jews in Israel "replaces" the number lost in World War II? But what is the point of it all?

The Jews are God's chosen people. Israel is the apple of His eye. (Deuteronomy 32:10) God's plan prophetically told us of the reinstatement of Israel as a nation. Yet His plan did not end there. The time is coming when Israel and the Jews will once again get the opportunity to receive the Messiah. They passed on Jesus the first time, but one third of the Jews alive in the tribulation will accept Jesus as Lord and Savior (Zechariah 13:9.) God will protect the Jews from their surrounding enemies. That is what He is doing right now, as the world gathers against this tiny nation. The United States has been an ally since 1948, but the current presidential administration has been the first to walk away from that alliance. Israel will find itself all alone.

And that is how God works. God used a small boy to slay a giant! When Israel was surrounded by Sennacherib and the Assyrian troops, an angel killed 185,000 soldiers in the middle of the night. Gideon pared down his army to 300 at the Lord's request in Judges 7 before proving victorious against a much bigger enemy. Why? Because large armies, big men and powerful weapons point to man's power. God's power is much greater. What if Mahmoud Ahmadinejad and Iran finish the project of obtaining weapons-grade plutonium? God has Israel's back! Even nuclear bombs pale in comparison to God and the power of God. Which side are we on? Before answering that question, ponder on God's promise:

[1] **Now the Lord had said to Abram:**
"Get out of your country,
From your family
And from your father's house,
To a land that I will show you.
[2] **I will make you a great nation;**
I will bless you
And make your name great;
And you shall be a blessing.
[3] **I will bless those who bless you,**
And I will curse him who curses you;
And in you all the families of the earth shall be blessed."
Genesis 12:1-3 (NKJV)

If we curse Israel, we will be cursed! Israel is the land where our Savior walked and someday will be the most important place on the planet!

May 4: God waters the vineyard all the time!

When we are walking in sin, it is overwhelmingly sad and scary to know that God is watching us all the time. Yet on the other side, it sure is comforting that God watches us all the time when we are hurting, in need, or walking strongly with Him. He waters His vineyard all the time!

[2] In that day sing to her,
"A vineyard of red wine!
[3] I, the LORD, keep it,
I water it every moment;
Lest any hurt it,
I keep it night and day.
[4] Fury *is* not in Me.
Who would set briers *and* thorns
Against Me in battle?
I would go through them,
I would burn them together.
Isaiah 27:2-4 (NKJV)

What great pictures that He washes us in His Word and that we once were scarlet, but now are white as snow! Often, when we do laundry, all of the stains are not removed. There is just too much dirt in the cloth for that launderer's soap to completely win the battle! It does not matter how badly stained we are when we come to Jesus. He is able to remove the stains made from our past, along with those of our present and our future! Sometimes, we continue to walk in that stained and soiled feeling of our broken past. But the Lord tells us that His yoke is easy and His burden is light. If it does not seem easy, if we are heavily burdened, it is because we are not allowing Him to shoulder the burden for us!

Isaiah 27 specifically speaks of Israel, the nation of His chosen people. Why is Israel such a special place? The Lord loves that land so much that He cannot take His eyes off of it. He prepared it for the Jews before they ever entered, and made it a land flowing with milk and honey. Though the Jews through disobedience were removed from the land, at no time did the Lord remove the land deed He gave them. Even in the 1,878 years when the Jews were spread to the four corners of the earth, the land was theirs. Though the Arabs surrounding the Jews on all sides desire that land, it is a gift given to the Jews by God. We know that when God called the Jews to remove the existing people from the land initially, the failure of the Jews to do so continues to have an impact to this very day with the descendants of those people still causing trouble to the Jews. But if we ever get confused which group to side with, rather than consulting the world newspapers, consult God!

I will plant them in their land, And no longer shall they be pulled up From the land I have given them," Says the LORD your God.
Amos 9:15 (NKJV)

If anyone hurts the land of Israel, they will have to answer to God, for He keeps it night and day. Sounds like that land is pretty secure, regardless of what the newspapers say!

May 5: Fruit inspectors?

Sometimes, Christians believe they have the right to be "fruit inspectors." Based on a specific verse in Matthew, God tells us how we can tell if someone truly is walking with Him:

[17] Even so, every good tree bears good fruit, but a bad tree bears bad fruit. [18] A good tree cannot bear bad fruit, nor *can* a bad tree bear good fruit. [19] Every tree that does not bear good fruit is cut down and thrown into the fire. [20] Therefore by their fruits you will know them.
Matthew 7:17-20 (NKJV)

It is easy for God to judge the fruit, as He and only He can see what lies within. That would be the heart, the motives and the changes that have occurred in each of our lives. Remember, when we come to the Lord, He does not immediately perfect us, but sends in the Holy Spirit cleaning service to start sweeping out the mess in our lives. Many sermons state that we are not to judge non-believers, but based on the methodology that the Bible gives us how to confront someone who sins against us, we are to judge other believers. Yet there is a huge difference between someone sinning and someone who sins directly against us. If we address the person who sins directly against us in love and forgiveness, the other steps would not have to happen as often. Once again, there are always three points of view in any given situation, ours, theirs and God's, and only His is accurate. In the verses above, we can see whether or not their fruit is good or bad, but that does not mean we need to confront them or judge them! We need to love them anyway! Other verses in Matthew highlight this:

¹ "Judge not, that you be not judged. ² For with what judgment you judge, you will be judged; and with the measure you use, it will be measured back to you. ³ And why do you look at the speck in your brother's eye, but do not consider the plank in your own eye? ⁴ Or how can you say to your brother, 'Let me remove the speck from your eye'; and look, a plank *is* in your own eye? ⁵ Hypocrite! First remove the plank from your own eye, and then you will see clearly to remove the speck from your brother's eye.
Matthew 7:1-5 (NKJV)

Most of us realize that the characteristics of others that bother us the most are typically our own attributes. The 2 X 4 often has taken up residence in our eyes, and it is not because we are bored. We are blinded by our own sins, and cannot see the forest through the trees because of that sin. Let's look at 1 John for another perspective:

⁵ This is the message which we have heard from Him and declare to you, that God is light and in Him is no darkness at

all. ⁶ If we say that we have fellowship with Him, and walk in darkness, we lie and do not practice the truth. ⁷ But if we walk in the light as He is in the light, we have fellowship with one another, and the blood of Jesus Christ His Son cleanses us from all sin.

⁸ If we say that we have no sin, we deceive ourselves, and the truth is not in us. ⁹ If we confess our sins, He is faithful and just to forgive us *our* sins and to cleanse us from all unrighteousness. ¹⁰ If we say that we have not sinned, we make Him a liar, and His word is not in us.
1 John 1:5-10 (NKJV)

There are many people who claim to be walking with the Lord still straddling the fence between God's Law and man's "right" to live as he pleases. Some live with their girlfriends, go out and get drunk, curse like sailors or sin in a variety of ways. Are we supposed to tell them all the ways they are failing? Certainly, there are times when God might open a door to share with them personally where we have walked in our lives. Usually, that door opens with a question from the other person, not a caustic comment from a judging believer!

We have to be careful judging others, as God is the only fruit inspector. We might be able to see the fruit, but only He can taste it! Some of the sweetest fruits we have eaten did not look so great on the outside. If we spend more time loving our neighbors as ourselves and loving the Lord with all of our heart, soul, mind and strength, then the Holy Spirit will open doors where we can share loving language with those struggling with sins. Just like driving a car, it is much easier for someone else to see our blind spots, as it is easier for us to see their blind spots.

May 6: What is your retirement plan?

With stock values decreasing, retirement plans losing value and savings accounts depleting rapidly, here are some comforting words.

As Christians, our Boss has the greatest retirement plan! In our future, we will have no pain, no sadness and no crying. Our bodies will not wear out, break down or fall apart. Our minds will not become unclear, insane or inane. We will not find ourselves lonely, longing or left out. We never will die, decline or drift away from the purpose we were created for. Why? Because God has promised us all these things in His word! Being that He never has broken His Word, we can take that promise to the bank, unless it is an American bank, for those banks will fail!

Our future is not sitting on a cloud, playing a harp, as many people picture. Neither is it eternity that borderlines on boredom. Instead, God has promised that we will rule and reign with Him, as kings and priests, and Jesus told us when He left the earth almost 2,000 years ago that He went to prepare a place for us. His Father's house has many mansions. If He created the world in six days, what will our heavenly homes look like with 2,000 years of preparation? We will be learning His Word for all of eternity and serving Him for the same duration. Imagine what it will be like to be in His presence and feel His love forever!

On this earth, we talk of our 401 K's, how much interest income we receive each year, and whether or not our homes are paid for. Yet God has not just given us a future and a hope in His Son while in heaven. He has given us a Comforter to walk with us every moment! Even when the Jews were wandering in the wilderness, He made this promise:

"For the LORD your God has blessed you in all the work of your hand. He knows your trudging through this great wilderness. These forty years the LORD your God *has been* with you; you have lacked nothing." '
Deuteronomy 2:7 (NKJV)

If we ever find ourselves in a wilderness in our lives, the Lord will continue to provide our needs. Those needs might not match our desires, but know that God will take care of His own perfectly, just as He does everything! Part of that blessing is to be a part of His family, the body of Christ! His promises cover our times on this earth when we are working for Him, but those promises also include the greatest retirement plan ever! God will hire us if we apply! He will not reject our applications! Come to Him, all who are labored and are heavy laden. Oh, and He will also give us rest!

May 7: Follow the Leader!

Freshmen at the United States Air Force Academy have rigid requirements, which become stricter when outside the confines of their own rooms. They have to be dressed immaculately from the top of the head to the shine on the shoes. They have to walk at attention, saluting everyone who outranks them (that is everyone)! They have five responses to any question: "Yes, sir;" "No, sir;" "No excuse, sir;" "Sir, may I make a statement;" and "Sir, may I ask a question." They never are to make eye contact with anyone, as they are not good enough to do that. At the end of that first year, they earn the right to look, hear, interact and walk freely. Within a matter of months, the next class of freshmen has to endure the same treatment.

Once sophomore year begins, those who endured the extreme hazing only months before become the ones doing the hazing. One of the quotes the freshmen have to memorize comes from German Field Marshall Erwin Rommel:

> "Be an example to your men in your duty and in private life. Never spare yourself and let the troops see that you don't in your endurance of fatigue and privation. Always be tactful and well-mannered and teach your subordinates to be the same. Avoid excessive sharpness or harshness of voice, which usually indicates a man who has shortcomings of his own to hide."

Ironically, sophomores scream at the freshmen to recite Rommel's quote, somehow forgetting the point of the statement.

When we are training others, it should be "do as I do," rather than "do as I say!" Paul was a great example to others. It was not with pride and arrogance that he said,

Therefore I urge you, imitate me.
1 Corinthians 4:16 (NKJV)

Imitate me, just as I also imitate Christ.
1 Corinthians 11:1 (NKJV)

Paul knew that because he was following Jesus, he was becoming a reflection of the Lord. If people followed Paul, they would also reflect Jesus.

Beloved, do not imitate what is evil, but what is good. He who does good is of God, but he who does evil has not seen God.
3 John 11 (NKJV)

that you do not become sluggish, but imitate those who through faith and patience inherit the promises.
Hebrews 6:12 (NKJV)

When we read the Bible, we can see Jesus on every page. Consequently, we can imitate Him. As Christians, we all have people God has placed into our lives, who have made great impacts on our walks with the Lord, and we can imitate those Christians. Remember, though, every single man, no matter how strongly he walks with the Lord, will let us down, and God never will let us down. When we are imitating a Christian man, understand that God's work in him has not been completed yet, either.

May 8: Tail-wagging happiness!

> A dog is the only thing on this earth that loves you more than he loves himself.
> --Josh Billings (19th-Century American humorist)

Dogs are incredible companions, and unlike humans, cannot hide their emotions. Instead, that wagging tail demonstrates absolute pleasure. It thumps against our legs like a metronome, and based on the height of the dog, can sweep a coffee table clean of dust and decorations. God could have given us wagging tails, but instead, chose to give us smiles. Yet unlike wagging tails, those smiles can be authentic or feigned:

27 If I say, 'I will forget my complaint,
I will put off my sad face and wear a smile,'
28 I am afraid of all my sufferings;
I know that You will not hold me innocent.
29 *If* **I am condemned,**
Why then do I labor in vain?
Job 9:27-29 (NKJV)

In truth, the smile that becomes a billboard on our faces should reflect our future, rather than our present condition. We live in a broken world, but we are only visitors here. Never let the present get in the way of the promise!

And Hannah prayed and said:
"My heart rejoices in the LORD;
My horn is exalted in the LORD.
I smile at my enemies,
Because I rejoice in Your salvation.
1 Samuel 2:1 (NKJV)

It all depends what holds our attention, what we are watching! If our eyes are focused on heaven, we will not see the mess around us!

Lewis Grizzard said, "Life is like a dogsled team. If you ain't the lead dog, the scenery never changes." For most of us, who are not leading the pack, that scenery deserves a change.

May 9: Do you crave those neon lights?

Everywhere we turn, people are looking to fill their own appetites, desires and lusts. As Christians, we are not perfect, either, but hopefully, we are at least looking to follow what the Lord tells us in His Word, as He reminded us in John 14:15 when He said, **"If you love Me, keep My commandments."** Newspapers continuously run stories of pastors caught in sexual sins, without making mention that none of us are perfect, just forgiven. Even so, it is still sad when our choices destroy the witness the Lord has given us. Sometimes, it is a huge blessing not to be a public figure, as most of us certainly have made bad decisions in our Christian walks that could have damaged the Lord's witness in our lives to a greater degree.

When God created the world, He certainly saw what it was going to become. He saw each choice that every individual would make throughout eternity. And though He made us to know Him and to love Him as He loves us, He also knew how few actually would come to that place in their lives. On a typical Saturday or Sunday morning, we see fewer and fewer people attending church. Included in that number are many people who attend church but do not know the Lord at all. There are surely more people in a bar on a Saturday night than a church on Sunday morning. And still, the Lord allows it all to continue! How much it must sadden God to know what blessings He could bestow upon everyone who came to Him!

He created us all, yet most do not even acknowledge they were created. They would rather take credit for their own beauty, talents or accomplishments, as if they had anything to do with His gifts. He gave us all that we are. God is so big, and though we can see Him everywhere, most cannot find Him!

[13] **"Enter by the narrow gate; for wide *is* the gate and broad *is* the way that leads to destruction, and there are many who go in by it.** [14] **Because narrow *is* the gate and difficult *is* the way which leads to life, and there are few who find it.**

Matthew 7:13-14 (NKJV)

They say the neon lights are bright on Broadway, but the stars in the sky that God created are much brighter. Would we rather walk down the broad way that leads to financial success, stardom and ego-building, or would we rather follow the quiet, narrow path that points to God? A friend once took his children up on the top of a mountain at night, looking down to the city lights below. He asked them what was more beautiful, the lights man created, with the hand of the prince of this earth, or the lights above, which God created. We need to keep our eyes on the things of God and desire what He has for us! That is all we could ever want or need!

May 10: Is it worth it?

We all have friends in the Lord who seem to struggle immensely. Do we attribute that suffering to the bad decisions they have made? Most of us have friends who seem to suffer greatly and others who do not seem to suffer at all. Yet we know that every Christian will suffer at some time in their walks, for we are baptized into the suffering of Jesus Christ.

Any time we need an example of how to live our lives, a great place to start is the life of Jesus. Certainly, He suffered greatly so that we might live, and He told us that because He was hated, we shall be hated, too. Job certainly suffered greatly, too, and though many erroneously believe that the Book of Job is about why the just suffer, the book is more about the fact that we will suffer. Did Job bring that suffering on himself? No, God removed the hedge of protection from his most trusted servant and allowed Satan access to both Job and Job's family! The only stipulation that the Lord gave Satan was that he was not allowed to kill Job. Yet, in one day, Job's 10 children died! Through that suffering, God drew Job closer than before. In the midst of that trial, Job summed up his feelings about God in Job 13:15: **"Though He slay me, yet will I trust Him."**

Paul was another who endured a lot while on this earth. Why?

¹² **But I want you to know, brethren, that the things** *which happened* **to me have actually turned out for the furtherance of the gospel,** ¹³ **so that it has become evident to the whole palace guard, and to all the rest, that my chains are in Christ;** ¹⁴ **and most of the brethren in the Lord, having become confident by my chains, are much more bold to speak the word without fear.**
Philippians 1:12-14 (NKJV)

For I consider that the sufferings of this present time are not worthy *to be compared* **with the glory which shall be revealed in us.**
Romans 8:18 (NKJV)

Is it worth it to endure difficult times for the Lord? If God told us that we were going to have to endure 10 years of extreme physical pain, but would use our difficulties to bring others to the Him, would we joyfully do it? All of us are not called to be martyrs, but if that is our calling, the Lord will walk with us along the entire path. When we cannot walk, He will carry us. All of the apostles but John died martyrs' deaths, and even John was plunged into burning oil, but did not die. Are we willing to die for our beliefs? If not, we really do not believe! If Jesus is everything to us, then the love of our lives will not get in the way. Neither will the worry of handling the pain of death. He is with us always!

May 11: Comfortable or comforted?

Many people in the United States purchased homes at a much higher value than the current value of the home. For some of those people, who borrowed against their perceived equity, they find themselves completely upside-down, unable to continue the immense mortgage payments. Though in the past, they seemingly had it all, without God, they had nothing. Wealth often gets in the way of a relationship with God, for when we believe we can supply our own needs, we fail to look to Him as our provider.

Ask an exceedingly wealthy person about their status and they usually will state that they are "comfortable," for they are comparing themselves to the richest of the rich. The oil barons of the Middle East certainly have more. We lose sight of what it really means to be poor, and for that matter, what it really means to be rich. Poor is not driving around in a new SUV. Poor is not owning a home, regardless of its size. Poor is not curbing spending habits to eating out no more than once a week. Poor is not a closet filled with designer clothes. Poor is when each meal becomes a challenge, keeping any roof overhead is a blessing and clothing is a pair of jeans that must be washed a few times a week to keep clean. Yet, why is it that there are more poor people following the Lord than rich people?

[24] **And when Jesus saw that he became very sorrowful, He said, "How hard it is for those who have riches to enter the kingdom of God!** [25] **For it is easier for a camel to go through the eye of a needle than for a rich man to enter the kingdom of God."**
Luke 18:24-25 (NKJV)

When we attribute our earthly possessions to our own talents, our own decisions and our own intelligence, we are sidestepping the One who gave us everything! Jesus told us in the Sermon on the Mount, **"Blessed are the poor in spirit, for theirs is the kingdom of heaven."** "Poor in spirit" is a term that goes hand-in-hand with humbleness. It is giving God the glory for all He has given us, rather than taking credit for any of it ourselves! What would God have us do with our 6,000-square foot home? Fill it with the best of the best, or would He rather see us help people in need? That does not mean that God cannot bless His people, but do His people bless Him by helping others, or bless themselves, by desiring more? Do we really need a luxury car?

[1] **"Comfort, yes, comfort My people!"**
Says your God.
[2] **"Speak comfort to Jerusalem, and cry out to her,**
That her warfare is ended,

That her iniquity is pardoned;
For she has received from the LORD's hand
Double for all her sins."
Isaiah 40:1-2 (NKJV)

When Jesus came, He comforted the people, giving them rest from their burdens. On the cross, He shouldered each of our sin burdens, and then left us with His Holy Spirit, the Comforter, to be with us every moment. Do we really need anything else? When we look around and see the economic hardships of a majority of the people around the world, trust that God is giving them that opportunity to come to the end of themselves, the end of the place where they believe they can do it on their own. Pray for a harvest of new believers in the world! The time is right! And in the meantime, thank Him for all that He has given us!

May 12: Comfort zone

> "The greatest enemy to human potential is your comfort zone."

In Southern California, most people are aware of the tradition of "Taco Tuesday." We all have Mexican restaurants that are personal favorites. Las Golondrinas is one of those, and their daily price of $2.70 per taco is cut in half every Tuesday. Is it possible there are better places out there? Yes, but when we have found contentment, we hesitate to look anywhere else.

As Christians, we often find ourselves in similar situations. Whether it be the comfort of our job, our home, our church or even the town that we live in, it is easy to stay within the confines of the boundaries we have imposed on ourselves. Sometimes though, God wants to stretch us. It is in those times when we are most apt to grow. Yet left to our own decisions, most of us would choose the sameness, rather than yearn for the potential ups and downs of a constantly changing environment.

It is amazing how Joshua handled difficulties. When he was preparing to lead the Israelite army of 600,000 at the Battle of Jericho, a visitor approached Joshua:

[13] And it came to pass, when Joshua was by Jericho, that he lifted his eyes and looked, and behold, a Man stood opposite him with His sword drawn in His hand. And Joshua went to Him and said to Him, "*Are* You for us or for our adversaries?"
[14] So He said, "No, but *as* Commander of the army of the LORD I have now come."
And Joshua fell on his face to the earth and worshiped, and said to Him, "What does my Lord say to His servant?"
[15] Then the Commander of the LORD's army said to Joshua, "Take your sandal off your foot, for the place where you stand *is* holy." And Joshua did so.
Joshua 5:13-15 (NKJV)

This is not an appearance by an angel, but by Jesus, called a *theophany* or *christophany*, as that term refers to an appearance by God in the form of man. Similar to the time when Moses confronted God in the burning bush, both men were told to take off their sandals as they were on holy ground. When an angel truly appears, and man attempts to worship the angel, the angel always instructs them not to do that, as they are not God. Notice that when Joshua asks the Lord the initial question, "Are You for us or for our adversaries," the answer is neither. Instead, He announces His position as the Commander of the army, basically telling Joshua that he is to relinquish his position as leader and let the Lord handle the battle. Joshua worships his Commander on the spot.

The next question is, "What message does my Lord say to His servant?" This sounds similar to the question Paul asks in Acts:

So I said, 'What shall I do, Lord?' And the Lord said to me, 'Arise and go into Damascus, and there you will be told all things which are appointed for you to do.'
Acts 22:10 (NKJV)

Often in our walks and talks with the Lord, we are quick to tell the Lord what our will is in a situation. "Lord, this is how I want You to answer my prayer!" Yet, to be in the center of His will, we need to listen and ask. "Lord, what shall I do?" It is in those places outside of our comfort zones where God can teach us the most. It is rare when we feel like taffy from being pulled and stretched so much. Yet know that the Lord stretches us for the purpose of drawing us closer to Him. Without being stretched, we tend to rely on our own power rather than His.

Do we want to operate in the center of His will or in the center of our own wills? There is no greater place to be than where He wants us!

May 13: Happy Mother's Day!

When there only are three pieces of pie remaining and four people at the dinner table, mothers announce that they do not like dessert. Our society seems to have fewer full-time mothers, yet we know that all mothers are working mothers. An anonymous quotation reminds us, "Mothers hold their children's hands for a short while, but their hearts forever."

God specifically designed our system of procreation. Though Adam was a direct creation of God, the rest of us are sons of man, and woman. Job's friend, Bildad the Shuhite, had this to say:

How then can man be righteous before God?
Or how can he be pure *who is* born of a woman?
Job 25:4 (NKJV)

Bildad thought he understood the system, but was missing a major point. Jesus was both righteous and born of a woman! It is extremely difficult for us to understand what Mary endured with her Son being the Messiah. She trusted in the Father, who protected her even in `pregnancy. By the Law, she should have been stoned to death for her pre-marriage pregnancy. What must it have been like to raise and rear the Son of God? Yet the deepest aspect of Mary's testimony involves her presence at her son's death.

²⁶ When Jesus therefore saw His mother, and the disciple whom He loved standing by, He said to His mother, "Woman, behold your son!" ²⁷ Then He said to the disciple, "Behold your mother!" And from that hour that disciple took her to his own *home*.
John 19:26-27 (NKJV)

Mary had other children, yet Jesus handed the godly responsibility to love His grieving mother to His trusted friend, John. Mary understood that her Son came to save the world from their sins, yet as any human, certainly had doubts. In those doubting moments, John could be a great reminder.

Yet on this Mother's Day, we all should be thankful for our mothers. God never makes mistakes and carefully chose each of our mothers for His perfect reasons. We have no idea of the sacrifices that have been made for our lives, though those who have become parents surely can see that sacrifice from a different perspective.

> I remember my mother's prayers and they have always followed me. They have clung to me all my life. – Abraham Lincoln

Those prayers brought many of us to salvation! For those who are presently motherless, reflect upon the past. Otherwise, take the time to be grateful for the mother God chose in our lives.

May 14: Don't be one of the frozen chosen!

A favorite song by Keith Green says, "My eyes are dry, my faith is old, my heart is hard, my prayers are cold. And I know how I ought to be alive to You and dead to me." Though God has given us peace that passes understanding in the midst of the greatest trial, we have to trust Him for that peace to occur.

When we fail to trust in His promises, we become Christian popsicles, cold and hard. Soft and pliable are better attributes as Christians.

"The same sun that softens the butter hardens the clay."

Though the Jews are God's chosen people, each one of us who walks with the Lord has been chosen by God, too. He does not hang us out to dry as believers, but goes before us in all we do:

29 "Then I said to you, 'Do not be terrified, or afraid of them. 30 The LORD your God, who goes before you, He will fight for you, according to all He did for you in Egypt before your eyes, 31 and in the wilderness where you saw how the LORD your God carried you, as a man carries his son, in all the way that you went until you came to this place.'
Deuteronomy 1:29-31 (NKJV)

After the Jews disobeyed God when He told them to conquer the people in the Land of Canaan, afraid of their enormous size, He punished them. While being punished, the Jews opted to try and fix it their own way, but God's hand was not in their attempt. He warned the disobedient Jews that He was not with them in the endeavor, but they went anyway, and were defeated:

41 "Then you answered and said to me, 'We have sinned against the LORD; we will go up and fight, just as the LORD our God commanded us.' And when everyone of you had girded on his weapons of war, you were ready to go up into the mountain.
42 "And the LORD said to me, 'Tell them, "Do not go up nor fight, for I *am* not among you; lest you be defeated before your enemies." ' 43 So I spoke to you; yet you would not listen, but rebelled against the command of the LORD, and presumptuously went up into the mountain.
Deuteronomy 1:41-43 (NKJV)

We can find ourselves in similar circumstances when we choose to disregard God's Word and walk in sinful practices. Yet remember that God does not punish us to destroy us. He only chastises the ones He loves! One of God's greatest promises, and reminders, comes in a subsequent verse:

"For the LORD your God has blessed you in all the work of your hand. He knows your trudging through this great wilderness. These forty years the LORD your God *has been* with you; you have lacked nothing." '
Deuteronomy 2:7 (NKJV)

When we are His and He is ours, God will bless ALL the work of our hands! We will lack nothing! This is not the prosperity gospel, preaching wealth and earthly prosperity. Yet our needs certainly will be fulfilled by the God who loves us so much that He cannot take His eyes away from us! If we find ourselves enduring cold streaks in our walks as Christians, we need to come back to the cross and that place of trust. Let God soften our hearts. If He shapes it while it is frozen, it will shatter! Even at the hands of the Master Potter, the clay needs to be warm and soft to sculpt!

May 15: God's will

An old proverb reminds us that the will of God never will take us where the grace of God will not protect us. Though we can differentiate between God's perfect will and His permissive will, the most important aspect is that He has a plan. He allows us to stray from His perfect will and have our way, yet He always brings us back to His path for our lives.

> We're not necessarily doubting that God will do the best for us; we are wondering how painful the best will turn out to be."—C.S. Lewis

Many misquote the following verse by avoiding the beginning requirement:

Delight yourself also in the LORD,
And He shall give you the desires of your heart.

Psalm 37:4 (NKJV)

Notice the conditional statement: if our hearts are in line with the heart of God, then He will give us the desires of our hearts! That is similar to the way prayer works. Prayer does not change God; it changes us. God changes our hearts, and changes our desires to accept whatever He chooses to give. Even in the midst of difficulties, He continues to provide, though often at the eleventh hour, building our faith, just as He built the faith of Abraham. When praying specifically, we should pray for specific people and even their specific needs, but we should not ask for specific answers to that prayer. God is bigger and wiser than all of us combined. How would our ordinary requests ever compare to God's extraordinary solutions?

[16] Rejoice always, [17] pray without ceasing, [18] in everything give thanks; for this is the will of God in Christ Jesus for you. 1 Thessalonians 5:16-18 (NKJV)

We serve a God that cannot conflict His nature, and part of that nature is to provide the needs of His children. That is how much He loves us! Yet we often erroneously desire more than He gives, or fail to be thankful for what we surmise is a less-than-perfect answer to our prayer. God gave in to Hezekiah's request for extra years of life (2 Kings 20), but that turned out to be problematic, as the son born to Hezekiah in that "extra time" became the worst king ever! We should pray for God to change our hearts to be in line with His heart, in His will, and in His perfect timing!

May 16: Mirror, mirror on the wall...

Most of us have been slowed by other drivers, whose eyes are looking at themselves in the rearview mirrors rather than focusing on the road. Mirrors are incredible tools, invented early in man's history, mostly for personal grooming. Though there were less clear versions of the mirror early on, around the time of Jesus they began making metal-coated, glass mirrors in Sihon (what is now Lebanon). Since that time, mirrors additionally have been used in decoration, architecture and in scientific instruments. Yet the initial usage is still the most common.

Before the invention of the mirror, it is doubtful that people cared quite as much about every hair being in place. Questioning a companion, "How's my hair look," would be the closest thing to a mirror, other than gazing into a still, pool of water! Upon reflection, how much more valuable would a mirror be if it revealed what was on the inside of a person rather than what was on the outside!

It is a true challenge to each believer to see ourselves the way God sees us! There are certainly two sides to that coin, as usually, we think too highly of ourselves, knowing that God has told us in His Word that our hearts are desperately wicked and deceitful at best. Yet when we have received salvation from the Lord, the Father sees the righteousness of His Son when He looks upon us!

I will praise You, for I am fearfully *and* wonderfully made; Psalm 139:14 (NKJV)

Though most people would choose to have Hollywood looks, that is not the beauty that we should desire. In Isaiah 53:2 when prophetically describing Jesus, Isaiah says, **"He has no form or comeliness and when we see Him, there is no beauty that we should desire Him."** The beauty of Jesus is on the inside, just as it should be for all of us as believers.

[1] **"Take heed that you do not do your charitable deeds before men, to be seen by them. Otherwise you have no reward from your Father in heaven.** [2] **Therefore, when you do a charitable deed, do not sound a trumpet before you as the hypocrites do in the synagogues and in the streets, that they may have glory from men. Assuredly, I say to you, they have their reward.** [3] **But when you do a charitable deed, do not let your left hand know what your right hand is doing,** [4] **that your charitable deed may be in secret; and your Father who sees in secret will Himself reward you openly.**

Matthew 6:1-4 (NKJV)

God created us exactly the way we are, so He certainly loves the outside. He also made the inside and easily sees our hearts and motives.

**³Who may ascend into the hill of the LORD?
Or who may stand in His holy place?
⁴He who has clean hands and a pure heart,
Who has not lifted up his soul to an idol,
Nor sworn deceitfully.
⁵He shall receive blessing from the LORD,
And righteousness from the God of his salvation.
Psalm 24:3-5 (NKJV)**

Clean hands demonstrate our actions, while pure hearts demonstrate our motives. If we spent as much time developing those godly motives instead of focusing on the tone of every muscle and the placement of every hair, we might start to reflect our Lord, whose beauty was on the inside! Mirror, mirror on the wall…why focus on the outside, ya'll?

May 17: Filled with the Holy Spirit

Some people believe that Christians are filled with the Holy Spirit until they sin, and then are "un-filled," until confession of that sin. After confession, they are filled again. Yet that is not what the Bible says. In Acts 1:8, we see that God gives believers the Holy Spirit to imbue them with power and become witnesses for Him. In Acts 2:4, the Day of Pentecost arrived. In Acts 1:12-15, 120 people in the upper room all were filled with the Spirit. In Acts 4:8, Peter was in front of the Sanhedrin, and Peter was filled with the Holy Spirit. In all of these, the word "filled" is in the aorist tense in the Greek, πλησθεις (*plēstheis*, or the passive participle *pimplēmi*). **The aorist tense signifies an event that occurred at one time in the past.** This tense alone tells us that God fills us with the Holy Spirit at one time!

In Acts 4:31, we see that believers prayed and all were filled with the Holy Spirit. In Acts 6:3, there is a need of distribution of food to the widows. The requirement of the men for this job is that they must be filled with the Spirit. Do they lose that job when they commit a sin, and then gain the job back after they have asked for forgiveness? This sure puts more emphasis on our works than on the work that Jesus did in our behalves on the cross! As long as we live on this earth, we will continue to sin. That brings to mind Paul's words:

For what I am doing, I do not understand. For what I will to do, that I do not practice; but what I hate, that I do. Romans 7:15 (NKJV)

Lastly, in Acts 6:5, we see that Stephen was full of the Holy Spirit, while in Acts 11:24, we see the same description of Barnabas. What is the significance of being filled with the Holy Spirit? All of God exists inside of each of us as believers, rather than a small portion of God in each of us. That is hard for our finite minds to conceptualize! Rather than removing a portion of Himself when we sin, He remains in us as the Comforter. And when do we need that comfort more than after we have sinned?

Confessing our sins is an important aspect of walking with the Lord, but we cannot wrongly put too much emphasis on our own failures. If we are not aware of our sin, or forget a sin we committed, the Lord is still faithful to forgive our sin if He is our Messiah. As much as we want to take control of our own lives, we are richly blessed that God is truly the One in control!

May 18: Called by His name!

If a man has his name on a building, he really has made it. If his name is on his desk, he still is pretty important. Yet if his name is on his shirt, he probably could have made some better career choices! Titles can be pretty important to men, especially in the workplace. In Philemon, we see five titles or descriptions of people in the first sentence:

¹ Paul, a prisoner of Christ Jesus, and Timothy *our* brother, To Philemon our beloved *friend* and fellow laborer, ² to the beloved Apphia, Archippus our fellow soldier, and to the church in your house:
Philemon 1-2 (NKJV)

First, Paul is described as a prisoner of Jesus Christ. Instead of calling attention to himself and his title of apostle, we see a more humble extreme. Some scholars think that Paul was describing the fact that he was incarcerated, but it is deeper than that. Knowing that Paul chose his words carefully when he wrote or spoke, we know that he meant exactly what he said. How was Paul a prisoner of Jesus? Jesus certainly captured his heart. Additionally, Paul was in jail not because men had placed him there. Instead, Paul was in jail because it was God's will for him to be there. Once Jesus has purchased our lives with His blood, He owns us. That is what redemption is all about. Then our lives are for His glory, rather than for our own self-aggrandizing glorification!

Next, Timothy is described as "our brother." What a great reminder that all of us in the family of God are related. It should not surprise us how often we argue and battle with fellow brothers and sisters in the Lord. Those who have grown up in larger families realize that battles constantly arise. Yet the bigger part of those battles is the phrase that blood is thicker than water. Even though we fight, we love each other, forgive each other and support each other. A brother may argue with his sister, but if a stranger attacks her, he will break down walls to come to her defense. We often can lose sight of the fact that each of us serving the Lord has been chosen by Him. Why should we fight with people He chose for His purposes? We should love our Christian family, our brothers from different mothers and our sisters from different misters!

Both Philemon and Apphia are described as "beloved." This is the Greek word *agapetos*, ἀγαπητός, which comes from another Greek word used for the most selfless and spiritual love, *agape*. This is a strong reminder that the Father looks upon each of us as believers with an unconditional love. God's love is not based on our ever-changing performance. He's not a lover, plucking petals from a flower. "He loves me. He loves me not. He loves me. He loves me not." Instead, just realize, He loves us! He chose us for His purposes!

Philemon is also described as a laborer. For all who belong to the Lord, He gave us at least one spiritual gift. Additionally, He calls us to use our gifts for His glory, laboring for Him. That labor is to bring more people to know Him by sharing His love with others and it is also in helping other believers to know Him better through teaching, encouragement, etc. Remember, a successful ministry has nothing to do with size. We all have seen small ministries filled with God's power and large ministries that seem to glorify man more than God. If we are willing to work for Him, He will use us.

Lastly, Archippus is described as a fellow soldier. There is a battle that has been raging on this earth since the fall of Adam. It involves powers and principalities, the host of angels. When Lucifer sinned, he departed heaven with one third of the heavenly host, yet there are two thirds remaining on God's side. This battle is waged around us constantly, and with the angels outnumbering the grains of sand in the sea, it is a large battle. When we accepted Jesus as Messiah, we changed sides. Never forget that Satan wants to destroy us for leaving him and turning to Jesus! He also wants to destroy our testimony so that God will not use us to further His kingdom.

There are many titles that we honor as men: president, chief executive officer, senator, and others. Yet in this short book, the Lord shares with us five titles that each believer has. Never forget that our titles are not so important. It is the title of the God we serve that matters.

He is Wonderful, Counselor, Mighty God, Everlasting Father, Prince of Peace. He is the King of Kings and the Lord of Lords. He is the Chief Cornerstone, the Holy One of Israel, the Rock of my strength and my Hiding Place. He is my Deliverer, my Savior, the Lord of all the earth. He is *Elohim, El Shaddai,* and *Jehovah-jireh.* He is the Living God, Lord of all the Armies, the Most High God!

May 19: Bird brains!

One of the strange behaviors to watch in the animal kingdom involves birds. Sometimes, they preen in the side-view mirror of parked cars. Additionally, they peck at the mirror, and bird poop covers the side of the car. The internet reveals a wealth of people enduring this same, odd-bird behavior. An on-line ornithologist gave an interesting explanation. Male robins and cardinals are prone to this behavior, though it is not limited to only those birds. Springtime seems to be the most common time for it, but what is the consensus opinion is that the bird is doing battle with another male…in the mirror. The poop trail is his marking of territory. Suggested solutions are varied and involve putting a bag over the mirror, a car cover, or even dishwashing soap placed on the mirror to make it more opaque. Of course, the easiest solution is to hit the stupid bird with a broom until it quits breathing!

Birds are not known for their incredibly large brains! As humans, our brains are much closer to the capacity of those birds than they are to the capacity of God's brain. God probably looks at us in much the same way that we look at those silly birds. "You are fighting against yourself again!" How often do we fall into that same trap? With God's perfect plan for our lives, He still allows us to choose our own ways. Yet when we choose the wrong path, He faithfully and patiently brings us back to the path He designed especially for each of us. Just like the bird, our biggest mistakes usually take place when we pridefully are looking at ourselves! If we keep our eyes on God, we will not even begin to worry about our enemy in the mirror.

Yes, we do fight against powers and principalities, the powers of Satan. Yet it does not really matter what battle lies ahead. If our eyes are on ourselves rather than God, we are destined to lose the battle every time.

You must not fear them, for the LORD your God Himself fights for you.'
Deuteronomy 3:22 (NKJV)

Though we seem to think that the battles in our own lives are so big that we deserve to worry about them, in truth, we are no better than the bird pecking against a mirror. Trust God! He loves us so much that He desires to protect us and do battle for us! We are soldiers in His army and He has the power to defeat anyone and anything!

May 20: Whose advice do you value?

Philip Calvin McGraw sure does love to tell people what they should do with their lives. Better known as Dr. Phil, he makes an inordinate amount of money dispensing advice to a variety of guests with a bigger variety of problems on his television show. His simple language and Southern drawl seem to convince his guests that he cares and never would mislead them. A song called "Wear Sunscreen" offers us this scintillating wisdom concerning advice:

> Be careful whose advice you buy, but be patient with those who supply it. Advice is a form of nostalgia. Dispensing it is a way of fishing the past from the disposal, wiping it off, painting over the ugly parts and recycling it for more than it's worth.

Why are we so quick to listen to a man's advice, and hesitant to listen to the advice that the Lord offers? His Word is filled with advice! If we follow His Word, our lives would be so much easier. Isaiah shared this passage with us:

[1] **"Woe to the rebellious children," says the LORD,**
"Who take counsel, but not of Me,
And who devise plans, but not of My Spirit,

That they may add sin to sin;
² Who walk to go down to Egypt,
And have not asked My advice,
To strengthen themselves in the strength of Pharaoh,
And to trust in the shadow of Egypt!
³ Therefore the strength of Pharaoh
Shall be your shame,
And trust in the shadow of Egypt
Shall be *your* humiliation.
Isaiah 30:1-3 (NKJV)

Dr. Phil is not the first person to dispense advice that does not involve biblical truth. He is on a long list of psychologists, psychiatrists and psychobabblers who cannot share the truth if they do not follow the truth. Jesus is the Truth and the only Way! It does not matter if we believe in the power of positive thinking. Norman Vincent Peale was appalling in the same manner that Paul is appealing! If our advisor does not follow Jesus, we should be very careful how closely we adhere to their advice. The answer is not blowing in the wind; it is in the pages of God's Word! Beware of the hot air of most dispensing that advice!

May 21: Tires!

Regardless of how old a car is, or even how expensive, it sure drives well with a new set of tires. Without a good set of tires, it is not going to take us very far. Though even new tires can have blowouts, we tend to trust that new tire much more at high speeds or on bumpy terrains. It is like the feeling of wearing an old, worn out pair of tennis shoes. They make knees ache, joints hurt and by the end of the day, add to leg exhaustion. In the same manner, a new set of tires gives new life to the car. It corners better, gets better traction in the snow or rain and makes the ride so much smoother.

Jesus is more concerned with the way we walk than the way we ride! Our walks with Him should not wear out like a set of tires or a pair of shoes. Instead, daily, they should improve by drawing closer to Him.

Draw near to God and He will draw near to you. Cleanse *your* hands, *you* sinners; and purify *your* hearts, *you* double-minded.
James 4:8 (NKJV)

It is amazing to think of the relationship Adam had with God in the pre-sin Garden of Eden. He walked with God and talked with God. There is not a better way to get to know someone than the close fellowship of a walk together. When we walk with God, we spend time talking to Him and listening to Him. How can we know Him without that communication? Yet after sin entered the picture, man never had that same relationship with God again. Moses could talk to God, but not look upon the Lord. We can walk with God, as He is living inside of each of us as believers.

Someday, we will see His face. We cannot begin to imagine what He will look like, but we know that His eyes will have a sweetness and gentleness far-surpassing anything in our imaginations.

"And I will pour on the house of David and on the inhabitants of Jerusalem the Spirit of grace and supplication; then they will look on Me whom they pierced. Yes, they will mourn for Him as one mourns for *his* only *son*, and grieve for Him as one grieves for a firstborn.
Zechariah 12:10 (NKJV)

We all were present at the crucifixion of our Lord as our sins put Him there. Sounds like in the future, He will retain those scars of the wounds He received instead of us. We should keep our walks with Him, our eyes upon Him and never depart! He will put air in our tires and soles on our shoes, as Jesus is the only Soul Man! That is where the rubber meets the road!

May 22: What is the worst kind of cancer?

Cancer is a frequent worry in the lives of most people. Some doctors guess we each get cancer 7-10 times in our lives, yet most of the time, our bodies fight off the cancer with a healthy immune system, without any knowledge that cancer infiltrated the normally healthy cells. When those healthy cells turn into rogue cells, a compromised immune system has difficulty reversing them back to a healthy status. At that time, cancer grows and spreads, and kills a person from the inside out. There are treatments, such as chemotherapy and radiation, that can help fight the battle. With chemotherapy, they slowly drip poison into the body, with the hopes of killing the cancer before killing the host!

Sin is a cancer. Similar to cancer, sin will kill us from the inside out. While the dermatologist has to freeze the precancerous spots over and over again, sin has only one remedy. When Jesus died on the cross, He carried the burden of all of our sins. That means our past, present and future sins! When we ask Him into our hearts and lives, that burden is removed forever!

[14] But each one is tempted when he is drawn away by his own desires and enticed. [15] Then, when desire has conceived, it gives birth to sin; and sin, when it is full-grown, brings forth death.
James 1:14-15 (NKJV)

[1] My little children, these things I write to you, so that you may not sin. And if anyone sins, we have an Advocate with the Father, Jesus Christ the righteous. [2] And He Himself is the propitiation for our sins, and not for ours only but also for the whole world.
1 John 2:1-2 (NKJV)

Propitiation is one of those three-dollar words. It means to appease the wrath of divine judgment. The death of Christ fully satisfied all the righteous demands of God toward the sinner, as sin must be punished, but it must only be punished once.

How sad that the world puts more emphasis on the cancers that destroy our bodies than the cancerous sins that destroy our eternal lives! Remember that we need not struggle with making an appointment. God will meet us right where we are and will take that deathly sin away from us immediately, if only we ask! Even if we are Christians, we should walk in the freedom of having that burden removed by confessing our sins to Him.

If we confess our sins, He is faithful and just to forgive us *our* sins and to cleanse us from all unrighteousness.
1 John 1:9 (NKJV)

May 23: Proof!

The greatest evidence in a court of law is an eyewitness and certainty grows in correlation to the number of eyewitnesses. In the case of Jesus, His life has been historically documented. In addition to many different authors of the Bible, the Jewish historian Josephus also speaks of Him. Paul reminds us in 1 Corinthians 15:5-6 that Cephas (Peter), the rest of the apostles and a collective group of over 500 people all saw the risen Jesus. While the life and death of Jesus was important, without His resurrection it all was for nothing, for if He could not conquer death, how could we? Paul also mentions James and all the apostles seeing the risen Jesus in 1 Corinthians 15:7. Why is it important that James saw Jesus? Well, if anyone would know if the risen Jesus was an imposter, his brother James surely would know. Additionally, James was not a believer at the time of his brother's death, but came to believe after the resurrection. Talk about a convincing event! God has given us many eyewitnesses to corroborate the evidence given in His Word.

[16] For we did not follow cunningly devised fables when we made known to you the power and coming of our Lord Jesus Christ, but were eyewitnesses of His majesty. [17] For He received from God the Father honor and glory when such a

voice came to Him from the Excellent Glory: "This is My beloved Son, in whom I am well pleased." [18] And we heard this voice which came from heaven when we were with Him on the holy mountain.
[19] And so we have the prophetic word confirmed, which you do well to heed as a light that shines in a dark place, until the day dawns and the morning star rises in your hearts;
2 Peter 1:16-19 (NKJV)

This passage in 2 Peter reminds us of the fact that the fulfilled prophecies in and of themselves demonstrate the power of God. Certainly, if one prophecy came true it would be a miracle, but over 300 Old Testament prophecies concerned the birth of Jesus. All of them came true! Some people argue that Jesus simply knew the Scriptures and acted in a way to fulfill those prophecies. Self-fulfilling prophecy might be possible in an event like riding down the Palm Sunday road on a foal of a donkey, but can an infant decide where to be born? Think of some of the prophecies completely out of the hands of Jesus. In Psalm 22:18, it reads, **"They divide My garments among them, and for My clothing, they cast lots."** If simply trying to fulfill all of the prophecies, how could Jesus have controlled the actions of those crucifying Him? He could not! In the same manner, Psalm 22 speaks of crucifixion before it ever had been invented…**"they pierced My hands and My feet."**

2 Peter 1:18 reminds us that we have been given a **"more sure word of prophecy."** In Greek, the word for "more sure" is *bebaios*, which literally means firm, steadfast or secure. God's fulfillment of prophecy is just as secure as His promise to us of salvation. Our belief as Christians stands on the foundation of God's Word, and more specifically, God's promises! Peter was present at the transfiguration of Jesus, heard the voice of the Father, and states that the fulfillment of prophecy is just as important to us as believers. This should remind each of us to stand on those promises without wavering! Prophecy does not come from man, but from God, as when a man utters one false prophecy, he is a false prophet. This should give us awareness of God's presence in the lives of some claiming to be prophets.

Has every prophecy given by them come true? If not, flee from them! Additionally, it should remind us not to predict the future. We know from God's Word what prophecies still are to be fulfilled, but we surely do not know the specific way He will accomplish that fulfillment. God has no chance of being wrong, for being outside of time, He can see the beginning, the end and every point in between!

And I fell at his feet to worship him. But he said to me, "See that you do not do that! I am your fellow servant, and of your brethren who have the testimony of Jesus. Worship God! For the testimony of Jesus is the spirit of prophecy."
Revelation 19:10 (NKJV)

Most importantly, the number of prophecies and fulfillments demonstrates His love for us. He went to great lengths to not only get our attention, but convince us of His love. As Isaiah reminded us, **"Yet it pleased the Lord to bruise Him."** The Father gladly allowed Jesus to endure the agony, humiliation and loneliness of the cross so that we could have relationship with the Father!

May 24: How do you hear God?

"The Lord told me that you are going to marry Amy." What should we do if we hear a Christian make a comment of this nature? Wow, that is a lot of power being given to a person! Simply by not marrying Amy, this person could make God into a liar in the perspective of the message-giver, yet the truth of the situation is, this bearer of a prophecy is a false prophet. God is never wrong, never lies and never puts more emphasis on our words than His!

"You shall not take the name of the LORD your God in vain, for the LORD will not hold *him* guiltless who takes His name in vain.
Exodus 20:7 (NKJV)

Of all the 10 Commandments, this is the one that is probably the least understood. Many people think it refers to using the Lord's name in a curse word. Certainly, that is part of it, but that does not touch on the enormity of this command. "In vain," means in any empty manner. That could mean cursing or swearing using the Lord's name, yet it also could apply to our previous situation of someone saying, "The Lord told me to…"

The Bible is the finished version of God's Holy Word. He is not adding to the Bible. Neither is He subtracting from it. If God tells us to do something, is it through His Word that He is speaking? Remember, God never will conflict His Word. Humans all suffer with pride, and though we can feel the prodding of the Holy Spirit leading us, the phrase, "God told me" is certainly overused in Christian circles. Is it possible that it was not God's voice, but our own? Is it something that we desperately want and we feel that God wants us to have it? Additionally, if God is speaking to one person and not another, is the one going to be prideful of his advanced spirituality? What does the Bible say about the voice of God?

³The voice of the LORD *is* over the waters;
The God of glory thunders;
The LORD *is* over many waters.
⁴The voice of the LORD *is* powerful;
The voice of the LORD *is* full of majesty.
⁵The voice of the LORD breaks the cedars,
Yes, the LORD splinters the cedars of Lebanon.
⁶He makes them also skip like a calf,
Lebanon and Sirion like a young wild ox.
⁷The voice of the LORD divides the flames of fire.
⁸The voice of the LORD shakes the wilderness;
The LORD shakes the Wilderness of Kadesh.
⁹The voice of the LORD makes the deer give birth,
And strips the forests bare;
And in His temple everyone says, "Glory!"
Psalm 29:3-9 (NKJV)

Additionally, the Holy Spirit speaks to us in a still, small voice, and Jesus told us that His sheep know His voice, but God the Father spoke loudly (Deuteronomy 5:22) when giving the 10 Commandments to the wandering Jews. God speaks loudly in His Word. If we do not read it, how can we hear Him? If God told us something, what verse did He use?

May 25: World religions

Last week, there was a news report of a man driving 140 miles per hour down the interstate. The police chase ended when he blew an engine in his Corvette, earning him a one-month jail sentence. The late night speedster believes that he has been reincarnated 700 or so times, and that he had once been Leonardo Da Vinci. Why do all these people who believe in reincarnation think they were someone famous in a past life? It is much more romantic than being a garbage collector. Would this man treat this life with more esteem if he thought it was his only shot?

This world has many beliefs and many religions. Muslims believe in an afterlife. In fact, according to the Qu'ran, warriors who die fighting in the cause of Allah, the god of Islam, are ushered immediately to Allah's presence. Additionally, enemies of Islam are sentenced immediately to hell upon death. In Islam, sin is anything that goes against the will of Allah and sin is an act, not a state of being. Heaven, or paradise, is something that must be earned.

Buddhism is quite different, putting an emphasis on karma. Karma is the force that drives the cycle of suffering and rebirth for each being, based on action and motive. By accomplishing good deeds, a person will be reincarnated as a higher being. Bad deeds cause the opposite effect. Want 500 tries at getting it right? This is the perfect religion! After numerous tries, if a person keeps progressing, he might become an enlightened being.

Though Judaism has much of the same fundamentals as Christianity, humanists seem to be setting the standards rather than God's Word. Jews believe in *mitzvahs*, which are basically "good deeds." On *Yom Kippur* or the Day of Atonement, Jews spend the day fasting in the temple while reflecting on the actions of the previous year. If a person has performed more good deeds than bad, he is a good person. Most Jews do not believe in an afterlife.

Christianity is quite different. Unlike Buddhism, a person only gets one chance, unless that person is a Catholic and their friends or relatives pay a priest to pray them into heaven from purgatory, both concepts that are not to be found in the Bible. Unlike Judaism, heaven is a place of reward for forgiven sinners, rather than "good people," as the Bible teaches that all of us are sinners and even one sin makes a man a sinner. Unlike Islam, Christianity teaches its followers to love their enemies, rather than kill them. Islam is also a religion that teaches that lying is wrong, though when speaking to your enemies, lying is required.

There are many other religions out there, as well. How do we decide what is right? Some people believe that all paths lead to the same result, or that all religions lead to the same God. But that involves a very limited world view, for if we wanted to go from Los Angeles to Paris, we would not just get on-board any airplane to take us there! What a ludicrous philosophy! The truth of Christianity lies in the Bible. It is an integrated document written by many different authors in a lengthy time period of a few thousand years. Yet one statement never conflicts another when read in context. Historically, it has proven itself not just accurate, but perfectly accurate. As prideful as men are, authors write about themselves and their own exploits. Instead, in the Bible, the variety of authors wrote about God, most notably, Jesus Christ, who humbled them all with His love, honesty and miracles. No other document associated with any religion makes predictions or prophecies that come true. In the Bible, they all either have come true or will. Jesus is not one answer. He is the only answer. He does not expect us to be perfect. To be forgiven, we only have to acknowledge who He is and what He did for us. He does all the rest. Repent and follow Him!

⁶ Jesus said to him, "I am the way, the truth, and the life. No one comes to the Father except through Me.
⁷ "If you had known Me, you would have known My Father also; and from now on you know Him and have seen Him." John 14:6-7 (NKJV)

God tells us in His Word exactly who He is. When we accept parts of that and change the parts we find more difficult to believe, does it change God? He is what He is. Accept Him or not, He cannot change and will not change! Any god we could invent would not hold a candle to the One we have who loves us. Get to know Him better today! He cared enough to send His very Best!

May 26: Fight or flight?

All of us have those polarizing moments of emphasis. Even our euphemisms describe those points in time: "when the rubber meets the road," "when push comes to shove," "when your back is up against the wall," or "it is now or never." Those phrases describe the timing of "when to throw in the towel," which is a description of surrender. In boxing, the side has retired when the coach tosses a white towel into the ring. It is a smaller scale of an army hoisting a white flag. God allows each of us to fall into situations that will test our faith, if we are believers. He also allows people to fall into situations that will bring us to faith, if we are not believers.

Most of us easily can remember the point of surrender in our own lives, when we finally found that point of brokenness and decided to try God's way rather than continue to flounder by doing it our way. With our faces in the gutter, there is nowhere to look but upward. At that point, it either is time to run away from Him or run into His comforting arms!

³ Blessed *be* the God and Father of our Lord Jesus Christ, who according to His abundant mercy has begotten us again to a living hope through the resurrection of Jesus Christ from the dead, ⁴ to an inheritance incorruptible and undefiled and that does not fade away, reserved in heaven for you, ⁵ who are kept by the power of God through faith for salvation ready to be revealed in the last time.
⁶ In this you greatly rejoice, though now for a little while, if need be, you have been grieved by various trials, ⁷ that the genuineness of your faith, *being* much more precious than gold that perishes, though it is tested by fire, may be found to praise, honor, and glory at the revelation of Jesus Christ, ⁸ whom having not seen you love. Though now you do not see *Him,* yet believing, you rejoice with joy inexpressible and full of glory, ⁹ receiving the end of your faith—the salvation of *your* souls.
1 Peter 1:3-9 (NKJV)

How can we tell if our faith in Jesus Christ is fake or real? Does it stand the test of trial? When we are in the darkest places, do we run to the light of His love or do we blame the darkness on Him? Yes, our God allows the difficulties in our lives, but He does not cause them! Yet He always is there to comfort us if we turn to Him. Often as believers, we have to deal with the ramifications of our sin, which might involve some definite hardship. He has promised never to leave us or forsake us. He will carry us when we cannot walk! Nothing compares to the glory of God's love, and the salvation that He promises never will perish.

We rarely remember to be thankful for the hardships, but those hardships are part of the road that brought us to the present. Be thankful in everything!

May 27: Pentecost

Pentecost is a Greek word meaning "fifty." In the Old Testament, this Jewish feast week was called *Shavuot,* which in Hebrew means "weeks." Beginning on the second day of

Passover, the "counting of the *omer*" began, referring to a sacrifice of an *omer*-measure of barley. The second day of Passover was also called "First Fruits," and was the beginning of the barley harvest. After seven weeks elapsed, the wheat harvest began, signifying the start of *Shavuot*. On the Hebrew calendar, this feast began on the first day of *Sivan*, and was one of the three feasts of Moses that required for every Jewish man twenty years of age or older to make a pilgrimage to Jerusalem.

Additional significance lies in the fact that during the exodus of the Jews from Egypt to the Promised Land, *Shavuot* marks the day when the Jews received the Law. Having departed Egypt in haste, with Pharaoh's soldiers in hot pursuit, the Jews carried their emancipation from slavery with the requirement of following God's Law. In the Bible, seven is symbolic of completeness, and not ironically, after seven weeks of seven days, God shared His Law with them. According to tradition, King David was born and died on *Shavuot*, which is the only one of the seven feasts of Moses using leavened bread instead of unleavened bread. Leaven points to sin, as it causes bread to puff up, while prideful sin causes man to puff up.

A deeper significance of the day involves another anniversary, as *Shavuot* is also the day that the Church began. The resurrection of Jesus occurred on the day of First Fruits, that second day of Passover, as He was the first fruit of the resurrection. The resurrection is a category, rather than an event. To explain that further, just as Jesus was resurrected, each of us as believers will be in the first resurrection, concluding with the following verse:

[16] For the Lord Himself will descend from heaven with a shout, with the voice of an archangel, and with the trumpet of God. And the dead in Christ will rise first. [17] Then we who are alive *and* remain shall be caught up together with them in the clouds to meet the Lord in the air. And thus we shall always be with the Lord. [18] Therefore comfort one another with these words.
1 Thessalonians 4:16-18 (NKJV)

After He was resurrected, Jesus appeared to His disciples before He departed from the Mount of Olives and returned to heaven in a cloud. A Sabbath's journey away, according to the Book of Acts, the disciples left the Mount of Olives for the upper room. Just as Jesus promised, when He departed the believers, He left them with the Holy Spirit:

15 "If you love Me, keep My commandments. 16 And I will pray the Father, and He will give you another Helper, that He may abide with you forever— 17 the Spirit of truth, whom the world cannot receive, because it neither sees Him nor knows Him; but you know Him, for He dwells with you and will be in you. 18 I will not leave you orphans; I will come to you.
John 14:15-18 (NKJV)

The word for "another" Helper, is *allos* (ἄλλος), which differs from *heteros*. *Allos* signifies another of the same sort, while *heteros* signifies another of a different sort. This tells us that the Holy Spirit is like Jesus. Yet there is a difference. Jesus walked with His followers, and was with them for three years, but only part of the time. The Holy Spirit is a gift to believers that will be with us at all times, as He dwells inside of us:

Nevertheless I tell you the truth. It is to your advantage that I go away; for if I do not go away, the Helper will not come to you; but if I depart, I will send Him to you.
John 16:7 (NKJV)

So on that first Pentecost Sunday many years ago, celebrating the anniversary of the giving of the Law, the first believers were filled with the Helper, who will teach us and bring to remembrance all things. He will imbue us with power. He came in as a rushing wind! What a gift we have been given! God is dwelling in us!

May 28: Remembrance

Today is Memorial Day, a day of picnics and the opening of many swimming pools around the country. Additionally, the day also is associated with huge sales in the department stores. Sadly, as a nation, we have lost sight of the real reason for this holiday. On Thanksgiving, we bow in thanks of the things we have, and on Memorial Day, we bow in thanks to the people who gave their lives for what we have. Even the men who fought without dying sacrificed, leaving home and homeland to defend our way of life, not knowing if they ever would return.

Those who have served in the military understand the sacrifices that have been made for us all. No matter how much reading and studying we do about the historical events in reference, we typically cannot picture those events as accurately as a first-hand observer would. In the movie "Saving Private Ryan," the opening scene involves the assault on the beaches of Normandy. The brutality of that scene is overwhelming, along with the inevitability of countless deaths of teenage men. A visit to the cemetery at Omaha Beach is one of the most chilling days, for someone who understands the historical significance. Walking from gravestone to gravestone in the pristinely maintained cemetery, with grass a lush green even on a cold, winter day, is an unforgettable memory. Most of the dead there were under 20 years of age. There are close to 10,000 Americans buried at Normandy.

Remember!

God told the Israelites to do the same:

[9] Only take heed to yourself, and diligently keep yourself, lest you forget the things your eyes have seen, and lest they depart from your heart all the days of your life. And teach them to your children and your grandchildren, [10] especially concerning the day you stood before the LORD your God in Horeb, when the LORD said to me, 'Gather the people to Me,

and I will let them hear My words, that they may learn to fear Me all the days they live on the earth, and *that* they may teach their children.'
Deuteronomy 4:9-10 (NKJV)

"Take heed," reminds us to watch out over our own lives. It takes work to guard over our own hearts, but each moment we are capable of sinning. If we reflect on His commandments, His merciful hand in our lives and His miracles, we will not forget! The Lord performed many miracles for the children of Israel. They even heard His voice on Mount Horeb, giving them the 10 Commandments. In this passage, the Lord reminds us to remember what our eyes have seen or those memories will depart from our hearts forever.

What have we seen? We have seen His mighty hand of miraculous power in each of our lives. Each of us following Him was blind and now sees; was deaf and now hears; was dead and now lives! On this Memorial Day, remember the ones who sacrificed for our lives, for our freedom. But more importantly, remember God's hand in it all, personally! As the passage above says, we must teach our children and our grandchildren, so they will not forget, either!

Remember!

May 29: Have you packed your parachute?

Faith is a decision to trust, and in the case of Christianity, it is a decision to trust in God. We are trusting that the many promises that He has made to us through His Word all will be fulfilled. Everyone has faith, but not everyone has faith in God. If a person turns on a light switch, he has faith that the room instantly will become brighter. To understand this with more of a life-or-death point of view, a skydiver can take all the steps to make his journey safer by packing his own parachute, checking it multiple times and following all the guidelines of how to make a safe jump. Yet when it comes down to the last moment of taking that one step out of the airplane, he must have faith that the parachute will open and bring him safely to the ground. When Paul wrote to the church members of Thessalonica, he commented on their faith:

³ We are bound to thank God always for you, brethren, as it is fitting, because your faith grows exceedingly, and the love of every one of you all abounds toward each other, ⁴ so that we ourselves boast of you among the churches of God for your patience and faith in all your persecutions and tribulations that you endure, ⁵ which is manifest evidence of the righteous judgment of God, that you may be counted worthy of the kingdom of God, for which you also suffer; ⁶ since it is a righteous thing with God to repay with tribulation those who trouble you, ⁷ and to give you who are troubled rest with us when the Lord Jesus is revealed from heaven with His mighty angels, ⁸ in flaming fire taking vengeance on those who do not know God, and on those who do not obey the gospel of our Lord Jesus Christ.
  2 Thessalonians 1:3-8 (NKJV)

Paul was known for his long sentences, and the verse above is another of those, so take time wading through the various clauses! He begins with a testament of his compliment of the faith of the church members, which was growing exceedingly. What causes faith to grow in abundance? Is it ease of situation or smoothness of life? How about prosperity or wealth? If we go to a gym, our muscles are not going to grow by watching others exercise. Instead, the muscle has to be worked hard in order to build it. No pain, no gain. Similarly, this philosophy applies to the faith of believers. We grow when tested.

Could answered prayer have anything to do with increased faith? It certainly can, yet do not forget that our prayers are not supposed to be Christmas wish lists made to the great Santa Claus. The sweetest prayers are the ones made on behalf of others, which are intercessory prayers. That has more to do with hardship, trial or tribulation, as we support our fellow believers by asking the Lord to come to their rescue. Though each of us seem to run from trouble, sometimes that is right where God wants us to be in order to force us to trust in Him above self! A book called "The Body in Pain," explains that to a person who has not experienced pain, a pin prick will be so excruciatingly painful that the person will think they are about to die. Yet after experiencing different levels of pain, we realize that our pain tolerance has grown and that the pin prick was nothing.

God draws us closer to Himself through various trials. When we look back on the situations He has pulled us through, our faith grows. The more difficult the trial, the greater testimony we have of His merciful hand in our lives. If we remember what He has accomplished in our lives, our faith will grow. Additionally, if we want our faith to grow, we should read His Word:

So then faith comes by hearing, and hearing by the word of God.
Romans 10:17 (NKJV)

What it comes down to is a life-or-death decision, like that of the skydiver. Do we truly believe in Jesus Christ as our Lord and Savior? Our eternal lives are based on that one step. Have we packed our eternal parachutes properly?

May 30: The balance of your Christian walk

Living in this world after becoming a Christian is like walking on top of a fence. On one side of the fence is the world while on the other side is heaven. Hebrews tells us that we are seated in the heavens already, for God is outside of time and sees us in our future home. Yet while we are in this temporary dwelling place, and in these earthly tents, we are being constantly attacked through the lust of the eyes, the lust of the flesh and the pride of life. (1 John 2:16) There are times when we fall from the precarious position of balance into the world, but the Lord pulls us back, just as Jesus reached His hand down to rescue a drowning Peter, after Peter had walked on water like the Lord.

Having saved us from the world, the Lord does not want us to feel the pressure of following the Law, as even though the 10

Commandments were perfect, they were designed as a tutor to show us that we could not follow them all the time. Instead, the Lord gave us a system designed with our flaws in mind. That system is Jesus, the only perfect man, who died for our sins, spilling His innocent blood instead of ours to pay the price for each of us. If we have accepted the Lord as our personal Savior, we are no longer slaves to sin, but we will continue to sin until the day we are in His presence. Some people who claim to be Christians miss the point, and continue in their sinful practices, knowing the Lord will forgive them. That dishonors the work on the cross of Jesus rather than honoring Him!

[15] To the pure all things are pure, but to those who are defiled and unbelieving nothing is pure; but even their mind and conscience are defiled. [16] They profess to know God, but in works they deny Him, being abominable, disobedient, and disqualified for every good work.
Titus 1:15-16 (NKJV)

We honor Jesus through our works and through our lives. Yes, we are sinners, saved by His grace, and we will continue to make mistakes. Yet Jesus will teach us through those mistakes. Each day, we should become more like Him. There are many Christians who argue about sin. Is it a sin to smoke? Is it a sin to drink? With half of Christian couples in the United States getting divorced, is that a sin? If we feel that it is wrong, it is!

I know and am convinced by the Lord Jesus that *there is nothing unclean of itself; but to him who considers anything to be unclean, to him *it is* unclean.
Romans 14:14 (NKJV)

Be careful not to venture into "moral relativism," or the belief that we decide what is right or wrong by how we feel about an issue, though. That is not what the Lord is telling us in His Word:

It is good neither to eat meat nor drink wine nor *do anything* by which your brother stumbles or is offended or is made weak.
Romans 14:21 (NKJV)

Instead, understand the bigger picture. If anything we do causes a fellow Christian to stumble, we are to walk away from it. It does not matter if the Bible specifically mentions that action as sin or not. Smoking is certainly a great example, as it never is mentioned in the Bible. We know the addictiveness of nicotine, and the fact that smoking is frowned upon by even a majority of non-Christians. We also are aware of the fact that the body is the temple of God, and smoking certainly is bad for that body. Recent statistics show that one-third of all smokers will die because of that habit. When a fellow Christian sees another smoking, can it cause them to stumble? Could they rationalize their own sinful behaviors through that action? "If he can smoke cigarettes, than I can smoke pot. God never mentions marijuana in the Bible and it is grown naturally."

There is an easy answer to those weak arguments. Do not do it if it causes your brother to stumble. If this sounds a little black and white, it is! Through the writings of Paul, God took the gray areas and brought them to His side. Walk in the light for God is Light! We should desire to resemble Jesus rather than the Madison Avenue idea of what is cool or acceptable.

May 31: Eight

Eight is an interesting number. It appears the same whether it is backwards or upside down. While there may be eight maids a 'milking in the "12 Days of Christmas," the number eight is very significant in the life of a baby, particularly in the Old Testament. That was the day that an infant boy was to be circumcised in the Hebrew custom (Genesis 17:12). Circumcision was a symbolic event pointing to the cutting away of the flesh, as the greatest challenge to each child of God is to walk in the Spirit, not in the flesh. It also demonstrated that the Jews were set apart by God. Certainly, when Moses was raised in Pharaoh's court, he always could be identified as Jewish by anyone who saw him naked. Customarily, eight seems to stand for new beginnings in the Bible. In addition to the rite of circumcision occurring on that eighth day, children were dedicated to the Lord at that time, including the baby girls. Jesus was circumcised on the eighth day (Luke 2:21) and taken to the temple in Jerusalem in dedication to the Lord. John the Baptist also was circumcised on the eighth day (Luke 1:59).

Many of the Levitical rites dealing with impurity also occurred upon the eighth day, including a sacrifice of two turtledoves by women after their monthly cycle (Leviticus 15:29). Though Leviticus can be a very difficult book to understand, so many rites occur on that all-important eighth day that significance is obvious. Remember, God gave these Laws to the Jews as a tutor. Covering sins and impurities with sacrifices took much time and energy. When Jesus died, and earned for us forgiveness of sins through His selfless act, His grace radiated throughout, especially with the reminder that because sin must be covered by the spilling of innocent blood, He had taken away the difficult rituals.

One of the earliest references to the importance of new beginning occurs in Genesis. When God destroyed the earth with the Great Flood, He spared only eight people upon the ark. Those eight people gave a new beginning to the world we know today and our blood runs from the bloodlines of Noah's family, just as it does from Adam and Eve:

[4] For if God did not spare the angels who sinned, but cast *them* down to hell and delivered *them* into chains of darkness, to be reserved for judgment; [5] and did not spare the ancient world, but saved Noah, *one of* eight *people*, a preacher of righteousness, bringing in the flood on the world of the ungodly;
2 Peter 2:4-5 (NKJV)

who formerly were disobedient, when once the Divine longsuffering waited in the days of Noah, while *the* ark was

being prepared, in which a few, that is, eight souls, were saved through water.
1 Peter 3:20 (NKJV)

While it is simple to search for the numeral eight with Bible software, the most interesting aspects of that number in the Bible occur in regard to repetitive actions. One of the most unusual of that variety is the fact that eight people miraculously were brought back to life in the Bible. Of course, that number does not pertain to Jesus, for the eight resurrected people tasted of death twice in their lives. Jesus only died once! Those eight resurrected people are the widow's son by Elijah (1 Kings 17:17-25), the son of the Shunammite woman by Elisha (2 Kings 4:32-37), the man placed in the tomb of Elisha (2 Kings 13:20), The widow of Nain's son by Jesus (Luke 7:11-18), the daughter of Jairus by Jesus (Luke 8:41-56), Lazarus by Jesus (John 11), Dorcas by Peter (Acts 9), and Eutychus by Paul (Acts 20). Talk about a new beginning! The words of Jesus to Lazarus should resonate with us all, "Lazarus, come forth!" If Jesus had not used his friend's name, it is easy to assume that all the dead would have emerged from their tombs by the power of Christ! Someday, we should all hope to hear those same words when He calls us home!

Interestingly, there are eight miracles of Elijah mentioned in the Bible: the shutting up of the heavens, multiplying the widow's meal, raising the widow's son, causing rain to come down from heaven, causing fire to come down from heaven, causing fire to come down from heaven again and lastly, dividing the Jordan River. When Elijah's mantle passed to Elisha, Elisha asked for the following in 2 Kings 2:9: **And so it was, when they had crossed over, that Elijah said to Elisha, "Ask! What may I do for you, before I am taken away from you?" Elisha said, "Please let a double portion of your spirit be upon me."** Then in the life of Elisha, he performed 16 miracles, exactly double the amount done by Elijah!

There are times when each of us yearns for a new beginning, especially those who do not know Jesus as Lord and Savior.

When playing backyard baseball, when a batter hit the ball into a tree in the playing field, and it did not come down, it was a "do-over." We can have a "do-over" by God's gift whenever we are willing to come to Him in repentance, willing to lay our sin at the foot of the cross and willing to allow Jesus to remove and carry that sin away from our slumping shoulders. Resurrection gives us a new beginning in Christ. Even as Christians, there are times when we fall back into the sin God has removed from us. Our Lord always is willing to give us another chance, another new beginning. If our legs are buckling due to the heavy burden that we are carrying, we can walk free, fresh and new whenever we are ready. Want a new beginning? Jesus is willing to walk beside us anywhere we go!

^{33} There he found a certain man named Aeneas, who had been bedridden eight years and was paralyzed. ^{34} And Peter said to him, "Aeneas, Jesus the Christ heals you. Arise and make your bed." Then he arose immediately. ^{35} So all who dwelt at Lydda and Sharon saw him and turned to the Lord. Acts 9:33-35 (NKJV)

June 1: Grow up!

When we are in our comfort zones, we are not growing. Growth is one of those aspects of life that should begin at birth and not finish until death. Oliver Wendell Holmes once said,

> "The great thing in the world is not so much where we stand, as in what direction we are moving."

Certainly, this applies to each of us even more strongly in our Christian walks. Peter was one who displayed an inordinate amount of growth. When he was walking with Jesus, Peter often acted rashly or spoke without thinking. He is known for bragging that he loved Jesus more than the rest, and then Jesus revealed to Peter that Peter would deny Jesus three times within the next few hours. In the Garden of Gethsemane, Peter was ready to defend Jesus from the mob of Jewish leaders, took out his sword, and sliced off the ear of Malchus. If Jesus had not healed Malchus, Peter would not have written any books in the New Testament. Tradition tells us that when Peter was to be martyred, he asked to be crucified upside down, for he did not feel worthy to suffer the same death as his Savior. Peter grew immensely, and we can see that growth in the words of 1 Peter and 2 Peter.

[5] But also for this very reason, giving all diligence, add to your faith virtue, to virtue knowledge, [6] to knowledge self-control, to self-control perseverance, to perseverance godliness, [7] to godliness brotherly kindness, and to brotherly kindness love. [8] For if these things are yours and abound, *you will be* **neither barren nor unfruitful in the knowledge of our Lord Jesus Christ. [9] For he who lacks these things is shortsighted, even to blindness, and has forgotten that he was cleansed from his old sins.**
[10] Therefore, brethren, be even more diligent to make your call and election sure, for if you do these things you will never stumble; [11] for so an entrance will be supplied to you abundantly into the everlasting kingdom of our Lord and Savior Jesus Christ.
2 Peter 1:5-11 (NKJV)

We come to the Lord with faith, and should add virtue to that faith. Virtue can be moral excellence or chastity. Next, comes knowledge, and the important knowledge is of the Word of God. Following knowledge is self-control, the ability to abstain from the lust of the flesh, the lust of the eyes and the pride of life. We add perseverance to self-control, finding the ability to keep on keeping on, through whatever struggle God allows in our pathways. Now we are getting to the advanced aspects of the Christian walk, as godliness comes next, with the outpouring of that godliness becoming brotherly kindness. It all ends in the greatest attribute, love! Love is everything! When people treat us badly, do we respond in love? When we do not, it shows that our growth has not yet been completed. Remember to not let love in your life be like a tennis term, where love is nothing. It needs to be the beginning and the end, the best of us and the worst of us, the greatest gift. Love is God and God is love.

June 2: Israel against the world!

It is interesting that every news story about Israel makes it to the front page, though the country is incredibly small. Certainly, the story concerning the flotilla of international aid workers made worldwide headlines. Seventy miles from Israel's coastline, Israeli commandos dropped from helicopters to board the ships, to turn them away from the coast of Israel. Why? Israel is not a cruel nation. In fact, any time a world crisis occurs, Israel is the first nation to send aid workers, for any natural disaster. Israel carries food, medicine and other supplies to the West Bank on a daily basis, even though hated by the people they are helping. In regard to the flotilla, Israel offered to escort the ships to the port of Ashdod and have the aid supplies checked through the proper channels before delivering those to the West Bank. Yet the organizers of the flotilla had ulterior motives, of breaking the embargo and re-opening a pipeline that Israel had closed. This was about weaponry. Israel stopped another flotilla from Lebanon months before in a similar manner.

In parts, Israel is only eight miles across. From the West Bank, the rockets fired by the Muslims continue to wreak havoc on the Jews of Israel. Since the nations of the world never take the side of Israel, Israel must defend itself. That is something Israel is known for, as its commandos are the most highly trained in the world. That should tell us something about the Arab claims of this flotilla, who asserted they were unarmed, and said that the Israeli forces fired upon them before boarding. Hmmm. The best-trained commandos in the world board a ship of unarmed peacekeepers and suffer severe injuries? Someone was lying. In the videos taken by the Israeli Defense Forces, impossible to fake, mobs of Arabs were beating the Israeli soldiers with metal rods and stabbing them with knives. Cases of slingshots and heavy rocks were also found on board.

Were there aid workers on board concerned for the people of the West Bank? Absolutely, as a small representation of truth will fool the masses into thinking there is only truth. The Muslims do not want the West Bank. They want all of Israel. They want the extinction of every Jew on the planet. That is what the Qu'ran teaches, to kill the infidel. It is difficult for those of us in the western world to understand that mentality, for we believe that if we treat our enemies with respect, that enemy will treat us in the same manner. That is not the case with the Muslims! They look upon that behavior as a sign of weakness. Treat them blindly with respect, and they will look for an opening to kill us! Do not be fooled! God told us about this in His Word. In the passage below, the Lord appears to Hagar, the concubine of Abraham, and makes promises to her:

⁹ The Angel of the LORD said to her, "Return to your mistress, and submit yourself under her hand." ¹⁰ Then the Angel of the LORD said to her, "I will multiply your descendants exceedingly, so that they shall not be counted for multitude." ¹¹ And the Angel of the LORD said to her: "Behold, you *are* with child,
And you shall bear a son.
You shall call his name Ishmael,
Because the LORD has heard your affliction.
¹²He shall be a wild man;
His hand *shall be* against every man,
And every man's hand against him.
And he shall dwell in the presence of all his brethren."
Genesis 16:9-12 (NKJV)

Mohammed, the founder of Islam, came from Ketar, who was the second son of Ishmael's 12 sons, though there were more than 2,500 years between Mohammed and Ketar. Just as God promised, He has multiplied the descendants of Ishmael exceedingly, with a number approaching 2 billion in the world today! Verse 12 above translated directly says, **"He will be like a wild donkey of a man."** Certainly, their hands are against every man, and they also live among their brethren!

The other part of this incident that is interesting is the participation of Turkey. Up until recently, Turkey has been Israel's closest ally in the Muslim world. Over the years, the two nations even have participated in joint military exercises. Yet that relationship was strained before the events of the flotilla, but has been further strained by the death of nine Turks in the flotilla. Why is that important? In Ezekiel 38, God tells us the nations which will join together in a major battle against the nation of Israel. One of those nations is Togarmah, widely accepted by Bible scholars as a reference to southern Turkey, near the Syrian border. Additionally, the Bible tells us that in the latter days, all the nations of the world will gather against the apple of His eye:

^{1} **Behold, the day of the LORD is coming,
And your spoil will be divided in your midst.
^{2}For I will gather all the nations to battle against Jerusalem;
Zechariah 14:1-2 (NKJV)**

It all comes down to the Western Bank. The Arabs referred to it as Palestine, but they call all of Israel by that name. That word is offensive, as God named the nation Israel, just as He gave Jacob that name! The word Palestine comes from the biblical word "Philistine." These were the people God told the children of Israel to cast out when He gave them the Promised Land. Yet instead of following God's mandate, the Israelites allowed some of the Philistines to remain in the Promised Land. The giant Goliath was a Philistine! To this day, those same people continue to be thorns in the side of the Jews. Israel's disobedience to God's order still has ramifications. Are we ready for the show to come? Trust His Word! It never has been wrong! Whatever we do, we should bless Israel. God gave that land to Israel, with a deed of trust. It does not matter how bad the Arabs desire it, God will not let go!

June 3: Exceedingly, abundantly

Without God, we are powerless. While this earth seems to be a battleground for those driven by power, wanting to rise above the masses, we know that it is the Lord who appoints kings and countries (Romans 13:1-2). As believers, it is God's power that works within us:

[20] Now to Him who is able to do exceedingly abundantly above all that we ask or think, according to the power that works in us, [21] to Him be glory in the church by Christ Jesus to all generations, forever and ever. Amen.
Ephesians 3:20-21 (NKJV)

These verses occur in a chapter that deals with why believers should pray. For many believers, prayer is the least utilized gift of all God has given. Most of us have fallen into that trap, thinking that God's will is going to occur regardless of our participation. Yet that participation sweetly involves us in the process! Additionally, answered prayer helps to build our faith, drawing us even closer to the Lord! Prayer gives us comfort when in distress, encouragement when facing a trial, compassion when grieving for a loved one and hope when faced with a world opposed to God. Paul also gave us these sweet words of encouragement:

[16] Rejoice always, [17] pray without ceasing, [18] in everything give thanks; for this is the will of God in Christ Jesus for you.
1 Thessalonians 5:16-18

Our lives should be prayers to the Lord. Those prayers exalt the work of God in our hearts. The verses from Ephesians 3 reveal that God's ability is greater than what we ever could imagine. God is able to do whatever we ask, so ask and we shall receive. God is able to do all that we think. God is able to do all we ever can ask or think. He is able to do above all we ever can ask or think. He is able to do abundantly above all we ever can ask or think. He is able to do exceedingly, abundantly, above all we ever can ask or think! Does this put it in better perspective?

This passage is about prayer. What is being exposed in us is that we do not usually believe, but our lack of belief does not stop

God. He loves to bless us with answered prayer, but our prayers should not be like a Christmas wish-list from Santa Claus! We should pray for God's will to be accomplished. We know from His Word that He sent His Son because "God so loved the world." Our prayers for salvation for our unbelieving friends and family members should be at the top of our prayer lists. God is intricately woven into all aspects of our lives. He is not a God way up there. He is God with us! Immanuel!

June 4: Perfection in imperfection!

Professional athletics often can show us the worst aspects of worldly behavior, especially when it comes to pride and egotism. Most professional athletes make so much money that it is disgusting, especially when compared to the salaries of manual laborers. That being said, occasionally we get to see the other side of the coin. Due to the visible nature of professional athletics, when something special happens, many people share in the experience.

In a baseball game between the Detroit Tigers and New York Yankees, Armando Galarraga found himself in rare territory. Not only was he pitching a no-hitter against the Yankees, Galarraga was one out away from a perfect game. A no-hitter is when no batter reaches base safely with a hit during the game. On the other hand, a perfect game not only has zero hits, but no batter reaches base in any manner, whether it be a hit, error or even a walk. Galarraga was in a zone. Though he had completed two seasons at the major league level, after a disappointing 2009 season he had been dropped to the Tigers' AAA minor league team to begin the 2010 season. In May of 2010, Galarraga returned to the big leagues. In a game soon after, he had retired 26 batters in a row, and was one out away from a perfect game. To put this in perspective, in almost 400,000 completed games in Major League baseball, there have been 20 perfect games.

The 27th batter grounded a ball between second and first bases, fielded by the first baseman. Galarraga covered first and received the throw from a jubilant first baseman, with the pitcher's foot firmly planted on the base. Both started to celebrate, and then realized the umpire had called the batter safe. The batter, knowing he was out, was holding his head with both hands, disappointed in the unfairness of the play, though the call went in his favor. Galarraga looked at umpire Jim Joyce, smiled and walked back to the pitcher's mound. After retiring the next batter, the game ended with a one-hit shutout, with Tiger manager Jim Leyland in Joyce's face, angrily spewing venom. Joyce left the field, and immediately went to see the replay. The play was close, but it was easy for Joyce to see that he had blown the call. He started crying, knowing that he had changed baseball history and taken away an extremely rare accomplishment with his error. Immediately, Joyce went to find Galarraga. Still crying, Joyce apologized and explained that he had seen the tape. Galarraga told Joyce that everybody makes mistakes! So in a game that should be remembered as one of the few perfect games in baseball history, we saw imperfection. Though no fielders made errors, the umpire did. Though no batters really had hits, the pitcher was a hit, with anyone who watched or heard about the game. Though Galarraga will not be credited with a perfect game, we saw a glimpse of perfection in his reaction.

As Christians, how would we have reacted in the same situation? Forgiveness would not be at the top of most of our lists, though anger and resentment would be. Yet God only allows events to occur in our lives for His reasons.

[14] **"For if you forgive men their trespasses, your heavenly Father will also forgive you.** [15] **But if you do not forgive men their trespasses, neither will your Father forgive your trespasses.**
  Matthew 6:14-15 (NKJV)

[21] **Then Peter came to Him and said, "Lord, how often shall my brother sin against me, and I forgive him? Up to seven times?"**

²² **Jesus said to him, "I do not say to you, up to seven times, but up to seventy times seven.**
Matthew 18:21-22 (NKJV)

God is awesome! Nothing is beyond His control. Galarraga certainly will not be remembered for pitching a perfect game, as Baseball Commissioner Bud Selig refused to reverse the call. Yet Galarraga will be remembered as being the only man ever to throw a perfect game and have it taken from him. Sadly, the umpire will not be remembered for 30 years of good calls. His name always will be remembered for the bad call, though just as Galarraga, Joyce handled the situation perfectly. He asked for forgiveness, admitted his mistake, and cried tears of contrition. We should all be that soft-hearted dealing with our own sins, and just as gracious dealing with the sins of others. What a lesson!

June 5: Trinity!

There are many parts of the Bible that are difficult for our human brains to understand. Additionally, there are many parts of the Bible that people argue about. Typically, if we have trouble grasping a subject, or if it does not make logical sense to our world-limited minds, we tend to discount the subject as being impossible. A great example would be the virgin birth of our Savior. Sadly, there are many people who believe in God that do not believe Mary was impregnated by the Holy Spirit. They rationalize that because each of us has an earthly parent, everyone must. Anyone who struggles with the acceptance of the Immaculate Conception must believe in a very small God! If He is powerful enough to have created all that we can see and all that we cannot see, why is He limited to do what we can logically concede? Another of those quarrelsome categories is the existence of a Trinity! We are told in the Ten Commandments that there is one God. So how could there be three?

In the beginning God created the heavens and the earth.
Genesis 1:1 (NKJV)

**In the beginning was the Word, and the Word was with God, and the Word was God. ² He was in the beginning with God.
John 1:1**

**That which was from the beginning, which we have heard, which we have seen with our eyes, which we have looked upon, and our hands have handled, concerning the Word of life—
1 John 1:1 (NKJV)**

Three verses written thousands of years apart fit succinctly together! In the first verse above, the word for God is *Elohim*. In Hebrew, the suffix "im" signifies male and plural. The apostle John gives Jesus a title at the beginning of his gospel, and that is the Word. Who was with God the Father at creation? Jesus, the Word of God! John expounds on that in the third verse above from 1 John, when he reminds us that Jesus was in the beginning before creation. We know he is referring to Jesus because John saw Jesus with his own eyes and touched Him with His own hands!

One of the most important verses for all Jews is the *Shema*. The verse is repeated at each visit to temple. Additionally, it is written on a tiny scroll and placed into a mezuzah, which is attached to the door frame. Some Jews place this at the entrance to every room, while others place it outside the door most commonly used to enter their homes. The verse inside says:

**⁴ "Hear, O Israel: The LORD our God, the LORD *is* one! ⁵ You shall love the LORD your God with all your heart, with all your soul, and with all your strength.
Deuteronomy 6:4-5 (NKJV)**

Interestingly, the word for one is אחד, pronounced *echad*. The word *echad* actually means one, but can mean more than one. There is another Hebrew word meaning "one and only one," *yachid*, but that is not the word here. In fact, the word *yachid* never is used in reference to One God! In the following verse, *echad* is also the word used for one:

Therefore a man shall leave his father and mother and be joined to his wife, and they shall become one flesh.
Genesis 2:24 (NKJV)

If two people can be one, then God also can be one God in three persons. Many people try to explain the triune nature of God through water, stating that it can be in solid form, liquid form or gas form. Others try to explain it through an egg, which has a yolk, albumen and a shell. Truthfully, neither of those helps us picture the triune nature of God.

Throughout the Bible, we see the presence of God the Father, God the Son and God the Holy Spirit. When studying the attributes of God, we see that He is omnipotent, omniscient and omnipresent, and all three representations of the one God are all of those attributes. They work together and relationally speaking, all have order. Jesus always does the will of the Father. Additionally, the Holy Spirit always testifies of Jesus. So the Holy Spirit draws us to accept Jesus and once we accept the Son, we are allowed access into the throne room of God the Father. We can come to the Father any time we want in prayer! They never conflict each other. All three are living inside of us as believers. It is hard for our minds to completely grasp, but someday we will. If we invited God to dinner, we only would set one place for Him, though He is Father, Son and Holy Spirit!

Yet one of the greatest lessons is that God tells us who He is in His Word. If those words do not resonate perfectly, the limit is our own finite brains rather than the Bible. God loves to teach the teachable, so even when we do not understand initially, by seeking Him, our understanding will increase!

June 6: Well done, good and faithful servant!

Former UCLA basketball coach John Wooden died at the age of 99, four months short of his 100th birthday. While at UCLA,

Wooden guided the Bruins to 10 NCAA titles in 12 years, a feat unheard of and completely unmatched. Additionally, he was the first person to be inducted into the Basketball Hall of Fame as a player and as a coach. As a player, he led his Purdue Boilermakers to the NCAA title in 1932. Coach Wooden stayed connected in college basketball circles and was highly-esteemed by everyone. The elderly Wooden retained the characteristic twinkle in his eyes even in later years. Though he was quiet about his Christian beliefs, he certainly was not silent about them, stating that if he was accused of being a Christian, he wanted to ensure there was enough evidence to be convicted! Here are some of his quotations over the years:

> "Be more concerned with your character than your reputation, because your character is what you really are, while your reputation is merely what others think you are."
>
> "You can't live a perfect day without doing something for someone who will never be able to repay you."
>
> "Material possessions, winning scores, and great reputations are meaningless in the eyes of the Lord, because He knows what we really are and that is all that matters."
>
> "Talent is God-given. Be humble. Fame is man-given. Be grateful. Conceit is self-given. Be careful."
>
> "I have always tried to make it clear that basketball is not the ultimate. It is of small importance in comparison to the total life we live. There is only one kind of life that truly wins, and that is the one that places faith in the hands of the Savior."

What does God think of His followers?

[20] "So he who had received five talents came and brought five other talents, saying, 'Lord, you delivered to me five talents;

look, I have gained five more talents besides them.' ²¹ His lord said to him, 'Well *done,* good and faithful servant; you were faithful over a few things, I will make you ruler over many things. Enter into the joy of your lord.'
Matthew 25:20-21 (NKJV)

This verse fits into the life of John Wooden, being that there are five players on a basketball team. Yet it does not just take the starters to win a collegiate championship! God may have given Wooden the first five players. Yet through his hard work, teaching skills and most importantly, the way he loved his players with the love of the Lord, Wooden had players on the bench better than the starters of most teams! Wooden's wife died in 1985 of cancer and every month since then, on the 21st of the month, he wrote a love letter to her and carried it to her grave. Now, he has been reunited with her, but more importantly, with his Savior!

Well done good and faithful servant. Enter into the joy of your Lord! Looking forward to meeting you in eternity, Coach!

June 7: God lives!

The fact that God lives is not news to many of us on the planet right now. Yet a majority of the 6 billion people going to and fro all over this earth do not believe in a God who has an active part in our lives. Though there are a small percentage of people who claim to be atheists, sadly, that number is growing. While not atheists, there are an abundance of people who consider themselves agnostic. That means they just cannot figure it all out. Most of them want to believe that they are the god of their own lives, but since they have been hard-wired in creation that there is a God, they sense a conflict in their souls.

As we can see in Genesis, God spoke to Noah many years before the flood, and told Noah to make a boat, for it was going to rain. "Rain, what is that," Noah likely asked, as up to that time, God watered the plants upward, from the springs of the earth. Even in those days not so long after Adam had strolled in the Garden of Eden, people were living their lives as if God did not exist, did not live. Yet by looking at the ages of the first generations, when they died and when they had sons, we find that Lamech, the father of Noah, was 56 when Adam died, nine generations later! Though there were many people alive on the earth around the time of the Flood, there was a survivor whose father knew the first man, a survivor whose father knew a man who walked and talked with God!

When reading the passage in Deuteronomy discussing the Ten Commandments, we can see that the Jews in the wilderness did not see God, but they certainly heard His voice. That voice scared them.

[4] The LORD talked with you face to face in the mount out of the midst of the fire, [5] (I stood between the LORD and you at that time, to shew you the word of the LORD: for ye were afraid by reason of the fire, and went not up into the mount;) saying,
Deuteronomy 5:4-5 (NKJV)

[23] And it came to pass, when ye heard the voice out of the midst of the darkness, (for the mountain did burn with fire,) that ye came near unto me, *even* all the heads of your tribes, and your elders; [24] And ye said, Behold, the LORD our God hath shewed us his glory and his greatness, and we have heard his voice out of the midst of the fire: we have seen this day that God doth talk with man, and he liveth. [25] Now therefore why should we die? for this great fire will consume us: if we hear the voice of the LORD our God any more, then we shall die.
Deuteronomy 5:23-25 (KJV)

Verse 24 above tells us that God talks with man and He lives! He wants to talk to each of us now. Each of us has the same 24 hours a day to get it all done. We are busier than we should be and unfortunately, do not always put that relationship with the Living God as the priority of our lives.

A time management consultant met with a college class. He pulled out a wide-mouthed jar and a handful of large rocks. After fitting all the large rocks in the jar that he could, he asked the class, "Is the jar full?" One student responded, "Yes." The consultant pulled out some pebbles and poured them into the jar, having demonstrated that the jar was not full. "Is it full now," he asked. Unsure, no one answered, and he pulled out sand and poured it into the jar, then water to the point where finally, the jar was full. "What's the lesson," he asked. The same young man who had answered the original question incorrectly, once again piped in, "You can fit more things in than you think you can." "I am sorry," said the consultant, "but that is not the lesson at all. The lesson is that you all have the same amount of room in your jars and you have to put in the big rocks first."

We as Christians serve the One God, the Living God. Our faith is built on the Rock of our salvation, Jesus Christ. He is the biggest Rock, which we need to fit in first. Why do we spend so much time spinning our wheels, worrying about finances, jobs, careers, hobbies, vacations, possessions, even television…the list goes on and on. This life is a proving ground, in which we are called to find that relationship with God! We cannot have closeness in any relationship without much time spent with the other! God gives us an assignment to teach our children and grandchildren about Him. That is our next biggest rock. Is God the priority of our lives? Should He be? Just like Adam, we can walk with God and talk with God any time we desire, as He lives in each of us. He created us just so He could share His love with us, and most of the time, we give Him the moments that are left over at the end of the day…if we even give Him that.

Spend some time with the Lord today! He so wants us to share time with Him! Though we cannot see His face, we can feel His presence!

June 8: Is the honey worth the sting?

If a man reaches into a beehive, he may find some honey, but also is likely to acquire a sting. Afterwards, he will be able to make the judgment of whether or not the sweetness of the honeycomb was worth the pain of the sting. Is the glass half empty or half full? Interestingly, bees give their lives to protect that hive and that honeycomb, as the female honeybee tears her abdomen in order to deposit the stinger. Rarely will that bee choose to sting when not protecting the hive.

There are many life lessons in that example. As Christians, we should be optimists, as regardless of life's difficulties, the sweetness of our blessed hope in Jesus Christ overrides any trial or tribulation that we must endure while on this earth. In fact, any sting that Satan has to offer is comparatively nothing.

^{55}"O Death, where is your sting?
O Hades, where is your victory?"
^{56} The sting of death is sin, and the strength of sin is the law.
^{57} But thanks be to God, who gives us the victory through our Lord Jesus Christ.
1 Corinthians 15:55-57 (NKJV)

We need not fear Satan's knockout punch as believers. He can attempt to stumble us, and in so doing, damage our testimonies for the Lord. God's enemy also may kill us, but to do that, God must both allow and plan that timely demise. But at the worst, it is physical death, not spiritual death. It is a simple blink of the eyes when we transition from present with the body to present with the Lord! Many people have a strong fear of death, but as believers, death has no sting! That death momentarily could be painful, but it pales in comparison to life in Jesus! "Foxe's Book of Martyrs" describes the deaths of some of God's followers. What is most apparent is that God miraculously helped those martyrs in the process, just as He remained with Stephen in Acts 7:59.

Life upon this earth can be difficult, yet regardless how much pain exists, God's sweetness will override any bitterness!

A satisfied soul loathes the honeycomb,
But to a hungry soul every bitter thing *is* sweet.

Proverbs 27:7 (NKJV)

God's promises can carry us through the greatest difficulty. Taste the sweetness of His Word. Honey lasts indefinitely in a sealed container. We are sealed by the Holy Spirit, who teaches us all things. How long will God's words last in us?

[103] **How sweet are Your words to my taste,**
Sweeter **than honey to my mouth!**
[104] **Through Your precepts I get understanding;**
Therefore I hate every false way.
Psalm 119:103-104 (NKJV)

June 9: Little miracles!

When the Jews fled Egypt, feverishly pursued by Pharaoh's soldiers, God remained between the two forces as a pillar of cloud by day and a pillar of fire by night. As the Jews approached the Red Sea, God rolled back the waters with the hand of Moses and the Jews crossed the sea on dry land. When the Jews had reached the other side safely, Pharaoh's army was walking on the same miraculous path that should be covered in salt water. Moments later it was, as the waves came crashing down, destroying every last soldier. At the bottom of the Red Sea, chariot wheels thousands of years old still sit, a testament to the Lord's miraculous hand. A short time later, with Moses on Mount Horeb receiving the 10 Commandments from God, those same Jews who had seen two of the Lord's most ostentatious miracles were creating a golden calf to worship! How can we forget His miracles so quickly?

Most if not all of us who walk with the Lord can look back and see similar behavior in our own lives, when God delivered us yet again with a miracle, and shortly after, we once again wallowed in sin. Just as a pig loves to wallow in mud, our desperately wicked hearts continue to be drawn to sin.

As a dog returns to his own vomit,
So **a fool repeats his folly.**

Proverbs 26:11 (NKJV)

The verse from Proverbs is a graphic, yet representative example of our relationship with sin. Sin does not taste good, and there certainly is not any nutritional value in it. As much as it hurts us, we find ourselves in that position often. Yet our God of mercy and grace keeps forgiving us. That is a miracle in itself! It is difficult to understand that kind of unconditional love, as it is so far removed from the kind of love we typically have for each other.

[2]"I have loved you," says the LORD.
"Yet you say, 'In what way have You loved us?'
Was not Esau Jacob's brother?"
Says the LORD.
"Yet Jacob I have loved;
[3]But Esau I have hated,
And laid waste his mountains and his heritage
For the jackals of the wilderness."
Malachi 1:2-3 (NKJV)

God chose us before the foundations of the earth. He did not choose us for what we would accomplish for Him. He could have chosen anyone for any task, or simply, done the task Himself. He chose us for His reasons. If we are His, we have won the lottery! Yet it does not end there. Not only are we forgiven. Not only do we get to spend eternity with Jesus. Not only is He living inside of us even now. Yet He continues to perform miracles in our lives every single day. Seemingly small miracles can have greater impacts than the larger miracles. Think of the mobs that witnessed the healings of Jesus, and then remember how few people were following Jesus at the time of His crucifixion. This testifies to the fickle nature of humans. Signs and wonders point to the power of the Lord, but the sweetest time is when He does something special, personal and small. It is a reminder of how intricately He is woven into our lives. It also tells us how well He knows us and how much He loves us.

¹O LORD, You have searched me and known *me*.
²You know my sitting down and my rising up;
You understand my thought afar off.
³You comprehend my path and my lying down,
And are acquainted with all my ways.
⁴For *there is* not a word on my tongue,
But behold, O LORD, You know it altogether.
⁵You have hedged me behind and before,
And laid Your hand upon me.
⁶*Such* knowledge *is* too wonderful for me;
It is high, I cannot *attain* it.
⁷Where can I go from Your Spirit?
Or where can I flee from Your presence?
⁸If I ascend into heaven, You *are* there;
If I make my bed in hell, behold, You *are there*.
⁹*If* I take the wings of the morning,
And dwell in the uttermost parts of the sea,
¹⁰Even there Your hand shall lead me,
And Your right hand shall hold me.
¹¹If I say, "Surely the darkness shall fall on me,"
Even the night shall be light about me;
¹²Indeed, the darkness shall not hide from You,
But the night shines as the day;
The darkness and the light *are* both alike *to You*.
¹³For You formed my inward parts;
You covered me in my mother's womb.
¹⁴I will praise You, for I am fearfully *and* wonderfully made;
Marvelous are Your works,
And *that* my soul knows very well.
¹⁵My frame was not hidden from You,
When I was made in secret,
And skillfully wrought in the lowest parts of the earth.
¹⁶Your eyes saw my substance, being yet unformed.
And in Your book they all were written,
The days fashioned for me,
When *as yet there were* none of them.
¹⁷How precious also are Your thoughts to me, O God!
How great is the sum of them!

¹⁸ *If* I should count them, they would be more in number than the sand;
When I awake, I am still with You.
¹⁹ Oh, that You would slay the wicked, O God!
Depart from me, therefore, you bloodthirsty men.
²⁰ For they speak against You wickedly;
Your enemies take *Your name* in vain.
²¹ Do I not hate them, O LORD, who hate You?
And do I not loathe those who rise up against You?
²² I hate them with perfect hatred;
I count them my enemies.
²³ Search me, O God, and know my heart;
Try me, and know my anxieties;
²⁴ And see if *there is any* wicked way in me,
And lead me in the way everlasting.
Psalm 139:1-24 (NKJV)

We have never been loved like this before! Truly, what do we have to fear?

June 10: Are you thirsty?

Living in the desert changes our frame of mind in reference to heat, especially with days when the temperature soars above 120 degrees. Even with dry heat, most would not choose to live in an oven. It is difficult to remain hydrated, as heat makes us thirsty.

When the Jews were wandering in the wilderness, the Lord supplied every need, just as He does with us. Having been to Jordan, it is easy to picture the desolate, red sand in every direction. Somehow, when we see desert, we automatically become thirstier. Even though the Lord was supplying manna for them to eat on a daily basis, the Jews still struggled with their trust of the Lord.

¹ Then all the congregation of the children of Israel set out on their journey from the Wilderness of Sin, according to the commandment of the LORD, and camped in Rephidim; but *there was* no water for the people to drink. ² Therefore the

people contended with Moses, and said, "Give us water, that we may drink."
So Moses said to them, "Why do you contend with me? Why do you tempt the LORD?"
³ And the people thirsted there for water, and the people complained against Moses, and said, "Why *is* it you have brought us up out of Egypt, to kill us and our children and our livestock with thirst?"
⁴ So Moses cried out to the LORD, saying, "What shall I do with this people? They are almost ready to stone me!"
⁵ And the LORD said to Moses, "Go on before the people, and take with you some of the elders of Israel. Also take in your hand your rod with which you struck the river, and go. ⁶ Behold, I will stand before you there on the rock in Horeb; and you shall strike the rock, and water will come out of it, that the people may drink."
Exodus 17:1-6 (NKJV)

In the New Testament, we see the bigger picture with the revelation of this event. Jesus is the Living Water and the Rock of our salvation. Without the Rock being struck, with the crucifixion of Jesus at Calvary, we would not have eternal life. Through His death, our life has meaning. Without Him, our souls thirst for the Living God. Yet even with Him, we endure dry spells when we struggle to hear His voice. At those times, we should make sure that we are giving Him the opportunities to speak to us! Are we attending church services? Are we reading His Word? We are not camels, able to store water up to be used when we are thirsty. Instead, we need to eat daily and drink daily.

O God, You *are* my God;
Early will I seek You;
My soul thirsts for You;
My flesh longs for You
In a dry and thirsty land
Where there is no water.
Psalm 63:1 (NKJV)

Remember, seven days without Jesus makes one weak!

June 11: Tears of a Savior

One of the most powerful scenes in "The Passion of the Christ" occurs at the moment when Jesus surrenders His Spirit and dies. At that instant, a great teardrop falls from heaven and lands as a giant drop of rain. When the rain makes contact with the earth, an earthquake splits the temple veil and opens our access into the throne room of the Father. When considering the emotions of God, we know that He feels joy, anger and sadness, yet His emotions are certainly different than our own. When we feel sadness, we are experiencing the moment without knowledge of the future. On the other hand, God sees the past, the present and the future. Yet when Jesus came to earth as a man, He experienced all of the emotions that we experience.

Isaiah tells us:

He is despised and rejected by men,
A Man of sorrows and acquainted with grief.
Isaiah 53:3 (NKJV)

This verse points prophetically to the tears of our Lord. In Luke, we see the tears of Jesus due to that rejection:

[41] Now as He drew near, He saw the city and wept over it, [42] saying, "If you had known, even you, especially in this your day, the things *that make* for your peace! But now they are hidden from your eyes. [43] For days will come upon you when your enemies will build an embankment around you, surround you and close you in on every side, [44] and level you, and your children within you, to the ground; and they will not leave in you one stone upon another, because you did not know the time of your visitation."
Luke 19:41-44 (NKJV)

This event occurred on Palm Sunday, soon after Jesus was honored as King. He rode on the colt of a donkey from the

Mount of Olives toward the Garden of Gethsemane, fulfilling Zechariah 9:9. It is a beautiful view from that road of the holy city of Jerusalem, and looking upon that city, Jesus began to weep. What made Jesus cry? The people He came to save did not see His love! He loved them so much that He came to die for them, but they blindly looked away. Even those aware of the Old Testament prophecies were looking for a conquering warrior rather than a suffering servant. Jesus also saw their future, for in A.D. 70, the Romans would surround God's city and level it, casting the Jews to the four corners of the earth. Because they did not see Him, their eyes were blinded for future generations, as well. Those blinders remain for the most part, though God does allow some Jews to see Jesus now. We know that in the Great Tribulation, He will open their eyes. Yet there was another prophetic event that the words of Isaiah applied to, when Lazarus died:

[35] **Jesus wept.** [36] **Then the Jews said, "See how He loved him!"** [37] **And some of them said, "Could not this Man, who opened the eyes of the blind, also have kept this man from dying?"** [38] **Then Jesus, again groaning in Himself, came to the tomb. It was a cave, and a stone lay against it.** [39] **Jesus said, "Take away the stone."**
Martha, the sister of him who was dead, said to Him, "Lord, by this time there is a stench, for he has been *dead* four days."
[40] **Jesus said to her, "Did I not say to you that if you would believe you would see the glory of God?"** [41] **Then they took away the stone *from the place* where the dead man was lying. And Jesus lifted up *His* eyes and said, "Father, I thank You that You have heard Me.** [42] **And I know that You always hear Me, but because of the people who are standing by I said *this*, that they may believe that You sent Me."** [43] **Now when He had said these things, He cried with a loud voice, "Lazarus, come forth!"** [44] **And he who had died came out bound hand and foot with graveclothes, and his face was wrapped with a cloth. Jesus said to them, "Loose him, and let him go."**
John 11:35-44 (NKJV)

This section begins with the shortest verse in the Bible, and one of the most powerful. **Jesus wept**. If Jesus knew that He was going to resurrect Lazarus momentarily, why did He cry? There are many answers to that question. Part of it has to do with what love really is. Love is filled with compassion and empathy, which is the ability to feel someone else's pain. Jesus certainly felt the pain of the sisters of Lazarus, who were His friends. Additionally, remember that this was before the death of Jesus. We are told of another Lazarus, a beggar who died, and then went to Abraham's Bosom (Luke 16:20-31). At that time, all the dead went to *Gehenna*, which had a large chasm separating those bound for heaven and those bound for eternal damnation. It was not a pleasant place, and Lazarus was there after he died. After His death on the cross, Jesus went to the same place, and took the righteous souls with Him to heaven! Though Jesus was 100% God when He walked on the earth, He was also 100% man! Lazarus had been dead four days, and according to the Scriptures, he stunk!

How does our sin smell? Sometimes, we seem to focus on the stench of the sin of others rather than our own sin. This is part of the human condition, as with the gift of smell, we grow accustomed to our own assault of the olfactory senses, and are much more offended at the offensive odors we are not so accustomed to! But the truth is, each of us are stinkers. Just as He did with Lazarus, Jesus took the dead, stinking man in each of us as Christians and brought us back to life. In that moment, He gave us the everlasting gift of life with Him! The stench is gone, not because we do not continue to sin, but because He forgave us and took the punishment in our places.

It should humble us to know that our Savior cried for us in our trespasses. The God who created all loves us so much that He cries for us! He hears each of our tears, especially, the tears of contrition. Remember, not all of our tears come from a contrite heart. Esau cried to his father Isaac when he lost his birthright in Genesis 27:38. Additionally, Judas wept bitterly before hanging himself.

For godly sorrow produces repentance *leading* to salvation, not to be regretted; but the sorrow of the world produces death.
2 Corinthians 7:10 (NKJV)

Sorrow can be worldly sorrow when things do not work out the way we want them to. That sorrow is not repentance, it is feeling sorry for ourselves. It would be a true step of growth if we would allow our sin to break our hearts, just as it breaks God's heart! When we get to that point, Jesus will cry out to us, "Come forth!"

June 12: Put on the brakes!

Hills certainly are completely different, whether we are ascending or descending. Though a drive uphill challenges the power of an engine, a drive downhill challenges the power of our brakes. We should replace brake pads often, as stopping power is paramount to daily safety.

We also need stopping power in our Christian walks. Without the power of the Holy Spirit, we simply do not have the power to turn away from sin. Once that truck begins to roll down the hill, without brakes, it will not come to a stop until it runs into a solid object. As the saying goes, something has got to give! Interestingly, when we have a locomotive on a train track pulling 50 cars, it takes just as much power for the engine to pull those cars uphill as it takes for the engine to bring all of those cars to a stop. The key word is momentum!

Can we have momentum in our Christian walks? Certainly! Every aspect of life is habit forming. Sometimes, we focus more on bad habits than good habits. Yet it is not only nicotine, drugs and alcohol that cause addictive responses in us. For example, if we get accustomed to getting up early on Sundays to attend church services, we will miss that service when we do not attend. One of the best habits that we can create is to surround ourselves with godly people:

Do not be deceived: "Evil company corrupts good habits."
1 Corinthians 15:33 (NKJV)

Additionally, the Bible says:

Learn to do good;
Seek justice,
Rebuke the oppressor;
Defend the fatherless,
Plead for the widow.
Isaiah 1:17 (NKJV)

When we commit our lives to the Lord, He meets us where we are. That does not mean that He perfects us on the spot. Some people demonstrate noticeable about-faces in their lives, while others seem to struggle through the muck and mire. What is the difference? It has to do with brokenness. When we truly come to the end of ourselves and see that our way was a complete failure, then and only then are we willing to do it God's way. Each step forward is a part of that learning curve. God knows us all so well. After all, He made us exactly the way we are! We learn the best from positive reinforcement rather than negative reinforcement. When we do something God's way, it feels good inside!

"Learn to do good." God realizes that we have lived many years as sinners. Our habits are certainly not in doing it His way. Yet He does not tell us to never make a mistake! If we do something right once, it will become easier the next time. Part of our walk with Him is learning new habits. When we err and do it the old way, He reminds us that is not the way He intended. He reminds us softly at first, but it can get louder or more painful if we ignore Him.

[1] I beseech you therefore, brethren, by the mercies of God, that you present your bodies a living sacrifice, holy, acceptable to God, *which is* your reasonable service. [2] And do not be conformed to this world, but be transformed by the

renewing of your mind, that you may prove what *is* that good and acceptable and perfect will of God.
Romans 12:1-2 (NKJV)

Following God's Law is not an unreasonable request. In fact, Paul writes that it is our reasonable service. Behavior changes begin with changes in attitude. It always begins in the mind. Knowing that we are going to need brakes is the first step of stopping! That is the knowledge that we need a Savior in a broken and dying world. The next stage is learning how to apply those brakes, which is learning to rely on the Holy Spirit to power our walks. As we grow in the Lord, we should not be surprised if Satan's attack gets stronger. The closer to the Lord we walk, the more the evil one will despise us. But even in those difficulties, we can look back and see the number of times the Lord has delivered us in the past. He never will leave us or forsake us, even when we seem to be barreling down the hill without brakes!

June 13: Who provides for our families?

Not so many generations ago, the man of the house was the only wage earner. Typically, the woman of the house remained at home, taking care of the children and the household. In the United States, this began to change during World War I. With their husbands oversees, many women had to work outside the home to make ends meet for their families, and the war effort created many jobs in manufacturing. The number of women in the workplace has continued to increase, and consequently, motherhood has become less of a priority. Currently, with a rise in the cost of living, providing for a family seems to require two salaries, rather than one. In 2010, for the first time women outnumbered men in the U.S. workforce!

All of these factors have greatly increased the pressure on a new father, who sees the extra mouth to feed with accelerated challenges. Not only are the daily costs greater, but the potential for future health care and education adds to that burden. As Christians, we should be aware of these challenges but should not let them overwhelm us, in any way. With unemployment increasing around the globe, sometimes we need to remember, who is the real provider?

In Genesis, God tells Abraham to take Isaac to Mt. Moriah and offer his son as a burnt offering. This may seem like a strange request, but the Lord always has ample reasons. Abraham was a man of faith and knew that God already had promised him that He would multiply the descendants of Isaac exceedingly. Having already performed a miracle by having the 100-year-old Abraham father a child with the 90-year old Sarah, Abraham knew that God would perform another miracle here. With prior knowledge of God's loving hand, Abraham obeyed. At the last moment, God provided a substitute sacrifice:

[13] Then Abraham lifted his eyes and looked, and there behind *him was* a ram caught in a thicket by its horns. So Abraham went and took the ram, and offered it up for a burnt offering instead of his son. [14] And Abraham called the name of the place, The-LORD-Will-Provide; as it is said *to* this day, "In the Mount of the LORD it shall be provided."
Genesis 22:13-14 (NKJV)

Here, we see one of the redemptive names of God in the Old Testament, *Jehovah-jireh*. The event carried huge, prophetic significance for it pointed to another Father who would sacrifice His Son on the same spot. God's Holy City of Jerusalem is known for its ridge system, with Mt. Moriah, Mt. Zion and the Mount of Olives being the three highest peaks. Jesus was crucified outside the city, on Mt. Moriah. Notice that in the Genesis account, Isaac carried the wood up the mountain, just as Jesus carried His own cross. Instead of Isaac, a ram (a male lamb) was killed. Years later on Calvary, the Lamb of God would die and take away the sins of the world. Most depict Isaac as a young lad, but likely, he was 33-years-old, the same age as Jesus when our Lord endured the cross.

If God provided a sacrifice for His servant Abraham, it is also a simple task for Him to supply the needs of His people, in regards to food, shelter, medical expenses and any other potential requirement. Though we are called to work and pay for our food through the "sweat of our face" according to Genesis 3:19, we should not forget who the Great Provider really is! If we feel like our backs are up against the wall, we should know that the God who created us loves us so much that He cares for our every need. Just as He did with Job, sometimes the Lord puts us in extremely difficult circumstances to draw us closer to Him. If we are struggling, we should focus on the fact that He is with us, if we only will turn to Him.

⁸ Draw near to God and He will draw near to you. Cleanse *your* hands, *you* sinners; and purify *your* hearts, *you* double-minded. ⁹ Lament and mourn and weep! Let your laughter be turned to mourning and *your* joy to gloom. ¹⁰ Humble yourselves in the sight of the Lord, and He will lift you up. James 4:8-10 (NKJV)

June 14: Pray without ceasing!

Regardless of our political affiliation, if given the opportunity to speak personally with the President of the United States, we would be excited. Most likely, we would tell all of our friends about the experience. Even if we disagree with the President's policies, we could use that time to share with him the errors that he is making. In this nation's history, there only have been 44 presidents. As powerful as the American president is in the world, there is only one God, and He appointed all of the presidents and kings. Should we not find it even more amazing that we get to speak with God?

Prayer is such an interesting gift. When Jesus died, being our High Priest according to Hebrews, the temple veil split. In the Old Testament days of the tabernacle and the sacrificial system, the high priest was able to enter the Holy of Holies once a year. The Holy of Holies, the dwelling place of God on earth, was behind the veil, with man allowed to enter the other places of the tabernacle. That partition symbolized man's separation from God because of sin. Because Jesus was punished for our sins and His innocent blood was shed instead of ours, it opened our access into the throne room of God, as long as we ask for His forgiveness. At any moment, we can speak to the One who created us through the gift of prayer. It is an amazing way to deal with stress, anger and frustration.

[16] Confess *your* trespasses to one another, and pray for one another, that you may be healed. The effective, fervent prayer of a righteous man avails much. [17] Elijah was a man with a nature like ours, and he prayed earnestly that it would not rain; and it did not rain on the land for three years and six months. [18] And he prayed again, and the heaven gave rain, and the earth produced its fruit.
James 5:16-18 (NKJV)

It is interesting who Paul chose as an example of a righteous man offering effective prayers. Elijah lived at a time when the Jews certainly were not following God's Laws or hearing His voice. Instead, the country was being controlled by Ahab, Jezebel and their 850 false prophets. The prayer of Elijah created a three and a half year drought on the nation. Yet the most important part of that prayer to notice is that it created hardship for Elijah, as well. This was not a prayer for wealth, ease of passage or physical healing. It was a prayer of sacrifice! Elijah wanted the Jews to return to the Lord with fervor, and knew that they would not look up until they had been humbled. With no rain, the food would not be plentiful. Remember, this was not like today when we have thousands of bottles of water on every shelf. Drinking water came from underwater springs and rivers. Rain water was a part of that supply. Elijah prayed for personal hunger and thirst, along with God's saving hand!

Are we willing to suffer for the salvation of others as Elijah was? Jesus died for us to have the gift of prayer. Do we take it for granted? When we are angry, instead of lashing out, we are to pray. When we are frustrated, instead of worrying, we are to pray. When we are sick, instead of struggling, we are to pray. That does not mean that God will take away the obstacles, but He will carry us through them. We know that prayer does not change God's heart, but it brings our hearts into alignment with His. That is why we pray for His will to be done. Once we are able to have peace in the midst of turmoil, we are closer to His will. Yet the bulk of our prayer time should be spent praying for others. Jesus gave us a great example of that in John 17, though He was about to endure the cross. He mentioned His own needs, and then spent the bulk of His time praying for His disciples and all of the believers yet to come.

If there is a box under the Christmas tree with our name on it, we cannot get the benefit of the gift without opening it. In the same manner, we do not get the benefit of the gift of prayer without using it. God gave the gift because He wants to hear the desires of our hearts!

Yet you do not have because you do not ask.
James 4:3 (NKJV)

June 15: Peace, be still!

Looking at the ocean reminds us of the repetitious nature of waves. No matter what, after one wave crashes to the shore, within moments, another wave follows. Even the seemingly small waves generate so much power. Power does not always come from a burst of energy; it also can come from slow, continuous motion. We can picture the way a river flows downstream, as well. It does not matter how quickly the water is flowing. It can carry objects great distances and in a similar fashion, can change what appears to be a solid object forever. Rocks are shaped into a smooth, glass-like finishes with that continuous flow.

The world we live in seems to have waves of sin, continuously crashing around us. Sadly, that continuous sin can shape us in a way we did not desire and carry us into places we did not envision going. We know that God gave Satan the dominion over this earth for the time being, and with the evil one in charge, our world is becoming more sinful by the day.

**"When the waves of death surrounded me,
The floods of ungodliness made me afraid.
2 Samuel 22:5 (NKJV)**

Even though we may feel that we are under constant attack, God can say, **"Peace, be still,"** and remove those obstacles from our paths, if He so chooses. Additionally, He can leave those obstacles to test us, and draw us closer to Him!

**You rule the raging of the sea;
When its waves rise, You still them.
Psalm 89:9 (NKJV)**

Yet as much as the waves of sin continue, those of us who follow Jesus are covered by the waves of His mercy. Nothing is more constant than God! Even when we are faithless, He is faithful. He is faithful to His own promises, and He has promised to never leave us or forsake us. We can demonstrate our love by following His commandments. Are we truly following God, or are we living with the Burger King philosophy (Have it your way)?

**Oh, that you had heeded My commandments!
Then your peace would have been like a river,
And your righteousness like the waves of the sea.
Isaiah 48:18 (NKJV)**

When we are riding on top of a wave, there is peace, through His righteousness. Yet when we are in the direct, line-of-fire of that wave, there is destruction. We should want to walk on the waves as Peter did. There is only one way to do that and it is to walk beside Jesus, not ahead of Him or behind Him, but right with Him!

**He alone spreads out the heavens,
And treads on the waves of the sea;
Job 9:8 (NKJV)**

**But let him ask in faith, with no doubting, for he who doubts is like a wave of the sea driven and tossed by the wind.
James 1:6 (NKJV)**

June 16: How long have we suffered?

Driving in daily, Southern California traffic tests anyone's patience. Half of the people are in the left lane, going slower than the speed limit and the other half are dangerously swerving in and out of traffic, trying to beat the system. It seems that everyone has much more to do than the prescribed amount of activities in a 24-hour day. Most people are running late, rushing in and rushing out. It seems that all the advancements in technology created to save us time are causing the opposite effect. We desperately need patience to get through each day. Patience is closely related to another attribute.

One of the fruits of the Spirit is longsuffering, *makrothymia* in Greek and *erekh appayim* in Hebrew. The Hebrew word reveals the deeper meaning, as the literal translation of that phrase is "long of nose" or "long of breathing." When angry, most people breathe quickly through their nostrils, as if snorting. Yet the Lord is described as "slow to anger," in Nehemiah 9:17, Psalm 103:8, Psalm 145:8, Joel 2:13 and Nahum 1:3. With His ability to wipe us out in a moment without any effort at all, coupled with our propensity to mess up, His longsuffering may be the attribute of God we should be most thankful for!

As Christians, we are to emulate our Creator.

**But those who wait on the LORD
Shall renew *their* strength;
They shall mount up with wings like eagles,
They shall run and not be weary,
They shall walk and not faint.
 Isaiah 40:31 (NKJV)**

Waiting on the Lord involves walking beside Him, not running ahead of Him. There are times when we pray about an issue, and when we do not hear an immediate answer from God, decide to step out in faith. Yet God's timing is so different from ours, with a thousand years being like a day and a day being like a thousand years in His sight, according to Psalm 90:4.

Be still, and know that I *am* **God;**
I will be exalted among the nations,
I will be exalted in the earth!
Psalm 46:10 (NKJV)

Remember playing "frozen statues" as a kid? One person would spin others around and let go, and then yell, "Freeze." Those being spun would lock themselves rigidly into that random pose of a statue. There are times when God is telling us to freeze. How long do we need to be still? Until He answers, for God opens the doors and closes them. We should wait on Him patiently and know that His longsuffering has given us the greatest gift.

…and consider *that* **the longsuffering of our Lord** *is* **salvation…**
2 Peter 3:15 (NKJV)

Are we willing to suffer for the salvation of others?

He who is **slow to anger** *is* **better than the mighty,**
And he who rules his spirit than he who takes a city.
Proverbs 16:32 (NKJV)

June 17: Happy Father's Day!

According to some sources, 2010 was the 100th anniversary of the day we began to honor fathers in this country, though 54 other countries also celebrate this day on the third Sunday in June each year. To God, every day is Father's Day, from both a heavenly and earthly perspective.

Honor your father and your mother, that your days may be long upon the land which the LORD your God is giving you.

Exodus 20:12 (NKJV)

In the Lord's fifth commandment, we see the first of His Laws that deals with man's relationship with man, rather than with man's relationship with God. Additionally, it is the first commandment that offers an additional blessing for following it. If we honor our fathers and mothers, we will live more than the prescribed time. Yet it is faulty logic to think that anyone who lives a long time must have honored their parents! Somehow, most of us put our own spin on that simple verse, thinking that we only need to honor our parents if they have earned it, or in our eyes, if they deserve that honor. On the contrary, God does not put any spin on that commandment. Simply by the fact that God has chosen our earthly parents, we are to honor them!

God places each of us in families, and He chose the perfect place for us all. Certainly, there are times when we would question that, as families can bring much frustration and sadness to our lives. Yet that can be part of the brokenness that God uses to bring us to Him! It is much easier to understand how our heavenly Father loves us when given the example of our earthly father, at least most of the time. Once our relationship with the heavenly Father is on solid ground, we begin to understand the relationship with our earthly fathers.

We should continue to pray for growing our relationships with our earthly fathers and heavenly Father. It is never too late to repair either relationship and both are the most important we can have in our lives. Happy Father's Day!

To understand the deepest example of a Father's heart, we turn to Luke:

[11] Then He said: "A certain man had two sons. [12] And the younger of them said to *his* father, 'Father, give me the portion of goods that falls *to me.*' So he divided to them *his* livelihood. [13] And not many days after, the younger son gathered all together, journeyed to a far country, and there wasted his possessions with prodigal living. [14] But when he

had spent all, there arose a severe famine in that land, and he began to be in want. ¹⁵ Then he went and joined himself to a citizen of that country, and he sent him into his fields to feed swine. ¹⁶ And he would gladly have filled his stomach with the pods that the swine ate, and no one gave him *anything*.
¹⁷ "But when he came to himself, he said, 'How many of my father's hired servants have bread enough and to spare, and I perish with hunger! ¹⁸ I will arise and go to my father, and will say to him, "Father, I have sinned against heaven and before you, ¹⁹ and I am no longer worthy to be called your son. Make me like one of your hired servants." '
²⁰ "And he arose and came to his father. But when he was still a great way off, his father saw him and had compassion, and ran and fell on his neck and kissed him. ²¹ And the son said to him, 'Father, I have sinned against heaven and in your sight, and am no longer worthy to be called your son.'
²² "But the father said to his servants, 'Bring out the best robe and put *it* on him, and put a ring on his hand and sandals on *his* feet. ²³ And bring the fatted calf here and kill *it*, and let us eat and be merry; ²⁴ for this my son was dead and is alive again; he was lost and is found.' And they began to be merry.
Luke 15:11-24 (NKJV)

No matter what we have done, the Father is willing to welcome us into His arms. That is the heart of our Father, who sent His only Son to earth to die for our sins. Though the Father loves Jesus will all of His being, He wanted to show His love for us:

Yet it pleased the LORD to bruise Him;
He has put *Him* to grief.
When You make His soul an offering for sin,
He shall see *His* seed, He shall prolong *His* days,
And the pleasure of the LORD shall prosper in His hand.
Isaiah 53:10 (NKJV)

Happy Father's Day to our earthly fathers, who God appointed for each of us, and to our heavenly Father!

⁴Sing to God, sing praises to His name;
Extol Him who rides on the clouds,
By His name YAH,
And rejoice before Him.
⁵A father of the fatherless, a defender of widows,
Is God in His holy habitation.
⁶God sets the solitary in families;
He brings out those who are bound into prosperity;
But the rebellious dwell in a dry *land.*
Psalm 68:4-6 (NKJV)

June 18: Know your strengths and weaknesses!

Strategy in tennis is similar to playing chess on a moving chessboard. One of the interesting challenges involves hiding weaknesses while accentuating strengths. It comes down to the weakest link in the chain. With a world-class forehand and a high school level backhand, it will not take long to figure out where to hit the ball in order to win.

As Christians, we also have strengths and weaknesses to battle an opponent with a well-trained army. That army is trained to search for a way to defeat us, and in so doing, to damage our testimonies for the Lord. Yet unlike tennis, where we attempt to disguise our weaknesses, in our Christian walks we should hand those weaknesses over to Jesus.

⁷ And lest I should be exalted above measure by the abundance of the revelations, a thorn in the flesh was given to me, a messenger of Satan to buffet me, lest I be exalted above measure. ⁸ Concerning this thing I pleaded with the Lord three times that it might depart from me. ⁹ And He said to me, "My grace is sufficient for you, for My strength is made perfect in weakness." Therefore most gladly I will rather boast in my infirmities, that the power of Christ may rest upon me. ¹⁰ Therefore I take pleasure in infirmities, in reproaches, in needs, in persecutions, in distresses, for Christ's sake. For when I am weak, then I am strong.
2 Corinthians 12:7-10 (NKJV)

The Lord chose Paul to write a majority of the New Testament. Yet along with that great challenge and blessing was a "thorn in the flesh." Theologians have argued over what sin or issue caused Paul to suffer. Many opine that it had to do with a physical affliction, but God chose not to reveal what caused Paul to struggle. To me, that is so each of us can associate our own struggle with the one Paul endured. Each Christian understands what it is like to fail. In that failure, we not only let ourselves down, but feel as though we have failed the God who saved us. First, know there is nothing we can do that surprises God. He saved each Christian knowing each sin and mistake we ever would make. Most of our sins occur when our pride gets in the way. Instead of relying on Jesus, as we often do with our weaknesses, we fool ourselves into believing that we are strong enough to handle the demonic attacks alone.

Peter was a great example for us in that his attacks and failures came in his strengths, rather than in his weaknesses. Known as a courageous man, Peter was the only disciple to get out of the boat and attempt to walk on the water with Jesus. He sliced off the ear of Malchus, an assistant to Caiaphas, when the Jewish high priest came to arrest Jesus in the Garden of Gethsemane. When Jesus warned the disciples the night before His crucifixion that they would all be scattered, Peter bragged that he loved Jesus more than the others. Jesus told Peter that before the night was over, Peter would deny Jesus three times.

Sadly, in the hours to come, Peter's courage shrank into nothingness, even lying to a young girl about his association with Jesus. Why did Peter fail? Because when we brag, it is our own strengths and accomplishments that we are calling attention to. We need the full armor of God spoken of in Ephesians to fight in God's army. One of the obvious aspects of the parts of armor mentioned is that there is nothing covering the backside. God arms us for a face-to-face battle, not a retreat!

We are strongest in the areas that we hand over to the Lord. But God uses our weaknesses to demonstrate His power. We should take pleasure in our weaknesses, as they point to the grace and mercy of our God, who loves us! Whose battle is it?

Then all this assembly shall know that the LORD does not save with sword and spear; for the battle *is* the LORD's, and He will give you into our hands."
1 Samuel 17:47 (NKJV)

June 19: Obedience

Working with children gives us a better grasp of obedience. When drawing a proverbial line and instructing children not to cross that line, instantaneously, someone is going to test us. With the ensuing step nearing the line, the challenger keeps a watchful eye on the one in charge to see if they will ignore the challenge or react as promised. Additionally, bystanders focus keenly on the situation to glean information for their future challenges to authority. The initial reaction will set the tone instantly. Whether or not we choose to acknowledge it, all of us do better once we know the rules.

Though this resembles our relationships with God, there is a major difference. Unlike us, when God draws a line, He will not threaten punishment or ramification and then choose to forget or ignore what he said. In human relationships, we are told to choose our battles, as sometimes those battles are simply not worth it. Yet God cannot change; nor should He, as He is perfect. So when God gives us instructions or commandments, they are based on His perfect knowledge of what is best for us. If an atheist followed the commandments of the Lord, even his life would benefit from that obedience.

Obedience has been defined as carrying out the word and will of another person, particularly, the Word and will of God. Henry Ward Beecher said, "True obedience is true freedom."

So Samuel said:
"Has the LORD *as great* delight in burnt offerings and sacrifices,

As in obeying the voice of the LORD?
Behold, to obey is better than sacrifice,
And to heed than the fat of rams.
1 Samuel 15:22 (NKJV)

God's greatest desire for us is our obedience, as it is a demonstration of our love for Him. Jesus said, if you love Me, obey My commandments (John 14:15). One of the ways that God demonstrates His love for us is through His discipline. If He simply ignored our failures and sins, it would reflect that He did not desire for us to improve, and in so doing, draw closer to Him and His ways.

[5] **And you have forgotten the exhortation which speaks to you as to sons:**
"My son, do not despise the chastening of the LORD,
Nor be discouraged when you are rebuked by Him;
[6] *For whom the LORD loves He chastens,*
And scourges every son whom He receives."
[7] **If you endure chastening, God deals with you as with sons; for what son is there whom a father does not chasten?** [8] **But if you are without chastening, of which all have become partakers, then you are illegitimate and not sons.** [9] **Furthermore, we have had human fathers who corrected** *us,* **and we paid** *them* **respect. Shall we not much more readily be in subjection to the Father of spirits and live?**
Hebrews 12:5-9 (NKJV)

Discipline is never easy to endure. It must have broken the heart of Moses to not get to enter into the Promised Land, because he disobeyed the Lord by striking the rock rather than speaking to it to produce water in the wilderness (Numbers 20:11). Yet when Moses brought the situation up to God, the Lord told Moses not to mention it again (Deuteronomy 3:26). Are there situations in our lives where we are choosing not to listen to the commandments of the Lord? All of us have problematic areas, whether it is pride, gossip, sexual immorality, deceitfulness or a variety of other sins. Though we continue to struggle with sin, the repetitious sins demonstrate an unwillingness to listen.

We know that the joy of the Lord is our strength and that one of the greatest gifts He has given His children is the peace that passes all understanding. If we are walking in disobedience, the joy and peace will evade us until we choose to obey Him. God provided us all with the rule book, called the Holy Bible. With 613 commandments in the Bible, we all know what He expects. He even sees our motives, so it does not make much sense to challenge Him. If we want to be happy, we should obey Him!

**"Behold, happy *is* the man whom God corrects;
Therefore do not despise the chastening of the Almighty.
Job 5:17 (NKJV)**

June 20: Intelligence

There have been many studies done demonstrating that more people of lower intelligence believe in God. One of those was completed by Danish professor Helmuth Nyborg, whose 2008 study showed that atheists scored 1.95 IQ points higher than agnostics, who in turn, scored 3.82 points higher than people with a belief in God, though with a liberal persuasion. Finally, the dogmatic folks who believe in a God along with a literal interpretation of the Bible scored lowest on the IQ test, another 5.89 points down the scale.

A common interpretation of those statistics states that people of a lower intelligence also have lower economic means, due to that intelligence. With increased financial hardships comes the need to have a belief in a time when those challenges will be gone. So in this interpretation, religion gives hope to the hopeless. Truthfully, religion does not give us anything, but relationship does. Without Jesus Christ, all of us are without hope. For those who now feel stupid, this is what God has to say:

[27] But God has chosen the foolish things of the world to put to shame the wise, and God has chosen the weak things of the world to put to shame the things which are mighty; [28] and the base things of the world and the things which are despised

God has chosen, and the things which are not, to bring to nothing the things that are, [29] that no flesh should glory in His presence.
1 Corinthians 1:27-29 (NKJV)

Many brilliant people carry a strong belief in God. Yet the Bible tells us to have the faith of a little child, and most little children are sweetly naïve. In comparison to the intelligence of God, even Albert Einstein would be naïve! God's existence is a simple fact, and often, adults have a more difficult time seeing simplicity, choosing instead to complicate it all. The acronym K.I.S.S. reminds us to keep it simple, stupid.

[18] For the wrath of God is revealed from heaven against all ungodliness and unrighteousness of men, who suppress the truth in unrighteousness, [19] because what may be known of God is manifest in them, for God has shown *it* to them. [20] For since the creation of the world His invisible *attributes* are clearly seen, being understood by the things that are made, *even* His eternal power and Godhead, so that they are without excuse, [21] because, although they knew God, they did not glorify *Him* as God, nor were thankful, but became futile in their thoughts, and their foolish hearts were darkened. [22] Professing to be wise, they became fools, [23] and changed the glory of the incorruptible God into an image made like corruptible man—and birds and four-footed animals and creeping things.
Romans 1:18-23 (NKJV)

Simply by seeing the intricacies of the universe, of the human body and of the balance of nature, we can see that there has to be a Creator. The next step is to find out that the Creator desires a relationship with each of His creations! Most atheists and agnostics choose to emphasize their own intelligence, as truthfully, they desire to be the god of their own world. If we want to be an elephant, that does not make us elephants, though, does it? Additionally, the people who believe in God but do not acknowledge Him are just as misguided, for if He is powerful enough to have created all that we can see, He is powerful enough to have men write His words in a book. In our youth, we think we know it all, but with age comes awareness of how little we actually know! Then it becomes a comfort that the God who knows all is in charge of our lives.

C.S. Lewis said, "I believe in Christianity as I believe that the sun has risen: not only because I see it but by it, I see everything else." What is the Bible's definition of foolish?

The fool has said in his heart, *"There is* no God."
They are corrupt,
They have done abominable works,
There is none who does good.
Psalm 14:1 (NKJV)

[16] All Scripture *is* given by inspiration of God, and *is* profitable for doctrine, for reproof, for correction, for instruction in righteousness, [17] that the man of God may be complete, thoroughly equipped for every good work.
2 Timothy 3:16-17 (NKJV)

June 21: What does it mean to be a good soldier?

Entrance into West Point, the Naval Academy and the Air Force Academy all require congressional appointments. But compared to the training, the rigid entrance requirements are nothing at the service academies. The best education in leadership comes from following a good leader. Good leaders make wise decisions based on changing conditions; good leaders never panic under pressure; good leaders work on the weaknesses of their subordinates, rather than focusing on a single strength. The leaders-to-be at the service academies witness a variety of leadership styles and are able to choose which style to emulate.

Although most of us never will experience warfare in the army representing our countries, all of us as believers are soldiers in a much more important war. God wants us to follow Him, and the more we emulate Him, the more He will use us in leadership roles. He has all of the best leadership qualities to emulate! To be soldiers in God's army, we need to forget about the cares of this world!

³ You therefore must endure hardship as a good soldier of Jesus Christ. ⁴ No one engaged in warfare entangles himself with the affairs of *this* life, that he may please him who enlisted him as a soldier. ⁵ And also if anyone competes in athletics, he is not crowned unless he competes according to the rules.
2 Timothy 2:3-5 (NKJV)

What an interesting battle it is for believers, who are fighting powers and principalities, the heavenly host of fallen angels, rather than flesh and blood. That battle wages all around us non-stop, and if we are not following orders from our Supreme Commander, will remain in a state of constant loss. God certainly has demonstrated to us through His Word and through His Son what it takes to be a soldier in His army. Rather than destroy the opposing forces through anger, we are to change them through God's love. What's the best way to win a war? Have all of them want to be on our side!

⁷ I have fought the good fight, I have finished the race, I have kept the faith. ⁸ Finally, there is laid up for me the crown of righteousness, which the Lord, the righteous Judge, will give to me on that Day, and not to me only but also to all who have loved His appearing.
2 Timothy 4:7-8 (NKJV)

Our Lord does not need us to further His Kingdom. It is not a numbers game with the winning side being the one with the most people on it. Instead, God desires for everyone to have the opportunity to accept Him or deny Him. He does not need us to fight, as He has the power to create or destroy with His breath! When a man enlists in the military, He is called to serve, and that is what God asks from each of us. We are to serve Him, serve our fellow believers and even serve our enemies.

⁴⁴ **And whoever of you desires to be first shall be slave of all.**
⁴⁵ **For even the Son of Man did not come to be served, but to serve, and to give His life a ransom for many."**
Mark 10:44-45 (NKJV)

This charge I commit to you, son Timothy, according to the prophecies previously made concerning you, that by them you may wage the good warfare,
1 Timothy 1:18 (NKJV)

June 22: Freedom

One of the most poignant moments of the movie "Braveheart" occurred when the main character, William Wallace, was being tortured. His captors gave him a chance to ease his own suffering by altering his rigid stance against them. Instead, he screamed, "Freedom," and that word and belief resonated throughout the crowd, with their amazement of his strength even in death. Though Wallace was beheaded for his beliefs, those beliefs were not forgotten.

Freedom is such an important word to Americans, who began this country because our founding fathers were not allowed to worship God in the freedom desired while in England. Sadly, freedom here has been strongly infused with political correctness, as we have lost sight of the reason that democracy carried such significance. What does the Bible say about freedom?

Stand fast therefore in the liberty by which Christ has made us free, and do not be entangled again with a yoke of bondage.
Galatians 5:1 (NKJV)

Most people look at the commandments and laws of the Bible as an infringement on their freedom. Yet in government, there is always a limit on freedom. Each government simply chooses which limits they will impose. In regards to limits, complete freedom is anarchy, with each person doing anything they want.

To understand this further, if we believe it is our right to kill another person, that conflicts the other person's right to live. When we are walking in sin, breaking God's commandments, we are as closely bound to those sins as a prisoner weighed down by a ball and chain. That ball and chain are the "yoke of bondage." To be free from that ball and chain does not mean that we have no limits. Instead, it means that we can move around without the weighted burden of our sin.

Each man after Adam was born into sin, with sin being our nature. Do we have to teach a child to lie or to be selfish? On the contrary, those actions come just as easily as breathing for the child. Being born into sin, each of us will continue to sin, even as Christians. Yet God's promise to us is that if we choose to honor Him and serve Him, He will make us free from the bondage of sin. Each time we sin as a believer, instead of being weighed down by that action, we receive God's forgiveness the moment we ask!

As Christians, it is no longer about us as individuals. We are surrounded by Christ! Additionally, we are free in Christ, free with Christ and free because of Christ. We have been redeemed by the blood of the Lamb! Redemption is a word difficult to understand for a non-believer, as they fail to see the importance of the sacrificial system. God, being perfect, cannot just ignore sin. He has to punish it and because one sin makes a man a sinner, we are all guilty and due His punishment. Yet when God sent His Son to live a perfect life and be the scapegoat for each of us, God put in place a system where we can be cleaned. Redemption means "purchased," and that is exactly what Jesus did. He purchased our dirty lives with His innocent blood. What a cost!

As Christians, that ball and chain no longer weighs us down. We have the freedom not to sin! When Jesus returned to heaven, He promised us the gift of the Holy Spirit to live inside each of us as believers. Each time we consider sinning, the Holy Spirit reminds us of our sins beforehand, during and afterwards. Being God, the Holy Spirit cannot ignore sin, either.

Therefore, if anyone is in Christ, he is a new creation; old things have passed away; behold, all things have become new.
2 Corinthians 5:17 (NKJV)

The greatest difficulty is walking as that new creation in Christ, and realizing that the old man is dead. Satan often reminds us of the pleasures involved in our old sinful lives, but smartly, he does not remind us of the brokenness caused by that sin. Having had many years to craft his lies, Satan does his job very well. Yet with God living in us, surrounded by Christ, how can we lose? Walk in the freedom He has given us! It cost Him so much! Once He has cut us loose from the "yoke of bondage," we should stay away from the sins that controlled us. Why do we desire to be broken when He wants us to be whole?

But if we walk in the light as He is in the light, we have fellowship with one another, and the blood of Jesus Christ His Son cleanses us from all sin.
1 John 1:7 (NKJV)

June 23: Pray without doubting!

Faith makes all things possible, but love makes all things easy, according to an anonymous quote. Jesus told His disciples that faith the size of a mustard seed is enough to move a mountain (Matthew 17:20), which would be a pretty creative way to make mountains out of mole hills!

[7] "Ask, and it will be given to you; seek, and you will find; knock, and it will be opened to you. [8] For everyone who asks receives, and he who seeks finds, and to him who knocks it will be opened. [9] Or what man is there among you who, if his son asks for bread, will give him a stone? [10] Or if he asks for a fish, will he give him a serpent? [11] If you then, being evil, know how to give good gifts to your children, how much more will your Father who is in heaven give good things to those who ask Him!

Matthew 7:7-11 (NKJV)

Where does faith come from? Many Christians answer that question by quoting the following verse:

[8] For by grace you have been saved through faith, and that not of yourselves; *it is* **the gift of God, [9] not of works, lest anyone should boast.**
Ephesians 2:8-9 (NKJV)

Yet the verse above in the proper context is not saying that faith is a gift from God. Salvation by grace is the gift of God! He saved us because of His grace, not because of anything we did or ever would do. As believers, we all have different degrees of faith and it is ever-changing, often based on the situation and our closeness to the Lord. That walk with Jesus is not on a flat, easy path. There are hills to climb, curves to maneuver and places where we even feel out of breath. Yet to believe without seeing is a true blessing (John 20:29). Romans 10:17 gives us a better understanding of faith and how it increases. Faith comes by hearing God's Word. The Bible is not an old book to place on a nightstand, where it will gather dust. Neither is it only the book our grandmothers read. The Bible is the living, breathing Word of God! It holds every answer to every situation in our lives. When discussing people's different interpretations of God's Word, one friend shockingly said that he wished there was not a Bible! It is not God's Word causing the problems, but man's difficulties in understanding, and that typically comes from deductive rather than inductive study. Deductive study is when a person already has a point of view and tries to prove that point when studying, rather than looking at the verses in context with an open mind, to see where God leads. When we see what the Lord has done in our lives individually and compare those actions to the promises He makes to us in His Word, that is where faith is affected. God never will leave us or forsake us, as He has demonstrated that faithfulness to our lives, through His Word.

[22] So Jesus answered and said to them, "Have faith in God. [23] For assuredly, I say to you, whoever says to this mountain, 'Be removed and be cast into the sea,' and does not doubt in his heart, but believes that those things he says will be done, he will have whatever he says. [24] Therefore I say to you, whatever things you ask when you pray, believe that you receive *them,* and you will have *them.*
Mark 11:22-24 (NKJV)

Faith is not a belief in self or the powers of man. It is faith in God! All of us have situations in our lives that send us to our knees. Sometimes, that is when we are relying on our own power, and as soon as we regain enough strength, will try to stand on our own power again. Yet God desires for us to fall to our knees in prayer, knowing that we need Him desperately. There is no problem small enough that we can handle it alone, and no problem big enough that God cannot handle it alone!

And whatever we ask we receive from Him, because we keep His commandments and do those things that are pleasing in His sight.
1 John 3:22 (NKJV)

June 24: Are you faithful?

Mother Teresa said, "Be faithful in small things for it is in them that your strength lies." That quotation seems to reflect the parable of the talents shared by Jesus:

[14] "For *the kingdom of heaven is* like a man traveling to a far country, *who* called his own servants and delivered his goods to them. [15] And to one he gave five talents, to another two, and to another one, to each according to his own ability; and immediately he went on a journey. [16] Then he who had received the five talents went and traded with them, and made another five talents. [17] And likewise he who *had received* two gained two more also. [18] But he who had received one went and dug in the ground, and hid his lord's

money. ¹⁹ After a long time the lord of those servants came and settled accounts with them.

²⁰ "So he who had received five talents came and brought five other talents, saying, 'Lord, you delivered to me five talents; look, I have gained five more talents besides them.' ²¹ His lord said to him, 'Well *done,* good and faithful servant; you were faithful over a few things, I will make you ruler over many things. Enter into the joy of your lord.' ²² He also who had received two talents came and said, 'Lord, you delivered to me two talents; look, I have gained two more talents besides them.' ²³ His lord said to him, 'Well *done,* good and faithful servant; you have been faithful over a few things, I will make you ruler over many things. Enter into the joy of your lord.'

²⁴ "Then he who had received the one talent came and said, 'Lord, I knew you to be a hard man, reaping where you have not sown, and gathering where you have not scattered seed. ²⁵ And I was afraid, and went and hid your talent in the ground. Look, *there* you have *what is* yours.'

²⁶ "But his lord answered and said to him, 'You wicked and lazy servant, you knew that I reap where I have not sown, and gather where I have not scattered seed. ²⁷ So you ought to have deposited my money with the bankers, and at my coming I would have received back my own with interest. ²⁸ So take the talent from him, and give *it* to him who has ten talents.

²⁹ 'For to everyone who has, more will be given, and he will have   abundance; but from him who does not have, even what he has will be taken away. ³⁰ And cast the unprofitable servant into the outer darkness. There will be weeping and gnashing of teeth.'
Matthew 25:14-30 (NKJV)

Interestingly, the parable begins with the traveling man, who is symbolic of the kingdom of heaven. He gives money to three different servants, and the amount of money given reflects the abilities of the recipients. It is ironic that the currency used is the talent. God gives each of us talents and abilities. Often, we lose sight of the fact that everything that we are came from Him. If our talent is singing, it is not our hard work or desire to succeed that made us that way. God gave the gift, and He also gave the work ethic to improve that gift. Take the greatest athletes in the world and draw the identical conclusions. Because He has a plan for each of us, that plan includes every aspect of our personalities. Are we being faithful in how we are utilizing the gifts He has given us?

Hananiah is the only man in the Bible referred to as faithful:

[1] Then it was, when the wall was built and I had hung the doors, when the gatekeepers, the singers, and the Levites had been appointed, [2] that I gave the charge of Jerusalem to my brother Hanani, and Hananiah the leader of the citadel, for he *was* a faithful man and feared God more than many. Nehemiah 7:1-2 (NKJV)

Certainly, each of us has moments of faithfulness. Faithful is the Greek word *pistos* (πιστός), and just like it sounds, it is to be filled with faith. According to Easton's Bible Dictionary, faith is "the persuasion of the mind that a thing is true." Since there are different amounts of faith, the pinnacle of belief would be blind faith, the act of completely believing without seeing. A common misconception is that "seeing is believing," but our eyes can be deceived just as easily as any of our other senses. Instead, it is quite the opposite. Believing is seeing! Once we believe that Jesus Christ came to save us from our sins, we can see the meaning of every aspect of life. It all makes sense.

But if we were truly faithful, would we ever have moments of doubt? Certainly not! Sometimes, we are not even aware of the times when the doubt creeps in. It is doubt when we are struggling to pay our bills and we worry if we are going to make it. It is doubt when we worry whether or not we will get the job we applied for, not knowing what we will do without it. It is doubt when we worry about our Christian friend who has made some bad choices. The key word is worry. When we worry, we are forgetting the size of our God, who is big enough to create all that we can see and all that we cannot see. Even with His enormous power, He cares about each hair on our heads.

Be anxious for nothing, but in everything by prayer and supplication, with thanksgiving, let your requests be made known to God;
Philippians 4:6 (NKJV)

When Mother Teresa reminded us that our strength lies in being faithful in small things, it is to see that God exists in the smallest increment of our lives. The gifts that He has given us do not need to be used in coliseums or stadiums to make an impact. The biggest impacts occur in one-on-one relationships. That is where it all begins. Who is around us desperately needing to hear about Jesus? For those gifted as cooks, take that friend a meal and share with them the Bread of life! For those gifted in encouragement, tell a friend who is struggling about God who does miracles. For those gifted in hospitality, invite a friend who needs a place to sleep, but do not forget to tell them about the God who supplies every need. Do not bury the talent God gave. Let God use it for His glory. It is why He gave it! And most importantly, we should use those gifts with love in our hearts!

But remember who really is faithful:

If we are faithless,
He remains faithful;
He cannot deny Himself.
2 Timothy 2:13 (NKJV)

[22] ***Through*** **the LORD's mercies we are not consumed,**
Because His compassions fail not.
[23] ***They are*** **new every morning;**
Great *is* **Your faithfulness.**
Lamentations 3:22-23 (NKJV)

June 25: Temptation

Irish writer Oscar Wilde said, "The only way to get rid of temptation is to yield to it." That summarizes the way that most of the world looks at temptation. Christian apologist C. S. Lewis offered a different perspective:

> "A silly idea is current that good people do not know what temptation means. This is an obvious lie. Only those who try to resist temptation know how strong it is…A man who gives in to temptation after five minutes simply does not know what it would have been like an hour later. That is why bad people, in one sense, know very little about badness. They have lived a sheltered life by always giving in."

Many think that temptation is greater today than ever before, yet history repeats itself, and since the days of Adam, man has not changed. Yet through technology, the opportunities to engage in sexual sin certainly have increased. Women in the biblical era wore loose-fitting clothing, and it was rare when men other than their husbands saw any of their skin. Contrast that to the form-fitting clothing of today, along with the ability to meet a variety of partners on-line, simply a few clicks of the mouse away from an otherwise impossible meeting. Yet unlike Oscar Wilde, the words of Paul tell us God's stance on our abilities as Christians to "Just say no!"

No temptation has overtaken you except such as is common to man; but God *is* faithful, who will not allow you to be tempted beyond what you are able, but with the temptation will also make the way of escape, that you may be able to bear *it*.
1 Corinthians 10:13 (NKJV)

Though we might feel that attacks are individually based, Paul points out to us that we all stumble in the same ways. Additionally, our abilities to reject temptation have little to do with our own faithfulness and everything to do with the faithfulness of God. He protects us. That does not mean He separates us from all temptation with a hedge of protection. God allows us to be tempted for His purposes. What good could possibly come from our temptations and subsequent failures? They both demonstrate to us how weak we truly are without Him! God allowed Satan to tempt Jesus in the wilderness, and if the Father allowed the evil one access to His Son, He certainly will allow temptations in each of our lives. As we grow as Christians, we learn how to rely on God's power instead of our own when rebuffing the wily weapons of the slimy serpent. Yet what happens when we give in to temptation and fail? Look at the life of King David, described in 1 Samuel as a "man after God's own heart:"

[2] Then it happened one evening that David arose from his bed and walked on the roof of the king's house. And from the roof he saw a woman bathing, and the woman *was* very beautiful to behold. [3] So David sent and inquired about the woman. And *someone* said, "*Is* this not Bathsheba, the daughter of Eliam, the wife of Uriah the Hittite?" [4] Then David sent messengers, and took her; and she came to him, and he lay with her, for she was cleansed from her impurity; and she returned to her house. [5] And the woman conceived; so she sent and told David, and said, "I *am* with child."
2 Samuel 11:2-5 (NKJV)

King David had grown somewhat lethargic in his kingly duties, having sent his army into battle without his leadership. If he had been leading rather than lazing, King David would not have found the time to be tempted by Bathsheba. Yet his sin was worse than giving in to his lustful urges. Additionally, Bathsheba was the wife of Uriah, a soldier in King David's army. Unlike David, Uriah was faithful in his duties to king and country. Bathsheba was equally guilty and the two conceived a child. King David compounded his initial mistake with more bad decisions. He first attempted to make Uriah think he had fathered the child by bringing his general home for a respite. Yet Uriah would not go into his wife, as his men had not been given the same opportunity. Finally, King David wrote a letter to his lead general, Joab, instructing the general to place Uriah in the most intense battle, then to have support troops leave Uriah unprotected. Sadly, King David had Uriah hand deliver the note requesting his own murder.

It does not matter how many steps we take to disguise our sin, or hide it. The Lord sees inside the heart, and consequently, sees our motives. God revealed His displeasure to David through Nathan the prophet, and both David and Bathsheba suffered with the death of their newborn child. Though David prayed for the child to be saved, when the Lord did not choose to answer David's prayer in that manner, David moved forward, rightly not blaming the Lord.

Sin has ramifications. Giving into temptation is sin. God understands our weaknesses, just as we need to understand His strength. Though David and Bathsheba certainly suffered in their punishment, the most important aspect to see is that the Lord forgave them. If we are struggling in sin, with temptation continuing to win in our daily battles, know that the Lord continues to love us. Yet if we do not seem to be learning from repetitive failures, a logical conclusion would be that we are operating under our own power rather than the power of the Lord.

I say then: Walk in the Spirit, and you shall not fulfill the lust of the flesh.
Galatians 5:16 (NKJV)

[13] **Let no one say when he is tempted, "I am tempted by God"; for God cannot be tempted by evil, nor does He Himself tempt anyone.** [14] **But each one is tempted when he is drawn away by his own desires and enticed.** [15] **Then, when desire has conceived, it gives birth to sin; and sin, when it is full-grown, brings forth death.**
James 1:13-15 (NKJV)

June 26: Who is the authority of your life?

Science fiction author Robert Heinlein said, "No statement should be believed because it is made by an authority." On the other side of the coin is Robert E. Lee, who said, "Obedience to lawful authority is the foundation of manly character." These are radically different philosophies from two intelligent men.

The truth is we often believe what we are told by authorities. For example, none of us fought in the battles of World War I. If all we did was read about the Great War in history books, does it make the event any less factual because we were not eyewitnesses? Certainly, what needs to occur in choosing who to believe is the credibility of the witness. Politicians fall into the category of who not to believe, regardless of political party. Look up the word politician in the dictionary and there is a picture of Pinocchio, he of the long nose! Especially in our two-party system, both sides have the propensity to spin a story in order to elevate themselves and their own party. Somewhere along the lines, the good of the people became lost by the wayside.

Part of the problem has to do with the human condition along with the desire to be the authority of our own lives. In that regard, each of us retains the ability to make our own choices, and more importantly, to act on those choices. Yet the heart of the problem is that whether we like it or not, we will answer to a much higher authority than ourselves because of those choices.

[5] **Let this mind be in you which was also in Christ Jesus,** [6] **who, being in the form of God, did not consider it robbery to be equal with God,** [7] **but made Himself of no reputation, taking the form of a bondservant, and coming in the likeness of men.** [8] **And being found in appearance as a man, He humbled Himself and became obedient to the point of death, even the death of the cross.** [9] **Therefore God also has highly exalted Him and given Him the name which is above every name,** [10] **that at the name of Jesus every knee should bow, of**

those in heaven, and of those on earth, and of those under the earth, [11] **and that every tongue should confess that Jesus Christ is Lord, to the glory of God the Father.**
Philippians 2:5-11 (NKJV)

Our choice becomes a simple one. We can acknowledge Jesus Christ as Lord while we are walking on this earth, or we can choose to wait and make that acknowledgment on Judgment Day. In the verse above, it does not say that most of the knees will bow, but that **"every knee should bow."** The next verse highlights the fact that this does not just refer to humanity, but every created being. That would include the heavenly host of angels, as well as the demons under the control of Satan.

Because God created us in His image, we have His Laws written on our hearts. Without studying the 10 Commandments, each of us instinctively knows the difference between right and wrong. Even though we have a tendency to rationalize the reasoning behind our sinful choices, it does not change the sin. In addition to the Laws being written on our hearts, God has given us the Bible so that we might know Him.

[16] **All Scripture is given by inspiration of God, and is profitable for doctrine, for reproof, for correction, for instruction in righteousness,** [17] **that the man of God may be complete, thoroughly equipped for every good work.**
2 Timothy 3:16-17 (NKJV)

We only have two directions to go after reading the above verse. Is it true or false? Was Paul a reliable source, an authority worth trusting? Is the Bible a reliable source? Archaeologists have proven without fail that historically, the Bible is accurate. Naysayers continue to assault the Bible's authenticity, but more proof continues to be discovered. Sadly, even Christians seem to lose sight of the importance of God's love letter to us all. Some polls have shown that less than 10% of Christians have read the Bible in its entirety. Does this have to do with its length or difficulty to grasp? Or does it have more to do with our laziness? It certainly is much easier to turn on the television than to pick up the Bible after a day of work! But if we believe in God, do we truly want to know Him?

St. Augustine said, "If you believe what you like in the Bible, and reject what you do not like, it is not the Bible you believe but yourself!" Every story in the Bible points to God's attributes. For someone who does not believe in God, it is worth reading the entire Bible just to make sure. Certainly it is the most important choice of our lives!

[20] **knowing this first, that no prophecy of Scripture is of any private interpretation,** [21] **for prophecy never came by the will of man, but holy men of God spoke as they were moved by the Holy Spirit.**
2 Peter 1:20-21 (NKJV)

June 27: Sheep

It is interesting that in Bible analogy, Jesus is the Shepherd and we are the sheep. Sheep are not the most intelligent of animals. Look at the way sheep meander when grazing, from one grass clump to another, without looking up. They are so focused on the continuous feeding of their bellies that they can get lost easily. Additionally, we know the way they defend themselves. If a wolf finds its way into the herd, even if all the sheep unite together, the wolf will not leave until his stomach is full. Better make sure that the sheep are not near a cliff, for in their game of follow-the-leader, there will be more sheep guts at the bottom of that cliff than in a tennis string factory! Water is another protective concern, as if those thick, woolen coats are submerged, the sheep will often drown as they become too heavy to stay afloat. Why is it that a sheep in water will not shrink like a wool sweater when it is washed? Here is some food for thought: the sheep might produce useful wool, but they are either food for wolves or food for people. One way or another, they are going to be eaten! The truth is, without a shepherd, those sheep are wolf snacks!

> "A dead cow or sheep lying in a pasture is recognized as carrion. The same sort of a carcass dressed and hung up in a butcher's stall passes as food." --John Harvey Kellogg, who invented Kellogg's cornflakes

Certainly, sheep need a shepherd, and as Isaiah the prophet said, **"All we like sheep have gone astray. We have turned everyone to his own way."** We need to follow a Shepherd who will protect us and get us back on the right path!

**[11] "I am the good shepherd. The good shepherd gives His life for the sheep. [12] But a hireling, *he who is* not the shepherd, one who does not own the sheep, sees the wolf coming and leaves the sheep and flees; and the wolf catches the sheep and scatters them. [13] The hireling flees because he is a hireling and does not care about the sheep. [14] I am the good shepherd; and I know My *sheep*, and am known by My own. [15] As the Father knows Me, even so I know the Father; and I lay down My life for the sheep. [16] And other sheep I have which are not of this fold; them also I must bring, and they will hear My voice; and there will be one flock *and* one shepherd.
John 10:11-16 (NKJV)**

If we follow Jesus, our Shepherd, we never will get lost. Additionally, the Lord has given the gift of teaching to His followers through the Holy Spirit. Though some might have stronger gifts of teaching, we are all teachers. Pastors are to provide spiritual food for those under their care, and protect the flock. Emulating Jesus, pastors are to lead in a godly manner. Also, each Christian father is supposed to be the spiritual leader of his family, teaching his wife and his children. Yet each of us will find ourselves in situations where we are to instruct others in God's Word and in God's ways.

> "Shepherds do not produce sheep. Sheep produce sheep." --Earl Radmacher, former president of the Western Conservative Baptist Seminary.

There is nothing better than a great meal, but it is just as rewarding to prepare a wonderful meal for someone else. We should ensure that we are feeding others, rather than just getting fed. Fat sheep cannot run fast enough to evade predators and they make the most plentiful meals!

And Jesus, when He came out, saw a great multitude and was moved with compassion for them, because they were like sheep not having a shepherd. So He began to teach them many things.
Mark 6:34 (NKJV)

June 28: Forgiveness

Most of us can look back on our lives and see numerous decisions that could have ended those lives. Additionally, most of us are equally amazed that the people we have involved in our horrendous decisions have forgiven us! One of the most difficult aspects of life is to accept the failures of others as easily as we accept our own failures. Certainly, the behaviors of others that typically bother us the most are those that we readily exhibit! How many times have we made comments about a driver's failure to signal, when moments later, we fail to do the same?

The greatest biblical example we have of forgiveness on this earth is not surprisingly, Jesus. Our Lord knew that Judas was going to betray Him, and still, loved Judas like a brother. We have all heard the term "forgive and forget." In truth, while forgiveness can be a supreme challenge for all of us, the second part of that phrase is even more difficult. What did Jesus teach us about forgiveness?

[21] Then Peter came to Him and said, "Lord, how often shall my brother sin against me, and I forgive him? Up to seven times?"
[22] Jesus said to him, "I do not say to you, up to seven times, but up to seventy times seven.
Matthew 28:21-22 (NKJV)

Many people say that we do not have to forget, only forgive. Yet can we truly forgive someone who has sinned against us without forgetting the past? In order to have the same negative action happen to us often, we have to put ourselves back into that vulnerable position of love and trust. We do that even if we know the possible, or even probable outcome. To put it in perspective, how many times has God forgiven us for the same sins?

[14] **"For if you forgive men their trespasses, your heavenly Father will also forgive you.** [15] **But if you do not forgive men their trespasses, neither will your Father forgive your trespasses.**
Matthew 6:14-15 (NKJV)

There is another aspect of forgiveness that we often overlook. Have we ever not forgiven a person because they hurt us so badly that they did not deserve it? Or maybe they did not apologize, and in the same manner, they did not deserve forgiveness. The true blessing occurs when we forgive the unforgivable. The burden that is removed is from our own shoulders, as until we are able to forgive, we carry the weight. Often, those who sin against us do not remember the sin, do not think of the sin and do not acknowledge the sin. To forgive them is freedom for us!

> "To forgive is to set a prisoner free and discover that the prisoner was you." –Lewis B. Smedes

Therefore I say to you, her sins, *which are* many, are forgiven, for she loved much. But to whom little is forgiven, *the same* loves little."
Luke 7:47 (NKJV)

June 29: Help!

Most of us are familiar with the phrase, "The Lord helps them who helps themselves." Just hearing it makes us want to pick ourselves up by the bootstraps and be strong. If wondering where in the Bible that well-known saying occurs, or even the verse that it is based on, we will not find either. In fact, God does quite the opposite. He loves the unlovable. He helps the helpless. He rescues the lost. Never forget that we were all dead in our trespasses until God made the dead alive again; He made the broken whole; He made the lame walk; He made the blind see; and He made the deaf hear.

[14] not giving heed to Jewish fables and commandments of men who turn from the truth. [15] To the pure all things are pure, but to those who are defiled and unbelieving nothing is pure; but even their mind and conscience are defiled. [16] They profess to know God, but in works they deny Him, being abominable, disobedient, and disqualified for every good work.
Titus 1:14-16 (NKJV)

To those people young in the faith, this saying is an example of one of those fables and commandments that could lead someone far astray from the place God wants them. Our Lord desires for us to remain on the straight and narrow path that leads directly to Him. For those having difficulty finding that path, God tells us about that walk in His Book, which is filled with examples of how to live our lives. Though our salvation certainly is not based on our works, but instead, on the work that Jesus already has accomplished on our behalves at Calvary, the verse above in Titus demonstrates to us that our works should be of a godly nature if we are walking with Jesus. Our Lord gives us some great examples of how to treat others through His deeds and through His words:

[41] "Then He will also say to those on the left hand, 'Depart from Me, you cursed, into the everlasting fire prepared for the devil and his angels: [42] for I was hungry and you gave Me no food; I was thirsty and you gave Me no drink; [43] I was a stranger and you did not take Me in, naked and you did not clothe Me, sick and in prison and you did not visit Me.'
[44] "Then they also will answer Him, saying, 'Lord, when did we see You hungry or thirsty or a stranger or naked or sick

or in prison, and did not minister to You?' [45] Then He will answer them, saying, 'Assuredly, I say to you, inasmuch as you did not do *it* to one of the least of these, you did not do *it* to Me.' [46] And these will go away into everlasting punishment, but the righteous into eternal life."
Matthew 25:41-46 (NKJV)

Many people, Christians included, walk past homeless beggars as if they were invisible. Part of that behavior has to do with our life experiences, seeing, hearing and even reading about the number struggling with substance abuse. Often, we make sweeping judgments that their plight has to do with laziness. Often, God opens doors in our lives and places us in ministry opportunities with the down-trodden. Most are desperate to get back on their feet, yet are bound to sin. Certainly, there have been bad decisions all along the way in their lives, yet most Christians can reflect upon equally bad decisions in their own lives.

The passage above in Matthew does not say help those who deserve our help. Instead, Jesus tells us to help those in need. Give them food, give them clothing and give them water. Even if they are guilty of a heinous crime, visit them in prison! Notice that the passage does not say to give them money. That money might be a stumbling block used for the purchase of a substance that keeps them homeless. Remember, Jesus was homeless. Would we help Him? All of us desire the basics of food, shelter and companionship! Every person we come in contact with was perfectly and marvelously created by God. He does not make losers! They have eternal souls that badly need a Lord to guide them, and without Him they are captives of the same one who controlled us before we came to the Lord!

And Jesus said to him, "Foxes have holes and birds of the air *have* nests, but the Son of Man has nowhere to lay *His* head." Luke 9:58 (NKJV)

June 30: Perfection!

Seven might be the most frequent combination on a roll of two dice, but it is not just a crap shoot that the same number is the one most frequently seen in the Bible, standing for spiritual perfection. Since only God is perfect, we can see His perfection in each occurrence! Entire books have been written about the usage of seven in the Bible, so it is certain that the explanation of seven in a devotional will be far from complete. One of the greatest oddities of seven in the Bible is that in the Old Testament, different forms of the word all occur in multiples of seven: "seven" occurs 287 times, which is 7 X 41; "seventh" occurs 98 times, or 7 X 14; "sevenfold" occurs 7 times, obviously, 7 X 1; "seventy" occurs 56 times, or 7 X 8; "seventy" in combination with other numbers occurs 35 times, or 7 X 5; "seven" in combination with other numbers (like one hundred and seven) occurs 112 times, which is 7 X 16. God gives us a clue into the significance of seven in the word's first usage:

[2] And on the seventh day God ended His work which He had done, and He rested on the seventh day from all His work which He had done. [3] Then God blessed the seventh day and sanctified it, because in it He rested from all His work which God had created and made.
Genesis 2:2-3 (NKJV)

In six days, God completed His work of perfection, preparing a place for man before creating man. On the seventh day, God rested, not because He was tired, but to give us an example of a Sabbath day in our lives. After completing our week of work, God desires for His creation to rest their tired bodies and restore their souls by worshipping Him. Looking at other "seven's" will reveal that perfection:

There are seven promises in God's covenant to Abraham in Genesis 12:2-3:
    1. "I will make you a great nation."
    2. "And I will bless you."

3. "And make your name great."
4. "And you shall be a blessing."
5. "I will bless those who bless you,"
6. "And curse those who curse you."
7. "And in you, all the families of the earth shall be blessed."

In Exodus 6:6-8, God gives us seven "I will" statements concerning His covenant with Israel:
1. "I will bring you out from under the burdens of the Egyptians."
2. "I will rescue you from their bondage."
3. "And I will redeem you with an outstretched arm and with great judgments."
4. "I will take you as my people."
5. "And I will be your God."
6. "I will bring you into the land that I swore to give to Abraham, Isaac and Jacob."
7. "I will give it to you as a heritage: I am the Lord."

In the Gospel according to John, there are seven "I am" statements by Jesus:
1. "I am the bread of life." John 6:35 and John 6:48
2. "I am the light of the world." John 8:12 and John 9:5
3. "I am the door." John 10:7
4. "I am the good shepherd." John 10:11-14
5. "I am the resurrection and the life." John 11:25
6. "I am the way, the truth and the life." John 14:6
7. "I am the true vine." John 15:1 and John 15:5

Jesus made seven statements from the cross:
1. "Father, forgive them, for they know not what they do." Luke 23:34
2. "Assuredly, I say to you, today you will be with Me in Paradise." Luke 23:43
3. "My God, My God, why have You forsaken Me?" Matthew 27:46
4. "Woman, behold your son." Then He said to the disciple, "Behold your mother." John 19:26-27

5. "I thirst." John 19:28
6. "Father, into Your hands I commit My spirit." Luke 23:46
7. "It is finished." John 19:30

Those sevens culminate in Revelation, a book concerning events yet to come in the earth's existence. The title of the book means "unveiling," as it is the unveiling of Jesus Christ, who returns in judgment to a sinful world. Many people misunderstand the wrath and judgment of God, thinking that it somehow conflicts His love. Yet even in judgment, He loves perfectly, offering His grace to a dead and dying world, which refuses to believe and follow Him. Three different waves of seven judgments increasing in severity mark that time. In Revelation, there are seven churches, seven letters, seven Spirits, seven golden lampstands, seven stars, seven seals, seven horns, seven eyes, seven angels, seven trumpets, seven thunders, seven thousand people, seven heads, seven crowns, seven plagues, seven golden bowls, seven hills, seven kings and seven last visions. There are 55 "sevens" and 5 "sevenths" in Revelation alone. Is it ironic that in the book that discusses the end of this world and the beginning of the one that never will pass away that God uses seven so frequently, with seven standing for spiritual perfection?

We can find sevens everywhere in the Bible. A favorite occurs in Isaiah, referring to the Holy Spirit:

[1] **There shall come forth a Rod from the stem of Jesse,
And a Branch shall grow out of his roots.**
[2] **The Spirit of the LORD shall rest upon Him,
The Spirit of wisdom and understanding,
The Spirit of counsel and might,
The Spirit of knowledge and of the fear of the LORD.
Isaiah 11:1-2 (NKJV)**

In this verse, there are seven, perfect attributes of the Holy Spirit:
1. The Spirit of the Lord
2. The Spirit of wisdom

3. The Spirit of understanding
4. The Spirit of counsel
5. The Spirit of might
6. The Spirit of knowledge
7. The Spirit of the fear of the Lord

Those attributes should be a part of each of our walks, as the Holy Spirit dwells inside of us, giving us His attributes. When we feel like we are not walking in God's power or wisdom, it is not because we are too weak or too dumb. Instead, it is because we are walking in the flesh, rather than in the Spirit. When we rely on our own power, we are certain to bog down, but when we rely on God, we always will proceed, "full steam ahead." It is the difference between riding in a toy powered by rubber bands and riding in a rocket! Let God power our walks! Just because God is in us does not mean that we always are in God! Sometimes, we choose to walk away from His love, His grace and His power! Look to Him, the author and finisher of our faith, who has shared so many sevens to demonstrate His perfection. Those sevens demonstrate to us the perfection of God's Word, for with 40 different authors writing the 66 different books over thousands of years, how did they all know to follow that same theme? It is because the Holy Spirit led them and in the same manner, He will perfect His followers!

The LORD will perfect *that which* **concerns me;**
Your mercy, O LORD, *endures* **forever;**
Do not forsake the works of Your hands.
Psalm 138:8 (NKJV)

July 1: I told you so!

There probably is not a phrase that cuts us to the quick as easily as the oft-uttered "I told you so!" It is the upscale, adult-version of "Neener, neener," and certainly rankles men and women in their marriages, friendships and business relationships. It calls attention to two sides of the same problem. When we feel the need to highlight our own intellectual superiority each time a friend, partner or colleague crashes and burns, it points to our pride. On the other hand, the simple fact that it bothers us when someone mentions the errors in our decision-making capabilities points to pride from a different direction. The biblical key is admonition alongside encouragement.

Look at how Paul handled a similar situation when on board a ship as a prisoner:

[21] But after long abstinence from food, then Paul stood in the midst of them and said, "Men, you should have listened to me, and not have sailed from Crete and incurred this disaster and loss. [22] And now I urge you to take heart, for there will be no loss of life among you, but only of the ship. [23] For there stood by me this night an angel of the God to whom I belong and whom I serve, [24] saying, 'Do not be afraid, Paul; you must be brought before Caesar; and indeed God has granted you all those who sail with you.' [25] Therefore take heart, men, for I believe God that it will be just as it was told me. [26] However, we must run aground on a certain island."
Acts 27:21-26 (NKJV)

Talk about getting someone's attention! After Paul addressed their misguided plan, he promised that all would survive. He must have spoken with authority for they all believed him, choosing to eat the existing food on board ship before lightening the load in preparation for the impending shipwreck.

[42] And the soldiers' plan was to kill the prisoners, lest any of them should swim away and escape. [43] But the centurion, wanting to save Paul, kept them from *their* purpose, and commanded that those who could swim should jump *overboard* first and get to land, [44] and the rest, some on boards and some on *parts* of the ship. And so it was that they all escaped safely to land.
Acts 27:42-44 (NKJV)

God carries us through the hardships of life. Some are able to swim, while others cannot get to shore safely without a board or part of the ship to keep them afloat. Sometimes the remnants of our destructive lives carry us to a safer place, with God's helpful hand guiding all the way. We are continuously barraged by growth challenges, and not surprisingly, they all come back to pride. We should listen to the people God has placed into our lives and weigh the advice they give with God's wisdom. Additionally, we should remember that the failures of others do not make us any more special. Most importantly, we should trust God and His promises. He can carry us through situations that even make our survival look impossible. Nothing is impossible with God!

[10] Reject a divisive man after the first and second admonition, [11] knowing that such a person is warped and sinning, being self-condemned.
Titus 3:10-11 (NKJV)

July 2: Who is your Nineveh?

Even when we are following the Lord, He puts us in places where we are not following our hearts. That should not surprise us as the heart is suspect, at best. Jeremiah described it as deceitful and desperately wicked. When we decide to walk away from the cares of the world and put our trust in Jesus Christ, He gives us new hearts. Yet the old memories and the problematic sin nature still can rear their ugly heads and lead us down paths of unrighteousness for our own name's sake.
When God called Jonah to go to the people of Nineveh, Jonah made a beeline in the opposite direction.

[1] Now the word of the LORD came to Jonah the son of Amittai, saying, [2] "Arise, go to Nineveh, that great city, and cry out against it; for their wickedness has come up before Me." [3] But Jonah arose to flee to Tarshish from the presence of the LORD. He went down to Joppa, and found a ship going to Tarshish; so he paid the fare, and went down into it, to go with them to Tarshish from the presence of the LORD.
Jonah 1:1-3 (NKJV)

Having been to Joppa, a quaint city on the Mediterranean Sea just south of Tel Aviv, it is easy to picture Jonah's point of departure. Nineveh was not a port city, and therefore, could not be reached by ship. It was a three-day journey from the coast, and Jonah chose to evade the Lord. That is hard to do with an omnipresent God! What was it about this request from God that sent Jonah spiraling in the opposite direction? Jonah did not want the people of Nineveh to find the Lord's grace and salvation. It was the equivalent of the Lord asking a USC grad to share His love with a UCLA supporter. If this analogy is not explanatory, place any rivals in those two spots!

Jonah gives us a great example of the lengths that God will go to if He wants to get us back on His path, the path of righteousness for His name's sake. We know the rest of the story: Jonah boarded a ship and it seems to have been more than a three-hour tour; the weather started getting rough and the tiny ship was tossed; if not for the intelligence of the fearless crew who figured that Jonah was the cause of the storm, the ship would have been lost; they threw him overboard; Jonah was swallowed by a giant fish; Jonah prayed for three days; the fish vomited Jonah onto the shore. After much thought, Jonah decided to make the trip to Nineveh. When he told the people that the Lord was going to destroy the city and the people in 40 days, they decided to follow the Lord, much to Jonah's dismay!

Do we have any Nineveh's in our lives? Any people in our lives are not there by chance or coincidence, but are there because the Lord placed them there. Do we have rivals or enemies that make fun of our faith? Are there people who at every step seem to be trying to trip us? All of us have people we meet who are very difficult to love. Often, we choose the slow boat to China rather than the long walk of a servant in dealing with them! Learn a lesson from Jonah. Would we rather be blanched white from the stomach acid of a giant fish, or make the journey the Lord requests? We have the gift of free choice, but God's will overrules any choice we can make! When we venture from the path of His righteousness, He has the power, creativity and ability to put us right where He wants us. It is much easier to just do what He says!

Bless those who persecute you; bless and do not curse. Romans 12:14 (NKJV)

July 3: The Prodigal Son

[17] "But when he came to himself, he said, 'How many of my father's hired servants have bread enough and to spare, and I perish with hunger! [18] I will arise and go to my father, and will say to him, "Father, I have sinned against heaven and before you, [19] and I am no longer worthy to be called your son. Make me like one of your hired servants."' [20] "And he arose and came to his father. But when he was still a great way off, his father saw him and had compassion, and ran and fell on his neck and kissed him. [21] And the son said to him, 'Father, I have sinned against heaven and in your sight, and am no longer worthy to be called your son.' [22] "But the father said to his servants, 'Bring out the best robe and put *it* on him, and put a ring on his hand and sandals on *his* feet. [23] And bring the fatted calf here and kill *it,* and let us eat and be merry; [24] for this my son was dead and is alive again; he was lost and is found.' And they began to be merry.
Luke 15: 17-24 (NKJV)

In this chapter, Luke describes three lost items, a sheep, a coin and a son. We all know the feeling of panic when we are lost, or when we have lost something of value. While it may be devastating to lose a wallet, nothing compares to a lost life. From the point of view of a parent, there are no limits to what they would trade for the life of that child to be restored again. Our heavenly Father grieves when His children walk in the ways of the world rather than in the ways of the Lord, yet He can see the end of the story just as easily as He sees the beginning. That being said, the miracle in raising Lazarus from dead to live is no more powerful than what God did in our lives!

And we know that all things work together for good to those who love God, to those who are the called according to *His* purpose.
Romans 8:28

All things? How is that even possible? How can God take our worst decisions and cause good to come from them? That is exactly what He did in the life of the Prodigal Son, who made a conscious choice to leave his family and explore the world of sin. In the process, he spent all of his inheritance. Finally, brokenness surrounded him on every front. Pigs ate better than he did. God did not create robots and force His creation to love Him in return, but He does want our love. His plan allows us to find brokenness of our own choosing, and return to Him, of our own choosing.

In those years away from Him, our understanding of sin and forgiveness deepen. When Jesus asked Peter who of two debtors would love the man the most after he who lent the sum forgave the debts, Peter said, "the one who had the greater debt forgiven." (Luke 7:43) Many of us know exactly how the Prodigal Son felt, as we have had the greater debt forgiven. When God has removed the burden of death and brokenness from our shoulders that we both have earned and deserved, we walk with a freedom from that burden and a love that understands the enormous gift.

God changes our lives! He makes the lame to walk, the blind to see, the deaf to hear and the dead to live again, all because of what occurred on Calvary. Why did God choose us? Because:

[27] But God has chosen the foolish things of the world to put to shame the wise, and God has chosen the weak things of the world to put to shame the things which are mighty; [28] and the base things of the world and the things which are despised God has chosen, and the things which are not, to bring to nothing the things that are, [29] that no flesh should glory in His presence.
1 Corinthians 1:27-29

This speaks of His mercy! God calls men who feel as Paul felt, who called himself the chief of sinners (1 Timothy 1:15). As we see in the other parables of Luke 15, God always seeks after the lost. He leaves the 99 to go after the one lost sheep, and all of heaven rejoices when that which was lost is found. What a heart our Father has! It is hard to fathom the depth of His love!

July 4: America, Bless God!

While most Christians seem to focus on the New Testament, the Old Testament is also special, particularly for the history, the poetry and the prophecy. A pilgrimage to Israel can open a believer's eyes to those biblical places. Though Israel has certainly changed drastically in 2,000 years, a journey there offers more understanding in regard to the distances between cities, the topography and the people. The circuitous relationship between God and the Jews, His chosen people, is heartbreaking. When He selected them as His people, the apple of His eye, the Jews followed and loved Him. Then they fell into idolatry, far away from God and His ways. He punished them, and the Jews came crawling back, asking for His forgiveness. Of course, He forgave them. He always does! They would walk in His ways again, and then another generation would fall into idolatry. After centuries of this behavior, they rejected Jesus as Messiah. At that time He cast them to the four corners of the world. According to the Bible, He is not finished with them yet, as the fullness of the Gentiles will occur before the time of the Jews begins anew.

Many Christians cannot understand why the Jews do not see Jesus as their Messiah, but Jesus explained that to us all in Luke 19:41-43 when He said that their eyes have been blinded. That will change. Sadly, many Christians see the Jews as completely different from themselves. Yet those Old Testament stories are not for our entertainment, but our admonition, as we struggle in exactly the same ways:

¹ Moreover, brethren, I do not want you to be unaware that all our fathers were under the cloud, all passed through the sea, ² all were baptized into Moses in the cloud and in the sea, ³ all ate the same spiritual food, ⁴ and all drank the same spiritual drink. For they drank of that spiritual Rock that followed them, and that Rock was Christ. ⁵ But with most of them God was not well pleased, for *their bodies* were scattered in the wilderness.
⁶ Now these things became our examples, to the intent that we should not lust after evil things as they also lusted. ⁷ And do not become idolaters as *were* some of them. As it is written, *"The people sat down to eat and drink, and rose up to play."* ⁸ Nor let us commit sexual immorality, as some of them did, and in one day twenty-three thousand fell; ⁹ nor let us tempt Christ, as some of them also tempted, and were destroyed by serpents; ¹⁰ nor complain, as some of them also complained, and were destroyed by the destroyer. ¹¹ Now all these things happened to them as examples, and they were written for our admonition, upon whom the ends of the ages have come.
1 Corinthians 10:1-11 (NKJV)

What does this have to do with the United States? Turn on the television, surf the internet, go to a movie, go shopping at the mall or take a stroll on the beach! Everywhere that we look is sexual immorality, in addition to all forms of idolatry. What is idolatry?

Therefore put to death your members which are on the earth: fornication, uncleanness, passion, evil desire, and covetousness, which is idolatry.
Colossians 3:5 (NKJV)

Money has become the god of the United States, though this nation was founded because people wanted to worship the One and Only God freely. The authors of the Constitution were believers, who wrote the principles of Christianity into that document. Just like the Jews, though, our country has been going in the wrong direction. Prayer was banned from public schools in 1962, and along with it, Bible reading. Now, we argue about removing the 10 Commandments from our courts and eliminating "in God we trust" from our money. Atheism and agnosticism are growing, and more importantly, Christianity is being watered down. Pastors are preaching without even using the Bible, as they do not want to offend those attending! Is there any question why the United States is declining in world power? What can we do?

If my people, which are called by my name, shall humble themselves, and pray, and seek my face, and turn from their wicked ways; then will I hear from heaven, and will forgive their sin, and will heal their land.
2 Chronicles 7:14 (NKJV)

Interestingly, the verse above does not tell us that the unbelievers need to turn to the Lord. In Nineveh, when Jonah warned the people of God's impending judgment, the unbelievers all turned to Him. Yet before God destroyed Sodom and Gomorrah, the Lord promised Abraham that He would spare the city if there were even 10 righteous men in the cities. God desires for us to lead the way through our prayer and our humbleness! For those who do not like our president or his policies, we still should pray for him. Do we pray specifically for his salvation? How this nation would change if our president accepted Jesus Christ as his Lord and Savior! It would be a miracle, but God performed that same miracle in our lives. There are so many Christians walking with one foot in the world and one with the Lord. That is not really a walk, but a hop! A pogo stick is not going to get us to heaven! If we seek the Lord diligently, He will hear us!

The phrase, "God Bless America gets old." God has blessed America for so many years. It is time for us to cry out together, "America Bless God!"

Stand fast therefore in the liberty by which Christ has made us free, and do not be entangled again with a yoke of bondage.

Ephesians 5:1 (NKJV)

July 5: Wait on the Lord

Most married couples are on slightly different schedules when it comes to going somewhere. Typically, women take longer to get ready, which probably has more to do with their appearance, though getting the children ready also can add a huge variable to the equation. It certainly takes longer for any woman to fix her hair than it does for a bald man! Yet there are marriages where the men do the dilly-dallying, and the women do the waiting. Some people are always early, while others are always late!

God's time is certainly different than ours, as we are told that to Him, a thousand years are like a day and a day is like a thousand years (2 Peter 3:8 and Psalm 90:4). But we know that the omniscient God cannot act too early or too late. He only can be perfectly on time, and accomplish the perfect task. In the meantime, God requires us to wait on Him. He is not doing His hair; but mostly, He is getting His children ready! Notice this verse written by King David:

**[1]I waited patiently for the LORD; And He inclined to me, And heard my cry.
[2]He also brought me up out of a horrible pit,
Out of the miry clay,
And set my feet upon a rock, *And* established my steps.
Psalm 40:1-2 (NKJV)**

Often, we equate ease of life with success. Yet we seem to draw closer to God when fully stretched. True happiness occurs when our feet are firmly planted on the Rock, rather than shifting sand. Most of us have difficulties facing us right now. We might have spent many hours talking to the Lord upon our knees, feeling like He is not listening, or not answering. He always hears and always answers, either yes, no or not now. Trust Him. He provides all that we need. God fed the Jews manna in the wilderness for 40 years. Not one sandal or garment wore out on that journey, as God does not just provide, but provides miraculously. God wants us to rely on Him!

And He said to me, "My grace is sufficient for you, for My strength is made perfect in weakness." Therefore most gladly I will rather boast in my infirmities, that the power of Christ may rest upon me.
2 Corinthians 12:9 (NKJV)

July 6: Praise the Lord!

Whenever we feel down, or that the world is taking us for a rough ride, it is good to reflect on the Book of Job, which Bible scholars postulate was the first book of the Bible ever written. God described Job as His most righteous servant on the earth, yet the Lord allowed him to be attacked strongly by Satan. Most of us know the pain associated with burying a parent, someone who brought us into this world and shared every step of our walks while here. Yet the exception to that rule occurs with the people who have to bury their children. There is no greater pain on this earth. That being said, Job's 10 children died one fateful afternoon in a tornado. What was Job's response? He praised the Lord! No wonder he was called the most righteous servant on the earth! Most of us struggle to praise the Lord when the slightest issues arise in our lives! We should praise the Lord in everything, as we know that God has a perfect plan in each of our lives!

^{8}Oh, give thanks to the LORD!
Call upon His name;
Make known His deeds among the peoples!
^{9}Sing to Him, sing psalms to Him;
Talk of all His wondrous works!
^{10}Glory in His holy name;
Let the hearts of those rejoice who seek the LORD!
^{11}Seek the LORD and His strength;
Seek His face evermore!
1 Chronicles 16:8-11 (NKJV)

We can praise the Lord in our words to Him, yet we also can praise the Lord in our actions to others. It glorifies God when we speak of His wondrous deeds! If the Lord lives in our hearts, we cannot help but tell others of the miracles He has performed! Jesus told us about the relationship that exists between the mouth and the heart:

Brood of vipers! How can you, being evil, speak good things? For out of the abundance of the heart the mouth speaks.
Matthew 12:34 (NKJV)

When the verse in 1 Chronicles 16 reminds us to "Seek His face evermore," it speaks of the closeness that God desires from each of us. Face-to-face relationship is what God desires from all of us. He wants intimacy! If we know God in an intimate way, we will understand the lengths that He went to so that we would feel His love, even though we should be separated from Him because of our sin. That gives us the greatest reason to praise Him, that He forgave us!

It is interesting that one of the Hebrew words for praise is also the same word used for confession, *yadah* (ידה). While praise and confession may appear to be unrelated, they are closely related when we understand that confession does not really refer to the daily sins, but instead, our confessions to God that we are completely overrun by sin and unworthy to be allowed into His presence. That certainly makes us feel more like praising Him, for our access to Him has nothing to do with who we are and everything to do with who He is. It has nothing to do with what we have done and everything to do with what He did!

We love Him because He first loved us.
1 John 4:19 (NKJV)

Agape is the word used for love both times in the verse above, which is a self-sacrificing love, contrasting to brotherly or sexual love. Yet the most telling part of that verse is the first occurrence of the word, reflecting our love for God, is in the active tense. The second occurrence, reflecting God's love for us, is in the Greek aorist tense. That tense refers to an event that happened at one moment in the past. When was the time that God demonstrated His love for us? It was at the cross! That is why we praise Him. He died so that we might have abundant life. If we love Him, we should tell someone about that love! And most importantly, praise Him for everything!

O LORD, *there is* none like You, nor *is there any* God besides You, according to all that we have heard with our ears.
1 Chronicles 17:20 (NKJV)

July 7: Grace like rain

We tend to pull out umbrellas in torrential downpours, but when it is only misting, often ignore the dampness in the air. Yet it is not the size of the raindrop that causes wetness. Even a light mist can soak us to the bone! Being soaked might not have a positive connotation to us, but there are benefits:

[25] Husbands, love your wives, just as Christ also loved the church and gave Himself for her, [26] that He might sanctify and cleanse her with the washing of water by the word, [27] that He might present her to Himself a glorious church, not having spot or wrinkle or any such thing, but that she should be holy and without blemish.
Ephesians 5:25-27 (NKJV)

In this passage, we are given the example of how husbands are to love their wives, with the same sacrificial love that Jesus had for His church. Jesus has sanctified and cleansed us by washing us with the water of His Word. Walking through this dirty world, we cannot help but have some of the world rub off on us, and sometimes, it stays on us for a while. Each day, we need to hose that dirt off by reading the Bible, allowing God to cleanse us! We never would consider going to work covered in dirt and mud, as we would be embarrassed to have our co-workers see us in such an unclean state. We rarely focus on the fact that our spiritual condition is much more important than our physical condition. God's desire for us is that we are holy and without blemish, but He knows us better than we know ourselves, and understands that we cannot live sin-free lives. He has given us a way of escape, as He always does! He wants to wash the sin away before that dirt becomes so encrusted on us that it becomes a part of us! If the dirt stays on us too long it will cake, and change our appearance. We do not want to become the creature from the black lagoon.

When the rain begins, it mixes with the oil and makes roadways incredibly slippery. In the same manner, sin is a slippery slope that leads to a toppling fall. Without the sin remedy of Jesus Christ, that sin always will lead us to exactly the same place. Though there are many people in this world who believe they live charmed lives with all of their possessions, vacations and riches, without a Savior they are lost! We should not get so caught up in this world that we forget who put us here, and why He still has us here. It is for His glory. Stay in His Word and share with others the amazing answers He gives to the questions of life! Just as the mist that soaks us to the bone, a little bit of God's Word every day will wash us clean!

[5] To Him who loved us and washed us from our sins in His own blood, [6] and has made us kings and priests to His God and Father, to Him *be* glory and dominion forever and ever. Amen.
Revelation 1:5-6 (NKJV)

July 8: Let your light shine!

One of the most beautiful national parks is Bryce Canyon in Utah, where the rock formations, called hoodoos, are other-worldly. Another amazing attribute there is that it offers one of the darkest places in the United States with a 7.4 magnitude night sky, which is advantageous for star-gazing. It is incredible how clear those distant lights become with the absence of light pollution.

When God created the heavens and the earth, "darkness was on the face of the deep," according to the second verse of the Bible, Genesis 1:2. Yet God created light, and added it to the darkness, separating the two with night and day. Over night, He placed the lesser lights, the moon and the stars, with the sun providing the light of day. Is it any wonder that most crimes are committed in the dark of night? Without being seen, criminals are less apt to be caught, and even the best eyewitness has trouble giving a perfect description in the darkness. Light removes shadows and exposes evil, pointing to God!

[15] that you may become blameless and harmless, children of God without fault in the midst of a crooked and perverse generation, among whom you shine as lights in the world, [16] holding fast the word of life, so that I may rejoice in the day of Christ that I have not run in vain or labored in vain. Philippians 2:15-16 (NKJV)

A May 2004 TIME Magazine article discussed scientific documentation that while the sun is not growing weaker, the earth is getting darker. According to scientists, solar radiation reaching the earth's surface has declined by as much as 10%. At the same time that the earth is growing physically darker, we as Christians are cognizant of the fact that the earth is growing spiritually darker by the day. While the oppressive nature of Satan's God-given dominion of the earth may heighten our awareness of the brokenness of the world, it should in the same regard excite us to be lights for the Lord! With increasing darkness, even the smallest lights will shine brightly!

[14] "You are the light of the world. A city that is set on a hill cannot be hidden. [15] Nor do they light a lamp and put it under a basket, but on a lampstand, and it gives light to all *who are* in the house.[16] Let your light so shine before men, that they may see your good works and glorify your Father in heaven.
Matthew 5:14-16 (NKJV)

As Christians, we are not covert spies operating in secret. We do not need to beat people over the head with the message of God, but when others see the love He has given us, and that same love being given from us to others, they will want to know more about the God we worship! Just as Jesus came as the Light of the world, we are to reflect His light as our lives become mirrors of His. Just as a moth is drawn to a flame, diurnal people (creatures of the daytime as opposed to nocturnal people, those of the night) are drawn to any source of light. We should not hide our lights but should let them shine. We can polish our mirrors through repentance and forgiveness!

The people who walked in darkness
Have seen a great light;
Those who dwelt in the land of the shadow of death,
Upon them a light has shined.
 Isaiah 9:2 (NKJV)

July 9: Home is where we hang our hats!

The old phrase that "home is where you hang your hat" is certainly a truth in many ways. Though vacations are fun, it is always a blessing to go home, to sleep in the bed most accustomed to. Additionally, home is where all of our "stuff" is, the boxes and boxes of possessions that evoke memories of our lives. Yet it is interesting that when a fire, landslide or other disaster is drawing nigh, the objects that we desire the most are the photos of our dearest family and friends. "Things" can be replaced, but memories have to be created anew.

Most of us have friends who recently have lost their homes, as the economy remains unstable. Additionally, the number of homeless seems to be increasing. Though God has promised to supply our needs, Jesus was homeless. Regardless of whether or not we have a roof over our head, we have a home. It is with the Lord:

[1] **"Let not your heart be troubled; you believe in God, believe also in Me.** [2] **In My Father's house are many mansions; if** *it*

were not *so,* I would have told you. I go to prepare a place for you. ³ And if I go and prepare a place for you, I will come again and receive you to Myself; that where I am, *there* you may be also. ⁴ And where I go you know, and the way you know."
John 14:1-4 (NKJV)

If God created the universe in six days, imagine how amazing our home in heaven will be, as Jesus has been preparing it for almost 2,000 years! On this earth, we put so much emphasis on our homes. They need to be just right for entertaining, as we do not want others to see the house in disarray. Yet the truth is, God can provide for us whether we are in a mansion, a studio apartment or on a bus bench! What is most important is that we all realize this is not our home! God is outside of the dimension of time, and according to Hebrews, sees us as seated in the heavens already. We are travelers on this earth, not residents, as our home is with God. Home is not really where we hang our hats. Home is where we hang our hearts!

Life's difficulties remind us of the unselfish prayer of Elijah. He prayed for a three-and-a-half-year drought to occur on the nation of Israel. That prayer was unselfish because the ensuing drought and famine would affect Elijah, too. Yet he was willing to endure the hardship so that others would be drawn to the Lord. All of us find the Lord in our brokenness. That is because of pride. When we finally realize that we cannot do it on our own, we turn to the only One who can do it for us, Jesus! We should be willing to endure hardship so that others will come to know Jesus Christ as their Lord and Savior.

We dwell in Jesus Christ and the Holy Spirit dwells in us! We should hang our hearts on God. He will never let us down!

But as it is written:
"Eye has not seen, nor ear heard,
Nor have entered into the heart of man
The things which God has prepared for those who love Him."

1 Corinthians 2:9 (NKJV)

July 10: Strong and courageous!

Physical strength is an attribute that has been honored by men throughout history. Being that we are by nature competitive, pointing to our pride, that strength has been measured throughout time. Certainly, this is an age-old occurrence, though we can mark its history easily by the Olympic Games, a competition of bigger, stronger and faster. While muscle might define outer strength, inner strength is called courage. Courage is not defined in terms of size, though the ability to face larger adversaries certainly points to someone bigger on the inside. Think of David, when he was still a lad, and faced the giant Goliath! As Christians we are called to be both strong and courageous.

[8] **"Therefore you shall keep every commandment which I command you today, that you may be strong, and go in and possess the land which you cross over to possess,** [9] **and that you may prolong *your* days in the land which the LORD swore to give your fathers, to them and their descendants, 'a land flowing with milk and honey.'**
Deuteronomy 11:8-9 (NKJV)

In the verses above, Moses is re-telling the words of the Lord to the children of Israel, before they enter the Promised Land. In his oration, Moses reminds them to be strong. After 40 years of wandering in the wilderness, what should have been an 11-day journey from Egypt to Israel, the Jews could look back and see where they had failed. Upon Moses sending spies into the Promised Land, the people were afraid, as the spies returned with stories of giants in the land, comparing the size of the Israelites to grasshoppers. Only Joshua and Caleb had the courage to follow the Lord into battle. So in punishment, the Lord forced the Jews to roam the desert sands until every unbeliever had died. Entering the Promised Land called for courage, as the Jews knew the size of the enemy. Additionally, to fight the giant inhabitants would take strength.

Interestingly, there are nine verses in the Bible using the phrase, "Be strong and of good courage." They are: Deuteronomy 31:6, Deuteronomy 31:7, Deuteronomy 31:23, Joshua 1:6, Joshua 1:9, Joshua 1:18, Joshua 10:25, 1 Chronicles 22:13 and 1 Chronicles 28:20. In the three verses in Deuteronomy, Moses prepares Joshua. Though Moses was not allowed to enter the Promised Land, the Lord selected Joshua to lead the people. Three times, Moses encouraged Joshua with the phrase, "Be strong and of good courage." In Joshua, the Lord speaks those same words to Joshua three times. So Joshua heard that phrase six times and then he gave the same advice to the people after capturing the five kings, in the verse from Joshua 10. Finally, the last two times we read this phrase, King David speaks to his son, Solomon, who was to take David's place as king.

Is the Lord asking us for the same strength and courage? Strength does not just refer to a physical attribute. Strength is the resolve to wholly lean on Jesus' name. This world is a difficult place. We cannot do it alone. We need Him, yet most of the time, the situations He places us in call for our courage. The Lord will win the battles but we need the courage to stand alongside Him. Watch and see what He accomplishes! It does not matter how large the enemy is. It does not matter how many soldiers are in the army surrounding us. It does not matter what small odds for survival the world would give us. God is bigger. He lives inside us. Just as the pillar of cloud by day and the pillar of fire by night, He goes before us!

You must not fear them, for the LORD your God Himself fights for you.'
Deuteronomy 3:22 (NKJV)

What or who are the giants in our lives? Be strong and of good courage…and trust in God!

To You, O my Strength, I will sing praises;
For God *is* my defense,
My God of mercy.

Psalm 59:17 (NKJV)

July 11: The Way

A common misconception in religion is that there are many paths to God. Whether it is Buddhism, Islam, Shintoism, Hinduism, Judaism, Christianity, or a mix of any of those, many people hold to the notion that a belief in God is virtually the same. Yet by studying world religions, though there might be some similarities, the differences are much more apparent. God created each of us, and in every one of His creations is a gaping hole that only He can fill. Many try to fill that hole with that which will not satisfy: drugs, alcohol, fame, fortune, possessions, sex, family or anything apart from God that we could add to that endless list. Is God easy to find?

[13] **"Enter by the narrow gate; for wide *is* the gate and broad *is* the way that leads to destruction, and there are many who go in by it.** [14] **Because narrow *is* the gate and difficult *is* the way which leads to life, and there are few who find it. Matthew 7:13-14 (NKJV)**

While the gate that leads to God might be narrow and difficult to find, it is not hidden. God's desire is that all of us might come to know Him, and He wants us to find Him. Finding God is not like searching for a needle in a haystack. Instead, seeking the Lord is like searching for something that is so huge that we have a tendency to take it for granted and overlook it. God is as plain as the nose on our faces, as the saying goes.

One of the most eye-opening stops in the Middle East is Petra, Jordan. Bible scholars believe that Petra will be the haven in the wilderness that will house the Jews in the second half of the tribulation, prophesied about in Revelation. Petra is a city carved into sandstone, as the outside walls are ornately decorated into the soft rock, and the caves inside are large enough to house millions of people. Yet the most interesting part of Petra involves the journey in. There is only one way into Petra. A pathway leads between the granite walls hundreds of feet tall, and winds for miles, curving like a bow. At times, that pathway is fairly wide, but it narrows to the width of six feet in places. Without knowing the city exists, it would be easy to completely miss it. Interestingly, the pathway into the city is called the *Siq* in Arabic, meaning, the Way.

Jesus said to him, "I am the way, the truth, and the life. No one comes to the Father except through Me.
John 14:6 (NKJV)

Jesus did not claim to be one of many paths to God. He insisted that He was the only way. Early believers in Christianity were called by that moniker, "The Way." Those who believe in many paths to God should think of what occurs at an airport.

If we are in Houston, Texas, and want to fly to Paris, France, if we get on a plane to Buenos Aires, Argentina, we certainly will not be in Paris when the plane arrives. In fact, we will be much farther from our intended destination than when we began. Certainly, all paths do not have the same destination. That being said, another series of airplane flights can correct the erroneous part of our journey, getting us to Paris eventually. In the same way, even if we start our journey to God by going in the wrong direction, we can stop wherever we are and point ourselves in His direction. We do not have to be near an airport to start that journey; we just need to point ourselves back towards God if we have been seeking the world.

And you will seek Me and find *Me*, when you search for Me with all your heart.
Jeremiah 29:13 (NKJV)

[7] **"Ask, and it will be given to you; seek, and you will find; knock, and it will be opened to you.** [8] **For everyone who asks receives, and he who seeks finds, and to him who knocks it will be opened.**
Luke 11:7-8 (NKJV)

July 12: Help, I need somebody!

A memorable television commercial depicts a young man standing on the dock of a lake. In the lake is a drowning friend calling for help, yet the young man on the dock ignores the cries. The advertisement was attempting to demonstrate that when we have a friend with a drug problem and we do not tell parents or friends, we are no different than the young man on the dock. People who are jeopardizing their lives need help.

In the same manner, we all need a Savior. Salvation is the deliverance from destruction, and every person born is on a fast path toward destruction. Yet salvation is not only the deliverance, but the Deliverer from that destruction! Jesus gives us the gift of salvation, but He also is our salvation! The gift that He gives to us is Him! It says in John:

"Greater love has no one than this, than to lay down one's life for his friends.
John 15:13 (NKJV)

That is exactly what Jesus did for us; He died so we do not have to!
Remember, salvation is:
- Something we cannot do alone.
- Something we cannot do for others.
- A debt paid. Because sin must be paid for, Jesus paid it for us.
- Blood money! His blood is worth more than any amounts of gold or silver.
- Enough to satisfy all of our debts.
- Something that cannot be received without asking for it!

Jesus is the Door, the Gate and the Way. Notice that all of those nouns are singular. He is the only path for us to heaven.

"Behold, I stand at the door and knock. If anyone hears My voice and opens the door, I will come in to him and dine with him, and he with Me.

Revelation 3:20 (NKJV)

Anyone can come into the presence of Jesus by accepting Him into their hearts. He stands at the door of our hearts and knocks, and we decide whether or not to let Him in. If we ask Him in, He is not like a visiting relative. They say that visiting relatives and fish both will go bad in three days. Jesus comes in and stays forever! God died for man. That is not legend—it is truth. If He is the truth and He lives in us, we are keepers of the truth. Are we missing Jesus in our lives? Do we have friends that desperately need a Savior? Are we afraid to tell them, as they might think we are crazy? If they were drowning, would we give them a hand?

**"There is none righteous, no, not one;
Romans 3:10 (NKJV)**

**So he answered and said, " 'You shall love the LORD your God with all your heart, with all your soul, with all your strength, and with all your mind,' and 'your neighbor as yourself.' "
Luke 10:27 (NKJV)**

July 13: Do your duty!

Duty has been described as reverence, respect for authority, regard, or more specifically, the social force that binds us to our obligations and the courses of action demanded by that force. Cadets at the United States Air Force Academy memorize a quotation about duty:

> "Duty, then, is the sublimest word in the English language. You should do your duty in all things. You can never do more. You should not wish to do less."
> --General Robert E. Lee

General Lee applied the subject of duty to a soldier, and we should understand that application, as we are all soldiers. Jesus said, "He who is not with Me is against Me," in Luke 11:23, summing up the two opposing sides of the spiritual battle. Soldiers understand that they are mere representatives of their commander in chief, who makes decisions with lives on the line. Those decisions have nothing to do with their rights.

As Christians, we are representing our Commander in Chief, who has purchased our lives at a great cost, with His own precious blood. In fact, by looking at the life and death of Jesus, we can better understand what it means to carry out our duties regardless of our desires. On the night before the crucifixion, when in the Garden of Gethsemane, Jesus prayed to the Father three times that if there was any other way to accomplish this great task, to please, let it be done. Then He lovingly and nobly took the most difficult steps that gained our salvation and His death! So what is our duty?

¹ I beseech you therefore, brethren, by the mercies of God, that you present your bodies a living sacrifice, holy, acceptable to God, *which is* your reasonable service. ² And do not be conformed to this world, but be transformed by the renewing of your mind, that you may prove what *is* that good and acceptable and perfect will of God.
Romans 12:1-2 (NKJV)

In the same manner that Jesus accepted the Father's will, our duty is identical. We are to do the will of the Father. Paul's explanation points us to the fact that we are to become living sacrifices to the Lord. That is such a vivid picture, as in the Old Testament sacrificial system, the animals being sacrificed died on the altar. Yet in this analogy, our bodies are not dead sacrifices, but alive. Most of us have promised the Lord to walk away from a sin, and then found ourselves involved in that sin again.

The sacrifice we made to the Lord crawls off the altar and lives again! Yet God forgives each time we ask for that forgiveness. Do not take that forgiveness for granted. According to the verses in Romans, it is our "reasonable service" to give the Lord our bodies. That means to walk away from fornication, drunkenness or any other sin that makes our bodies dirty. Remember, the Lord lives inside that body! When we become Christians, God changes our hearts, yet our brains still retain the old memories of our sinful lives. By following God's Laws, our behaviors change to match His ways. Over time, those old sinful memories do not carry such a magnetic attraction to us.

Reasonable service is duty, just like in General Lee's description. That duty is reasonable, for we cannot do more. We should not wish to do less, especially when we remember what Jesus did for us!

It pleased them indeed, and they are their debtors. For if the Gentiles have been partakers of their spiritual things, their duty is also to minister to them in material things.
Romans 15:27 (NKJV)

Stay this night, and in the morning it shall be *that* if he will perform the duty of a close relative for you—good; let him do it. But if he does not want to perform the duty for you, then I will perform the duty for you, *as* the LORD lives! Lie down until morning."
Ruth 3:13 (NKJV)

July 14: Where did it all go wrong?

There are certainly many different religious beliefs on the planet earth. We all need something to believe in, as we understand the frailty of life. A view of world religions reveals an emphasis on rituals. Practitioners of Islam face Mecca and pray five times daily. Catholics use rosary beads to assist in counting the number of Hail Mary's prayed. Most Buddhists ritually stand before a Buddha or Bodhi-tree daily with clasped hands, in personal worship. Hindus perform a daily *puja* ceremony, first, looking at a picture of the family's god; next, the family offers flowers, food or fruit to the god; and last, the family retrieves the food and eats it. Judaism emphasizes the *mitzvah*, which is a good deed. On the Day of Atonement, Jews reflect on the previous year to decide if they have done more good deeds than bad. Christianity is quite different than the rest, emphasizing relationships, not performance or ritual.

Islam teaches that it is a Muslim's duty to kill the infidel, which is anyone who does not believe that Mohammed is the only god. They have chosen to worship a child molester, who at the age of 53, married a 6-year-old girl, and had "relations" with her until he died at the age of 62. Travel to a Muslim country gives us more insight into their rituals. The first "call to prayer" comes from the minaret around 5 a.m., and there is a "snooze alarm." Ten minutes or so after the original cacophony subsides, it begins again. Those poor people need more sleep!

Even as Christians, we can lose sight of God's goal. When His Word is not taken literally, and man intersperses his own ideas into the mix, problems occur. Buddhists and Hindus worship an object constructed by the hands of man, an idol. What kind of a god can man create? What is a piece of shiny metal going to do when we pray to it? Jews are close to grasping the truth, as there is nothing wrong with good deeds. Yet there is not a place in the Old Testament where God teaches that He grades on a curve. The Lord's sliding scale is not an accountant's balance sheet, with good deeds marked in black as assets and sins marked in red as liabilities. Instead, one sin makes a man a sinner, we are all sinners (1 John 1:10 and Romans 3:23) and the wages of sin is death (Romans 6:23).

There is only one mark that will override the sins on our balance sheets, the mark that says we have decided to follow Jesus. When that occurs, all of our sins are washed away.

"Come now, and let us reason together,"
Says the LORD,
"Though your sins are like scarlet,
They shall be as white as snow;
Though they are red like crimson,
They shall be as wool.
Isaiah 1:18 (NKJV)

The Master Accountant blots out our sins with White-out. It even can cover the scarlet ink made from blood used to keep track of our sins! How can we tell that Christianity is the only way to God? The Bible is the only document that teaches absolute truth. It does not sugarcoat how great man is, but emphasizes that all men are sinners and need a Savior! We all know that men love to talk about themselves and their own accomplishments. Is it not ironic that the Bible records the life of Jesus, written by men who believed with every fiber of their beings that He was and is the Living God? Some of the men doing the writing accomplished quite a bit with the hand of God ruling their lives, but the stories where not about them! Instead, they wrote of a humble Rabbi who taught them to love their enemies, not kill them. He is worth knowing! For those who already know Him, He is worth knowing better! Spend time making that relationship closer today!

[37] Jesus said to him, *'You shall love the LORD your God with all your heart, with all your soul, and with all your mind.'* [38] This is *the* first and great commandment. [39] And *the* second *is* like it: *'You shall love your neighbor as yourself.'* [40] On these two commandments hang all the Law and the Prophets." Matthew 22:37-40 (NKJV)

July 15: Where can you hide?

One of the greatest difficulties that we face as believers is how to stay separate from the world while living in it. God does not desire for us all to be monks and hermits, or for that matter, to live in a Christian commune where the only people we see are fellow believers. Someday, we will worship God and be surrounded by only others doing the same! Yet while on this earth, believers in the Father, the Son and the Holy Spirit are in the minority. Do the world and the trappings of the world keep us so busy that we do not take time for God? If we truly love the Lord, would we rather spend time with Him or worshipping an American Idol?

[1]**Blessed *is* the man**

Who walks not in the counsel of the ungodly,
Nor stands in the path of sinners,
Nor sits in the seat of the scornful;
²But his delight *is* **in the law of the LORD,**
And in His law he meditates day and night.
Psalm 1:1-2 (NKJV)

The verse above from Psalms covers the bases. It begins with the word "Blessed," pointing to our salvation. Literally, the word means, "Oh, how happy," and that is the ongoing feeling that salvation brings. Next, we see places we are not to go as Christians. When a believer walks in the counsel of the ungodly, it is a slow, progressive path. An ungodly man might not be sinning all the time, but he certainly does not ask for God's advice before acting. Additionally, notice that it is not a one-time meeting, but continuing contact. Next, we see that we are not to stand in the path of sinners. We are all sinners, but this refers to those who are blatantly contradicting the laws of God. In the first example, we were walking, and in this one, we are standing. It sounds like we are going to spend even more time with the sinners. Who would stand in the middle of the road with a drunk driver barreling toward us? Without thought, they are going to mow us down!

God is not telling us to avoid non-believers, for that would conflict what He has told us in other places in the Bible. How else would they hear about Jesus if we did not share that love with them? Yet, we also know that it takes an enormous amount of strength to refrain from joining in their sin. In the Old Testament, God warned the children of Israel not to marry foreigners, as He knew the Israelites would fall away from worshipping Him and would worship the idols of the foreigners. As the verse in Psalms continues, we are told not to sit in the seat of the scornful. The verse progresses from walking, to standing, to sitting. In the last example, the believer has become comfortable with the sinner, and the sin. The word "scornful" means someone who mocks God.

Standing on an icy slope facing downhill gives us a picture of the ease of falling into sin. It is much more difficult to remain stopped then to come to a stop on the way down the hill. While expert skiers may control their downward progress, it is much more difficult to ski uphill to our original destination, as the forces are pushing us downward. That is similar to the force of sin in our lives. God's solution is to stay away from situations that will make us stumble. He is the only one who can pick us up when we fall! It might seem like there is not a place to hide from the stench of the world, but we have the Lord living inside of us. He cleans us! Turn to Him!

Do not love the world or the things in the world. If anyone loves the world, the love of the Father is not in him.
1 John 2:15 (NKJV)

July 16: Compromise means promise together!

Sometimes, it seems like all of life is a compromise. Compromise is defined as a settlement in which each side makes concessions. Lawyers spend hours negotiating compromises to ease time spent in litigation. One of the best biblical examples of compromise comes from the wisdom of King Solomon. Two harlots from the same house gave birth to children three days apart. When one of the newborn infants died in the night, the mother of that baby took the other woman's baby. Of course, she denied those claims. Solomon, gifted in God's wisdom, had to make a judgment though he was not there at the time.

And the king said, "Divide the living child in two, and give half to one, and half to the other."
1 Kings 3:25 (NKJV)

Of course, the thieving mother was fine with that result, as her baby already had died. Yet the actual mother revealed her honesty when she acknowledged that she would rather have the other mother raise the child than to see her child die. Solomon gave the true mother her child back.

American news reporter Jane Wells said, "Learn the wisdom of compromise for it is better to bend a little than to break." That might be wisdom when it comes to settling differences within a family or marriage, yet it is ignorance when it comes to compromising principles! Elbert Hubbard, a 20th-century American writer, had a different perspective when he said, "It's the weak man who urges compromise, never the strong man."

God does not compromise. One of His attributes is that He cannot change, so consequently, getting involved in deal-making would demonstrate that He did not know what He was doing to begin with. Additionally, we know that God always keeps His side of the bargain, which makes the only cheaters on the other side of the bargaining table. When God makes a promise, we can take that covenant to the bank. Do our promises hold that same strength?

As Christians, we face compromise on a daily basis. Do we compromise our integrity at work? Are our business ethics different from our ethics when dealing with fellow believers at church? "Everyone else does it," should not be an excuse, as we are not accountable to everyone else. Yet we are accountable to God. Do we compromise our Christian values when watching television, attending movies or even telling a dirty joke? Certainly, we all make mistakes. But God does not want us to compromise the Christian values He has given us.

When the Lord calls us out of the world to serve Him, most of us walk away from behaviors that we are not proud of. Sadly, many people claiming to be Christians either continue in the old ways, or fall back into those lives. Those compromises never work out well. In fact, when we compromise the Lord's calling on our lives, we are no better off than a baby cut in half! If there are compromises in our Christian walks we should turn around and take a step back in God's direction!

For if, after they have escaped the pollutions of the world through the knowledge of the Lord and Savior Jesus Christ,

they are again entangled in them and overcome, the latter end is worse for them than the beginning.
2 Peter 2:20 (NKJV)

July 17: Whose church is it?

Driving down the highways and byways of the towns in the United States, it is apparent that there are more churches than Starbucks, in a variety of shapes, sizes and denominations. Most people attending church think that their own denomination is the only one that believes correctly. The word "church" first appears in Matthew 16:18, when Jesus says, **"And I also say to you that you are Peter, and on this rock I will build My church, and the gates of Hades shall not prevail against it."** Even that verse causes a schism as Catholics believe it is speaking of Peter being the foundation of their church, while evangelical Christians believe that the Rock is Jesus, contrasting the name of Peter, or Cephas, meaning "little stone," with the Rock of our salvation, Jesus, who is certainly not a little stone.

In Greek, the word church is *ecclesia*, meaning "called out ones." We have been called out of the world by God to minister to others with the gifts God gives us. Church is not a building, but the people inside the building. Whether or not we believe in a pre-tribulation rapture, a mid-tribulation rapture or a post-tribulation rapture, we are members of the same church. It is not when we go to heaven that is important, but who we see when we get there! It better be Jesus! Whether we believe in full-immersion baptism, sprinkling or dipping, we are members of the same church. Sprinkled, dipped and dunked are more important terms at Dunkin' Donuts!

God's church is the body of Christ! Some people like to hang out with Tonto, for they are the Lone Rangers, who shy away from situations where they will be hurt again, as most have suffered critical wounds from inside the church. Those pains inflicted by fellow church members or even church leaders hurt much more deeply than the ones that come from unbelievers, as we expect the abuse from the world (John 15:18). Typically, those wounds occur when the church is being run like a corporation rather than like a hospital. If the pastor thinks he is the CEO, he has forgotten whose church it really is!

Church is a place of worship, fellowship and food, and the food should be a double blessing, as each person attending has the opportunity to feed and be fed. Sadly, the food in our churches today resembles the restaurants of the world. Some offer little more than a homily, not much more than the thought of the day. Many people in these churches complain if the sermon goes too long, as their diet is entirely fast food. Pastors pick and choose which aspects of the Bible they will teach and which they will avoid. Rather than being fed a healthy, balanced diet, the people attending those churches fill up on dessert (stories that make them feel good about themselves) and completely sidestep the entrée and the vegetables (anything that makes the people feel uncomfortable with their own sins). Then there are the churches similar to all-you-can-eat Chinese buffets. The people eat so much they cannot get up, and never would take the first step in preparing a plate for someone else. MSG goes to the brain! It is hard to find the perfect fit, but God wants us to remain in fellowship.

**[23] Let us hold fast the confession of *our* hope without wavering, for He who promised *is* faithful. [24] And let us consider one another in order to stir up love and good works, [25] not forsaking the assembling of ourselves together, as *is* the manner of some, but exhorting *one another,* and so much the more as you see the Day approaching.
Hebrews 10:23-25 (NKJV)**

Those gifts that God gives are not for our own edification, but to minister to others. Some pastors think that the Bible is meant to be taught simply. Yet, God created us all, and He made us so marvelously and wonderfully different. Some people desire simplicity, while others desire depth. There are pastors at every level of the spectrum in that regard, using the gifts that God has given them in exactly the way He desires. As Christians we never grow to the point where we no longer need to be fed. Yet it does not take a pastor to feed us.

But the Helper, the Holy Spirit, whom the Father will send in My name, He will teach you all things, and bring to your remembrance all things that I said to you.
John 14:26 (NKJV)

It might take some time, but find a church that teaches the Word of God. Find a church with a pastor who teaches the depth of the Bible that our hearts desire. Just like manna in the wilderness, God continues to feed us daily! Find a church where we can serve others. If hurt, forgive and turn the other cheek. God wants us all to be in fellowship with others who will love us as we love them. He did not say it was going to be easy!

And He is the head of the body, the church, who is the beginning, the firstborn from the dead, that in all things He may have the preeminence.
Colossians 1:18

July 18: Leadership and the family

Most people fall into the categories of followers or leaders, yet there also are a small number of people not willing to follow, though no one wants to follow them, either! Leaders are not self-appointed. The best way of discovering whether or not we are leaders is by looking behind to see if anyone is following. As Christians, first and foremost, we should be followers of Jesus Christ. Unless our walk closely resembles His, leadership is the worst place we could be. We have all heard the common parental retort when faced with the child's answer that someone else did it first: "If someone else jumped off a cliff, would you follow them?" That is exactly what occurs when we follow another person who is not following Jesus. All other roads lead to death and destruction!

In 1 Timothy, Paul explains the attributes required of leaders within the church, bishops and deacons. Bishops, according to Paul, must be:

[2]"blameless, the husband of one wife, temperate, sober-minded, of good behavior, hospitable, able to teach; [3] not given to wine, not violent, not greedy for money, but gentle, not quarrelsome, not covetous; [4] one who rules his own house well, having *his* children in submission with all reverence [5] (for if a man does not know how to rule his own house, how will he take care of the church of God?); [6] not a novice, lest being puffed up with pride he fall into the *same* condemnation as the devil. [7] Moreover he must have a good testimony among those who are outside, lest he fall into reproach and the snare of the devil. "
1 Timothy 3:2-7 (NKJV)

Included in this section of verses is an example of God's first assignment to the majority of Christians as leaders. We are to be leaders in our own families. When God blesses a couple with a child, their first responsibility is to lead that child to the Lord through teaching and upbringing. This is not exclusively a New Testament philosophy, as God instructed the Israelites to remember the past and to remind their children of the events that occurred in the exodus from Egypt:

[20] "When your son asks you in time to come, saying, 'What *is the meaning of* the testimonies, the statutes, and the judgments which the LORD our God has commanded you?' [21] then you shall say to your son: 'We were slaves of Pharaoh in Egypt, and the LORD brought us out of Egypt with a mighty hand; [22] and the LORD showed signs and wonders before our eyes, great and severe, against Egypt, Pharaoh, and all his household. [23] Then He brought us out from there, that He might bring us in, to give us the land of which He swore to our fathers. [24] And the LORD commanded us to observe all these statutes, to fear the LORD our God, for our good always, that He might preserve us alive, as *it is* this day. [25] Then it will be righteousness for us, if we are careful to

observe all these commandments before the LORD our God, as He has commanded us.'
Deuteronomy 6:20-25 (NKJV)

Part of teaching our children is to remind them of God's Laws, God's miraculous and merciful hand and God's promises. Yet this cannot be accomplished without the fear of the Lord. Fearing God means exactly what it says, and is a reverence for the Lord's unending power. In Proverbs, God gives us further instructions on how we are to lead in our families:

Train up a child in the way he should go,
And when he is old he will not depart from it.
Proverbs 22:6 (NKJV)

If we have not taught our children the way of the Lord, how will they know it? "Train" is the same word for *Chanukah*, which means to dedicate. We are to dedicate our children to the way of the Lord. God's promise does not say that they never will stray from His ways, but "when he is old he will not depart from it." There are many people whose parents did their duty, only to see their children follow the ways of the world. Sometimes, it is painfully difficult to watch the erroneous steps of those adults on the path to destruction, though they were taught God's Laws as children. Sometimes, we lose sight of God's promise that they will return to Him. This is a sweet promise from the Lord that should bring comfort to godly parents!

Are we fulfilling our duty as the leader God called us to be? The first priority is to follow God, the next is to lead in our family and only then, will God use us to lead in other areas. It all starts with the words to the old song, "I have decided to follow Jesus, no turning back!" Remember, a leader does not need a following mob to make his position more important. A leader only needs one follower to do his job perfectly!

His lord said to him, 'Well *done,* good and faithful servant; you have been faithful over a few things, I will make you ruler over many things.

Matthew 25:23 (NKJV)

July 19: Let it shine!

Many people seem to resemble their dogs! Partly, that has to do with the breed of dog we choose as our dogs reflect the choices of our lives. Similarly, after spending a lifetime together, many husbands and wives seem to look alike, as well. That has more to do with the single-mindedness of the couple, along with the amount of time spent together. Who do we spend the most time with?

[29] Now it was so, when Moses came down from Mount Sinai (and the two tablets of the Testimony *were* in Moses' hand when he came down from the mountain), that Moses did not know that the skin of his face shone while he talked with Him. [30] So when Aaron and all the children of Israel saw Moses, behold, the skin of his face shone, and they were afraid to come near him.
Exodus 34:29-30 (NKJV)

Moses spent enough time with God that he reflected the Lord when he was around others. As Christians, we have Jesus living inside of us and the Light of the world is being reflected to others in the same manner that the moon reflects the sun's light in God's magnificent creation. When God created light, He made the sun as the greater light and the moon as the lesser light (Genesis 1:16). Can the people walking in darkness see the light that shines on our faces?

Now when they saw the boldness of Peter and John, and perceived that they were uneducated and untrained men, they marveled. And they realized that they had been with Jesus.
Acts 4:13 (NKJV)

Each of us as believers can picture the face of a fellow Christian in our lives that radiates Jesus. There is not a little piece of Jesus in each of us, but instead, all of God is inside of each of us. If

He is not reflecting from our faces, it is because too much of the dirt of the world is blocking the light. If we are not spending time with the Lord, that glow wears off! The life of Jesus continues to be written in the lives of believers. There is no greater compliment that can be paid to any of us as believers than when people say we have been with Jesus! It should show on our faces, in our walks, in our language, in our choices and in our growth.

Where is the strongest light in a world of darkness? It is radiating from the faces of the people who have been with Jesus. We should let our lights shine!

[14] "You are the light of the world. A city that is set on a hill cannot be hidden. [15] Nor do they light a lamp and put it under a basket, but on a lampstand, and it gives light to all *who are* in the house.[16] Let your light so shine before men, that they may see your good works and glorify your Father in heaven.
Matthew 5:14-16 (NKJV)

July 20: That is just lame!

A favorite Bible story is about Mephibosheth, the lame son of Jonathan and grandson of King Saul. Though David had been a faithful servant to King Saul, playing the lyre to soothe the King's nerves, slaying a giant to save the King's land and lifting a sword to support the King's battles, King Saul wanted David dead. At the same time, David and Jonathan became the closest of friends. When King Saul and Jonathan died together in battle and were beheaded, it solved one of David's problems yet created another. King Saul no longer would be trying to kill David, but the new King was broken-hearted for the loss of his dearest friend. When David became King of Israel, all of King Saul's supporters went into hiding. After searching, King David found the closest descendant, Mephibosheth. Once found, Mephibosheth ate at the King's table for the remainder of his life. Additionally, King David ensured that the servants cared for the land with the profits going to Mephibosheth.

What is the significance of a lame man feasting with a king? Each of us suffers the same walk as a crippled man. Our walks point to the direction of our lives, and without God, they always are pointed the wrong way. Yet even as believers, we continue to trip and fall. Every man's battle seems to be sexual temptation, as Jesus pointed out that lusting is identical to committing adultery. While that sin is common to man, there is a long list of sins that continues to trip up even the strongest believers. Without God leading us in the paths of righteousness, we will quickly find ourselves in the paths of unrighteousness.

For You have delivered my soul from death.
***Have You* not *kept* my feet from falling,**
That I may walk before God
In the light of the living?
Psalm 56:13 (NKJV)

God knows that we are sinners. Being omniscient, He never is surprised by our mis-steps or sins. God is quick to forgive when we ask for His forgiveness, though He desires for us to understand the ramifications of our sins.

The sacrifices of God *are* a broken spirit,
A broken and a contrite heart—
These, O God, You will not despise.
Psalm 51:17 (NKJV)

If our sins broke our own hearts as much as they broke God's heart, we might begin to walk closer to Him. Yet the most amazing aspect is that He comes to wherever we are with as little as each of us has to offer. We do not earn His love or His salvation. That is His gift, and because of that gift, we will eat at the King's table for all of eternity! Though we cannot earn the gift, we certainly should be thankful for it!

[8]For You have delivered my soul from death,
My eyes from tears,
***And* my feet from falling.**

⁹**I will walk before the L**ORD
In the land of the living.
Psalm 116:8-9 (NKJV)

July 21: Hard clay

One of God's often overlooked miracles is how He continues to re-work the clay of our hearts!

But now, O LORD**,**
You *are* **our Father;**
We *are* **the clay, and You our potter;**
And all we *are* **the work of Your hand.**
Isaiah 64:8 (NKJV)

A favorite quotation states, "The same sun that melts butter hardens the clay." We can see that in effect all around us as to most people, the name of Jesus is a stumbling block, yet to those who believe the Bible, Jesus is the name above every name, and just by hearing His name, our hearts are softened. Yes, the cares of the world get in the way. If there was no pleasure associated with sin, there certainly would not be a lure. Living in the midst of a sinful world, it is easy to yearn for what appears to be relative ease in the lives of many. Yet with earthly prosperity comes a greater responsibility to use that wealth for God's purposes, rather than for self-aggrandizement. Sadly, too often we turn our eyes to the world and others we know, coveting what God has given them, and in so doing, we break the tenth commandment. Rather than questioning what God has chosen to give us, we should accept His wisdom in the gifts He has given.

Surely you have things turned around!
For shall the thing made say of him who made it,
"He did not make me"?
Or shall the thing formed say of him who formed it,
"He has no understanding?"
Isaiah 29:16 (NKJV)

Clay that is hard cannot be bent or molded. Instead, it must be pressed, rolled and crushed. Only then does it warm up, and only then can it be shaped into whatever the potter desires. That is what God does with each of our hearts. Cold hearts cannot be broken, and only a broken heart can find the Lord. It is in that point of brokenness when we can see the nothingness of our existence without God that we finally can see the need for a Savior. He pressed us into those situations; He rolled us to the edge of despair; He crushed our hearts so that they could learn how to truly love. He will make us the people He wants us to be, and will not complete the work until we see Him face to face.

We often complain to God about the situations of our lives. It seems a little ridiculous when we understand the depths He went to in order to give us abundant life. Do we believe He would do anything that is not intended to be the best in our lives? It is all for the greatest purpose, and He is using everything that He accomplishes in our lives simultaneously in the lives of others. Trust Him, for He loves us so much!

[5] **Then the word of the LORD came to me, saying:** [6] **"O house of Israel, can I not do with you as this potter?" says the LORD. "Look, as the clay *is* in the potter's hand, so *are* you in My hand, O house of Israel!**
Jeremiah 18:5-6 (NKJV)

July 22: Discarded pottery

It is difficult to drink from a cup with a crack or hole in it. If the crack is on the side, the liquid drips all over us. If there is a hole in the bottom, even if that hole is very small, it does not take long for all of the liquid to drain from the cup. In the same manner, we are vessels for the Lord:

that each of you should know how to possess his own vessel in sanctification and honor,
1 Thessalonians 4:4 (NKJV)

God does not use a dirty vessel. If there is unrepentant sin in our lives, we need to be clean before we are ready to serve the Lord. Aimee Semple McPherson, a pioneer for using multimedia in evangelism, had an extramarital affair, faked her own death as a cover, and later died from an overdose of barbiturates. Though married, Ted Haggard, founder of a mega-church in Colorado and leader of the National Association of Evangelicals, was caught in a homosexual affair, and requested for the hustler to bring illegal drugs to their tryst. Sadly, the list of pastors and teachers who have stumbled is long: Paul Crouch, Jim and Tammy Bakker, Jimmy Swaggart, Lonnie Frisbee, etc. Just because a person has the gift of teaching does not exclude them from the temptations of sin. Additionally, pride can stumble those who begin to believe they are above rebuke. God does not need the greatest preacher or teacher, as He gave the gift. He easily can raise someone else up in their places. In the same manner that a cracked drinking vessel cannot hold water, a sinful vessel cannot hold Living Water!

Yet God knows that we are sinners, and does not desire for us to be broken pieces of pottery, cast away, never to be used again. In Job 2:8, Job uses a broken piece of pottery, called a potsherd, to scrape the boils from his skin. In the most prophetic psalm of Jesus on the cross, Jesus says:

My strength is dried up like a potsherd,
And My tongue clings to My jaws;
You have brought Me to the dust of death.
Psalm 22:15 (NKJV)

On the cross, while Jesus was enduring the greatest pain imaginable for our benefits, He felt like He was all used up, like a discarded piece of pottery. Without God, we are all potsherds. Satan has used us for his deceitful plans and his benefit. Without serving God, even unknowingly, we serve God's enemy, the one who has been given dominion over the earth for a time. Yet those of us as believers, who found ourselves discarded from the world, lying in the dirt and dust, were rescued by the Master Potter. He took that old discarded and broken clay and melded it back together. Previously filled with cracks and holes, we are now capable of being filled by Him with Living Water.

We should not lose sight of the fact that our vessels still can sustain cracks, but those can be filled by our repentance and His forgiveness. We are on this earth to share God's love with others. Why would God use a dirty vessel? Simply be reading the newspapers about the pastors who have fallen into temptation, we can understand how Satan continues to battle by trying to destroy the testimony of God's people. Be aware of the battle that he fights, as it certainly is not a new or original strategy. We must possess our vessels in holiness by honoring the Lord with our lives and our life's work!

I am forgotten like a dead man, out of mind;
I am like a broken vessel.
Psalm 31:12 (NKJV)

July 23: Hoist it and carry it!

When hiking, it is amazing how light the backpack feels at the beginning of the journey in contrast to how heavy that same backpack feels at journey's end. In a similar manner, until the day each of us accepted Jesus as our Lord and Savior, we carried the enormous burden of our own sins on our narrow shoulders. In that moment when we decide to follow Jesus, the burden is lifted from us, and placed on the shoulders of the only One who can handle that burden. Jesus died so that we might live. But what did He tell us to do?

[24] Then Jesus said to His disciples, "If anyone desires to come after Me, let him deny himself, and take up his cross, and follow Me. [25] For whoever desires to save his life will lose it, but whoever loses his life for My sake will find it.
Matthew 16:24:25 (NKJV)

What was the cross to Jesus? First, it was the instrument of His death. One of the most important aspects of His death is that He was not murdered, as Jesus gave His life for us. Willingly. At any moment, He could have chosen to perform a miracle and exit stage right. Yet because He understood what the cross would do for us and because He loved us, He endured the cross. Secondly, the cross was a place of humiliation for Jesus. The Roman soldiers stripped Jesus of His clothing, placed a crown of thorns on His head, and made fun of Him. With the crowd of bystanders chiming in, along with one of the criminals being crucified beside Jesus, there were few present who did not despise Him.

As Christians, we have to be willing to die to self in order to live in Jesus. Are there aspects of our lives that we are not willing to part with? How about our husbands or wives? Would we still follow Jesus if that spouse did not join us in our pursuit? If we lost every possession, would we still be willing to follow Him? When a rich, young ruler came to Jesus and asked what it would take to follow Him, Jesus responded by telling the young man to sell all his possessions and distribute the money to the poor (Luke 18:18). Unable to walk away from his wealth, the young man chose a path that did not involve Jesus. At the heart of the matter is the matter of the heart. Jesus knew right where that young man's heart was, just as He knows all about our hearts, as He shaped them!

[19] "Do not lay up for yourselves treasures on earth, where moth and rust destroy and where thieves break in and steal; [20] but lay up for yourselves treasures in heaven, where neither moth nor rust destroys and where thieves do not break in and steal. [21] For where your treasure is, there your heart will be also.
Matthew 6:19-21 (NKJV)

Picking up our own crosses demonstrates a willingness to let our old lives completely pass away, without regard to pride, possessions or position. Picking up our crosses daily involves carrying a weighty burden continuously, but do not forget that Jesus never would allow us to shoulder those burdens alone. We might have times of humiliation, with people making fun of us for our belief in what they cannot see, though we see Him clearly. Certainly, we will face many difficulties, as our Lord faced so much more in our places.

It is difficult to imagine the weight of the burden of each of our sinful lives that Jesus was willing to carry! God tells us to pick up our crosses and follow Him. He is right ahead of us, and every step of the way, He carries that burden with us. We might think we have the heaviest part of the load, but God does all the work. All He wants is our willingness! He is with us always.

⁴He shall call to the heavens from above,
And to the earth, that He may judge His people:
⁵"Gather My saints together to Me,
Those who have made a covenant with Me by sacrifice."
⁶Let the heavens declare His righteousness,
For God Himself *is* Judge.
Psalm 50:4-6 (NKJV)

July 24: Deeper than the deepest ocean

When exploring the outdoors, most people occasionally find themselves in places where they have to cross water, be it river, lake or stream. Without being able to see the bottom, we never can be certain of the depth of the body of water. By poking a long stick toward the bottom, we sometimes can make an educated guess of that depth, but it can change drastically with one step. In those cases, we go from mostly dry to drenched without any warning. Depth certainly cannot be seen simply by looking at the surface.

Christians should carry similar attributes to those streams. When walking in the Spirit, relying on God, our depth should be bottomless. God gives us our depth, whether it is strength, character, patience or love. Additionally, by looking at a person, we have no idea what lies within. That same depth also occurs in God's Word. What an amazing gift God gave us in the Bible. We always can find the depth we are seeking when reading His Word. The Bible may appear to be shallow to new believers interested in learning the basics about God. Yet at the same time and by looking at the same verse, the depth can be immeasurable. Look for the depth in the following story.

As powerful as the Roman Consul Pontius Pilate was in Israel and Jerusalem, he allowed Jesus to be crucified, even though he did not find any wrong in the Man. We also know Pilate was a learned man, as he knew Hebrew, Greek and Latin. He personally wrote this title and placed it upon the cross, and when Jewish leaders asked him to change it, Pilate would not alter it in any way.

[19] **Now Pilate wrote a title and put** *it* **on the cross. And the writing was:**
JESUS OF NAZARETH, THE KING OF THE JEWS.
[20] **Then many of the Jews read this title, for the place where Jesus was crucified was near the city; and it was written in Hebrew, Greek,** *and* **Latin.**
[21] **Therefore the chief priests of the Jews said to Pilate, "Do not write, 'The King of the Jews,' but, 'He said, "I am the King of the Jews." ' "**
[22] **Pilate answered, "What I have written, I have written."**
John 19:19-22 (NKJV)

In Hebrew, that title says, "ישוע הנצרי ומלך היהודים" and is pronounced *"Yeshua HaNazarei v'Melek HaYehudim."* Specifically, the title placed on the cross by Pilate states, "Jesus the Nazarene, and King of the Jews." We do not know if Pilate knew the acrostic written inside his statement, or if it was only an inside comment on the proceedings of the crucifixion by the Father, but notice the first letter of each word:

יַשׁוּעַ	הַנצרי	וַמלך	הַיהודים
Yeshua	The Nazarene	And the king	Of the Jews

Remember, Hebrew reads from right to left. Those four characters are יהוה. This is the *tetragrammaton*, which in Greek, means "a word having four letters. It refers to the unpronounceable name of God in the Old Testament. As Hebrew was written without vowels, there is no one left alive who can pronounce it. Hence, we have shortened it in English to YHWH, and it is where we get *Yahweh, Jehovah,* etc. When Jews see these letters, they pronounce it "*Adonai,*" meaning "Lord." Additionally, as they do not even attempt to pronounce the name of God, they also substitute "*HaShem,*" meaning "the name." Written on the cross was the name of God! The name of God is powerful, and we know that name from the story of Moses and the burning bush.

**[13] Then Moses said to God, "Indeed, *when* I come to the children of Israel and say to them, 'The God of your fathers has sent me to you,' and they say to me, 'What *is* His name?' what shall I say to them?" [14] And God said to Moses, "I AM WHO I AM." And He said, "Thus you shall say to the children of Israel, 'I AM has sent me to you.' "
Exodus 3:13-14 (NKJV)**

When Jesus identifies Himself as the "I AM" in the Garden of Gethsemane, as He can pronounce the unpronounceable name, we see what happens:

**Now when He said to them, "I am *He,*" they drew back and fell to the ground.
John 18:6 (NKJV)**

Notice that the word "He" is italicized, as that word has been placed into the passage to make it more readable or understandable in our language. It is perfectly understandable that He said, "I AM," and they fell to the ground! God has written a love letter to us all called the Bible. With immeasurable depth, we will be studying His Word for all of eternity. While Paul Harvey might say, "And that is the rest of the story," the truth is, that is just the beginning of the story!

July 25: Wisdom

Often we come across well-educated people who seem to be completely lacking in common sense. On the far end of that spectrum are idiot savants, people who have one or more areas of absolute expertise, though that brilliance is in stark contrast to their overall lack of intelligence. An example would be a quantum physicist standing outside barefooted in a blizzard with his mind on solving a challenging equation. The simplicities of daily life are rigors to those people. Certainly there is a difference between intelligence and wisdom. While intelligence can be gained by reading books and studying, wisdom only can be gained by life experiences. Obviously, those life experiences take much longer to acquire and to amass.

When God offered any gift requested to King Solomon, the son of David asked the Lord for wisdom (1 Kings 3). Ironically, the King demonstrated that he already had a large quantity of wisdom, as he understood its significance in relation to a king and his kingdom. A man with less wisdom would have asked for wealth, longevity or safety.

**[29] And God gave Solomon wisdom and exceedingly great understanding, and largeness of heart like the sand on the seashore. [30] Thus Solomon's wisdom excelled the wisdom of all the men of the East and all the wisdom of Egypt. [31] For he was wiser than all men— than Ethan the Ezrahite, and Heman, Chalcol, and Darda, the sons of Mahol; and his fame was in all the surrounding nations. [32] He spoke three thousand proverbs, and his songs were one thousand and five. [33] Also he spoke of trees, from the cedar tree of Lebanon even to the hyssop that springs out of the wall; he spoke also of animals, of birds, of creeping things, and of fish. [34] And men of all nations, from all the kings of the earth who had heard of his wisdom, came to hear the wisdom of Solomon.
1 Kings 4:29-34 (NKJV)**

Though Solomon was the wisest man of all, he also had blind spots in his wisdom. With 700 wives and 300 concubines, King Solomon fell away from the Lord and into idolatry, as he began to follow the gods of his foreign women. It is difficult to imagine that King Solomon was able to keep 1,000 women happy in any facet, and by numbers alone, it is apparent that this decision by an otherwise wise king was very selfish. Those decisions to marry could be called, "King Solomon's Mines," as he seemed to keep saying, "Mine, mine and mine" when selecting additional brides! How can we as Christians gain wisdom?

[13] Who *is* wise and understanding among you? Let him show by good conduct *that* his works *are done* in the meekness of wisdom. [14] But if you have bitter envy and self-seeking in your hearts, do not boast and lie against the truth. [15] This wisdom does not descend from above, but *is* earthly, sensual, demonic. [16] For where envy and self-seeking *exist,* confusion and every evil thing *are* there. [17] But the wisdom that is from above is first pure, then peaceable, gentle, willing to yield, full of mercy and good fruits, without partiality and without hypocrisy. [18] Now the fruit of righteousness is sown in peace by those who make peace.
James 3:13-18 (NKJV)

Interestingly, the phrase "meekness of wisdom" in James 3:13 above seems to point to the most important attribute of wisdom. When combined with humbleness or meekness, wisdom is much more palatable. This is the contrast of the "pride of wisdom," as we all understand that when combined with arrogance, advice from a wise man potentially would be ignored. Wisdom is not self-serving, but for the benefit of others. Without loving others, how can we demonstrate God's love for us? As Christians, God allows us to endure intense stretching. Just as an athlete stretches his muscles before using them in competition, God prepares us for future usage by stretching us. We learn from those difficult life experiences. If we are focused on the Lord, through that stretching comes great wisdom. Additionally, God can help us to use that wisdom when ministering to others enduring similar circumstances.

When enduring those stretches by the Lord, the greatest challenge is to learn through the challenge, to increase wisdom and understanding, rather than just complain. God never makes mistakes and consequently, there is a reason for each aspect of our lives. Never lose sight of His guiding hand in the midst of each circumstance, as what we often think of as punishment easily could be construed as blessing in His eyes!

That He would show you the secrets of wisdom!
For *they would* double *your* prudence.
Know therefore that God exacts from you
***Less* than your iniquity *deserves*.**
Job 11:6 (NKJV)

July 26: Are you listening?

Greek philosopher Epictetus said, "We have two ears and one mouth so that we can listen twice as much as we speak." That seems to be an infrequent occurrence in the modern world where listening is a lost art. Living in a society that pushes the philosophy that the squeaky wheel gets the oil, we are surrounded by squeakers. We keep our ears busy with iPods blaring noise nearly every moment of every day. Television fills most of our evenings, and certainly, it is not the quality of the programming that lures us, but the mindless filling of time. Rare are the times when we actually sit in peace…and listen!

Each day, we can find God in our lives. This really has nothing to do with God's daily appearance. He is omnipresent. Instead, it has more to do with heightening our awareness of His voice, His hand and His orchestration of every aspect of our lives. How often do we think that God speaks? In William Shakespeare's play "Julius Caesar," Mark Antony says, "Friends, Romans, countrymen, lend me your ears!" Our lives would be much simpler if instead of lending our ears to what the Lord says, we would keep our ears on His words!

He who has ears to hear, let him hear!"
Matthew 13:9 (NKJV)

He who has an ear, let him hear what the Spirit says to the churches.
Revelation 2:7 (NKJV)

That statement and sentiment are repeated over a dozen times in the New Testament alone. God created us all with a pair of ears, yet when we come to the Lord, He gives us spiritual eyes and spiritual ears. When Jesus spoke in parables, it was so that only those He intended to receive the message would understand:

And He said, "To you it has been given to know the mysteries of the kingdom of God, but to the rest *it is given* in parables, that
'Seeing they may not see,
And hearing they may not understand.'
Luke 8:10 (NKJV)

We should not be confused by the Bible, as God is not the author of confusion (1 Corinthians 14:33). For the person confused by God's Word, the greater possibility is that they have not acquired the spiritual ears to hear or the spiritual eyes to see the wonders of His works! By taking any event in our lives, and reflecting upon the event, we will see that God is there, in the midst of it all. We carry Him into our sin, in addition to those times when we carry Him into church! He is with us always. If we want to hear His voice, we should read the Bible out loud!

For the hearts of this people have grown dull.
Their ears are hard of hearing,
And their eyes they have closed,
Lest they should see with their eyes and hear with their ears,
Lest they should understand with their hearts and turn,
So that I should heal them.'
Matthew 13:15 (NKJV)

July 27: What is more important than listening to God?

In 1 Kings 19:12, Elijah hears a "still, small voice." Many Christians refer to that phrase when discussing the voice of God, trying to explain our internal prodding to follow the Lord's instructions. Yet a "still, small voice" will not always get our attention with the tumult and clamor surrounding us. Do we think God stops speaking if we do not hear Him? Or do we think He speaks louder until we hear Him? Whereas it is important to have spiritual ears and spiritual eyes, what is more important to us as believers is to have spiritual feet! Hearing the voice of God is not nearly as important as following the voice of God!

^{22} But be doers of the word, and not hearers only, deceiving yourselves. ^{23} For if anyone is a hearer of the word and not a doer, he is like a man observing his natural face in a mirror; ^{24} for he observes himself, goes away, and immediately forgets what kind of man he was. ^{25} But he who looks into the perfect law of liberty and continues *in it,* and is not a forgetful hearer but a doer of the work, this one will be blessed in what he does.
James 1:22-25 (NKJV)

We often hear fellow believers say something along the lines of, "God told me to do such and such." Did they truly hear God's voice out loud? Certainly, the Lord orchestrates even the smallest situations in our lives and if we are paying attention, those situations can remind us of His Word. Yet without having read His Word, how can God bring those verses to remembrance? Does He say: "Buy that car!" "Eat Spaghetti-O's for lunch today!" "Don't drive Interstate 5 this morning as it is going to be backed up!" Instead, God's revelation is complete in the Bible. Yet God can speak to us in strange ways: through the words of a song we are listening to on the radio, through different people sharing the same Bible verse with us, etc.

Often, we can confuse what we are feeling in our hearts with what God is telling us! As we know from the words of Jeremiah, the heart is desperately wicked and deceitful at best. Many times, we can tell it is not the voice of God as what our hearts are telling us to do conflicts His Word. God never will do that. Sadly, when we attribute the prodding of our hearts to the voice of God and tell others, we are walking in spiritual pride. "God speaks to me louder than He speaks to you! I must be more spiritual than you are!" More than not, to hear God's voice is to hear His Word, and to follow God's voice is to follow His Word. Consequently, we need to spend lots of time reading the Bible. Yet that can lead to spiritual pride, as well.

[1] Now concerning things offered to idols: We know that we all have knowledge. Knowledge puffs up, but love edifies. [2] And if anyone thinks that he knows anything, he knows nothing yet as he ought to know. [3] But if anyone loves God, this one is known by Him.
1 Corinthians 8:1-3 (NKJV)

God wants us to study His Word, and humbly with love, to apply His Word to our own lives. Additionally, the Lord desires for us to share His truths by ministering to others. That does not mean we need to stand in a pulpit and preach to others, though that is perfect for those called into that ministry. The key is to share with the people He brings into our lives. Yet most importantly, God wants us to walk in the ways of His Word. People do not need to hear the Bible; they need to see the Bible in each of our lives!

Be diligent to present yourself approved to God, a worker who does not need to be ashamed, rightly dividing the word of truth.
1 Timothy 2:15 (NKJV)

July 28: Where is our refuge?

Jack Tatum, a retired safety for the Oakland Raiders, died recently at the age of 61. In the last few years before his death, he had suffered from diabetes and corresponding complications, including the amputation of toes and a leg. Known in the National Football League as "The Assassin" for his crippling hits, Tatum's philosophy was that if receivers worried about the hit that was coming, they would not be able to focus on catching the ball. On an incomplete pass over the middle of the field in a 1978 pre-season game against the New England Patriots, Tatum lowered the boom on receiver Darryl Stingley. The hit paralyzed Stingley, who became a quadriplegic. Tatum never apologized and wrote three books capitalizing on the hit: "They Call Me Assassin," "They Still Call Me Assassin," and "Final Confessions of NFL Assassin Jack Tatum." Here is what he said concerning an apology:

> "It could have happened to anybody," said Tatum. "People are always saying, 'He didn't apologize.' I don't think I did anything wrong that I need to apologize for. It was a clean hit."

By NFL rules at the time, the hit was legal. In fact, Tatum did not receive a penalty on that day in 1978, though he would have with today's rules. Sadly though, Tatum never grasped that intent to cripple was not the issue. His life basically ended the life of another man. Stingley died in 2007 from complications associated with his paralysis, having struggled through every aspect of life for almost 30 years. Whether or not Tatum wanted to take any responsibility, a godly man would have reached out to Stingley. In a 1985 game when Hall-of-Fame linebacker Lawrence Taylor hit quarterback Joe Theismann so hard that Theismann's leg snapped in two and protruded from the skin, Taylor's first look was a sickened expression calling for a stretcher in deep concern. There is a difference between doing one's job while playing a sport involving extreme physical contact and trying to seriously hurt another player. Though Stingley's death was not immediate, his life changed in so many ways.

Unlike man, God is able to look inside the heart and see intent. The obvious difference between manslaughter and murder is intent, or more specifically, premeditation. God set aside six cities of refuge, three on the east side of the Jordan River (Golan, Ramoth and Bosor) and three on the west side (Kadesh, Shechem and Hebron).

^{25} So the congregation shall deliver the manslayer from the hand of the avenger of blood, and the congregation shall return him to the city of refuge where he had fled, and he shall remain there until the death of the high priest who was anointed with the holy oil. ^{26} But if the manslayer at any time goes outside the limits of the city of refuge where he fled, ^{27} and the avenger of blood finds him outside the limits of his city of refuge, and the avenger of blood kills the manslayer, he shall not be guilty of blood, ^{28} because he should have remained in his city of refuge until the death of the high priest. But after the death of the high priest the manslayer may return to the land of his possession.
Numbers 35:25-28 (NKJV)

Specifically, the "avenger of blood" is the closest relative who acts in revenge or retaliation because of the spilled blood. Once the intent of the crime had been decided, a murderer was put to death while a manslayer was sent to a city of refuge. He was allowed to remain in that city until the death of the high priest. At that time, the manslayer was allowed to return to his home, without threat of harm from the avenger of blood. Tradition says that the mother of the high priest supplied the clothes and food for the manslayer, as in that regard, the manslayer would not desire for the high priest to die. Yet this story pertains to each of us. God is the "Avenger of Blood," as He will put to death all the murderers. This is not a physical death, but a spiritual one. Additionally, Jesus is both our High Priest and our City of Refuge. We live in Jesus and He lives in us!

…where the forerunner has entered for us, *even* **Jesus, having become High Priest forever according to the order of Melchizedek.**
Hebrews 6:20 (NKJV)

This verse in Hebrews reminds us that we can dwell in the City of Refuge forever, because our High Priest never will die! When Jesus died on the cross, every person there was responsible for His death. Though none of us were alive at that time, we were responsible, as well, for He carried our sins as His burden on that day. Yet fortunately for us, we are not guilty of murder in His eyes, though we are guilty of manslaughter. How do we know? Because He told His Father from the cross:

Then Jesus said, "Father, forgive them, for they do not know what they do."
Luke 23:34 (NKJV)

We did not kill Jesus with intent or premeditation. Still, repentance is sorrow for that sin. Sadly, Jack Tatum had no sorrow for the actions of his life. Though only God can judge the heart, Tatum's actions up until death did not appear to be those of a repentant man. When a celebrity dies, the "cool" thing to say is R.I.P., standing for "rest in peace." Sadly, neither rest nor peace are in store for those who did not follow Jesus. Once again, when what we believe is reflected in how we live, others will see both our love and our repentance! We should let our love and life change the lives of others!

Then he knelt down and cried out with a loud voice, "Lord, do not charge them with this sin." And when he had said this, he fell asleep.
Acts 7:60 (NKJV)

July 29: Keep on keeping on!

Listening to God is such an important aspect of our lives, but putting those instructions to work defines our lives. One of the greatest difficulties of being a Christian is to keep that walk pointed toward Jesus and never to look back. Paul did an amazing job, having turned away from persecuting early Christians; he stayed the course, though in turn, Paul was persecuted more than any other Christian. Much of his focus stemmed from his past:

¹² And I thank Christ Jesus our Lord who has enabled me, because He counted me faithful, putting *me* into the ministry, ¹³ although I was formerly a blasphemer, a persecutor, and an insolent man; but I obtained mercy because I did *it* ignorantly in unbelief. ¹⁴ And the grace of our Lord was exceedingly abundant, with faith and love which are in Christ Jesus. ¹⁵ This *is* a faithful saying and worthy of all acceptance, that Christ Jesus came into the world to save sinners, of whom I am chief.
1 Timothy 1:12-15 (NKJV)

Paul realized that if God did nothing more for him than give him eternal salvation, it was much more than Paul deserved. He walked in that grace and mercy. Grace is getting something we do not deserve, while mercy is not getting what we deserve. We do not deserve God's forgiveness, yet He gives it if we ask Him. We deserve death as payment for those sins, yet He gives us abundant life.

Most of us likely have known someone who seemed to brag about their sin when giving their testimony. "I was really bad! Let me tell you the horrible things I did before I became a Christian!" That is not the heart that Paul had in telling us about his past. Paul's past broke him and every time he thought about it, the past broke him a little bit more. Paul understood the abject poverty of his own spiritual condition without Jesus, and therefore, understood the enormity of the gift that had been given. Most of us know that feeling. So how do we balance the memories of the past with our present walks and our future hopes?

Therefore, if anyone *is* in Christ, *he is* a new creation; old things have passed away; behold, all things have become new.
2 Corinthians 5:17 (NKJV)

Salvation changes every aspect of our beings, though our memories are still there. Yet no matter how painful our past was, we can look at that past through the glasses of perception. It is difficult to walk in sadness, regardless of our current hardships, knowing that we have an eternity with our Savior. It is difficult to beat ourselves up over our sinful pasts knowing that God forgave everything and used our brokenness to bring us to His feet. It is difficult to walk again as an unbeliever when we understand what Jesus did by dying for our sins. Bobby McFerrin gave good advice to us as Christians, "Don't worry! Be happy!" We should let the joy of the Lord be our strength, and that joy stems from the burden that He carried for each of us. If we want to be blessed, we must not stray from our walks with the Lord!

[13] Brethren, I do not count myself to have apprehended; but one thing *I do,* forgetting those things which are behind and reaching forward to those things which are ahead, [14] I press toward the goal for the prize of the upward call of God in Christ Jesus.
Philippians 3:13-14 (NKJV)

July 30: Separate, but not equal!

One of the precepts of Constitutional law was "separate, but equal." This concept referred to the early acceptance of segregation based on race. Though the effect of this segregation was far-reaching, it was most apparent in the American South, where there were separate schools, restaurants, pools, bathrooms, drinking fountains and more for whites and blacks. Separation was obvious, but there was nothing that even bordered on equality. Though these laws were overturned in 1954, it took 10 years to begin to see a difference.

Most people over 50 can remember at least some of the ramifications of those laws, while for people over 60, they lived it! We all can imagine what it must feel like to be on the other side looking in. It would be devastating to wonder why some people have it so easy, and why based on skin color, others have it so difficult. As Christians, we also seem to have problems with separation anxiety. We are called to be separate from the world. Jesus explained this concept to His disciples:

And He said to them, "You are from beneath; I am from above. You are of this world; I am not of this world.
John 8:23 (NKJV)

It can be difficult to walk the fine line of existing in this world, but realizing that this is not our home, anymore than it was the home of Jesus. We are called to be holy:

...^{15}but as He who called you *is* holy, you also be holy in all *your* conduct, ^{16} because it is written, *"Be holy, for I am holy."*
1 Peter 1:15-16 (NKJV)

Holiness can be defined as wholeness. We cannot have wholeness without Jesus living inside of us, completing us. Holiness also can be defined as righteousness, and without Jesus being punished for our sins, we have no chance at holiness. Without holiness, we are separated from God.

The world we live in seeps into every aspect of our lives. Think about an average day. We go to work, eat a couple meals and watch television. If we turn on the television, almost every show has at least some part that flaunts the acceptance of the world's ways, and at the same time, violates the laws of God. That list would include premarital sex, drunkenness, marital infidelity, foul language, or even scantily-clad actors and actresses that leave little to the imagination. Opening a magazine reveals the same. Conversations with co-workers often cross the line with dirty jokes or gossip. As Christians, we are called to glorify God in all that we do. That means to remain separate from the world. But do not confuse separation with isolation. There are things we should not do and places we should not go. It is highly doubtful that drunken revelers in a bar are going to glean anything from our conversation about God, but our neighbors might notice there is something different about us, in a positive way. Think of the song, "They'll know we are Christians by our love."

God is going to separate the wheat from the chaff and the sheep from the goats, and while on this earth, we are to be separate from those who do not follow Him. Is it that important to fit in? Sometimes it feels important, but we should prefer to fit in with God and God's people. We are to be separate, and thankfully, not equal, especially when it comes to eternity! Should we prefer to be separate from the world or separated from God?

July 31: Six

When God created the heavens and the earth, it was on the final day that He created Adam. Consequently, that sixth day carries the significance of man, and throughout the Bible, the symbolism of six being the number of man continues. Whether or not we are six feet under or one beer short of a six-pack, man has demonstrated that without God, all of us are incomplete and have no chance of perfection.

Then God saw everything that He had made, and indeed *it was* very good. So the evening and the morning were the sixth day.
Genesis 1:31 (NKJV)

Even with our lack of perfection, God is not disappointed in His creation. God commented on all of His other creative days saying that they were good, but after creating man, His comment was that it was "very good." God created us without sin, but Adam brought imperfection upon us all with his choice to disobey the Lord. After Adam, sin is pervasive in all mankind, but there is no sin that highlights man's hatred against his brother more than murder. As God gives life to us all, when one man takes that gift away from another, it demonstrates a complete disregard for God, God's laws and others. When God gave His laws to Moses on Mount Sinai, it was not accidental that the law against murder was number six on the list.

**⁸ Now Cain talked with Abel his brother; and it came to pass, when they were in the field, that Cain rose up against Abel his brother and killed him.
⁹ Then the LORD said to Cain, "Where *is* Abel your brother?"
He said, "I do not know. *Am* I my brother's keeper?"
¹⁰ And He said, "What have you done? The voice of your brother's blood cries out to Me from the ground. ¹¹ So now you *are* cursed from the earth, which has opened its mouth to receive your brother's blood from your hand.
Genesis 4:8-11 (NKJV)**

That first murder was so heinous that Abel's blood cried out to the Lord. Even though Cain was aware of God's omniscience, he lied in a weak attempt to cover his sin. Perhaps the most interesting representation of six being the number of man occurs in reference to the man indwelt by Satan in the tribulation:

**Here is wisdom. Let him who has understanding calculate the number of the beast, for it is the number of a man: His number *is* 666.
Revelation 13:18 (NKJV)**

Many Bible prophecy aficionados have attempted to apply this numerical equivalent to world leaders with different political views than their own. Hence Ronald Wilson Reagan was thought by some to be the coming world leader representative of Satan based on six letters in each of his three names. Hollywood attempted to solve this in its own way, by giving a child a birthmark with three sixes in the movie, "The Omen." Presently, how this number might apply does not make much sense to us, but for Christians alive in the tribulation, it could make perfect sense. Mathematicians have tried to "solve this equation," and some have pointed out that Roman numerals carry an interesting property along these lines. Where I=1, V=5, X=10, L=50, C=100 and D=500, totaling those numbers comes to 666.

Just as God operates in the tri-unity of Father, Son and Holy Spirit, the beast is associated with Satan, the antichrist and the false prophet. All biblical representations of the antichrist, whether historical or prophetic, follow with the symbolism of six standing for man. Goliath, an avowed enemy of God and God's people, was six cubits in height and carried six pieces of armor including an iron spear that was 600 shekels in weight (1 Samuel 17:4-7). Revelation 19:17-18 speaks of the "supper of the great God," when the carnivorous birds of the air eat the flesh of those killed in Armageddon. We see a similar occurrence after David slays Goliath:

This day the LORD will deliver you into my hand, and I will strike you and take your head from you. And this day I will give the carcasses of the camp of the Philistines to the birds of the air and the wild beasts of the earth, that all the earth may know that there is a God in Israel.
1 Samuel 17:46 (NKJV)

In Revelation, the antichrist creates an image of himself and places it in the Jewish temple in Jerusalem. In the same manner, Nebuchadnezzar created a statue of himself that was 60 cubits high and 6 cubits wide, in Daniel 3:1.

Man is a sinner and with God, is capable of having that sin removed. There is only one God, and mathematically speaking, $6 + 1 = 7$. Take man's sin and add God and perfection occurs. God will perfect us. Sadly, many people seem to grade their own behavior like a CPA, with good deeds counted in the black and sins counted in the red. On that grading scale, a good person is one who has more good deeds than bad deeds. Unfortunately, God is the one doing the judging, and He has told us that one sin makes a man a sinner. Without a Savior, punished for our sins, it does not matter how many good deeds are on our balance sheets! If we have not accepted Jesus as our Lord and Savior, that event is the only remedy for our great sin debt. If we have accepted Him, the removal and atonement of our sin should bring great joy!

For the wages of sin *is* death, but the gift of God *is* eternal life in Christ Jesus our Lord.

Romans 6:23 (NKJV)

August 1: Busy, busy body, too busy for God!

As the world keeps spinning around, it seems like we keep spinning faster with it. Most of our lives have spun out of control in many facets. Though men used to work six days a week instead of the present custom of five, it appears we are working more hours now. The weekend got its beginning based on the difference between the Christian Sabbath and the Jewish Sabbath. While Jews rested on Saturday, Christians rested on Sunday. The owner of a New England cotton mill gave his workers both days off, as not to offend either group. Henry Ford followed suit for all of his factories in 1926, and then some unions began asking for both days off in 1929. In 1940, the two-day weekend became a standard practice in the United States.

Even within the church, many have a tendency of putting in many hours of work. Part of this has to do with being people pleasers. As Christians, we do our best not to let our church families down. While God does call each of us into a ministry, He does not want us spinning out of control. Think of the difference between Mary and Martha, probably the best known sisters in the Bible. Luke and John both describe these two sisters as friends of Jesus, and we also know that they were sisters of Lazarus, the man who Jesus raised from the dead. Though both women loved Jesus immensely, they had different relationships with Him. Through this story, God gives us an example of the kind of relationship that He desires with each of us.

[38] Now it happened as they went that He entered a certain village; and a certain woman named Martha welcomed Him into her house. [39] And she had a sister called Mary, who also sat at Jesus' feet and heard His word. [40] But Martha was distracted with much serving, and she approached Him and said, "Lord, do You not care that my sister has left me to serve alone? Therefore tell her to help me."

⁴¹ And Jesus answered and said to her, "Martha, Martha, you are worried and troubled about many things. ⁴² But one thing is needed, and Mary has chosen that good part, which will not be taken away from her."
Luke 10:38:42 (NKJV)

What does it mean to be "distracted with much serving?" How can serving the Lord be a distraction? We all know what it feels like to develop habits. While not all habits are bad, even the good habits can involve much mindless repetition. Martha had a guest in her home, and while He was a guest she knew very well, she still felt obligated to ensure that everything was perfect. Who knows what task kept her busy, but it could have been cooking, cleaning or even serving a meal. She was angry at Mary, her sister, who instead of assisting with the chores, sat at the feet of Jesus.

Each of us have tasks in our lives, ones that we feel obligated to accomplish, which can take away from the time we should be devoting to the Lord. Just like Martha, sometimes those tasks even can be ones we feel like we are doing for the Lord. Brother Lawrence, who served as a monk in a Carmelite monastery in Paris in the 17th century, wrote a book entitled, "The Practice of the Presence of God." Brother Lawrence marvelously mastered the ability to worship God joyfully in the most menial of tasks, and as the title so aptly says, it takes practice! Yet never lose sight of the example God gave to each of us after He created the world in six days. He rested. He was not tired, but He knew that we needed His example.

Many followers of God still have different ideas of what day the Sabbath should occur. It does not really matter which day, but honor the Lord and His commandment to keep the Sabbath day holy. That commandment is for our benefit in so many ways. In addition to needing a day to spend with the Lord, we also need a day to rest our weary bones. Martha desired to serve the Lord, and worked hard to show Jesus exactly that, but Mary took the time to sit at His feet. That is where He wants us, as without that intimacy, we are just spinning our wheels.

Our Lord places each of us into a ministry to perform for Him, yet He never places us where we cannot rest. As Simon and Garfunkel told us, "Slow down, you move too fast!" The key is how to be Mary in a Martha world.

Do not labor for the food which perishes, but for the food which endures to everlasting life, which the Son of Man will give you, because God the Father has set His seal on Him." John 6:27 (NKJV)

August 2: Climb every mountain!

Mt. Whitney is a 14,505-foot tall mountain in central California. It is the highest mountain in the contiguous United States. The trail meanders through forests, meadows, brooks and lakes. Within moments from the trailhead, it is more common to see what God made, rather than what man has made. Roads disappear from view. Occasionally, a fellow hiker comes into sight, with man-made supplies on his back. Yet sitting down beside a crisply cool mountain lake reveals no trash or pollution. Sometimes, in those moments away from man, we can have an easier time finding God and God's voice. What is most apparent on an expansive mountain is that we serve a huge God, who made it all. That largeness in comparison to our smallness can make some feel inconsequential, yet as insignificant as we might feel in the grand scheme of it all, God cares so much for each of us!

[1] **I will lift up my eyes to the hills— From whence comes my help?**
[2] **My help *comes* from the LORD,**
   Who made heaven and earth.
[3] **He will not allow your foot to be moved;**
   He who keeps you will not slumber.
[4] **Behold, He who keeps Israel**
   Shall neither slumber nor sleep.
[5] **The LORD *is* your keeper;**
   The LORD *is* your shade at your right hand.

⁶ **The sun shall not strike you by day,**
  Nor the moon by night.
⁷ **The L**ORD **shall preserve you from all evil;**
  He shall preserve your soul.
⁸ **The L**ORD **shall preserve your going out and your coming in**
  From this time forth, and even forevermore.
Psalm 121 (NKJV)

Though God created all of the earth's topographies, there is something special about mountains. They are visible from incredible distances, and the steep, jagged edges give the impression that there is no way under, over, through or around them. Yet as big as the mountains are, God is so much bigger! In the Bible, all travelers go "up to Jerusalem." The word "up" does not designate north, as the same word is used when traveling from any direction. Jewish men were required to make three journeys yearly to God's Holy City for Passover, Pentecost and Tabernacles, and those making lengthy pilgrimages would sleep along the road of the mountainous terrain. They looked to God for protection, as He preserves our souls, along with our coming in and going out.

He loves us so much that He cannot take His eyes away from us; He never sleeps. He gives us such a solid foundation that our feet cannot be moved, nor our walks stumbled. In the brightest sunlight, He protects us. In the darkness of night, He is a lamp unto our feet and a light unto our paths. God is not the man upstairs, a bigger, better one of us. He is the Creator of all, yet He cares about every single aspect of our lives. For those who feel small or insignificant, remember that God's attention to detail keeps His focus right upon each of us. It is a miracle that He loves us in the midst of our failures, and that He wants us to know His love. If we seek Him, we will find Him. If we want to hear His voice, we will! If we want to see Him, He will help us. Yet it has to be our choice to climb that mountain! Once we are His, He will keep us forever!

But from there you will seek the LORD your God, and you will find *Him* if you seek Him with all your heart and with all your soul.
Deuteronomy 4:29 (NKJV)

August 3: Only you can prevent forest fires!

Driving past a fire station, it is easy to forget how important of a task those firemen play in our society. We often take them for granted until we need them to put out a fire. Interestingly, our relationship with God can be similar. Certainly, our prayers become more necessary when faced with trials, at least in our own minds. We often take God for granted when all is running smoothly. Yet there also are other spiritual lessons in regard to fire. It is amazing how quickly a fire can devastate an area from the moment it begins. While there is a science to putting out a forest fire, if the fire runs out of combustible material, it goes out. It is not a new science, as even King Solomon was aware of that:

[20] Where *there is* no wood, the fire goes out;
And where *there is* no talebearer, strife ceases.
[21] *As* charcoal *is* to burning coals, and wood to fire,
So *is* a contentious man to kindle strife.
Proverbs 26:20-21 (NKJV)

Being that we are not perfected when we become Christians, gossip is a stumbling block for all of us at times. Gossip is any language that does not edify, or build up, the person we are talking about. Truthfully, most of us rationalize our discussions, thinking that we are part of the solution rather than part of the problem. Even the conversations that begin with the right intent can quickly turn into gossip with the slightest misstep.

[8] But no man can tame the tongue. *It is* an unruly evil, full of deadly poison. [9] With it we bless our God and Father, and with it we curse men, who have been made in the similitude of God. [10] Out of the same mouth proceed blessing and cursing. My brethren, these things ought not to be so. [11] Does

a spring send forth fresh *water* and bitter from the same opening?
James 3:8-11 (NKJV)

When we get hurt, or when that pain affects our close friends and family, we seem to have the need to talk it out. That is exactly what God wants us to do, with one stipulation. Talk it out with Him instead! He is the solution to the problem. For those who have been hurt, He is the Healer. If we have been wronged, He is the truth. God will set us free. Sometimes it takes time, but the solutions always occur perfectly in God's time. Otherwise, the words we speak perpetuate the forest fire, and that fire continues to burn and destroy all in its path.

A perverse man sows strife,
And a whisperer separates the best of friends.
Proverbs 16:28 (NKJV)

August 4: One rule book

Interpersonal relationships are one of life's greatest blessings, and at the same time, one of life's greatest challenges. None of us are immune to the powerful highs and lows that are companions to those relationships. Certainly, the behaviors that bother us the most are typically, behaviors that we would see in a mirror if we looked closely enough. Regardless of what difficult situation we find ourselves in, it is obvious that we would not be in those positions unless God had allowed those occurrences. Yet His calling to us is that in any difficulty, we are to treat others with love. That love is not just any love; it is the same love that enabled the Father to sacrifice His only Son so that we might have eternal life.

There is only one set of rules. God treats His greatest enemy with the same love that He treats His Son. That is one of the many attributes of God. He <u>is</u> love, and consequently, is incapable of being anything but completely loving. That might be difficult for our finite brains to comprehend, as even in His wrath, God only can love perfectly. To see an example of this, the Book of Revelation shares many prophetic statements of God pouring out His wrath on a sinful earth, though we also can see the purpose behind God's wrath. First, it is a response to man completely ignoring the Creator and His laws, yet at the same time, in His judgments, God will attempt to get man's attention and have as many as possible turn to Him. In His love, He wants us to know Him.

**7 Beloved, let us love one another, for love is of God; and everyone who loves is born of God and knows God. 8 He who does not love does not know God, for God is love. 9 In this the love of God was manifested toward us, that God has sent His only begotten Son into the world, that we might live through Him. 10 In this is love, not that we loved God, but that He loved us and sent His Son *to be* the propitiation for our sins. 11 Beloved, if God so loved us, we also ought to love one another.
1 John 4:7-11 (NKJV)**

Just as God loved His Son Jesus, each of us has someone in our lives that we treat better than others. It might be a child, a parent, a best friend or even a co-worker. Typically, that better treatment comes from a long, track record of that person desiring to please and protect us. At the same time, we might treat others with less regard, as we believe we can see their hearts and understand their motives. Yet is that truly the case?

**But the LORD said to Samuel, "Do not look at his appearance or at his physical stature, because I have refused him. For *the* LORD does not *see* as man sees; for man looks at the outward appearance, but the LORD looks at the heart."
1 Samuel 16:7 (NKJV)**

The key to our interpersonal skills dwells in our love. We are called by God to love them as He loved us. That is not because they have done anything to deserve that love, as we did not deserve His love. Yet God demonstrates to us that love changes everything. Have one set of rules in how to treat others! We are called to treat them as we would treat the most special person in our lives. It is not hypocritical to love our son, parent or friend, but it is hypocritical not to love our enemies or detractors with that same love. It is God's calling on each of our lives. The one rule book is the Bible! God loves us in the same way that He loves Jesus, and treats us the same.

There is a wonderful analogy of the shepherd, who when his sheep begin to stray, gently pulls them back with the crook of his staff. If they continue to stray, he turns the staff around and pops them on the hindquarters. If that does not get their attention, he may choose to break their back legs and carry them until the legs heal. While carrying them, the shepherd draws much closer to them, to the point where they do not desire to stray. Jesus is our Shepherd. Sadly, men claiming to be shepherds tend to break the legs at the first mistake of the sheep, and along with that, are not willing to carry the sheep. Instead, the sheep are cast aside where wolves may prey on them. We are called to come alongside our brothers, to build them up. When this is done, the body of Christ functions as intended, with each person able to use and grow in the gifts that God has given. The answer is to love others just as we love our favorite person.

[43] **"You have heard that it was said, *'You shall love your neighbor* and hate your enemy.'** [44] **But I say to you, love your enemies, bless those who curse you, do good to those who hate you, and pray for those who spitefully use you and persecute you,** [45] **that you may be sons of your Father in heaven; for He makes His sun rise on the evil and on the good, and sends rain on the just and on the unjust. Matthew 5:43-45 (NKJV)**

August 5: Earth, Wind and Fire

How is it possible to walk in the flesh so soon after God does a miracle in our lives? A classic example happened when Moses was on top of Mt. Sinai receiving the 10 Commandments, while the Jews were worshipping a golden calf fashioned by Aaron, only a brief time after God had parted the Red Sea, killing Pharaoh's pursuing army in the process. Another example involved Elijah, days after he killed 850 false prophets on Mt. Carmel (1 Kings 18). Elijah began running and did not stop for a long time. While King Ahab rode to Jezreel, Elijah ran and arrived before Ahab. Yet Elijah did not stop there. Ahab's wife Jezebel threatened Elijah's life, and somehow, Elijah lost sight of the miracle the Lord had performed days earlier on Mt. Carmel. He ran from Jezreel to Beersheba, 130 miles, to escape the clutches of Jezebel. Instead of walking in the Spirit, Elijah seemed to be running in the flesh! Why would a man who understood God's limitless power run from an evil queen?

Aaron, Elijah and the children of Israel are not alone in their fickle nature. Each of us can reflect upon disappointing ventures back into sin after becoming Christians. God promises that He will complete His work in us, but He did not promise to do that instantaneously. Part of our growth with Him is to understand His continuing presence in our lives and His comfort even when we fail. Look at what He accomplished in the life of Elijah:

⁴ But he himself went a day's journey into the wilderness, and came and sat down under a broom tree. And he prayed that he might die, and said, "It is enough! Now, LORD, take my life, for I *am* no better than my fathers!" ⁵ Then as he lay and slept under a broom tree, suddenly an angel touched him, and said to him, "Arise *and* eat." ⁶ Then he looked, and there by his head *was* a cake baked on coals, and a jar of water. So he ate and drank, and lay down again.
1 Kings 19:4-6 (NKJV)

The "angel" was a *theophany*, an Old Testament appearance of Jesus, who comforted the exhausted Elijah. Jesus touched Elijah, spoke to him, and then gave him food and water. When we are exhausted, rest, food and drink give us energy. We can rest in the Lord, and we also know that Jesus is the Bread of Life and the Living Water! It must have been powerful food (angel food cake?), for Elijah arose and journeyed 40 days to Mt. Horeb, the mountain in Arabia where Moses had received the Law from God. At Mt. Horeb, the miracles continued. The Lord came to Elijah in a cave and asked, "What are you doing here,

Elijah?" (We can remove Elijah's name and insert our own, as there are so many times when we carry ourselves to such extremes that no one but God can find us or rescue us)! There is not anger in that simple question, designed to put Elijah back on track.

¹¹ Then He said, "Go out, and stand on the mountain before the LORD. ' And behold, the LORD passed by, and a great and strong wind tore into the mountains and broke the rocks in pieces before the LORD, *but* the LORD *was* not in the wind; and after the wind an earthquake, *but* the LORD *was* not in the earthquake; ¹² and after the earthquake a fire, *but* the LORD *was* not in the fire; and after the fire a still small voice.
1 Kings 19:11-12 (NKJV)

With Earth, Wind and Fire performing, Jesus spoke to Elijah, while God the Father passed by, and finally, the Holy Spirit demonstrated His presence in the still, small voice. What is most apparent in this story is that regardless of Elijah's failure to trust in the Lord, God continued to feed Him, to comfort Him, to speak to Him, and to remain with Him. It is not about Elijah's faithfulness, or ours for that matter. But it is about God's faithfulness. God performs so many miracles in each of our lives. Sometimes, we forget. Other times, we tend to ignore those miracles, or even to focus on the fear we might have of people, created by an omnipotent God who loves us. Do we have anything to be afraid of with God on our side?

For we do not wrestle against flesh and blood, but against principalities, against powers, against the rulers of the darkness of this age, against spiritual *hosts* of wickedness in the heavenly *places*.
Ephesians 6:12 (NKJV)

August 6: Show me!

Missouri often is referred to as the "Show-Me State." Though the unofficial state motto might seem strange, it reflects the stalwart quality of Missourians, and has a better ring to it than the "Talk is Cheap State!" Yet the concept that actions speak louder than words is not unique to a Midwestern state. James offers us a similar sentiment:

For as the body without the spirit is dead, so faith without works is dead also.
James 2:26 (NKJV)

Do we really believe what we claim to believe? Interestingly, as Charles Darwin approached death, the confirmed agnostic who showed strong signs of atheism in his "science apart from God" theories, considered embracing the Christ that he had denied for all of his adult years. Finally, Darwin decided that a conversion to Christianity would be hypocritical, and would refute all of his life's work, and consequently, he died without making peace with God. As hypocritical as Darwin might have appeared, Christians can appear even more hypocritical when they espouse the view that God's will is both paramount and beneficial, yet moan whenever life gets a little bit rocky.

It is not uncommon to talk to a Christian with a fear of death. Satan's deceit can cause doubt to seep into a Christian's belief system, and one doubt can rock a stable ship. Sadly, there are people claiming to be Christians who go through the Bible as if it were a grocery list, picking and choosing which aspects they want to believe. "Everyone has sex before marriage, so that cannot be wrong." "I am too young to raise a baby alone, so I am going to have an abortion. I know that until birth, it is not really a life anyway." "If I tell the truth, it will hurt her feelings, so I do not understand why it is wrong to lie." If God is powerful enough to have created all that we can see, and all that we cannot see, is He not powerful enough to have errant men write His inerrant words in a book? It takes more faith to believe that all of this exists without God! How could all the intricacies of the universe, our planet or our bodies have happened randomly?

When we look at the Hall of Fame of Faith in Hebrews 11, we see a cast of characters including Abel, Enoch, Noah, Abraham, Sarah, Isaac, Jacob and Joseph. Yet there is another name in that list:

[30] By faith the walls of Jericho fell down after they were encircled for seven days. [31] By faith the harlot Rahab did not perish with those who did not believe, when she had received the spies with peace.
Hebrews 11:30-31 (NKJV)

One of the people in Faith's Hall of Fame is a prostitute, who God chose to be in the bloodline of Jesus, as she was the great grandmother of King David! Why was what she did so important to be mentioned centuries later? Rahab lived in Jericho where the people did not worship the One God, yet when Pharaoh's army broke the world record for swimming underwater, many people in the region took notice of a God who did not just slumber, but lifted His mighty hand to save His people. Then Rahab demonstrated that her belief was not just words, but actions, as she hid the Israelite spies, then said,

[9] "...I know that the LORD has given you the land, that the terror of you has fallen on us, and that all the inhabitants of the land are fainthearted because of you. [10] For we have heard how the LORD dried up the water of the Red Sea for you when you came out of Egypt, and what you did to the two kings of the Amorites who *were* on the other side of the Jordan, Sihon and Og, whom you utterly destroyed. [11] And as soon as we heard *these things,* our hearts melted; neither did there remain any more courage in anyone because of you, for the LORD your God, He *is* God in heaven above and on earth beneath."
Joshua 2:9-11 (NKJV)

Rahab did not see God's miracle, but instead, she heard about it and acted. In the same manner, we please God when we demonstrate that our beliefs go much deeper than words. It is easy to go to church or to check a box next to the word

"Christian" on a survey. It is simple to pray when a spouse is in the hospital or to say "thank You, God" after getting a raise at work. It is more difficult to notice that a family down the street seems to be dropping lots of weight soon after the parents lost their jobs. It is also more difficult to thank God when we cannot pay our bills at the end of the month. Yet we are not called to follow God when it is easy; we are called to follow Him wherever He may lead. We are going to walk through the valley of the shadow of death, but we are not going to be walking there alone. God is telling us all, "If you truly believe what you say you believe, show Me!"

Jesus answered and said to them, "This is the work of God, that you believe in Him whom He sent."
John 6:29 (NKJV)

August 7: It is a matter of the heart!

"Young at heart" refers to people who might not be so young in age, yet still love with reckless abandon. Typically, as we age, love involves a different level of trust, as most people know what it feels like to have their hearts broken. Consequently, to completely give our heart to another, we must feel strongly that they will not rip it out and trample upon it. In the Bible, there are many aspects of the heart. It has emotion, will, intellect and conscience. While emotion is the ability to love, will is the ability to fully carry out a plan, regardless of circumstance. Intellect involves the ability to reason, and finally, conscience is the ability to distinguish right from wrong, based on feeling. David often wrote of the heart in Psalms. Here is a favorite example:

[10] Create in me a clean heart, O God,
And renew a steadfast spirit within me.
[11] Do not cast me away from Your presence,
And do not take Your Holy Spirit from me.
[12] Restore to me the joy of Your salvation,
And uphold me *by Your* generous Spirit.
[13] *Then* I will teach transgressors Your ways,

**And sinners shall be converted to You.
Psalm 51:10-13 (NKJV)**

For God to clean our hearts, it is first apparent that we are unclean. Certainly, it is easy to understand how the filth and slime of the world can cause us to love incompletely, to reason without logic, to change course on our legitimate plans and lastly, to vacillate on matters of morality. Even as Christians, our hearts become soiled, yet God has the ability and the desire to make them clean again. It is also obvious that a heart does not clean itself, like a self-cleaning oven. Instead, the process involves breaking. Only God can clean a heart!

**The sacrifices of God *are* a broken spirit,
A broken and a contrite heart—
These, O God, You will not despise.
Psalm 51:17 (NKJV)**

What breaks our hearts as Christians? Sadly, our sin accomplishes that task, as when we realize the burden that each transgression places on the shoulders of Jesus, we understand that we are no different than the Jewish officials who falsely convicted Him, the Roman soldiers who crucified Him, or the on-lookers who made fun of Him. If our sin does not break our hearts, then we are walking in ignorance of the work that Jesus accomplished on our behalves. David seemed concerned that God would take the Holy Spirit from him. Understand that the role of the Holy Spirit was not the same in the time of David as it is for us in the Church Age. When Jesus returned to heaven, He left the Comforter in His place, to be with us always. Though we can ignore the voice of the Holy Spirit, as believers, He continues to reside within us. Still, the issue remains of whether we choose to walk in the Spirit or walk in the flesh. When we are walking in the Spirit, the joy of salvation is obvious.

Each of us can remember what it was like to walk in the new freedom of forgiveness after becoming Christians. God desires for us to hold that thought dear in our hearts. It is sweet to notice a couple in their advanced years, walking hand-in-hand along the beach. Occasionally, we get the benefit of seeing how real love actually grows in time. While the physical expression of that love might not be as strong, there are couples who finish the sentences when the other speaks. Deep love involves deep knowledge and understanding of the recipient of that love. On the other hand, we also can picture a couple out to dinner, where no word is exchanged between the two. Love has evolved into a bitter struggle, for they both have lost sight of what drew them together to begin with.

Which relationship do we have with God? His heart has the same aspects of emotion, will, intellect and conscience, yet God's heart never changes. If the relationship is struggling, it has everything to do with the mistakes of **our hearts**! We cannot have true joy in the Lord without obedience to God and His laws. It might seem like the opposite, but true freedom does not occur until we walk in His will. God is the only one we truly can give our hearts to without having Him let us down. That was the beauty of the cross. When God chose to depart heaven, to come to this sinful earth and die for us so that we could know His love, He demonstrated that to us all. If we have lost our joy, we need to follow Him more closely and He will restore unto us the joy of salvation! Broken hearts might involve pain, but without that brokenness, we cannot know God! If we want restoration, it is certainly God's desire for each of us!

Nevertheless I have *this* against you, that you have left your first love.
Revelation 2:4 (NKJV)

August 8: Oil press

Not surprisingly, one of the most memorable aspects of a trip to Israel is the city of Jerusalem. It is amazing to walk where Jesus walked, and even though centuries have passed since then, in some ways it is as if time stood still. For Christians who never have been to Israel before, it still feels like home. New-agers would refer to that as "déjà-vu," but the truth is, it feels like home because the One living inside of us was born there! God loves Jerusalem so much that He cannot take His eyes off it. Of all the places on the earth He created, He chose Jerusalem!

⁵ 'Since the day that I brought My people out of the land of Egypt, I have chosen no city from any tribe of Israel *in which* to build a house, that My name might be there, nor did I choose any man to be a ruler over My people Israel. ⁶ Yet I have chosen Jerusalem, that My name may be there, and I have chosen David to be over My people Israel.'
2 Chronicles 6:5-6 (NKJV)

For now I have chosen and sanctified this house, that My name may be there forever; and My eyes and My heart will be there perpetually.
2 Chronicles 7:16 (NKJV)

Just outside the city walls at the bottom of the Mount of Olives is a magnificent garden, filled with incredibly old, olive trees. It is called the Garden of Gethsemane, which comes from the Hebrew word *Gat-Shemanim,* meaning "oil press." Jesus and His disciples spent much time in this garden, and were there the night before His crucifixion. In fact, this is where Judas brought the guards when he betrayed Jesus with a kiss. Jesus prayed three separate times that if it was the Father's will, to let this cup pass from Him. Anticipating the events to come, our Lord sweated blood.

In the Bible, olive oil is emblematic of the Holy Spirit. We are to keep oil in our lamps to keep those lamps lighted (Matthew 25). Even the process of making olive oil points to our Lord, as when the olive is crushed, the oil remains. When Jesus was crushed, beaten and bruised, He left the Holy Spirit in His place. We never should lose sight of what our Savior endured for us, accepting His Father's will to suffer in our places by becoming a man, for God cannot suffer. Though the physical pain was great, it was the separation from His Father that pained Jesus the most. He did not just carry our sins, He became sin for us. When we find ourselves in troublesome situations and feel alone, we should remember that Jesus will join us in our Gardens of

Gethsemane. He will never leave us, or forsake us. How much oil do we have in our lamps?

For He made Him who knew no sin *to be* sin for us, that we might become the righteousness of God in Him.
2 Corinthians 5:21 (NKJV)

August 9: With sanctification and honor

One of the greatest lures of the world is sex. We see it every time we open a magazine, turn on a television, go to a movie, and in the United States, every time we walk down the street. In the days of Jesus, people wore clothing that hid their bodies, but today, some of our clothing does not leave much to the imagination. According to a recent survey, 95% of Americans have had sexual relations prior to marriage, and surprisingly, that number has remained the same since the 1950s. This is possibly the biggest hurdle for Christians who believe in God and believe that the Bible is the Word of God. When we pick and choose which parts of the Bible that we believe, we are creating God in our image, deciding what the God we worship should be like. In His Word, He tells us who He is. Our thoughts or hopes cannot and will not change that!

When Christians weigh the world's opinion when deciding the validity of verses in the Bible, huge problems arise. Yet sadly, that is exactly what occurs when it comes to premarital sex and extramarital sex. Certainly, King Solomon struggled in the same manner, with his 700 wives and 300 concubines. Sex is a creation of God to populate the earth, hence His command to, "Be fruitful and multiply," in Genesis 1:22. Additionally, God had other reasons for the act of sexual intercourse. He designed it for husbands and wives to share intimacy. That intimacy is an example for us of the relationship that He desires with each of us as believers. No, that does not mean that we will have sexual relations with God, but as the brides of Christ, He wants to know us in a very intimate and special way. Interestingly, of all the sins mentioned in the Bible, sexual sin is the only one where we sin against our own bodies.

¹⁸ **Flee sexual immorality. Every sin that a man does is outside the body, but he who commits sexual immorality sins against his own body.** ¹⁹ **Or do you not know that your body is the temple of the Holy Spirit** *who is* **in you, whom you have from God, and you are not your own?** ²⁰ **For you were bought at a price; therefore glorify God in your body and in your spirit, which are God's.**
1 Corinthians 6:18-20 (NKJV)

Paul writes of the sacredness of the bodies of believers, and in the same manner that a husband becomes one with his wife, we as believers have become one with God. If we have sexual relations with another person, we share our soul with them. It would be similar to carrying an idol into church and worshipping that idol alongside Jesus. Our bodies are the temple of the Holy Spirit, and we should not defile God's sacred home. God tells us often that He is a jealous God. He chose us. He sent His Son to die for our sins. He purchased us with His blood. We are His!

Sex is a wonderful and unique gift given by God, and we know how Satan loves to corrupt God's gifts as much as possible. Sadly, the focus that the world puts on sex demonstrates the worship of the gifts of God, rather than the worship of God, Himself. As Christians, we are called to be His, and His alone. Our jealous God does not want us having more conversations with the world than we have with Him. We should let our relationship with God become more intimate in our prayers and in the way that we desire to please Him. Possess the temple of the Holy Spirit with honor! God loves us so much and He wants us to love Him back, intimately!

⁴ **that each of you should know how to possess his own vessel in sanctification and honor,** ⁵ **not in passion of lust,**
1 Thessalonians 4:4-5 (NKJV)

August 10: How do we please God?

Possibly the best known verse in the New Testament is John 3:16. It is quoted often, but even many non-Christians would be able to repeat the book, chapter and verse, based on the placard seen at many, popular sporting events. Beginning in 1977, Rollen Stewart donned a multi-colored, afro wig and held up a sign with "John 3:16" written on it, always in a strategically-located position that made every sports fan envious. Stewart was known by fans as either "Rainbow Man" or "Rock-n-Rollen," and after becoming a born-again Christian, the publicity stunts were his way of getting the word out about God. Sadly, while Stewart got the word out, he did not get the Word in. He carried out a string of stink-bomb attacks on Trinity Broadcasting Network, the Crystal Cathedral and others to demonstrate that in God's eyes, the recipients of the attacks offered less than sweet-smelling aromas to God. Currently, Stewart is serving three consecutive life sentences for attempted kidnapping, with the whole incident surrounding the charges being completely bizarre. While Stewart found his own unique ministry, he seemed to lose sight of how to please God.

How can we please God? Is that not what intimacy is all about? True intimacy exists when we care more about pleasing our spouse than ourselves. At the same time, if our spouse cares in the same selfless manner for us, that relationship thrives. God has given us the truest example of that intimacy in how He loves each of us, knowing that our love for Him always will lack in comparison. While God's love is constant, our love vacillates. Once again, that is based on our own, ever-changing behaviors. Additionally, God's love for us involves only the best for us, though our love for Him is sadly lacking in its focus.

[16] For God so loved the world that He gave His only begotten Son, that whoever believes in Him should not perish but have everlasting life. [17] For God did not send His Son into the world to condemn the world, but that the world through Him might be saved.

John 3:16-17 (NKJV)

God sent His Son to die for each of us, for He loved "the world." While some people have difficulty understanding how God could love each of us without regard to our own works or behaviors, our first step is in grasping that He created each of us. Is it possible to hate the works of our own hand? He was not surprised by our sinfulness, our destructive nature or our propensity to ignore Him. Instead, God continues to reveal Himself to us by loving us. Whether or not we choose to acknowledge that love is a decision each of us must make. That is the only decision of merit in our lives! Once we make the decision to follow God, the next decision is how to please Him.

Pleasing God may seem impossible to the mortal man, yet God has simplified that process for each of us as believers. He has given us the Holy Spirit to dwell within us. A perfect God is deeply offended by sin, but when we sin, God does not call us out as losers, failures or heathens. Instead, the Holy Spirit softly reminds us of our sin, and as we grow closer to the Lord, we seem to improve at listening to Him. God does not expect us to follow perfectly, but through the Holy Spirit, we learn how to follow Him better. Though our sin earns death as a penalty (Romans 6:23), He took the penalty for us (2 Corinthians 5:21). In the Bible, God has given us His instructions on how to live in a pleasing manner. Additionally, His Son came to live in a way that glorified the Father as an example to us all. We also please Him through prayer and through fellowship with others.

Never forget that we are unique creations of the Most High God. He made us in His image, which does not mean that we have His nose or smile. Instead, it means that He made us to know Him. Without that knowledge, we will not be complete. He has a plan for our lives, and His plan involves us and Him together. If our day does not begin with Him, end with Him and include Him all throughout, the intimacy that God desires in that relationship is missing. Do not worry. He is patient and is waiting for each of us to draw nearer to Him today!

⁸ **Draw near to God and He will draw near to you. Cleanse** *your* **hands,** *you* **sinners; and purify** *your* **hearts,** *you* **double-minded.** ⁹ **Lament and mourn and weep! Let your laughter be turned to mourning and** *your* **joy to gloom.** ¹⁰ **Humble yourselves in the sight of the Lord, and He will lift you up.**
James 4:8-10 (NKJV)

We all get lost occasionally, just as "Rainbow Man" lost sight of God's plan in his own life while attempting to point others in God's direction. But God never loses sight of us! In fact, He sees us from the inside out!

¹⁵ **"If you love Me, keep My commandments.** ¹⁶ **And I will pray the Father, and He will give you another Helper, that He may abide with you forever—** ¹⁷ **the Spirit of truth, whom the world cannot receive, because it neither sees Him nor knows Him; but you know Him, for He dwells with you and will be in you.** ¹⁸ **I will not leave you orphans; I will come to you.**
John 14:15-18 (NKJV)

August 11: Dave in a cave

A favorite biblical character for most of us is David. Though he is described by the Lord as a man after God's own heart (1 Samuel 13:14, Acts 13:22), the simple fact that God said that about David should be an encouragement to us all. After all, David was imperfect like the rest of us. In fact, when King David had an adulterous affair with Bathsheba, and subsequently, had her husband killed in battle to hide the sin due to her pregnancy, David demonstrated the level of the Lord's forgiveness in each of our lives. Yet there was another side to David that appealed to God. What does it mean to be a man after God's own heart?

David wrote over half of the psalms, with the title of that book meaning "praises" in Hebrew. At least 78 of the 150 Psalms have been attributed to David, who in his songs to the Lord, carries us through all the highs and lows of life. Yet the common thread in those poetic psalms is the consistency of David's praise. He praises the Lord in his happiness and he praises the Lord in his sadness. Certainly, he understood as we all should that the Lord is worthy of our praise! David was a simple shepherd boy and a musician, as we read in the Bible that he was very skillful with the lyre. In fact, David played the lyre for King Saul, though Saul was threatened by the presence of the Lord in David's life, which was obvious to all after David killed the giant Goliath when the rest of Israel shook in fear.

[6] Now it had happened as they were coming *home*, when David was returning from the slaughter of the Philistine, that the women had come out of all the cities of Israel, singing and dancing, to meet King Saul, with tambourines, with joy, and with musical instruments. [7] So the women sang as they danced, and said:
"Saul has slain his thousands,
And David his ten thousands."
[8] Then Saul was very angry, and the saying displeased him; and he said, "They have ascribed to David ten thousands, and to me they have ascribed *only* thousands. Now *what* more can he have but the kingdom?" [9] So Saul eyed David from that day forward.
1 Samuel 18:6-9 (NKJV)

David did not immediately flee from King Saul's angry hand, but tried to earn Saul's respect by his loyalty. When David did decide to flee, it was not in fear, for if David understood the power of God when facing Goliath, he also was aware of that same power when facing an enemy of a different stature. While Goliath might have been large in size, King Saul was large in power. Yet David fully accepted that God was larger in every sense than any enemy.

Still, David fled to the caves of *En Gedi*. In Hebrew, *En Gedi* means the springs of the wild goats, and to this day, wild goats are prevalent in that area. With Dave in a cave, King Saul and his army were seeking to find the lad and kill him. Saul separated from his army to find a little privacy in a cave. (They did not have Porta-Potty's back then)! When Saul's robe fell to the ground to cover his feet, David crawled to a spot near enough to kill Saul, and instead, cut a piece away from the hem of Saul's garment. Now we know why caves smell so musty! Once outside the cave, David confronted King Saul.

**[8] David also arose afterward, went out of the cave, and called out to Saul, saying, "My lord the king!" And when Saul looked behind him, David stooped with his face to the earth, and bowed down. [9] And David said to Saul: "Why do you listen to the words of men who say, 'Indeed David seeks your harm'? [10] Look, this day your eyes have seen that the LORD delivered you today into my hand in the cave, and *someone* urged *me* to kill you. But *my eye* spared you, and I said, 'I will not stretch out my hand against my lord, for he *is* the LORD's anointed.' [11] Moreover, my father, see! Yes, see the corner of your robe in my hand! For in that I cut off the corner of your robe, and did not kill you, know and see that *there is* neither evil nor rebellion in my hand, and I have not sinned against you. Yet you hunt my life to take it. [12] Let the LORD judge between you and me, and let the LORD avenge me on you. But my hand shall not be against you.
1 Samuel 24:8-12 (NKJV)**

David's trust in God was apparent. He was not promoted to be the King of Israel because of his own pride, but instead, because he was God's anointed. For God understood David's heart. Though just like the rest of us, David made good and bad decisions, his heart loved and followed God completely. That is what it means to be a man after God's own heart! When David's son died, the result of his adultery with Bathsheba, David responded differently than most of us in adversity.

**So David arose from the ground, washed and anointed himself, and changed his clothes; and he went into the house of the LORD and worshiped.
2 Samuel 12:20 (NKJV)**

We have the tendency to blame God for the difficulties we find ourselves in, though most of the time, those situations are the result of our own bad decisions. God loves us so much that He is incapable of hurting us, and if we are in extreme circumstances, they have been designed by the Most High for our own benefit. Trust Him and praise Him. God has the power to bring every situation to the close He desires, even if we find ourselves sequestered in a random cave in the wilderness. If He delivered Dave in the cave, He will deliver us!

And he said: "The LORD *is* my rock and my fortress and my deliverer;
2 Samuel 22:2 (NKJV)

August 12: What is your foundation?

In modern construction, we always dig down before building up. In fact, modern buildings have either a shallow foundation or a deep foundation. With a shallow foundation, we dig down three feet or so into the ground, while the deep foundation varies in relation to the size of the building, and goes much deeper than three feet in most architectural plans. Basically, the foundation disperses the weight, enabling even structures the size of the Empire State Building to stand strong. After laying the foundation, another essential step occurs in the laying of the cornerstone, also known as the foundation stone. In a foundation of a building using masonry, the first stone placed is the most important, as every other stone is set in relation to that cornerstone, which in turn, determines the layout of the entire building. What is our faith built on?

[46] **"But why do you call Me 'Lord, Lord,' and not do the things which I say?** [47] **Whoever comes to Me, and hears My sayings and does them, I will show you whom he is like:** [48] **He is like a man building a house, who dug deep and laid the foundation on the rock. And when the flood arose, the stream beat vehemently against that house, and could not shake it, for it was founded on the rock.** [49] **But he who heard and did nothing is like a man who built a house on the earth without**

a foundation, against which the stream beat vehemently; and immediately it fell. And the ruin of that house was great."
Luke 6:46-49 (NKJV)

This basic, construction knowledge was even known in biblical times, as they knew that a rock foundation was much more solid. The true test of a foundation never occurred on an average day, but when a storm arose, was the foundation solid enough to support the house? In the same manner, our faith is important on a daily basis, but when difficulties arise, our faith will not sustain us unless that faith is built on a solid rock of a foundation. As Jesus reminded us in Luke above, if we follow His instructions, our house will not fall. Those instructions resonate throughout the Bible. Reading the Bible haphazardly certainly does not offer the same benefit. Do we wait until the end of the day to open God's Word, only to find that after reading 10 words, our heads hit the pillow? Instead, if we want that house of faith to stand, we must dig deeply when reading God's Word, as we must dig down before building up. Romans 10:17 reminds us that "faith comes by hearing, and hearing by the Word of God." Deeper knowledge of the Bible increases faith, and consequently, solidifies that foundation!

Jesus said to them, "Have you never read in the Scriptures:
'The stone which the builders rejected
Has become the chief cornerstone.
This was the LORD's doing,
And it is marvelous in our eyes' ?
Matthew 21:42 (NKJV)

Jesus is the foundation of our faith and additionally, He is the stone that the builders rejected who has become the chief cornerstone. Without the life, death and resurrection of our Savior, our lives and faith would be useless. Where else could we turn?

If the foundations are destroyed,
What can the righteous do?
Psalm 11:3 (NKJV)

Howling winds, torrential downpours, cataclysmic floods and powerful earthquakes will all cause destruction in our houses of faith, unless that faith is founded on Jesus Christ. Our hope is built on nothing less than Jesus' blood and righteousness. I dare not trust the sweetest frame, but wholly lean on Jesus' name. On Christ the solid Rock I stand. All other ground is sinking sand! If we feel like our faith is shaky, we must spend more time in God's Word. He is the answer to all of our questions!

Therefore thus says the Lord GOD:
"Behold, I lay in Zion a stone for a foundation,
A tried stone, a precious cornerstone, a sure foundation;
Whoever believes will not act hastily.
 Isaiah 28:16 (NKJV)

[19] Now, therefore, you are no longer strangers and foreigners, but fellow citizens with the saints and members of the household of God, [20] having been built on the foundation of the apostles and prophets, Jesus Christ Himself being the chief corner*stone*, [21] in whom the whole building, being fitted together, grows into a holy temple in the Lord, [22] in whom you also are being built together for a dwelling place of God in the Spirit.
Ephesians 2:19-22 (NKJV)

August 13: Tommy, can you hear Me?

Most of these devotionals have come from personal life lessons, though they are written in third-person narrative. Today, that narrative changes to first person, as I would like to share a miracle that happened. Most importantly, that miracle is encouraging to all of us as believers!

One day, I received an email from a man in Georgia I never had met. He was looking for a part-time job for his son, who had been a college tennis player and teaching tennis professional in North Carolina. His son, who had grown up in a Christian household and at one time had a relationship with the Lord, had developed a substance abuse issue somewhere along the way. He was in treatment in Orange County, California, and was seeking the Lord again. Though I did not have enough tennis lessons to hire a second teaching pro, I told the father that I would be glad to talk with his son, Tommy. The father and I exchanged a few emails, and he forwarded my email address to Tommy.

Two weeks later, I received an email from Tommy's mother. From the tone of the email, it did not sound like she knew that Tommy's father and I had corresponded. She, too, found my tennis web site, yet she also noticed that I spoke of my relationship with the Lord. By that time, Tommy had moved to a sober-living house in Laguna Beach. After a few email exchanges, she forwarded my phone number to Tommy and his to me. But I dropped the ball. In the midst of summer, tennis camps take all of my time, and by week's end, my body is completely out of energy. I thought about Tommy often, and knew that one way to get to know him would be to go play tennis with him. Yet with my 50-year-old body already struggling, I was not excited about hitting with a 26-year-old former collegiate tennis player! I decided to wait until my camps had ended before calling him. My excuses sound like those from Moses when the Lord asked Him to lead the Israelites!

On the last day of camps, I arrived at the grocery store at 7:00 a.m. to pick up supplies for the day. A young man noticed my tennis attire and initiated a conversation:

"Are you a tennis pro," he asked.
"Yes," I said, "Do you play tennis?"
"I do play tennis," he responded. "I played in college, but I also used to teach tennis in North Carolina. I just moved to Laguna Beach. I moved into a sober-living house near here."
"Hi, Tommy," I said, with tears in my eyes. "Your parents both contacted me recently and gave me your phone number. I think God really wanted us to meet!"

The look on Tommy's face was just as incredulous as the one on mine. We had a brief conversation after that. He had gotten up later than he wanted, as he was on his way to an Alcoholics Anonymous meeting. It was not his custom to go to the grocery store, but because he was behind schedule, he rushed over to get a cup of coffee. Tommy might have been late on his own time schedule, but in God's eyes, he was perfectly on time. In the same regard, I might have been late calling Tommy, but I also was perfectly on time, for that chance meeting at a grocery store!

I had tears rolling down my cheeks all the way to the tennis courts. God is so awesome! We all lose sight of the daily miracles that He performs in each of our lives.

I called Tommy later in the day, as I wanted to remind him of God's little miracles. Truly, no miracle is small in effect, yet when God raises a man from the dead as He did with Lazarus or parts the Red Sea to clear a dry path of escape for the Jews, many people see the signs and wonders and marvel at God's power. Yet in what seem to be little miracles, He reminds us of how intertwined He truly is in the lives of His people! His scarlet thread weaves throughout our lives! How much does He love us? He knows everything about us, including what time we will get up, where we will go, what clothes we will put on, what words we will choose when we speak, and how all that will impact more than one person at the same time. All things worked together, just as God promised.

For the next six months, Tommy brought two of his housemates, also battling addiction, to my house for a weekly Bible study. God's miracles continued, and the relationships with Tommy, Aaron, Matthew and their families continue to enrich my life. Never forget:

And we know that all things work together for good to those who love God, to those who are the called according to *His* purpose.
Romans 8:28 (NKJV)

Really? All things? God is so big that He can orchestrate every single event to bless us and to glorify His name! Thanks, God, for yet another miracle, and along with it, another reminder of Your guiding hand in my life and in the lives of Your followers!

The humble He guides in justice,
And the humble He teaches His way.
Psalm 25:9

For I know the thoughts that I think toward you, says the LORD, thoughts of peace and not of evil, to give you a future and a hope.
Jeremiah 29:11(NKJV)

August 14: Thankfulness

Not surprisingly, most of our prayers are not consistent. We can pray for a specific outcome, and then when God answers that prayer exactly as we asked, we find that it is not the answer we really desired. Certainly, we can picture God hearing our prayers and saying, "What do you want this time? It never is enough for you, is it?"

> There is no greater difference between men than between grateful and ungrateful people. ~R.H. Blyth

Prayers should not be a shopping list of items we desire, that we visualize would make our lives so much easier. Instead, our prayers should be for the needs of others, and most importantly, praises to God for all He has chosen to give us in His infinite wisdom. Instead of complaining that a beautiful rose has thorns, we should be thanking Him for those thorns. Thankfulness is not an act, but an attitude. Part of the attitude adjustment that needs to occur is an assessment of our spiritual condition. That assessment acknowledges that without God, we are spiritually deceased! Our sins have created a wide separation between man and our God, who in His perfection cannot look upon sin. Yet the Father sent His only Son to bridge that gap.

What do we have to be thankful for? First of all, God chose us! So many Christians get this mixed up, by thinking that God chose us based on who we would become. No! That is unequivocally wrong! He chose us for His own reasons, and those reasons had everything to do with showing His mercy upon those who did not deserve it. If we become anything special, it is all because of God. Any abilities are gifts that He has given. A gift is not practiced, learned or perfected. It is opened and used! If we really desire to please God, we should use the gifts that He has given for His glory rather than for our own benefits!

**[13] But we are bound to give thanks to God always for you, brethren beloved by the Lord, because God from the beginning chose you for salvation through sanctification by the Spirit and belief in the truth, [14] to which He called you by our gospel, for the obtaining of the glory of our Lord Jesus Christ. [15] Therefore, brethren, stand fast and hold the traditions which you were taught, whether by word or our epistle.
2 Thessalonians 2:13-15 (NKJV)**

Once again, what should we be thankful for? Everything! There is not a part of our pasts that was not at least partially responsible for bringing us to this exact point. And lest any of us forget, if we are Christians, this exact point involves the greatest gifts…God living inside of us, the calling to serve Him and eternal life with Him! Is life too difficult for us at times? The greatest difficulty of our lives might be facing us right this very moment. If not a Christian, there is a solution. That solution is to accept Jesus as Lord and Savior. If we are a Christian, the solution is to reflect on our spiritual condition without Him. Regardless of where we are, praise Him, for He is in control. When Paul and Silas were in prison, chained, possibly tortured, but most certainly not in the location they would desire to be in, what did they do?

**But at midnight Paul and Silas were praying and singing hymns to God, and the prisoners were listening to them.
Acts 16:25 (NKJV)**

Then God performed miracles! No matter what we are enduring, God is not blind to it. In fact, He put us right where we are for His reason. Many question that if we have free will, how is it that God has placed us in these positions? To simplify that answer just a bit, God is outside of time and knows each decision that every man ever will make. Additionally, when we make the wrong decision, one that leads us away from God, He allows us to walk that path. At the same time, He puts detour signs in our lives to bring us back to the path He has planned for us. If we are His, He never will let go of us!

Be thankful for everything, but most importantly, be thankful for having God in our lives!

Now thanks *be* to God who always leads us in triumph in Christ, and through us diffuses the fragrance of His knowledge in every place.
2 Corinthians 2:14 (NKJV)

August 15: How well do you know the Bible?

When it comes to the availability to read and study the Bible, it is certainly easier today than ever in history. In the days of Jesus, there were a limited number of hand-written scrolls, not books, yet knowing the *Tanakh* (the Hebrew Old Testament) was an important task for the Jewish men. After the completion of the New Testament, scribes copied the Bible. According to legend, any time the scribe wrote the word "God," he would bathe and clean himself thoroughly beforehand. A passage mentioning God's name more than once would be an arduous process. If a scribe misspelled a word, he started the page over again, as there was no white-out and the copy needed to be perfect. Consequently, there were not that many copies of the Bible in its entirety.

When Johannes Gutenberg invented the printing press, it all changed. In 1455, Gutenberg published the Bible. After that time, many Christians began to read the Bible, instead of relying on a priest to read it to them in Latin. Today, we have the freedom to read whenever and wherever we like. Additionally, we have many different versions of the Bible along with computer software to help us to read the Bible in the original languages of Greek and Hebrew. Yet in some ways, there are fewer people studying the Bible than ever before.

Why is it important to know the Bible? In addition to teaching us about the words and deeds of Jesus, God's own Son who walked this earth, the Bible teaches us about God's dealings with man throughout time. Because God does not change, His Laws do not change. The Bible gives us instructions of how to live in a godly manner, and how to know God. Additionally, God wants us to know His Word well enough to share it with others:

[15] But sanctify the Lord God in your hearts, and always *be* **ready to** *give* **a defense to everyone who asks you a reason for the hope that is in you, with meekness and fear; [16] having a good conscience, that when they defame you as evildoers, those who revile your good conduct in Christ may be ashamed. [17] For** *it is* **better, if it is the will of God, to suffer for doing good than for doing evil.**
1 Peter 3:15-17 (NKJV)

This verse is not instructing us to go door-to-door like the Jehovah's witnesses, but as misguided as that group may be in some regards, they are typically better instructed in defending their faith. We are to be prepared to defend our faith whenever naysayers come our way. Yet the heart is a key to it all, as we are to have both meekness and fear when sharing our faith with others. Meekness has been described as power under control, with the picture coming to mind of a stallion, which runs both gracefully and powerfully. Certainly, meekness is not a synonym of weakness. Additionally, Jesus overturning the tables of the money changers in the temple gives us a better picture, as it took strength to completely intimidate a group, yet He did it as humbly as possible.

Many Christians attempt to argue another person to the Lord, but rare are the times when an argument actually changes someone's mind. Most of us have come to our beliefs based on our upbringing, our education, our life experiences and our own thought processes. Middle-Easterners admire a man capable of a logical argument, but in the Western world, an argument is more of a sign of disrespect. Consequently, if we are prepared when someone asks a question about the Bible, we honor God in our humbleness and fear. We do not lead someone to Jesus; He draws them:

No one can come to Me unless the Father who sent Me draws him; and I will raise him up at the last day.
John 6:44 (NKJV)

Sometimes, we lose heart when the person we share with does not seem ready to walk away from the cares of the world. Yet every word about God is a planted seed. With that being said, if someone sees the joy in our lives, especially in the midst of hardship, and asks questions about God based on what they see in our lives, we need to be ready.

So shall My word be that goes forth from My mouth;
It shall not return to Me void,
But it shall accomplish what I please,
And it shall prosper *in the thing* **for which I sent it.**
Isaiah 55:11 (NKJV)

But the Helper, the Holy Spirit, whom the Father will send in My name, He will teach you all things, and bring to your remembrance all things that I said to you.
John 14:26 (NKJV)

August 16: The limitations of the human brain

One of the quotations that cadets are required to memorize at the United States Air Force Academy is engraved on a statue of an eagle and its fledglings at the terrazzo level of the campus:

> "Man's flight through life is sustained by the power of his knowledge." ---Austin "Dusty" Miller

Unless the quotation is referring to man's knowledge of God, Miller and the believers in that statement are placing undue emphasis on the power of man, rather than He who created man. While man's knowledge certainly has increased throughout history, we continue to find that scholars throughout each generation knew much less than thought at the time. The "practice of medicine" is a prime example, as it certainly would not be deemed a practice if it was perfect! If man's knowledge was so important, Ponce de Leon would not have been searching for a fountain of youth.

In regard to God, the limitations of the human brain always seem to have man putting God in a box. Because man's abilities and knowledge are finite, even Christians sometimes operate as if God is only a bigger, better man. Yet to truly understand God is to grasp that He has no limits, other than His own nature! Yes, there are some things that God cannot do. He cannot lie, nor sin in any way. Nor can He change. God does not continue to learn; He always has known all there is to know. It occurred to me that God never has uttered the line, "It occurred to Me!" Most beneficial to us as believers is that God never can let us down, leave us or forsake us!

Along these lines, Christians seem to struggle most in the area of prayer. The amazing ways that God answers prayer are rarely in the mundane manner we ask for His answers!

[17] that Christ may dwell in your hearts through faith; that you, being rooted and grounded in love, [18] may be able to comprehend with all the saints what *is* the width and length and depth and height— [19] to know the love of Christ which passes knowledge; that you may be filled with all the fullness of God.
Ephesians 3:17-19 (NKJV)

Without God's help, man has no chance in comprehending God's dimensions, but as we grow as Christians, He stretches us. Those stretches occur in every way, with one of those being a deeper understanding of who He is. It is much like other relationships as the more time we spend with God, the better we will know Him. Consequently, the better we know Him, the more likely we are to ask for His will to be done when we pray, rather than a specific answer. God cannot answer our prayer just as we request if it is contrary to His will! We should desire for God to stretch us to have a deeper understanding of who He is!

that by two immutable things, in which it *is* impossible for God to lie, we might have strong consolation, who have fled for refuge to lay hold of the hope set before *us*.
Hebrews 6:18 (NKJV)

August 17: Everyone needs compassion

Compassion has been described as feeling someone else's pain. Enduring this world, we all are certain to be in a plethora of painful positions. Pain can be emotional, physical or spiritual, though there are times when we are suffering a combination of the three. One of the interesting attributes of pain is that we tend to forget it to some degree, once we have seen the proverbial light at the end of the tunnel. Yet our body never forgets. That is a gift of sorts, for once we have endured a great difficulty, we retain a confidence of survival when faced with another trial. To the man who never has experienced a pinprick, it feels insurmountable, while a woman having a baby would understand how the two would not be worthy of comparison. Rather than making fun of the man for his ignorance involving pain, a compassionate person would understand that as tiny as it is, his pain is very real to him.

One of the best biblical revelations of pain and compassion comes from the Book of Job. Certainly Job endured more physical pain than any of us, yet it was the accompanying spiritual and emotional pain of feeling separated from God that hurt the worst. Imagine what Job endured! His seven sons and three daughters died on one day; his entire body was impacted by painful boils, that Job scratched and scraped with a discarded piece of broken pottery; Job's wife advised him to "Curse God and die;" Job prayed, but did not feel God's presence anymore in his life; Job's best friends spent hours telling him that God was condemning him for sin, though Job knew that was not the case. He felt completely alone. If his friends would have sat beside Job and cried with him, without any condemnation, it would have helped him more. Yet Job felt like they were piling on to an already difficult situation.

> "Compassion will cure more sins than condemnation."---
> Henry Ward Beecher

We know that God is compassionate. In fact, it is easy to understand how God can feel our pain, as He created us. In Isaiah 53, Jesus is described as a Man of sorrows and acquainted with grief. He knows our pain, and everything else about us!

But You, O Lord, *are* a God full of compassion, and gracious, Longsuffering and abundant in mercy and truth.
Psalm 86:15 (NKJV)

A synonym for compassion is mercy, with the best description of mercy being "not getting what we deserve." Certainly, from God's perspective, we are deserving of death for our sin, yet God has devised a way of escape. Simply by asking His Son to be the Lord of our lives, the work that Jesus accomplished on the cross will satisfy each of our sin debts. He took the pain that we earned with our lives and in exchange, we receive the blessings that He earned with His life. Some people question how a just and loving God does not just forgive everyone. Would that be love? If a daughter was raped and murdered, would any father want to forgive and forget when the case came before a judge? Punishment is just as loving as forgiveness.

[14] What shall we say then? *Is there* unrighteousness with God? Certainly not! [15] For He says to Moses, *"I will have mercy on whomever I will have mercy, and I will have*

compassion on whomever I will have compassion." ¹⁶ **So then** *it is* **not of him who wills, nor of him who runs, but of God who shows mercy.**
Romans 9:14-16 (NKJV)

Yet because we are not endowed with God's unlimited knowledge or His heart, we are called to follow the examples set by the Father in His forgiveness of us, and by Jesus in His life upon this earth. Numerous times in the Gospel, we see Jesus pouring out compassion on the people.

But when He saw the multitudes, He was moved with compassion for them, because they were weary and scattered, like sheep having no shepherd.
Matthew 9:36 (NKJV)

And when Jesus went out He saw a great multitude; and He was moved with compassion for them, and healed their sick.
Matthew 14:14 (NKJV)

Even when Jesus was suffering upon the cross, He compassionately looked upon the pain of Mary, His mother, and John, His disciple and friend. Jesus ignored His own great pain and still continued ministering to others. He told John to take care of Mary as a son would and told Mary to love John as she would love a son, filling a need in both of their hearts (John 19:27). At that time, Jesus also asked for forgiveness for those who crucified Him, and saved a wayward thief who was dying beside Him (Luke 23:43).

Each day, we are faced with situations involving friends, co-workers, family members and even strangers. It is easy to condemn people in their sinful pride, and more difficult to love them in the midst of turmoil. Yet that love can cover a multitude of sins. If someone hurts us deeply, and our response is compassion and love, that action will speak louder than words. Most of us can look back on our own lives and remember the voluminous effect that someone else's compassion had on our lives. If we follow God, we will learn to love more like Him, in that "agape" way.

Should you not also have had compassion on your fellow servant, just as I had pity on you?
Matthew 18:33 (NKJV)

August 18: Do you know His voice?

When someone else calls the dog we own, a well-trained dog looks to us first, to see if we approve. Dogs have an acute sense of smell, but their sense of hearing is also phenomenal. Even when we whisper, our dogs know our voices, especially if we have spent much time together. That is a great analogy to our relationship with the Lord. Depending on the amount of time we spend with Him, we should know His voice. Quality time with Him is through Bible study, prayer and fellowship. It could include time spent in church or time spent completely alone.

[1] **"Most assuredly, I say to you, he who does not enter the sheepfold by the door, but climbs up some other way, the same is a thief and a robber.** [2] **"But he who enters by the door is the shepherd of the sheep.** [3] **"To him the doorkeeper opens, and the sheep hear his voice; and he calls his own sheep by name and leads them out.** [4] **"And when he brings out his own sheep, he goes before them; and the sheep follow him, for they know his voice.** [5] **"Yet they will by no means follow a stranger, but will flee from him, for they do not know the voice of strangers."** [6] **Jesus used this illustration, but they did not understand the things which He spoke to them.**
John 10:1-6 (NKJV)

The Holy Spirit is the doorkeeper and Jesus is the door. Do we know His voice? That is one of the most important questions that each of us has to answer. We do not become sheep by believing; we believe by becoming sheep. Is this confusing? If we believe in Jesus Christ, it is because He chose us as sheep from the foundations of the earth. He called Lazarus by name,

Zacchaeus by name, Mary Magdalene by name at the tomb... and we all will hear Him call us by name, too, if we are true believers!

The voice of our Lord could crumble rocks into tiny bits, but is the voice of a peaceful river, restoring our souls. Though His voice could send every enemy sprawling, it is the voice of sweet forgiveness when we repent of our sin and turn toward Him. His voice can be still and small, but we can hear that whisper loudly, deep in our souls, as if He is speaking with the world's largest megaphone. Lazarus was dead and still could hear the voice of his Lord:

[43] Now when He had said these things, He cried with a loud voice, "Lazarus, come forth!" [44] And he who had died came out bound hand and foot with graveclothes, and his face was wrapped with a cloth. Jesus said to them, "Loose him, and let him go."
John 11:43-44 (NKJV)

If we desire to hear His voice, we will hear His voice, for the Lord has promised that anyone who seeks Him, will find Him. But without the desire to hear His voice *above all others*, there is no point in listening. Voices of the world will conflict God's voice of reason, and the world's voice will focus on our pride, accomplishments, financial goals, etc. God's voice will focus on following His Word, edifying others with His love, and drawing nearer to Him. He who has an ear should hear what the Spirit is saying!

And you said: 'Surely the LORD our God has shown us His glory and His greatness, and we have heard His voice from the midst of the fire. We have seen this day that God speaks with man; yet he *still* lives.
Deuteronomy 5:24 (NKJV)

August 19: What is your excuse?

Freshmen at the United States Air Force Academy are allowed five responses during the first year when "conversing" with upper classmen. Those responses are "Yes, sir," "No, sir," "Sir, may I ask a question," "Sir, may I make a statement," and the final response, which was required any time anyone asked a why question, "No excuse, sir!" The system is designed to break the individual mentality, and have every cadet think with a focus on the group. All who endured that first year would remember it as senseless and demoralizing, but certainly, the goal of getting a group to act collectively as one is met, for the most part.

One of the greatest lessons has to do with making excuses. In the military, there is no excuse for a foul up. No matter how much explaining was accomplished by the culprit, the situation only seemed to worsen. As Christians, an excuse is even more ludicrous, for instead of giving that excuse to a superior ranking official of varying intelligence, we are giving that excuse to our omniscient Creator. God is not fooled for a moment. Instead, He knows much more about the situation than anyone directly involved. In any disagreement, there are always three points of view: ours, theirs and God's. Which one of those is the only correct one? In the Gospel of John, when Jesus heals a paralytic man, the man is filled with excuses:

[1] **After this there was a feast of the Jews, and Jesus went up to Jerusalem.** [2] **Now there is in Jerusalem by the Sheep *Gate* a pool, which is called in Hebrew, Bethesda, having five porches.** [3] **In these lay a great multitude of sick people, blind, lame, paralyzed, waiting for the moving of the water.** [4] **For an angel went down at a certain time into the pool and stirred up the water; then whoever stepped in first, after the stirring of the water, was made well of whatever disease he had.** [5] **Now a certain man was there who had an infirmity thirty-eight years.** [6] **When Jesus saw him lying there, and knew that he already had been *in that condition* a long time, He said to him, "Do you want to be made well?"**

⁷ The sick man answered Him, "Sir, I have no man to put me into the pool when the water is stirred up; but while I am coming, another steps down before me."
⁸ Jesus said to him, "Rise, take up your bed and walk." ⁹ And immediately the man was made well, took up his bed, and walked.
John 5:1-9 (NKJV)

In his short statement, the paralytic man offered three excuses: "I have no man to put me into the pool," "the water is stirred up," and "another steps down before me." Each of those excuses sounds similar to the ones we make. His first excuse echoes when we say there is no one around to help us. It points to a reliance on other men rather than a reliance on God. His second excuse sounds like when we erroneously believe that conditions are not right for a miracle, pointing to a dependence on circumstances, rather than dependence upon the Lord. Lastly, his third excuse sounded similar to us saying that others always get in our way. That points to us blaming others rather than trusting God.

Even when we make excuses, that does not mean that God will not continue to use us. Instead of looking at the life of a paralytic sinner, we can look into the life of a man selected by God to lead His chosen people, Moses. When the Lord called him to lead the children of Israel, Moses made seven excuses to God, with the last two being identical. It appears he was running out of excuses, but still the Lord used him mightily. Here are those excuses:

1. But Moses said to God, "Who am I that I should go to Pharaoh, and that I should bring the children of Israel out of Egypt." **Exodus 3:11 (NKJV)**
2. Then Moses said to God, "Indeed when I come to the children of Israel and say to them, 'The God of your fathers has sent me to you,' and they say to me, 'What is His name?' what shall I say to them?" **Exodus 3:13 (NKJV)**

3. Then Moses answered and said, "But suppose they will not believe me or listen to my voice; suppose they say, 'The Lord has not appeared to you.'" Exodus 4:1 (NKJV)
4. Then Moses said to the Lord, "O my Lord, I am not eloquent, neither before nor since You have spoken to Your servant; but I am slow of speech and slow of tongue." Exodus 4:10 (NKJV)
5. But he said, "O my Lord, please send by the hand of whomever else You may send." Exodus 4:13 (NKJV)
6. And Moses spoke before the Lord, saying, "The children of Israel have not heeded me. How then shall Pharaoh heed me, for I am of uncircumcised lips?" Exodus 6:12 (NKJV)
7. But Moses said before the Lord, "Behold, I am of uncircumcised lips, and how shall Pharaoh heed me?" Exodus 6:30 (NKJV)

Are we making excuses to God? Frequently in the lives of believers, those excuses have to do with sins we are not willing to walk away from. Additionally, we also have the tendency to make excuses involving ministry opportunities, just as Moses did. If God asks why we did something without Him or against Him, our answer should be a resounding, "No excuse, Sir!" Yet even with our failures and excuses, He continues to love us. But He certainly desires our willingness!

[1] And Jesus answered and spoke to them again by parables and said: [2] "The kingdom of heaven is like a certain king who arranged a marriage for his son, [3] and sent out his servants to call those who were invited to the wedding; and they were not willing to come.
Matthew 22:1-3 (NKJV)

August 20: Love God in everything!

Purity is the state of being undiluted, or unmixed with extraneous materials. Additionally, purity in a spiritual sense has to do with freedom from sin or guilt, combining with the sexual aspect of chastity. Certainly, we never will be free from sin while on this earth, yet with the forgiveness of God, we are free from guilt. As Christians, we are brides of Christ, and He desires all of our love! That sounds like a level of requirement that we simply cannot uphold, yet that is not God's point of view. Because an omniscient God created us, He comprehends every false desire in the minds and hearts of His sheep. Instead of condemnation, God's desire for us is that through the journey, we will learn to trust Him more, to follow Him more and most importantly, to love Him more.

³ We give no offense in anything, that our ministry may not be blamed. ⁴ But in all *things* we commend ourselves as ministers of God: in much patience, in tribulations, in needs, in distresses, ⁵ in stripes, in imprisonments, in tumults, in labors, in sleeplessness, in fastings; ⁶ by purity, by knowledge, by longsuffering, by kindness, by the Holy Spirit, by sincere love, ⁷ by the word of truth, by the power of God, by the armor of righteousness on the right hand and on the left, ⁸ by honor and dishonor, by evil report and good report; as deceivers, and *yet* true; ⁹ as unknown, and *yet* well known; as dying, and behold we live; as chastened, and *yet* not killed; ¹⁰ as sorrowful, yet always rejoicing; as poor, yet making many rich; as having nothing, and *yet* possessing all things. 2 Corinthians 6:3-10 (NKJV)

The list above does not paint the Christian life as a simple walk in the park. Instead, the words spoken by Paul point to a higher calling in the midst of turmoil. There is no great difficulty in loving those who love us, but when we treat our enemies with love, it demonstrates that our hearts are operating under a higher power, the power of the Holy Spirit. If we cannot love others, we cannot love God. Sometimes as believers, we have the audacity to judge where unbelievers are walking, especially in regard to their sinful ways and lives. Yet the ugliness that we perceive in their lives is truly, ugliness in our own lives. God created them just as He created us. Instead of judging them, we are called to love them, as that love may be the shining light in their world of darkness, pointing them just as it did us to a God who loves!

Though I speak with the tongues of men and of angels, but have not love, I have become sounding brass or a clanging cymbal.
1 Corinthians 13:1 (NKJV)

One of the greatest challenges as believers is to keep that love of God at the forefront of our minds and hearts. Sometimes, the Lord will reveal locked doors, protecting areas of our lives that we are holding onto, unwilling to give Him the key. Those areas may be different in each of our lives. Examples would be the desire for more money, more status or more accolades from men. Are our business ethics identical to our ethics at church? God does not want parts of us. He does not even desire to have most of us. Instead, God desires all of us! Whether we want to give Him the key or not, He is going to open that door! That is the Christian journey summed up in a nutshell.

He must increase, but I *must* decrease.
John 3:30 (NKJV)

John the Baptist's statement speaks volumes. As we grow in the Lord, we should become more like God. Our Lord does not accomplish that transformation by turning a light switch, though if He desired, He could. Yet He wants us to desire more of Him in our lives.

[12] Therefore, my beloved, as you have always obeyed, not as in my presence only, but now much more in my absence, work out your own salvation with fear and trembling; [13] for it is God who works in you both to will and to do for *His* good pleasure.
Philippians 2:12-13 (NKJV)

> "That all things are possible to him who believes, that they are less difficult to him who hopes, they are more

easy to him who loves, and still more easy to him who perseveres in the practice of these three virtues."
--Brother Lawrence, from "The Practice of the Presence of God"

Believing is more than thought; it is belief in action, also called faith. Hope is the desire to be with Jesus, along with the expectation of obtaining that desire, with joy being the companion of both the desire and expectation. Yet those will pass away, for when we see Jesus face-to-face, faith and hope will no longer be necessary. Love, though, will remain for all of eternity! By loving others now, we also love God. We can love Him through every aspect of our lives, not just Bible study, fellowship and prayer. Are there moments of our lives when God departs from us? No, as He has set up His tabernacle in our souls, never to depart. As He never will leave us, how can we leave Him? We should worship the Lord in every part of our lives, and let our love for others (and for Him) be at the forefront!

[4] Love suffers long *and* is kind; love does not envy; love does not parade itself, is not puffed up; [5] does not behave rudely, does not seek its own, is not provoked, thinks no evil; [6] does not rejoice in iniquity, but rejoices in the truth; [7] bears all things, believes all things, hopes all things, endures all things. [8] Love never fails. But whether *there are* prophecies, they will fail; whether *there are* tongues, they will cease; whether *there is* knowledge, it will vanish away. [9] For we know in part and we prophesy in part. [10] But when that which is perfect has come, then that which is in part will be done away.
1 Corinthians 13:4-10 (NKJV)

But I say to you, love your enemies, bless those who curse you, do good to those who hate you, and pray for those who spitefully use you and persecute you,
Matthew 5:44 (NKJV)

August 21: A servant to all!

In our culture, the words "slave" and "servant" carry negative connotations. Especially in the history of the United States, slavery reminds us of a time when our ancestors uprooted families from African nations and sold them to do manual labor for others, without pay. Other nations were involved in the slave trade, too. One of the best depictions of that time is the movie, "Amazing Grace," which celebrates the life of William Wilberforce, a transformed Christian and Member of Parliament who devoted his life to ending slavery in England. Additionally, the movie touches on the life of John Newton, a former slave trader who wrote the words to our best known hymn, using his painful past to understand God's love and forgiveness. It is difficult to imagine how painful it must have been to be living freely, working and supporting a family, only to be kidnapped, taken across the world, and forced to work for others...or die.

There is a difference between a slave and a servant. A servant is paid for his work, while a slave is not, but is purchased from someone else. As negative as the word "servant" is, the Bible refers to Paul, Peter, James, Jude and Epaphras as bondservants of Jesus Christ. "Bondservant" is *duolos* in Greek. In the Old Testament, a servant would work for six years, and then be set free. Yet if the servant wanted to remain, he would place his ear against a wooden door, have his ear pierced by an awl and would stay with the master by choice. The earring placed through the servant's ear was a sign that he belonged to the master forever (Exodus 21:1-6). As Christians, we are no different from the other bondservants mentioned in the Bible. We have chosen to remain with our Master forever, and certainly, we are paid handsomely! We have been given eternal life! What would cause a servant to desire to remain with the master? Certainly, they would have to think they were well taken care of, but they really would have to love the master! Look at another servant in the Bible:

**¹² So when He had washed their feet, taken His garments, and sat down again, He said to them, "Do you know what I have done to you? ¹³ You call Me Teacher and Lord, and you say well, for *so* I am. ¹⁴ If I then, *your* Lord and Teacher, have washed your feet, you also ought to wash one another's feet. ¹⁵ For I have given you an example, that you should do as I have done to you. ¹⁶ Most assuredly, I say to you, a servant is not greater than his master; nor is he who is sent greater than he who sent him. ¹⁷ If you know these things, blessed are you if you do them.
John 13:12-17 (NKJV)**

When Jesus washed the feet of His disciples, He performed a task that only the lowest in class would attempt. Knowing that, Peter told the Lord that he would not allow Him to serve in that manner. Yet Jesus told Peter without Peter allowing that to happen, He would have no part of Peter. That changed Peter's mind very quickly! Peter always seemed to be the one who said what he thought. We can see that as courage or brashness, but it had to be uncomfortable to have Jesus, who was God on earth, washing the dirtiest part of the disciples' bodies. Envision how nasty their feet would be, wearing sandals and walking around on the unpaved roads. Yet that is exactly the lesson the Lord wanted them, and us, to learn.

**For who *is* greater, he who sits at the table, or he who serves? *Is* it not he who sits at the table? Yet I am among you as the One who serves.
Luke 22:27 (NKJV)**

A servant is not concerned with his own needs, but a good master will take care of those needs. Jesus served His disciples and us, knowing that the Father would take care of His needs. In turn, Jesus calls us to serve others. That is the kind of love that will speak loudest to a broken world. If we are busy serving others, God certainly will take care of our needs! But we need to be careful that we do not serve to be seen! Each of us knows a special friend with a servant's heart, who always is working behind the scenes. The Bible tells us not to even let our left hand know what our right hand is doing! Are we servants to all? Jesus was! If God can lower Himself, we certainly can!

33 Then He came to Capernaum. And when He was in the house He asked them, "What was it you disputed among yourselves on the road?" 34 But they kept silent, for on the road they had disputed among themselves who *would be the* greatest. 35 And He sat down, called the twelve, and said to them, "If anyone desires to be first, he shall be last of all and servant of all."
Mark 9:33-35 (NKJV)

August 22: The glory of God in nature

One of the comments we make to workaholics is, "Stop and smell the roses." At a glance, everyone notices the physical beauty of the rose, though many different varieties of God's majestic flower have aromas that are more surprising than even the physical beauty. We cannot appreciate that aspect without getting up close and personal with the rose, which takes time, energy and proximity. God has intricately woven His creative hand through everything upon the earth, but to notice, it might involve getting away from shopping centers and Starbucks!

**20 For since the creation of the world His invisible *attributes* are clearly seen, being understood by the things that are made, *even* His eternal power and Godhead, so that they are without excuse, 21 because, although they knew God, they did not glorify *Him* as God, nor were thankful, but became futile in their thoughts, and their foolish hearts were darkened.
22 Professing to be wise, they became fools,**
Romans 1:20-22 (NKJV)

We can see God in nature! And yes, we even can smell God in nature. Consider the flowers, to paraphrase what Jesus said. Every single flower has its own perfume! How amazing that just as humans have different fingerprints, flowers each have their own smell. God's handiwork is so amazing that it is obvious how awkward and clumsy man's creative hand is in comparison.

Try walking through a lush forest at night. Without our visual senses, that sense of smell is heightened.

²⁷ "Consider the lilies, how they grow: they neither toil nor spin; and yet I say to you, even Solomon in all his glory was not arrayed like one of these. ²⁸ "If then God so clothes the grass, which today is in the field and tomorrow is thrown into the oven, how much more *will He clothe* you, O *you* of little faith?
Luke 12:27-28 (NKJV)

Taking the time to smell the roses also can apply to the rest of God's creations. Do we take the time to get up close and personal with the people God has dropped into our lives? There are no coincidences, as God has a purpose and a plan for each of us. Consequently, He places people in our paths for a reason. It does not matter if they are Christians or atheists, God has a design behind it all. Sometimes, we have a tendency to portray joyfulness while at church, when in reality, there are some real difficulties facing us. On a similar note, rather than just smile at a church acquaintance, take the time to discover where they are hurting. Sometimes a simple hug can do wonders, but most of the time, our impact on their lives will take time, energy and proximity. Smell the roses, and do not forget, we are going to a city where the roses never fade!

¹ The heavens declare the glory of God;
And the firmament shows His handiwork.
² Day unto day utters speech,
And night unto night reveals knowledge.
Psalm 19:1-2 (NKJV)

August 23: Are you being deceived?

Paraphrasing another saying, American author Carolyn Wells said, "Actions lie louder than words." Certainly, lying is a part of our condition and our culture. We tell our children all about Santa Claus, the Easter Bunny and the Tooth Fairy, knowing that down the road, they will discover the truth, and then will pass on the lie when they have children. We think of that as harmless, sometimes referred to as a white lie. On the surface, some lies do appear to be harmless, but in actuality, all lies cause harm. Though God tells us in His commandments that lying is a sin, we all find ourselves trapped in perpetuating many of the lies in our lives.

When Satan was cast out of heaven, before Adam and Eve had children, he had become the great deceiver, spinning his tales to serve his own purposes. By taking a small part of the truth that God had spoken to Adam, Satan twisted the words to confuse Eve. Yet Eve would not have taken the advice of the slimy serpent without her own problematic desire to "be like God." Satan appealed to her pride in his plan to trip her up. That should not be a surprise to any of us, as he continues to use that ruse with each of us. Yet we know that Jesus not only speaks truth, but is the truth!

Jesus said to him, "I am the way, the truth, and the life. No one comes to the Father except through Me.
John 14:6 (NKJV)

The great deceiver operates against the truth of Jesus. We cannot be deceived unless we are led away from the truth unknowingly, otherwise it would be a choice rather than deception. Logic reveals that there is no one being deceived who believes they are being deceived. All of us are subject to deception, but as Christians, our protection remains as long as we are relying on the power of God, rather than operating under our own prideful, power supply. Once again, the same issue that tripped up Satan makes us stumble. If we have desires for power, notoriety, or money – basically, the trappings of the world – then we also have the potential to be fooled. Satan preys on human weakness, and he has spent all of man's history practicing his craft. Though the old adage says that "practice makes perfect," Satan never will be perfect, though he certainly is powerful. Yet, God, who dwells in us, is much greater than any of the beings He created!

**There is a way *that seems* right to a man,
But its end *is* the way of death.
Proverbs 14:12 (NKJV)**

There are few people who choose the wrong path, knowing that it leads to destruction. But when we put emphasis on our own intelligence, rather than relying on God's omniscience, we have entered the wide gate.

**[13] "Enter by the narrow gate; for wide *is* the gate and broad *is* the way that leads to destruction, and there are many who go in by it. [14] Because narrow *is* the gate and difficult *is* the way which leads to life, and there are few who find it.
Matthew 7:13-14 (NKJV)**

When Jesus was teaching His disciples about the latter days, referring to the end times, he warned of false christs and false prophets, members of Satan's army.

**For false christs and false prophets will rise and show great signs and wonders to deceive, if possible, even the elect.
Matthew 24:24 (NKJV)**

Is it possible to deceive the elect? When Jesus walked the earth as a man, He performed miracles. In the form of the antichrist, Satan will attempt to copy the miracles of Jesus. Those miracles will cause many to follow, yet the elect should know His Word, and His prophetic warning of not allowing those signs and wonders to amaze and deceive them. The word "elect" in the Bible refers to two separate groups, the children of Israel and the church. When Jesus is speaking to His disciples, the context of the verses seems to relate to the Jews. Yet it is apparent from the verse that God will not allow His followers to be deceived at this time.

We should ensure that our actions and our lives do not lead others astray. We can be seed planters or seed waterers, but our greatest calling is to love others by speaking truth. Jesus is the truth that will set us free! Without knowing Jesus, we are being deceived! Yet even as Christians, we can lose sight of what God wants us to do, by choosing to do what "seems right." One key is not to allow the praises of men to become spiritual barometers in our lives. We should measure ourselves against God's Word, not public or private opinion or approval!

It is **not good to eat much honey;**
So to seek one's own glory *is not* **glory.**
Proverbs 25:27 (NKJV)

August 24: Recharging your batteries

Life is a series of victories and defeats, peaks and valleys, joy and sadness. Interestingly, the line of delineation between each of those apparent opposites reveals that each are closely related. In defeat, there is always victory. Each valley contains a highest point in that valley. In the lowest degree of sadness, there is a joy that we have survived and can go no lower.

> "Everyone wants to live on top of the mountain, but all the happiness and growth occurs while you are climbing it." – Anonymous

Certainly, we all desire the "mountaintop" experience with God, yet sometimes, we forget what that period at the pinnacle entails. Moses spent two consecutive, 40-day periods of fasting alone with God on Mount Sinai. It was a time of powerful and memorable fellowship with the Lord, but during the second period, Moses was pouring out His soul to the Lord to save and not destroy the children of Israel, who had fallen into almost immediate idolatry when Moses journeyed up the mountain to receive the Law. More specifically, Moses ached for the life of his brother Aaron, who had fashioned the golden calf.

[18] And I fell down before the LORD, as at the first, forty days and forty nights; I neither ate bread nor drank water, because of all your sin which you committed in doing wickedly in the sight of the LORD, to provoke Him to anger.
[19] For I was afraid of the anger and hot displeasure with

which the LORD was angry with you, to destroy you. But the LORD listened to me at that time also. [20] **And the LORD was very angry with Aaron *and* would have destroyed him; so I prayed for Aaron also at the same time.** [21] **Then I took your sin, the calf which you had made, and burned it with fire and crushed it *and* ground *it* very small, until it was as fine as dust; and I threw its dust into the brook that descended from the mountain.**
Deuteronomy 9:18-21 (NKJV)

Moses prayed for Aaron, <u>also</u>. We know that God listened to Moses at other times, as well, and it sounds as though Moses prayed for the people first, and his own family second. How many in our Christian leadership feel that way about those God has entrusted them with? How many are willing to give up food and water for even a day? What this passage reveals is that our prayer should be to never give up on anyone! It does not matter what we have done, or how we have sinned against God. Each of us has our secret closet filled with awful sins, and only God knows the sins behind that door. Fortunately for us, if we repent, God casts those sins deep into the ocean, and He never dredges them up again. Sadly, we sometimes have trouble letting go of the sins that God has forgiven. Instead, we should be more concerned with allowing God to break our hearts because of our sin, for without that effect upon our hearts, the same sin will continue!

> "Nobody trips over mountains. It is the small pebble that causes you to stumble. Pass all the pebbles in your path and you will find that you have crossed the mountain." – Anonymous

Each journey is a series of highs and lows. We have moments of high energy and moments when we cannot envision taking another step. But as long as we are walking with the Lord, He recharges our batteries, preparing us for another journey, and another battle. Interestingly, unless we have some distance from the mountain, we cannot even see it! That "alone time" with the Lord on top of the mountain is something to treasure, but as He remains with us throughout every step and every battle, the valleys and ascents are just as special. We need to be content wherever the Lord has us, for the place He desires for us to be is definitely a special place!

Let your conduct *be* without covetousness; *be* content with such things as you have. For He Himself has said, *"I will never leave you nor forsake you."*
Hebrews 13:5 (NKJV)

Now godliness with contentment is great gain.
1 Timothy 6:6 (NKJV)

August 25: Training

Championship athletes may be born with God-given abilities of speed, power and agility, but without proper training, those abilities are useless. To perform like a champion involves much repetition and muscle memory, fine tuning those same muscles. Additionally, without endurance, all but the shortest races will end with failure.

> "Excellence is an art won by training and habituation. We do not act rightly because we have virtue or excellence, but we rather have those because we have acted rightly. We are what we repeatedly do. Excellence, then, is not an act but a habit." – Aristotle

While these fundamentals directly apply to physical conditioning, they are also analogous to spiritual conditioning. Imagine a lengthy race that not only has many spectators lining the course, but additionally, an army of naysayers trying to trip us up and wipe us out of the race. That would make marathon running more enjoyable to watch! Satan and his demonic host have spent all of man's history plotting against and deceiving God's saints. His goal is to ruin our testimonies for the Lord.

²⁴ Do you not know that those who run in a race all run, but one receives the prize? Run in such a way that you may obtain *it*. ²⁵ And everyone who competes *for the prize* is temperate in all things. Now they *do it* to obtain a perishable crown, but we *for* an imperishable *crown*. ²⁶ Therefore I run thus: not with uncertainty. Thus I fight: not as *one who* beats the air. ²⁷ But I discipline my body and bring *it* into subjection, lest, when I have preached to others, I myself should become disqualified.
1 Corinthians 9:24-27 (NKJV)

According to Paul, we are to run with certainty. That certainly is the knowledge of God's Word. In the Bible, we are given many promises, and as God is incapable of breaking a promise, we can be certain that what He has promised will come to fruition. He has promised that any temptation in our paths is one we can handle, and along with that He will give us a way of escape (1 Corinthians 10:13). He has promised that He never will leave us or forsake us (Hebrews 13:5). He has promised that the work that He began in us, He will complete (Philippians 1:6). It sounds like much of the race has to do with God's power in our lives.

God did His part. He took a blind man and gave him vision. He took a dead man and gave him life. He took a lame man and gave him powerful legs. Those are the spiritual conditions of each of us without God. People in wheelchairs see others running, and yearn to run beside them. God gave us legs to run the race, and we should run for His glory. We already have received the Prize and that is God's Son in our lives! If we finish the race strongly, we will receive a crown, yet that crown belongs to Jesus, and at the Bema Seat, we will cast the crown at His feet.

So what are we responsible for? Keeping the faith and finishing strongly. The repetition necessary in our lives involves Bible study, fellowship and prayer. Yet God has a ministry for each of us and we are to serve Him and serve others in that ministry. Do not get confused by the world's philosophy that bigger is better.

One person is enough to make a successful ministry if that is God's will. There are plenty of ministries with thousands of followers who are being misled. How many people were still following Jesus when He was on the cross?

We should commit ourselves to holiness. God would not keep us here unless He had people for us to love. Most of the time, those people will be the down-trodden, the ones the world might call unlovable. Remember, God put people in our lives to love us!

[1] Therefore we also, since we are surrounded by so great a cloud of witnesses, let us lay aside every weight, and the sin which so easily ensnares *us,* and let us run with endurance the race that is set before us, [2] looking unto Jesus, the author and finisher of *our* faith, who for the joy that was set before Him endured the cross, despising the shame, and has sat down at the right hand of the throne of God.
Hebrews 12:1-2 (NKJV)

August 26: Endurance

One of the children's tales all of us remember is Aesop's Fable concerning the tortoise and the hare. Our Christian lives typically are distance races, rather than sprints. Endurance is one of the greatest requirements of the Christian walk. While many who come to the Lord hope for ease and prosperity in their new lives, that is not God's promise. Instead, He promises that He never will leave us or forsake us (Hebrews 13:5). Jesus also promises that we will continue to suffer!

These things I have spoken to you, that in Me you may have peace. In the world you will have tribulation; but be of good cheer, I have overcome the world."
John 16:33 (NKJV)

The walk of a Christian is similar to climbing a mountain. Each difficult step up that mountain carries us closer to the Lord, though we have no idea what it will look like when we get to the top. We do know that God will be there, and that is enough reason to climb! Additionally, we can look back and see the view of where we came from. When we look down the mountain, the journey does not appear to be as steep or painful as it did when we were climbing that section, but we remember the journey. There are times when we might slip or even fall, yet God will pick us up, help us to dust the world off and get back on the journey again. One of the keys is not to quit, as nothing worth having is easy!

As Jesus reminded us, we all have mountains to face in our lives. He certainly did when He walked on this earth, and a servant is not greater than his Master. (John 15:20). When we feel like our mountain is insurmountable, we should remember that God already has promised that anything He puts into our paths we can handle (1 Corinthians 10:13), not alone, but with Him in control of our lives. Are we walking with Him in our trials, or walking alone? He wants to help shoulder the burden, if we only will let Him!

[13] Brethren, I do not count myself to have apprehended; but one thing *I do,* forgetting those things which are behind and reaching forward to those things which are ahead, [14] I press toward the goal for the prize of the upward call of God in Christ Jesus.
Philippians 3:13-14 (NKJV)

August 27: Fatigue

Some days, all of us suffer from a complete lack of energy! Part of the human condition is having bodies that need rest. Most of us tend to find our balance more on the side of tired than of rested. If that negative balance continues for long enough, we cross the line from fatigue to exhaustion. That feeling of absolute fatigue may begin with physical signs, but the root is typically much deeper than physical strain.

> "Our fatigue is often caused not by work, but by worry, frustration and resentment." ---Dale Carnegie

Carnegie's statement carries a ring of truth, for when faced with difficult decisions, many times, it affects our sleep. All have found their minds racing when they should be dreaming of eating banana splits. What a nice dream of ice cream!

⁶ Be anxious for nothing, but in everything by prayer and supplication, with thanksgiving, let your requests be made known to God; ⁷ and the peace of God, which surpasses all understanding, will guard your hearts and minds through Christ Jesus.
Philippians 4:6-7 (NKJV)

God's promise to us on this matter is a conditional one. *If* we do not worry, but instead, hand the issues over to Him to resolve and trust that He will, *then* He will fill us with a peace that is beyond what others could understand in the middle of that turmoil. It comes down to a matter of trust. When we worry, we are calling God a liar, as He already has promised many times that He will not let us down in any way. He never will leave us or forsake us. He always will work out all things together for the benefit of those whom He has chosen. He cannot lie for it is against His nature. Trust Him!

Worry causes a snowball effect in our sleep pattern. Miss one night of rest, and grumpiness affects actions throughout the day and other relationships, which will add to the worry in our lives. That gives the worrywart more issues to worry about!

"Fatigue makes cowards of us all." ---Vince Lombardi

But those who wait on the LORD
Shall renew *their* strength;
They shall mount up with wings like eagles,
They shall run and not be weary,
They shall walk and not faint.
Isaiah 40:31 (NKJV)

Remember, God will handle our issues in His time! That is what it means to wait on Him! Somehow, in the heat of the battle, we can lose sight of the fact that not only is God's answer the perfect one, but His timing is perfect, as well. When we are able to hand the issue over to the Lord, our strength will be renewed. That is because we then are operating under His power, rather than our own. Instead of carrying the burdens of the world upon our narrow shoulders, we run unfettered. Unfortunately, it sounds easier than it is, due to our sinful nature. For most of us, it becomes a process. First, we understand what it says in God's Word, so our brain grasps the concept. Yet sometimes we have to endure some fatigue and maybe even some exhaustion before that message travels the 18-inches between our heads and our hearts. Once we accept in our hearts that God is as always, in control, the burden is lifted.

[18] **And to whom did He swear that they would not enter His rest, but to those who did not obey?** [19] **So we see that they could not enter in because of unbelief.**
Hebrews 3:18-19 (NKJV)

August 28: The journey

Today, I drove back from Mt. Whitney with Tommy. Our group of climbers began with eight, but after a strenuous day-hike on Wednesday, we were down to four. Thursday morning at 3:30, we began the 22-mile journey, and as we approached Trail Crest at 13,600 feet, could see the conditions deteriorating rapidly. Tommy was hurting with a cramp in his side and lagged behind a little, while three of us approached the summit. Every seasoned climber that we passed cautioned us to turn back. We anxiously watched the darkening clouds to see which direction they were moving. Could we sneak up to the summit, take a quick photo and hurry down? While making the decision, we saw a bolt of lightning crash on the summit, less than a half mile away. . Unfortunately, that side of the mountain is completely exposed.

We turned around and began to descend rapidly. In less than a half mile, we met up with Tommy, who was continuing toward the summit at 14,000 feet. All four of us were mentally and physically able to go to the top, but that was not our destiny that day. Having been on the summit many times before, I hurt for the three who were disappointed to get that close without reaching the peak. For the first five miles down the mountain, hail pummeled us. It felt like we were being shot continuously with BB's. Moving at different paces, all four of us arrived at the bottom alone and exhausted. Driving back to Southern California today, Tommy and I conversed about the journey.

Tommy is living in a sober, recovery house with others on the same path (see the devotional from August 13). Having been controlled by substances until 90 days ago, he has been humbled and is now seeking the Lord. The trek up Mt. Whitney reminded him of his walk with Jesus, and his walk without those substances. He spoke of the physical difficulty of ascending the mountain. Though I had attempted to describe how difficult the climb would be, the exhaustion of muscles coupled with the thinning air as we ascended became an internal argument. "Stop now; it hurts too bad!" OR "You can do this, Tommy. Just put one foot in front of the other!" One was the voice of God, reminding Tommy that even though it was difficult, he should not quit. Tommy stopped looking at the summit, which was tantalizingly within view. Instead, he took one step at a time, seemingly alone. In rehabilitation, Tommy has been surrounded by other people with the same struggle. Sometimes, it is easier to move as a group, and that support can be very helpful. Yet because God made us all to be different, we do not always move at the same pace. Tommy found that moving at his own pace was synonymous with his path to recovery. There would be times when he would need that individual strength, without the support of a group. What we sometimes forget, though, is that even when there are not people around us to encourage us, God is always there!

All Christians are on that same path. It does not matter if God has rescued us from substance abuse or other bondages common to man. Our journey is _to_ God, _with_ God and _because of_ God. There are times when we get ahead of Him, traveling at our own pace, while the opposite also occurs, with us moving more slowly than He desires. Regardless, God brings us to the place He wants us to be, and there is no more peaceful feeling than doing it all in God's perfect timing. When we look to Him, His hand will guide us.

**¹I will lift up my eyes to the hills— From whence comes my help?
²My help *comes* from the LORD,
Who made heaven and earth.
³He will not allow your foot to be moved;
He who keeps you will not slumber.
Psalm 121:1-3 (NKJV)**

Not reaching the summit reminded Tommy that his journey was not yet over. Many struggles remain in his path, and in ours, but with God guiding us, protecting us, and sometimes even carrying us, we will complete the journey with Him! There are mountains to climb, giants to slay and crosses to bear.

**"I am the vine, you *are* the branches. He who abides in Me, and I in him, bears much fruit; for without Me you can do nothing.
John 15:5 (NKJV)**

**²⁸ Come to Me, all *you* who labor and are heavy laden, and I will give you rest. ²⁹ Take My yoke upon you and learn from Me, for I am gentle and lowly in heart, and you will find rest for your souls. ³⁰ For My yoke *is* easy and My burden is light."
Matthew 11:28-30 (NKJV)**

August 29: Are you sleeping?

Often, in the middle of the night, a noise or movement can wake us from the deepest of slumbers. Sleep is a wonderful gift. That nightly slumber can rejuvenate the body, soul and spirit. Additionally, it is a perfect balance. Sleep too many hours and lethargy seems to mark each step throughout the day. Sleep too little and the day is equally difficult. Many people suffer from insomnia, having trouble falling asleep, trading that rejuvenation for worry and doubt. Safety while sleeping helps each of us to rest peacefully, without fear of robbery or assault.

²For you yourselves know perfectly that the day of the Lord so comes as a thief in the night. ³ For when they say, "Peace and safety!" then sudden destruction comes upon them, as labor pains upon a pregnant woman. And they shall not escape. ⁴ But you, brethren, are not in darkness, so that this Day should overtake you as a thief. ⁵ You are all sons of light and sons of the day. We are not of the night nor of darkness. ⁶ Therefore let us not sleep, as others *do*, but let us watch and be sober. ⁷ For those who sleep, sleep at night, and those who get drunk are drunk at night.
1 Thessalonians 5:2-7 (NKJV)

As Christians, there is no fear of the Lord's coming, for it is neither a surprise nor a curse. Yet to an unbelieving world, the return of Jesus will not be pleasant, as His wrath and judgment will be upon them. In this passage, Paul is not telling us that sleep is detrimental, but sleeping blindly is problematic. To sleep soberly is to be aware of potential dangers, all the while trusting God for His protective hand of guidance. Is a thief in the night a concern if we anticipate the thief's arrival? Even while sleeping, we are to keep a watchful eye on attacks from many directions. While awaiting arrest in the Garden of Gethsemane, Jesus awoke His disciples:

⁴⁵ When He rose up from prayer, and had come to His disciples, He found them sleeping from sorrow. ⁴⁶ Then He said to them, "Why do you sleep? Rise and pray, lest you enter into temptation."
Luke 22:45-46 (NKJV)

When we wake up in the middle of the night, do we think of it as a rude interruption to a peaceful night or as a call to prayer? When Elijah battled the 850 prophets of Baal and Asherah, when their "god" did not respond, Elijah called attention to the false god's lack of power:

And so it was, at noon, that Elijah mocked them and said, "Cry aloud, for he *is* a god; either he is meditating, or he is busy, or he is on a journey, *or* perhaps he is sleeping and must be awakened."
1 Kings 18:27 (NKJV)

We serve a God who never sleeps! He keeps a watchful eye upon each of His children, protecting us, guiding us and caring for us. He tucks us in and wakes us up when it is time. He loves us so much that He cannot take His eyes off of us! Many people believe in a God who is too busy to hear our prayers and consequently, too busy to answer those prayers. Yet our God is so powerful that He has time for us all! If He interrupts our sleep, He probably wants to talk! If we are His, we can rest assured that He will take care of us!

[1] "Then the kingdom of heaven shall be likened to ten virgins who took their lamps and went out to meet the bridegroom. [2] Now five of them were wise, and five *were* foolish. [3] Those who *were* foolish took their lamps and took no oil with them, [4] but the wise took oil in their vessels with their lamps. [5] But while the bridegroom was delayed, they all slumbered and slept.
[6] "And at midnight a cry was *heard:* 'Behold, the bridegroom is coming; go out to meet him!' [7] Then all those virgins arose and trimmed their lamps. [8] And the foolish said to the wise, 'Give us *some* of your oil, for our lamps are going out.' [9] But the wise answered, saying, '*No,* lest there should not be enough for us and you; but go rather to those who sell, and buy for yourselves.' [10] And while they went to buy, the bridegroom came, and those who were ready went in with him to the wedding; and the door was shut.
[11] "Afterward the other virgins came also, saying, 'Lord, Lord, open to us!' [12] But he answered and said, 'Assuredly, I say to you, I do not know you.'

[13] "Watch therefore, for you know neither the day nor the hour in which the Son of Man is coming.
Matthew 25:1-13 (NKJV)

August 30: What is your point of view?

In the early years of settlers coming to the shores of what would become America, many people died of starvation, or at the hands of the existing residents of the land, the Indians. Sadly, most of the men on the initial voyages to the new land were gentry. Consequently, none of the men were willing to work. Planting, building, clearing land...in their minds, these were tasks for a lower class of people. The only work they were willing to do involved digging for gold or searching for gems, minerals or ores that could add to their wealth. Not even starvation changed their minds about manual labor!

When the Pilgrims landed at Plymouth Rock, it was a different situation entirely. Even the motive of coming to this new land was opposite, focused on sharing Jesus Christ with people who never had heard His message. Prior to the voyage, this strong body of believers solidified its bonds to the Lord, as well as the bonds to one another. Their suffering on the three-month voyage was similar to those on previous expeditions, but how they handled that suffering was exemplary, with joy and thanksgiving. Upon arrival, everyone pitched into the effort of building a settlement and growing enough food for survival, trade and profit. All along the way, they looked to God for their provisions, and with their hearts right, He provided.

Additionally, God provided help from the Indians to teach the Pilgrims survival skills in this new land. After a few years, the Pilgrims began to see major improvements. With winter approaching, the Pilgrims were prepared, having enough corn to last until the next harvest. But God threw a wrench into their plans. A ship arrived without food, carrying an additional group of settlers. Instead of an abundance of food for the winter, the Pilgrims severely rationed their supplies. Yet with God in their focus, not one Pilgrim died of starvation that year. In the spring, the leaders decided to employ a new strategy. Instead of planting, tending and harvesting collectively, they told the people to select a plot of land and grow their own corn. People worked even harder to grow more than necessary. Yet again, something went wrong with their plans. A drought occurred on the land. None of the local Indians could remember a longer period without rain. Once again, the Christian leadership took it to the Lord, and upon reflection, decided that their motives had changed. Instead of asking the Lord for provision, the people had become more concerned with profit. It did not matter if Satan used gold bars or corn to trip up God's people; it was the same issues of greed and pride. Collectively, the people gathered together and repented to the Lord. Not surprisingly, the Lord opened the skies with a gentle rain that saved all of the crops.

What does it mean to repent? It is a complete change in point of view. Instead of looking at the world and our own sins through our own eyes, when we repent, we look through God's eyes. Sin is a cancer that separates us from God, and without a remedy, one sin would kill us. Yet repentance urges us to turn around and see that sin from a different perspective. Satan urges us to give in to sin, and when we sin, we are serving him. By doing that "about-face," we face God. When we see our own sin through God's perspective, it repulses us in the same manner that it repulses God. That change is a matter of the heart. Instead of saying, "Sorry for sinning, God," and then continuing in the same manner, repentance alters our hearts to the point that we no longer desire to continue in that brokenness. Instead of pleasing Satan, we begin pleasing God.

[8] If we say that we have no sin, we deceive ourselves, and the truth is not in us. [9] If we confess our sins, He is faithful and just to forgive us *our* sins and to cleanse us from all unrighteousness.
1 John 1:8-9 (NKJV)

Confess is the Greek word *homologeo* in the passage above, meaning to "speak the same thing" or "to come in agreement with." It is the same word used in the following passage, as well:

> ⁹ that if you confess with your mouth the Lord Jesus and believe in your heart that God has raised Him from the dead, you will be saved. ¹⁰ For with the heart one believes unto righteousness, and with the mouth confession is made unto salvation.
> **Romans 10:9-10 (NKJV)**

This confession does not involve going to a human intermediary. Instead, our High Priest is Jesus Christ. Yet even though we can confess with our mouths and in our hearts that He is Lord, sin remains a concern. As believers, we need to continue to repent of our sins. The moment we are saved, Jesus forgives us of all past, present and future sins, yet our part in that is the ongoing confession of those sins. This involves reflection upon our lives. God punishes us because He loves us. That punishment of drought caused the Pilgrims to reflect and find sin in their lives. In a similar way, we should be reflecting on the sin in our lives, and through confession, to change our points of view. Once we see our sin through the Lord's eyes, He can draw us closer!

> **But without faith *it is* impossible to please *Him,* for he who comes to God must believe that He is, and *that* He is a rewarder of those who diligently seek Him.**
> **Hebrews 11:6 (NKJV)**

> **testifying to Jews, and also to Greeks, repentance toward God and faith toward our Lord Jesus Christ.**
> **Acts 20:21 (NKJV)**

August 31: Grace

Of all the significant numbers in the Bible, five appears to be the most special in relation to man, standing for grace. Grace is unmerited favor, or receiving a gift that was not earned. The gift given by God was not earned, but additionally, could not be earned in any way, shape or form. Interestingly, if six is the number of man, if we take one away we are left with five, the number of grace. What is the one thing being taken away? Our sin! God's removal of that sin should give each believer the greatest joy, relief and need to praise the One who accomplished that feat.

The fifth letter of the Hebrew alphabet also reveals much to us. It is the letter *"hey,"* which looks like this, ה. In Hebrew, letters are also pictographs, as each letter also has a word that it stands for. Interestingly, *"hey"* means "behold," which is the Old Testament rendering of revelation. In that letter, God announces to us all, "Look at the gift I have given you!" The pictograph of this letter has a man standing with arms raised! Additionally, Jewish mystics of ancient times assigned this letter to represent the breath or Spirit of God.

God chose Abraham and told him that He would bless the families of all nations through Abraham. Abraham did not earn that blessing by his own perfection. Instead, God showed favor through His grace. In Genesis 15:9, God requests a five-fold sacrifice from Abraham: a 3-year-old heifer, a 3-year-old female goat, a 3-year-old ram, a turtledove and a young pigeon. Once again, five points to the grace of God!

[1] When Abram was ninety-nine years old, the LORD appeared to Abram and said to him, "I *am* Almighty God; walk before Me and be blameless. [2] And I will make My covenant between Me and you, and will multiply you exceedingly." [3] Then Abram fell on his face, and God talked with him, saying: [4] "As for Me, behold, My covenant is with you, and you shall be a father of many nations. [5] No longer shall your name be called Abram, but your name shall be Abraham; for I have made you a father of many nations. [6] I will make you exceedingly fruitful; and I will make nations of you, and kings shall come from you. [7] And I will establish My covenant between Me and you and your descendants after you in their generations, for an everlasting covenant, to be God to you and your descendants after you.

Genesis 17:1-7 (NKJV)

Abraham was not the only one to receive a name change, as his wife, Sarai, became Sarah. In our culture, the most significant time for a name change is in marriage, and in the same manner, Abraham and Sarah took the name of God. The Lord placed that Hebrew *"hey"* into the midst of their names, filling them with His grace, His Spirit!

Certainly, it is no accident that Deuteronomy is the fifth book of the Bible, with one of the most important themes of the book being the grace of God. Is it any wonder that this is the book quoted most often by Jesus while on this earth? Even the title in Hebrew, *"Devarim,"* means "words." God gifted us with His words, and through those words, with the ability to know Him! That is grace, for even though He created us, God could have retained that separation from His creation!

being justified freely by His grace through the redemption that is in Christ Jesus,
Romans 3:24 (NKJV)

The same Greek word used for "freely," *dorean*, applies to a gift given "without a cause." It is the same word used by Jesus when He said, "They hated me without a cause," in John 15:25. Just as there was no cause for people to hate Jesus, there is no cause in us that God would love us! We are justified without a cause by His grace!

David, when only a lad, picked up five, smooth stones to face the giant Goliath in battle, yet he needed only one of those stones. With One Rock pointing to the Rock of our salvation and five pointing to the grace of God, the Lord delivered David and all of Israel that day!

Five of you shall chase a hundred, and a hundred of you shall put ten thousand to flight; your enemies shall fall by the sword before you.
Leviticus 26:8 (NKJV)

Notice that the verse above does not say "five shall chase a hundred," but "five **of you** shall chase a hundred," referring to five people being filled with the grace and Spirit of God. Our power is from God, not from ourselves! When Jesus was speaking at length to the multitudes, and desired to feed them, the disciples brought five fish and two loaves. Through His grace, 5,000 men ate that day, a gift from the Bread of life (Matthew 14:17).

Throughout the Bible, five points to the grace of God, who gave the greatest gift to each willing to receive it. To walk in His grace is to understand the immensity of His gift. Though He gave it freely, without cause, it did not come cheaply, costing Jesus death on the cross and a temporary separation from His Father because of our sins. When we continue to walk in sin, we act as if His gift means nothing! Just as the Hebrew pictograph of the fifth Hebrew letter reveals a man with arms raised, the revelation of grace should have each of us behold the Lord, who has gone to great lengths to save us. With the fifth commandment pointing to honoring our parents, we should first honor the Father who gave us life and relationship in Him. He is worthy of all of our praises and we are so unworthy of His grace!

[14] **"For *the kingdom of heaven is* like a man traveling to a far country, *who* called his own servants and delivered his goods to them.** [15] **And to one he gave five talents, to another two, and to another one, to each according to his own ability; and immediately he went on a journey.** [16] **Then he who had received the five talents went and traded with them, and made another five talents.**
Matthew 25:14-16 (NKJV)

September 1: Declaration of dependence

Our nation's history involves a time when men laid it all on the line for the sake of religious freedom. Though our population continues to argue about that freedom, we never should lose sight of the fact that the United States began as a Christian nation. Our founding fathers were not fighting for the right to worship Satan, Allah or a host of other false gods. The religious freedom yearned for was to worship God deeper than the desires of the existing church, rather than less intensely. Yet as the nation grew, children and grandchildren replaced the men with that longing, who had not known the same difficulties, and we know that God only has children, not grandchildren. Consequently, instead of relying on God to be their Provider, the ensuing generations relied on their own knowledge and hands for survival. God warned His people of exactly that:

[11] **"Beware that you do not forget the Lord your God by not keeping His commandments, His judgments, and His statutes which I command you today,** [12] **lest—when you have eaten and are full, and have built beautiful houses and dwell in them;** [13] **and when your herds and your flocks multiply, and your silver and your gold are multiplied, and all that you have is multiplied;** [14] **when your heart is lifted up, and you forget the Lord your God who brought you out of the land of Egypt, from the house of bondage;** [15] **who led you through that great and terrible wilderness, in which were fiery serpents and scorpions and thirsty land where there was no water; who brought water for you out of the flinty rock;** [16] **who fed you in the wilderness with manna, which your fathers did not know, that He might humble you and that He might test you, to do you good in the end—** [17] **then you say in your heart, 'My power and the might of my hand have gained me this wealth.'**
Deuteronomy 8:11-17 (NKJV)

Although most of us complain about the difficulties life has to offer, in truth, those difficulties are more of a conduit to God than our many blessings. In God's blessings, the tendency for most of us might be an initial prayer of thanksgiving, yet the typical follow-up is the feeling that either we deserved the blessing or that we gave ourselves that blessing with our own intelligence, talents or hard work. Sometimes, it becomes obvious that our definitions of blessing and curse are reversed in many ways. For if hardship brings us to the Lord, is not that truly a blessing? And in the same manner, if earthly prosperity and gain carry us away from the Lord, are not those truly curses? It all depends upon point of view, and along with that, the way we serve the Lord. If those monetary blessings are used entirely for our own earthly comfort, it only can lead us down a slippery slope away from the Lord. Our God gives and takes away according to His own plan, and if He gives to us, it is so that we will give back to Him by helping others.

Many Bible-believing pastors feel that we are either approaching or in the end times prophesied in God's Word. Jesus told His disciples in Matthew 24 about difficulties that would occur just before the judgments of Revelation, and many of those difficulties seem very similar, though less intense than the judgments of Revelation. Each judgment will increase in intensity, just as a symphony approaches a mighty crescendo. How should we as believers view these challenges?

We, the people of God, in order to form a more perfect union with Him, make this declaration of dependence upon Him! He is our Provider, who will give us all we need. Often, He provides at the last moment to increase our faith. Our Lord blesses us more than we ever could ask. If the world seems to be getting difficult all around us, we should be thankful to God. He supplied every need for His chosen people in their exodus from Egypt to the Promised Land. Additionally, He supplied every need for our founding fathers, the Puritans and Pilgrims, walking in a covenant relationship with the Lord. In the same manner, He will supply the needs of His followers, for He is *Jehovah-jireh*, the Lord who provides. If we truly love Him, we should follow His commandments, and trust Him!

"How shall I pardon you for this?
Your children have forsaken Me
And sworn by *those* that are not gods.
When I had fed them to the full,
Then they committed adultery
And assembled themselves by troops in the harlots' houses.

Jeremiah 5:7 (NKJV)

September 2: If it is not broken...

A common point of view on intervention is "If it is not broken, do not fix it!" Certainly, when we tinker with what is working smoothly, we often can put a wrench in the works. Truly though, the times are rare when we are not facing a battle on at least one front. God's goal in us is perfection, yet His intervention in our lives is ongoing. One, small step at a time, our Lord brings us closer to His completed work in us. Each step along that way involves brokenness. Certainly, without brokenness, we cannot take that first step away from the world and toward God. When God breaks us, it is often a cause-and-effect scenario based on our pride, but sometimes, it has little to do with our own failures and everything to do with God's timing and His perfect plan.

If we reflect upon the life of Job, we see that not only was he referred to as God's most faithful servant, but Job praised the Lord. Even after his 10 children died on one day, Job continued that praise. It is not like Job had been backsliding, or involved in idolatry. Yet the Lord carried Job to a level of brokenness that none of us ever have experienced. Joseph is another wonderful example. Sold into slavery by his brothers, Joseph spent 13 years either in prison or serving in the household of Potiphar. Amazingly, Joseph's faith never wavered, as he waited for God's hand in fulfilling His promise in Joseph's life. With a miraculous wave of His hand, the Lord lifted Joseph from prisoner to second in command of Egypt.

David is another example. As the eighth son of Jesse, David saw few opportunities to learn leadership skills. Being the youngest in his family, David constantly remained at the beck and call of his parents, as well as his older brothers. Yet God had a different plan, placing David in a role of overseeing sheep instead of people. Willing to sacrifice his own life for those sheep, David perfected his sling skills when killing a threatening bear, seemingly, in preparation for a giant named Goliath soon to join David's path. David also succeeded in his praise to the Lord, accomplished with heartfelt words and a lyre. God chose David to reign as King of Israel, though King Saul ruled in fear of David's God-touched life. Instead of a meteoric rise to power, David first was subjected to his own brokenness, running away and hiding from the King who desired to take that life.

In order to lead, teach or love others in a godly manner, there must first be brokenness. Baptism is a symbolic act of obedience to the words of Jesus for each of us as believers, pointing to the old man dying and the new man rising up. That new man is filled with God's will rather than the will of a sinful man. But while our brokenness might begin with that act, it certainly does not end there. Our walks with the Lord are not along a flat pathway, but instead, involve many different terrains. We must be broken continuously. Otherwise, pride continues to seep into our lives, as we forget that everything we are is a gift from God.

[24] Most assuredly, I say to you, unless a grain of wheat falls into the ground and dies, it remains alone; but if it dies, it produces much grain. [25] He who loves his life will lose it, and he who hates his life in this world will keep it for eternal life. John 12:24-25 (NKJV)

When we reflect upon our sinful pasts, we exude much more compassion for those walking in sin. Seeing the sin of others continues to break our hearts, just as it does the heart of the Lord, as we know that only He can heal them. When others feel that compassionate love, they are much more likely to hear the tale we have to tell of a God who saves, heals and restores. We run away from hardships, though in all truth, those are the times when we rely on the Lord the most. Brokenness should be a daily part of each of our lives. Because daily sin is still with us, daily repentance should be its companion.

Though Jesus died for our sins, not a bone was broken, as He did not need to be humbled. Still, He chose death, even the death of the cross. And we complain about losing a job, having our cars break down or having a friend betray us. Sometimes, our lives are going so smoothly that we lose sight of the fact that we are relying on our own power, rather than the power of God. In reality, our saying should be, "If it's not broken, it's not God's!" Are we His?

[11] **My son, do not despise the chastening of the LORD,
Nor detest His correction;**
[12] **For whom the LORD loves He corrects,
Just as a father the son *in whom* he delights.
Job 3:11-12 (NKJV)**

[17] **"Behold, happy *is* the man whom God corrects;
Therefore do not despise the chastening of the Almighty.**
[18] **For He bruises, but He binds up;
He wounds, but His hands make whole.
Job 5:17-18 (NKJV)**

September 3: Every day is Labor Day!

Today is Labor Day in the United States, a holiday that began in New York City in 1882 and began its national celebration in 1894, to exhibit "the strength and *esprit de corps* of the labor organizations." Those organizations served a definite purpose in our nation's history, especially in regard to enacting child labor laws. In the 1950s, labor unions were at their peak, while today, there are still 16.1 million Americans who are members. Most fall under the umbrella of the American Federation of Labor and Congress of Industrial Organizations (AFL-CIO). Rather than representing the workers, those labor unions now have become more of an attempt at acquiring political power. While Labor Day continues, most celebrators have no interest in honoring those labor organizations, and instead, think of it as the end of summer.

As Christians, we are members of the only perfect labor union. We are united in Jesus Christ and as members of His body, are called to work for the kingdom of God, while He takes care of all of our needs. Whatever area of brokenness that the Lord pulled us out of will often become a ministry in our lives. Yet God typically gives us time to walk with Him in strength before calling us back to the place that tripped us up. Why would the Lord send an alcoholic into a bar to witness to drunks, a week after walking away from alcohol? God is without limit, and consequently, so is His choice of potential workers. Typically, the compassionate love demonstrated by those who can see their own past in the sin of others speaks the loudest message.

**[1] After these things the Lord appointed seventy others also, and sent them two by two before His face into every city and place where He Himself was about to go. [2] Then He said to them, "The harvest truly *is* great, but the laborers *are* few; therefore pray the Lord of the harvest to send out laborers into His harvest. [3] Go your way; behold, I send you out as lambs among wolves. [4] Carry neither money bag, knapsack, nor sandals; and greet no one along the road.
Luke 10:1-4 (NKJV)**

It is interesting that the Lord sent them out in pairs. A fellow Christian is wonderful support when it comes to study, prayer and encouragement. Additionally, the Lord sent men without possessions or weapons. Certainly, they would be easy prey to those who wanted to rob them, but there was nothing to take! "Lambs among wolves" is a wonderful picture, as the ravenous wolves could tear the sheep into bits if it was not for the Shepherd protecting the sheep. When God calls us into a ministry, we should walk in faith, wherever He has called us.

At times, God calls us into some dark and dreary places to speak His Word. Regardless of where we are, He is with us, and there is no reason to fear. Jesus is the Shepherd that protects His sheep in the midst of those wolves, and the Light that illuminates the darkness. Why do we question Him?

As we celebrate Labor Day, we should reflect upon our ministries for the Lord. Are we feeding others, or just being fed? Remember, there are many jobs involved to grow a healthy plant. Someone plows or cultivates the land, plants the seed, waters it, keeps the weeds from choking the plant, and is there for the harvest. Our Lord has workers all along that process, and each are just as important. What job do we have on God's farm?

[34] Jesus said to them, "My food is to do the will of Him who sent Me, and to finish His work. [35] Do you not say, 'There are still four months and *then* comes the harvest'? Behold, I say to you, lift up your eyes and look at the fields, for they are already white for harvest! [36] And he who reaps receives wages, and gathers fruit for eternal life, that both he who sows and he who reaps may rejoice together.
John 4:34-36 (NKJV)

[5] Who then is Paul, and who *is* Apollos, but ministers through whom you believed, as the Lord gave to each one? [6] I planted, Apollos watered, but God gave the increase. [7] So then neither he who plants is anything, nor he who waters, but God who gives the increase. [8] Now he who plants and he who waters are one, and each one will receive his own reward according to his own labor.
1 Corinthians 3:5-8 (NKJV)

September 4: We shall overcome!

Robert Collier said, "The mere fact that you have obstacles to overcome is in your favor." Somehow, we lose sight of the fact that ease of passage does not equate to quality of the experience, as growth occurs when we are pulled, pushed, prodded and stretched. We often think that trial by fire signifies an endurance of pain, though that would depend on the level of faith of the one being tested. Shadrach, Meshach and Abednego waltzed through the fiery furnace of Babylon, which was so hot that it cremated a guard who opened the door. Yet those three warriors of God danced in the flames beside the Lord, who did not even allow them to smell of smoke when they emerged unscathed from Nebuchadnezzar's site of their intended deaths. That trio walked in faith, even when facing the fire.

What does it mean to overcome? In the Old Testament, the word is used often in times of battle, signifying total defeat of an enemy. Additionally, the word also can apply to drunkenness, as the imbiber is completely overcome by the wine. Most of us who have lived in a worldly manner before coming to the Lord might remember the complete personality change that could occur because of alcohol. While the connotation of drunkenness may give us a negative understanding of the word, we can apply that comprehension in a positive manner.

Each of us as believers has obstacles to overcome, with the reasons behind those obstacles being at least two-fold. Satan desires to destroy our testimonies. He despises us for the commitment that we have made to serve the Lord. Certainly, he and his demonic host place many of those obstacles in our paths, trying to trip us up. Yet lest we forget, our sovereign God has the right to approve each of those occurrences. God uses those obstacles to draw us closer to Him, by stretching our preconceived ideas of what we are able to handle. Obviously, we can handle much more with God living inside of us than we could when battling alone.

[4] For whatever is born of God overcomes the world. And this is the victory that has overcome the world— our faith. [5] Who is he who overcomes the world, but he who believes that Jesus is the Son of God?
1 John 5:4-5 (NKJV)

When we endure tribulation, our faith increases. In that way, all who believe in Jesus Christ as their Lord and Savior will overcome the world. It is His victory for us, and we receive the benefit. Jesus told us in John 16:33 that we will have tribulation in this world, but He has overcome the world. What must we overcome? Satan is well familiar with the statistics of what obstacles trip us up the most often. Yet it does not matter if our past is alcohol abuse, drug abuse, sexual immorality, anger, stealing, lying, etc. If our present is with the Lord, then our future dwells with Him, as well.

I write to you, fathers,
Because you have known Him *who is* from the beginning.

I write to you, young men,
Because you have overcome the wicked one.
I write to you, little children,
Because you have known the Father.
1 John 2:13 (NKJV)

To be overcome by God is to be totally given over to Him. Is there something we are holding back? He desires for us to serve Him wholeheartedly, and in our walk with Him, the Lord continues to uncover parts of our hearts and aspects of our lives that we are selfishly holding onto. Yet He has promised that we shall overcome. It is God's gift to each of us as believers, and it comes with the crown of life!

Blessed *is* the man who endures temptation; for when he has been approved, he will receive the crown of life which the Lord has promised to those who love Him.
James 1:12 (NKJV)

These will make war with the Lamb, and the Lamb will overcome them, for He is Lord of lords and King of kings; and those *who are* with Him *are* called, chosen, and faithful.
Revelation 17:14 (NKJV)

September 5: Vitamin deficiency

In years past, many sailors on long-distance voyages died of scurvy, though it was not until 1932 that scientists were able to associate the disease with Vitamin C deficiency. Typically, scurvy occurs when a person has been deprived of Vitamin C for around 90 days. On those lengthy voyages, cured meats and grains outlasted the fresh fruits and vegetables that contained the essential vitamin. Similarly, Vitamin D deficiency causes rickets, which is a softening of the bones. This occurs mostly in children, and leads to deformity and fractures.

Obviously, all food does not give the same degree of sustenance. In 1978, Danish scientists created the Food Guide Pyramid, which was accepted by the United States Department of

Agriculture (USDA) in 1992. The pyramid emphasizes that we need carbohydrates, vegetables, fruits, fats, dairy products and proteins on a daily basis, further breaking down the specific amounts necessary for a healthy body.

Certainly, God draws a correlation between our physical needs and our spiritual ones. He designed our bodies along with the nutrients, vitamins and food items to supply those needs. In the same manner that our bodies cannot survive without those vitamins or nutrients, our spiritual nature cannot grow in a healthy manner without the right food:

So He humbled you, allowed you to hunger, and fed you with manna which you did not know nor did your fathers know, that He might make you know that man shall not live by bread alone; but man lives by every *word* that proceeds from the mouth of the LORD.
Deuteronomy 8:3 (NKJV)

God demonstrated His miraculous hand by supplying the manna daily in the wilderness, yet additionally, He performed another miracle in that the heavenly food supplied every physical need of the wandering Jews. In a similar manner, Noah and his family of seven had no complaints of scurvy after spending 377 days aboard the ark. (Noah was told to enter the ark seven days before the rain, as the rains began on the 17th day of the second month according to Genesis 7:11-13, and they left the ark on the 27th day of the second month the following year). Fruits and vegetables certainly did not grow instantaneously once the water subsided, so Vitamin C would not be prevalent for even more time. Yet God miraculously carried them through.

He takes care of us spiritually in the same manner, if we are willing to open His Word. Sometimes, we complain that the sermons at church contain more milk than meat, yet as Christians, we should be able to open the Bible and receive meat from the Holy Spirit. That does not mean it is wrong to desire some meat from the pulpit, but if we are spiritual carnivores, church should not be the only place we are eating!

⁹ "Whom will he teach knowledge?
And whom will he make to understand the message?
Those *just* weaned from milk?
Those *just* drawn from the breasts?
¹⁰For precept *must be* upon precept, precept upon precept,
Line upon line, line upon line,
Here a little, there a little."
Isaiah 28:9-10 (NKJV)

Just as an infant does not feed on meat, but obtains the necessary nutrients from the mother's milk, baby Christians do not begin with the meat of the Word. As we grow in the Lord, we should reflect Him more, and that growth comes from a deeper understanding of God and God's Word. Those home-cooked meals typically taste better than eating out at restaurants! Similarly, God desires to feed us at home, not just at church. We should open up His Word if we desire the spiritual meat that will make us walk strongly in Him! The Bread of Life will give us all that we need!

¹³ **For everyone who partakes *only* of milk *is* unskilled in the word of righteousness, for he is a babe. ¹⁴ But solid food belongs to those who are of full age, *that is*, those who by reason of use have their senses exercised to discern both good and evil.**
Hebrews 5:13-14 (NKJV)

September 6: Power

By picking up a sports page in a newspaper or tuning in to any sporting event on television, it is easy to see the emphasis we place on power. Football is a physical battle from start to finish. Baseball involves more finesse, but spectators still are drawn to the home run hitters and the fastball pitchers, giving us the idea that bigger is better. Powerful dunks fill the highlight reels in basketball, while at the same time, we discuss in amazement the power of Andy Roddick's serve in tennis and the distance of a Tiger Woods' drive in golf. Athletes are not much different than the spectators, as we see a corps of competitors drawn to anabolic steroids, in an attempt to grow physically stronger, regardless of adverse effects to health. Sadly, our emphasis on physical strength continues to grow, while ignoring the more important aspect of spiritual strength.

Christianity is all about power. God has the power of creation. Not only does He create us physically, mentally and spiritually, but He has the power to create us anew when we choose to follow Him. That speaks highly of the power of God, for no man has the power to walk away from addictions or a life of sin by relying on his own strength. Additionally, as Christians, we learn almost instantly that there is a strong power battling against us, but our God, who created Satan and allows Satan's temporary dominion over the earth, is omnipotent.

You are of God, little children, and have overcome them, because He who is in you is greater than he who is in the world.
1 John 4:4 (NKJV)

God's power is most helpful to us in regard to our sin. Without His power of forgiveness, each of us would receive the death that we have earned with our lives. Yet because of God's grace and mercy, He is able to forgive our sin.

But that you may know that the Son of Man has power on earth to forgive sins"—then He said to the paralytic, "Arise, take up your bed, and go to your house."
Matthew 9:6 (NKJV)

The New Testament story of the woman with the blood issue demonstrates to us another aspect of God's power:

[27] When she heard about Jesus, she came behind *Him* in the crowd and touched His garment. [28] For she said, "If only I may touch His clothes, I shall be made well." [29] Immediately the fountain of her blood was dried up, and she felt in *her* body that she was healed of the affliction. [30]

And Jesus, immediately knowing in Himself that power had gone out of Him, turned around in the crowd and said, "Who touched My clothes?"
³¹ But His disciples said to Him, "You see the multitude thronging You, and You say, 'Who touched Me?' "
Mark 5:27-31 (NKJV)

When the power had gone out of Jesus, in Mark 5:30 above, it does not mean that the power of Jesus was dissipated in any way. Before the event, He was all powerful, and that omnipotence remained both during and after the healing. When we are touched by the Lord, He gives us His power. Without that power, we cannot walk away from the sins of our lives, nor will we be reminded of our sins and the confession necessary to receive His forgiveness.

How do we walk in the power of Jesus? To rely on the Holy Spirit dwelling inside of us, we are to turn away from the lusts of the flesh. But in order to have that close, personal relationship with Jesus Christ, we must be touched by Him. That involves closeness, and as we all understand from interpersonal relationships, closeness comes from time and focus. When we spend more time in prayer, Bible study and Christian fellowship, we get to know more about our Lord. By focusing on a deeper relationship with God, we grow more powerful in Him. That does not mean that we rely more strongly on our own power, but that we learn how to rely on the power of God. He is our strength; with Him, we cannot fail!

God *is* my strength *and* power,
And He makes my way perfect.
2 Samuel 22:33 (NKJV)

¹⁶ **I say then: Walk in the Spirit, and you shall not fulfill the lust of the flesh.** ¹⁷ **For the flesh lusts against the Spirit, and the Spirit against the flesh; and these are contrary to one another, so that you do not do the things that you wish.** ¹⁸ **But if you are led by the Spirit, you are not under the law.**

Galatians 5:16-18 (NKJV)

September 7: Transparency

Gerry Adams said, "One man's transparency is another's humiliation." Scientifically, transparency is the ability to completely see through an object, while in regard to people, transparency is to see someone as they really are, without façade, deceit or disguise. Humiliation comes from the same root as the word "humble," and that lack of pride is the most central part of transparency. Most Christians can see two lives when looking at their past, as God changes lives drastically. Typically, new believers have much transparency, for they are excited to have the great gift of a sin burden removed from their shoulders. Yet sadly, many Christians fail to love in a Christ-like manner, and see the sinful pasts of fellow Christians as less than lovable. That behavior is reminiscent of Jonah, who refused to go to Nineveh because he did not want the Lord to save those heathens. The pain of unacceptance can cause some jaded Christians to put mirrors on their once, transparent lives, in an attempt to reflect what the viewer wants to see.

There is a noticeable difference between sharing our sinful pasts and bragging about our sin. When we speak of our lives before Jesus changed us, it should be in the heart that Paul had when he spoke of his sin:

[12] And I thank Christ Jesus our Lord who has enabled me, because He counted me faithful, putting *me* into the ministry, [13] although I was formerly a blasphemer, a persecutor, and an insolent man; but I obtained mercy because I did *it* ignorantly in unbelief. [14] And the grace of our Lord was exceedingly abundant, with faith and love which are in Christ Jesus. [15] This *is* a faithful saying and worthy of all acceptance, that Christ Jesus came into the world to save sinners, of whom I am chief.
1 Timothy 1:12-15 (NKJV)

Was Paul bragging that he was the chief of sinners? On the contrary, he knew that all he deserved was death, yet Jesus had given him eternal life! The Greek word for *insolent* in the passage above actually means "violently arrogant," so Jesus had changed Paul from being filled with pride to an abject, spiritual poverty and humbleness. Paul was ashamed of his past, but he transparently shared it with many generations of Christians. He did not worry about his detractors, as Paul knew that God's will would be accomplished. God chose Paul, just as He has chosen each of us!

Transparency is not our only goal. Looking into a lake with two feet of water might enable us to see every object on the bottom, yet that is not transparency as much as it is lack of depth! Instead, we should set a goal of becoming like the Caribbean Sea with crystal, clear water of enormous depth, yet still allowing someone on the surface to see the bottom clearly.

We have a tendency to respect people, rather than respect God. Desiring respect, many Christians act differently at church than they do at home or at work. Yet God sees the heart. Consequently, the most gifted teachers are not the ones who try to act "holier than thou." Certainly, there is a great difference between acting holy and being holy. Someone who has sinned and repented can have a much different perspective than another who has yet to stumble.

Through our transparency, others who care to look may see the miracles that God has accomplished. While fellow believers might have difficulty forgiving our sin, God has no difficulty. God's love is the guideline, as all of us are in need of a Physician! Transparency involves humbleness, wisdom and accepting God's will, yet all those require depth of character, rather than shallowness. If it hurts to be transparent, do not lose sight of the fact that the Lord's love is deeper than the deepest ocean! He will sustain us, even when others fail!

I have been crucified with Christ; it is no longer I who live, but Christ lives in me; and the *life* which I now live in the

flesh I live by faith in the Son of God, who loved me and gave Himself for me.
Galatians 2:20 (NKJV)

September 8: Silence of the Lamb!

Novelists, politicians, defense attorneys and those in public relations spend their careers spinning stories. Though the best stories have ties to truth, most are not written or spoken with complete honesty. Part of the problem is perspective, as none of us see the absolute truth. Only God has the proper point of view. When Jesus was on trial the night before His crucifixion, He completely understood each person's perspective. Yet, we see prophetically in the words of Isaiah what Jesus had to say on that night:

He was oppressed and He was afflicted,
Yet He opened not His mouth;
He was led as a lamb to the slaughter,
And as a sheep before its shearers is silent,
So He opened not His mouth.
Isaiah 53:7 (NKJV)

Certainly, Jesus did not need a defense attorney to represent Him with the truth, as John 14:6 reminds us that Jesus **is** the Truth. Being God, Jesus had the power and knowledge to extricate Himself from the situation, but steadfastly remained, for He desired to be there.

And they made His grave with the wicked—
But with the rich at His death,
Because He had done no violence,
Nor *was any* deceit in His mouth.
Isaiah 53:9 (NKJV)

At times in our lives, we can find ourselves in precarious positions, and can feel the need to extricate ourselves with some verbal, fancy footwork. As difficult as it might be, most of us never have tried silence as a strategy. There are times when God leads us into the battle, just as He went before the Israelites with the Ark of the Tabernacle. He certainly led David to pick up five, smooth stones and face a giant. Typically, the biblical stories involving God's people in battle involved odds tipping strongly in favor of the enemies! That is how God reveals His power, just as He had Gideon pare down his army from 32,000 to only 300.

Then the LORD said to Gideon, "By the three hundred men who lapped I will save you, and deliver the Midianites into your hand. Let all the *other* people go, every man to his place."
Judges 7:7 (NKJV)

With that small army, Gideon's men were part of a miracle, whereas if 32,000 men would have won the battle, we would be pointing to their power, rather than the power of God. In similar fashion, we will be soldiers in the Lord's army at Armageddon, though God will fight the battle without any of us lifting a hand!

You must not fear them, for the LORD your God Himself fights for you.'
Deuteronomy 3:22 (NKJV)

When we feel backed into a corner, or have a major battle on our hands, we should remember that God has the ability and the power to take care of us. If the odds are strongly against us, He might have us face our enemies. Yet just as easily, He might decide the battle while we are sleeping. There are also times when we dig the hole deeper by opening our mouths. If there is any deceit in our mouths, stick some duct tape over it! If our silence is of the Lord, that silence is golden!

But Jesus kept silent. And the high priest answered and said to Him, "I put You under oath by the living God: Tell us if You are the Christ, the Son of God!"
Matthew 26:63 (NKJV)

September 9: Have you seen Him?

In any court case, an eyewitness can sway the jury, especially if his testimony is believable. When there are multiple eyewitnesses, regardless of minor differences in points of view, it can become an open-and-shut case. As modern-day Christians, we certainly are in a different place than the disciples who walked with our Lord, yet with our spiritual eyes, we still have been given the gift of sight. Yet we who believe trust their words and visions of the resurrection of Jesus.

[26] And after eight days His disciples were again inside, and Thomas with them. Jesus came, the doors being shut, and stood in the midst, and said, "Peace to you!" [27] Then He said to Thomas, "Reach your finger here, and look at My hands; and reach your hand *here,* and put *it* into My side. Do not be unbelieving, but believing."
[28] And Thomas answered and said to Him, "My Lord and my God!"
[29] Jesus said to him, "Thomas, because you have seen Me, you have believed. Blessed *are* those who have not seen and *yet* have believed."
John 20:26-29 (NKJV)

Jesus did not berate Thomas for his "seeing is believing" mentality, instead choosing to give Thomas that physical evidence desired. Yet Jesus called attention to the blessing of all modern-day Christians, who did not physically see the risen Savior walking the earth. If Thomas was the only person to see Jesus after His crucifixion, especially with the fact that we could not cross-examine him, we might not believe as readily. Instead, God gave us many eyewitnesses, according to the words of Paul:

[3] For I delivered to you first of all that which I also received: that Christ died for our sins according to the Scriptures, [4] and that He was buried, and that He rose again the third day according to the Scriptures, [5] and that He was seen by Cephas, then by the twelve. [6] After that He was seen by over

five hundred brethren at once, of whom the greater part remain to the present, but some have fallen asleep. [7] After that He was seen by James, then by all the apostles. [8] Then last of all He was seen by me also, as by one born out of due time.
1 Corinthians 15: 3-8 (NKJV)

With the list of those to see the risen Savior including the brother of Jesus, in addition to His closest disciples, we can rest assured that it was not a case of mistaken identity with someone who looked like Jesus! Also notice that Jesus did not choose to appear to only His close friends, as Paul was last on the list. Paul believed Jesus to be a blasphemer, who earned His death by claiming to be God. Convinced by his contact with a post-crucifixion Jesus, Paul became the leading spokesman in the spread of Christianity. Additionally, the resurrection of Jesus was not the only miracle witnessed. That list was a lengthy one that contained healings as well as restoration of life to the dead. Those witnessed miracles included participation of Moses, Elijah and God the Father at the transfiguration (Mark 9, Luke 9 and Matthew 16).

[16] For we did not follow cunningly devised fables when we made known to you the power and coming of our Lord Jesus Christ, but were eyewitnesses of His majesty. [17] For He received from God the Father honor and glory when such a voice came to Him from the Excellent Glory: "This is My beloved Son, in whom I am well pleased." [18] And we heard this voice which came from heaven when we were with Him on the holy mountain.
2 Peter 1:16-18 (NKJV)

We live almost 2,000 years after the events witnessed by our Christian forefathers. Though we cannot cross-examine them, we can determine the veracity of their testimonies based on the relevance of their changed lives. Were the disciples willing to die for their beliefs in the risen Savior? Certainly, and other than John, each of the disciples died a martyr's death. Confronted with recanting their testimonies as eyewitnesses, or suffering a painful death, the disciples chose death. If it was only one person, we could ascertain that mental instability could be in effect, but over 500 saw the risen Savior.

Through the Holy Spirit, God has given us the ability to see His miracles on a daily basis. We as believers have entered into a relationship that differs only slightly from that of early Christians, as all of us can see the miracle of the lives He has changed. Those miracles encompass each person who has accepted Jesus as Lord and Savior. If we desire to see Jesus, He will reveal Himself to us. If we have seen Him, are we living lives that would honor Him? Our changed lives could be the evidence that someone else notices that leads them to Jesus. Our lives are the eyewitness testimony!

Men of Israel, hear these words: Jesus of Nazareth, a Man attested by God to you by miracles, wonders, and signs which God did through Him in your midst, as you yourselves also know—
Acts 2:22 (NKJV)

September 10: Pearls of wisdom

Bonnell Thornton said, "Some often repent, yet never reform; they resemble a man traveling in a dangerous path, who frequently starts and stops, but never turns back." Sin surely is the most dangerous path, for it leads to certain death. Paul wrote:

For the wages of sin *is* death, but the gift of God *is* eternal life in Christ Jesus our Lord.
Romans 6:23 (NKJV)

In that statement, Paul summarized that the deserved toll for the work we do on the highway of sin requires us to pay with our own lives. God, though, has offered an escape clause in the contract. If we repent of our sin, then He forgives us, and instead of our death being the payment, God receives payment in full from the death of His Son, Jesus.

In addition to that forgiveness, God gives us pearls of His wisdom! Our repentance becomes the pearl in the oyster. A grain of sand, a parasite or even damage to the mollusk can create the beginning of a pearl, as the oyster covers that external stimuli with nacre, or mother of pearl. In the same manner, repentance is an entirely external stimulus. Without God, we would have no reason to turn from sin. Our desperately wicked hearts are content serving ourselves, rather than serving God, and through that love, serving others.

Beloved, let us love one another, for love is of God; and everyone who loves is born of God and knows God.
1 John 4:7 (NKJV)

God has imprinted His ways and laws onto each of us, as He created us. We know the difference between right and wrong, and without God, we choose to do the wrong thing most of the time. Without God, why would our sin break our hearts, just as it breaks God's heart?

As Christians, the Holy Spirit affects our consciences. After sinning, He causes us to reflect upon our sin, and think how our actions hurt others, too. That becomes the grain of sand in the oyster, an irritation. The more we reflect upon our sins, we begin to cover that irritation with mother of pearl. After enough time, that reflection grows into repentance, when we ask for God's forgiveness and turn away from the sin, as we can see how badly the sin affected ourselves and others. Sin becomes a pearl in the life of a Christian. From failure comes success due to the hand of God, who makes something beautiful out of something ugly! That sin being removed from us additionally teaches us love for God, who forgave so great a debt.

Yet we need to remember that reformation is the last stage of repentance. If we continue to sin, without learning from those mistakes, we will find ourselves on a dangerous road. More time might elapse between steps, but if the one-way road is headed to destruction, eventually, we will arrive right where we are aimed.

To reform is to learn from our sin, and put ourselves on a path with a different end!

But go and learn what *this* means: '*I desire mercy and not sacrifice.*' For I did not come to call the righteous, but sinners, to repentance."
Matthew 9:13 (NKJV)

September 11: Free will

People with the gift of evangelism always look for an opportunity to share the Lord's love with friends, neighbors and even the random acquaintances that God puts into their lives. One evangelist gave a Bible to a friend, asking the man to read the Gospel of John. At the bottom of the Bible was a commentary, and when the friend did not completely understand the passage he had read, he looked to the commentary for clarification of the words of Jesus:

The wind blows where it wishes, and you hear the sound of it, but cannot tell where it comes from and where it goes. So is everyone who is born of the Spirit."
John 3:8 (NKJV)

When the commentary discussed God "controlling" us, the friend felt unable to continue reading. "I was controlled by my parents growing up," he said, "and have spent my life with everyone trying to control me. I am not about to allow God to control me." The evangelist reminded him that the commentary included man's words, while the Bible contained God's words. He offered to get a different Bible, without a commentary, and further instructed that "control" might give the wrong connotation, trying to get him to put "guide" or "lead" into the same sentence. But the word "control" became the excuse of not reading the Bible.

We all talk about free will, as God has given us the ability to make our own choices. Yet just as "wind blows where it wishes," and God knows where it will blow before it does, each one of our choices fits into God's all-inclusive plan. In a Bible study of men in substance abuse rehabilitation, another seems to be in that same place. When asked to explain his belief, he spoke with honesty. "I believe in God, but I guess I am not willing for Him to be in control of my life." God did not create us to be robots, following Him because He requires it. Instead, God desires for us to understand His love, and because He loves us, follow Him out of our love for Him.

We love Him because He first loved us.
1 John 4:19 (NKJV)

Anyone who thinks that God is not in control does not understand the size and power of God! There is nothing that He is incapable of. Paul certainly understood God's power, when on the road to Damascus, Jesus spoke to Paul out of the clouds. Paul's companions all saw a bright light, but only Paul heard what Jesus had to say:

[3] As he journeyed he came near Damascus, and suddenly a light shone around him from heaven. [4] Then he fell to the ground, and heard a voice saying to him, "Saul, Saul, why are you persecuting Me?"
[5] And he said, "Who are You, Lord?"
Then the Lord said, "I am Jesus, whom you are persecuting. It *is* **hard for you to kick against the goads."**
[6] So he, trembling and astonished, said, "Lord, what do You want me to do?"
Then the Lord *said* **to him, "Arise and go into the city, and you will be told what you must do."**
Acts 9:3-6 (NKJV)

Paul's life before that day involved his own choices. He chose to persecute Christians. He chose to believe that Jesus was not God; nor was He the Messiah written about in the Scriptures. Paul chose to walk in pride, based on his pedigree of studying under Gamaliel. Yet after that day, Paul's life changed drastically. Yes, he chose to follow Jesus. From that point on, Paul asked, "Lord, what do You want me to do?" Hearing God is a life-changing experience. We relinquish control of our own lives because that is what we desire to do. Yet God can place us in situations where it would be very difficult to ignore Him, just as He did with Paul on that dusty road.

The man discussed at the beginning, who stopped reading after John 3 because he did not want anyone else to control his life, had some life-changing situations soon after his introduction to the Bible. Making his own decisions, he chose to take illegal drugs, drive 130 MPH on the freeway and attempt to rape a woman he was stalking, all under the influence of drugs. He is now in jail, where he likely will be in a small cell for a very long time. Does he think he is still in control of his own life? He is going to have ample time to finish reading John's Gospel. Just like God did with Paul, He could be reaching out to change another man's life. Until we are willing to hand it over to Jesus, our choices will lead us to death, but God always leads us to life! Truly, we do not get to choose whether or not to honor God. Our only choice is when we will do that!

[10] **that at the name of Jesus every knee should bow, of those in heaven, and of those on earth, and of those under the earth,** [11] **and** *that* **every tongue should confess that Jesus Christ** *is* **Lord, to the glory of God the Father.**
Philippians 2:10-11 (NKJV)

[10] **In this is love, not that we loved God, but that He loved us and sent His Son** *to be* **the propitiation for our sins.** [11] **Beloved, if God so loved us, we also ought to love one another.**
1 John 4:10-11 (NKJV)

September 12: Who will our neighbors in heaven be?

Ask any Christian to talk about the greatest pain they have experienced in their Christian walks and most stories will involve an event that occurred at church, at the hand of a fellow believer. We expect to be hurt by non-believers, but those we share the deepest love with can blindside us. Does this go conjointly with the philosophy that "you only hurt the ones you love?" Though we are called by God to love others, including our enemies, most would say that we are not called to like everyone else. Yet truthfully, if God has chosen another for His kingdom, why do we struggle in sharing the kingdom with them? Are we planning on asking for a mansion in a different neighborhood of heaven if God places them next door? Though heaven is a gated community, the point is not to separate the neighbors! What if God decided to surround us in heaven with the people we could not learn to love while we were here? Just as Jonah felt about the people of Nineveh, most of us have people we do not click with easily. But who said it was supposed to be easy?

Jesus did not give us the easy way out. Even in situations where we feel ethical or moral superiority, we still are called to forgive, and to do that continuously.

[21] Then Peter came to Him and said, "Lord, how often shall my brother sin against me, and I forgive him? Up to seven times?"
[22] Jesus said to him, "I do not say to you, up to seven times, but up to seventy times seven.
Matthew 18:21-22 (NKJV)

Forgiveness is the release of a debt. In order to forgive a brother, we must get to the place in our hearts where we no longer feel they owe us anything. God places the burden securely on our backs when he shares this analogy with us:

But if you do not forgive, neither will your Father in heaven forgive your trespasses."
Mark 11:26 (NKJV)

It is easy to get high-handed when noticing the shortcomings of others, yet the smelling salts that bring us back to consciousness typically involve self-reflection. "Let he who is without sin cast the first stone," comes to mind, as we are all sinners, saved by grace. Is it time to release a burden? One of the greatest gifts of forgiveness is that it not only frees the person being forgiven, but it also frees the one forgiving. Let go and let God! When a fisherman releases his catch, the fish swims with such exuberance when freed. Release someone today, and feel the same release from God!

¹ Though I speak with the tongues of men and of angels, but have not love, I have become sounding brass or a clanging cymbal. ² And though I have *the gift of* prophecy, and understand all mysteries and all knowledge, and though I have all faith, so that I could remove mountains, but have not love, I am nothing. ³ And though I bestow all my goods to feed *the poor,* and though I give my body to be burned, but have not love, it profits me nothing.
⁴ Love suffers long *and* is kind; love does not envy; love does not parade itself, is not puffed up; ⁵ does not behave rudely, does not seek its own, is not provoked, thinks no evil; ⁶ does not rejoice in iniquity, but rejoices in the truth; ⁷ bears all things, believes all things, hopes all things, endures all things.
⁸ Love never fails. But whether *there are* prophecies, they will fail; whether *there are* tongues, they will cease; whether *there is* knowledge, it will vanish away. ⁹ For we know in part and we prophesy in part. ¹⁰ But when that which is perfect has come, then that which is in part will be done away.
¹¹ When I was a child, I spoke as a child, I understood as a child, I thought as a child; but when I became a man, I put away childish things. ¹² For now we see in a mirror, dimly, but then face to face. Now I know in part, but then I shall know just as I also am known.
¹³ And now abide faith, hope, love, these three; but the greatest of these *is* love.
1 Corinthians 13 (NKJV)

September 13: Light of the world, You stepped down into darkness

Regardless of how dark it is in the middle of the night, when we wake from a deep slumber and walk the programmed path between bed and bathroom, we typically choose to remain in the dark. Though the light would awaken others in the house, more of our reasoning of not turning on the light has to do with the painful adjustment our eyes would need to make.

People walking in darkness are typically content in that darkness. If someone turns on the light, most will scream at them to turn it off. Yet once our eyes have adjusted to the light, life becomes much easier, alleviating the need to spend countless time and energy groping for items that could not be found in the darkness. Additionally, light exposes evil.

Is it any wonder why those walking in sin are often unwilling to hear about Jesus Christ, the Light of the world? The light of Jesus exposes the darkness of sin. Similar to the physical realm, in the spiritual realm, our eyes must adjust. Yet once we see it through God's eyes, as He enlightens us to understand sin from His perspective, we no longer desire to walk in darkness. Instead, He places the Light inside of us, in the person of the Holy Spirit, who enables us to love others with God's love. He also empowers us to walk away from the sin that had enslaved us! That new walk is not instantaneous; it is an adjustment of our new vision. In His light, our beauty is revealed, as it is a reflection of God's light.

> People are like stained-glass windows. They sparkle and shine when the sun is out, but when the darkness sets in their true beauty is revealed only if there is light from within.
> ~Elisabeth Kübler-Ross

The people who sat in darkness have seen a great light, And upon those who sat in the region and shadow of death Light has dawned."
Matthew 4:16 (NKJV)

Sadly, most people fear the light more than a child fears the dark! Most of us have stubbed a toe in the middle of the night. That would not have happened if we had turned on the light!

Jesus shines His Light, illuminating our walks and our lives. It does not matter how widely we open our eyes, in the darkness, we cannot see. We should turn on the light of Jesus in our lives!

**To give light to those who sit in darkness and the shadow of death,
To guide our feet into the way of peace."
Luke 1:79 (NKJV)**

September 14: Calling all teachers!

Ever seen a 6-year-old boy teaching his 4-year-old sister how to tie her shoes? It is one of those times when being a fly on the wall brings a huge smile, as the simplicity of that teaching ability typically reflects the person who taught him, probably moments before.

As Christians, we are all teachers. Some teach by words, while others teach by deeds. Yet boldness is a key. Certainly, there are times when God desires for even the most gifted teachers to be students. Additionally, no matter how much head or heart knowledge that a teacher has, even the simplest of students still has subjects they can teach the teachers.

In Acts 18, we see an example of an eloquent speaker in the early days of Christianity:

[24] Now a certain Jew named Apollos, born at Alexandria, an eloquent man *and* mighty in the Scriptures, came to Ephesus. [25] This man had been instructed in the way of the Lord; and being fervent in spirit, he spoke and taught accurately the things of the Lord, though he knew only the baptism of John. [26] So he began to speak boldly in the synagogue. When Aquila and Priscilla heard him, they took him aside and explained to him the way of God more accurately. [27] And when he desired to cross to Achaia, the brethren wrote, exhorting the disciples to receive him; and when he arrived, he greatly helped those who had believed through grace; [28]

for he vigorously refuted the Jews publicly, showing from the Scriptures that Jesus is the Christ.
Acts 18:24-28 (NKJV)

Apollos spoke boldly and with great eloquence, but he was missing the end of the story. He preached the Old Testament Scriptures and the baptism of John, but Apollos had not changed his teaching to reflect the life, death and resurrection of the Messiah, along with the continuous presence in each believer of the Holy Spirit! If the Bible mentions his power as a teacher, Apollos must have been extremely gifted, yet two humble servants stepped up to the plate to set him right. That speaks of the humbleness of Apollos, as he was able to receive the instruction from Priscilla and Aquila, a couple of tentmakers. Surely, that change in the teaching of Apollos blessed all in earshot!

Are we willing to teach any time God brings someone into our lives with less understanding? Even new believers have more understanding of God's Word than people who do not believe. Lack of pride is one of the greatest attributes of a gifted teacher. Those teachers filled with pride will attempt to answer questions beyond their knowledge or experience, though humble teachers often will respond with, "I don't know the answer to your question, but let me pray about it, study it and I will get back to you!"

Be willing to step up like Aquila and Priscilla to set those straight, who are missing the big picture. Additionally, we should be willing to teach those God places in our paths, for they need to hear His Word. Teach with humbleness, knowing that God can use students to teach just as easily. Lastly, do not be intent on following a talented orator, as without truth, the speech will be nothing more than entertainment. Remember, the best teacher is typically the best student. Jesus was the greatest teacher, and He knew the Word backwards and forwards! By learning from the Greatest Teacher, we should all be teachers in some facet. At the very least, we should be teaching our family members! Are we willing to do that?

13 Till I come, give attention to reading, to exhortation, to doctrine. **14** Do not neglect the gift that is in you, which was given to you by prophecy with the laying on of the hands of the eldership. **15** Meditate on these things; give yourself entirely to them, that your progress may be evident to all. **16** Take heed to yourself and to the doctrine. Continue in them, for in doing this you will save both yourself and those who hear you.
1 Timothy 4:13-16 (NKJV)

September 15: I 'toed' you so!

Our bodies are intricately-engineered systems of machinery that pose a scientific quandary to those believing in evolution, especially in a world governed by the law of entropy, the Second Law of Thermodynamics. How could this have occurred by accident? While that exquisite detail points to God, the uses of the body also remind us of our Creator. The human brain might be the central location of the body, helping all parts to work together, but when any of the parts fails to work correctly, the entire body suffers.

God has given that example for each of us to understand, as it applies directly to the Body of Christ, all Christians working together for God's glory. While there are many gifts and talents in the Body of Christ, none are greater or lesser in comparison to each other. What would the gift of teaching matter if there was no one to be a student? Additionally, to a man living alone in the outer reaches of the desert, who would be there to encourage him?

12 For as the body is one and has many members, but all the members of that one body, being many, are one body, so also *is* Christ. **13** For by one Spirit we were all baptized into one body— whether Jews or Greeks, whether slaves or free—and have all been made to drink into one Spirit. **14** For in fact the body is not one member but many.

[15] If the foot should say, "Because I am not a hand, I am not of the body," is it therefore not of the body? [16] And if the ear should say, "Because I am not an eye, I am not of the body," is it therefore not of the body? [17] If the whole body *were* an eye, where *would be* the hearing? If the whole *were* hearing, where *would be* the smelling? [18] But now God has set the members, each one of them, in the body just as He pleased. [19] And if they *were* all one member, where *would* the body *be?* [20] But now indeed *there are* many members, yet one body. [21] And the eye cannot say to the hand, "I have no need of you"; nor again the head to the feet, "I have no need of you." [22] No, much rather, those members of the body which seem to be weaker are necessary. [23] And those *members* of the body which we think to be less honorable, on these we bestow greater honor; and our unpresentable *parts* have greater modesty, [24] but our presentable *parts* have no need. But God composed the body, having given greater honor to that *part* which lacks it, [25] that there should be no schism in the body, but *that* the members should have the same care for one another. [26] And if one member suffers, all the members suffer with *it;* or if one member is honored, all the members rejoice with *it.*
1 Corinthians 12:12-26 (NKJV)

Just as the lust of the flesh, the lust of the eyes and the pride of life lead to sin, our lust and pride cause dissension in the Body of Christ. What happens when the big toe decides to forego his "little job," as he desires to be the mouth? That big toe gives us strength in walking, and without him, we weakly would limp along. Even the smallest toe has an individual job, giving us balance. Thumbs are not just used for hitchhiking, either. Remember, there are no small jobs in the Body of Christ, only a small understanding of what God is accomplishing with those jobs.

Willingness to use those gifts for the benefit of the Body is a major part of the problem. Most televangelists exemplify the wrong behavior, desiring to be in that position for wealth and attention. God has given us the greatest example in the Holy

Spirit, though equal with Father and Son, He always points to Jesus, not self. In the same manner, Jesus always does the will of the Father. They do not bicker and backbite concerning size of gift, but instead are One, just as the Body of Christ is supposed to be! Do we desire to use our gifts in a bigger way?

His lord said to him, 'Well *done,* good and faithful servant; you were faithful over a few things, I will make you ruler over many things. Enter into the joy of your lord.'
Matthew 25:21 (NKJV)

Instead of yearning for a different gift or talent, we should look for the opportunities that God places in our paths to use the gifts He has given. With priorities in order of using gifts for the benefit of others, rather than self, God will perform amazing miracles, even with the smallest of gifts. To bury the gift is offensive to He who gave it, as it is for His glory! Even if blessed with being the little toe of the body, helping others to walk in balance, we will fall without that toe! When we fall together, we all will say, "I 'toed' you so!"

[14] **"For *the kingdom of heaven is* like a man traveling to a far country, *who* called his own servants and delivered his goods to them.** [15] **And to one he gave five talents, to another two, and to another one, to each according to his own ability; and immediately he went on a journey.** [16] **Then he who had received the five talents went and traded with them, and made another five talents.** [17] **And likewise he who *had received* two gained two more also.** [18] **But he who had received one went and dug in the ground, and hid his lord's money.** [19] **After a long time the lord of those servants came and settled accounts with them.**
[20] **"So he who had received five talents came and brought five other talents, saying, 'Lord, you delivered to me five talents; look, I have gained five more talents besides them.'** [21] **His lord said to him, 'Well *done,* good and faithful servant; you were faithful over a few things, I will make you ruler over many things. Enter into the joy of your lord.'** [22] **He also who had received two talents came and said, 'Lord, you delivered**

to me two talents; look, I have gained two more talents besides them.' ²³ His lord said to him, 'Well *done,* good and faithful servant; you have been faithful over a few things, I will make you ruler over many things. Enter into the joy of your lord.'
²⁴ "Then he who had received the one talent came and said, 'Lord, I knew you to be a hard man, reaping where you have not sown, and gathering where you have not scattered seed. ²⁵ And I was afraid, and went and hid your talent in the ground. Look, *there* you have *what is* yours.'
²⁶ "But his lord answered and said to him, 'You wicked and lazy servant, you knew that I reap where I have not sown, and gather where I have not scattered seed. ²⁷ So you ought to have deposited my money with the bankers, and at my coming I would have received back my own with interest. ²⁸ So take the talent from him, and give *it* to him who has ten talents.
Matthew 25:14-28 (NKJV)

September 16: Power in the blood

Though many of us have great difficulties dealing with blood, it is certainly amazing. Our blood consists of red blood cells, platelets and white blood cells. Red blood cells sustain us through nourishment, carrying oxygen, calcium, potassium and amino acids, traveling through 60,000 miles of arteries, veins and capillaries in about 23 seconds. Wow! Additionally, those red blood cells help to keep the blood clean by removing waste. Platelets work with the red blood cells to ensure that we do not lose all of our blood if we are cut, through coagulation and clotting. White blood cells are the soldiers, fighting off disease along with antibodies, and some of those white blood cells die in battle.

It is all about the blood. Many of the laws of the Old Testament have to do with blood, including the ritual of the blood sacrifice. Many Christians and non-Christians alike struggle with what they view as an archaic, sacrificial system, yet God began teaching us about the power of the blood all the way back in the

Garden of Eden, when He covered the naked Adam and Eve with clothing, by killing an innocent ram (Genesis 3:21). Even then, the spilling of innocent blood covered sin.

For the life of the flesh *is* in the blood, and I have given it to you upon the altar to make atonement for your souls; for it *is* the blood *that* makes atonement for the soul.'
Leviticus 17:11 (NKJV)

It all was fulfilled in the life, death and resurrection of Jesus. He became the sacrificial Lamb when He died on the cross, in punishment of our sins. In John 6, Jesus tells His followers another aspect having to do with His blood:

[53] Then Jesus said to them, "Most assuredly, I say to you, unless you eat the flesh of the Son of Man and drink His blood, you have no life in you. [54] Whoever eats My flesh and drinks My blood has eternal life, and I will raise him up at the last day. [55] For My flesh is food indeed, and My blood is drink indeed. [56] He who eats My flesh and drinks My blood abides in Me, and I in him. [57] As the living Father sent Me, and I live because of the Father, so he who feeds on Me will live because of Me.
John 6:53-57 (NKJV)

That statement offended many of the Jews, who were taught in the Old Testament to eat the sacrifice, but never to drink the blood. This appeared to be cannibalism! Yet in communion, we are told that the wine is the blood of Christ, while the bread is His body broken for us. Communion is like the red blood cells that give us food and nourishment. Jesus feeds us! Additionally, Jesus cleanses us, just as the blood in our bodies removes waste.

But if we walk in the light as He is in the light, we have fellowship with one another, and the blood of Jesus Christ His Son cleanses us from all sin.
1 John 1:7 (NKJV)

To Him who loved us and washed us from our sins in His own blood,
Revelation 1:5 (NKJV)

Additionally, the blood of Christ can prevent infections from taking root and destroying us. Those infections are sin-based, and even Christians continue to sin. Yet through the covering of the blood of Christ, and the Holy Spirit dwelling inside of us, He attacks that sin in our lives. Just as the blood in our bodies continues to circulate, the blood of Jesus continues to flow within the Body of Christ, cleansing its members.

As God reminded us in the Old Testament, it is all about the blood, for there is life in the blood. Whether human or animal, without blood, we are dead. In the same manner, without the blood of Christ that feeds us, cleanses us and heals us, we are spiritually dead. If we are members of the Body of Christ, there is power in the blood!

And according to the law almost all things are purified with blood, and without shedding of blood there is no remission.
Hebrews 9:22 (NKJV)

For *it is* not possible that the blood of bulls and goats could take away sins.
Hebrews 10:4 (NKJV)

September 17: Staying power!

When we have goals in mind, occasionally they can be achieved by chance. If a man's goal is to make $50,000, one play on a slot-machine can change that future goal to an accomplishment, yet those occurrences are few and far between. Instead, most goals are met by consistent behavior, and without passion, a man cannot stay the course long enough for success. On the other hand, when that work ethic remains focused on others, rather than self, passion prevails.

Often, the goals we set for our own accomplishments revolve around money and possessions. Sadly, achieving those goals rarely brings satisfaction. Most of us are familiar with John D. Rockefeller's response to the question, how much money is enough. "Just a little more than I have," was his answer. People typically ascribe a future feeling of satisfaction to those lofty, financial goals, yet if achieved, find that more emptiness is waiting for them.

Paul had a different kind of motivation in achieving his goals. With a respected Jewish pedigree, Paul was from the tribe of Benjamin; had studied under the most-respected rabbi, Gamaliel, and thus, had much intellectual knowledge concerning the Old Testament; and worked strongly against Christians and the spread of Christianity. Yet when confronted from the heavens by the risen Savior while on the road to Damascus, Paul's life changed on the spot (Acts 9). Forced to question the intellectual decisions of his life to that point, Paul devoted the remainder of his life to sharing the gospel of Jesus Christ with everyone in his path. He preached to Jews and Gentiles alike. Scholars believe the hunchbacked Paul was short, had a speech impediment and suffered from eye problems. Regardless of his physical limitations, Paul spoke with the Lord's power. What did Paul receive from his resolve to share the love of the Lord? Hardship, torture, shipwrecks and imprisonment. When we travel, we ask about the amenities of the nicest hotels. Paul asked about the jails!

In regard to consistency, George Whitefield is worth studying, as well. An 18th-century, Anglican Protestant minister, Whitefield bridged the gap of Christian belief between those in pre-Revolution America, as Methodists, Baptists, Puritans, Quakers and followers of other religious denominations flocked to hear him preach. In 34 years of speaking God's truth, Whitefield preached over 18,000 sermons, an average of more than a sermon each day! Similar to Paul, Whitefield did not slow down as his health deteriorated. In 1770 at the age of 56, Whitefield's asthmatic breathing worsened, but he continued to preach and travel with fervor. One day when a friend told him he was more fit to sleep than preach, this was his response:

> "Lord Jesus, I am weary in Thy work, but not of it. If I have not finished my course, let me go and speak for Thee once more in the fields, and seal Thy truth, and come home and die."

That day, he had difficulty speaking, but paused in prayer, then preached with God's strength for two hours. The next morning, he left this broken world, having remained steadfast throughout.

Therefore, my beloved brethren, be steadfast, immovable, always abounding in the work of the Lord, knowing that your labor is not in vain in the Lord.
1 Corinthians 15:58 (NKJV)

Steadfast is a nautical term meaning to stay the course, regardless of wind or waves, trying to push and pull us in other directions. Unlike those external forces, the Holy Spirit does not push or pull us. Instead, He guides and leads us on God's path. If we feel like our walks with the Lord and work for the Lord are wavering, then our sails are billowed by self instead of Spirit. Remember the greatest commandments of Jesus, to love God with all of our hearts and to love others. When that love replaces our focus on personal goals and selfish ambitions, our lives take on a whole new meaning. When we are tired, He is our rest (Matthew 11:28). He is the Author and Finisher of our faith (Hebrews 12:2). Stay the course, with the Holy Spirit guiding all the way!

[5] For as the sufferings of Christ abound in us, so our consolation also abounds through Christ. [6] Now if we are afflicted, *it is* for your consolation and salvation, which is effective for enduring the same sufferings which we also suffer. Or if we are comforted, *it is* for your consolation and salvation. [7] And our hope for you *is* steadfast, because we know that as you are partakers of the sufferings, so also *you will partake* of the consolation.

2 Corinthians 1:5-7 (NKJV)

²¹ And you, who once were alienated and enemies in your mind by wicked works, yet now He has reconciled ²² in the body of His flesh through death, to present you holy, and blameless, and above reproach in His sight— ²³ if indeed you continue in the faith, grounded and steadfast, and are not moved away from the hope of the gospel which you heard, which was preached to every creature under heaven, of which I, Paul, became a minister.
Colossians 1:21-23 (NKJV)

¹Blessed *is* the man
Who walks not in the
counsel of the ungodly,
Nor stands in the path of sinners,
Nor sits in the seat of the scornful;
²But his delight *is* in
the law of the LORD,
And in His law he meditates
day and night.
³He shall be like a tree
Planted by the rivers of water,
That brings forth its fruit in its season,
Whose leaf also shall not wither;
And whatever he does shall prosper.
Psalm 1:1-3 (NKJV)

September 18: Target practice

While "innocent until proven guilty" might be the motto of the judicial system of the United States, front page news makes a much larger impact than a page-34 retraction. Major allegations against yet another televangelist/mega-church pastor came as Eddie Long, senior pastor of New Birth Missionary Baptist Church of Lithonia, Georgia, was accused by four, unrelated young men of sexual coercion. The leader of the 30,000+ member congregation vehemently denied the allegations, though he has admitted to taking the young men on trips to Africa and various other places in an attempt to widen their world visions. Certainly, without more proof, Long should not be guilty in our minds, yet his lifestyle and "prosperity gospel" messages make him an easy target for Satan's demonic host. A large, financial settlement out of court testifies more to his guilt than innocence.

Every believer has a target on his head. Knowing that Satan cannot take away God's greatest gift to us in our salvation, instead, demonic forces attempt to take away our greatest gift back to God, our testimonies of what He has accomplished in each of our lives. Paul writes to us in Ephesians of the spiritual battles that will continue for each believer while in this world:

[10] Finally, my brethren, be strong in the Lord and in the power of His might. [11] Put on the whole armor of God, that you may be able to stand against the wiles of the devil. [12] For we do not wrestle against flesh and blood, but against principalities, against powers, against the rulers of the darkness of this age, against spiritual *hosts* of wickedness in the heavenly *places*. [13] Therefore take up the whole armor of God, that you may be able to withstand in the evil day, and having done all, to stand.
Ephesians 6:10-13 (NKJV)

With truth, righteousness, peace, faith, salvation and God's Word protecting us in different facets, God is the one who keeps us safe. If Long is guilty of the allegations, it is easy to see how he could have lost that protection. Imagine the additional harm to his congregation if he denies the allegations if guilty, much less the harm to the young men! Adding sin to previous sin by lying certainly does not glorify our God who forgives. Righteousness does not include walking in ways contrary to the teaching of the Bible. Peace cannot flow like a river when we disregard God's truth. At the same time, faith involves God supplying our needs, while the hunger for earthly prosperity conflicts waiting on the Lord to resolve every conflict. Questioning a pastor's salvation is God's job, as only He can see inside the heart, yet if these allegations are true, at the very least, Long has lost sight of his own accountability. Lastly, God's

Word is at the center of it all. Satan knows the words of the Bible better than Long, and with years of practice, can trip any man not relying on God. Once again, preaching earthly prosperity when God only promises heavenly blessings demonstrates a desire to be like the world, and additionally, leads many others astray. Some sorrowfully say that thousands of people are relying on Long, yet therein lies the problem. If those people were trusting instead in Jesus, they would have enough spiritual acumen to see that following a pastor with a $3 million yearly salary, who drives a $350,000 Bentley and wears $5,000 suits, contradicts the words of Jesus:

For it is easier for a camel to go through the eye of a needle than for a rich man to enter the kingdom of God."
Luke 18:25 (NKJV)

Eddie Long is another member of a growing number of pastors, who (allegedly) have stumbled mightily, bringing to mind the well-known saying, "The bigger they are, the harder they fall." With a long list of other pastors in similar positions, we should not lose sight of the fact that God allowed this to happen for His purposes. Either He is discrediting a charlatan, who is preying on believers for his own financial stability while leading them down a path of lies (not to mention preying on impressionable young men), or God has allowed the allegations in order to strengthen the flock against attack. In the midst of the process, though, the name of God is dragged through the proverbial mud, as unbelievers look at Long's status and equate his message to that of all believers. Thinking we are all filled with the same hypocrisy, those unbelievers push further away from God. The difference between Christians and non-Christians is not the presence of sin in our lives; it is the forgiveness of that sin!

The lesson for all believers is the importance of our walks with the Lord. We can demonstrate God's love for us in how we reflect His love. Certainly, we all are sinners, saved by grace, and will continue to fall. Yet how we respond to the failure of our own sin points to God. Lest we forget, we are accountable to Him for every decision that we make, and certainly, pastors carry a greater accountability to God, as their words can lead others astray. Follow God, not man! Read God's Word daily to ensure that when pastors are not speaking truth we will not be led astray. Do not glorify man, but glorify God. Lastly, do not forget that there is a target on our heads, as well. The more work that we are doing for the kingdom of God, the larger that target will grow, as Satan will send more powerful, fallen angels to do battle with us! Yet never forget, the battle is the Lord's!

[1] My brethren, let not many of you become teachers, knowing that we shall receive a stricter judgment. [2] For we all stumble in many things. If anyone does not stumble in word, he *is* a perfect man, able also to bridle the whole body. [3] Indeed, we put bits in horses' mouths that they may obey us, and we turn their whole body. [4] Look also at ships: although they are so large and are driven by fierce winds, they are turned by a very small rudder wherever the pilot desires. [5] Even so the tongue is a little member and boasts great things.
James 3:1-5 (NKJV)

September 19: Do the weeds 'tare' us up?

Many people, Christians included, argue about the meaning of each passage in the Bible. Some interpret very literally, while others spiritualize each statement. One example is the belief in the rapture, the return of Jesus Christ to take His church to heaven. There are large groups of believers using Scripture to "prove" their personal viewpoint, but those diversely include a pre-tribulation rapture, a mid-tribulation rapture, a post-tribulation rapture, no rapture at all, and even the belief that the rapture already has occurred. It all can be very confusing, yet we know:

For God is not *the author* of confusion but of peace, as in all the churches of the saints.
1 Corinthians 14:33 (NKJV)

The Bible tells us what God wants us to know, but that does not mean that He tells us everything! For example, we do not know the time and day of our Savior's return. When Jesus came to earth as a man, even He did not know! (Matthew 24:36) As believers, we are meant to know and hear our Savior's voice, and to understand His words. Why did Jesus teach in parables?

¹⁰ And the disciples came and said to Him, "Why do You speak to them in parables?"
¹¹ He answered and said to them, "Because it has been given to you to know the mysteries of the kingdom of heaven, but to them it has not been given. ¹² For whoever has, to him more will be given, and he will have abundance; but whoever does not have, even what he has will be taken away from him. ¹³ Therefore I speak to them in parables, because seeing they do not see, and hearing they do not hear, nor do they understand.
Matthew 13:10-13 (NKJV)

We all know the feeling when people are picking apart every word that we speak. Certainly, the enemies of Jesus had that intent, but the parables confused them. Yet our Lord desires for us to understand His Word. Through the Holy Spirit, He reveals to us what the Bible says, though when we make our minds up what a passage means before we read it in context, we are not listening! The best interpretation of the Bible comes from other places in the Bible, as it is an integrated message woven together with the scarlet thread of the blood of Jesus. Each author was inspired by the Holy Spirit to write exactly what he wrote. Be careful not to use the Bible to prove a point, but instead, to read with an open mind. Jesus is the Great Teacher, who will lead us when reading His Word.

Sadly, there are many false teachers leading believers astray. If those believers were opening the Bible to ensure the teaching was accurate, that would not happen. Jesus told us that there were tares growing with the wheat. Instead of destroying the healthy plants when uprooting the weeds, the Lord will separate those plants in His harvest.

²⁴ Another parable He put forth to them, saying: "The kingdom of heaven is like a man who sowed good seed in his field; ²⁵ but while men slept, his enemy came and sowed tares among the wheat and went his way. ²⁶ But when the grain had sprouted and produced a crop, then the tares also appeared. ²⁷ So the servants of the owner came and said to him, 'Sir, did you not sow good seed in your field? How then does it have tares?' ²⁸ He said to them, 'An enemy has done this.' The servants said to him, 'Do you want us then to go and gather them up?' ²⁹ But he said, 'No, lest while you gather up the tares you also uproot the wheat with them. ³⁰ Let both grow together until the harvest, and at the time of harvest I will say to the reapers, "First gather together the tares and bind them in bundles to burn them, but gather the wheat into my barn." ' "
Matthew 13:24-30 (NKJV)

We are not responsible for uprooting the tares, destroying the false teachers who are sowing discord in God's harvest. As believers, our responsibility is to check the Scripture daily to ensure that our teachers are sharing the full counsel of God. That takes time and effort to study, but when we remember that the Bible is God's voice, speaking to us, what is there that is more important? If we allow the tares to choke the wheat away, it has to do with our apathy. Be aware of the tares among us, and do not let them 'tare' us up!

²³ "Then if anyone says to you, 'Look, here *is* the Christ!' or 'There!' do not believe *it*. ²⁴ For false christs and false prophets will rise and show great signs and wonders to deceive, if possible, even the elect. ²⁵ See, I have told you beforehand.
Matthew 24:23-25 (NKJV)

September 20: From the heart

Most of us have no difficulty remembering the best teachers in our lives. Personally, one of the most memorable was a political science professor teaching about South Africa and apartheid. He was one of the world's leading opponents of apartheid, in which all blacks in the nation were treated as sub-humans. Few saw the correlation between South African apartheid and the racial history of the American South. Yet on the first day of class, when the professor spoke, he wept. Hearing his passion, all students in the class instantly knew that we were going to receive a gift. When people speak from their intellect, we hear facts, figures and statistics. On the other hand, when people speak from their hearts, we hear about issues they would be willing to die for.

Many Christians have died for their beliefs. In fact, all of the apostles except for John died martyr's deaths. Though it might seem odd for God to allow many of His most zealous followers to die that way, we lose sight of the volumes spoken in those actions. How strongly did these men believe that they had walked with their risen Savior? Well, they believed so strongly that they were willing to lose their lives without hesitation or doubt! When Peter saw Jesus after the resurrection, Jesus told Peter how he would die:

[17] **Jesus said to him, "Feed My sheep.** [18] **Most assuredly, I say to you, when you were younger, you girded yourself and walked where you wished; but when you are old, you will stretch out your hands, and another will gird you and carry *you* where you do not wish."** [19] **This He spoke, signifying by what death he would glorify God. And when He had spoken this, He said to him, "Follow Me."**
[20] **Then Peter, turning around, saw the disciple whom Jesus loved following, who also had leaned on His breast at the supper, and said, "Lord, who is the one who betrays You?"** [21] **Peter, seeing him, said to Jesus, "But Lord, what *about* this man?"**
[22] **Jesus said to him, "If I will that he remain till I come, what *is that* to you? You follow Me."**
[23] **Then this saying went out among the brethren that this disciple would not die. Yet Jesus did not say to him that he would not die, but, "If I will that he remain till I come, what *is that* to you?"**

John 21:17-23 (NKJV)

Peter might have struggled when receiving those words from His Lord, comparing his own death to that of his friend John, but when it came time, the struggle was far behind him. Early church fathers Origen and Tertullian reveal to us in their writings that Peter was crucified in Rome. Yet, feeling unworthy to die the same death as Jesus, Peter asked to be crucified upside down!

When we speak of Jesus, do we speak with complete commitment? He gave His life, so that we could be a part of His inheritance. When we reflect on our lives without Him, and see the corresponding sadness and brokenness, it is a wonderful reminder of who He is in our lives. Yes, there are trials, severe at times. Yet the joy of the Lord is our strength. He carries us through each hardship, and draws us closer to Him in the process. We cannot argue someone to the Lord, but we certainly can love them to Jesus. More than any words can express, we should let His light shine in our lives so radiantly that people can see the love in our hearts, through every action. We lose sight of the immense gift He has given when we mindlessly and methodically go through each day. How would we feel if we won the lottery? The gift He has given is so much more valuable, and that gift should fill us with immense joy!

We might be willing to die for our dearest friends and relatives, but are we willing to die for our enemies? Jesus gave His life willingly for sinners, who did not even believe in Him. If we believe with the same conviction that the apostles did, the world should be able to see that we are set apart, for we have walked with Jesus. That walk includes the cross, for we were baptized into His death (Romans 6:3). Are we willing to endure the cross to follow Jesus?

Then Jesus said to His disciples, "If anyone desires to come after Me, let him deny himself, and take up his cross, and follow Me.
Matthew 16:24 (NKJV)

Greater love has no one than this, than to lay down one's life for his friends.
John 15:13 (NKJV)

September 21: Take heed!

When driving down a country road, if a sign said, "ROAD CLOSED AHEAD," ignoring that warning, or missing it entirely by not paying attention, could cause life to change drastically or end in a matter of moments. How we react to warnings falls into one of two categories. When being confronted with a yellow light at a traffic signal, people either will stop abruptly or hit the gas pedal and go even faster! That dichotomy of response certainly reflects two extremely different results, as well. Warnings remind us to proceed with caution, yet that involves listening very closely.

On a package of Dial Soap, a warning says to "use like regular soap." Some hair dryers contain the warning, "Do not use while taking a shower." Hershey's Almond Bars include this great piece of advice: "Warning, may contain traces of nuts." Nytol sleep aid reminds us: "May cause drowsiness." It is any wonder that the human race still continues with the way most of us listen to warnings, though many of those should be second nature to us by now. Yet as believers, the warnings that we should pay the closest attention to are the ones from God!

The phrase "take heed" occurs 54 times in the King James Version and 49 times in the New King James Version. The word for "heed" is *shamar* in Hebrew, and means to keep, tend, watch over or retain. In Greek, that same word is *epecho*, meaning to hold upon or to give attention to. Any time we come across that phrase in the Bible, it is a reminder to pay attention. It is saying, "guard yourself," for this is an area that trips many people! Our lives may depend upon these warning! Look at a few of those instances:

[9] Only take heed to yourself, and diligently keep yourself, lest you forget the things your eyes have seen, and lest they

depart from your heart all the days of your life. And teach them to your children and your grandchildren, [10] especially concerning the day you stood before the LORD your God in Horeb, when the LORD said to me, 'Gather the people to Me, and I will let them hear My words, that they may learn to fear Me all the days they live on the earth, and *that* they may teach their children.'
Deuteronomy 4:9-10 (NKJV)

In this passage, God reminds the Jews of the importance of His Law, which He gave to them on Mount Horeb. Teaching that law to the next generations will pass the warning forward, for we know that by walking in the fear of the Lord, we will honor His commandments, yet when we walk in complete disregard of His Law, we can have no relationship with Him. That is more deadly than a bridge out on a lonely stretch of road!

> "Mankind is notoriously too dense to read the signs that God sends from time to time. We require drums to be beaten into our ears, before we should wake from our trance and hear the warning and see that to lose oneself in all, is the only way to find oneself."
> —Anonymous

Fortunately for us, God created us and knows our limitations. Though most of us think we are much more intelligent than we really are, we demonstrate that lack of intelligence by not responding to God's warnings. Yet as believers, He continues to warn us. Typically, those warnings get louder or more painful as we continue to ignore His words. Yet if we ignore God long enough, those warnings are likely to cease:

Therefore take heed how you hear. For whoever has, to him *more* will be given; and whoever does not have, even what he seems to have will be taken from him."
Luke 8:18 (NKJV)

As believers, we need to quit accelerating through those yellow lights, the cautions that the Lord places in our paths.

Additionally, write those warnings on our hearts, as they will continue to have an effect on each of our lives! It is easier to stop when we are not moving so quickly, so the first step is to slow down! It is in those quiet places when we hear His voice the loudest!

Take heed to yourself and to the doctrine. Continue in them, for in doing this you will save both yourself and those who hear you.
1 Timothy 4:16 (NKJV)

September 22: Law or grace?

One of the most difficult issues to understand is why we continue to sin as Christians, yet each of us knows that we do. Paul reminded us in Romans 7 that we would not understand sin if it were not for the Law, the 10 Commandments and corresponding laws of the Old Testament (Galatians 3:24). Yet as we can see from the writings of Paul, we are no longer under the Law, but instead, we are now under grace (Romans 6:14).

God taught us through the Law, so we would know sin and the ramifications of sin. Before we accepted Jesus as Lord and Savior, we were slaves to sin. Without the presence of the Holy Spirit, we were unable to say no to the requests of sin in our lives. In ancient times, the galley slaves chained to the boat had no ability to leave that boat, and whenever the captain, their master, told them to row, they obeyed or faced death. Our pre-Christian days in sin resemble that analogy. Yet as believers, we are no longer bound by sin. Now it is a choice, as God has set us free!

When we approach sin as Christians, the Holy Spirit sends out a reminder to run away, just as Joseph did when Potiphar's wife made advances toward him (Genesis 39:12). Certainly, we do not always listen, and our bad choices cause much pain. Sin always has ramifications, hurting us and others along the wayside. Certainly, we feel like we have let God down when we fail, and additionally, are keenly aware that we just added another burden to the shoulders of Jesus to carry on Calvary. Just because He was crucified many years ago does not mean our present lives do not have further impact on His suffering, as Jesus carried ALL the sins of the world.

[16] I say then: Walk in the Spirit, and you shall not fulfill the lust of the flesh. [17] For the flesh lusts against the Spirit, and the Spirit against the flesh; and these are contrary to one another, so that you do not do the things that you wish. [18] But if you are led by the Spirit, you are not under the law. Galatians 5:16-18 (NKJV)

In comparison to being under the Law, being under grace gives us the ability to obey out of love for God, rather than out of fear of the consequences. Without the Holy Spirit, we can try as hard as we can not to sin, but we will fail over and over again. Yet it is not about us giving it our all; instead, it is about God giving it His all! That is grace, **G**od's **R**iches **A**t **C**hrist's **E**xpense. Getting what we do not deserve is the greatest gift from God! Grace should be the motivating factor in our response, as having had a great burden removed from our shoulders, and placed on the shoulders of Jesus, our love for Him should be immense!

[15] What then? Shall we sin because we are not under law but under grace? Certainly not! [16] Do you not know that to whom you present yourselves slaves to obey, you are that one's slaves whom you obey, whether of sin *leading* to death, or of obedience *leading* to righteousness? Romans 6:15-16 (NKJV)

Many carnal Christians continue in their sins. For if Jesus forgives them, what does it matter? Churches are filled with people who get drunk on Saturdays, and sit in the pew on Sundays. Additionally, many people professing Christ continue in their sexual sins, ignoring the laws that any sexual relations outside of marriage are against God, accepting the world's judgment of what is right instead of God's Law. Certainly, we all have blind spots and the Holy Spirit sees those with great ease. In His perfect time, He points them out to each of us. Just because the Holy Spirit is in us does not mean that we are in the Holy Spirit! Yet here is the big catch: if we are not feeling convicted of our sin, then we are not His! The battle lines are drawn in our own bodies, as our hearts serve the Lord, but our minds continue to struggle. God desires for us to attack those thoughts before they become actions.

casting down arguments and every high thing that exalts itself against the knowledge of God, bringing every thought into captivity to the obedience of Christ,
2 Corinthians 10:5 (NKJV)

Some Christians get confused, thinking that because we are not under Law but under grace, God changed, or at the very least, His requirements changed. God cannot change! He is perfect, and has no need to change. We changed! In the days of the Old Testament when believers were under the Law, they did not have the Holy Spirit dwelling inside of them. When Jesus returned to heaven after His resurrection from the dead, He left the Comforter with us to convict us of sin and point us to Jesus! What a powerful gift!

When we reflect upon the great gifts that God has given, taking away the sin weighing us down, living inside of us with constant conviction not to sin, and granting us eternal life with Him, we should walk in absolute joy! With corresponding love to our God that gives, we should begin to address and conquer the habitual sins of our lives.

[9] knowing this: that the law is not made for a righteous person, but for *the* lawless and insubordinate, for *the* ungodly and for sinners, for *the* unholy and profane, for murderers of fathers and murderers of mothers, for manslayers, [10] for fornicators, for sodomites, for kidnappers, for liars, for perjurers, and if there is any other thing that is contrary to sound doctrine, [11] according to the glorious gospel of the blessed God which was committed to my trust.
1 Timothy 1:9-11 (NKJV)

[22] For I delight in the law of God according to the inward man. [23] But I see another law in my members, warring against the law of my mind, and bringing me into captivity to the law of sin which is in my members. [24] O wretched man that I am! Who will deliver me from this body of death? [25] I thank God—through Jesus Christ our Lord!
Romans 7:22-25 (NKJV)

[4] For whatever is born of God overcomes the world. And this is the victory that has overcome the world— our faith. [5] Who is he who overcomes the world, but he who believes that Jesus is the Son of God?
1 John 5:4-5 (NKJV)

He who overcomes shall inherit all things, and I will be his God and he shall be My son.
Revelation 21:7 (NKJV)

September 23: "Sticks and stones..."

William Shakespeare said, "A rose by any other name would smell as sweet," meaning that it is more important what we are than what we are called. Additionally, names can be what we use in an attempt to hurt others. All are familiar with the saying, "Sticks and stones will break my bones, but words will never hurt me." Yet, words can cause much deeper scars than sticks or stones ever could.

Names carried much more significance in the past. Surnames, which tend to be our last names in the west but are usually the first names in the east, have not been around nearly as long as most of us would guess. In England, the practice became commonplace in the 13th and 14th centuries, mostly due to the large population and the need to differentiate between many people with the same birth name. Surprisingly, until the 19th century, no one but the aristocracy in Japan had a surname. Most surnames in all cultures seem to follow a similar line, utilizing a family occupation, personal characteristic, geographical feature, person descended from or even a mention of religious ties.

In the Bible, we see many lists of lineages, with the most important being that of Jesus, who, by the way, does not have the surname "Christ!" Luke, a doctor by trade, traces the bloodline of Jesus through His mother Mary in Luke 3:23-38, while Matthew follows a different line in many cases, based on an occurrence that happened in the days of Moses:

[1] Then came the daughters of Zelophehad the son of Hepher, the son of Gilead, the son of Machir, the son of Manasseh, from the families of Manasseh the son of Joseph; and these *were* the names of his daughters: Mahlah, Noah, Hoglah, Milcah, and Tirzah. [2] And they stood before Moses, before Eleazar the priest, and before the leaders and all the congregation, *by* the doorway of the tabernacle of meeting, saying: [3] "Our father died in the wilderness; but he was not in the company of those who gathered together against the LORD, in company with Korah, but he died in his own sin; and he had no sons. [4] Why should the name of our father be removed from among his family because he had no son? Give us a possession among our father's brothers."
Numbers 27:1-4 (NKJV)

While the sons were counted concerning the rights of inheritance, daughters did not retain the same rights. Preparing to occupy the Promised Land, the daughters of Zelophehad were being absorbed into another family in regard to inheritance, as their father had died in the wilderness. When the daughters of Zelophehad approached Moses on this issue, Moses carried that same issue to the Lord. God told Moses that the request of the young ladies should be honored as it was correct. From that time forward, when a man died with only daughters as his heirs, the rights passed to the daughters. Because of that law, Matthew 1:1-17 traces the bloodline of Jesus through his legal bloodline, which culminates with Joseph, the man God chose as the head of household for His own Son, though the Holy Spirit, not Joseph, had impregnated Mary. In the Greek language, there was not a word for "son-in-law," so "son" always was used. In each of the lists, the term "begot" occurs frequently. Though last names did not occur at that time, Solomon could very easily have been Solomon Davidson, as the son of David.

Biblically speaking, names also carried a great deal of significance. Though we are most familiar with the name of Jesus, our Savior had the same name as Joshua in the Old Testament. *Yeshua*, in the Hebrew, was transliterated into "*Iesous*" in the Greek, and was once again transliterated into Latin, becoming "*Iesus*." Finally, it moved into our English, Jesus. Though our Savior certainly was not called by the name Jesus when walking around Jerusalem, He certainly knows when we call out that name! Yet all versions of the name carry the same meaning, "The Lord saves."

When reading the Bible, it always is a worthwhile step to research the meaning of the names involved in each story. Though it is only one example among many, the names in the Book of Ruth tell their own story. Ruth (beauty) humbly takes her place as a destitute stranger, dependent upon the grace of Boaz (the strong one). He redeems her and binds her to himself in marriage. When beauty is married to strength, the house is filled with worship (the meaning of their son Obed's name.)

Now when He said to them, "I am," they drew back and fell to the ground.
John 18:6 (NKJV)

[10] **that at the name of Jesus every knee should bow, of those in heaven, and of those on earth, and of those under the earth,** [11] **and *that* every tongue should confess that Jesus Christ *is* Lord, to the glory of God the Father.**
Philippians 2:10-11 (NKJV)

How special is the name of Jesus in our ears, or on our tongues? He is the God who saves, and His name causes kings to bow. When He is in our lives, we cannot be hurt by sticks, stones, names or anything else! There is just something about that name, Jesus!

He who overcomes, I will make him a pillar in the temple of My God, and he shall go out no more. I will write on him the name of My God and the name of the city of My God, the New Jerusalem, which comes down out of heaven from My God. And *I will write on him* My new name.
Revelation 3:12 (NKJV)

September 24: Harvest moon

Every 20 years or so, a full moon illuminates the first night of autumn. The phenomenon is called the Super Harvest Moon, and in 2010, it occurred just six hours after the fall equinox. An equinox is a time when the sun is directly above Earth's equator, making the length of day and night identical. Each year has a harvest moon, which is the full moon closest to the autumnal equinox. Typically, harvest moons seem larger when rising than all of the rest, for as they pass the horizon, the particles in the air give them more color, though all celestial bodies look reddish when low in the sky.

Harvest is a special time of year, though as we get away from agrarian ways, we lose sight of what that meant for our ancestors. It was the culmination of all the year's labor, and regardless of the amount of that labor put in by man, without God's hand granting ample sun and rain, the crops would not grow. Jesus gives us a great reminder of the Father's part in that process, along with His, and the application to each of us as believers.

[1] "I am the true vine, and My Father is the vinedresser. [2] Every branch in Me that does not bear fruit He takes away; and every *branch* that bears fruit He prunes, that it may bear more fruit.
John 15:1-2 (NKJV)

Any gardeners in our midst understand the need for pruning trees. In the Old Testament, the Jews were instructed concerning the usage of trees, especially in times of battle or war. Interestingly, fruit-bearing trees were not to be used in any aspect of making war, other than feeding the soldiers from the fruits or nuts growing on their branches. Yet any tree that did not bear fruit could be uprooted and used in the battle, whether for battering ram, spear, fire, or any other need.

[19] "When you besiege a city for a long time, while making war against it to take it, you shall not destroy its trees by wielding an ax against them; if you can eat of them, do not cut them down to use in the siege, for the tree of the field *is* man's *food*. [20] Only the trees which you know *are* not trees for food you may destroy and cut down, to build siegeworks against the city that makes war with you, until it is subdued. Deuteronomy 20:19-20 (NKJV)

God looks at us in the same manner. This world is a battleground, as Satan and his fallen, heavenly host continue to wage war on the children of God. Constantly, Christians are being attacked, whether by an assault on ethics and morals, or a more direct frontal assault of a personal nature. Yet if we are walking with the Lord, we will be fruit-bearing. That fruit can have an impact by offering food to a world starving for the ways of God. If we are not bearing fruit as believers, God will prune us, giving our branches His strength to grow and produce edible fruit. Unbelievers cannot bear fruit, and will be uprooted and burned in the battles.

**Therefore every tree which does not bear good fruit is cut down and thrown into the fire.
Matthew 3:11 (NKJV)**

God's ways are not our ways, nor are His thoughts our thoughts. Hence, many of us complain when the pruning takes place. Does a tree cry out when he loses a branch? If we are walking strongly with the Lord, even when faced with the most difficult challenges, we should remember that it is God who stretches us,

God who causes us to grow and God who prunes us! He wants us to have the sweetest fruit, giving strength and sustenance to many others!

[22] But the fruit of the Spirit is love, joy, peace, longsuffering, kindness, goodness, faithfulness, [23] gentleness, self-control. Against such there is no law.
Galatians 5:22-23 (NKJV)

[43] "For a good tree does not bear bad fruit, nor does a bad tree bear good fruit. [44] For every tree is known by its own fruit. For *men* do not gather figs from thorns, nor do they gather grapes from a bramble bush. [45] A good man out of the good treasure of his heart brings forth good; and an evil man out of the evil treasure of his heart brings forth evil. For out of the abundance of the heart his mouth speaks.
Luke 6:43-45 (NKJV)

September 25: Queen of the night

We often hear those who have been seeking a lost object say that it was in the last place they looked. That should be the case in every search, for what is the point in continuing to look once an item has been found? In the same regard, each inhabitant of our planet is seeking that missing piece to complete the puzzle. Once that piece has been discovered, and the puzzle is solved, what need is there to find another piece? Jesus is the final piece, who gives us peace, and He is the solution to every problem.

Some may believe that to be an oversimplification, as our finite minds continue to complicate our lives. Yet whether we trust Him or not, each problem that arises has an answer in Jesus. Sometimes, we have to leap a hurdle, and He is the spring in our step. Other times, we have to evade an enemy, when the Holy Spirit reminds us to run away from sin. Still, there are times to stand and fight, when victory comes against all odds, by His hand.

Just as the Lord utilized a lad with five, smooth stones to defeat the towering giant, Goliath, God demonstrates His power when we are outnumbered by the enemy. Israel entered a land flowing with milk and honey, yet it also was flowing with inhabitants. Though the Israelites were smaller in stature and in number, the Lord led them in battle, granting the land to His chosen people. While in control of the land many years later, King Hezekiah felt pressure from his own people to prepare a plan of defense. The Assyrians had conquered the northern tribes of Israel, and taken them into captivity. Though Hezekiah was a godly king, his first line of defense was to bribe the Assyrians:

13 And in the fourteenth year of King Hezekiah, Sennacherib king of Assyria came up against all the fortified cities of Judah and took them. 14 Then Hezekiah king of Judah sent to the king of Assyria at Lachish, saying, "I have done wrong; turn away from me; whatever you impose on me I will pay." And the king of Assyria assessed Hezekiah king of Judah three hundred talents of silver and thirty talents of gold. 15 So Hezekiah gave *him* all the silver that was found in the house of the LORD and in the treasuries of the king's house. 16 At that time Hezekiah stripped *the gold from* the doors of the temple of the LORD, and *from* the pillars which Hezekiah king of Judah had overlaid, and gave it to the king of Assyria.
2 Kings 18:13-16 (NKJV)

Instead of asking God for help, Hezekiah stripped gold from the doors of the temple, the Lord's house. Rather than solving the problem, that gold added fuel to the fire of the Assyrians, desiring all of the gold of Israel. Hezekiah's desire to protect his people added pressure to an already stressful situation. Next, he attempted an alliance with Egypt, thinking that if both nations combined armies, their numbers would rival that of the advancing Assyrian army. Though Hezekiah's motive was valiant, he made plans without consulting God. Isaiah the prophet spoke harshly to Israel:

1 "Woe to the rebellious children," says the LORD,

> "Who take counsel, but not of Me,
> And who devise plans, but not of My Spirit,
> That they may add sin to sin;
> ²Who walk to go down to Egypt,
> And have not asked My advice,
> To strengthen themselves in the strength of Pharaoh,
> And to trust in the shadow of Egypt!
> Isaiah 30:1-2 (NKJV)

Israel's position seemingly worsened, as the Assyrian army advanced and surrounded Jerusalem. Finally, Hezekiah handed the battle to the Lord, encouraging the people that God's hand held the power. With the citizens of God's great city preparing to die, the Lord sent a mighty angel to the enemy troops, killing 185,000 in the night, without help from any Israeli soldiers. While we sleep, the Lord protects us. If we are His, He desires for us to bring our problems to Him, and then wait for His perfect timing.

In Israel, there is a cactus called the Queen of the Night, which blooms only for a few nights in September each year. Its beautiful bloom opens widely around midnight, and then closes for the remainder of the year. Few people see its beauty, but even without being realized, its beauty is just as special. How many of our battles are won by the Lord while we sleep? How many times do our battles disappear, though we fail to acknowledge Him who wins the battles for us? When battles arise in the lives of His children, God frequently steps in to save us. After all, He is the God who saves! Yet sometimes our odds of success have to decrease before God gets involved. That points to His power, rather than the power of man.

We need to lay our concerns, problems and battles at the foot of the cross, and hand them over to Jesus. The next step is typically the most difficult one. Trust Him, and He will accomplish His will in His time. Though His timing usually is later than we would desire, nonetheless, it is perfectly in His will. He is incapable of making a mistake. Whether or not we see what He is accomplishing on our behalves, it is as beautiful as an unseen bloom in the midst of darkness.

⁷ "Be strong and courageous; do not be afraid nor dismayed before the king of Assyria, nor before all the multitude that *is* with him; for *there are* more with us than with him. ⁸ With him *is* an arm of flesh; but with us *is* the LORD our God, to help us and to fight our battles." And the people were strengthened by the words of Hezekiah king of Judah.
2 Chronicles 32:7-8 (NKJV)

September 26: *Yom Kippur*

In the Jewish faith, today is *Yom Kippur*, the Day of Atonement. Of all the Jewish feasts, this is the most solemn. Look at the Lord's description of the day:

²⁶ And the LORD spoke to Moses, saying: ²⁷ "Also the tenth *day* of this seventh month *shall be* the Day of Atonement. It shall be a holy convocation for you; you shall afflict your souls, and offer an offering made by fire to the LORD. ²⁸ And you shall do no work on that same day, for it *is* the Day of Atonement, to make atonement for you before the LORD your God. ²⁹ For any person who is not afflicted *in soul* on that same day shall be cut off from his people. ³⁰ And any person who does any work on that same day, that person I will destroy from among his people. ³¹ You shall do no manner of work; *it shall be* a statute forever throughout your generations in all your dwellings. ³² It *shall be* to you a sabbath of *solemn* rest, and you shall afflict your souls; on the ninth *day* of the month at evening, from evening to evening, you shall celebrate your sabbath."
Leviticus 23:26-32 (NKJV)

Atonement describes how humans can be reconciled to God. In Old Testament times, the atonement was accomplished through the blood sacrifice. It was the only day when the high priest could enter the Holy of Holies and sprinkle the blood of the atonement sacrifice on the altar in payment for the sins of the

Jews committed in ignorance that year (Hebrews 9:7). Additionally, the sacrifice covered the sins of the high priest. From A.D. 70 until today, in the Jewish tradition, prayer has replaced the sacrifice, as there is no temple to accomplish the ritual of sacrifice. In the Christian faith, on the other hand, we understand that the accomplishment of Jesus on the cross was sufficient to cover all of the sins of the world, past, present and future. Additionally, Jesus is the High Priest, and unlike the man in that role in Old Testament times, our High Priest is without sin.

Therefore, in all things He had to be made like *His* brethren, that He might be a merciful and faithful High Priest in things *pertaining* to God, to make propitiation for the sins of the people.
Hebrews 2:17 (NKJV)

The only time the word "atonement" is used in the New Testament, it is translated reconciliation, in the following verse:

And not only *that*, but we also rejoice in God through our Lord Jesus Christ, through whom we have now received the reconciliation.
Romans 5:11 (NKJV)

Reconciliation is a return to balance, or bringing two things together. In this case, it removes our separation from God due to our sin. By accepting the work done by Jesus, His blood covers our sin. Sadly, the Jews spend this day doing a mental balance sheet of the events in their lives in the previous year. They believe that if more good deeds (*mitzvahs*) are done than bad, it makes them good people, and they will continue to hold a place in the Lord's Book of Life. Yet we understand that one sin is enough to make us sinners, and even one sin is punishable by death through God's law. Additionally, all the good within us is Him, while all the bad comes from our flesh! Without the work of Jesus, we all would be lost.

As Christians, we are not required to observe the Jewish traditions of this day, yet it is a wonderful anniversary to honor God for the reconciliation He allowed His Son to accomplish on our behalves. We should solemnly reflect upon our sins of the previous year, but rejoice in the fact that we serve a risen Savior, who was punished willingly for those sins with the spilling of His own precious blood. Happy *Yom Kippur*!

Then you shall cause the trumpet of the Jubilee to sound on the tenth *day* of the seventh month; on the Day of Atonement you shall make the trumpet to sound throughout all your land.
Leviticus 25:9 (NKJV)

September 27: Who is the scapegoat?

Though many years have passed, one of my most vivid memories from childhood involved some fudge brownies that my father had purchased for a special occasion. He put them on top of the refrigerator for the next day, but when morning came, someone had eaten them. When questioned, my older sister told him that she had seen me do it. Her angelic face convinced my parents, though I insisted it was not me. In my opinion, a bad situation became worse as the punishment did not fit the crime. In addition to the physical pain of a spanking, I spent the next two weeks in my room, other than the time spent in school. My parents were not only punishing the crime of stealing the brownies, but the more serious crime of lying about it. Years later, my sister revealed to my mother that she had eaten the brownies and lied about me. It sure was difficult receiving the punishment for someone else's crime.

Today, the word "scapegoat" applies to a person who is made to bear the blame of others. In the Bible, we have an Old Testament story of the scapegoat, along with its New Testament revelation. In order to understand the concept, we need to be familiar with Leviticus 16:

⁶ "Aaron shall offer the bull as a sin offering, which *is* for himself, and make atonement for himself and for his house. ⁷ He shall take the two goats and present them before the LORD *at* the door of the tabernacle of meeting. ⁸ Then Aaron shall cast lots for the two goats: one lot for the LORD and the other lot for the scapegoat. ⁹ And Aaron shall bring the goat on which the LORD's lot fell, and offer it *as* a sin offering. ¹⁰ But the goat on which the lot fell to be the scapegoat shall be presented alive before the LORD, to make atonement upon it, *and* to let it go as the scapegoat into the wilderness.

¹¹ "And Aaron shall bring the bull of the sin offering, which is for himself, and make atonement for himself and for his house, and shall kill the bull as the sin offering which *is* for himself. ¹² Then he shall take a censer full of burning coals of fire from the altar before the LORD, with his hands full of sweet incense beaten fine, and bring *it* inside the veil. ¹³ And he shall put the incense on the fire before the LORD, that the cloud of incense may cover the mercy seat that *is* on the Testimony, lest he die. ¹⁴ He shall take some of the blood of the bull and sprinkle *it* with his finger on the mercy seat on the east *side;* and before the mercy seat he shall sprinkle some of the blood with his finger seven times.

¹⁵ "Then he shall kill the goat of the sin offering, which *is* for the people, bring its blood inside the veil, do with that blood as he did with the blood of the bull, and sprinkle it on the mercy seat and before the mercy seat. ¹⁶ So he shall make atonement for the Holy *Place,* because of the uncleanness of the children of Israel, and because of their transgressions, for all their sins; and so he shall do for the tabernacle of meeting which remains among them in the midst of their uncleanness. ¹⁷ There shall be no man in the tabernacle of meeting when he goes in to make atonement in the Holy *Place,* until he comes out, that he may make atonement for himself, for his household, and for all the assembly of Israel. ¹⁸ And he shall go out to the altar that *is* before the LORD, and make atonement for it, and shall take some of the blood of the bull and some of the blood of the goat, and put it on the horns of the altar all around. ¹⁹ Then he shall sprinkle some of the

blood on it with his finger seven times, cleanse it, and consecrate it from the uncleanness of the children of Israel. [20] "And when he has made an end of atoning for the Holy *Place,* the tabernacle of meeting, and the altar, he shall bring the live goat. [21] Aaron shall lay both his hands on the head of the live goat, confess over it all the iniquities of the children of Israel, and all their transgressions, concerning all their sins, putting them on the head of the goat, and shall send *it* away into the wilderness by the hand of a suitable man. [22] The goat shall bear on itself all their iniquities to an uninhabited land; and he shall release the goat in the wilderness.
Leviticus 16:6-22 (NKJV)

Who is the scapegoat? Different pastors seem to present this section in extremely different ways, as many call attention to Jesus being the sacrifice for sin, as His blood was spilled on Calvary for our sins. Additionally, as He was punished for our sins, and we "escaped," many believe that we are the scapegoats, yet we are misunderstanding that term based on the modern-day usage of the word. Instead, in the Hebrew, the scapegoat is *azazel,* which contains the root word of forgiveness; this is the goat of entire removal, though alive. By biblical definition, a scapegoat did not take the blame, but instead, took away the sin to a separated place. When the high priest placed his hands upon the scapegoat, he transferred all of the sins of the people onto that goat before it was sent into the wilderness. At that time, the scapegoat took away the sins of the people.

**The next day John saw Jesus coming toward him, and said, "Behold! The Lamb of God who takes away the sin of the world!
John 1:29 (NKJV)**

John the Baptist helped us to understand the role of Jesus in the sin removal of Leviticus. Jesus was the scapegoat, who took away the sins of the world, yet at the same time, He was the sacrificial Lamb of God, whose blood was spilled upon the altar! The sacrificial system of the Old Testament taught us about the importance of blood, for life is in the blood. In Hebrews, we are reminded of that process:

And according to the law almost all things are purified with blood, and without shedding of blood there is no remission.
Hebrews 9:22 (NKJV)

Additionally, on *Yom Kippur* there was a goat sacrificed upon the altar, to cover the sins of the people. This first goat had to die, unlike the second goat. In the modern-day definition, this was the scapegoat, as he received the punishment deserved by others. Yet this is the sin offering. That blood must be sprinkled on the mercy seat, and the word for mercy seat is the same one we use for propitiation, which is the satisfaction of God's wrath against sin. Notice that in Leviticus 16:17, the high priest made atonement for his own sins, as well as the sins of the people. The word used for atonement is the same word used in Genesis 6:14 when Noah "covered" the ark with pitch. While the blood sacrifice can **cover** our sins, it was not capable of **taking away** our sins. So as goats could not be resurrected, two were necessary to complete the tasks. Yet Jesus became both goats. His blood covered our sins when He died upon the cross, spilling His innocent blood for our redemption. Additionally, all of our sins were placed upon Him as our scapegoat, as He took away the sins of the world.

He also had another role in this process for us! Jesus is the High Priest doing the work of atonement, according to Hebrews:

where the forerunner has entered for us, *even* Jesus, having become High Priest forever according to the order of Melchizedek.
Hebrews 6:20 (NKJV)

Unlike the high priests of the Old Testament, Jesus will be High Priest forever! Additionally, He is without sin, so He does not need to offer sacrifice for His own sins. Lastly, because Jesus lived as a perfect man, He does not need to offer a yearly sacrifice. His death was sufficient to cover our sins once and for all, and additionally, was sufficient to take away our sins once and for all!

Matthew 25:31-36 tells us about the judgment of the sheep and goats that occurs after Jesus returns. Sheep are the believers, who will be separated to the right hand of the Lord, while the goats, whose sin has not been taken away, will be placed on the left hand of Jesus. The Lamb of God became a goat for us!

**For He made Him who knew no sin *to be* sin for us, that we might become the righteousness of God in Him.
2 Corinthians 5:21 (NKJV)**

Jesus did not just carry our sin. He became sin for us! If we are believers, God has nothing against us! Jesus propitiated not only believer's sins but the sins of the whole world. **Only believers are redeemed but the whole world is propitiated.** Did Christ die for the whole world? Yes, His death was **sufficient** to pay the price for every sin. But it is only **efficient** if we believe. "Redeemed" refers to believers. "Propitiation" refers to believers and unbelievers. The ceremony using these two goats is the root meaning of forgiveness in the New Testament. There is no reason to dig up our old sins. He has removed them! Rejoice, and quit dredging up old sin. If He can let it go, why is it we cannot?

**As far as the east is from the west,
So far has He removed our transgressions from us.
Psalm 103:12 (NKJV)**

September 28: The proving ground

A proving ground is a United States military installation to test weaponry. In the implementation stage, though theoretical scientists have strategized and discussed seemingly every aspect of the new weapon, thorough testing is necessary before using that weaponry. As technology has advanced, so has the killing power of those weapons. Ironically, in the name of technological advancement, humans could have developed the technology that will eventually lead to their destruction. During testing for the atomic bomb, the United States completed a portion at the Pacific Proving Grounds, a name describing various sites in the Marshall Islands, in the middle of the Pacific Ocean.

Along those lines, God has used the earth as a proving ground of His own design, though not for destructive power. Instead, He sent His Son to earth to perfect Him:

[10] For it was fitting for Him, for whom *are* all things and by whom *are* all things, in bringing many sons to glory, to make the captain of their salvation perfect through sufferings. [11] For both He who sanctifies and those who are being sanctified *are* all of one, for which reason He is not ashamed to call them brethren,
Hebrews 2:10-11 (NKJV)

Does that mean that Jesus was imperfect before coming to earth as a man? That is a fallacy in every way, shape and form. Instead, the perfection that was being completed was His life lived to perfection. Jesus dotted every "i" and crossed every "t" on His way to the cross. By living a perfect life, without sin, though being tested in every possible sin, Jesus demonstrated His love for God's creation, us. He was pushed, pulled, stretched, beaten, bruised, bloodied and betrayed, all to prove to us what He was willing to do for each citizen of the earth. When the military tests weaponry, its scientists have postulated what exactly will happen, yet there always are surprises. When God sent His Son to this proving ground, there were no surprises. It was not to "see what happened" with the idea of tweaking it all to work perfectly. Instead, He sent His Son to demonstrate that love to us, that we might believe and love Him back!

[8] though He was a Son, *yet* He learned obedience by the things which He suffered. [9] And having been perfected, He became the author of eternal salvation to all who obey Him,
Hebrews 5:8-9 (NKJV)

Though Jesus is equal with God, the Father, He willingly subjected Himself to act in the will of the Father. Was Jesus disobedient before coming to earth? No, He was perfect then, too. By turning away from every temptation, Jesus showed us the power of God. That power is immense, for any of us walking this earth cannot even imagine one day in complete righteousness! By accepting such a painful death, Jesus showed us the power of His love, for as God, He never would have been subjected to death, even the death of the cross. With false witnesses testifying against Him, and many who did not understand the reason for His life, Jesus endured the pain and humiliation of the cross to bear the burden of our sins. Amazingly, Isaiah reminds us that "it pleased the Lord to bruise Him." Though the Father's love for Jesus surpasses any love we can understand, God the Father was pleased by the event on that hilltop outside of the city of Jerusalem. For the death of Jesus on the cross opened the door of relationship for each of us willing to repent of our sins. At that moment of repentance, God removes the sin burden from each of our shoulders and places it upon the shoulders of His Son, on that day almost 2,000 years ago!

This earth is a proving ground for each of us, as well. Sometimes, we become more earthly-minded, though we are called to be heavenly-minded. Three score and 10 years might seem like a lengthy period of time, yet most people approaching the age of 70 cannot believe that the time passed so quickly. Our time spent on earth will not equate to a breath in the time we will spend in heaven! Yet we are here to prove our allegiance to God, who created us. Once we have made the decision to follow Jesus, the most important part of our work already has been achieved. Yet after that decision has been made, the remainder of our time spent here is to share that process with others walking in brokenness.

If God knows the outcome of each of our lives beforehand, why put us through it all? Just as He did with His only Son, the Father is offering proof to the world, that they might see Him through Jesus and through us as believers, as we should reflect Him.

[10] **that at the name of Jesus every knee should bow, of those in heaven, and of those on earth, and of those under the earth,** [11] **and** *that* **every tongue should confess that Jesus Christ** *is* **Lord, to the glory of God the Father.**
Philippians 2:10-11 (NKJV)

God's greatest desire is that all He created would know His love, yet many will not choose to follow Him. At Judgment Day, everyone will acknowledge His work, and His personal attempt at proving His love for each of us.

Are we willing to suffer in order to prove our faith, as Jesus did? Often, we complain when merely uncomfortable, yet it might be our joy in the midst of trial that speaks the loudest to our unbelieving friends and neighbors. If we truly love Jesus we should be willing to prove it!

[3] **Blessed** *be* **the God and Father of our Lord Jesus Christ, who has blessed us with every spiritual blessing in the heavenly** *places* **in Christ,** [4] **just as He chose us in Him before the foundation of the world, that we should be holy and without blame before Him in love,** [5] **having predestined us to adoption as sons by Jesus Christ to Himself, according to the good pleasure of His will,** [6] **to the praise of the glory of His grace, by which He made us accepted in the Beloved.**
Ephesians 1:3-6 (NKJV)

September 29: Soft-hearted

Walking through this world, each of us has that tendency of majoring in the minors, making mountains out of mole hills. When that occurs, our hearts can move from a soft and supple place to being as hard as kryptonite, which nothing can penetrate. In the "Wizard of Oz," the Wizard tells the Tin Man, who felt incomplete because he did not have a heart, "Hearts will never be made practical until they are unbreakable." On the contrary, a broken heart is the only way that we can find God.

Otherwise, that heart is not ready to hear what the Lord has to say.

God speaks to us all, yet not everyone is listening. In fact, all of us are not listening most of the time. Yet God loves us so much that He keeps talking to us, whether we are listening or not. What does He tell us? His words have to do with matters of the heart. God, the Creator of all, is telling us how much He loves us! Just like any relationship, after telling us that He loves us, what the Lord desires is that we will love Him in return.

[6] Oh come, let us worship and bow down;
Let us kneel before the LORD our Maker.
[7] For He *is* our God,
And we *are* the people of His pasture,
And the sheep of His hand.
Today, if you will hear His voice:
[8] "Do not harden your hearts, as in the rebellion,
As *in* the day of trial in the wilderness,
[9] When your fathers tested Me;
They tried Me, though they saw My work.
Psalm 95:6-9 (NKJV)

In the Psalm above, King David gives us an example of people who God spoke to, but did not hear His voice. The Jews took 40 years to make an 11-day journey, wandering through the wilderness because of their lack of listening to God. In this case, He spoke through actions, vanquishing their enemies in the Red Sea with a miracle that no one could have missed. He provided water for them to drink out of a flinty rock, and heard their voices crying out. They could see His presence constantly through a pillar of cloud by day and a pillar of fire by night, protecting them and guiding their way. Additionally, God provided daily food through manna, and they even complained about that! Yet it was not just His actions that spoke to the Jews. On Mount Horeb (Sinai), every Jew heard God's voice as He gave the Law. Yet that still was not enough for them.

After enduring their constant complaints, sinful behavior and lack of trust, God's long fuse had finally reached its end. When it was time to enter the Promised Land, Moses sent in a group of spies on a reconnaissance mission. Rather than returning with glowing reports of the beauty of the land that the Lord was giving them, or jumping for joy with the size and quantity of the provisions God had prepared for them, the spies were defeated in heart by the giant inhabitants. Only Joshua and Caleb were soft-hearted enough to understand God's words that He would fight their battles for them.

Just as Pharaoh's heart hardened when God performed miracles through the hands of Moses and Aaron, the Jews had allowed the cares of the world to place a wedge between their hearts and God. Still a God who saves, He disallowed the ability of anyone over the age of 20 to enter the Promised Land, other than Joshua and Caleb. All of the people who had started the journey in Egypt, apart from those two trusting souls, would die before crossing the Jordan River. Yet with the children below the age of accountability, who likely emulated their parents in those complaints, God completed His promise and carried the Jews into Israel.

God created each of us, and speaks to each of us. Yet He leaves it up to us whether or not we desire to listen. Those of us who follow Him tired of hearing the broken, enticing words of the world, speaking of self, success and strength. The world's words are lies, leading to death and destruction. Yet when goals are not achieved or happiness is non-existent when we arrive in that place that we thought would solve it all, our hearts get broken. It is then that Christians turn to God! If He has called out and we have not heeded His voice, He will keep speaking. But just like Pharaoh and the Jews in the wilderness, there is a point when He will stop reaching out to a cold, calloused, Kryptonite heart. If He cannot penetrate that heart, nothing can.

> "Have a strong mind and a soft heart." –Anthony J. D'Angelo

¹⁸ **And to whom did He swear that they would not enter His rest, but to those who did not obey?** ¹⁹ **So we see that they could not enter in because of unbelief.**
Hebrews 3:18-19 (NKJV)

Belief is a choice, but it is not "blind faith." God reveals Himself though words and deeds, that we would hear and see Him. If we have heard His voice or seen His hand, then we should follow Him! Every other path leads to destruction! Instead, find the narrow path that leads to God. There are few who find it. Yet the journey begins with a soft, broken heart!

¹² **Beware, brethren, lest there be in any of you an evil heart of unbelief in departing from the living God;** ¹³ **but exhort one another daily, while it is called** *"Today,"* **lest any of you be hardened through the deceitfulness of sin.**
Hebrews 3:12-13 (NKJV)

September 30: Four and the world

With the number three pointing directly to the trinity of Father, Son and Holy Spirit, the fourth number is what the Trinity added, when "in beginning, God created!" He created the world, and all that is in it. We can see that significance of four in the Bible, yet it is also apparent by looking at the world God created.

The earth *is* the LORD's, and all its fullness,
The world and those who dwell therein.
Psalm 24:1 (NKJV)

On the fourth day, God finished creating the world, while on the next two days He furnished it! This would be similar to building a house, which has to occur before filling it with curtains, furniture and people. We can see four throughout God's creation. There are four directions or regions: north, south, east and west. Similarly, there are four elements: earth, wind, fire and water. Additionally, there are four seasons: spring, summer, fall and winter. Most animals are four-legged. Mathematically, four is the first number that is not a prime, the first number that can be divided and the first square. Biblically, there are too many occurrences of four to mention in a devotional, but here are a few:

² **Daniel spoke, saying, "I saw in my vision by night, and behold, the four winds of heaven were stirring up the Great Sea. ³ And four great beasts came up from the sea, each different from the other.**
Daniel 7:2-3 (NKJV)

Noted preacher J. Vernon McGee said that, "The 'winds' speak of agitation, propaganda, public opinion, and disturbance. The 'sea' suggests the masses, the mob, and the peoples of the Gentiles." God granted Satan dominion over this earth for a time and in this dream, we can see what exists in Satan's world, strife and division. In this prophetic dream, the Lord gave Daniel a picture of all of the kingdoms of the world to come, including a more powerful version of the Roman Empire just before this world ends.

In references to heaven, the perfect number of seven applies. In Revelation, when speaking of Jesus, 10 million voices speak loudly together:

"Worthy is the Lamb who was slain
To receive power and riches and wisdom,
And strength and honor and glory and blessing!"
Revelation 5:12 (NKJV)

Notice seven different aspects of that praise: power, riches, wisdom, strength, honor, glory and blessing. Yet in the next verse of Revelation, when the earth creatures praise Him, it involves only four aspects: blessing, honor, glory and power.

And every creature which is in heaven and on the earth and under the earth and such as are in the sea, and all that are in them, I heard saying:
"Blessing and honor and glory and power
***Be* to Him who sits on the throne,**

And to the Lamb, forever and ever!"
Revelation 5:13 (NKJV)

Once again, four points to the world. When God pours out His wrath upon a sinful earth, the judgments of Revelation will begin with another four: the four horsemen of the apocalypse (Revelation 6). Additionally, there are many other fours throughout the Bible. Here are a few of those:

In the tabernacle, there are four rings of gold on the ark of the covenant, one on each corner (Exodus 25:12); there are four ornamental bowls on the lampstand (Exodus 25:33); there are four pillars in the gate of the court of the tabernacle (Exodus 27:16); when Nehemiah is rebuilding the wall surrounding Jerusalem, the enemies of Israel send him four messages concerning the wall, and Nehemiah responds four times that he will not meet with them, which would cause the work to cease (Nehemiah 6:3-4); and finally, there are four, strange beasts mentioned in both Ezekiel 1:5 and Revelation 4:5.

By adding one, pointing to God, to the number four, pointing to the world, we see the number for grace. By taking one away from the number of the world, all that remains is three, significant of the Trinity! If the significance of all these numbers shows us anything it is that our God is a God or order. He speaks to us through the Holy Spirit living inside of us; He speaks to us through the words of the Bible; and He even speaks to us through all of creation. How can people not believe in Him, or more importantly, how can people not trust in Him? He is so big that He breathed all that we can see and all that we cannot see into being. By looking at the immensity of that creation in the stars, planets and galaxies, we see His enormous power. Yet by looking through a microscope, we can see the attention to detail. Just by studying a strand of DNA boggles the minds of the earth's greatest scientists. When we see the world, we should know above all else that He is above all else. He is worthy of all praise in power, riches, wisdom, strength, honor, glory and blessing!

¹⁸ For the wrath of God is revealed from heaven against all ungodliness and unrighteousness of men, who suppress the truth in unrighteousness, ¹⁹ because what may be known of God is manifest in them, for God has shown *it* to them. ²⁰ For since the creation of the world His invisible *attributes* are clearly seen, being understood by the things that are made, *even* His eternal power and Godhead, so that they are without excuse, ²¹ because, although they knew God, they did not glorify *Him* as God, nor were thankful, but became futile in their thoughts, and their foolish hearts were darkened. ²² Professing to be wise, they became fools,
Romans 1:18-22 (NKJV)

October 1: *Sukkot*, the Feast of Tabernacles

Last night at sundown began the Feast of Tabernacles, one of the seven feasts of Moses in the Jewish faith. Passover (*Pesach*), Unleavened Bread (*Matzos*) and First fruits *(Bikkurim)* occur in the spring, in the month of *Nisan*. Forty days later, Pentecost (*Shavuot*) occurs. Then in the fall, there are three more feasts all in the month of *Tishri*, Trumpets (*Rosh Hashanah*), the Day of Atonement (*Yom Kippur*) and Tabernacles (*Sukkot*). Here is a biblical description of the eight-day fall feast, also called Booths:

³⁹ 'Also on the fifteenth day of the seventh month, when you have gathered in the fruit of the land, you shall keep the feast of the LORD *for* seven days; on the first day *there shall be* a sabbath-*rest*, and on the eighth day a sabbath-*rest*. ⁴⁰ And you shall take for yourselves on the first day the fruit of beautiful trees, branches of palm trees, the boughs of leafy trees, and willows of the brook; and you shall rejoice before the LORD your God for seven days. ⁴¹ You shall keep it as a feast to the LORD for seven days in the year. *It shall be* a statute forever in your generations. You shall celebrate it in the seventh month. ⁴² You shall dwell in booths for seven days. All who are native Israelites shall dwell in booths, ⁴³ that your generations may know that I made the children of Israel dwell in booths when I brought them out of the land of Egypt: I *am* the LORD your God.' "

⁴⁴ So Moses declared to the children of Israel the feasts of the LORD.
Leviticus 23:39-44 (NKJV)

This feast is reminiscent of the Jews wandering in the wilderness for 40 years. Jews construct shelters in their backyards, though in the high-rise condominiums and apartments of Jerusalem and New York City, it is easy to spot *sukkahs* (booths) on the small patios, as well. Modern-day technology has changed this tradition, as many Jews order a pre-made *sukkah* to erect, rather than needing the skills of basic carpentry. Yet rabbis have requirements for a kosher *sukkah*, especially in regard to the roofing (*s'chach*). The branches must be earth-grown, from the plant kingdom, and unattached to the ground. For example, branches still attached to a tree would not suffice. One of the requirements is to ensure that there is space between the branches placed on top of the shelter, to reveal the stars in the sky, allowing wind to blow through and remind the Jews of the wilderness.

Lastly, there are four species in the procession, which are often used in the roofing. Many believe these species point to the four types of Jews: Citrus (*etrog*), which has a good fragrance and taste, represents a person with both wisdom and good deeds. Myrtle (*hadassim*) has a good fragrance, but cannot be eaten, representing a person with good deeds, but who lacks wisdom. Palm (*lulav*) is edible, but has no scent, representing a person with wisdom but without good deeds. Lastly, willow (*aravah*) has neither taste nor smell, thus representing the person who lacks both good deeds and wisdom. This sounds similar to the soils of Matthew 13!

Sukkot was one of three compulsory, yearly pilgrimages to Jerusalem for all able-bodied men. Any booth shorter than 31 inches would not allow people to sit comfortably, so would not meet the requirements, while a structure larger than 31 feet tall would make it too much of a permanent structure, as it needs to be temporary. Interestingly, Peter offered to build booths for Jesus, Moses and Elijah on the Mount of Transfiguration!

²⁸ Now it came to pass, about eight days after these sayings, that He took Peter, John, and James and went up on the mountain to pray. ²⁹ As He prayed, the appearance of His face was altered, and His robe *became* white *and* glistening. ³⁰ And behold, two men talked with Him, who were Moses and Elijah, ³¹ who appeared in glory and spoke of His decease which He was about to accomplish at Jerusalem. ³² But Peter and those with him were heavy with sleep; and when they were fully awake, they saw His glory and the two men who stood with Him. ³³ Then it happened, as they were parting from Him, *that* Peter said to Jesus, "Master, it is good for us to be here; and let us make three tabernacles: one for You, one for Moses, and one for Elijah"—not knowing what he said.
³⁴ While he was saying this, a cloud came and overshadowed them; and they were fearful as they entered the cloud. ³⁵ And a voice came out of the cloud, saying, "This is My beloved Son. Hear Him!" ³⁶ When the voice had ceased, Jesus was found alone. But they kept quiet, and told no one in those days any of the things they had seen.
Luke 9:28-36 (NKJV)

As Christians, we are not required to keep the Jewish feasts, though this sounds like a fun one! Sleeping under the stars can be so peaceful, though rain is much more of a concern for the Jews around the world than it was for those in the desert. Most Bible scholars believe that the Jewish feast days are incredibly significant, especially in symbolic fulfillment, pointing out that the three spring feasts were fulfilled in the first coming of Jesus, the middle feast was fulfilled in the beginning of the church, and the three fall feasts will be fulfilled in the second coming of Jesus.

¹⁶ So let no one judge you in food or in drink, or regarding a festival or a new moon or sabbaths, ¹⁷ which are a shadow of things to come, but the substance is of Christ.
Colossians 2:16-17 (NKJV)

Some Bible scholars believe the Feast of Tabernacles points to the rapture, the return of Jesus for His church, as those celebrating this feast leave their temporary dwellings for permanent ones on the 8th day, but most scholars believe that the Feast of Trumpets points more accurately to the rapture, while the Feast of Tabernacles points to the return of Jesus at the end of the Great Tribulation for all remaining believers. At that time, every remaining person on the earth will have a relationship with the Lord. John taught us:

And the Word became flesh and dwelt among us, and we beheld His glory, the glory as of the only begotten of the Father, full of grace and truth.
John 1:14 (NKJV)

The word used for "flesh" in the passage above is tabernacle. The Word became flesh and was "tabernacled" among us is what the verse says more specifically. Jesus lives with us. Jesus dwells inside of us, as believers. That is the most exciting part of the Feast of Tabernacles. While the Jews commemorate a time when the Lord led them as a pillar of cloud by day and a pillar of fire by night, as Christians, this is a festive week to remember that Jesus not only lives, but He lives inside each of us! What trials can conquer us with God dwelling in us, leading our defense? Jesus was crucified on the Feast of Passover, buried on the Feast of Unleavened Bread and was resurrected on the Feast of First Fruits! The Holy Spirit came to empower us and remain with us on the Feast of Pentecost. What will happen on the three fall feast days? No wonder many Christians are filled with anticipation this time of year!

For whatever things were written before were written for our learning, that we through the patience and comfort of the Scriptures might have hope.
Romans 15:4 (NKJV)

October 2: Shadows

One of the most common dog names in the United States is Shadow, and we all know how many dogs love to follow right behind their masters! If we only would follow Jesus that closely! On sunny days, it is impossible to get away from our shadows.

Shadows offer coolness on a hot day, and can lengthen or shorten depending upon the location of the sun in the sky. Even little men can cast long shadows, and with that in mind, imagine the size of God's shadow, when the train of His robe filled the temple with glory! There are four verses in Psalms about us dwelling in the shadow of His wings.

Be merciful to me, O God, be merciful to me!
For my soul trusts in You;
And in the shadow of Your wings I will make my refuge,
Until *these* calamities have passed by.
Psalm 57:1 (NKJV)

What an amazing picture that gives us of God's covering upon each believer! Instead of us riding upon His wings from place to place, God desires for us to walk through the battleground upon the earth. Yet in that walk, we are sheltered by His mighty wings. Without nearness to God, we would not be in His shadow. When calamities are upon us, God has apportioned a safe haven, shielding us from the fiery darts of the evil one.

[37] **"O Jerusalem, Jerusalem, the one who kills the prophets and stones those who are sent to her! How often I wanted to gather your children together, as a hen gathers her chicks under *her* wings, but you were not willing!** [38] **See! Your house is left to you desolate;** [39] **for I say to you, you shall see Me no more till you say, *'Blessed* is *He who comes in the name of the* LORD*!'* "**
Matthew 23:37-39 (NKJV)

Jesus spoke these words from the Mount of Olives, the site of His departure to heaven as well as the site of His future return to earth. We serve a Lord who desires to protect us, but without our willingness to follow Him, we walk unprotected through a world that chews us up and spits us out. Yet, as believers, not even death can harm us.

Yea, though I walk through the valley of the shadow of death,
I will fear no evil;
For You *are* **with me;**
Your rod and Your staff, they comfort me.
Psalm 23:4 (NKJV)

We are not walking through a valley of death, but only a shadow of death. That shadow offers no more than a silhouette, which has no power to harm us! When facing the sun, shadows are behind us, and when facing the Son, the shadows of our burdens are behind us. We are going to a place where there will be no darkness. As God is everywhere, and God is the Light of the world, our heavenly home will offer no shadows!

[23] **The city had no need of the sun or of the moon to shine in it, for the glory of God illuminated it. The Lamb** *is* **its light.** [24] **And the nations of those who are saved shall walk in its light, and the kings of the earth bring their glory and honor into it.** [25] **Its gates shall not be shut at all by day (there shall be no night there).**
Revelation 21:23-25 (NKJV)

We dwell in the shadow of the Lord's wings, where He offers His protection. Yet in our future home, there will be no need of protection. With open gates and a city without walls, there will no longer be an enemy desiring to capture us, as once the Lord has captured our hearts, we are safely in His grasp for all of eternity! Though the cares of the world can give us moments of fear, that fear is not of the Lord, as He guides us, protects us and loves us! Fear not! There is not a shadow that can harm us and that is the closest to darkness we ever can come once we belong to the King of kings!

[1] **He who dwells in the secret place of the Most High
Shall abide under the shadow of the Almighty.
[2] I will say of the LORD,** *"He is* **my refuge and my fortress;
My God, in Him I will trust."
Psalm 91:1-2 (NKJV)**

October 3: Preserve me, Lord!

Jellies and jams sure do taste great on toast or biscuits. With those jellies made from fruit juices, and jams and preserves made from actual fruit, most of our grandmothers had cupboards filled with their own canned goods. It seems simple to can with pectin, sugar or honey used as a gelling agent, to prepare the fruit while canning for long-term storage.

Certainly, some fruit preserves are better than others, and typically, if the canning process is done correctly, it depends on the taste of the fruit before canning. Basically, the sweeter the fruit, the better it will continue to taste, even when preserved. What a wonderful analogy that is to believers, who are given the fruits of love, joy, peace, longsuffering, kindness, goodness, faithfulness, gentleness and self-control, according to Galatians 5:22. Unlike the gifts of the Spirit, in which the Lord gives us at least one of the gifts, but may give more depending on circumstance, prayer or His desire, all believers will exhibit all of the fruits of the Spirit at least some of the time. What does He do with that sweet-tasting fruit? Well, the same as our grandmothers did. He preserves it!

**So Jacob called the name of the place Peniel: "For I have seen God face to face, and my life is preserved."
Genesis 32:30 (NKJV)**

When studying the Bible, the "Rule of First Mention" can be applied most of the time. The way that a word is used in its first appearance in the Bible typically will be the way it is used throughout. In the verse above, we can see that "preserved" in its first mention applies to the preservation of a believer's life. As every man eventually will experience physical death, God's preservation certainly applies to our spiritual lives. Notice the difference between the first death of a physical nature and the second death of a spiritual nature in the following verses:

"He who has an ear, let him hear what the Spirit says to the churches. He who overcomes shall not be hurt by the second death." '
Revelation 2:11 (NKJV)

But the cowardly, unbelieving, abominable, murderers, sexually immoral, sorcerers, idolaters, and all liars shall have their part in the lake which burns with fire and brimstone, which is the second death."
Revelation 21:8 (NKJV)

What event must take place for that spiritual life to occur? According to Genesis 32:30 quoted above, that happened once Jacob had seen God's face! Once again, do not get caught up in the physical realm, when God operates in the spiritual realm. Though many men saw the face of Jesus, no one has seen the face of the Father, physically. Yet God reveals Himself to man spiritually. Jesus told His disciples that we can know the Father by knowing the Son. Once we have seen the Father, we never will be the same, but without Jesus introducing us, we cannot see the Lord's face:

All things have been delivered to Me by My Father, and no one knows the Son except the Father. Nor does anyone know the Father except the Son, and *the one* to whom the Son wills to reveal *Him.*
Matthew 11:27 (NKJV)

We are preserved from the wiles of the demonic host, as God will not allow anything or anyone to pry us out of His loving hands. Additionally, we are preserved for eternity, when we will share the fruits God has given us with all other believers!

²³ Now may the God of peace Himself sanctify you completely; and may your whole spirit, soul, and body be preserved blameless at the coming of our Lord Jesus Christ.
²⁴ He who calls you *is* faithful, who also will do *it.*
1 Thessalonians 5:23-24 (NKJV)

We cannot be blameless without God's cleansing, for each believer is deserving of the same spiritual death that unbelievers will receive. Yet by God's mercy and grace, we have been given eternal life through Him. That gift should give each believer a better perspective when trials seem to darken our paths. Does it really matter, if we are His, knowing that He only allows those trials for us to draw closer to Him? Nothing can harm us when we have been preserved by the Lord! Walk in His power, even in the midst of great difficulty!

¹ **Jude, a bondservant of Jesus Christ, and brother of James, To those who are called, sanctified by God the Father, and preserved in Jesus Christ:**
² **Mercy, peace, and love be multiplied to you.**
Jude 1-2 (NKJV)

October 4: Works!

As we age, it is interesting what minutiae seem to fill our brains, with childhood memories surprisingly being the most vivid. Personally, those memories are the family trips to see different Walt Disney movies. Returning from the theater, Dad would sing the songs with us. "Whistle While You Work" from "Snow White and the Seven Dwarfs" was a favorite. Work is the event that fills the majority of each day, and the majority of our lives. Though there certainly are times when we become weary in our work, that work should be a labor of love.

The dictionary is the only place where success comes before work, yet that success is relative. Unfortunately, most of us place too high of a priority on financial gain. Instead, we should look at our jobs as opportunities to let our lights shine for the Lord, and measure our success accordingly. God places each of us right where He wants us to be. Though we tend to complain about work, we should be tireless workers for God's kingdom, regardless of pay scale, location or difficulty.

> Pray like everything depended on God. Work like everything depended on you." --Saint Augustine

Yet we understand and acknowledge that our works have nothing to do with our salvation. When Jesus died on the cross, He said, "It is finished," reminding us that He accomplished all the work on our behalves to save us. Instead, our work as believers is to glorify God. As Christians, that work should include helping believers and unbelievers. While God desires to use us in the spread of the gospel, we also can glorify Him by edifying other members of the body of Christ. The Greek word for "edify" comes from the root *oikos*, meaning "to build." Just as in construction, building is a process that begins with a strong foundation. Not until that foundation is laid can a building begin to take shape. Jesus is our firm foundation, and He desires for us to encourage, teach and love fellow believers through His gift of ministry and our edification.

[10] For God *is* not unjust to forget your work and labor of love which you have shown toward His name, *in that* you have ministered to the saints, and do minister. [11] And we desire that each one of you show the same diligence to the full assurance of hope until the end, [12] that you do not become sluggish, but imitate those who through faith and patience inherit the promises.
Hebrews 6:10-12 (NKJV)

Any work that we accomplish on God's behalf should not be for reward, or even a pat on the back. There is no greater joy than operating in the gift(s) that God has given us. Yet as we can see from the verse above, God remembers our work. Rather than desiring earthly accolades, we should revel in the fact that our work brings pleasure to God. Our focus never should stray from the work that Jesus accomplished on the cross, which gave each of us eternal life. His job involved an inordinate amount of pain and discomfort, culminating in death. As Christians, there should be no job below our station or too uncomfortable. It is time to roll up our shirt sleeves, get our hands dirty and serve others, diligently. And along the way, be ready for God to perform miracles in the lives around us!

remembering without ceasing your work of faith, labor of love, and patience of hope in our Lord Jesus Christ in the sight of our God and Father,
1 Thessalonians 1:3 (NKJV)

October 5: "But God..."

Often in our Christian walks, we seem surrounded by the enemy. With odds insurmountably stacked against us, our chances of survival seem to increase based upon the fact that escape points to God's hand rather than our own. We are surely in trouble, but God...

"But God!" There are few, two-word phrases that offer such power. No matter what the world demonstrates, God's hand can change it all in a second. Ever since the covering angel Lucifer rebelled against God and fell from heaven with one-third of the heavenly host of angels, he has been battling against God on this earth. Our mighty Lord allows that battle for His own purposes, yet Satan's pride makes him think that he has a chance at victory against the God who created him.

[26] **"Men *and* brethren, sons of the family of Abraham, and those among you who fear God, to you the word of this salvation has been sent.** [27] **For those who dwell in Jerusalem, and their rulers, because they did not know Him, nor even the voices of the Prophets which are read every Sabbath, have fulfilled *them* in condemning *Him*.** [28] **And though they found no cause for death *in Him*, they asked Pilate that He should be put to death.** [29] **Now when they had fulfilled all that**

was written concerning Him, they took *Him* down from the tree and laid *Him* in a tomb. [30] **But God** raised Him from the dead.
Acts 13:26-30 (NKJV)

God had a plan for salvation before the foundation of the world, and that plan included the life, death and resurrection of His Son on the cross. When Jesus died, Satan and his demons certainly began to celebrate, and that celebration continued for three days. **But God** resurrected Jesus from death, opening the door for our relationships with Him. God turned Satan's greatest victory into his greatest defeat in that moment! In 45 different verses in the New King James Version, and 47 verses in the King James Version, the phrase, "But God," is included. Throughout the Bible, God takes defeat and turns it into victory in the lives of believers. Joseph's brothers sold him into slavery, but God elevated Joseph to be the second most powerful man in Egypt, and then used Joseph to supply food for God's chosen people in the midst of drought:

**But as for you, you meant evil against me; but God meant it for good, in order to bring it about as *it is* this day, to save many people alive.
Genesis 50:20 (NKJV)**

Through the writings of Paul, God reminds us that we walk by faith, not by sight (1 Corinthians 5:7). In a nutshell, when we are trusting in God, it does not matter how strongly the odds are stacked in favor of the enemy. It does not matter if we look outside of our windows and see a destructive storm of immense proportions. It does not matter if an attacking army has us in its sights. God is capable to deliver us from anything. Battles, diseases and any other obstacles are nothing in His path, yet He may choose to deliver us by taking us home. Additionally, He might desire for us to endure those trials to draw us closer to Him in the process. We can do nothing without Him! But God? With Him, all things are possible!

My flesh and my heart fail;

But God *is* the strength of my heart and my portion forever.
Psalm 73:26 (NKJV)

No temptation has overtaken you except such as is common to man; but God *is* faithful, who will not allow you to be tempted beyond what you are able, but with the temptation will also make the way of escape, that you may be able to bear *it.*
1 Corinthians 10:13 (NKJV)

October 6: Goal!

In hockey, one of the greatest achievements is a hat trick, one player scoring three goals in the same game. Goals are not the only achievements recorded for a player, as "assists" is another important category. Hockey is such a fast-moving sport that two assists can be recorded for one goal, with the assist being a pass of the puck that leads directly to that goal. For Christians, God always gets the goals, but we can get assists through prayer. Unlike hockey, there is no limit on the number of play-ers (or pray-ers) getting assists in God's book!

What or who is at the top of our prayer lists? Prayer is such an untapped source among believers, involving us in the processes of God! Even though it is obvious that Paul was a powerful preacher, precious pastor and talented theologian, if we read between the lines, it is also obvious that he was a devoted man of prayer. When reading through the epistles, there is constant mention of people on Paul's prayer list. Paul understood that anyone in his life had been divinely placed there, so Paul encouraged them, yet also asked God for His guidance and protection in their lives.

One of the best examples of prayer in the Bible is commonly called the Lord's Prayer, in which Jesus gives His disciples a lesson in how to pray. Located in both Matthew 6:9-13 and Luke 11:2-4, Jesus shows us what our prayers should include:

[9] **In this manner, therefore, pray:**

Our Father in heaven,
Hallowed be Your name.
¹⁰ Your kingdom come.
Your will be done
On earth as *it is* **in heaven.**
¹¹ Give us this day our daily bread.
¹²And forgive us our debts,
As we forgive our debtors.
¹³ And do not lead us into temptation,
But deliver us from the evil one.
For Yours is the kingdom and the power and the glory forever. Amen.
Matthew 6:9-13 (NKJV)

The prayer begins with an acknowledgment of God and praise to Him. Notice that the prayer continues by asking for the Lord's will to be done, and proceeds with a request for Satan's dominion over this broken earth to come to an end, with the Lord's kingdom to come in its place. Next, Jesus teaches us to ask for the Lord to feed us. Daily bread can be enough physical food to survive, yet the spiritual food of God's Word is imperative to our healthy growth as Christians! Additionally, we should ask for the Lord's forgiveness, while acknowledging that God also requires us to forgive others who have sinned against us. We also should ask for God's protection, keeping us from temptation. The prayer finishes with another acknowledgment of our God; He rules over us, has all power and deserves every bit of the glory, eternally. "So be it," is the meaning of "amen," the way we end our prayers.

That prayer does not remotely resemble the prayer of the typical believer, who instead of concentrating on the needs of others, uses prayer in the same way that a greedy child writes his Christmas wish list for Santa Claus. "I want this and this and this and this!" Though there is nothing wrong with praying for our own needs, God already has promised that He will supply every need! Obviously, the distance between our needs and our perceived needs can be as wide as the Grand Canyon! Why was each and every prayer of Jesus answered immediately? Jesus always prayed in the will of the Father!

There is one God manifested in three persons, the Father, Son and Holy Spirit. All three persons are equal, but have different roles. Jesus always submits to the will of the Father. Consequently, He did not need the heart change that we do when praying. That is the greatest aspect of prayer in the life of a believer, bringing our hearts in line with God's heart.

Delight yourself also in the LORD,
And He shall give you the desires of your heart.
Psalm 37:4 (NKJV)

In this conditional statement, to delight ourselves in the Lord refers to our love relationship with Him. What is the greatest desire our hearts would have if our relationship with Jesus was paramount in our lives? To draw even closer to Him! He loves us so much that He prays for our needs before we even are aware that they are needs!

Who *is* he who condemns? *It is* Christ who died, and furthermore is also risen, who is even at the right hand of God, who also makes intercession for us.
Romans 8:34 (NKJV)

Knowing that God supplies our needs, our greatest prayers as believers are for our friends and families who do not know the Lord! Many of us are indebted to other believers, who prayed for us when we had no knowledge of God or relationship with Him. Additionally, when our fellow believers are under attack, God desires to hear from us. That demonstrates our love for His saints, and pleases God! Lastly, when we are asking for God's will to be done, we should pray with faith, for we serve a God who listens, cares and answers!

[16] **Confess *your* trespasses to one another, and pray for one another, that you may be healed. The effective, fervent prayer of a righteous man avails much.** [17] **Elijah was a man**

with a nature like ours, and he prayed earnestly that it would not rain; and it did not rain on the land for three years and six months. [18] And he prayed again, and the heaven gave rain, and the earth produced its fruit.
James 5:16-18 (NKJV)

October 7: Knowledge of Him

From 1966 until 1974, The Newlywed Game appeared on ABC television, with emcee Bob Eubanks asking a variety of leading questions to four young couples, to see how well they knew each other. In any relationship, the time spent early on can be the sweetest, before little habits like forgetting to replace the toothpaste cap or leaving the toilet seat in the wrong position can begin to grate on nerves. When the honeymoon ends and the drudgery of everyday life begins to take effect, how badly does a couple desire to continue growing closer together?

As Christians, we are a part of the most important love relationship, with our Savior, Jesus. Do we know more about Him than we did a year ago? That is what it is all about. Even Christians who have walked with Jesus for decades should continue to grow in His ways and in His Word!

[17] that the God of our Lord Jesus Christ, the Father of glory, may give to you the spirit of wisdom and revelation in the knowledge of Him, [18] the eyes of your understanding being enlightened; that you may know what is the hope of His calling, what are the riches of the glory of His inheritance in the saints,
Ephesians 1:17-18 (NKJV)

If we are Christians, Jesus has revealed Himself to us. The Greek word for revelation is *apocalypso*, meaning "unveiling," where we get our word apocalypse. The word "enlightened" in the verse above does not refer to the flip of a light switch, giving us all absolute knowledge of God. Instead, it is the removal of the veil covering our spiritual eyes, opening the door for us to see God. Instead of opening our intellect, He opens the eyes of our hearts. That is an introduction, but seeing God is not the same as knowing God. Knowledge of Him takes time, energy and effort.

but grow in the grace and knowledge of our Lord and Savior Jesus Christ.
1 Peter 3:18 (NKJV)

God continues to reveal Himself to us through the world He breathed into existence and all of His creation, nature. Each believer is also a part of nature, and sometimes, God reveals Himself through His people, Christians. God has revealed Himself to man through His audible voice at times, and additionally, through angels, dreams and visions. Additionally, God can reveal Himself to us through our consciences, inner voices distinguishing between right and wrong. Surely, He also reveals Himself through miracles, and the size of those miracles can offer the believer insight into the depth of God's contact into our lives. While those without spiritual vision chalk many events up to coincidence, believers in the omnipotent God realize that He works everything according to His intricately-woven plan. Nothing occurs accidentally!

Certainly, God revealed Himself to us by sending His Son to live on this earth. That was the culmination of His revelation, as it all points to Jesus! Without Him, we would have no access to relationship with God. Additionally, God has revealed Himself to us through the Holy Spirit, who lives inside every believer, pointing us to the Messiah. Finally, God has revealed Himself to us through His Word, telling us all that we need to know about Him.

Reading the Bible should be a passion for each believer, as it is God's love letter to His creation. Each time we read the Bible, it deepens our understanding of who God is and what He accomplished on our behalves! We should not get caught in the trap of deciding who God is before reading the Bible, for He wants to tell us about His actions and attributes! Look for Jesus on every page of the Bible, whether Old or New Testament. His name might not be apparent, but Jesus is there, even if concealed.

[1] God, who at various times and in various ways spoke in time past to the fathers by the prophets, [2] has in these last days spoken to us by *His* Son, whom He has appointed heir of all things, through whom also He made the worlds;
Hebrews 1:1-2 (NKJV)

It is easy to get caught up in the trappings of this world. There is so much to keep us occupied, and time seems to slip by so quickly. Yet God placed each of us here for a purpose. The greatest priority is to find that personal relationship with Him who created us. Next on that list is the responsibility of teaching our own families about God, which includes His Laws, attributes and words. Additionally, our Christian love can affect everyone whom God places in our paths. As we spend more waking hours in our jobs than anywhere else, that could be our most important ministry. We are holy because He is holy, and that word means "set apart." Do others sense that there is something different about us? Can they see the joy of our salvation, the peace that passes understanding and the hope of an eternity to spend with our Savior?

Emphasize drawing closer to God every single day! There is nothing more important! God is so big that He created all that we can see and all that we cannot see, yet He loves us so much that He wants to have a personal relationship! "Draw me close to You! Never let me go!"

[18] For on the one hand there is an annulling of the former commandment because of its weakness and unprofitableness, [19] for the law made nothing perfect; on the other hand, *there is the* bringing in of a better hope, through which we draw near to God.
Hebrews 7:18-19 (NKJV)

October 8: Set apart!

Noted 18th-century American pastor George Whitefield said, "It is an undoubted truth that every doctrine that comes from God, leads to God; and that which doth not tend to promote holiness is not of God." Holiness is not an action, but a way of life; not a moment, but a progression; not a musical note, but a series of symphonies. The word "holy" means to be set apart, separated. As Christians, we walk that fine line of being in the world, but not of the world. Sadly, when we look around today, we see that the church resembles the world more than the world resembles the church. Yet God has not called us to fit in.

"Holier than thou" may be the perception that the world has of the attitudes of Christians, but without Jesus, Swiss cheese is more holy than we are! Holiness is separation from evil, and in that sense, we understand that God is the only one without sin, without evil. Yet He has called us to be holy!

For I *am* the LORD who brings you up out of the land of Egypt, to be your God. You shall therefore be holy, for I *am* holy.
Leviticus 11:45 (NKJV)

Without the death and resurrection of Jesus, we have no chance at holiness. Every Christian continues to sin, regardless of desiring perfection. Yet through our redemption, God looks upon our lives and instead of seeing our sin, sees the perfect life of His Son in our places. He was punished for our transgressions instead of us. Yet God desires for us to demonstrate our love for Him by desiring to resemble Him, rather than resembling the world. We cannot set ourselves apart, but Christ Himself sets us apart!

> "Perfect holiness is the aim of the saints on earth, and it is the reward of the saints in heaven." –Joseph Caryl

In Paul's letter to Titus, he gives us a reminder of some of the ways that we can be separated from the world:

[1] Remind them to be subject to rulers and authorities, to obey, to be ready for every good work, [2] to speak evil of no one, to be peaceable, gentle, showing all humility to all men. [3] For we ourselves were also once foolish, disobedient, deceived, serving various lusts and pleasures, living in malice and envy, hateful and hating one another. [4] But when the kindness and the love of God our Savior toward man appeared, [5] not by works of righteousness which we have done, but according to His mercy He saved us, through the washing of regeneration and renewing of the Holy Spirit, [6] whom He poured out on us abundantly through Jesus Christ our Savior, [7] that having been justified by His grace we should become heirs according to the hope of eternal life. [8] This is a faithful saying, and these things I want you to affirm constantly, that those who have believed in God should be careful to maintain good works. These things are good and profitable to men.
Titus 3:1-8 (NKJV)

We are to glorify the Lord in body and in spirit. That is accomplished by becoming a living sacrifice to Him. While God gives us new hearts as believers, we retain the old brains, filled with memories of sinful pasts. In that transformation from worldliness to holiness, we need to separate ourselves from the hurdles that caused us to stumble. While one drink might not cause drunkenness, that small taste could lead an alcoholic on a binge of immense proportions. Paul reminds us that the gray areas, not regarded as sin, also should be left behind if there is any potential in causing someone else to stumble.

All things are lawful for me, but all things are not helpful. All things are lawful for me, but I will not be brought under the power of any.
1 Corinthians 6:12 (NKJV)

When the Lord is living inside of us, we always are standing on holy ground. Do we desire to carry Him into the dens of iniquity or would we rather have Him carry us into the Promised Land? Be holy, for He is holy!

And you shall be holy to Me, for I the LORD *am* holy, and have separated you from the peoples, that you should be Mine.
Leviticus 20:26 (NKJV)

[1] I beseech you therefore, brethren, by the mercies of God, that you present your bodies a living sacrifice, holy, acceptable to God, which is your reasonable service. [2] And do not be conformed to this world, but be transformed by the renewing of your mind, that you may prove what is that good and acceptable and perfect will of God.
Romans 12:1-2 (NKJV)

October 9: King me!

Many Americans are fascinated with royalty. In 1981, 750 million people worldwide watched the televised wedding between Princess Diana and Charles, Prince of Wales. Though many viewers were women yearning for the "perfect wedding," another element involved the desires of "ordinary" people to marry royalty. Whether that attraction stems from a hope for power, notoriety, wealth or ease of life, it is seemingly selfish in nature.

As Christians, we are betrothed brides of the King of kings. Additionally, we are joint heirs of Jesus, who will inherit all, with a future promise of becoming kings and priests in the Lord's kingdom. For believers, the Bible offers other specific promises of the crowns we can obtain through our Christian walks.

In James 1:12 and Revelation 2:10, those who suffer for the Lord's sake and endure temptation are promised the Crown of Life. The Crown of Righteousness is promised in 2 Timothy 4:8

to those who look for the glorious appearing of the Lord. Believers who feed the sheep will receive the Crown of Glory, according to 1 Peter 5:4. The Crown of Rejoicing, referred to by many Bible scholars as the soul winner's crown, is promised to participants in the growth of God's kingdom. Paul describes a fifth crown, the imperishable or incorruptible crown:

^{24} Do you not know that those who run in a race all run, but one receives the prize? Run in such a way that you may obtain *it*. ^{25} And everyone who competes *for the prize* is temperate in all things. Now they *do it* to obtain a perishable crown, but we *for* an imperishable *crown*. ^{26} Therefore I run thus: not with uncertainty. Thus I fight: not as *one who* beats the air. ^{27} But I discipline my body and bring *it* into subjection, lest, when I have preached to others, I myself should become disqualified.
1 Corinthians 9:24-27 (NKJV)

To be disqualified in the race we run as Christians involves giving in to the flesh, rather than walking in the Spirit, yet since it is the Lord who will complete His work in us, He will get us to the finish line. The analogy of an Olympic athlete gives us a better grasp of the discipline necessary to achieve the highest prize. Yet what is the motive? Today, most professional athletes are driven by money. What is the purpose of winning a crown from our Lord? The 24 elders cast their crowns at the feet of Jesus:

^{9} Whenever the living creatures give glory and honor and thanks to Him who sits on the throne, who lives forever and ever, ^{10} the twenty-four elders fall down before Him who sits on the throne and worship Him who lives forever and ever, and cast their crowns before the throne, saying:
^{11}"You are worthy, O Lord,
To receive glory and honor and power;
For You created all things,
And by Your will they exist and were created."
Revelation 4:9-11 (NKJV)

Living in this competitive world, even Christians fall prey to the pitfalls of one-upmanship. Yet, we tend to lose sight of the fact that any of the crowns given by Jesus are the direct result of His creation. If we have a deep desire to feed the sheep, did not Jesus place that desire within us? If we are gifted as teachers, it is a direct result of the spiritual gift He gave us! In his book "Church History in Plain Language," author Bruce Shelley writes of an early church leader named Clement:

> "Clement insists that spiritual insight comes to the pure in heart, to those humble enough to walk with God as a child with his father, to those whose motive for ethical behavior goes far beyond fear of punishment or hope of reward to a love of the good for its own sake. It is an ascent from faith through knowledge to the beatific vision beyond this life, when the redeemed are one with God. The basis for this possibility is the image of God implanted by creation."

Motive is the defining aspect of it all. Are we performing to please God or to stand before the procession of fellow Christians proudly receiving a prize? Our Lord desires humbleness from each of us. To stand before Him, we need a change of heart:

³ Who may ascend into the hill of the LORD?
Or who may stand in His holy place?
⁴He who has clean hands and a pure heart,
Who has not lifted up his soul to an idol,
Nor sworn deceitfully.
Psalm 24:3-4 (NKJV)

While clean hands display godly actions, pure hearts signify godly motives. The most important motive of our lives should be to do it all for God's glory and pleasure. To worship Him is to love Him in return for all that He has done for us. That should be the driving influence of our Christian lives and walks, to honor Him, who wore a crown of thorns because of our sins! Do we desire a crown to give back to Him for all He has done for us? The way up is down. Through humbleness, God will use us for His kingdom. When our pride, competitiveness and ego get in the mix, the Lord puts us on the bench. Would we rather be kings or court jesters?

Behold, I am coming quickly! Hold fast what you have, that no one may take your crown.
Revelation 3:11 (NKJV)

October 10: If under the Law, the yoke's on us!

Most of us have spent time with the Lord early in the morning and desired to go an entire day without sinning just to please Him. Yet even if we cloister ourselves from the rest of the world where we are less apt to find conflict, we continue to sin. It might be anger when stubbing a toe on the corner of the sofa or impatience when we forget to save the file we have been typing on the computer, but it seems that sin always creeps in. While Satan may look at that sin in a believer's life as a small victory, God never looks upon it as a defeat. Why? Because our Father already has won the war!

After we have accepted Jesus as our Savior, He already has forgiven us for all past, present and future sins. Certainly, that is a part of what Paul refers to when he says that we have received all of the spiritual blessings (Ephesians 1:3). In a society where chaos would exist without rules, it is extremely difficult for us to understand that we are not living under the rules any longer. What occurs when 99.9% of the drivers adhere to the rules of the road, but one decides that green, yellow and red lights all mean, "Go?" There is going to be at least one wreck involving the Lone Ranger and those following the rules!

When Jesus died on the cross, He carried each believer on His shoulders to the place of grace, rather than the Law. That work He accomplished involved great physical pain in addition to the most painful aspect, His separation from the Father when the sins of the world were placed on the shoulders of Jesus. The 10 Commandments were given to us as a tutor, to demonstrate the impossibility of living a life without sin. Additionally, once we learn those commandments, we have a much deeper understanding of which of our actions cross into that sinful realm. In the Old Testament, that awareness of sin became heightened as the remedy of the sin offering was extremely time consuming. Awareness of sin is a great attribute in the life of the believer, but defeat from sin is not where God desires for us to be.

[1] Stand fast therefore in the liberty by which Christ has made us free, and do not be entangled again with a yoke of bondage. [2] Indeed I, Paul, say to you that if you become circumcised, Christ will profit you nothing. [3] And I testify again to every man who becomes circumcised that he is a debtor to keep the whole law. [4] You have become estranged from Christ, you who *attempt to* be justified by law; you have fallen from grace. [5] For we through the Spirit eagerly wait for the hope of righteousness by faith. [6] For in Christ Jesus neither circumcision nor uncircumcision avails anything, but faith working through love.
Galatians 5:1-6 (NKJV)

As Christians, we are no longer bound to sin, or bound to the Law, as Jesus has set the captives free! The "yoke of bondage" discussed in the passage above was easy to picture for those in an agricultural setting. If that yoke was not carved correctly, it would cause the oxen to put the strain on soft muscle tissue rather than the more solid bone structure. Additionally, other problems occurred when the oxen pulled in teams. When an ox was alone, he pulled straight, but when there was more than one pulling from the same yoke, it was difficult to move in a straight path due to the unequal strength of the oxen.

Do not be unequally yoked together with unbelievers. For what fellowship has righteousness with lawlessness? And what communion has light with darkness?
2 Corinthians 6:14 (NKJV)

Paul gave us this example to understand close relationships with unbelievers, whether it be in marriage or business. While a believer is bound to grace, an unbeliever is bound to the Law. Those bound to the Law will continue to be judged by the Law, where one sin makes a man a sinner and the wages of sin is death. As Christians, God does not desire for us to walk in defeat, but instead, to know the joy of the Lord as Jesus won that battle for us! That does not mean that we are to ignore the 10 Commandments. In fact, our world will not allow that to happen in cases of murder and robbery. Yet we are to live in a manner pleasing unto the Lord. The rules have now become principles, as we desire to obey God because of our love for Him, not because of the ramifications of breaking those rules. Obey Him out of love, not out of fear of punishment!

That brings a freedom to the lives of believers, who will not be defeated. Sometimes, believers make bad decisions and feel bound to their sins, once again. Yet that occurs when we are not allowing God to pull the yoke for us. When a believer is bound to Satan, the straight and narrow path no longer can be followed! With God's gift of the Holy Spirit to dwell within us, we are no longer self-powered. Instead, we are powered by God, if we allow Him to be the Lord of our lives. If we are struggling under our own power we should turn our lives over to God!

[13] **"Enter by the narrow gate; for wide** *is* **the gate and broad** *is* **the way that leads to destruction, and there are many who go in by it.** [14] **Because narrow** *is* **the gate and difficult** *is* **the way which leads to life, and there are few who find it. Matthew 7:13-14 (NKJV)**

[20] **I have been crucified with Christ; it is no longer I who live, but Christ lives in me; and the** *life* **which I now live in the flesh I live by faith in the Son of God, who loved me and gave Himself for me.** [21] **I do not set aside the grace of God; for if righteousness** *comes* **through the law, then Christ died in vain."**
Galatians 2:20-21 (NKJV)

October 11: A disappearing God?

When the Lord destroyed the earth with the Great Flood in the days of Noah, belief in God was different than it is now. In fact, with the longevity of those early lives, Noah's father knew Adam, though nine generations separated the two men. Consequently, in the generation before the Flood, people could speak with a man who had walked with God in the Garden of Eden. While belief in God may have existed in a different state, relationship with God was not evident in the actions and attitudes of the people:

[11] The earth also was corrupt before God, and the earth was filled with violence. [12] So God looked upon the earth, and indeed it was corrupt; for all flesh had corrupted their way on the earth.
Genesis 6:11-12 (NKJV)

Even in the new world, as man "progressed," relationship with God seemed to deteriorate. While the Romans and Greeks remained theists, retaining belief in deities, most in those civilizations were polytheists, believing in many gods. Citizens of those cultures paid for festivals to please the plethora of gods, yet those misinformed failed to understand the One True God's desire for a relationship. It was in ancient Greece that the term atheism first was seen, though it was not until the 1800s that people began to associate themselves with that term.

God's existence is evident in each direction we can see, hear or feel. Yet most people do not desire a relationship with their Creator, with the potential of having God in control of their lives. Instead, most people choose to serve themselves, as if they were the gods of their own worlds. While God honors humbleness, the world honors knowledge, power and wealth.

[23] Thus says the LORD:
"Let not the wise *man* glory in his wisdom,
Let not the mighty *man* glory in his might,

Nor let the rich *man* glory in his riches;
²⁴But let him who glories glory in this,
That he understands and knows Me,
That I *am* the LORD, exercising lovingkindness, judgment, and righteousness in the earth.
For in these I delight," says the LORD.
Jeremiah 9:23-24 (NKJV)

The prophet Jeremiah spoke the verses above to people who had rejected God's Word, which continues to be just as problematic today, if not more so. Atheism has become more prevalent, while agnosticism, the belief that the existence or non-existence of any deity is unknowable, has increased even more rapidly. While some may term this "the disappearance of God," instead, it is the disappearance of faith. Is it any wonder that depression, divorce and suicide rates continue to increase? Technology can help us to move around this world faster, higher and stronger, but not happier. We need God for our peace, our happiness and our joy! In comparison to the omniscience of God, our increasing intelligence is nothing.

**¹⁸ For the wrath of God is revealed from heaven against all ungodliness and unrighteousness of men, who suppress the truth in unrighteousness, ¹⁹ because what may be known of God is manifest in them, for God has shown *it* to them. ²⁰ For since the creation of the world His invisible *attributes* are clearly seen, being understood by the things that are made, *even* His eternal power and Godhead, so that they are without excuse, ²¹ because, although they knew God, they did not glorify *Him* as God, nor were thankful, but became futile in their thoughts, and their foolish hearts were darkened. ²² Professing to be wise, they became fools,
Romans 1:18-22 (NKJV)**

An elderly woman shopped for a new television and insisted it had to be black-and-white, as she did not have cable. No family member or sales associate could convince her that the two issues were unrelated. She would not accept expert opinion, as she thought she knew better. In the same manner, people are most dangerous when they overestimate their own intelligence. As Christians, most of us would agree that the more we study the Bible, the less we know, as we can see how much more there is to learn. God is so big and so complex, that we can study His Word for all of eternity and still, continue to learn.

Transformation involves that appearance of faith. Faith is not the opposite of science, but the knowledge that God created science! Even as Christians, we have different levels of faith given by God. Yet it is simple to increase our faith in the all-mighty God. Read His Word! The more we know Him, the more we will see Him in every aspect of our lives. If we seek God, we will find Him. He has promised that, and wants to reveal Himself to us all!

[10]"For you have trusted in your wickedness;
You have said, 'No one sees me';
Your wisdom and your knowledge have warped you;
And you have said in your heart,
'I *am*, and *there is* no one else besides me.'
[11]Therefore evil shall come upon you;
You shall not know from where it arises.
And trouble shall fall upon you;
You will not be able to put it off.
And desolation shall come upon you suddenly,
Which you shall not know.
Isaiah 47:10-11 (NKJV)

October 12: Are we foolish?

[27] But God has chosen the foolish things of the world to put to shame the wise, and God has chosen the weak things of the world to put to shame the things which are mighty; [28] and the base things of the world and the things which are despised God has chosen, and the things which are not, to bring to nothing the things that are, [29] that no flesh should glory in His presence. [30] But of Him you are in Christ Jesus, who became for us wisdom from God—and righteousness and

sanctification and redemption— ³¹ that, as it is written, *"He who glories, let him glory in the LORD."*
1 Corinthians 1:27-31 (NKJV)

The word for "foolish" in Strong's Concordance is *"moros ,* (μωρός,)* which primarily denotes "dull, sluggish, stupid, and foolish; it is used of persons." This verse says that God chose morons to confound the wise. In the same manner, the word for weak is *asthenos* (ἀσθενής), meaning "without strength" (*a* means "negative," and *sthenos*, "strength"). It is specifically translated "feeble." This refers to having no ability or strength whatsoever. So God is showing us that we are morons and people with no ability, without Him. That continues as "base" means that we are despised. Why? So that no flesh would glory in His presence! God has given us examples of this throughout the Bible:

When David was just a boy, the people of Israel found themselves facing a major obstacle in the 9-foot-9-inch Goliath. The entire army was afraid to fight him, yet God encouraged a young man to face Goliath. For David understood that the battle was not his; the battle belonged to the Lord. David grabbed five, smooth stones for his sling, not because he expected to miss. Instead, David understood that Goliath had four, giant brothers who might seek revenge. With one small stone, David through God defeated Goliath! (1 Samuel 17)

When facing the Midianites, Gideon had an army of 32,000 men. Yet the Lord spoke to Gideon, and said,

"The people who *are* with you *are* too many for Me to give the Midianites into their hands, lest Israel claim glory for itself against Me, saying, 'My own hand has saved me.'
Judges 7:2 (NKJV)

That army was first pared down to 10,000, and then through a test of how they drank water from *Ein Harod*, the springs of Gideon, the final number reached only 300! With those 300, the

Lord defeated the much larger army of Midianites, and in so doing, gave us a lesson on how He works!

After the Jews of the northern tribes had been taken captive by the Assyrians, the southern tribes of Jerusalem found themselves fearful when surrounded by the advancing Assyrian army. Led by Sennacherib, God destroyed Sennacherib's troops numbering 185,000, by the hand of an angel in the night. When little conquers big, man cannot take credit for the power, as we have a tendency of doing. We more easily attribute it to God!

Even the men God called to follow Jesus demonstrated this verse. Most were fishermen. Matthew was a tax collector, one of the most hated professions of the day. (Things have not changed that much)! Yet God gave those uneducated men all the education they would need to begin His Church! Even the name that God gave to Saul demonstrates this as "Paul" means "little one!"

Though many modern-day Christians seem to get lost in the prosperity gospel, believing in a "name-it-and-claim-it" or "blab-it-and-grab-it" promise of earthly wealth, God has given us the information in His Word that it is more difficult for a rich man to enter heaven than for a camel to pass through the eye of the needle. God typically does not call the rich, powerful, famous, etc., for those people already have their god, money.

No servant can serve two masters; for either he will hate the one and love the other, or else he will be loyal to the one and despise the other. You cannot serve God and mammon." Luke 16:13

As followers of Jesus, we remain in the overwhelming minority, but power and wealth are not necessary when God is in our side! When faced with situations we are certain to lose, that is when God displays His miraculous hand the most often. Trust Him!

**Some *trust* in chariots, and some in horses;
But we will remember the name of the LORD our God.**

Psalm 20:7

October 13: Inner conflict

When a well-oiled machine is working smoothly, the continuous hum of the engine is like music. That machine can be a piece of equipment, but also can be a group or individual. Regardless of size of the equipment or the number of parts involved, lubrication minimizes friction to the point where all work together, smoothly. While it might be easier to grasp this concept by picturing an engine, each of us operates daily in the same manner. Often, we seem to forget that we are more than a body, as it constantly requires food, water and maintenance to keep it going. Yet as Christians, that machinery involves body, soul and spirit.

For you were bought at a price; therefore glorify God in your body and in your spirit, which are God's.
1 Corinthians 6:20 (NKJV)

Because God dwells within us in the form of the Holy Spirit, we are aware of His presence in our lives. God has not split Himself up into tiny increments, and placed that tiny increment of Himself within each believer. Instead, all of God is within each of us! Even with God's constant presence in our lives, our bodies seem to have times when they work against the Spirit, rather than with the Spirit. Yet oil lubricates the machinery! Is it ironic that the word oil in the Bible is emblematic of the Holy Spirit? He makes all things work together for our benefit!

And we know that all things work together for good to those who love God, to those who are the called according to *His* purpose.
Romans 8:28 (NKJV)

Often in the Bible, we see anointing with oil, and in the following verse, we can see that God anoints us with His Spirit. That covering empowers each believer with might that far surpasses our own strengths and abilities.

> [18]"The Spirit of the LORD is upon Me,
> Because He has anointed Me
> To preach the gospel to the poor;
> He has sent Me to heal the brokenhearted,
> To proclaim liberty to the captives
> And recovery of sight to the blind,
> To set at liberty those who are oppressed;
> [19] To proclaim the acceptable year of the LORD."
> Luke 4:18-19 (NKJV)

Additionally, that power enables us to present our bodies to the Lord for His purposes. Paul reminds us that if we feed the flesh, the flesh grows, but if we feed the Spirit, the Spirit grows. To walk in God's power is to ignore the cravings of the flesh. That does not mean that we should give up food and water, but that our focus should remain on God, not self.

> **[1] I beseech you therefore, brethren, by the mercies of God, that you present your bodies a living sacrifice, holy, acceptable to God, *which is* your reasonable service. [2] And do not be conformed to this world, but be transformed by the renewing of your mind, that you may prove what *is* that good and acceptable and perfect will of God.**
> **Romans 12:1-2 (NKJV)**

One of the most powerful words in the verse above is "reasonable." God does not view this request as a great accomplishment, but what is rational in exchange for all that He has accomplished on our behalves. Notice, though, that this is not a commandment. Instead, Paul begins by saying, "I beseech you," which means, "I beg you to do this." Paul begs us, as he understands the blessing that will come to each believer who submits in this way to God!

When the "machinery" of body, soul and spirit is well-oiled, there are no limits to what God may accomplish through us! Additionally, when the body of believers is also lubricated by the Holy Spirit, our Lord empowers the body to work together in the same facet. To be a hypocrite is to be in conflict within ourselves. *Hupokrites* is the Greek word for actors, literally, "to answer back." When an actor received a cue, he was expected to respond in a prescribed way. Instead of a situation-comedy, God desires for us to be a reality show! If God truly is dwelling within us, then our words, deeds and motives should reflect His attributes! Do not let the cravings of the flesh overpower the desires of the Spirit. Without oil, our machine will seize up, making our engines into paperweights for the rest of eternity!

**^{24} And those *who are* Christ's have crucified the flesh with its passions and desires. ^{25} If we live in the Spirit, let us also walk in the Spirit.
Galatians 5:24-25 (NKJV)**

October 14: Drawing lines

Living in a beach community, the constant ebb and flow of the tides offers many visual analogies to life as we know it. In the middle of the night, the sound of crashing waves becomes a distant drum roll that soothes the soul. As the tide rises, each wave seems to redraw a line of advancement in the darkening sand, highlighting the lighter color and dryness of the sand yet to be touched by water.

What a great reminder that is of our lives in the world. Every man continues in his battle against sin, with the major difference between believers and unbelievers being forgiveness of that sin. Yet with the onslaught of temptations coming at each of us in waves, we often discover that the line we originally drew in the sand has been redrawn. Just as the tide continues to rise, we all can look back on our lives and see that many of the sins we were certain to avoid are now a part of our past. Similarly, glancing back to the beach reveals that what was intended to be a line of defense has been annihilated by the advancing enemy. This is what James, the brother of Jesus, had to say about those trials:

^{2} My brethren, count it all joy when you fall into various trials, ^{3} knowing that the testing of your faith produces

patience. ⁴ But let patience have *its* perfect work, that you may be perfect and complete, lacking nothing. ⁵ If any of you lacks wisdom, let him ask of God, who gives to all liberally and without reproach, and it will be given to him. ⁶ But let him ask in faith, with no doubting, for he who doubts is like a wave of the sea driven and tossed by the wind. ⁷ For let not that man suppose that he will receive anything from the Lord; ⁸ he is a double-minded man, unstable in all his ways.
James 1:2-8 (NKJV)

Watching those forceful waves crash against the shoreline demonstrates the power of the ocean, but we often lose sight of the power of the wind, either knocking the waves down to nothingness or lifting them up to epic proportions. In the same manner, God in the form of the Holy Spirit has the power to lessen or completely erase the trials facing us. In Greek, the word for wind and the Holy Spirit is the same, *"pneuma."* Though God has the ability to eradicate our trials, that is not His purpose, for through testing, we grow closer to Him. Additionally, the trials increase our patience, wisdom and faith.

³⁵ On the same day, when evening had come, He said to them, "Let us cross over to the other side." ³⁶ Now when they had left the multitude, they took Him along in the boat as He was. And other little boats were also with Him. ³⁷ And a great windstorm arose, and the waves beat into the boat, so that it was already filling. ³⁸ But He was in the stern, asleep on a pillow. And they awoke Him and said to Him, "Teacher, do You not care that we are perishing?"
³⁹ Then He arose and rebuked the wind, and said to the sea, "Peace, be still!" And the wind ceased and there was a great calm.
Mark 4:35-39 (NKJV)

In the verse above, the disciples were riding in a boat above the waves. Though Jesus was in the boat with them, they feared death. Ironically, there is no record of anyone dying when in the presence of Jesus, but fear is not driven by logic. Yet these were seasoned fisherman; the fact that this storm scared them reveals that it could have been a strong attack from the enemy! Our travels through life entail many windstorms, darkening clouds and stormy seas. Yet with Jesus in our boats, do we have any reason to fear? The waves of His mercy can overwhelm any trial, attack or difficulty. Feel His peace. Be still…and know that He is God!

⁶ In this you greatly rejoice, though now for a little while, if need be, you have been grieved by various trials, ⁷ that the genuineness of your faith, *being* much more precious than gold that perishes, though it is tested by fire, may be found to praise, honor, and glory at the revelation of Jesus Christ, 1 Peter 1:6-7 (NKJV)

October 15: Slip-sliding away

There is nothing more challenging than the Christian walk. It is not a run, a crawl or even a soar, as the term "walk" denotes a slow, forward progression. Yet there are times when that walk either takes an extremely circuitous route, or even goes in the opposite direction. That is when we are no longer standing on solid ground, the Foundation of our salvation. In the Bible, it is called backsliding, and it cannot happen to unbelievers, as there is no blessing of fellowship to slide away from. Instead, this describes a person who knows God, yet chooses his old, sinful habits.

Picture a man on ice skates in a powerful windstorm. Striving to move ahead, when the strongest gusts hit him in the face, he proceeds with "one step forward, two steps back." When he loses his footing and falls onto his backside, that wind can cause him to slide backward, from whence he came.

As Christians, we have the hope of our walks with the Lord being continuous and straight, yet there are times when we become too self-confident, beginning to operate under our own power and direction, rather than being led, and fed, by Jesus. Sin can cause us to stumble in a way that may seem surprising in its ostentatious manner. When we stumble, we will be humble!

Throughout the Bible, we see godly men failing. Yet, the good news is that while all men fail, God never fails!

Your own wickedness will correct you,
And your backslidings will rebuke you.
Know therefore and see that *it is* **an evil and bitter** *thing*
That you have forsaken the LORD your God,
And the fear of Me *is* **not in you,"**
Says the Lord GOD of hosts.
Jeremiah 2:19 (NKJV)

Our wisdom begins with that fear of the Lord, but there are times when ignorance takes hold of our lives. When God destroyed the world by flood, Noah was one of only eight spared. Yet soon after, he lay uncovered, drunk in his tent (Genesis 9:20). King David was a man after God's own heart, yet his lust of Bathsheba led him to be responsible for the murder of her husband to disguise the adultery. Perhaps the best example for us all involves Peter, who soon after bragging to Jesus of his unwavering, undying love, denied his Lord three times.

Then He said, "I tell you, Peter, the rooster shall not crow this day before you will deny three times that you know Me."
Luke 22:34 (NKJV)

Notice that Peter, the only disciple brave enough to walk on water with Jesus, who sliced off the ear of Malchus in the Garden of Gethsemane in defense of Jesus, failed in his strength rather than in his weakness. Satan attacked Peter's courage immediately after the Lord's arrest, but the outcome was no surprise to Jesus. When we think that we are strong enough to handle Satan's attacks alone, we are destined for failure. In the same manner, we tend to hand our weaknesses to the Lord, knowing without Him we will fail. Yes, even Peter failed, but Jesus restored Peter soon after His resurrection. Is there any sin worse than denying the Lord? Yet this was the same Peter who wrote part of the New Testament, led many people to Christ, and was crucified upside down as a martyr for the Lord.

When a young boy disobeys his parents, that action might affect his fellowship, but not his son-ship. We cannot lose our relationship with the Lord! That is not based on our strengths, but on His! Certainly, there are times when all of us as Christians adversely affect our fellowship with the Lord, but through His restoration, we will regain that fellowship! If sin has taken away the blessing of our fellowship with the Lord we should ask for His forgiveness! God never desires to be far from us, yet at those times when we walk away, He cries out, "Where are you? I miss fellowshipping with you!"

Be strong and of good courage, do not fear nor be afraid of them; for the LORD your God, He *is* the One who goes with you. He will not leave you nor forsake you."
Deuteronomy 31:6 (NKJV)

October 16: How do we measure wealth?

Though economists have announced that the recession is over, most of the working class would disagree strongly. Credit card debt is at an all-time high. Foreclosures dot every neighborhood, while new construction has slowed to a crawl. At the same time, many churches continue to be weakened by the "prosperity gospel" seeping into the simplicity and truth of God's Word, confusing many Christians. With money-conscious pastors leading the way, the "name it and claim it," "blab it and grab it" mentality points to people who desire financial growth above a closer walk with the Lord.

While God has promised that He will take care of the needs of His people, those needs do not include an abundance of financial resources. The God of a thousand hills (Psalm 50:10) has the ability to bless His children in any way He desires, and sometimes that blessing can be of a financial nature. Yet typically, those He chooses to bless in that manner desire to use their blessing for the spread of the gospel, rather than to living higher on the hog!

Listen, my beloved brethren: Has God not chosen the poor of this world *to be* rich in faith and heirs of the kingdom which He promised to those who love Him?
James 2:5 (NKJV)

Comprehension of the symbiotic relationship between poverty and faith involves God as the provider, *Jehovah-jireh* (Genesis 22:14). Those faithful servants of the Lord without financial stability frequently are blessed by God's provision at the last moment. When rent is due, and there is not enough in the coffers to write the check, miracles happen. Certainly, God calls for us to be good stewards of what He provides, and some of those financial straits arise when our stewardship is questionable. Yet many times, God desires to increase the faith of His people by having them to wait upon His provision.

[41] Now Jesus sat opposite the treasury and saw how the people put money into the treasury. And many *who were* rich put in much. [42] Then one poor widow came and threw in two mites, which make a quadrans. [43] So He called His disciples to *Himself* and said to them, "Assuredly, I say to you that this poor widow has put in more than all those who have given to the treasury; [44] for they all put in out of their abundance, but she out of her poverty put in all that she had, her whole livelihood."
Mark 12:41-44 (NKJV)

There are places in the United States that are as impoverished as any third-world nation. It is commonplace to see the poor assist the poor in those areas, reminiscent of the widow, who gave out of her poverty. It is impossible to out-give God. Sacrifice is the greatest example of love, especially toward unbelieving neighbors. Living in such a wealthy country, it is simple to fall into the trap that "more is better" or "he who dies with the most toys wins." Yet God's truth shares with us that true wealth is having God in control of our lives. Eternity at the feet of Jesus is worth so much more than silver and gold.

Then Peter said, "Silver and gold I do not have, but what I do have I give you: In the name of Jesus Christ of Nazareth, rise up and walk."
Acts 3:6 (NKJV)

God has given us so much more than material wealth. He has given us spiritual legs to walk with Him, for all of eternity. Trust in Him. There is no need that God will not fill in the lives of His children! Just do not get needs confused with wants!

[26] For you see your calling, brethren, that not many wise according to the flesh, not many mighty, not many noble, *are called.* [27] But God has chosen the foolish things of the world to put to shame the wise, and God has chosen the weak things of the world to put to shame the things which are mighty; [28] and the base things of the world and the things which are despised God has chosen, and the things which are not, to bring to nothing the things that are, [29] that no flesh should glory in His presence. [30] But of Him you are in Christ Jesus, who became for us wisdom from God—and righteousness and sanctification and redemption— [31] that, as it is written, *"He who glories, let him glory in the LORD."*
1 Corinthians 1:26-31 (NKJV)

October 17: Rumble strips

Anyone who drives a car understands how easy it is to drift into another lane when eyes fail to remain focused ahead. Yet even if that occurs, on the freeways there are bumps between the lanes called rumble strips, which can alert the driver if slightly off course, or wake him if dozing. Focus is the key, as every action is the response of what holds our attention. If we are focused on achieving nothing, we are certain to accomplish exactly that.

God has placed each of us in a world that offers almost an infinite number of items to gain our focus. As Christians, our primary focus needs to remain on Jesus. Certainly, there are many other important aspects of our lives, including our families, jobs and ministries, yet with a primary focus on the

Lord, all else can be seen peripherally. Peter gave us one of the greatest biblical examples of the miracles that can occur when our eyes remain focused on Jesus.

[22] **Immediately Jesus made His disciples get into the boat and go before Him to the other side, while He sent the multitudes away.** [23] **And when He had sent the multitudes away, He went up on the mountain by Himself to pray. Now when evening came, He was alone there.** [24] **But the boat was now in the middle of the sea, tossed by the waves, for the wind was contrary.**
[25] **Now in the fourth watch of the night Jesus went to them, walking on the sea.** [26] **And when the disciples saw Him walking on the sea, they were troubled, saying, "It is a ghost!" And they cried out for fear.**
[27] **But immediately Jesus spoke to them, saying, "Be of good cheer! It is I; do not be afraid."**
[28] **And Peter answered Him and said, "Lord, if it is You, command me to come to You on the water."**
[29] **So He said, "Come." And when Peter had come down out of the boat, he walked on the water to go to Jesus.** [30] **But when he saw that the wind *was* boisterous, he was afraid; and beginning to sink he cried out, saying, "Lord, save me!"**
[31] **And immediately Jesus stretched out *His* hand and caught him, and said to him, "O you of little faith, why did you doubt?"** [32] **And when they got into the boat, the wind ceased. Matthew 14:22-32 (NKJV)**

One of the greatest lessons of Peter walking on water has to do with his failure. Yet a larger lesson is that no one else was willing to step out of the boat. During the time that Peter's focus remained on Jesus, he was not confined by the natural laws of the earth. When Peter fell beneath the water, Jesus reached down and saved him. We all have boisterous waves in our lives competing for attention, yet with our eyes focused on Jesus, miracles will occur.

Jesus said, "O you of little faith, why did you doubt," but could easily have said to the other disciples, who remained in the boat,

"O you of even less faith, why were you unwilling to follow Me?" When our faith wavers, the Lord will stretch out His hand and come to wherever we are to rescue us and lead us back to safety. Listen for the rumble strips. The Holy Spirit will wake us, alert us and remind us that our eyes have drifted from the Son of God. He has a plan and a purpose in our lives. Once we have seen Him, why do we desire to look anywhere else? Whatever the Lord has for us to do, we should do it intensely!

Now if God so clothes the grass of the field, which today is, and tomorrow is thrown into the oven, *will He* not much more *clothe* you, O you of little faith?
Matthew 6:30 (NKJV)

October 18: What God do you believe in?

Ask someone to name a genius and Albert Einstein would be at the top of the list. The 20th-century, theoretical physicist is considered to be the father of modern physics. Scientifically-gifted, Einstein was spiritually blind. He said, "I do not believe in the God of theology who rewards good and punishes evil." Additionally, he wrote, "I do not believe in a personal God and I have never denied this but have expressed it clearly." Yet Einstein certainly had the intelligence to comprehend that his belief had nothing to do with God's existence. For example, if we do not believe in electricity, and then stick a finger into an electrical socket, disbelief will not stop the ensuing shock! Obviously, more important than belief is adherence to that belief.

While there certainly are many different polls on the subject, with highly subjective results, one poll found that 97.5% of the world's population believes in God. That number sounds shockingly high when the amount of evil in the world is taken into consideration. That being said, there is an ever-widening gap between those who believe and those who act upon that belief. Additionally, belief in God in those polls does not differentiate between the God of the Bible and the gods of Hinduism, Islam, etc. Disappointingly, an increasing number of people claiming to be Christians believe that all religions worship the same God.

> "Whether they be Muslim, Christian, or any other religion, [They all] pray to the same God."---former U.S. President George W. Bush, November, 2003

Surprisingly, other well-known evangelical Christians adhere to that same philosophy, including Billy Graham, though that strongly conflicts what the Bible teaches. While universalists might believe there are many paths to salvation, God tells us in His Word that there is only one path:

[10] **let it be known to you all, and to all the people of Israel, that by the name of Jesus Christ of Nazareth, whom you crucified, whom God raised from the dead, by Him this man stands here before you whole.** [11] **This is the *'stone which was rejected by you builders, which has become the chief cornerstone.'* ** [12] **Nor is there salvation in any other, for there is no other name under heaven given among men by which we must be saved."**
Acts 4:10-12 (NKJV)

Certainly, belief in God is a springboard to following Him, yet simple belief without works is a path that leads away from God. After receiving the gift of salvation, God desires for us to demonstrate His love in our actions.

[14] **What *does it* profit, my brethren, if someone says he has faith but does not have works? Can faith save him?** [15] **If a brother or sister is naked and destitute of daily food,** [16] **and one of you says to them, "Depart in peace, be warmed and filled," but you do not give them the things which are needed for the body, what *does it* profit?** [17] **Thus also faith by itself, if it does not have works, is dead.**
[18] **But someone will say, "You have faith, and I have works." Show me your faith without your works, and I will show you my faith by my works.** [19] **You believe that there is one God. You do well. Even the demons believe—and tremble!** [20] **But**

do you want to know, O foolish man, that faith without works is dead? ²¹ Was not Abraham our father justified by works when he offered Isaac his son on the altar? ²² Do you see that faith was working together with his works, and by works faith was made perfect?**
James 2:14-22 (NKJV)

Works cannot earn salvation for anyone, yet works can be a measure of that belief. They will know we are Christians by our love! If we claim to be followers of Christ, but have not love, we are clanging cymbals. God increases the faith in His children by revealing Himself in their Bible reading. Additionally, answered prayer increases faith, and part of that has to do with God's provision in difficult circumstances. God's power saves us, restores us and provides for us. Yet if we look at Christianity through the one-dimensional eyes of what is in it for us, we have lost focus of the bigger picture. How can we touch the lives of others? Those are the works that must combine with faith to complete the circuit in the life of the believer. Yet do not lose sight of the fact that our salvation is not earned by our limited works. Our salvation came from the work that Jesus accomplished on Calvary. Seeing God has nothing to do with intelligence, and everything to do with spiritual eyes. It does not take a genius to see Him, but if God opens our eyes, we can see Him clearly, and serve Him by reaching out to others!

Jesus said to him, "I am the way, the truth, and the life. No one comes to the Father except through Me.
John 14:6 (NKJV)

October 19: Be loved!

Though shelter, water and food are essential ingredients to the overall health of an individual, love might be the most important item on a list of needs. Loneliness can be much more oppressive than starvation. John Donne summed up the human condition aptly with his statement that, "No man is an island."

When God formed Adam, the first man was given the opportunity to name all of the animals, which God also had created. Yet God knew that was not enough for Adam, and formed Eve as a helper to share his life. Adam did not spend countless hours in Garden of Eden singles' bars, or lose an abundance of sleep chatting on EdenHarmony.com, looking for the perfect fit. Instead, God supplied Adam's needs before Adam knew that the needs existed!

As Christians, we serve a God of love. He created us not as playthings or because He was lonely. Instead, He wanted to share His love with us! How sad it is that the majority of God's creation has no interest in His love. That love involved sending His only Son to die in our places, so that we might have a relationship with the Father. As difficult as it was for God to watch His Son suffer the ignominy of the cross, that event pleased God according to Isaiah 53, for it enabled the bridge of relationship to be constructed between God and man, taking us from bedeviled to beloved.

One of the sweetest words in the Bible is "beloved," which occurs in the Old Testament 46 times in 39 different verses in the New King James Version, with 27 of those verses coming from the Song of Solomon. Additionally, "beloved" occurs 66 times in 64 different verses in the New Testament. In the New Testament, "beloved" first applies to Jesus at His baptism, when the Father speaks:

And suddenly a voice *came* from heaven, saying, "This is My beloved Son, in whom I am well pleased."
Matthew 3:17 (NKJV)

In Greek, the word is *agapetos*, which comes from the root *agape*, designating a perfect love that is much different than sexual or brotherly love. To understand the sacrificial nature of *agape* is to grasp the willingness of Jesus to give His life for us. Amazingly, the same term that the Father used to describe His love for Jesus also describes His love for all believers:

To all who are in Rome, beloved of God, called *to be* saints: Grace to you and peace from God our Father and the Lord Jesus Christ.
Romans 1:7 (NKJV)

Yet it is an oversimplification to even begin to comprehend God's perfect love. He does not just love us; He is love, according to John. He loves us not because we are so lovable, but because that is His nature. While we were still sinners, Christ died for us. It is impossible for God to do anything less than love us completely. When life gets a little bumpy, or stays that way, remember that we serve a God who already has demonstrated how far He will go to love us. That love does not just supply some of our needs, but all of our needs, for just as He did with Adam, God is aware of those needs before we begin to have a clue.

As His beloved, we have the duty to share that same kind of love with those He places in our paths. Just as God loves the unlovable, often the people He wants us to reach are the downtrodden and lonely. We need to let Him use us to rescue the lonely, as all anyone wants is to "Be-loved!"

[7] Beloved, let us love one another, for love is of God; and everyone who loves is born of God and knows God. [8] He who does not love does not know God, for God is love. [9] In this the love of God was manifested toward us, that God has sent His only begotten Son into the world, that we might live through Him. [10] In this is love, not that we loved God, but that He loved us and sent His Son *to be* the propitiation for our sins. [11] Beloved, if God so loved us, we also ought to love one another.
1 John 4:7-11 (NKJV)

October 20: Honor God!

Honor is an interesting term that denotes giving high respect or credit to another. We can honor others through our words, deeds and motives. Additionally, honor designates moral integrity, and that term is often applied to a soldier.

An analogous relationship exists between honoring God and honoring parents. Leviticus 20:9 tells us that any child who curses his parents should be put to death! With the first half of the 10 Commandments dealing with man's relationship with God, He explicitly tells us how to honor Him by acknowledging that He is the only God, by not letting idols get in the way of our relationship with Him and by respecting His name and His holy day. The second half of the 10 Commandments deals with man's relationship with man, and the first relationship God highlights is that between a child and parent. Notice that there in not any stipulation following the words, "honor your father and your mother." It does not say, IF! The honor we are called to give our parents has nothing to do with whether or not we agree with them, whether or not we view them as honorable or whether or not we feel indebted to the life they have given us. Additionally, there is no time limit on the commandment, as this honor is to continue throughout our lives.

Roman philosopher Seneca said, "Nothing is more honorable than a grateful heart." That statement demonstrates the inward sign of the outward effect of the honor we should give to our Lord and to our parents. God's plan placed us exactly where He wanted us. It does not matter if our parents abandoned us as infants; without them, we would not have life. In the same manner, each of us as believers understands that without God, we are spiritually dead. Though we have the tendency to see the failures and mistakes made by our parents, God desires for us to focus on the gift of life they have given, along with the sacrifices. Most children do not respect the amount of those sacrifices until they have children of their own.

Honor is not lip service, but heart service, as actions speak louder than words. God certainly understands the difference!

Therefore the Lord said:
"Inasmuch as these people draw near with their mouths

And honor Me with their lips,
But have removed their hearts far from Me,
And their fear toward Me is taught by the commandment of men,
Isaiah 29:13 (NKJV)

Children can physically resemble their parents, yet similar traits can extend to personality, character and interests, depending on the amount of time spent together. Christians can resemble God in the same manner, yet without time spent with Him, the similarities will be minimal. Our first step to honoring God is through the thankfulness of what He has given us. Additionally, we can honor Him by obeying His commandments. Along those lines, honoring our parents also is honoring God. Yet there is no greater honor than desiring to be more like Him. He is worthy of our praise! As soldiers of God, Christians should walk upright morally, as representatives of the Lord. Additionally, when our parents bring us into this world, they give us a solid reputation. We cannot improve on that reputation, but by our actions, can ruin it. We honor our parents and honor God through our lives.

Do we want to resemble our Father? If we want to be a chip off the old block, know that God is the Ancient of Days, the Rock of Ages, the Chief Cornerstone and our Foundation!

^{22}**For the Father judges no one, but has committed all judgment to the Son, ^{23} that all should honor the Son just as they honor the Father. He who does not honor the Son does not honor the Father who sent Him.**
John 5:22-23 (NKJV)

October 21: Pray with belief!

Bible scholars refer to the 400-year period from the end of Malachi to the beginning of the Gospels as the "silent years," as in that time, God did not speak to the people through the prophets as He had from the days of Moses. Yet when God's prophetic words of a coming Messiah were about to come to fruition, He sent His angel Gabriel to the temple in Jerusalem to speak with Zacharias.

Zacharias was an old man, a Levitical priest of the order of Abijah. His wife Elizabeth, related to Aaron according to Luke 1:5, was old and barren, which for a Hebrew woman was a great sadness. Certainly, a Levitical priest and his wife knew the Old Testament Scripture that said:

³Behold, children *are* a heritage from the LORD,
The fruit of the womb *is* a reward.
⁴Like arrows in the hand of a warrior,
So *are* the children of one's youth.
⁵Happy *is* the man who has his quiver full of them;
They shall not be ashamed,
But shall speak with their enemies in the gate.
Psalm 127:3-5 (NKJV)

If children were a reward, then faulty, reverse logic would dictate that lack of children was a punishment, though God could have many reasons to not give children to a righteous couple. When Jesus healed a blind man, He told the disciples that the man's blindness had nothing to do with his sin or the sin of his parents; instead, the man was blind for that moment when Jesus would heal him (John 9). In the same manner, Zacharias and Elizabeth were childless for that time when God would perform a miracle.

While Zacharias was in the temple performing his duties at the altar of incense, the place of prayer, Gabriel greeted the priest, telling him in Luke 1:13 that his prayer for a son had been answered. Yet Gabriel's words were not enough to convince Zacharias. Even after an angelic promise, Zacharias remained incredulous.

And Zacharias said to the angel, "How shall I know this? For I am an old man, and my wife is well advanced in years."
Luke 1:18 (NKJV)

"How shall I know this?" Well, when she delivers little John the Baptist, Zacharias might figure it out! When Elizabeth's womb started to grow, he might have an inkling. What a sad lesson this is to all believers! Zacharias was called righteous in Luke 1:6, yet his faith in God's power was lacking. How many times do we pray without believing God is capable of answering our prayer? For years, Zacharias had prayed for a son, yet when God answered the prayer, his lack of faith was revealed. "We are too old to have children," was his response, though moments beforehand, he had been asking for exactly this answer to his prayer! Often, the answers we ask for are not in God's will. In the case of Zacharias and Elizabeth, their answer to prayer coincided with God's plan.

While the name Zacharias means "God remembers" and Elizabeth means "God's oath," by putting those names together, we are reminded that "God remembers God's oath." His oath was that the line of David would rule and reign on the throne:

^{34}**My covenant I will not break,**
Nor alter the word that has gone out of My lips.
^{35}**Once I have sworn by My holiness;**
I will not lie to David:
^{36}**His seed shall endure forever,**
And his throne as the sun before Me;
^{37}**It shall be established forever like the moon,**
Even *like* **the faithful witness in the sky."**
Psalm 89:34-37 (NKJV)

Yet, when Gabriel told Zacharias that his prayer had been answered, God had made an additional oath! When John the Baptist was born to this aged couple, it spoke of God's grace, for John means "God has been gracious." God answers our prayers because of His grace, giving us much more than we deserve. If our prayers involve our needs and the needs of others, in addition to the will of the Lord, rather than an advanced shopping list, God will answer. However, we should be careful that doubt does not seep into our prayers, or that we pray so repetitiously, that we no longer expect an answer from God. Never forget that we serve a God who answers our prayers!

> **Therefore I say to you, whatever things you ask when you pray, believe that you receive *them*, and you will have *them*.**
> **Mark 11:24 (NKJV)**

October 22: Sometimes, it is okay to lose our heads!

Each day, we are faced with many opportunities to speak to people who are lacking a relationship with Jesus Christ. More often than not, our lives and opinions will have little in common with those in the world, especially if we are focused on the spiritual realm, rather than the physical realm. Sometimes, we can offend others with our view of biblical truth. That offense can lead to severed relationships, yet even in the midst, God is in charge. We should not measure success against the cares of the world, as God will win any battle we are involved in. Many who originally are offended by someone sharing God's love and laws comes to know Him!

John the Baptist is a wonderful, biblical example of a man who failed by all earthly standards, yet gained victory by heavenly standards. While still in the womb, John was filled with the Holy Spirit, according to Luke 1:15. Elizabeth, a cousin of Mary the mother of Jesus, was six months pregnant with John when Mary came to share her news, and at that time, Elizabeth also was filled with the Spirit. John adhered to the vows of a Nazirite from birth, as he never drank wine or cut his hair, spending his life following God. Thirty years is a long time to go without a haircut!

> **[6] Now John was clothed with camel's hair and with a leather belt around his waist, and he ate locusts and wild honey. [7] And he preached, saying, "There comes One after me who is mightier than I, whose sandal strap I am not worthy to stoop down and loose. [8] I indeed baptized you with water, but He will baptize you with the Holy Spirit."**

Mark 1:6-8 (NKJV)

Pointing to the coming of Jesus, as the "Lamb of God who takes away the sins of the world," John baptized others and Jesus in the Jordan River. Yet, he likely appeared as a homeless man to others of his day. Additionally, he witnessed all three manifestations of God present at that event, as while Jesus was baptized, the Holy Spirit descended upon our Messiah like a dove. At the same time, the Father spoke, saying, "You are My beloved Son, in whom I am well pleased. (Mark 1:11)." That event began the ministry of the Messiah, and ended the ministry of John. Soon after, John spoke out against the marriage of Herod Antipas. Herod was not an autonomous king of Israel. In fact, the Romans were in power, and Herod was not much more than a figurehead to the Jews. Yet by paying tribute to the Romans, Herod enabled himself to flex an occasional muscle.

Though Herod was recognized by Mark Antony as the Jewish national leader, he did not adhere to Mosaic Law. Upon divorcing his wife to marry Herodias, his niece and the wife of his brother, Herod's actions received strong condemnation from John the Baptist. Threatened by that condemnation, Herod had John arrested and imprisoned. Salome, the daughter of Herodias and both Herod's niece and step-daughter, danced in a way to please Herod. He promised her anything, and prodded by her mother, Salome asked for the head of John the Baptist on a platter.

Was it a mistake for John to be outspoken concerning Herod's disobedience of God's Law? Regardless of severed relationships or severed heads, John spoke with the truth of the Lord. Though his life ended abruptly, God's plan continued in John's absence. As John died, the era of the prophets ended. How great was John? Jesus tells us that of all the Old Testament prophets, He was the greatest!

Assuredly, I say to you, among those born of women there has not risen one greater than John the Baptist; but he who is least in the kingdom of heaven is greater than he.

Matthew 11:11 (NKJV)

Though John had baptized for the repentance of sins, the baptism of the Holy Spirit given by Jesus empowered believers to walk away from sin. Those of us alive in the Church Age have been given an amazing gift, as the Holy Spirit remains with us every moment of our walks. We can lose sight of the fact that serving God may include difficult choices, yet we never should be severed from the truth. Though heads will roll, the Head of our Church is Jesus Christ!

**"Behold, I send My messenger,
And he will prepare the way before Me.
And the Lord, whom you seek,
Will suddenly come to His temple,
Even the Messenger of the covenant,
In whom you delight.
Behold, He is coming,"
Says the LORD of hosts.
Malachi 3:1 (NKJV)**

October 23: Where is your joy?

Certainly, it is impossible to go through life with a smile on our faces every moment of every day, but one of the keys to life is how to retain joy in the midst of trial. While happiness depends upon circumstance, joy depends upon our emotional well-being. Happiness is a fleeting emotion and joy is a way of life. Perhaps our greatest examples of joyfulness come from Jesus while He walked on this earth as a man.

**[17] Then the seventy returned with joy, saying, "Lord, even the demons are subject to us in Your name."
[18] And He said to them, "I saw Satan fall like lightning from heaven. [19] Behold, I give you the authority to trample on serpents and scorpions, and over all the power of the enemy, and nothing shall by any means hurt you. [20] Nevertheless do not rejoice in this, that the spirits are subject to you, but rather rejoice because your names are written in heaven."**

Luke 10:17-20 (NKJV)

When Jesus sent the 70 disciples out in pairs to share the gospel, He sent them without money, food or other supplies. In the verses above, we see that they returned, filled with joy. Though the disciples seemed to emphasize that even the demons were unable to hurt them while preaching in the name of Jesus, the foundation of their joyfulness was not in power, but in obedience. When God assigns a task to a believer, obedience to God always will bring joyfulness. One of the greatest blessings is for God to use the broken and battered lives which have come to Him. God could use anyone or anything to accomplish His plan, so when He chooses to use believers, it is an obvious gift! One of the best known verses on joy tells us:

Then he said to them, "Go your way, eat the fat, drink the sweet, and send portions to those for whom nothing is prepared; for *this* day *is* holy to our Lord. Do not sorrow, for the joy of the LORD is your strength."
Nehemiah 8:10 (NKJV)

It does not matter how dark the road ahead seems to be; certainly, by turning around and looking back on life without the Lord, the pathway seems much darker. No matter how difficult the trials we are facing, the Lord walks with us. If we are on His errand, He will give us power, peace and joy along the way. Imagine the difficulty of the task that the Father assigned to Jesus to accomplish for us!

looking unto Jesus, the author and finisher of *our* faith, who for the joy that was set before Him endured the cross, despising the shame, and has sat down at the right hand of the throne of God.
Hebrews 12:2 (NKJV)

Jesus joyfully endured the cross, though when in the Garden of Gethsemane, He prayed three times that if there was any other way that the Father would let this cup pass from Him. When God the Father did not open another door, Jesus obediently stepped through the door facing Him. Joy comes from obedience to God! It is not a fleeting emotion but a permeating peacefulness. It passes understanding. Joy is trusting that God will handle any obstacle in our paths because He loves us. Joy is not just for our own benefit, but for others around us, as well.

> "Grief can take care of itself, but to get the full value of a joy you must have somebody to divide it with." -- Mark Twain

Many of us tend to walk in sorrow rather than in joy. If that is the case, we should reflect upon our lives to discover the areas of disobedience to the Lord, as that failure to comply with God's plans will sap the joy from anyone. Many churches are familiar with the fact that 10% of the people do 90% of the work. Sadly, that means that 90% of the people are not serving. Our tasks do not need to be church-centered, as many Christians have ministries in their places of work, schools and neighborhoods. Yet without serving God, we are not being obedient to His calling. Without obedience, there is no joy. God's hope is for our joy to be so full that it speaks volumes to a broken and battered world!

These things I have spoken to you, that My joy may remain in you, and *that* your joy may be full.
John 15:11 (NKJV)

Therefore with joy
you will draw water
From the wells of
salvation.
Isaiah 12:3 (NKJV)

October 24: Reconciliation

Our modern world is spiraling out of control. According to George C. Kohn's "Dictionary of Wars," since 2925 B.C., this world has not had a day without war. In the 20th century, wars caused well over 100 million deaths. In fact, from 1910-2010, three times more people died in wars than the total number who died from 1410-1910. As the killing power of weaponry has increased, "might makes right" has become the creed of those in power, as well as those who yearn for that power.

Even without war, people have great difficulty getting along. Whether it is Muslims and Jews, Democrats and Republicans, rich and poor, black and white, labor and management, east and west or any other polarized group, people seem to have migrated far from the middle ground of co-existence. Marriages are suffering in the same capacity. In America, 50% of first marriages end in divorce, while 67% of second marriages and 74% of third marriages also end in the same manner. Even half of Christian marriages are destined for failure. Many families are destroyed by the prideful inability of husbands and wives to yield ever so slightly.

> "The worst reconciliation is better than the best divorce."—Miguel de Cervantes

Reconciliation is a perfect word to describe polar opposites coming together. When an accountant reconciles the books, he balances the assets and liabilities. That was the work that Jesus accomplished for us all. In Greek, the word *katallage* means both reconciliation and atonement, which is the same word for covering in Hebrew. Jesus paid the debt in full. He is the asset and we are the liabilities.

**[21] And you, who once were alienated and enemies in your mind by wicked works, yet now He has reconciled [22] in the body of His flesh through death, to present you holy, and blameless, and above reproach in His sight—
Colossians 1:21-22 (NKJV)**

As that verse in Colossians explains, we who were alienated from God have been given the great gift of acceptance in Jesus Christ. Though we were enemies of Him, serving Satan, He has paid the great debt owed by each of us. New believers walk in the joy of that freedom, as they are most aware of the sin that has been removed. As we continue to walk with the Lord, sometimes we forget the joy of that freedom! Rejoice in the Lord always, and again, rejoice! If He can reconcile the incredible gap between us and God, can we not forgive those in our lives? Even if they have wronged us greatly, it is nothing in comparison to what He forgave in each of us!

**[18] Now all things *are* of God, who has reconciled us to Himself through Jesus Christ, and has given us the ministry of reconciliation, [19] that is, that God was in Christ reconciling the world to Himself, not imputing their trespasses to them, and has committed to us the word of reconciliation.
2 Corinthians 5:18-19 (NKJV)**

Just as Jesus reconciled us to Himself, we are called to join in His ministry. The work of Jesus on the cross was sufficient to cover the sins of the world, though to be redeemed, we must ask Him to be the Lord of our lives. Yet in the same facet, we are called to carry on the ministry of reconciliation. Many come to the Lord with a long list of fractured relationships in their lives. By taking that first step of forgiveness, miracles are accomplished with the Lord's hand. When faced with someone who pushes our buttons, we should remember the debt forgiven in our own lives! But regardless of any reconciliation, we will continue to live in a broken world until Jesus rules and reigns in the Millennial Kingdom!

**And not only *that*, but we also rejoice in God through our Lord Jesus Christ, through whom we have now received the reconciliation.
Romans 5:11 (NKJV)**

October 25: Travel to and fro

A drive from Southern California to Yellowstone National Park passes through six states in 1,200 miles. California, Nevada, Utah, Idaho, Montana and Wyoming are vastly different in relation to topography, population and demographics. In relatively few hours, we can go from coastal splendor to high desert to majestic mountain terrain. Imagine how long this trip would have taken even 100 years ago! Though a brief airplane ride could cut the travel time even more, settlers in covered wagons certainly took many months to make the same journey.

It is amazing to think that a journey of that distance potentially involves going farther away from home than most people in biblical times ventured in their lives. When Jesus traveled throughout Israel, He walked! Additionally, all able-bodied Jewish men over the age of 20 were required to travel to Jerusalem three times per year for the feast weeks. Certainly, people of that time traveled, but it was much more time consuming and much more of a commitment. We tend to take so many of the modern-day conveniences for granted. By looking at one of the most prophetic books in the Old Testament concerning the end times, we get a glimpse into the state of the modern world.

"But you, Daniel, shut up the words, and seal the book until the time of the end; many shall run to and fro, and knowledge shall increase."
Daniel 12:4 (NKJV)

In the verse above, Michael the archangel instructs Daniel to seal the book until the end times. Two of the characteristics of the time period when the book would be unsealed are when people will be running to and fro and knowledge will have increased. Certainly, we have reached that time. There is more information in the Sunday New York Times than in an entire set of encyclopedias 20 years ago! Knowledge has grown exponentially. Many college students find that after learning state-of-the-art information in their fields of study, upon graduation, most of that information already is obsolete.

The Bible tells us what will occur in the end times, though no one knows when any of those events will begin. Yet in the meantime, we should continue to keep our eyes focused on Jesus. It is still easy to see Him in the splendor of His creation! Getting away from modern-day conveniences, if even for a short time, reminds us of a simpler life, where relationship with God did not have to compete with television, computers and iPods! Simplify!

[24]"Seventy weeks are determined
For your people and for your holy city,
To finish the transgression,
To make an end of sins,
To make reconciliation for iniquity,
To bring in everlasting righteousness,
To seal up vision and prophecy,
And to anoint the Most Holy.
[25]"Know therefore and understand,
That from the going forth of the command
To restore and build Jerusalem
Until Messiah the Prince,
There shall be seven weeks and sixty-two weeks;
The street shall be built again, and the wall,
Even in troublesome times.
[26]"And after the sixty-two weeks
Messiah shall be cut off, but not for Himself;
And the people of the prince who is to come
Shall destroy the city and the sanctuary.
The end of it *shall be* with a flood,
And till the end of the war desolations are determined.
[27]Then he shall confirm a covenant with many for one week;
But in the middle of the week
He shall bring an end to sacrifice and offering.
And on the wing of abominations shall be one who makes desolate,
Even until the consummation, which is determined,
Is poured out on the desolate."
Daniel 9:24-27 (NKJV)

October 26: Camping in the rain

Setting up camp in a rainstorm is a great way to get soaked to the bone. Fortunately, most campsites in national parks contain a layer of gravel to facilitate drainage. Otherwise, it would be incredibly uncomfortable sleeping in a tent filled with mud and water in a cold climate. Setting up the tent and campsite is certainly easier in dry conditions, but it is only an inconvenience, not an impossibility.

As Christians, it all has to do with a solid foundation. If our faith was built on ourselves, it would be very similar to putting up a tent in muddy water during a rainstorm. As the rain continues to fall, the tent pegs will loosen and the tent will fall. Once the inside of the tent is wet, nothing but heat and sun will dry it out. Yet instead, the foundation of our faith is Jesus Christ. Because He is rock solid, our lives are built on His stability!

Therefore thus says the Lord GOD:
"Behold, I lay in Zion a stone for a foundation,
A tried stone, a precious cornerstone, a sure foundation;
Whoever believes will not act hastily.
Isaiah 28:16 (NKJV)

Sadly, many Christians make that decision to follow Christ, but continue to walk with one foot in the world. The process of "one-foot walking" is neither comfortable nor effective. Following Jesus involves both feet.

[46] "But why do you call Me 'Lord, Lord,' and not do the things which I say? [47] Whoever comes to Me, and hears My sayings and does them, I will show you whom he is like: [48] He is like a man building a house, who dug deep and laid the foundation on the rock. And when the flood arose, the stream beat vehemently against that house, and could not shake it, for it was founded on the rock. [49] But he who heard and did nothing is like a man who built a house on the earth without a foundation, against which the stream beat vehemently; and immediately it fell. And the ruin of that house was great."
Luke 6:46-49 (NKJV)

What is apparent in the parable above is that storms will arise. Instead of the unrealistic promise that life will be filled with happiness and sunny skies, Jesus reminds us that trials will come and they will be difficult. Yet if Christ is the solid rock of our foundation, no storm will blow our house down. As Christians, we are strangers in a strange land. This world is not our home. Instead, we live in temporary homes. Our earthly bodies are nothing more than tents. Ironically, Paul worked as a tentmaker while preaching to his fellow believers in their earthly tents.

We should let our foundations be set in stone!

Nevertheless the solid foundation of God stands, having this seal: "The Lord knows those who are His," and, "Let everyone who names the name of Christ depart from iniquity."
2 Timothy 2:19 (NKJV)

October 27: God's plan

Knowing that sin separates us from God, does sin have any benefit? Certainly, we know that there is pleasure involved in sin or we would not be drawn to it just as cow manure draws flies! If we are tethered to sin, it remains destructive, but we can learn from sin in our past. In Romans 5 and 6, Paul offers many deep thoughts differentiating between being subject to the Law and being subject to grace.

[6] knowing this, that our old man was crucified with *Him*, that the body of sin might be done away with, that we should no longer be slaves of sin. [7] For he who has died has been freed from sin.
Romans 6:6-7 (NKJV)

All of us struggle with sin, even after becoming Christians. But as the apostle Paul taught in Romans, our bondage to sin has been cut once we have been justified in Christ. Our daily walks with Him include moment-by-moment choices whether or not to sin. That is the period of our sanctification. Before we were Christians, we sinned without thinking, yet now, it is a choice. When we choose to sin as Christians, we choose to glorify Satan, rather than to glorify God. And what we have to look forward to is glorification, when God will once and for all take sin away from us. Oh, what a day that will be!

God's plan rarely goes in the same directions as man's plans. At the same time, God's love was just as great in each of our lives, as He reveals to each of us what He has done and is willing to do on our behalves. Though our sins might seem unforgivable, God has no difficulty in forgiving. Sometimes, the people we have hurt retain that difficulty, though we typically have the hardest time forgiving ourselves. Once that burden has been lifted, and we can walk in the freedom and newness of life in Christ, our love for God increases immensely.

But God demonstrates His own love toward us, in that while we were still sinners, Christ died for us.
Romans 5:8 (NKJV)

God did not choose us because of what we would accomplish for His kingdom. He did not choose us because we earned it. He chose us to demonstrate His love for us. And what a demonstration it was! He died upon a cross of wood, but made the hill on which it stood! How wonderful it is to know that there is nothing we can do that God cannot forgive! All He wants is us to desire a relationship with Him.

He uses our brokenness in the past as a reminder of how great His love is, opening the doors for ministry opportunities. Look around. Where are we walking now? If there is not an opportunity to share God's love, we are not looking for it.

[1] Therefore be imitators of God as dear children. [2] And walk in love, as Christ also has loved us and given Himself for us, an offering and a sacrifice to God for a sweet-smelling aroma.
Ephesians 5:1-2 (NKJV)

October 28: Where the buffalo roam...

It is so strange to be in a place where buffalo roam freely; where elk congregate in herds of one hundred-fold, where man is in the minority, rather than the overwhelming majority. Driving around Yellowstone National Park in late October, there are not many cars on the road. Only 80 park workers are full-time, and once the snow begins, the season is past. Campgrounds are sparse, and the tent-campers are an especially rare commodity. Nights are cold, but there is something peaceful in the starry-skied nights; in hearing the wind and rain rippling against the tent; and in the first, blast of crisp air early in the morning.

Additionally, there is a spiritual benefit in living simpler. Modern-day conveniences have filled us with a cacophony of sound emanating from every direction. The younger generation cannot exist without continuous music from their iPods and even in Yellowstone National Park, the Verizon signal comes through strongly on cell phones. There does not seem to be a moment of silence as even the continuous clicking of fingers sending text messages to random places around the country goes on. Typing a devotional on a computer while sitting in the men's room, plugged into the only electrical adapter available for miles around falls into that same category! We have gotten so plugged in to electronics that we are losing the ability to be plugged in to God.

Be still, and know that I *am* God;
I will be exalted among the nations,
I will be exalted in the earth!
Psalm 46:10 (NKJV)

It is so much easier to hear God's voice when we are meditating on His Word, surrounded by chirping birds and whistling wind. People who claim they cannot hear God are either not reading the Bible or are not listening for His voice, instead choosing to fill the time by watching hours of television, surfing the internet or listening to music. Instead of filling time, should we not use the time for the glory of God? Each of us has the same 24 hours in each day. Certainly, there are some people who use that time much more wisely.

Is it really boring to return to a simpler form of life? There are modern-day conveniences all of us would miss greatly. A hot shower and indoor plumbing certainly would be at the top of many lists. Unplug! Take a trip to where the buffalo roam.

[12]Immediately the Spirit drove Him into the wilderness. [13] And He was there in the wilderness forty days, tempted by Satan, and was with the wild beasts; and the angels ministered to Him.
Mark 1:12-13 (NKJV)

The LORD your God in your midst,
The Mighty One, will save;
He will rejoice over you with gladness,
He will quiet *you* with His love,
He will rejoice over you with singing."
Zephaniah 3:17 (NKJV)

October 29: Walking in the world

It is interesting to discover the world view of people who cross our paths each day. Some of those world views involve a strong worship of money, possessions and gain. Others tend to focus upon nature, and worship God's creation rather than the Creator. Finally, a minority of people attempt to see the world through the eyes of God, and along with that, through the words of the Bible. Yet even Christians find a hard time avoiding the dirt and grime of the world. Sometimes, we need a refresher. Has the world view crept into our biblical world views while we were not paying attention?

[25] He who loves his life will lose it, and he who hates his life in this world will keep it for eternal life. [26] If anyone serves Me, let him follow Me; and where I am, there My servant will be also. If anyone serves Me, him *My* Father will honor.

John 12:25-26 (NKJV)

We look at our modern conveniences as time-savers. It may take less time to cut firewood with a chainsaw than with an axe, but what do we do with the saved time? Watch television? Would our lives be worse if we did not know which woman the Bachelor chose? There is satisfaction in completing a physical day of labor. That labor works our muscles and allows us to eat without getting fat. Our "conveniences" are creating more lethargy than time!

It is wonderful to get away from the world, and return to simpler times. Being away from the cares of home and job makes it easier to focus on God. Many Christians refer to the "mountain-top experience," a time when they feel an enormous closeness to God. Yet as Christians, those mountain-top experiences are not the norm. Instead, our daily walks with the Lord involve trials and tests, for without difficulties, we cannot be stretched or grow! If God did not desire for us to grow closer to Him, He would not leave us on this earth once we became Christians. If we descend from mountains, we always will find ourselves in valleys. All wars are fought in valleys. So what is the real benefit of the mountain top if we do not grow? Those times increase our love for the Lord and our faith in His power, in our lives. Without that strength, we would rely upon self in the midst of the battles and fail miserably!

[18] **"If the world hates you, you know that it hated Me before** *it hated* **you.** [19] **If you were of the world, the world would love its own. Yet because you are not of the world, but I chose you out of the world, therefore the world hates you.** [20] **Remember the word that I said to you, 'A servant is not greater than his master.' If they persecuted Me, they will also persecute you. John 15:18-20 (NKJV)**

Sometimes, we forget how important the world and the things of the world have become to us. Many Christians say they do not want to die until they have seen their grandchildren or mention another special goal. Yet truthfully, any time the Lord is ready for us to sit at His feet and worship would be the best time for that to take place. There is nothing this world has to offer that compares to the least that God has to offer. We need to let His Word clean us daily. There is nothing else that can take the grime of the world away!

[25] **Husbands, love your wives, just as Christ also loved the church and gave Himself for her,** [26] **that He might sanctify and cleanse her with the washing of water by the word,** [27] **that He might present her to Himself a glorious church, not having spot or wrinkle or any such thing, but that she should be holy and without blemish.**
Ephesians 5:25-27 (NKJV)

October 30: The road less traveled

While Europe has incredibly historic and beautiful buildings, which are older than anything in the United States, nothing compares to the national parks in America. With the dollar decreasing in value, more American families are discovering those parks instead of jet-setting around the world. Yosemite, Yellowstone and Glacier National Parks are seeing more visitors than ever before. Yet in a culture of ease, most people seem to drive to each site for a photo opportunity, rather than hike. Most wildlife strays from the beaten path. The prettiest pictures and best memories take extra work. Take a six-mile hike where the passersby are minimal and the sights will surpass those of the easy road.

How often do we miss opportunities in our Christian walks because we desire to take the easy road? Searching for simplicity rarely brings satisfaction. Tackling life exuberantly is a state of mind more than it is a daily choice, yet we fall into habits. Habits, as we all know, can be good or bad.

[13] **"Enter by the narrow gate; for wide *is* the gate and broad *is* the way that leads to destruction, and there are many who go in by it.** [14] **Because narrow *is* the gate and difficult *is* the way which leads to life, and there are few who find it.**

Matthew 7:13-14 (NKJV)

While the verse above applies closely to our abilities as believers to find salvation, it also applies to our daily walks. Many people find themselves following the neon lights of Broadway, but the daily blessings for Christians are more plentiful on the narrow way. We should take time to step out of our comfort zones occasionally. Try not to be so concerned with the easiest way to accomplish a goal, as God often can teach us more when the going gets tough. Walk through the mud, but do not let the glow of Jesus stop shining from us! There are many people in the dirtiest places of the world that desperately need to hear of a God who saves!

^{1}**Blessed *is* the man**
Who walks not in the counsel of the ungodly,
Nor stands in the path of sinners,
Nor sits in the seat of the scornful;
^{2}**But his delight *is* in the law of the LORD,**
And in His law he meditates day and night.
^{3}**He shall be like a tree**
Planted by the rivers of water,
That brings forth its fruit in its season,
Whose leaf also shall not wither;
And whatever he does shall prosper.
Psalm 1:1-3 (NKJV)

October 31: Three, the number of the Trinity

While three may be associated with the number of little piggies, the world that God created consists of many attributes separated in three parts. In the dimension of time, all exist in either past, present or future, with even the smallest increments of our lives broken down into yesterday, today and tomorrow. Every action will fall into the categories of thought, word and deed, while matter can be separated into mineral, vegetable and animal. Three is geometrically, the number of a cube, expressing length, width and height. Yet we never should limit God or His power to those three dimensions. While man plays on a three-dimensional chessboard, God plays on a chessboard with many more dimensions. When our problems seem too big for us to handle, God's solutions make our problems look inconsequential. Even that power of God can be summarized in His omniscience (God knows everything); His omnipresence (God is everywhere); and His omnipotence (God is all powerful).

There are four numbers standing for perfection in the Bible. While three is significant in terms of Divine perfection, seven points to spiritual perfection. Additionally, 10 relates to ordinal perfection, while 12 signifies governmental perfection. God is perfect in every way, unlike His creation. All of creation changed when Adam sinned, and groans for the return of the Son of God, who will perfect all vanity (Romans 8:22-23).

I have seen all the works that are done under the sun; and indeed, all *is* vanity and grasping for the wind.
Ecclesiastes 1:14 (NKJV)

Obviously, the greatest example of God's perfect divinity involves His existence as One God in three persons. While it is difficult for our human brains to completely grasp the ramifications of that fact, we first must understand that Father, Son and Holy Spirit operate in a completely unified way. That in itself is hard for us to comprehend, as whenever three people get together, even when formed in love, we lose sight of purposes, plans and goals. On the other hand, God's omnipotence ensures that there are no mistakes along the way.

Notice in the Scriptures that Jesus always accomplished the will of the Father. It was not because the Son was less powerful or less knowledgeable, yet He willingly submitted Himself to the Father, just as a wife is called to submit herself to her husband in Ephesians 5:22. Submission is not a master-slave relationship, but instead, is best understood in the military in terms of rank, involving order and chain of command. At the same time, the Holy Spirit always testifies of Jesus! Instead of calling attention to Himself, He remains the unnamed servant modeled in the Old

Testament when Abraham's servant journeyed to find a bride for Isaac (Genesis 24:4).

We can see that God exists in plural form in the first verse of the Bible, as the Hebrew word for God, *Elohim*, designates plurality, though its usage is singular. When reading Psalm 2, an interesting exercise is to identify the pronouns. Who does the psalmist refer to in each verse, Father, Son or Holy Spirit? By spending time in this psalm, what becomes apparent is the conversation among the Trinity:

[1] **Why do the nations rage,
And the people plot a vain thing?**
[2] **The kings of the earth set themselves,
And the rulers take counsel together,
Against the LORD and against His Anointed,** *saying,*
[3] **"Let us break Their bonds in pieces
And cast away Their cords from us."**
[4] **He who sits in the heavens shall laugh;
The LORD shall hold them in derision.**
[5] **Then He shall speak to them in His wrath,
And distress them in His deep displeasure:**
[6] **"Yet I have set My King
On My holy hill of Zion."**
[7] **"I will declare the decree:
The LORD has said to Me,
'You** *are* **My Son,
Today I have begotten You.**
[8] **Ask of Me, and I will give** *You*
The nations *for* **Your inheritance,
And the ends of the earth** *for* **Your possession.**
[9] **You shall break them with a rod of iron;
You shall dash them to pieces like a potter's vessel.' "**
[10] **Now therefore, be wise, O kings;
Be instructed, you judges of the earth.**
[11] **Serve the LORD with fear,
And rejoice with trembling.**
[12] **Kiss the Son, lest He be angry,
And you perish** *in* **the way,**

When His wrath is kindled but a little.
Blessed *are* all those who put their trust in Him.
Psalm 2 (NKJV)

Certainly, that significance of three as divine perfection can be seen throughout the Bible. In the tabernacle, the Holy of Holies was basically a cube, with specific length, width and height. Not surprisingly, the third book of the Bible, Leviticus, deals with true worship of God, with the Holy of Holies being the highest place of worship. Worship is not repeating the words to memorized songs. Instead, the best description of worship is to love God in return. He loved us first, and demonstrated that love in the most powerful way. Nails did not hold Jesus to the cross; it was His love for us, and the Father's love for us, as Jesus accomplished the Father's will. That accomplishment, though it was brutal for Jesus and the Father (Isaiah 53:10), brought us near to God and removed the separation.

[23] But the hour is coming, and now is, when the true worshipers will worship the Father in spirit and truth; for the Father is seeking such to worship Him. [24] God *is* Spirit, and those who worship Him must worship in spirit and truth."
John 4:23-24 (NKJV)

While walking as a Christian certainly has its difficulties, that life change is as easy as 1-2-3. When we come to the Lord, and surrender our lives to Him, He opens the doors and closes them. Any trial that comes our way, He helps us to endure. Every step of our journeys as Christians is a part of His plan, to instruct us in His ways and draw us closer to Him. We have an intimate relationship with the Father, who wants us to call Him Daddy in our childlike adoration (Romans 8:15). At the same time, we have an intimacy with Jesus, our Savior, who carried each of our sins upon His shoulders, punished with death instead of us (2 Corinthians 5:21). Lastly, how could God be any more intimate with us, as He has given us the Holy Spirit to dwell inside of us all the days of our lives? Divine perfection carries us through each aspect of our lives, if we are willing to hand those lives to Him!

²¹ **When all the people were baptized, it came to pass that Jesus also was baptized; and while He prayed, the heaven was opened.** ²² **And the Holy Spirit descended in bodily form like a dove upon Him, and a voice came from heaven which said, "You are My beloved Son; in You I am well pleased." Luke 3:21-22 (NKJV)**

November 1: Back to the battleground!

Vacations have been around since the English gave the legal courts a long, summer break. Today, many vacations coincide with particular holidays, and often point to recreation or tourism. Yet the term vacation can apply to relatively any departure from normal, day-to-day activities. In 1971, a McDonald's advertisement included the jingle, "You deserve a break today. So get up and get away to McDonald's." For housewives yearning to escape the monotony of cooking daily meals, the not-so-healthy fast food became a possibility. Obviously, all vacations are not improvements on what we view as daily drudgery!

Some of us head to the mountains for vacation. For some reason, mountains can speak to our souls differently than any other topography. While any of God's creation has its own unique beauty, the sights, smells and sounds of a mountain landscape appeal to all of our senses at the same time. Each journey is at least somewhat of an escape from the daily grind. Yet the first days back always occur with reluctance, as the "civilized" world seems to get in the way, desiring to change the rhythms of focus on God.

For an example of how one godly man in the Bible viewed vacation, we can look at Uriah the Hittite, the husband of Bathsheba. Soon after King David had committed adultery with Bathsheba and impregnated her, the king devised a plan to bring his soldier Uriah home for a vacation, hoping Uriah would sleep with Bathsheba and would not discover her infidelity with the king.

⁸ And David said to Uriah, "Go down to your house and wash your feet." So Uriah departed from the king's house, and a gift *of food* from the king followed him. ⁹ But Uriah slept at the door of the king's house with all the servants of his lord, and did not go down to his house. ¹⁰ So when they told David, saying, "Uriah did not go down to his house," David said to Uriah, "Did you not come from a journey? Why did you not go down to your house?"
¹¹ And Uriah said to David, "The ark and Israel and Judah are dwelling in tents, and my lord Joab and the servants of my lord are encamped in the open fields. Shall I then go to my house to eat and drink, and to lie with my wife? *As* you live, and *as* your soul lives, I will not do this thing."
2 Samuel 11:8-11 (NKJV)

Vacations are not meant to be escapes from duty. Confederate General Robert E. Lee once said,

> "Duty then is the sublimest word in the English language. You should do your duty in all things. You can never do more. You should never wish to do less."

Our duties as Christians are summed up in John 15, and those duties are threefold. First, we are to abide in Christ:

Abide in Me, and I in you. As the branch cannot bear fruit of itself, unless it abides in the vine, neither can you, unless you abide in Me.
John 15:4 (NKJV)

Next, we are to love one another:

This is My commandment, that you love one another as I have loved you.
John 15:12 (NKJV)

Thirdly, we are to carry the witness of Jesus to an unbelieving world:

[18] "**If the world hates you, you know that it hated Me before** *it hated* **you.** [19] **If you were of the world, the world would love its own. Yet because you are not of the world, but I chose you out of the world, therefore the world hates you.** [20] **Remember the word that I said to you, 'A servant is not greater than his master.' If they persecuted Me, they will also persecute you. If they kept My word, they will keep yours also.**
John 15:18-20 (NKJV)

God certainly has covered the bases in His assignments to us all, as we have a responsibility to Him first, then to ourselves, and finally, to the rest of the people we come in contact with on a daily basis. Notice that the relationship with God comes first, but many of us tend to focus on what we can see and touch physically. Instead of devoting the beginning of each day to God, we give Him the time that is left over, if any is. Most of us are great at taking care of our own needs, or at least trying to, though we often confuse the words "needs" and "desires." Putting those two words together gives us "deeds," and those deeds are for others, not self! We all know that it takes much patience and even more love to reach out to people who do not love us, but that is exactly what Jesus did! He loved each of us before we ever dreamed of loving Him, and we are to follow His example.

Since coincidences do not exist, we should look for someone whom God puts in our paths and share the Lord's love with them! Sharing God's love can sometimes involve words, but more often will involve deeds, fulfilling at least a portion of their needs and desires. When confronted with undeserved love, most people will reflect upon that action. That love changed the lives of each Christian, and God can use us to change other lives, too!

Now the purpose of the commandment is love from a pure heart, *from* **a good conscience, and** *from* **sincere faith,**

1 Timothy 1:5

November 2: Be a Barnabas!

Mount Everest is the highest mountain in the world, at 29,029 feet. With the first successful ascent by Sir Edmund Hillary and Tenzing Norgay in 1953, the feat has been celebrated as one of the most important accomplishments by mankind. Since that time, many others have reached the icy summit with the help of bottled oxygen. In fact, climbers began using oxygen on the mountain as early as 1922. When each step is a life-or-death struggle, a simple breath of fresh air can put just enough spring in a step to continue even the most difficult of tasks.

Oxygen to an extreme mountain climber is like encouragement to a believer. Each of us is faced with obstacles of seemingly epic proportions at times in our Christian walks. A well-placed comment or pat on the back from a fellow believer can sometimes be the difference between success and failure. All of us in the midst of struggle continuously question whether the task is too arduous and we should turn back. When that inner argument is taking place, a little encouragement can push us to the decision to continue in the task. Jesus, always the reflection of every godly behavior, gave us a great example of encouragement when He said:

These things I have spoken to you, that in Me you may have peace. In the world you will have tribulation; but be of good cheer, I have overcome the world."
John 16:33 (NKJV)

Without enduring a similar hardship, even the most encouraging words can fall upon deaf ears. Yet all of us know the hardship that Jesus endured for our behalves on the cross. Because He overcame, He will carry us through any trial or tribulation in our paths, as well. Another man in the Bible known for his encouraging nature was Barnabas. Even his name means "son of encouragement." When the disciples of Jesus were in their most trying circumstance, after their Savior had been crucified,

Barnabas brought Saul of Tarsus to meet them. Untrusting of the man who had formerly persecuted Christians, they were unwilling to meet with him until Barnabas encouraged them in the message Saul would bring.

But Barnabas took him and brought *him* to the apostles. And he declared to them how he had seen the Lord on the road, and that He had spoken to him, and how he had preached boldly at Damascus in the name of Jesus.
Acts 9:27 (NKJV)

Saul had seen Jesus and spoken with Jesus! For those who could not believe without seeing, like Thomas, the words lifted their spirits, enabling the disciples to proceed with the ministry. Another mention of Barnabas also tells us much:

[6] Now when they had gone through the island to Paphos, they found a certain sorcerer, a false prophet, a Jew whose name *was* Bar-Jesus, [7] who was with the proconsul, Sergius Paulus, an intelligent man. This man called for Barnabas and Saul and sought to hear the word of God.
Acts 13:6-7 (NKJV)

Barnabas and Saul were sought when people wanted to hear God's Word! Encouragement often can be an uplifting comment. "Hang in there; you are going to make it." Yet for those of us who seek the Lord, the most encouraging remark can be a well-placed verse from the Bible. What man says can be uplifting, yet what God says can save lives! Each of us has times when we need encouragement, and additionally, times when we can be an encouragement to those God places in our paths. Encouragement is a matter of the heart, both giving and receiving. Take heart!

[1] Therefore, when we could no longer endure it, we thought it good to be left in Athens alone, [2] and sent Timothy, our brother and minister of God, and our fellow laborer in the gospel of Christ, to establish you and encourage you concerning your faith, [3] that no one should be shaken by

these afflictions; for you yourselves know that we are appointed to this.
1 Thessalonians 3:1-3 (NKJV)

November 3: Fresh and new

What would it be like to receive a prison sentence of life without parole? Knowledge that all our freedoms for the remainder of life have evaporated would create desperation in the spirit. With living space confined, in addition to every imaginable choice, prisoners may not discuss the inner reflection upon the choices that brought them to that place, yet it is certain that every prisoner punishes themselves for the faulty choices.

It is amazing that we serve a God of forgiveness, who is willing to give each of us a fresh start every day! While we may still have to deal with the ramifications of our sin, God removes those sins as far as the east is from the west, when we come to Him in repentance.

**^{22}*Through* the LORD's mercies we are not consumed,
Because His compassions fail not.
^{23}*They are* new every morning;
Great *is* Your faithfulness.
Lamentations 3:22-23 (NKJV)**

Though God has given us the great gift of His grace, which is receiving something we do not deserve, He also fills us with His mercy. Mercy is not getting something we deserve. All we deserve is death, yet God in His mercy, gives us abundant life on this earth, as well as eternal life with Him! According to Lamentations, that mercy occurs on a daily basis. Most of us can think of someone in our lives who has committed suicide. Certainly, suicide is an act of desperation, when life is not working out with our hopes and dreams. Yet in God's eyes, each day can be a fresh start. Though the night may be filled with weeping, wailing and mourning, when the sun arises each morning, it sheds a new light on it all.

Is it any wonder that dawn is often the most beautiful time of the day? God's tender heart hears our cries. In fact, he collects our tears, for His safe keeping!

You number my wanderings;
Put my tears into Your bottle;
***Are they* not in Your book?**
Psalm 56:8 (NKJV)

Certainly, there are painful issues in each of our lives and some of the most difficult journeys in our pasts we never will forget. Yet the tears that seemed endless at the time fade into a distant memory. God never forgets. He keeps all of our pains near and dear to His heart. God's heart is tender and His mercies are tender, too!

Let Your tender mercies come to me, that I may live;
For Your law *is* my delight.
Psalm 119:177 (NKJV)

Depth of depravity and level of sin has no impact on the tender mercies of our Lord, who is willing and able to forgive if we are willing to repent. Even a serial killer in prison may come to know God's tender mercies! Those who come to the Lord can still walk in the freedom of forgiveness, though they will remain in prison as a result of their murderous pasts. Prison with the Lord is much better than freedom without Him!

When we are exhausted from carrying a burden that is too heavy for our shoulders, we can lay that burden down at the foot of the cross and let Jesus carry it for us! Each morning when the sun arises, remember that His mercies are fresh and new each day! Walk in His light and walk in His freedom!

[1]I will sing of the mercies of the LORD forever;
With my mouth will I make known Your faithfulness to all generations.
[2]For I have said, "Mercy shall be built up forever;
Your faithfulness You shall establish in the very heavens."

Psalm 89:1-2 (NKJV)

November 4: Acts of kindness

In 1995, "The Random Acts of Kindness Foundation" was established. Five years later, the movie "Pay It Forward" promoted people helping others altruistically. Each time our paths intersect with those of another person, we have the opportunity to display kindness. Certainly, most people instantly can feel the difference between true kindness and an action based on ulterior motives. In that regard, the phrase "what's in it for me" should have nothing to do with kindness.

British author Samuel Johnson once said, "Kindness is in our power, even when fondness is not." Johnson understood the deeper nuance of kindness, as it has nothing to do with affection, feeling or emotion. Instead, kindness is an action that speaks volumes. God has been teaching His children about kindness since the world began, and as the best teachers lead by example, God has demonstrated His kindness to each of us. At the same time, He expects His children to treat others with the same kindness, which includes the unbelieving world. Sadly, we even have difficulty treating our Christian friends with that kindness.

One of the greatest friendships in the Bible existed between David and Jonathan, with a relationship closer than brothers. Jonathan was the son of King Saul, who was trying to kill David. It must have been a true test of their friendship, as Jonathan found himself in the unenviable position of choosing between his best friend, a godly man, and his father, who had been God's anointed, but was no longer walking strongly with the Lord.

[11] And Jonathan said to David, "Come, let us go out into the field." So both of them went out into the field. [12] Then Jonathan said to David: "The LORD God of Israel *is witness!* **When I have sounded out my father sometime tomorrow,** *or* **the third** *day,* **and indeed** *there is* **good toward David, and I do not send to you and tell you,** [13] **may the LORD do so and much more to Jonathan. But if it pleases my father** *to do* **you**

evil, then I will report it to you and send you away, that you may go in safety. And the LORD be with you as He has been with my father. [14] And you shall not only show me the kindness of the LORD while I still live, that I may not die; [15] but you shall not cut off your kindness from my house forever, no, not when the LORD has cut off every one of the enemies of David from the face of the earth."
1 Samuel 20:11-15 (NKJV)

Jonathan demonstrated great kindness to David. Even knowing that his father was making horrendously bad choices, Jonathan continued to show loyalty to his father, too, yet not by jeopardizing the friendship with David. Sadly, Jonathan died on the battlefield alongside his errant father, King Saul. David subsequently became the king, and honored his promise to Jonathan by inviting Jonathan's son, Mephibosheth, to eat at the king's table, instead of eradicating the line of King Saul. Though the kindness exhibited between David and Jonathan was real, it is certainly easier to treat friends in that manner, rather than enemies. Without God's help, through the Holy Spirit dwelling within us, that kind of kindness is improbable, if not impossible.

[22] **But the fruit of the Spirit is love, joy, peace, longsuffering, kindness, goodness, faithfulness,** [23] **gentleness, self-control. Against such there is no law.**
Galatians 5:22-23 (NKJV)

While the Holy Spirit gives each believer at least one spiritual gift, all of the fruits of the Spirit will be exhibited by each believer, at least part of the time. Since God does not instantly perfect us once we become believers, utilizing the fruits of the Spirit occurs more frequently when we are walking in the Spirit.

> Kindness is a language that the deaf can hear and the blind can see. ---Mark Twain

Kindness can affect even the most jaded, softening the hardest hearts. Yet, we cannot truly understand kindness until we grasp the great kindness that God showed us, by sending His Son to die in our places while we were still sinners. Walking in the freedom of what Jesus accomplished for us should remind us of the kindness He would like us to exhibit to others. We should look for opportunities to share the Lord's kindness with others in our paths. Certainly, God will provide unlimited opportunities and challenge us with people we might see as undeserving of that kindness! Yet it is His calling on our lives.

³ For we ourselves were also once foolish, disobedient, deceived, serving various lusts and pleasures, living in malice and envy, hateful and hating one another. ⁴ But when the kindness and the love of God our Savior toward man appeared, ⁵ not by works of righteousness which we have done, but according to His mercy He saved us, through the washing of regeneration and renewing of the Holy Spirit, ⁶ whom He poured out on us abundantly through Jesus Christ our Savior, ⁷ that having been justified by His grace we should become heirs according to the hope of eternal life. Titus 3:3-7 (NKJV)

November 5: The sense of smell

When God created the human body, He gave us the senses of hearing, seeing, feeling, tasting and smelling. While they all work together to enhance our experience on this earth, some senses seem more important than others. The sense of smell would not be at the top of the list, as only half of the potential smells are pleasant ones. Yet it is difficult to imagine life without the smells of freshly-ground coffee, baking bread, puppy breath and a spring rain. On the other hand, in some cases, the loss of the ability to smell actually could be beneficial. It sure would make life easier if working at a sewer treatment plant or in the stockyards.

Paul wrote to the Corinthians of the juxtaposition between the stench of death and the sweet-smelling perfume of life in Christ:

¹⁴ Now thanks *be* to God who always leads us in triumph in Christ, and through us diffuses the fragrance of His knowledge in every place. ¹⁵ For we are to God the fragrance of Christ among those who are being saved and among those who are perishing. ¹⁶ To the one *we are* the aroma of death *leading* to death, and to the other the aroma of life *leading* to life. And who *is* sufficient for these things? ¹⁷ For we are not, as so many, peddling the word of God; but as of sincerity, but as from God, we speak in the sight of God in Christ.
2 Corinthians 2:14-17 (NKJV)

To spread the knowledge of Christ is a sweet perfume to a world of stench. Yet just as pigs do not realize how badly they smell, the world does not begin to comprehend the level of its odor. A week-long camping trip into the wilderness of Montana and Wyoming can reveal that analogy to us in a different way. When surrounded by others with a similar stench, that odor is not nearly as offensive. Yet when half of the stinkers shower, their soap-and-shampoo scents make the rest of us reek! Similarly, the knowledge of God is such a sweet-smelling aroma that it accentuates the dirt and grime of the world.

When men built God's tabernacle, which according to Hebrews 8:5 was a copy of the tabernacle in heaven, one of the parts was a golden altar of incense, which sat in front of the curtain of the Holy of Holies. The altar of incense was about three feet tall, and 1.5 feet square. According to the commands of God, the priests were to burn incense upon that altar every morning and evening, and then it remained burning throughout the day. The sweet-smelling aroma was symbolic of our prayers to God, as that is how He views our communication with Him. King David gave us many examples in his psalms of those prayers, reminiscent of Paul's admonishment in 1 Thessalonians 5:17 to "pray without ceasing."

Let my prayer be set before You *as* incense,
The lifting up of my hands *as* the evening sacrifice.
Psalm 141:2 (NKJV)

[3] Then another angel, having a golden censer, came and stood at the altar. He was given much incense, that he should offer *it* with the prayers of all the saints upon the golden altar which was before the throne. [4] And the smoke of the incense, with the prayers of the saints, ascended before God from the angel's hand.
Revelation 8:3-4 (NKJV)

How do we smell? Have we been washed clean in the Word of God, redeemed by the blood of the Lamb? Do we continuously talk to our Creator, knowing that He loves us and went to the farthest extremes to demonstrate His love for us? Any prayer we have for the Lord smells sweet to Him, for He created us to have a close relationship with Him. Just as He walked with Adam in the Garden of Eden, He desires to walk with us, surrounded by the sweet perfume of the most beautiful flowers. Yet if we are surrounded by the stench of the world, we might not recognize that the world's stench clings just as strongly to us. He wants to wash us in His Word, that we might be a sweet-smelling aroma unto Him!

Dead flies putrefy the perfumer's ointment,
And cause it to give off a foul odor;
So does **a little folly to one respected for wisdom** *and* **honor.**
Ecclesiastes 10:1 (NKJV)

November 6: Misery

Misery is not a state in the Midwest between Kansas and Illinois, but instead, is a state of extreme unhappiness, despondency or wretchedness. Sadly, if we look around, it is easy to find a large number of miserable people. Many of those feeling miserable are in better situations than happier people surrounding them. Consequently, misery also can depend upon the strength and fortitude of the inner man. We know that "misery loves company" and in our difficult economic times, that company has grown immensely.

> "It is by attempting to reach the top in a single leap that so much misery is caused in the world." --- William Cobbett, 18th-century English journalist

Misery occurs when expectation greatly exceeds the present condition, and additionally, when changes to that condition do not occur quickly enough to satisfy desires. Though we have been told that a spoonful of sugar helps the medicine go down, many people become disgruntled when the medicine still retains a slightly bitter taste. Those without God are destined for bitterness and misery, as life without hope is wretchedness.

[10] **As it is written:**
"There is none righteous, no, not one;
[11] *There is none who understands;*
There is none who seeks after God.
[12] *They have all turned aside;*
They have together become unprofitable;
There is none who does good, no, not one."
[13] *"Their throat is an open tomb;*
With their tongues they have practiced deceit";
"The poison of asps is under their lips";
[14] *"Whose mouth is full of cursing and bitterness."*
[15] *"Their feet are swift to shed blood;*
[16] *Destruction and misery are in their ways;*
[17] *And the way of peace they have not known."*
[18] *"There is no fear of God before their eyes."*
Romans 3:10-18 (NKJV)

With the hope of Jesus Christ, Christians have no reason to walk in misery, though when we lose sight of God's hand in our lives, we blindly can walk that route. Yet God is gracious, continuing to uplift us even when we fail to trust Him. Love is the answer. Without love, we cannot forgive others. Love cannot exist without forgiveness, and forgiveness cannot exist without love! Many of those walking in misery are carrying the burdens of unforgiveness. As Christians, we are called to forgive others just as Christ forgave us. All of us have been hurt by others. That pain seems to linger longer when caused by fellow believers, yet

God's mandate for us to release that burden applies just as strongly, if not more so, in those situations. Yet somehow, most of us feel the need to punish those whom have caused our pain, rather than trusting that God can handle it all much better. Instead of responding in judgment, God desires for us to respond in love. Love caused Paul to spend two years in Ephesus, sewing tents every morning, preaching and writing in the afternoon, and sewing tents every evening (1 Thessalonians 2:9). Paul financially supported his own ministry, and that ministry involved spreading the gospel to Jews and Greeks. Without complaint, Paul accepted his difficulties and trusted the Lord. His love for others was apparent in all he did.

> "Whoever is spared personal pain must feel himself called to help in diminishing the pain of others. We must all carry our share of the misery which lies upon the world." – Albert Schweitzer

We may have to carry the misery, but we do not have to let it envelop us. God's strength carries us and each of our burdens. How heavy can those burdens be, if He is shouldering all of them? While trust might be a very large step, when we reflect upon God's strength in our lives, all we can see is that He never lets us down. When the Lord continues to rescue us in each trial, it builds our faith to trust Him in the darkest times as well. Do not be a miserable Christian! We should let His joy radiate from our lives and from our faces! While misery might like company, we ought to leave the pity party and surround ourselves with the joy of the Lord!

[16] that He would grant you, according to the riches of His glory, to be strengthened with might through His Spirit in the inner man, [17] that Christ may dwell in your hearts through faith; that you, being rooted and grounded in love, [18] may be able to comprehend with all the saints what *is* the width and length and depth and height— [19] to know the love of Christ which passes knowledge; that you may be filled with all the fullness of God.

Ephesians 3:16-19 (NKJV)
November 7: What do you want?

Soccer fans are familiar with the calling of the announcer for Mexico's national soccer team when his players score a goal. The multi-syllabic droning can go on longer than the play that scored the goal! As unique (and irritating) as he can be, would it not be revealing if our own achieved goals were that easy to recognize? Certainly, the goals of most people are centered upon "things." We want more things! Bigger homes, bigger cars, bigger vacations and bigger bank accounts seem to grab the focus of our waking and sleeping hours. Those desires can apply to our children just as easily as they apply to us. We remind ourselves that it is all about additional security. Even Eve was not satisfied with the abundance of fruit God allowed her to eat, but desired more. Additionally, others in the Bible stumbled in a similar way, just as we do.

[20] Then the mother of Zebedee's sons came to Him with her sons, kneeling down and asking something from Him.
[21] And He said to her, "What do you wish?"
She said to Him, "Grant that these two sons of mine may sit, one on Your right hand and the other on the left, in Your kingdom."
[22] But Jesus answered and said, "You do not know what you ask. Are you able to drink the cup that I am about to drink, and be baptized with the baptism that I am baptized with?" They said to Him, "We are able."
[23] So He said to them, "You will indeed drink My cup, and be baptized with the baptism that I am baptized with; but to sit on My right hand and on My left is not Mine to give, but *it is for those* for whom it is prepared by My Father."
Matthew 20:20-23 (NKJV)

Instead of the wife of Zebedee asking Jesus for the elevation of her sons, the author of Mark 10 describes the "sons of thunder" asking Jesus directly. Regardless of who asked the question, the ambitious desires remained the same in all concerned. Desiring to be elevated to the left and right of Jesus gave all three a different picture soon after this event, as those elevated to His left and right were the thieves on the crosses beside Jesus! Would the wife of Zebedee have asked Jesus for her sons to be crucified along with the Lord?

Our ambitions often get in the way of how we serve God. Rather than asking the Lord for more power or money, we would benefit by asking Him for more humility or love. King Solomon could have asked God for anything, but asked for wisdom, as he desired to represent the people of Israel in a more godly way. Certainly, as Christians, our ambitions should be to serve the Lord more fully. Because we do not always see the big picture, as God does, we never understand the purposes that He is fulfilling in each of our lives. Some of the people that the Lord has used to impact us the most deeply remain unaware of God using them in the lives of others. Sometimes, our ministries can be seemingly silent and powerful through the Lord's hands.

What should we desire? The best answer to that question is for us to desire exactly what the Lord desires in our lives! When our will coincides with His will, miracles will occur. The biggest step that each of us must take to get to that place is contentment with whatever the Lord has in store for us, as difficult as it may seem! Our Father knows best!

**³ *Let* nothing *be done* through selfish ambition or conceit, but in lowliness of mind let each esteem others better than himself. ⁴ Let each of you look out not only for his own interests, but also for the interests of others.
Philippians 2:3-4 (NKJV)**

November 8: Grace or works?

In the 1980s, Smith-Barney ran an ad with John Houseman, the actor who played the difficult Harvard Law professor in "The Paper Chase." Houseman's dead-pan delivery portrayed the Smith-Barney tag line, "I made my money the old-fashioned way. I earned it!" For those not old enough to remember this advertisement, or too old to remember anything, speak those words with an over emphasis on the word "earned."

In the Bible, the old-fashioned way also was based on our earnings. God gave us the 10 Commandments as a tutor. Through those commandments, the Lord demonstrated to us that we were not righteous enough to keep all of His laws all of the time. Salvation only could be achieved by perfection. No matter how hard men would strive to follow the Lord's laws, everyone committed many sins. Additionally, God gave men a sin remedy in the form of blood sacrifices. Those were also based on works, man's actions as opposed to God's actions. The sacrificial system certainly reminded all of God's followers that covering their sins took a lot of work.

Then it all changed when Jesus came to earth to live as a man. Though He lived a perfect life, Jesus willingly died the brutal death of the cross, and then was resurrected. At that moment, God gave us a new-fashioned way to achieve salvation. No longer "works-based," the new way is "grace-based." Jesus completed the work, and then gave the gift of salvation to all who desired to receive it! Grace has been described as receiving what is unearned or even by the phrase, "God's riches at Christ's expense."

[8] For by grace you have been saved through faith, and that not of yourselves; *it is* **the gift of God, [9] not of works, lest anyone should boast. [10] For we are His workmanship, created in Christ Jesus for good works, which God prepared beforehand that we should walk in them.**
Ephesians 2:8-10 (NKJV)

"Workmanship," in the verse above is the Greek word *poiema*, which sounds like our word poem. When God created believers, He wrote a love sonnet in us! Many people misquote the verse above, stating that faith is a gift from God. Instead, the verse reminds us that grace is the gift from God! It is difficult to understand grace without emphasizing our spiritual condition without the Lord! King David wrote of that spiritual condition:

**¹³As a father pities *his* children,
So the LORD pities those who fear Him.
¹⁴For He knows our frame;
He remembers that we *are* dust
Psalm 103:13-14 (NKJV)**

From the dust He formed us, and from the dust we shall return. Somehow, we lose sight of the fact that we have no chance at anything but dirtiness and griminess without God's hand. Our dirty sins keep us separated from God.

**¹ Behold, the Lord's hand is not shortened,
That it cannot save;
Nor His ear heavy,
That it cannot hear.
² But your iniquities have separated you from your God;
And your sins have hidden *His* face from you,
So that He will not hear.
Isaiah 59:1-2 (NKJV)**

Works can be good or bad, yet God's works in our lives only can be perfect! As believers, our works do have an impact, as faith without works is dead according to James 2:20. Yet those works are not to earn our own salvation, but to glorify God with our lives, leading others to salvation. As believers, if we were doing an advertisement for God, we would say, "I got my salvation the new-fashioned way. God gave it to me!" Understanding the far-reaching depth of that gift should give each of us cause to jump for joy. Let the light of the Lord shine from our faces, far from Professor Kingsfield's deadpan delivery.

⁸ Therefore do not be ashamed of the testimony of our Lord, nor of me His prisoner, but share with me in the sufferings for the gospel according to the power of God, ⁹ who has saved us and called *us* with a holy calling, not according to our works, but according to His own purpose and grace which was given to us in Christ Jesus before time began,

2 Timothy 1:8-9 (NKJV)

November 9: There is a lot of room at the foot of the cross!

When Mary and Joseph were looking for a warm place to spend the night in Bethlehem with the birth of Jesus quickly approaching, there were no rooms at the inn. As the world's population continues to grow, we often find ourselves in positions where the innkeepers disappoint us, though Holiday Inn's advertisement says they are, "Pleasing people the world over." Pleasing people should not be at the top of our list, even if we are "the world's innkeeper."

For do I now persuade men, or God? Or do I seek to please men? For if I still pleased men, I would not be a bondservant of Christ.
Galatians 1:10 (NKJV)

Concerning the chain Motel 6, instead of having no rooms at the inn, National Public Radio announcer Tom Bodett reminded us, "We'll keep the light on for you." While the accommodations might not be as luxurious and the economy may have caused them to cut the electric bill by turning the lights off, it is nice to find a room, and one that allows pets! Certainly, any Motel 6 is much more comfortable than the manger where Jesus was born. It is wonderful that God never will tell us that there are no rooms at His inn. We can rest in Him and always can come to Him with every problem and concern.

[4] But God, who is rich in mercy, because of His great love with which He loved us, [5] even when we were dead in trespasses, made us alive together with Christ (by grace you have been saved), [6] and raised *us* up together, and made *us* sit together in the heavenly *places* in Christ Jesus, [7] that in the ages to come He might show the exceeding riches of His grace in His kindness toward us in Christ Jesus.
Ephesians 2:4-7 (NKJV)

Interestingly, in the verse above, when Paul speaks of God's great love "with which He loved us," the word "loved" is in the Greek aorist tense, which denotes an action that occurred at one specific time in the past. Though it is certain that God continues to love us, He demonstrated His love for us at the cross! God's mercy and grace occurred when Jesus willingly gave His life for us at Calvary. There is a lot of room at the foot of the cross. In fact, there is room for anyone who desires freedom from the bondage of sin. There is room for anyone who desires a life of strength and joy. There is room for anyone who desires the peace that passes understanding.

Sometimes, we erroneously believe that our problems are too small to matter to God, as He has much more important items on His agenda. Yet we are underestimating the size and power of God, who has enough of both to answer all of our prayers and supply all of our needs. Amazingly, He loves each of us so much that all of the issues of our lives matter to Him! It matters not how sinful our lives have been or how far away from God we have walked. He desires for us to come to the foot of the cross and receive His grace. When we are struggling, all we have to do is pick up the pieces and carry them to the place where Jesus accomplished it all on our behalves!

While Motel 6 might keep a light on for us, the Light of the world always will have room for us at the foot of the cross. Looking up at Jesus on the cross, seeing His blood-stained hands and feet, and feeling His tear-stained eyes will remind each of us of the love He demonstrated to show us the way.

[10]Yet it pleased the LORD to bruise Him;
He has put *Him* to grief.
When You make His soul an offering for sin,
He shall see *His* seed, He shall prolong *His* days,
And the pleasure of the LORD shall prosper in His hand.
[11]He shall see the labor of His soul, *and* be satisfied.
By His knowledge My righteous Servant shall justify many,
For He shall bear their iniquities.

Isaiah 53:10-11 (NKJV)

November 10: The "Bread of Life" is not fast food!

With the frantic pace of life in the modern world, we all seem to look for moments to fit in another activity. Even our eating habits have changed from sit-down, family meals of yesteryear to an energy bar on the run, or worse, frequent stops at the drive-through windows of fast food restaurants. With Thanksgiving approaching, that might be the last American meal when a family takes the time to eat, talk and share with one another.

Sadly, our family meals are not the only ones to suffer. Jesus reminded us when quoting Deuteronomy that our spiritual food is just as important as the physical food.

But He answered and said, "It is written, *'Man shall not live by bread alone, but by every word that proceeds from the mouth of God.'"*
Matthew 4:4 (NKJV)

In this verse, Jesus was speaking to Satan, who was misquoting God's Word by using it out of context. Surely, by applying only snippets of the Gospel to our lives, we can find ourselves far off course. Though Job's wife encouraged him to "Curse God and die," in Job 2:9, the verse is not teaching that action as a precept of the Christian doctrine. Yet to understand the verses in context, we have to study the Bible in its entirety.

Sadly, many people do not desire to chisel out five minutes of their days to devote to the Bible, desiring at the most a verse and a couple of sentences to give them a good feeling. Instead, God wants us to meditate on His Word throughout the day.

This Book of the Law shall not depart from your mouth, but you shall meditate in it day and night, that you may observe to do according to all that is written in it. For then you will

make your way prosperous, and then you will have good success.
Joshua 1:8 (NKJV)

Joshua highlighted the most important aspect of Bible study as it has more to do with following God's Word than knowing it. "Actions speak louder than words," and in the same manner, the Bible must travel the 18 inches between brain and heart before the words truly can affect lives. Yet without knowing God's Word, we cannot accomplish His desires in our lives. Just as a cow chews its food, we are to chew on the Word of God, ruminating on how to apply the Lord's philosophies and commandments personally. The most important part of our daily spiritual food is that it always points to Jesus.

And Jesus said to them, "I am the bread of life. He who comes to Me shall never hunger, and he who believes in Me shall never thirst.
John 6:35 (NKJV)

Certainly, without spending time in God's Word, how much of a priority can a relationship with Him be in our lives? Sadly, we have chosen to fill our time with aspects of this world that will pass away. Though we are called by God to earn a living by the sweat of our brows, work is not His only calling upon our lives. Additionally, we are called by the Lord to spend time with our families, yet God desires for us to teach His Word to them, as He has entrusted us with their lives. Yet many run through each day before collapsing in front of the television and falling asleep, with an empty bag from the nearest drive through still sitting atop the coffee table.

Jesus is not fast food. If we spend time at His table, He will fill us completely!

For the word of God *is* living and powerful, and sharper than any two-edged sword, piercing even to the division of soul and spirit, and of joints and marrow, and is a discerner of the thoughts and intents of the heart.

Hebrews 4:12 (NKJV)
November 11: Are you Velcro or Teflon?

In a group of 5-year-olds, some of them will have shoes with Velcro straps instead of laces, which makes perfect sense, as even the "bunny ear" method of tying shoelaces requires more manual dexterity than most little children have. Velcro sticks to everything and everything sticks to Velcro! Any article of clothing containing Velcro seems to attract every loose thread or piece of fuzz. On the other hand, modern-day technology also has given us Teflon and nothing sticks to Teflon. Scrambling eggs in a Teflon-coated pan will offer the opposite result of accomplishing the same task in an iron-skillet. That's why Bill Clinton was known as the Teflon president. Though becoming only the second president in our nation's history to be impeached, he was acquitted by the Senate in what was a largely-partisan vote. Public opinion on Clinton's presidency seemed unaffected by either guilt or evidence. Yet most politicians, regardless of party lines, are equally guilty!

As Christians, we need the properties of both Velcro and Teflon at different times. As we are called to be in the world, but not of the world, we continuously walk through the dirt and grime of a place governed by Satan and his demonic host. To walk through a sandstorm without getting a grain of sand on us would be miraculous, but that is exactly what Jesus did when He walked on this earth. He deflected sin as if He was wearing a Teflon coat. That being said, if Jesus attached Himself to a person, nothing could pull Him away. The key to Velcro's bond is the amount of surface area making contact, and with Jesus living inside of us, He grabs us from inside and out! The ministry of Jesus demonstrated His ability to be apart from the world while reaching out to those firmly in it.

[1]**Then *Jesus* entered and passed through Jericho.** [2] **Now behold, *there was* a man named Zacchaeus who was a chief tax collector, and he was rich.** [3] **And he sought to see who Jesus was, but could not because of the crowd, for he was of**

short stature. ⁴ So he ran ahead and climbed up into a sycamore tree to see Him, for He was going to pass that *way*. ⁵ And when Jesus came to the place, He looked up and saw him, and said to him, "Zacchaeus, make haste and come down, for today I must stay at your house." ⁶ So he made haste and came down, and received Him joyfully. ⁷ But when they saw *it*, they all complained, saying, "He has gone to be a guest with a man who is a sinner."
⁸ Then Zacchaeus stood and said to the Lord, "Look, Lord, I give half of my goods to the poor; and if I have taken anything from anyone by false accusation, I restore fourfold."
⁹ And Jesus said to him, "Today salvation has come to this house, because he also is a son of Abraham; ¹⁰ for the Son of Man has come to seek and to save that which was lost."
Luke 19:1-9 (NKJV)

Zacchaeus was a tax collector, and as a government worker, his pay certainly was not excessive, yet he was described as a rich man. His wealth came from ill-gotten gains, as Zacchaeus stole from the people. Matthew, one of the disciples of Jesus who wrote the first book in the New Testament, also had been a tax collector. Most people in biblical times put tax collectors in the same category as prostitutes, and with our similar sentiments toward the Internal Revenue Service, we can see that times have not changed that much!

¹⁵ **"Moreover if your brother sins against you, go and tell him his fault between you and him alone. If he hears you, you have gained your brother. ¹⁶ But if he will not hear, take with you one or two more, that *'by the mouth of two or three witnesses every word may be established.'* ¹⁷ And if he refuses to hear them, tell *it* to the church. But if he refuses even to hear the church, let him be to you like a heathen and a tax collector.**
Matthew 18:15-17 (NKJV)

Though Zacchaeus categorically was a heathen, Jesus reached out to him, uncaring of the amount of sin in the life of the chief tax collector. Jesus did not just speak to Zacchaeus on the street, but stayed as a guest in his home. Our Lord did not worry about how this appeared to others. How often do we avoid certain people, worrying that their sin will stick to us? Often, many Christians seem concerned with "the appearance of evil."

Abstain from all appearance of evil.
1 Thessalonians 5:22 (NKJV)

What is the appearance of evil? Crossing the line! If a Christian man shares his bed with a Christian woman before they marry, though they both report that they are "just cuddling," regardless of truth, the story does not seem believable! Yet often, we avoid ministry opportunities because of gossipers in the church. "Someone I know saw John outside of a bar," claims the gossiper on the telephone, in one of many calls, uncaring that her Christian brother had no interest in alcohol, but went there to share the Gospel with his wayward uncle.

As Christians, we are called to reach out to those walking in darkness. When God opens the door ever so slightly, we are to walk through the opening. That being said, God rarely places people in situations where they will fall. For example, the Lord would not ask a new believer struggling with alcoholism to go into that bar and share the Gospel with the drunken patrons. Certainly, the words would fall on deaf ears, and in our first steps as new believers, our coats are more Velcro than Teflon! Yet as we grow in our walks with the Lord, that Teflon coat easily can deflect the sins of the world, as we learn to rely on the strength of Jesus, rather than our own strength.

In the same manner, we should let our love be like Velcro. Though many of our closest friends and family members will let us down, our love for them should not waver! It is easy to get personal feelings interwoven with facts, yet it really does not matter who is at fault in any disagreement. By looking inward, it is obvious that each of us was at fault thousands of times, yet God continues to love and forgive us! He desires for us to love in that same manner. By reaching out to a sinful world, God continues to spread the good news of Jesus Christ. Never forget that we all were a part of that sinful world when God reached out to us!

We must let our coats be made of Teflon, repelling the sin of the world, but let our hearts be made of Velcro, attracting the lost who have no place to go!

Since you have purified your souls in obeying the truth through the Spirit in sincere love of the brethren, love one another fervently with a pure heart,
1 Peter 1:22 (NKJV)

November 12: Repentance: turn from the stench of sin

Typically, humans seem to have two rule books: one for self and one for everyone else! The human condition seems to affect us all, where we are disgusted by the behavior of others, but we easily can overlook the same behavior in ourselves. Christians are not left out in this behavior, either. Though God did not rank the 10 Commandments in order of which sins made Him the angriest, Christians have a tendency to weigh sins. An example would be the difference between venial sins and mortal sins in the doctrine of Catholicism, where venial sins are forgivable, not causing complete separation from God, and mortal sins will cause eternal damnation without forgiveness. There is not one Bible verse using either of those phrases; nor are there Bible verse teaching that God punishes sins differently. In God's eyes, a white lie is a lie, and carries the same punishment as a bold-faced lie.

[1] Therefore you are inexcusable, O man, whoever you are who judge, for in whatever you judge another you condemn yourself; for you who judge practice the same things. [2] But we know that the judgment of God is according to truth against those who practice such things. [3] And do you think this, O man, you who judge those practicing such things, and doing the same, that you will escape the judgment of God? [4]

Or do you despise the riches of His goodness, forbearance, and longsuffering, not knowing that the goodness of God leads you to repentance?
Romans 2:1-4 (NKJV)

Along the same lines, the Bible teaches that how we judge others is the same degree that God will judge us.

[37] "Judge not, and you shall not be judged. Condemn not, and you shall not be condemned. Forgive, and you will be forgiven. [38] Give, and it will be given to you: good measure, pressed down, shaken together, and running over will be put into your bosom. For with the same measure that you use, it will be measured back to you."
Luke 6:37-38 (NKJV)

One of the best examples that Jesus gave us involved the woman caught in adultery in the Gospel of John. It does not sound like there was any doubt that the woman had been caught in adultery. Certainly, it was not just catching her in a lie, with another man's message on her mobile phone. Instead, the scribes and Pharisees had caught this woman in the act. Yet as it takes two to tango, there is a missing piece to the puzzle. Where is the man who also had to be discovered at the same instant? Was it more of a sin for a woman to commit adultery than for a man to be in the same sin? Could the man have been part of a plot to trip up Jesus in the subsequent questioning? In that case, was it intended that he escape without acknowledgment while they took the woman for punishment (and death)? Obviously, there is more to the story, but when questioned, Jesus went directly to the heart of the matter when asked if she should be stoned, by the Old Testament law.

[5] Now Moses, in the law, commanded us that such should be stoned. But what do You say?" [6] This they said, testing Him, that they might have *something* of which to accuse Him. But Jesus stooped down and wrote on the ground with *His* finger, as though He did not hear.

⁷ So when they continued asking Him, He raised Himself up and said to them, "He who is without sin among you, let him throw a stone at her first." ⁸ And again He stooped down and wrote on the ground. ⁹ Then those who heard *it*, being convicted by *their* conscience, went out one by one, beginning with the oldest *even* to the last. And Jesus was left alone, and the woman standing in the midst. ¹⁰ When Jesus had raised Himself up and saw no one but the woman, He said to her, "Woman, where are those accusers of yours? Has no one condemned you?"
¹¹ She said, "No one, Lord."
And Jesus said to her, "Neither do I condemn you; go and sin no more."
John 8:5-11 (NKJV)

What did Jesus write on the ground? Many guess that it was the name of the missing man, but whatever He wrote, it had an immediate effect on the accusers. Jesus did not condemn the woman, though caught in sin, but instead, gave her encouragement in changing her ways. That is what repentance is all about, a change of direction. God does not snap His mighty fingers to perfect us when we decide to follow Him, but instead, a lengthy path begins. Along that path, He cleans us, convicting us to walk away from old, sinful habits. Sadly, many Christians look at their fellow, imperfect brothers and sisters and condemn them. "If you are still involved in that sin, you must not be saved." Sadly, even pastors are guilty of that judgment. Since only God can see inside of the heart, only God knows where each of us will spend eternity.

Therefore by their fruits you will know them.
Matthew 7:20 (NKJV)

We should be able to see the presence of God in the lives of mature believers, and along with that presence, should be able to see the fruits of the Spirit discussed in Galatians 5: love, joy, peace, longsuffering, kindness, goodness, faithfulness, gentleness and self-control. Yet lest we forget, even the strongest Christian has times in their walk with the Lord when none of those fruits are noticeable. That does not mean that the believer is destined for hell. Instead, it is part of the learning process as failure leads to brokenness, and brokenness, by the goodness of God, leads us to repentance.

By self-reflection, we can see many problematic areas in our lives and in our walks with the Lord. Yet we also can see sinful behaviors that Jesus has helped us to conquer. As we continue to walk with the Lord, there should be more of those areas! Unfortunately, sin will continue in each of our lives until we see our Savior face to face. That continuing presence of sin in our lives can sometimes feel like a heavy burden, but God wants us to let Him carry the load. It is a reminder of the brokenness of the present world, as well as a reminder of the blessing of an eternity when we no longer will have to worry about sin.

[9] Now I rejoice, not that you were made sorry, but that your sorrow led to repentance. For you were made sorry in a godly manner, that you might suffer loss from us in nothing. [10] For godly sorrow produces repentance *leading* **to salvation, not to be regretted; but the sorrow of the world produces death.**
2 Corinthians 7:9-10 (NKJV)

November 13: Using God

Sometimes, the stories making headlines in the national news are so depressing that they can cause us to avoid watching. Recently, the murder trial of Steven Hayes in the rape and murder of a mother with multiple sclerosis, along with her 17-year-old and 11-year-old daughters, deeply affected the jurors, who referred to the trial as a life-changing experience. Similar to a soldier who never can get those bloody pictures of war from his memory, what those jurors had to both see and hear never will be forgotten. Hayes was convicted and given the death sentence. Imagine the difficulty for the surviving husband and father who escaped, while the rest of his family died. To hear the expert testimony discussing the rape of his 11-year-old daughter would require more strength than most of us can imagine. Now his process begins again, as the accomplice of Hayes who planned the crime, Joshua Komisarjevsky, begins his trial.

Unlike Hayes, who as a lifelong criminal committed each dastardly act for drug money, Komisarjevsky seems bright and articulate. Surprisingly, he grew up in a strong Christian household, regularly attending church with his devoted family. As a teenager, Komisarjevsky claims that he was raped by a foster child staying in his family's home, and has blamed God for allowing that to occur. He claims that a loving God never would allow that kind of evil. Ironically, he attempted to prove that point by raping and murdering an 11-year-old girl. Regardless of his upbringing, evil rules his soul.

Certainly, these are extreme examples, yet all of us are affected by the evil of this world. We never should forget that Satan has been given dominion over this earth for now and he would love to destroy each of us who have personal relationships with Jesus. Though God does not cause evil, He allows evil. Certainly, Job's faith was tested when his 10 children died on the same day. God does not remove the hedge of protection between us and Satan to destroy us, but instead, desires for us to draw closer to Him. Often those difficulties reveal the status of our relationships with the Lord. Without enduring trials, our relationship may be only words, while being tested under fire strengthens us, just as heat strengthens metal.

In another recent news story, a Romanian man was suing God. It is easy for us to blame God for our difficulties. Even Job, God's most faithful servant upon the earth, played the "blame game." Yet suing God is using God, with a small rearrangement of the letters in those words. To blame our Creator demonstrates a pride in our own knowledge and intelligence. Are we all-knowing, like God? Can we tell what is going to happen 10 minutes from now, tomorrow, or 10 years from now? God never is surprised and has given us so many promises to stand on, including this one:

And we know that all things work together for good to those who love God, to those who are the called according to *His* purpose.
Romans 8:28 (NKJV)

Knowing that God is incapable of giving bad gifts to His children can carry us through the most difficult circumstances, yet our human nature can sometimes get in the way. C.S. Lewis, one of the most gifted Christian apologists, who certainly loved the Lord, had a desperate time in his relationship with God when his wife died of cancer. For a time, Lewis' anger surpassed his trust of the Lord. But God in His mercy reached out to Lewis and pulled him closer before his own death. There are times when all of us question God!

[1] Then the LORD answered Job out of the whirlwind, and said:
[2] "Who *is* this who darkens counsel
By words without knowledge?
[3] Now prepare yourself like a man;
I will question you, and you shall answer Me.
[4] "Where were you when I laid the foundations of the earth?
Tell *Me*, if you have understanding.
[5] Who determined its measurements?
Surely you know!
Or who stretched the line upon it?
[6] To what were its foundations fastened?
Or who laid its cornerstone,
[7] When the morning stars sang together,
And all the sons of God shouted for joy?
[8] "Or *who* shut in the sea with doors,
When it burst forth *and* issued from the womb;
[9] When I made the clouds its garment,
And thick darkness its swaddling band;
[10] When I fixed My limit for it,
And set bars and doors;
[11] When I said,
'This far you may come, but no farther,
And here your proud waves must stop!'

¹²"Have you commanded the morning since your days *began,*
And caused the dawn to know its place,
¹³That it might take hold of the ends of the earth,
And the wicked be shaken out of it?
¹⁴It takes on form like clay *under* a seal,
And stands out like a garment.
¹⁵From the wicked their light is withheld,
And the upraised arm is broken.
¹⁶"Have you entered the springs of the sea?
Or have you walked in search of the depths?
¹⁷Have the gates of death been revealed to you?
Or have you seen the doors of the shadow of death?
¹⁸Have you comprehended the breadth of the earth?
Tell *Me,* if you know all this.
Job 38:1-18 (NKJV)

When God questions Job in Job 38-40, we see the futility of that lack of trust. Being a Christian does not come with a promise of a simple and carefree life upon this earth. Instead, it comes with the promise that God never will leave us or forsake us for all of eternity. When Stephen died the death of a martyr at the hands of those who hated him, God never left his side.

⁵¹ "*You* stiff-necked and uncircumcised in heart and ears! You always resist the Holy Spirit; as your fathers *did,* so *do* you. ⁵² Which of the prophets did your fathers not persecute? And they killed those who foretold the coming of the Just One, of whom you now have become the betrayers and murderers, ⁵³ who have received the law by the direction of angels and have not kept *it.*"
⁵⁴ When they heard these things they were cut to the heart, and they gnashed at him with *their* teeth. ⁵⁵ But he, being full of the Holy Spirit, gazed into heaven and saw the glory of God, and Jesus standing at the right hand of God, ⁵⁶ and said, "Look! I see the heavens opened and the Son of Man standing at the right hand of God!"
⁵⁷ Then they cried out with a loud voice, stopped their ears, and ran at him with one accord; ⁵⁸ and they cast *him* out of the city and stoned *him.* And the witnesses laid down their

clothes at the feet of a young man named Saul. [59] And they stoned Stephen as he was calling on *God* and saying, "Lord Jesus, receive my spirit." [60] Then he knelt down and cried out with a loud voice, "Lord, do not charge them with this sin." And when he had said this, he fell asleep.
Acts 7:51-60 (NKJV)

If our faith is lip service, then we are using God. He is an excuse in our lives, rather than being the life in us! Following God involves faith in the midst of hardship, yet His promises abound in the Bible. Rather than using God as a crutch or an excuse, if we are trusting in Him, then He is using us! Do we want to be used by God for His purposes? Trust Him and step out in faith!

[1] Now faith is the substance of things hoped for, the evidence of things not seen. [2] For by it the elders obtained a *good* testimony.
[3] By faith we understand that the worlds were framed by the word of God, so that the things which are seen were not made of things which are visible.
Hebrews 11:1-3 (NKJV)

November 14: What does it take to get our attention?

With many sights, sounds and smells battling for our attention each moment of every day, what we choose to give our attention speaks more of who we are than anything else. Richard Moss said, "The greatest gift you can give another is the purity of your attention."

As Christians, how well do we pay attention to God? Think back to the time when God spoke to Moses. He spoke through a burning bush! Is that how we would expect God to appear? Think about it for a moment. He is the God who created everything we can see and everything we cannot see and He could have created a spectacle of any size or magnitude. Instead, He appeared to Moses in a burning bush. That bush caught the attention of Moses, for though he saw the same types of bush on a daily basis, this one was different. "I wonder what caused that bush to burn," probably thought Moses, looking at the clouds for signs of lightning. Yet the bush was not consumed!

In a similar way, God can capture our attention any time or place He desires. Though He has the ability to perform the greatest of miracles, He typically speaks in a way that we might look upon as ordinary, or unspectacular.

[21] So Balaam rose in the morning, saddled his donkey, and went with the princes of Moab. [22] Then God's anger was aroused because he went, and the Angel of the LORD took His stand in the way as an adversary against him. And he was riding on his donkey, and his two servants *were* with him. [23] Now the donkey saw the Angel of the LORD standing in the way with His drawn sword in His hand, and the donkey turned aside out of the way and went into the field. So Balaam struck the donkey to turn her back onto the road. [24] Then the Angel of the LORD stood in a narrow path between the vineyards, *with* a wall on this side and a wall on that side. [25] And when the donkey saw the Angel of the LORD, she pushed herself against the wall and crushed Balaam's foot against the wall; so he struck her again. [26] Then the Angel of the LORD went further, and stood in a narrow place where there *was* no way to turn either to the right hand or to the left. [27] And when the donkey saw the Angel of the LORD, she lay down under Balaam; so Balaam's anger was aroused, and he struck the donkey with his staff.
[28] Then the LORD opened the mouth of the donkey, and she said to Balaam, "What have I done to you, that you have struck me these three times?"
[29] And Balaam said to the donkey, "Because you have abused me. I wish there were a sword in my hand, for now I would kill you!"
[30] So the donkey said to Balaam, "*Am* I not your donkey on which you have ridden, ever since *I became* yours, to this day? Was I ever disposed to do this to you?" And he said, "No."
Numbers 22:21-30 (NKJV)

Causing a donkey to speak is certainly not ordinary, or what any of us would expect. At that time, God opened Balaam's eyes so that he, too, was able to see the Angel of the Lord along the path. In the same manner, God often opens our eyes to see Jesus along the way. When we are busy giving our attention to the things of the world, we easily can become blinded to the things of the Lord. Sometimes, we need to slow down, look around and see what is out of the ordinary. It might be something very small, but the smallest change can create the largest effect. Are our eyes open to see what God desires for us to see?

[2] And the Angel of the LORD appeared to him in a flame of fire from the midst of a bush. So he looked, and behold, the bush was burning with fire, but the bush *was* not consumed. [3] Then Moses said, "I will now turn aside and see this great sight, why the bush does not burn."
Exodus 3:2-3 (NKJV)

November 15: Why do Christians suffer?

Suffering is a part of life, and certainly, a part of death. When we look around, most of us picture the people surrounding us as living carefree and painless lives, but truthfully, suffering is the uninvited friend who gregariously introduces himself to us all, eventually. While God may desire for His followers to be "set apart" from the world, at the same time He does not ensure that our suffering disappears or even dwindles. In fact, that suffering potentially can increase as a believer.

> "God whispers to us in our pleasures, speaks in our conscience, but shouts in our pains: it is His megaphone to rouse a deaf world." – C.S. Lewis

By looking at how God responded to the Jews, His chosen people, we can draw a direct correlation of how He views each of us as believers.

[9]"For My name's sake I will defer My anger,

**And *for* My praise I will restrain it from you,
So that I do not cut you off.
¹⁰Behold, I have refined you, but not as silver;
I have tested you in the furnace of affliction.
¹¹For My own sake, for My own sake, I will do *it;*
For how should *My name* be profaned?
And I will not give My glory to another.
Isaiah 48:9-11 (NKJV)**

Affliction became God's furnace toward the Israelites, as He purified them under fire. In metallurgy, silver can be purified by either refining or smelting, with the major difference being that smelting slightly alters the chemical composition. Instead, heating silver purifies it without changing the chemical composition. In a similar manner, God allows us to be tested under fire to separate our flesh and our spirit. As we grow as Christians, that disobedient flesh should dissipate. At the same time, Christ dwelling in us, the Holy Spirit, becomes more pure, as less of our flesh is mixed with the final product. Yet we will not be perfected until God burns away the wood, hay and stubble of our lives. Then the precious gems will be all that remain.

**¹¹ For the grace of God that brings salvation has appeared to all men, ¹² teaching us that, denying ungodliness and worldly lusts, we should live soberly, righteously, and godly in the present age, ¹³ looking for the blessed hope and glorious appearing of our great God and Savior Jesus Christ, ¹⁴ who gave Himself for us, that He might redeem us from every lawless deed and purify for Himself His own special people, zealous for good works.
Titus 2:11-14 (NKJV)**

Purification can be a painful process because of our disobedience. There are times when we willfully choose to sin, regardless of God's laws or impact in our lives, and it in those times when we are destined to suffer. Yet we always cannot draw a correlation between suffering and our own disobedient decisions. Suffering is part of God's process of drawing us closer. When life is proceeding on a peaceful path, we often can take that ease for granted. When life is incredible, we often take responsibility for that success, based on our own talents, abilities and decisions. Paul gives us a perfect perspective in 1 Corinthians 1:29, "that no flesh should glory in His presence." Pride continues to get in the way, and we need a constant reminder that all we are, all we have and all we do are because of God's grace! On the other hand, when times are tough, we reach out to God. "Help me, Lord, for I cannot endure this without You!"

When we become Christians, all of our sins are forgiven. When we sin again, God carries us back to that place of repentance, so that He can make us fine again. In that way, we are "re-fined!" We need to humble ourselves in the eyes of the Lord. Regardless of where we are on the path of suffering, we should trust in Him, for He cares for us!

[8] Draw near to God and He will draw near to you. Cleanse *your* hands, *you* sinners; and purify *your* hearts, *you* double-minded. [9] Lament and mourn and weep! Let your laughter be turned to mourning and *your* joy to gloom. [10] Humble yourselves in the sight of the Lord, and He will lift you up. James 4:8-10 (NKJV)

But may the God of all grace, who called us to His eternal glory by Christ Jesus, after you have suffered a while, perfect, establish, strengthen, and settle *you*.
1 Peter 5:10 (NKJV)

November 16: Stand still!

Walking on a progressive journey, there are uphill segments, downhill segments, flatlands and rest. Each one of those puts stress on a different part of the body. Walking uphill tires the hamstrings, quadriceps and lungs. On the other hand, gliding downhill really works the knees. Even without hills, our bodies get tired, especially without endurance conditioning. Yet rest makes us weary, as well. If we sit on our bottoms long enough, they gets sore, while the leg muscles tighten. In those times, there is nothing that feels better than stretching those muscles out by continuing the journey. Each segment gives us a different perspective with the change of scenery. Analogous to the Christian walk, the journey has meaning from start to finish.

¹³ And Moses said to the people, "Do not be afraid. Stand still, and see the salvation of the LORD, which He will accomplish for you today. For the Egyptians whom you see today, you shall see again no more forever. ¹⁴ The LORD will fight for you, and you shall hold your peace."
Exodus 14:13-14 (NKJV)

Sometimes, the Lord desires for us to stand still. When faced with an enemy or battle, standing still is neither a retreat nor an advance. Many Christians fear confrontation, for it is in those situations when our flesh rears its ugly head. Most of the time, compromise is the key, when each side gives in to some degree. Yet God never desires for us to compromise our morals, principles or values. In those times, we need to stand firm.

Certainly, it is difficult to stand still and hold our peace when a war wages around us. It seems much simpler to run away. Interestingly, in the Bible's description of the armor of God, there is nothing covering the backside to protect us in a retreat. Peace to a believer is the knowledge that the Lord fights our battles for us. Our rest is in His salvation. Salvation is deliverance! In the Old Testament, though the word "salvation" is used frequently, rarely did people apply that concept to sin. Yet we know that the Lord has delivered us from sin, as well as from every difficulty that might arise. Sometimes, deliverance is death, a release from the bonds of this broken world. For example, when a Christian suffers from cancer, fellow Christians pray for healing. The healing given by the Lord may occur in the physical realm, but even if that believer dies, the Lord's healing occurs. Somehow we lose sight of the fact that when we are absent from the body, we are present with the Lord, as the words of Paul remind us in 2 Corinthians 5:8.

⁵Blessed *is* the man whose strength *is* in You,

Whose heart *is* set on pilgrimage.
⁶*As they* pass through the Valley of Baca,
They make it a spring;
The rain also covers it with pools.
⁷They go from strength to strength;
***Each one* appears before God in Zion.**
Psalm 84:5-7 (NKJV)

A pilgrimage was a requirement for every able-bodied Jewish man above the age of 20 to make three times yearly, at Passover (*Pesach*), Pentecost (*Shavuot*) and Tabernacles (*Sukkot*). It sure would be easier for those living in Jerusalem. Maybe God desired for His people to live in His chosen city! Depending upon where they lived, the pilgrimage could be a sizable journey, requiring both time and finances. Yet as the verse above reiterates, it was a journey of the heart. Though faced with difficulties along the way, those trusting in the Lord turned the challenging valleys into springs, adding life and sustenance to weary bodies along the journey. Just as the Jewish pilgrims, we are called to go from "strength to strength." That strength is a gift from God, who reminds us that when we are weak, then we are strong in Him! If life's journey had anything to do with our own strength, we would be destined for failure, but we continue our walks in the strength of the Lord. His strength is immeasurable!

No matter what battle is facing us, God is powerful enough to handle it exactly as He desires. He has a purpose and plan in our lives, and if we have chosen to follow Him, He will lead us beside still waters. He does not push us, pull us or drag us, yet leads us gently to the places He desires for our nourishment and growth. Before we knew Him, we were blind, and even then, He gently led us to the place where we would come to know His gentle hand of salvation upon our lives. If He did not lead us to a cliff's edge when we were blind, what makes us think He will lead us into danger now that we have been given spiritual sight? Trust Him! He never has let us down and He never will.

The LORD *is* my strength and song,

And He has become my salvation;
He *is* my God, and I will praise Him;
My father's God, and I will exalt Him.
Exodus 15:2 (NKJV)

November 17: Teach us to pray!

Of all the gifts God has given us, prayer is one of the most important as well as the least utilized. During the ministry of Jesus, we can see the emphasis that He placed on prayer, spending many nights crying out to His Father. Certainly, His disciples must have seen a direct correlation between the prayer life of Jesus and the power of His ministry, for they asked for help on how to pray. We do not see any similar requests from the disciples in the New Testament regarding other aspects of the Christian walk. For example, do any of the disciples ever ask Jesus to "teach us to teach," "teach us to heal," "teach us to perform miracles," or "teach us to cast out demons?"

Now it came to pass, as He was praying in a certain place, when He ceased, *that* one of His disciples said to Him, "Lord, teach us to pray, as John also taught his disciples."
Luke 11:1 (NKJV)

Without constant communication with God, we can lose sight of what He wants us to accomplish for Him. We must understand that the battlefield is changing all around us as we speak. For those who have soldiered in war, or more commonly, for those who have seen a movie involving war, we can picture the hurried communications between underlings and the generals in charge. If a general gives a command based on the situation at hand and the young lieutenant turns off the two-way radio immediately after receiving the order, what happens if the situation on the battlefield changes? Days later, should the lieutenant continue following the same order, or should he check in for new orders?

Prayer is only one side of the communication chain, involving our words and thoughts addressed to God. Yet to keep the lines of communication open, we must be able to hear God's instructions, too. His instructions come by reading His Word, as the Holy Spirit will teach us all things and bring to remembrance all He has taught us (John 14:26). Sometimes, God can speak to our hearts, but if His words do not involve Scripture, we should be careful that we are not listening to our own hearts or listening to the enemy. Satan is willing and able to pull verses out of context to trick us. Yet Jesus demonstrated to us how to fight that battle:

[1] Then Jesus was led up by the Spirit into the wilderness to be tempted by the devil. [2] And when He had fasted forty days and forty nights, afterward He was hungry. [3] Now when the tempter came to Him, he said, "If You are the Son of God, command that these stones become bread." [4] But He answered and said, "It is written, *'Man shall not live by bread alone, but by every word that proceeds from the mouth of God.'*" [5] Then the devil took Him up into the holy city, set Him on the pinnacle of the temple, [6] and said to Him, "If You are the Son of God, throw Yourself down. For it is written:
'He shall give His angels charge over you,'
and,
In their hands they shall bear you up,
Lest you dash your foot against a stone.' "
[7] Jesus said to him, "It is written again, *'You shall not tempt the LORD your God.'* " [8] Again, the devil took Him up on an exceedingly high mountain, and showed Him all the kingdoms of the world and their glory. [9] And he said to Him, "All these things I will give You if You will fall down and worship me." [10] Then Jesus said to him, "Away with you, Satan! For it is written, *'You shall worship the LORD your God, and Him only you shall serve.'* " [11] Then the devil left Him, and behold, angels came and ministered to Him.
Matthew 4:1-11 (NKJV)

As Christians, we are soldiers in God's army. Similar to any army, there is a chain of command, and the instructions for battle come from the commander-in-chief. Outside of the walls of Jericho, Joshua was confronted by an Old Testament appearance of Jesus, and there we learn one of His many titles:

¹³ And it came to pass, when Joshua was by Jericho, that he lifted his eyes and looked, and behold, a Man stood opposite him with His sword drawn in His hand. And Joshua went to Him and said to Him, "*Are* You for us or for our adversaries?" ¹⁴ So He said, "No, but *as* Commander of the army of the LORD I have now come."
Joshua 5:13-14 (NKJV)

In prayer, we should lift up our fellow soldiers in the battle for this world between God and God's enemy, who has been given dominion here for a time. In that ongoing prayer, we should ask for instructions of where and how He desires to use us as soldiers. We should ask for His strength, support and leadership, and most importantly, for His guidance. When we speak to God, we get much off our chests, but without hearing from Him, any battle we fight is misguided. We must search the Scriptures daily to hear what communication God has for us! Without both aspects of that communication, prayer and Bible study, we are cut off from the Commander of the Lord's army! Additionally, keep praying for our fellow soldiers. Our battles might be different, but we are a part of the same war, facing the same enemy!

¹⁷ And take the helmet of salvation, and the sword of the Spirit, which is the word of God; ¹⁸ praying always with all prayer and supplication in the Spirit, being watchful to this end with all perseverance and supplication for all the saints— ¹⁹ and for me, that utterance may be given to me, that I may open my mouth boldly to make known the mystery of the gospel, ²⁰ for which I am an ambassador in chains; that in it I may speak boldly, as I ought to speak.
Ephesians 6:17-20 (NKJV)

¹I will lift up my eyes to the hills— From whence comes my help?
²My help *comes* from the LORD,
Who made heaven and earth.
³He will not allow your foot to be moved;

He who keeps you will not slumber.
⁴Behold, He who keeps Israel
Shall neither slumber nor sleep.
Psalm 121:1-4 (NKJV)

November 18: By faith

As believers, God has given us the example of those who have gone before us. Throughout the Bible, we can read about other men and women of faith. Some of them lived in a time before Jesus came to earth as a man, while others were chosen by God as the foundation of the church. Additionally, there have been many faithful followers of the Lord in the years after the completion of the Bible. Regardless of the eras of those Christians, faith is a common denominator.

¹ **Now faith is the substance of things hoped for, the evidence of things not seen.** ² **For by it the elders obtained a *good* testimony.**
³ **By faith we understand that the worlds were framed by the word of God, so that the things which are seen were not made of things which are visible.**
Hebrews 11:1-3 (NKJV)

One of the men of faith who made the greatest impact on my life was Rusty Foster. Rusty spread the gospel for 60+ years, flying his plane over villages in other countries, and dropping translations of the Bible. Many of us seem to walk with an agenda strongly on our minds, though the Holy Spirit may desire for us to change course. Rusty had the ability to change course in midstream, as the Spirit led. If he saw an inebriated homeless man on the ground, Rusty sat down and began sharing the gospel with him in Spanish if necessary. Rather than resting on his laurels, Rusty always looked for God to open doors of ministry. When his wife died, Rusty became even busier, preaching numerous sermons each week in retirement homes. Certainly, when Rusty died, he joined the "Hall of Saints" spoken of in Hebrews 11.

Many men and women of God are mentioned in the list, each with an action highlighted with a description of how they accomplished their mighty feat, "by faith." Here is an example:

By faith Noah, being divinely warned of things not yet seen, moved with godly fear, prepared an ark for the saving of his household, by which he condemned the world and became heir of the righteousness which is according to faith.
Hebrews 11:7 (NKJV)

Without faith, we all are lost. Without faith, we are capable of no good work. Without faith, we cannot even stand!

Not that we have dominion over your faith, but are fellow workers for your joy; for by faith you stand.
2 Corinthians 1:24 (NKJV)

God has given us examples in the lives before us and the lives around us of what it means to walk in faith. Additionally, we are the examples for our friends and families! When reading the Bible, we should be encouraged in how those who lived before us finished the race, with God's merciful hand guiding the way. Just as He carried those believers to their rest in Him, He also will lead us! How can we continue with difficulties all around us? By faith!

knowing that a man is not justified by the works of the law but by faith in Jesus Christ, even we have believed in Christ Jesus, that we might be justified by faith in Christ and not by the works of the law; for by the works of the law no flesh shall be justified.
Galatians 2:16 (NKJV)

[9] **But, beloved, we are confident of better things concerning you, yes, things that accompany salvation, though we speak in this manner.** [10] **For God *is* not unjust to forget your work and labor of love which you have shown toward His name, *in that* you have ministered to the saints, and do minister.** [11] **And we desire that each one of you show the same diligence**

to the full assurance of hope until the end, [12] that you do not become sluggish, but imitate those who through faith and patience inherit the promises.
Hebrews 6:9-12 (NKJV)

November 19: Think about it...

Some people are naturally inquisitive, treating each step through life as a learning experience, while others seem to react anew in every situation, as if all they retain is water! Those who act before thinking are most dangerous with a loaded gun, especially with their ready, fire, aim philosophy of life. Certainly, there are times when our actions must be more of a reflex than a pondering thought followed by action, yet even that reflex comes from thought in training.

As Christians, God desires for us to spend time reading His Word, but more importantly, He desires for us to spend more time thinking about what we read. When those thoughts become actions, they have traveled full circuit. "Food for thought" takes priority over "food for flesh," with the defining difference being eating to live as opposed to living to eat. Most of us seem to be slaves to our stomachs, rarely missing meals. If we placed the same priority on not missing the daily bread of God's Word, our spiritual condition would be as healthy as our physical condition!

King Solomon, gifted with wisdom, shared some of that with us in Proverbs. One of his sayings was:

A satisfied soul loathes the honeycomb,
But to a hungry soul every bitter thing *is* sweet.
Proverbs 27:7 (NKJV)

The tastiest morsel can push a full man to Pepto-Bismol, while a starving man is never a gourmet. Yet every bit of the Bible is sweet, tasty and filling to a Christian. Reading the Bible never will leave a believer unsatisfied, as after eating the meat of God's Word, another nugget or morsel can be like a dessert of honeycomb.

[14] He causes the grass to grow for the cattle,
And vegetation for the service of man,
That he may bring forth food from the earth,
[15] And wine *that* makes glad the heart of man,
Oil to make *his* face shine,
And bread *which* strengthens man's heart.
Psalm 104:14-15 (NKJV)

God teaches us about the need for spiritual sustenance with the correlation of that physical nourishment, which He also supplies for us. Though we all have favorite meals and favorite restaurants, we always should look forward to each meal of God's Word. If the world's greatest chef brought a gourmet meal to the table, would we ignore it? That is what happens when we forget to read the Bible daily! Now there is some food for thought!

November 20: The King of glory

What a challenge it can be to live in a broken world, where the name of Jesus is used more often as a curse than in praise. Walking on the narrow way that leads to salvation can sometimes be a lonely road, as there are not many along the same path. Each of us has experienced what it is like to be in the minority in some facet. That might be based on race, gender, political belief or religious belief. Regardless, the imposed exile of being a minority can choke the breath from an otherwise acceptable condition.

As Christians, we have been called by God to be strangers in a strange land for the time being. Yet in our future, we will not only be in the majority, but there will be no minority! When Jesus returns to earth to rule and reign from the throne of David for 1,000 years, there will be no person remaining on the planet without a relationship with our Savior.

[1] The earth *is* the LORD's, and all its fullness,
The world and those who dwell therein.

² For He has founded it upon the seas,
And established it upon the waters.
³ Who may ascend into the hill of the LORD?
Or who may stand in His holy place?
⁴ He who has clean hands and a pure heart,
Who has not lifted up his soul to an idol,
Nor sworn deceitfully.
⁵ He shall receive blessing from the LORD,
And righteousness from the God of his salvation.
⁶ This *is* Jacob, the generation of those who seek Him,
Who seek Your face.   Selah
⁷ Lift up your heads, O you gates!
And be lifted up, you everlasting doors!
And the King of glory shall come in.
⁸ Who *is* this King of glory?
The LORD strong and mighty,
The LORD mighty in battle.
⁹ Lift up your heads, O you gates!
Lift up, you everlasting doors!
And the King of glory shall come in.
¹⁰ Who is this King of glory?
The LORD of hosts,
He *is* the King of glory.
Psalm 24 (NKJV)

With the poetic use of personification apparent in verse seven, it is easy to picture the gates lifting up their heads. Though we might envision a gate on a horizontal hinge, this gate is vertically-hinged, like a portcullis. In Medieval times, the portcullis kept enemies from entering a city, yet after the return of Jesus, there will be no need for gates or walls. Instead, all enemies will have been vanquished. That eastern gate of Jerusalem has remained sealed since 1541, when the Ottoman Sultan Suleiman I accomplished that task to ensure that the Messiah could not enter. Additionally, Muslims placed graves in the area outside the gate in the Kidron Valley, as the Old Testament teaches that a Jewish Rabbi must not be defiled by touching a grave. It is ironic that a man sealed a gate to stop a

Messiah he did not believe in. How could a grave or stone wall accomplish the feat that hell and death could not?

¹ Then He brought me back to the outer gate of the sanctuary which faces toward the east, but it was shut. ² And the Lord said to me, "This gate shall be shut; it shall not be opened, and no man shall enter by it, because the Lord God of Israel has entered by it; therefore it shall be shut. ³ As for the prince, because he is the prince, he may sit in it to eat bread before the Lord; he shall enter by way of the vestibule of the gateway, and go out the same way."
Ezekiel 44:1-3 (NKJV)

Though it might be challenging to feel alone in the crowd of this world, we rest in the hope of what will come. Imagine that day, surrounded by all believers in man's history, surrounded by the heavenly host of angels, all singing praises to Jesus Christ, our Lord and Savior, who will enter Jerusalem for the Millennial reign! With a choir of millions of voicing blending together sweetly, it will be glorious! Even those without beautiful singing voices on this earth will join in (they must have glorified voices as there are no tears in heaven)! No longer strangers in a strange land, each of us will find the destiny God has desired for us.

Open the gates,
That the righteous nation which keeps the truth may enter in.
Isaiah 26:2 (NKJV)

November 21: Addiction

According to reports, over 9 million Americans need treatment for drug addiction. Worldwide, the number of drug addicts is astounding. At the same time, there are an estimated 12 million alcoholics in the United States. Many term alcoholism as a disease, and certainly there are people who seem to have more of a propensity to fall into addiction when they take a drink. Yet the true addiction of the world is to sin.

> "All sin tends to be addictive, and the terminal part of addiction is what is called damnation." W.H. Auden

It all began with Adam and Eve disregarding the words of God, led by the silver-tongued serpent, confounding them with his misleading speech. Yet even that first sin pointed to the same aspects of our sinful behavior discussed in 1 John.

[16] For all that *is* in the world—the lust of the flesh, the lust of the eyes, and the pride of life—is not of the Father but is of the world. [17] And the world is passing away, and the lust of it; but he who does the will of God abides forever.
1 John 2:16-17 (NKJV)

Eve's flesh desired to savor the taste of the delicious fruit from the tree of the knowledge of good and evil. Her eyes noticed the beauty of the fruit. Yet Eve had another motive.

[2] And the woman said to the serpent, "We may eat the fruit of the trees of the garden; [3] but of the fruit of the tree which *is* in the midst of the garden, God has said, 'You shall not eat it, nor shall you touch it, lest you die.' "
[4] Then the serpent said to the woman, "You will not surely die. [5] For God knows that in the day you eat of it your eyes will be opened, and you will be like God, knowing good and evil."
Genesis 3:2-5 (NKJV)

Pridefully, Eve desired to be like God! When we approach sin, Satan lies to us about God's instructions, as well as His punishments associated with our sinful behavior. "It's not as big of a deal as you think it is," Satan reminds us, though in truth, our sinful behavior creates spiritual death and separation from God. Without repentance, we are destined for eternal damnation, just as Auden highlighted as the terminal point of addiction. Sadly, we are addicted to sin, and have no chance at conquering the addictions of our lives without the presence of the Holy Spirit dwelling within us. He reminds us, convinces us, and convicts us that what we are doing is not what God requires of us.

Addiction is the biggest liar. When involved in our sins, we lie to cover our tracks with family and friends. At the same time, we lie to ourselves, trying to convince ourselves that the addiction is controllable. Lastly, we lie to God! "If you help me out of this jam, I never will do that again." Atheist George Carlin said, "Just 'cause you got the monkey off your back doesn't mean the circus has left town." Without God, we cannot get the monkey off our back! All of us as Christians still fall prey to Satan's plots, tripping us up with sin. When people we love are struggling with sin it breaks our hearts, for we can look back and see similar struggles in our own lives. Without total surrender to God, we are destined for failure. But if we call on the name of Jesus, we will be saved!

The response of Jesus to the woman caught in the act of adultery reminds us of how God views our sin if we repent:

[10] When Jesus had raised Himself up and saw no one but the woman, He said to her, "Woman, where are those accusers of yours? Has no one condemned you?"
[11] She said, "No one, Lord."
And Jesus said to her, "Neither do I condemn you; go and sin no more."
John 8:10-11 (NKJV)

Our Lord desires for us to depart from the sin. That involves leaving our sinful past behind. Certainly, we all continue to struggle, but God desires for our sin to break our own hearts in the same manner that those sins break His heart. When we desire to please Him above all else, He will carry us through all difficulties. That being said, anyone struggling with the addiction of sin or the sin of addiction needs to turn it over to God. He is not there to condemn, but to love and forgive to those willing to bring it to Him.

Afterward Jesus found him in the temple, and said to him, "See, you have been made well. Sin no more, lest a worse thing come upon you."
John 5:14 (NKJV)

November 22: Gratefulness

When the Pilgrims were strangers in a strange land, much challenge and hardship greeted them upon every boundary. Yet they had come to this new land in order to worship in spirit and in truth. Though the hardships were great, the prior challenge of limited worship in their native country was greater, making almost any condition acceptable. No matter what obstacle seemed to appear in front of the Pilgrims, they remained steadfast in their trust of the Lord. In 1621, God had blessed their efforts, in farming and building, with perfect weather, and in that autumn, Governor William Bradford called for a public day of Thanksgiving. With the help of the local Indians and the Lord's hand with the weather, the corn crop never had been so bountiful, and for the first time, it looked as though there would be enough food to get them through winter. Bradford also invited Massasoit, chief of the Wampanoag tribe. Yet when that first day of Thanksgiving dawned, Massasoit arrived with 90 Indians, which threatened to deplete the abundant winter supplies. Yet rather than panic, the Pilgrims continued to trust in their Provider. *Jehovah-jireh* (the Lord who provides) had also provided for the guests, as the Indians arrived with five deer and a dozen fat, wild turkeys. Additionally, the Indian women assisted in preparation of the banquet, teaching the settlers much about the foods in the new land.

Since that time, Thanksgiving has become a national holiday and part of our nation's heritage, though in many households, gratefulness to the Lord who provides is not part of the celebration. First-century Roman philosopher Seneca said, "Nothing is more honorable than a grateful heart," yet we often ignore the bountiful blessings supplied by our Father like greedy children at Christmas, casting aside the new bicycle to see what other packages have our names upon them. There is nothing that grieves a parent more than an ungrateful child, and apparently, our Father knows that grief better than any.

^{16} Rejoice always, ^{17} pray without ceasing, ^{18} in everything give thanks; for this is the will of God in Christ Jesus for you.
1 Thessalonians 5:16-18 (NKJV)

Paul reminds us with the simply-stated verse above of many concepts that we tend to forget in our hearts. Our Father is incapable of giving bad gifts to His children, even if His children are ungrateful. "Rejoice always" and "in everything give thanks" should resonate in the hearts of all believers every day, not just on Thanksgiving, for we have a God who cares for us, always.

^{6} Therefore humble yourselves under the mighty hand of God, that He may exalt you in due time, ^{7} casting all your care upon Him, for He cares for you.
1 Peter 5:6-7 (NKJV)

Having been beaten with rods for casting the evil spirit of divination from a slave girl, Paul and Silas were imprisoned at Philippi and placed in stocks (Acts 16). At midnight, they were praying and singing hymns to God when a miraculous earthquake released them from bondage, along with all of the other prisoners. In those times, a jailer was responsible for the prisoners so completely, that if one escaped, the jailer had to serve the prisoner's sentence. If all prisoners escaped, that jailer would be destined for life in prison, serving each sentence. Yet Paul ensured that no prisoner left the jail, though there were no locks to bind them. Instead, he taught the jailer about the love of Jesus, bringing that man to the saving knowledge of our Lord. How often do we complain in our limited hardship, unaware of the miracles God is performing in our lives, as well as in the lives of others? Instead of showering Him with praise and thanksgiving, we exhibit the blackness of ungrateful hearts.

And of His fullness we have all received, and grace for grace.
John 1:16 (NKJV)

Our Lord does not shower us with partial blessings. Instead, we are granted the fullness of His love, the forgiveness of sin and the abundance of life in Him, through Him and with Him! On this Thanksgiving Day, rejoice, for we serve a God who loves us abundantly.

[20] Now to Him who is able to do exceedingly abundantly above all that we ask or think, according to the power that works in us, [21] to Him *be* glory in the church by Christ Jesus to all generations, forever and ever. Amen.
Ephesians 3:20-21 (NKJV)

He loves us more than we need and certainly, more than we deserve. Take time to notice the blessings and reflect upon the many ways He takes care of us. Most importantly, remember that even what appears to be a challenge or difficulty is a perfect blessing, for in those hardships, God draws us closer to Him. Let His love resonate in our souls this day, and every day! Happy Thanksgiving!

[4] Enter into His gates with thanksgiving,
***And* into His courts with praise.**
Be thankful to Him, *and* bless His name.
[5] For the LORD *is* good;
His mercy *is* everlasting,
And His truth *endures* to all generations.
Psalm 100:4-5 (NKJV)

November 23: Black Friday

Today officially begins the Christmas shopping season, as many retailers open as early as 5 a.m. to the bargain-hunting, American public. The name "Black Friday" originated in Philadelphia, where the foot and vehicle traffic increased to seemingly-epic proportions. Additionally, with debt defined as being in the red and profit defined as being in the black, the day begins the most profitable time for retailers throughout the year. Many retailers on the internet and in malls offer incredible specials on "Black

Friday," though in limited supply. For many, the day begins with a reminder of the Thanksgiving meal in leftovers, whether turkey sandwiches or turkey soup. After a meal commemorating our thankfulness to God, who blessed us with abundance, we now rush into a month-long process of buying gifts in over-abundance.

Yet we often lose sight of the most important gift being celebrated. When God sent His Son to earth to live as a man, He offered the only One who could endure this life without sin. When Jesus died, His precious blood was sufficient to cover the sins of all of humanity -- past, present and future. Instead of buying Chia pets and Snuggies for our friends and loved ones, we should tell them boldly about the Son of God. What better time to do that than in the season commemorating His birth! Even though scholars believe that Jesus was most likely born early in the fall, on one of the Jewish feast days, December 25 is the day our culture has set aside to celebrate His birth. Sadly, most Americans have become a part of the "Happy Holidays" generation, choosing to remove Christ from Christmas!

So for all the bargain-hunters, we can share the greatest gift, which ironically, is free. Salvation does not cost any of us a cent, yet it did not come cheaply, costing Jesus His life. As Christians, it is important to look for opportunities to share the gospel, when the Holy Spirit opens the door. When we push the door open, rarely do we find people willing to listen. But when they ask the questions, most people are receptive to our answers. "Why do you always have a smile on your face?" "You have a glow on your face; is there someone special in your life?" At the least, we can respond to their greeting of "Happy Holidays" with "Merry Christmas!"

[6] **For unto us a Child is born,**
Unto us a Son is given;
And the government will be upon His shoulder.
And His name will be called
Wonderful, Counselor, Mighty God,
Everlasting Father, Prince of Peace.

[7] Of the increase of *His* government and peace
There will be no end,
Upon the throne of David and over His kingdom,
To order it and establish it with judgment and justice
From that time forward, even forever.
The zeal of the Lord of hosts will perform this.
Isaiah 9:6-7 (NKJV)

[30] Then the angel said to her, "Do not be afraid, Mary, for you have found favor with God. [31] And behold, you will conceive in your womb and bring forth a Son, and shall call His name JESUS. [32] He will be great, and will be called the Son of the Highest; and the Lord God will give Him the throne of His father David. [33] And He will reign over the house of Jacob forever, and of His kingdom there will be no end."
Luke 1:30-33 (NKJV)

[4] He brought me to the banqueting house,
And his banner over me *was* love.
[5] Sustain me with cakes of raisins,
Refresh me with apples,
For I *am* lovesick.
Song of Solomon 2:4-5 (NKJV)

November 24: Connecting the dots

People who are immersed in details rarely can see the bigger perspective of what is taking place around them, as "you can't see the forest through the trees." Paraphrasing that thought, there are too many trees for us to grasp the size or usage of the forest. In the same manner, when we are focused on a problem, it is often difficult to see the solution. Correcting mistakes first involves awareness of making mistakes! Usually, it is about connecting the dots.

Another old adage says that history repeats itself, and with nothing new on the planet, we seem to cycle through age-old problems and concerns. Harry S Truman said, "The only thing new in the world is the history you don't know." With awareness of how others have solved problems, our passage can be simplified.

As Christians, we have a guidebook for life. In the Bible, God gives us rules of how to manage our lives. He began by giving us 10 Commandments, with the first half covering our relationship with Him and the second half covering our relationships with others. Additionally there are 603 other laws teaching us about life. Even without belief in God, His laws and commandments are for our benefit. Yet more important than the laws is what should occur when the laws are broken, as we all have the propensity to be rule breakers. Disobedience creates our difficulties and when looking for the solution, we can clear the field of vision by looking above the trees.

For we walk by faith, not by sight.
2 Corinthians 5:7 (NKJV)

Solutions to real problems do not involve critical thinking, as the world believes. Instead, those solutions come from God. He has promised us as His followers that He never will leave us or forsake us (Hebrews 13:5). He has promised that He will make all things work together to those who love Him, and to those who are the called according to His purposes (Romans 8:28). Only God can take our bad decisions and use them for our good as well as His glory! He has promised that He will not allow any temptation into our lives that we are not strong enough to escape from with His help (1 Corinthians 10:13). He has promised that if we confess our sins to Him that He will cleanse us from all unrighteousness (1 John 1:9). He has promised that when we finish the race on this broken earth that we will spend eternity with Him!

How bad can any situation be as a Christian? To find the solution to any problem, all we have to do is connect the dots!

[9] that if you confess with your mouth the Lord Jesus and believe in your heart that God has raised Him from the dead,

you will be saved. [10] For with the heart one believes unto righteousness, and with the mouth confession is made unto salvation. [11] For the Scripture says, *"Whoever believes on Him will not be put to shame."* [12] For there is no distinction between Jew and Greek, for the same Lord over all is rich to all who call upon Him. [13] For *"whoever calls on the name of the* LORD *shall be saved."*
Romans 10:9-13 (NKJV)

November 25: The attraction of sin

Back in the days when warfare had more to do with hand-to-hand combat and bows and arrows than missiles and nuclear bombs, there was a priority placed upon physical strength and dexterity. Men took pride in their ability to defend their families and their land. Consequently, they spent time developing those skills. At that time, when an archer aimed at the center of the target, if he was slightly off, the spotter would yell to him, "*Khatatha!*" The Aramaic word actually meant "missing the mark," and it was a reminder to the archer to concentrate harder while attempting again to hit the bull's-eye. In Greek, this word is *hamartia*, which is the same word used for sin in the New Testament. When we sin, we miss the standard that God has set for us. That standard is perfection.

Sin is any action that goes against the commandments the Lord has given us. In addition to the 10 Commandments, there are 603 other laws in the Old Testament. Why is sin such a draw for us all? Adam and Eve set the stage by disobeying the Lord, and suffered spiritual death for that sin. Because we are descendants of that initial couple, we also are born with sin nature. Sin is more natural to us than perfection. We can see that a toddler lies without us teaching the difference between truth and lie. The same toddler knows selfishness without our prodding, with one of his first words being, "Mine." Yet, the true draw of sin is its associated pleasure.

Some people erroneously think of God as a killjoy, not wanting us to experience the pleasure of sin. On the contrary, God's laws are all meant to protect us from the sins that hurt us. At the same time, Satan has taken all that is God's, and all God created, and tries to imitate God. Yet Satan's copies are nothing like God's originals. For example, God created sex as a blessing for married couples. More important than that blessing is the example it is meant to be of the intimacy that He desires with us. We are the brides of Christ, and our Lord yearns for us to have an intimate relationship with Him, with nothing to compare that relationship to. Instead, Satan has convinced the world that the pleasure of sex should be shared with anyone and everyone. Along the same lines, our relationship with God can carry us to the mountaintop. Satan, though, convinces the world to depart the mundane experience of life by enhancing that with drugs and alcohol. Under the influence of either, we no longer are communicating with the Lord who created us but with the prince of the power of the air, who has been given dominion over the earth for a time. God gave us His laws and commandments to demonstrate His love for us!

³ For this is the love of God, that we keep His commandments. And His commandments are not burdensome. ⁴ For whatever is born of God overcomes the world. And this is the victory that has overcome the world—our faith. ⁵ Who is he who overcomes the world, but he who believes that Jesus is the Son of God?
1 John 5:3-5 (NKJV)

Sadly, even as believers we continue to miss the mark of perfection, yet God reminds us sweetly to keep aiming at perfection. Additionally, He continues to cleanse us, any time we ask:

If we confess our sins, He is faithful and just to forgive us *our* sins and to cleanse us from all unrighteousness.
1 John 1:9 (NKJV)

Paul reminds us in Romans 7:15 that we continue to do what we hate, and the best part of that remark is that by hating sin, we demonstrate that at least a part of our hearts have grown to reflect the heart of the Lord. If we are struggling with sin, we must confess that sin to the Lord, that He may cleanse us from our unrighteousness. Keep in mind that God only wants the best for us all, and His commandments will lead us to that place. Do we really love Him? Keep aiming those arrows for the bull's-eye!

For the flesh lusts against the Spirit, and the Spirit against the flesh; and these are contrary to one another, so that you do not do the things that you wish.
Galatians 5:17 (NKJV)

November 26: Blessed are the flexible…

Trees certainly are resilient. Even in areas where tornadoes, hurricanes and other windstorms are prevalent, there still are many large and aged trees. Not surprisingly, God knew what He was doing when He created trees, with thicker branches near the trunk and thinner branches near the top. Trees are well-balanced, and even the material they are made out of is more flexible than we imagine. Think of a palm tree on an island during a hurricane. Rarely do the trunks snap regardless of wind, though the palms can bend almost to the ground! An old proverb reminds us that, "Trees that don't bend with the wind won't last the storm."

This principle can be applied just as easily to Christians. Many pastors have preached on the concept, "Blessed are the flexible, for they will not be broken." Brokenness is necessary when we are seeking the Lord, for it involves letting go of our pride. Pride is what keeps us from accepting Jesus into our hearts, for instead of following His plan in our lives, without that required humbleness, we still desire to control our own lives and destinies. Though after that brokenness occurs and we give our lives to Him, God desires for us to be flexible, like trees in the wind.

[1] **Blessed *is* the man**
Who walks not in the counsel of the ungodly,

Nor stands in the path of sinners,
Nor sits in the seat of the scornful;
² But his delight *is* in the law of the LORD,
And in His law he meditates day and night.
³ He shall be like a tree
Planted by the rivers of water,
That brings forth its fruit in its season,
Whose leaf also shall not wither;
And whatever he does shall prosper.
Psalm 1:1-3 (NKJV)

Notice in the psalm above that all seasons in the tree's life are not fruit-producing. Yet even when not producing fruit, the tree shall prosper, regardless of the occasional storms. Some trees have been subject to so many windstorms that instead of standing upright, their growth is in the leeward direction, a natural protection against the wind. In the same manner, God protects us by helping us to grow in different directions. Those differences help us to minister to different people. Some Christians in their rigidity draw sweeping generalizations that we all need to follow God in the same manner. That would be like Paul judging that everyone else must have a Damascus Road experience. Yet the Lord draws each of us to Him in a very unique and personal way. Whether we find that brokenness through addiction, another religion, a failed marriage, the death of a loved one or simply, the realization that we have been created by a God who loves us, the path to God begins when humbleness enters the picture.

¹² The righteous shall flourish like a palm tree,
He shall grow like a cedar in Lebanon.
¹³ Those who are planted in the house of the LORD
Shall flourish in the courts of our God.
¹⁴ They shall still bear fruit in old age;
They shall be fresh and flourishing,
¹⁵ To declare that the LORD is upright;
He is my rock, and *there is* no unrighteousness in Him.
Psalm 92:12-15 (NKJV)

God cannot change, as it is against His nature. His plan for our salvation has been in place since before the foundation of the world, yet He allows us freedom of choice. With that choice, each of us must decide whether to follow self or God, and as believers, even when our choices are erroneous, God leads us back to the path He has planned for us. Our Lord is resolute, but not rigid, and with that perspective, we need to bend. Without that flexibility, our trunks will snap in the storm. Though He cannot change, we have to change, and need to! When there are storms in our lives, we should remember that God never puts us anywhere to harm us, though He might use the wind to help us grow in a protective direction!

For he shall be like a tree planted by the waters,
Which spreads out its roots by the river,
And will not fear when heat comes;
But its leaf will be green,
And will not be anxious in the year of drought,
Nor will cease from yielding fruit.
Jeremiah 17:8 (NKJV)

November 27: Friendship

Friendship helps to make life special. Friends know our past, hope for our future and accept us just the way we are in the present. While God chooses our families, we choose our friends (hopefully with God's help). Categorically, there are friends for a reason, friends for a season and friends for a lifetime, and certainly, the numbers in each of those categories diminish from former to latter.

> Friendship is born at that moment when one person says to another, 'What! You too? I thought I was the only one." – C.S. Lewis

That sameness of thought, interest or personality can draw us near. Yet to have a good friend, we must be a good friend, and that takes time, effort and most importantly, heart. As time marches on, we all have friends who we would love to see more often, though regardless how much time passes in between visits, nothing changes. That love remains just as strong. No obstacle, including time or distance, could keep that friend away if a need presented itself.

One of the Bible's first examples of friendship is between Jonathan, the son of King Saul, and David, whom King Saul looked upon as his chief rival. Even though King Saul sought to murder David, the love and friendship between David and Jonathan increased.

Now when he had finished speaking to Saul, the soul of Jonathan was knit to the soul of David, and Jonathan loved him as his own soul.
1 Samuel 18:1 (NKJV)

That phrase reveals much, for love of self happens easily for prideful people. To treat another as well as we treat ourselves is quite a gift. Obviously, Jonathan loved his father in a different way than he loved his friend, David. Though Jonathan refused to betray David, he still chose to die on the battlefield in support of his misguided father. In the same manner, many of our family relationships remain close, as "blood is thicker than water." On the other hand, sibling rivalry can be intense. Look at the lives of Esau and Jacob, the sons of Isaac, to see the intensity regardless of brotherly love. Friends do not need to fight over parental love or standing.

A friend loves at all times,
And a brother is born for adversity.
Proverbs 17:17 (NKJV)

Yet our greatest example of friendship comes from Jesus. His life, deeds and words all exhibited the truest test of friendship.

[13] Greater love has no one than this, than to lay down one's life for his friends. [14] You are My friends if you do whatever I command you. [15] No longer do I call you servants, for a servant does not know what his master is doing; but I have

called you friends, for all things that I heard from My Father I have made known to you.
John 15:13-15 (NKJV)

We are the friends of God. Additionally, we are His children, as well. Yet the words of our Lord remind us that to be willing to die for a friend involves more love than dying for a family member. When Jesus died for us, we were not His friends, but strangers to Him. Still, He loved us that much.

Everyone seems to be on the go almost non-stop. To take the time to be a true friend involves dying to self and putting off perceived needs for the benefit of others. Sometimes we build walls, not to keep people out, but to see who cares enough to break those walls down. Is there someone around us who wants and needs our encouragement? It could be as easy as a phone call or email, or as difficult as a cross-country journey, but God desires for us to reach out to the people He has brought into our lives. We should reflect on the impact that friends have made in our lives! If we want to know how to reach someone else, we must think of what others could do, or have done, to reach us! But as Christmas approaches, the time of year with the most suicides due to loneliness, make the time to reach out to someone, and be the kind of friend to someone else that Jesus is to us!

[7] For scarcely for a righteous man will one die; yet perhaps for a good man someone would even dare to die. [8] But God demonstrates His own love toward us, in that while we were still sinners, Christ died for us.
Romans 5:7-8 (NKJV)

November 28: Peace and quiet

Sometimes, we all need a little peace and quiet. Often, home is the place where we find those much sought after commodities. Yet there also are times when home becomes a place with too much extraneous input, whether it is the difficulty of turning off the television, the constant ringing of the telephone or the continuous presence of needy people. Before complaining, realize that at times, we are the needy ones in the lives of our friends. That being said, man cannot supply our needs; only God can. God can and does use people to pass on His blessings, but He is the author and finisher of our faith.

[1] Therefore I exhort first of all that supplications, prayers, intercessions, *and* giving of thanks be made for all men, [2] for kings and all who are in authority, that we may lead a quiet and peaceable life in all godliness and reverence. [3] For this *is* good and acceptable in the sight of God our Savior, [4] who desires all men to be saved and to come to the knowledge of the truth.
1 Timothy 2:1-4 (NKJV)

One of the secrets to that peace and quiet is prayer. Peace has been described as the absence of external disturbances while quiet is the absence of internal disturbances. When believers in the Lord have hearts of prayer, instead of worrying about the battles raging, believers will hand the battles over to God. As David reminded King Saul and the Israelites in preparation of facing the giant, Goliath, the battle is the Lord's. Because Jesus is the Commander in Chief of the Lord's army, we are mere foot soldiers. As foot soldiers, we are not required to make life and death decisions, but instead, our single choice is whether or not to follow the Lord. He does not push us into battle or sit on a hillside watching us fight. Instead, He leads us into battle, protects us in the battle and leads us home in victory.

In addition to describing how we can achieve God's gift of peace and quiet, Paul gives us a better understanding of the necessary types of prayer that will lead us there. First, Paul mentions supplication, which comes from the Greek word *deesis*, meaning a wanting or a need. We all should comprehend what it is like to have needs, and the greatest need is for salvation. Through supplication, the Lord desires for us to pray for the needs of others, understanding that only God can supply the missing needs. Secondly, Paul talks of "prayers," the Greek word *proseuche*. We are reminded of what prayer entails by James, the brother of Jesus:

Confess *your* trespasses to one another, and pray for one another, that you may be healed. The effective, fervent prayer of a righteous man avails much.
James 5:16 (NKJV)

As believers, we should pray fervently for our friends, for our families, for our neighbors and even for our enemies. According to James, our prayers can bring healing, and that healing may be physical, spiritual or both. Thirdly, we see that another aspect of our prayer life should be as intercessors. The Greek word for intercessory is the word *enteuxis*, which comes from a root meaning "to draw in closely or intimately." Technically, it is a term for approaching a king, and we know that when Jesus died on the cross, the veil of the tabernacle was split, giving each believer access into the throne room of God.

Let us therefore come boldly to the throne of grace, that we may obtain mercy and find grace to help in time of need.
Hebrews 4:16 (NKJV)

Though God is the Creator of all, He does not desire for us to approach Him as the Cowardly Lion approached the Wizard of Oz, nervously shaking and holding his tail. Instead, we are to come boldly to His throne, because He is a God of grace. Through grace, He has released us from the immense debt owed due to our sin. While Jesus offers intercessory prayer to the Father on our behalves (Hebrews 7:25), we are called to perform the same role for the lost! Reflecting upon our own lives, each of us should be able to remember what it was like before we had the knowledge of grace. If surrounded by broken lives and broken people, we should have the understanding of the one step to mend the broken hearts and minds. Finally, Paul reminds us in 1 Timothy to be thankful for all men. It is easy to be thankful for people we think of as blessings, yet we are to be thankful for enemies, dishonest politicians and even the people who push our buttons. For God uses all things, positive and negative, to complete His work in us!

When a believer has an active prayer life, faith increases. Answered prayer reveals the Lord's intimate hand of guidance, as it reminds us that He is listening! When we learn to trust in His hand, we no longer waste precious time and energy in worry. Walking in that trust, we will find peace and quiet. Though we can have that peace and quiet in the noisiest situations, sometimes it is nice to get away to a place where birds are chirping, wind is blowing and raindrops are falling. It is then when it is easiest to be still and know that He is God (Psalm 46:10). Yet, even in the midst of turmoil, God can give us the peace that passes understanding. Though peace during turmoil might not make sense, it is certainly more of a miracle, pointing directly to God's hand!

If we really want peace and quiet, we should pray!

rather *let it be* the hidden person of the heart, with the incorruptible *beauty* of a gentle and quiet spirit, which is very precious in the sight of God.
1 Peter 3:4 (NKJV)

[11] that you also aspire to lead a quiet life, to mind your own business, and to work with your own hands, as we commanded you, [12] that you may walk properly toward those who are outside, and *that* you may lack nothing.
1 Thessalonians 4:11-12 (NKJV)

November 29: Contentment

Living in the United States, we often feel as though this country is the most blessed nation, as fewer people live below the poverty line. Statistics reveal that worldwide, 80% of people exist on less than $10 per day, with the poverty line being $1.25 per day. It is heartbreaking to think about people who cannot afford the basic needs of clothing and food. God has promised to provide both of those commodities for His children, but He also reminds us to be content in whatever station in life He places us.

⁶ Now godliness with contentment is great gain. ⁷ For we brought nothing into *this* world, *and it is* certain we can carry nothing out. ⁸ And having food and clothing, with these we shall be content. ⁹ But those who desire to be rich fall into temptation and a snare, and *into* many foolish and harmful lusts which drown men in destruction and perdition. ¹⁰ For the love of money is a root of all *kinds of* evil, for which some have strayed from the faith in their greediness, and pierced themselves through with many sorrows.
1 Timothy 6:6-10 (NKJV)

With Madison Avenue executives leading the way to entice us all to desire more gadgets, expensive automobiles, designer clothing and stylish accoutrement, it is easy to fall into the trappings of world philosophy. Yet God gave us the tenth commandment for a reason, not to covet the possessions or lives of others. "Keeping up with the Joneses" might involve a larger mansion or Mr. Jones' trophy wife, but God encourages us to trust Him as our Provider. That trust will give us contentment, as our Lord never makes mistakes. Our station in life does not come from hard work, random luck or guesswork by God, as He has a purpose and a plan in each of our lives.

¹⁰ But I rejoiced in the Lord greatly that now at last your care for me has flourished again; though you surely did care, but you lacked opportunity. ¹¹ Not that I speak in regard to need, for I have learned in whatever state I am, to be content: ¹² I know how to be abased, and I know how to abound. Everywhere and in all things I have learned both to be full and to be hungry, both to abound and to suffer need. ¹³ I can do all things through Christ who strengthens me.
Philippians 4:10-13 (NKJV)

Socrates said, "Contentment is natural wealth; luxury is artificial poverty." When our goals are merely of a financial nature, we are missing the greater importance of a personal relationship with our Creator.

> "Do not spoil what you have by desiring what you have not; remember that what you now have was once among the things you only hoped for." -- Greek philosopher Epicurus

Jesus traveled the length and width of Israel with one tunic, yet we fill whatever space we dwell in with possessions. If we move into a much larger home, it is only a matter of time before we fill that space with more possessions. God takes care of the needs of His children, yet our Savior was homeless during the time of His ministry. God also desires for us to be content in regard to marital status. Paul found that he was able to serve the Lord better as a single man, yet he also realized that it was just as right to be married for those called to be married. Sadly, many churches treat singles differently than they treat married couples or families. Along those lines, neither Jesus nor Paul would have gained acceptance in many churches!

[7] For I wish that all men were even as I myself. But each one has his own gift from God, one in this manner and another in that.
[8] But I say to the unmarried and to the widows: It is good for them if they remain even as I am; [9] but if they cannot exercise self-control, let them marry. For it is better to marry than to burn *with passion.*
1 Corinthians 7:7-9 (NKJV)

What is better, to want what we have or to have what we want? Our desires as Christians should be for closer walks with God rather than for bigger, better and more possessions. Money is not the root of all evil, as many misquote, but instead, the root of all evil is the **love** of money. Certainly, we all fight that battle and carry that love, at least to a certain degree. We do not need to take vows of poverty, but neither should we desire more than we have. We must be content wherever God has us, single, married, rich or poor. If He has chosen us to serve Him, we already have been given a gift greater than winning the lottery!

Let your conduct *be* **without covetousness;** *be* **content with such things as you have. For He Himself has said,** *"I will never leave you nor forsake you."*
Hebrews 13:5 (NKJV)

November 30: Two, the number of division

When riding upon a bicycle built for two, both aboard better have the same direction of travel in mind. In God's design of the human body, He gave us two eyes, two ears, two nostrils, two arms, two legs, two hands and two feet. If any of those pairs work against each other, no work gets done. Can we inhale through one nostril while exhaling through the other? What happens when one foot steps forward and the other backward? Without the agility of a cheerleader, who can do the splits, something is going to break!

[24] If a kingdom is divided against itself, that kingdom cannot stand. [25] And if a house is divided against itself, that house cannot stand. [26] And if Satan has risen up against himself, and is divided, he cannot stand, but has an end.
Mark 3:24-26 (NKJV)

As two is the first number that can be divided, it points to division. Even the second day of creation demonstrates division:

[6] Then God said, "Let there be a firmament in the midst of the waters, and let it divide the waters from the waters." [7] Thus God made the firmament, and divided the waters which *were* **under the firmament from the waters which** *were* **above the firmament; and it was so. [8] And God called the firmament Heaven. So the evening and the morning were the second day.**
Genesis 1:6-8 (NKJV)

The second book of the Bible also demonstrates division. With Egypt emblematic of the world, God separated the children of Israel from the world when He removed them from Egypt. The word "separated" denotes that Christians are set apart, which is the meaning of the word "holy." We are holy because He is holy (1 Peter 1:16)!

Additionally, the second of God's 10 Commandments deals with division, as in Exodus 20:4, the Lord spoke of His own jealousy, requiring His followers to follow Him instead of idols created by their own hands. Certainly, Jesus echoed those same sentiments when He said in Matthew 12:30 that anyone who is not for Him is against Him. Somehow, we forget that not following God is just as much of a choice as following Him! Along those lines, the choice to follow God is to pursue good and the choice not to follow God is to pursue evil. That sounds like a pretty expansive division! The eternal destinies of heaven or hell accompany that decision, with quite a division between the two.

By studying biblical pairs, we can see that two is the number of division. Obviously, Cain and Abel suffered so ostensibly from division that the first murder occurred. Because the Lord respected Abel's sacrifice of a firstborn lamb, and did not respect Cain's sacrifice of the fruit of the ground, Cain became jealous of his brother. Rather than trying to figure out how to better please the Lord, Cain chose to perform an act that could not have displeased the Lord any more, when he killed his brother. Brotherly jealousy also occurred between Esau and Jacob, the sons of Isaac. For a taste of lentil stew, the older Esau sold his birthright to Jacob. Yet those two fought for superiority when still in Rebekah's womb:

[24] So when her days were fulfilled *for her* to give birth, indeed *there were* twins in her womb. [25] And the first came out red. *He was* like a hairy garment all over; so they called his name Esau. [26] Afterward his brother came out, and his hand took hold of Esau's heel; so his name was called Jacob. Isaac *was* sixty years old when she bore them.
Genesis 25:24-26 (NKJV)

God chose the younger brother, Jacob, who became Israel, and through his offspring came the 12 tribes of the Jewish people. Similarly, God chose Isaac, rather than Ishmael, Abraham's oldest son. We still can see the ramifications of that division today, with the Jewish bloodline of Isaac and the Arab bloodline of Ishmael. Enmity exists between those two just as strongly as it did in biblical times. The division that occurred between all of these siblings offers a representative sample of what can occur between any two people, regardless of blood, friendship or commitment. When two people walk individually, they carry their own history, perception and desire.

Two only can be unified by God's hand. Though Adam walked with God in fellowship through the Garden of Eden, surrounded by all the animals he had named, God still understood Adam's need for a helper. The Lord created Eve by taking a rib from Adam's own body:

[21] And the LORD God caused a deep sleep to fall on Adam, and he slept; and He took one of his ribs, and closed up the flesh in its place. [22] Then the rib which the LORD God had taken from man He made into a woman, and He brought her to the man.
[23] And Adam said:
"This *is* now bone of my bones
And flesh of my flesh;
She shall be called Woman,
Because she was taken out of Man."
[24] Therefore a man shall leave his father and mother and be joined to his wife, and they shall become one flesh.
Genesis 2:21-24 (NKJV)

With the covenant of marriage, God demonstrated that by making the two into one, there would be no division. Sadly, half of Christian marriages end in divorce, mostly due to the fact that God and God's law do not retain primary importance in the life of the believer. Even Christians can forget that they lost their rights when purchased by the blood of Jesus! As the brides of

Christ, we follow that same example in our relationship with Jesus. We are one in the Spirit, as He lives in us and we are in Him! That oneness demonstrates a lack of division, as Christ removed the dividing line with His life, death and resurrection. To walk in that oneness is to follow His laws, for He chose us! Divisiveness in the body of Christ is far-reaching. Why should any of us be against someone the Lord has chosen for His kingdom? Put it to rest by handing it to the Prince of Peace! Lay that divisiveness at the foot of the cross.

[12] For as the body is one and has many members, but all the members of that one body, being many, are one body, so also *is* Christ. [13] For by one Spirit we were all baptized into one body— whether Jews or Greeks, whether slaves or free—and have all been made to drink into one Spirit. [14] For in fact the body is not one member but many.
1 Corinthians 12:12-14 (NKJV)

December 1: A man called Barnabas

One of the ways we can see how God works in a believer is to study a biblical character documented in the Bible. The Bible mentions Barnabas in 28 verses, with 23 of those coming in Acts. In Acts 4:36, Luke first mentions Barnabas, as Joses, a Levite from Cyprus. We also learn in that verse that the name Barnabas means "Son of Encouragement," and in that title, we get to see the strength that Barnabas is best remembered for. He encouraged others! We all have met people who have given us false encouragement, but the comments and actions of Barnabas came from the heart, edifying his fellow believers. Right after the conversion of Saul of Tarsus, Barnabas brought Saul to the other believers (Acts 9:27). Because Barnabas was highly respected, even the former "Christian killer" gained entrance into this close group of believers in the early church. By the acceptance of the man we know as Paul, we can see another attribute of Barnabas in his commitment to the Lord, along with his standing among peers. Sent to Antioch, Barnabas:

encouraged them all that with purpose of heart they should continue with the Lord. [24] For he was a good man, full of the Holy Spirit and of faith.
Acts 11:22-24 (NKJV)

It is difficult to find sweeter accolades. Barnabas encouraged the people, and that encouragement came straight from the heart. Additionally, the encouragement was about deepening their walks with the Lord. Luke describes Barnabas as a good man, and that goodness only can come from the Lord. Barnabas also had two other special attributes: he was filled with both faith and the Holy Spirit. Fullness means without any lack, as a vessel cannot be overfilled! From this comment, we know that God's presence was evident in the life of Barnabas!

In Acts 11:25, Barnabas departed for Tarsus to bring Paul back to Antioch to teach for a year. This demonstrates a lack of pride in Barnabas. He followed Jesus before Paul, but accepted his role without desiring to be more important than God desired for him to be. One of the biggest hurdles in the life of a Christian is that of spiritual pride, which causes us to covet the positions of power or fame where God places others. Think of Peter's conversation with Jesus after Jesus had restored him and told him of his future. "What will happen to John," was Peter's first question!

Next, with a worldwide famine occurring, we see in Acts 11:30 that the relief the disciples sent from their hearts to the struggling brothers in Judea went by the hands of Barnabas and Saul. This identifies Barnabas once again as a leader, but also shows his generosity. The next time we see Barnabas, he is returning from fulfilling his ministry in Jerusalem, again, along with Saul. This is after the martyrdom of James, the brother of Jesus (Acts 12:25). In Acts 13, we see that Barnabas is one of five men in Antioch appointed as a teacher and prophet. Then we see that of those five men, Saul and Barnabas were separated in an even more special way, sent out to preach. First they went to Seleucia, and then to Cyprus. In Salamis, they preached the Word at the temple to the Jews. In the island of Paphos, they came upon Bar-Jesus, a false prophet who was with Sergius Paulus, an intelligent man who wanted to hear God's Word from Saul and Barnabas. When the false prophet was blinded, Sergius Paulus became a believer!

Back in Antioch, in Acts 13:42, Paul and Barnabas persuaded some Jews and other devout men to follow the ways of the Lord. That is another attribute of Barnabas. To persuade someone demonstrates the ability to understand the point of view of that person, while explaining the need for change. This reveals compassion along with the ability to remember the brokenness of his own past. Nothing speaks louder than a changed life, and people certainly saw that in the life of Barnabas. Later in Acts 13, the Jews became angry at the words of Paul and Barnabas, who both realized that it was time for their ministries to focus on the Gentiles. At that time, they "shook off the dust of their feet," which shows the ability to change, another attribute of Barnabas. Sometimes, we get stuck in ruts. One person explained that a rut is a dent in the ground that becomes a ditch before too long, and that ditch becomes a grave with two ends gone! Being willing and able to hear the Lord's instructions enabled both Saul and Barnabas to avoid death, even if they did not avoid persecution!

Most of us could name a Barnabas in our own lives, yet the real challenge is to be a Barnabas in the lives of others. Of his own accord, Barnabas would not have any of those attributes and strengths, but when our attributes begin to reflect Jesus, lives change drastically!

December 2: Dangers of compromise

Compromise often brings a solution, yet also can cause problems, depending on the area of adjustment. In disagreements, compromise saves the day, while in morals, values and integrity, compromise is a first step on the slippery slope of sin.

> "Courage, not compromise, brings the smile of God's approval." –Thomas S. Monson.

With the Jews wandering on their 40-year journey from Egypt to Israel, two and a half tribes decided to ask for land on the east of the Jordan River, before entering the Promised Land. In so doing, Gad, Asher and half of Manasseh did not see what God had to offer before grabbing what was at hand. That situation is reminiscent of "Let's Make a Deal," when the contestant chose "coffee for a year" in the closest box, before seeing the car and recreational vehicle behind the curtain. If God has a gift prepared for us, it will be the perfect gift! Our choices and desires pale in comparison!

Additionally, Lot exhibited compromise in his walk. When strife occurred between the herdsmen of Lot and Uncle Abraham, Abraham gave his nephew a choice:

[8] So Abram said to Lot, "Please let there be no strife between you and me, and between my herdsmen and your herdsmen; for we *are* brethren. [9] *Is* not the whole land before you? Please separate from me. If *you take* the left, then I will go to the right; or, if *you go* to the right, then I will go to the left." Genesis 13:8-9 (NKJV)

Lot did not choose "Green Acres" as Abraham did, but instead, just adored a penthouse view, choosing Sodom to pitch his tent. Soon after, God destroyed the sinful city, sparing Lot before the judgment. Yet Lot's journey from God's path cost him his wife, as she was "a-salt-ed." Additionally, soon after the destruction of Sodom and Gomorrah, Lot's daughters worried that without a wife, their father's lineage would cease. They chose to solve that problem by getting their father drunk and sleeping with him, giving birth to children that began the lines of the Ammonites and the Moabites, both enemies of Israel.

Joshua, the replacement for Moses upon the elder statesman's death, had a different view of compromise, for God told Joshua:

Only be strong and very courageous, that you may observe to do according to all the law which Moses My servant

commanded you; do not turn from it to the right hand or to the left, that you may prosper wherever you go.
Joshua 1:7 (NKJV)

God desires for us to follow Him. While His path includes ascents and descents, with many hurdles along the way, true blessings occur when we do not compromise His calling on our lives. He does not want us so veer from His path, but instead, to follow Him through our obedience! As Jesus said,

"If you love Me, keep My commandments."
John 14:15 (NKJV)

December 3: Sent

After the battle of Marathon, Phidippides ran just over 26 miles to Athens and offered news of victory to concerned Athenian citizens. When the word, "Nike," departed his lips, Phidippides died on the spot. Today, that same distance is the length of the marathon. As Christians, our races sometimes feel longer and more exhausting than the race of that ancient Greek. Paul reminded us:

**^{24} Do you not know that those who run in a race all run, but one receives the prize? Run in such a way that you may obtain *it*. ^{25} And everyone who competes *for the prize* is temperate in all things. Now they *do it* to obtain a perishable crown, but we *for* an imperishable *crown*. ^{26} Therefore I run thus: not with uncertainty. Thus I fight: not as *one who* beats the air. ^{27} But I discipline my body and bring *it* into subjection, lest, when I have preached to others, I myself should become disqualified.
1 Corinthians 9:24-27**

A common phrase associated with working out is, "no pain, no gain." Even Christians endure pain, but God uses that to draw us closer to Him and get us in better shape for future events. When walking in the flesh, we often complain about the difficulty of the journey, even when our journeys do not stray far from the couch. Yet when walking in the Spirit, the Lord will send us on amazing errands:

Also I heard the voice of the Lord, saying:
"Whom shall I send,
And who will go for Us?"
Then I said, "Here *am* I! Send me."
Isaiah 6:8 (NKJV)

Isaiah was willing to go anywhere the Lord desired. The Lord blessed him with a prophecy of the virgin birth of the Messiah, but it was not an easy path. In fact, according to Justin Martyr and Tertullian, Isaiah's enemies sawed him in half, far from a magician's trick. God does not want us to sprint quickly from the start and run out of steam soon after. He wants us to run the race with endurance, ready to earn the prize. "On your marks, get set, go!"

December 4: Pleasing God...

One of the most interesting passages in the Bible involves Enoch, the seventh generation of mankind and the great-grandfather of Noah. With the number seven holding much biblical significance, denoting completeness, it is not ironic that Enoch uniquely did not taste of death. Yet prior to God taking Enoch, the special part of Enoch's life was that he "walked with God" for 300 years.

[21] Enoch lived sixty-five years, and begot Methuselah. [22] After he begot Methuselah, Enoch walked with God three hundred years, and had sons and daughters. [23] So all the days of Enoch were three hundred and sixty-five years. [24] And Enoch walked with God; and he *was* not, for God took him.
Genesis 5:21-24 (NKJV)

Walking with God is an intimate progression. Often as Christians, we seem to make our own plans, as we walk ahead of God. Instead of waiting on Him to operate in His will and in His perfect timing, we seem to be in a rush. Enoch seemed to enjoy the sweetness of walking alongside God, as his prime concern was to please the Lord.

⁵ For those who live according to the flesh set their minds on the things of the flesh, but those *who live* according to the Spirit, the things of the Spirit. ⁶ For to be carnally minded *is* death, but to be spiritually minded *is* life and peace. ⁷ Because the carnal mind *is* enmity against God; for it is not subject to the law of God, nor indeed can be. ⁸ So then, those who are in the flesh cannot please God.
Romans 8:5-8 (NKJV)

Certainly, Enoch was in the Spirit, even in those Old Testament times before the Holy Spirit came to dwell permanently within believers. When Jesus promised this gift to His followers, He spoke of "another" Helper, to abide with us forever (John 14:16). The Greek word for "another" in that verse is *allos*, referring to another of the same sort, which is much different from the other word for another, *heteros*, which means another of a different sort. This designation reminds us that the Holy Spirit is God, just as the Father and Son of God. What does it take to please God?

¹ Finally then, brethren, we urge and exhort in the Lord Jesus that you should abound more and more, just as you received from us how you ought to walk and to please God; ² for you know what commandments we gave you through the Lord Jesus.
1 Thessalonians 4:1-2 (NKJV)

If we love God, we are to keep His commandments (John 14:15). The word for "keep" is in the future indicative tense, which literally means, "you will keep," yet that word can be translated "guard," as well. Guarding God's commandments involves personal adherence, yet additionally, we are to protect those commandments. As the world around us continues to change in a direction away from God, we are to boldly protect the ways of the Lord. Though Enoch's life occurred early in the history of man, that life is still remembered and mentioned in the New Testament, first in the "Hall of Faith" of Hebrews 11. Paul honored Enoch for his faith in walking with God, and then drew a correlation between that faith and the act of pleasing God.

But without faith *it is* impossible to please *Him,* for he who comes to God must believe that He is, and *that* He is a rewarder of those who diligently seek Him.
Hebrews 11:6 (NKJV)

Unfortunately, many people erroneously think that God is involved in some grandiose game of Hide-and-Seek, making it difficult for us to find Him. On the contrary, God has given us every opportunity to see Him, whether it be through His creation all around us or His presence everywhere. He has promised that if we diligently seek Him, we will find Him (Deuteronomy 4:29). We all have played Hide-and-Seek with someone who instead of hiding, stood right in front of the seeker. When our minds are focused upon what is covert, we miss what is overt!

Enoch is mentioned an additional time in the New Testament, concerning prophetic words about apostates in the end times. Apostates are people who have fallen away from the Lord. Instead of walking beside Jesus, they are lagging far behind, sometimes to the point where they no longer can see Him. Interestingly, the words quoted in Jude 14-15 are from the Book of Enoch, an ancient, Jewish work attributed to Enoch, who existed before the Jewish religion began. While God may not have desired for the Book of Enoch to be included in the canonical version of the Holy Bible, He certainly wanted the verses about apostasy there!

God gave Enoch a special gift for his consistent walk alongside the Lord. That gift was that Enoch never would taste of death. According to polls, death is the second most common fear, behind public speaking. Even some Christians continue to fear death, though God has promised us that He has removed the sting. Instead of a fear of death, many hold a fear of dying, which involves the possibly painful process leading up to that last moment of being absent from the body and present with the Lord. Jesus explained to Nicodemus about being born again, and those who have been born twice only will taste of death once, while those who only have been born once will taste of death twice. To simplify that statement, physical birth plus spiritual birth equals physical death while physical birth without spiritual birth equals physical and spiritual deaths.

Whatever we fear, if we are walking with God there is no reason to fear. When walking alone on any pathway, we can be waylaid by those with evil intentions. When walking alongside God, He is there to protect us, yet when we choose to leave His side, that protection has disappeared. That being said, God has a special way of allowing calamity to strike those who have chosen to stray, and then continues to walk again as a companion as soon as those who have strayed are willing. But the true test as a believer is in the desire to walk beside God, filled in His Spirit, guarding His laws. Let Enoch be an example in each of our lives how to walk faithfully!

[12] **These are spots in your love feasts, while they feast with you without fear, serving** *only* **themselves.** *They are* **clouds without water, carried about by the winds; late autumn trees without fruit, twice dead, pulled up by the roots;** [13] **raging waves of the sea, foaming up their own shame; wandering stars for whom is reserved the blackness of darkness forever.** [14] **Now Enoch, the seventh from Adam, prophesied about these men also, saying, "Behold, the Lord comes with ten thousands of His saints,** [15] **to execute judgment on all, to convict all who are ungodly among them of all their ungodly deeds which they have committed in an ungodly way, and of all the harsh things which ungodly sinners have spoken against Him."**
Jude 12-15 (NKJV)

December 5: Where is your focus?

In Southern California and other border states, there are many residents who live locally, work locally and raise families locally, yet their hearts remain in the country of either their birth or their heritage. While it may appear that they should follow their hearts to the land of their choice, it is not as simple as that. Some live in the United States for purely financial reasons, while others simply no longer can survive in their homelands. Whatever the reasoning, there are many people who are essentially "strangers in a strange land."

As Christians, we should understand that feeling, for though we remain on this earth, our God, who is outside of the dimension of time, already sees us as seated in the heavens according to Ephesians 2:4-7. How can we be seated in heaven if we are still struggling on earth? According to Hebrews 12:23, the church already is registered in heaven. This is not like a hotel reservation, as though we might have plans, there are an infinite number of events that could change whether or not we actually stay in the hotel. Instead, as believers, we are registered in heaven and nothing can change that fact!

[2] Set your mind on things above, not on things on the earth. [3] For you died, and your life is hidden with Christ in God. [4] When Christ *who is* our life appears, then you also will appear with Him in glory.
Colossians 3:2-4 (NKJV)

The problem occurs when we focus on the world, rather than heaven. It is easy to do when we rely on our senses, what we can grasp, smell, taste, see and hear. Instead, God wants us to center ourselves on the work He has set aside for each of us. Rather than worrying about provisions, if we are busy in the Lord's work, He certainly will provide! Miraculously, He provides all we need, often in the hour we need it!

[19] "Do not lay up for yourselves treasures on earth, where moth and rust destroy and where thieves break in and steal; [20] but lay up for yourselves treasures in heaven, where neither moth nor rust destroys and where thieves do not break in and steal. [21] For where your treasure is, there your heart will be also.

Matthew 6:19-21 (NKJV)

Money is not the only stumbling block that trips us. Idolatry is anything that gets in the way of our relationship with God. Sadly, all of us stumble along those lines. Often, the treasure even can be a person, who we love so much that we cannot envision life without them. Yet no matter how special that love can be, it cannot compare to a heavenly life of dwelling with the Lord! Whenever God desires for us to join Him, it will be the perfect time!

Our challenge is how to dwell in a godly manner in a world that does not honor God. We still can honor Him in all we do! That includes all of our relationships – within our families, at school, at work, at church and at play! Even when we are confronted with people who do not believe in God, we remain His representatives. Additionally, we should make a special effort with strangers and aliens, for we are aliens on this earth, as well. Store up treasures in heaven, for the Bank of God gives much better interest! He remains interested in us!

The stranger who dwells among you shall be to you as one born among you, and you shall love him as yourself; for you were strangers in the land of Egypt: I *am* the LORD your God.
Leviticus 19:34 (NKJV)

December 6: The gift of prayer

If any of us ever received the opportunity to sit down with our favorite past or present President of the United States, it would be an event that we never would forget. Yet even if we received such a special opportunity, there is very little chance that man of power would receive any request or advice that we offered without simply laughing at us. Men of power have powerful advisors who likely have considered all the possibilities. That being said, we would brag to our friends and family of the meeting.

How much more amazing it is that we are invited into the throne room of God, not just for a once-in-a-lifetime meeting, but any time we desire to go there! Even more amazing than that is the fact that when we go there, God actually listens to us! Before the death of Jesus, one of the duties of the high priest was to enter the Holy of Holies once a year when he made atonement for the sins of himself and the people he represented. Individuals like us never could enter the dwelling place of God. When Jesus died, the temple veil was split in two, enabling each of us who follow the Lord access into His throne room. Paul explains that process to us in Hebrews:

[19] Therefore, brethren, having boldness to enter the Holiest by the blood of Jesus, [20] by a new and living way which He consecrated for us, through the veil, that is, His flesh, [21] and *having* a High Priest over the house of God, [22] let us draw near with a true heart in full assurance of faith, having our hearts sprinkled from an evil conscience and our bodies washed with pure water. [23] Let us hold fast the confession of *our* hope without wavering, for He who promised *is* faithful. [24] And let us consider one another in order to stir up love and good works, [25] not forsaking the assembling of ourselves together, as *is* the manner of some, but exhorting *one another*, and so much the more as you see the Day approaching.
Hebrews 10:19-25 (NKJV)

As the verses above state, the veil is symbolic of the flesh of our Savior, as it also was torn upon the cross. Jesus has become our High Priest, and He has given us access to come boldly before the throne of grace. "Boldness" is the Greek word *parrhesia*, coming from *pas* meaning "all," and *rhesis* meaning "speech." This pertains to "the absence of fear in speaking boldly." In non-biblical Greek literature, this is the same word used for "throwing up." Though that might be a disgusting picture, it reminds us that prayer is one place we do not need to be hiding anything. Hiding from God is ludicrous as He sees it all anyway! Prayer is one place where we need to throw it all up to God, and to give Him all the mess in our lives. In Old

Testament times, the Jews prayed in the temple. Today, the temple is within each of us!

**[20] Now to Him who is able to do exceedingly abundantly above all that we ask or think, according to the power that works in us, [21] to Him *be* glory in the church by Christ Jesus to all generations, forever and ever. Amen.
Ephesians 3:20-21 (KJV)**

Look at the verse above in a progressive manner. God is able to do **whatever** we ask. God is able to do **all** that we think. God is able to do **all we ever** can ask or think. He is able to do **above all** we ever can ask or think. He is able to do **abundantly** above all we ever can ask or think. He is able to do **exceedingly**, abundantly, above all we ever can ask or think! Does this put it in better perspective?

Often, we pray as if it is a shopping list, or worse, fail to pray as we believe God's will is accomplished without our input. Yet God desires to involve us in the process. God desires to bless us through prayer, more than we desire to be blessed. When we ask for God to accomplish something on our behalves, or for our friends and family, when He does, our faith increases. Through prayer, God reminds us that He is listening. Yet make sure that prayer life does not replace Bible study! Prayers are when we talk to God, but Bible study is when God talks to us, and we certainly need to hear what He has to say more than He needs to hear what we have to say!

Are we utilizing the gift of prayer, one of the most important gifts the Lord has given us? It took the death of Jesus on the cross, and the rendering of His flesh, for us to have access into the Father's throne room. Do not take that gift for granted, but use it the way God intended! Let prayer change our lives!

praying always with all prayer and supplication in the Spirit, being watchful to this end with all perseverance and supplication for all the saints—

Ephesians 6:18 (NKJV)

December 7: Change those dirty clothes

American author and humorist Mark Twain said, "Clothes make the man. Naked people have little or no influence on society." The naked Adam certainly influenced our society, but today, Twain's line holds truth. By looking at the clothes of a man, we often can see his profession, his personality and his prosperity. While there are people who spend more than they can afford on clothing, there are many more people who buy cheap clothing that does not last a season before disintegrating, discoloring or shrinking. Clothes do not change what is on the inside; they simply reflect the inner man.

As Christians, we should have a whole new wardrobe! It is like going through an intensive program through Weight Watchers. When we leave the program and re-enter the world, none of our old clothing should fit.

⁵ Therefore put to death your members which are on the earth: fornication, uncleanness, passion, evil desire, and covetousness, which is idolatry. ⁶ Because of these things the wrath of God is coming upon the sons of disobedience, ⁷ in which you yourselves once walked when you lived in them. ⁸ But now you yourselves are to put off all these: anger, wrath, malice, blasphemy, filthy language out of your mouth. ⁹ Do not lie to one another, since you have put off the old man with his deeds, ¹⁰ and have put on the new *man* who is renewed in knowledge according to the image of Him who created him, ¹¹ where there is neither Greek nor Jew, circumcised nor uncircumcised, barbarian, Scythian, slave *nor* free, but Christ *is* all and in all.
Colossians 3:5-11 (NKJV)

In verse 7 above, the word "walked" is in the Greek aorist tense, denoting that at one time in the past, the action took place. All of us walked in fornication, uncleanness, passion, evil desire, and covetousness, yet when we come to Christ, He teaches us to walk away from those ways. We all wish that walking away from sin was a one-time process, as brokenness is sin's companion each step of the way. Yet, there are times when we continue to walk away from sin as Christians. In verse 8, we see the clothing that we are to remove: anger, wrath, malice, blasphemy, filthy language and lying. All six of those actions destroy our relationships and reflect the evil from within.

Brood of vipers! How can you, being evil, speak good things? For out of the abundance of the heart the mouth speaks.
Matthew 12:34 (NKJV)

In the same manner that our friends, families and co-workers all would notice if we completely changed our style with a make-over, those same people also should notice when that make-over occurs on the inside! In the following passage from Colossians, we see the new clothing that is worn in place of the old:

[12] Therefore, as *the* elect of God, holy and beloved, put on tender mercies, kindness, humility, meekness, longsuffering; [13] bearing with one another, and forgiving one another, if anyone has a complaint against another; even as Christ forgave you, so you also *must do*. [14] But above all these things put on love, which is the bond of perfection. [15] And let the peace of God rule in your hearts, to which also you were called in one body; and be thankful. [16] Let the word of Christ dwell in you richly in all wisdom, teaching and admonishing one another in psalms and hymns and spiritual songs, singing with grace in your hearts to the Lord. [17] And *whatever* you do in word or deed, *do* all in the name of the Lord Jesus, giving thanks to God the Father through Him.
Colossians 3:12-17 (NKJV)

It would be easy for God to take us to heaven once we give our lives to Him. Instead, He leaves us here and changes our ways, so drastically that people who know us should be able to see that difference with ease. If accustomed to our destructive ways, when people see our newly-found constructive attributes of kindness, humility, meekness, longsuffering and tender mercies, they first will wonder what deceitful plans we have come up with to get ahead. Yet as time continues, and the change remains, that 180-degree turn will speak volumes to an unbelieving world. God uses our sinful past in His kingdom building!

Are there changes that the Lord is still making in our lives? If not, we are not listening to Him! We are not perfected until we see His face. In the meantime, expect God to continue cleaning, inside and out. Let the new attributes on the outside demonstrate those inner changes. If the changes only have occurred on the inside, then we are naked, and can have no effect on society!

[21] I find then a law, that evil is present with me, the one who wills to do good. [22] For I delight in the law of God according to the inward man. [23] But I see another law in my members, warring against the law of my mind, and bringing me into captivity to the law of sin which is in my members. [24] O wretched man that I am! Who will deliver me from this body of death? [25] I thank God—through Jesus Christ our Lord! Romans 7:21-25 (NKJV)

December 8: Have you been sanctified?

As a child, there were days spent running, jumping and digging in so much dirt that at the end of the day when it was time for a bath, the water was so murky that the bottom of the tub was obstructed from view. Though soap and water cleaned most of the dirt away, there always seemed to be some dirt that remained. It might be behind the ears, under the chin, on the small of the back or in another hard-to-reach area. Yet even without missing a spot, rinsing the soap from the body with dirty water left at least a slight residue of scum. Though baths might be relaxing, showers give us a better opportunity to wash the dirt away.

As Christians, God has washed all of the dirt away for we are sanctified the moment we receive salvation. No matter what we accomplish in our lives for the kingdom of God and no matter how much sin we commit after that point, we are not more or less clean than other believers in the eyes of God. At that moment of salvation, God takes our sin away. Because Jesus received the punishment that we deserved, that sin will not be punished again. That sounds similar to our criminal procedure of double jeopardy. Sanctification is the Greek word *hagiasmos*, which designates that we are set apart. When God takes His children by the hand and leads them to the cross, from that time forward, we are to be set apart from the world for His use. As we all know, though purchased by God with the blood of Jesus, we can still fail miserably.

Sexual sin is one of the most common ways that Satan trips believers. Stephen Arterburn wrote a book entitled, "Every Man's Battle," describing the far-reaching magnitude of the sins of the flesh. Sadly, we all can recount stories of pastors who have stumbled, whether it is from personal knowledge or newspaper articles in some of the more high-profile cases. Often, for a moment's pleasure, men trade the glory of God along with being used for His purposes.

**[3] For this is the will of God, your sanctification: that you should abstain from sexual immorality; [4] that each of you should know how to possess his own vessel in sanctification and honor, [5] not in passion of lust, like the Gentiles who do not know God; [6] that no one should take advantage of and defraud his brother in this matter, because the Lord *is* the avenger of all such, as we also forewarned you and testified. [7] For God did not call us to uncleanness, but in holiness. [8] Therefore he who rejects *this* does not reject man, but God, who has also given us His Holy Spirit.
1 Thessalonians 4:3-8 (NKJV)**

Paul uses strong language to remind us of the Lord's even stronger stance on His children being lured into the same sins that enslave the world. When we choose to satisfy the flesh, we reject God! Along with that rejection of God comes an acceptance of Satan! How horrifying our sin can be, with its far-reaching arms. Sexual immorality is defined as any sexual relations outside of the marriage between a husband and a wife. While some may think of sex as a physical act, God designed it as a spiritual union. That union should be an example to us of the intimate relationship God desires with each of us. He already knows everything about us and desires for us to know everything about Him! Though Paul uses sexual immorality as an example due to its pervasiveness, any sinful behavior to gratify the flesh falls into the same category. Drug and alcohol use and abuse also have become pervasive in our society. All of us have been affected by the destructive capabilities of these addictions. Yet God has promised us that because He purchased us at a price, we are no longer enslaved to our sins, but instead, are enslaved to Him.

The Greek word for servant is *duolos*. Unlike the negative connotation we immediately think of with the word "slave," in Old Testament times, servants were not taken against their will. Instead, they worked for the master of the house for a time period of seven years. If they chose to remain after that seven-year period, the master pierced their ears with an awl in a ceremony that demonstrated that they wanted to remain. In the same manner, we serve God, who only has His best for us. Why would anyone choose to serve a master who only will harm us, rather than a God who only will love us?

[9] Do you not know that the unrighteous will not inherit the kingdom of God? Do not be deceived. Neither fornicators, nor idolaters, nor adulterers, nor homosexuals, nor sodomites, [10] nor thieves, nor covetous, nor drunkards, nor revilers, nor extortioners will inherit the kingdom of God. [11] And such were some of you. But you were washed, but you were sanctified, but you were justified in the name of the Lord Jesus and by the Spirit of our God.
1 Corinthians 6:9-11 (NKJV)

If we have been washed clean by the power of God, why jump back into the world and roll in the dirt again? That sounds more like the behavior of pigs, described as unclean animals. We have been positionally sanctified, as Christ has been made sanctification for each of us as believers. We also have received practical sanctification, meaning that the Holy Spirit continues the process of cleaning us. Because we are imperfect, God continues to do a work in us, and that work will find completion in our total sanctification. That future event will occur when we see the eyes of our Lord and Savior! He will remove any ability to sin from our lives, and we will not have to struggle with sin ever again. Hallelujah!

[15] **but as He who called you *is* holy, you also be holy in all *your* conduct,**
[16] **because it is written, *"Be holy, for I am holy."***
1 Peter 1:15-16 (NKJV)

to open their eyes, *in order* to turn *them* from darkness to light, and *from* the power of Satan to God, that they may receive forgiveness of sins and an inheritance among those who are sanctified by faith in Me.'
Acts 26:18 (NKJV)

December 9: Increasing barrenness

According to statistics obtained from the 2010 Census, the number of American women who remain childless after their childbearing years has doubled since 1970. At that time, 10% of American women did not have children, while the number has now increased to 20%. While there may be scientific and cultural reasons behind that data, with one possibility being the increase of women in the workplace, a greater explanation involves the de-emphasis on God in the lives of Americans.

From the time that God created man and woman, and told them to "Be fruitful and multiply" (Genesis 1:28), our Lord has blessed those following Him with the promise of children. In agrarian economies, children helped to farm the land, and additionally, most spent their lives in proximity to one another. In addition to experiencing the blessing of life from their own loins, God's greatest calling to parents is into the ministry of teaching their children about Him. When God gave the Law to Moses and the children of Israel, His covenant contained a blessing to their children, as well.

[1] "Now it shall come to pass, if you diligently obey the voice of the LORD your God, to observe carefully all His commandments which I command you today, that the LORD your God will set you high above all nations of the earth. [2] And all these blessings shall come upon you and overtake you, because you obey the voice of the LORD your God:
[3] "Blessed *shall* you *be* in the city, and blessed *shall* you *be* in the country.
[4] "Blessed *shall be* the fruit of your body, the produce of your ground and the increase of your herds, the increase of your cattle and the offspring of your flocks.
Deuteronomy 28:1-4 (NKJV)

In biblical times, childless women felt cursed. A great example of that sadness can be seen in the life of Sarah, who passed her childbearing years without children. Equally sad for her husband, Sarah encouraged Abraham to sire a child with her maidservant.

[1] Now Sarai, Abram's wife, had borne him no *children*. And she had an Egyptian maidservant whose name was Hagar. [2] So Sarai said to Abram, "See now, the LORD has restrained me from bearing *children*. Please, go in to my maid; perhaps I shall obtain children by her." And Abram heeded the voice of Sarai.
Genesis 16:1-2 (NKJV)

Though God's covenant to Abraham had included that He would greatly bless Abraham's descendants, both Abraham and Sarah lost faith in the Lord's ability to make that event happen when Sarah's age increased. We often fail in the same manner, as we logically deduce what is possible and what is impossible. Yet with God, nothing is impossible (Luke 1:37)! Instead, the impossibility involves God breaking a promise, as He cannot go against His own nature. So after Abraham fathered Ishmael with Hagar, God performed the miracle of birth with 90-year-old Sarah giving birth to Isaac, blessing 100-year-old Abraham with the son of God's covenant. The failure of Abraham and Sarah to trust God created problems that still exist today, as Ishmael's 12 sons became the Arabic nations. Today, Israel is surrounded by those Arabic nations, also offspring of Abraham, which desire to annihilate the only Jewish state.

For a person to be physically barren can cause much sadness, yet the barrenness that leads to destruction is of a spiritual variety:

[5] But also for this very reason, giving all diligence, add to your faith virtue, to virtue knowledge, [6] to knowledge self-control, to self-control perseverance, to perseverance godliness, [7] to godliness brotherly kindness, and to brotherly kindness love. [8] For if these things are yours and abound, *you will be* neither barren nor unfruitful in the knowledge of our Lord Jesus Christ.
2 Peter 1:5-8 (NKJV)

The Greek word for "barren" in the passage above is *argos*, denoting utter uselessness. Another definition includes yielding no return because of inactivity. In our Christian walks, God has at least one ministry for each of us, as He desires for us to know the life that His love creates. Just as a mother desires to have children, Christians should desire to be used for the purposes God has created them for. Though ministry can include many difficult paths, there is no greater blessing than to be operating in the gifts God has given! Yet in order for that ministry to occur, Peter highlighted for each of us a progression of the growth in our walks that must occur first. We must diligently add virtue to our faith, continue to grow in knowledge, exhibit self-control, be able to persevere even in difficulties, to grow in godliness, to be kind to our brothers, and most importantly, to grow in love. Without love, God will not use us to further His kingdom! Just as no child desires to grow up in a home without parents who love him, God will not appoint us to be a part of a ministry accomplished without love. For those who have not found their ministries, step out in faith when God cracks the door open ever so slightly. Remember, it is not about our abilities, but His ability. God called the stuttering Moses to speak to a king and lead millions of people. There is nothing our Lord cannot accomplish. God does not need any of us, but He desires to use us for our blessing! Would we rather be a sandy desert or a fruit tree?

[25] "So you shall serve the LORD your God, and He will bless your bread and your water. And I will take sickness away from the midst of you. [26] No one shall suffer miscarriage or be barren in your land; I will fulfill the number of your days. Exodus 23:25-26 (NKJV)

December 10: Thorn in the flesh

Paul is a Bible hero, having written most of the New Testament. As Saul, before God gave him a new name, he was an educated man, and one of Gamaliel's best students. Gamaliel was a Pharisee and one of the leaders of the Sanhedrin. In a nutshell, because of his time with this rabbi, Saul knew the Old Testament scriptures very well, yet it was head knowledge instead of heart knowledge. In that head knowledge, he "righteously" persecuted the Christians of the early church, and was present at the stoning of Stephen. He pursued Christians until soon after, Saul was confronted by the Lord while on the road to Damascus, and called to be an apostle of the risen Christ. Paul's life changed instantly, as did his name, and it was so drastic of a change that the Christians initially perceived that it was nothing more than a ploy to become a mole of sorts.

With that pedigree and those amazing academic credentials, along with his diligence in doing the Lord's work, Paul had a great possibility of struggling with spiritual pride.

**Now concerning things offered to idols: We know that we all have knowledge. Knowledge puffs up, but love edifies.
1 Corinthians 8:1**

God gave Paul many gifts, yet at the same time, life was not so easy for Paul. He endured many physical hardships, in addition to his own continued persecution. Paul was stoned, beaten, shipwrecked and imprisoned, and also had an eye infirmity. Many of the actions on the previous list occurred multiple times, yet he counted it all loss for Christ. What is the thorn Paul is referring to?

**[7] And lest I should be exalted above measure by the abundance of the revelations, a thorn in the flesh was given to me, a messenger of Satan to buffet me, lest I be exalted above measure. [8] Concerning this thing I pleaded with the Lord three times that it might depart from me. [9] And He said to me, "My grace is sufficient for you, for My strength is made perfect in weakness." Therefore most gladly I will rather boast in my infirmities, that the power of Christ may rest upon me. [10] Therefore I take pleasure in infirmities, in reproaches, in needs, in persecutions, in distresses, for Christ's sake. For when I am weak, then I am strong.
2 Corinthians 12:7-10 (NKJV)**

Paul continued to cry out to the Lord to remove the "thorn," but it remained. Why? Does God not hear the prayers of those who love Him? Of course He does, yet He also is omniscient and knows what is best for each of us. How could struggling with a weakness or sickness be better for us? As Paul told us from what he learned in the situation, when we are weak, we are strong. When we rely upon our own strength, we are destined for failure, but God's power will help us to endure and conquer anything! It is interesting that Paul's "thorn" never was identified. Millions of Christians have found support in these verses. Because the "thorn" is not identified, many of us believe that our "thorn" is exactly the same as Paul's "thorn." Many scholars believe this is a direct reference to Paul's eye infirmity. Others believe that it may have been lust, as that certainly seems to be every man's battle. Yet regardless of what brought Paul to his knees, we know that it was a place he needed to be in order to draw closer to the Lord.

How many pastors in today's culture seem impressed with their own abilities, seemingly over the abilities of the Lord? This reminds us that one of the most special attributes of a godly man is humbleness! Even as Christians, sin continues to be an attraction, though we at least understand that when we choose to sin, there might be momentary pleasure, but there is going to be pain and brokenness in combination. When we sin, this verse should be a reminder that God can and will use our worst decisions to continue to teach us and draw us closer to Him. Without Him, we are lost, and it should still amaze us how much He is concerned with the smallest parts of our lives!

December 11: Conviction

In 2002, American prisons topped 2 million convicted criminals for the first time in history. Today, there are an estimated 2.3 million prisoners in our prisons, for a wide variety of crimes. In many ways, our society does not punish crimes as rigidly as it did in the early days of this nation's history. Additionally, our legal system has made it more difficult to convict a defendant in seemingly open-and-shut cases. The O.J. Simpson murder trial and the Casey Anthony trial would be perfect examples. Yet even when conviction occurs, our prisons are filled with innocent people, at least according to the majority of those incarcerated, who never will admit their guilt.

As Christians, the verb "convict" is quite different. The Greek word *elencho* designates a revelation of the fault of the convicted, with a strong suggestion of putting the person to shame. Unlike our legal system, the biblical system of conviction involves an admission of guilt. The biggest differences occur in those doing the judging as well as those being judged. In our legal system, those doing the judging are errant men, who if the tables were turned, often could be on trial for laws they have broken. Yet in the judgment of mankind, our sinless God is the judge and jury, and never will be fooled by lies or subterfuge, as only He can see the motives of each heart. Along the same lines, in our legal system, the criminal would prefer to be playing Monopoly, finagling to get a "Get out of jail free" card. An admission of guilt could undermine those plans greatly. Yet in the lives of Christians, an admission of guilt is the first step to forgiveness, demonstrating the humbleness necessary for God to do a work in us. That conviction is not a life sentence in the believer. Instead, it is the Holy Spirit's job to plant seeds in our hearts that will draw us closer to God!

**[7] Nevertheless I tell you the truth. It is to your advantage that I go away; for if I do not go away, the Helper will not come to you; but if I depart, I will send Him to you. [8] And when He has come, He will convict the world of sin, and of righteousness, and of judgment: [9] of sin, because they do not believe in Me; [10] of righteousness, because I go to My Father and you see Me no more; [11] of judgment, because the ruler of this world is judged.
John 16:7-11 (NKJV)**

Just as attorneys present evidence to convict a criminal, the Holy Spirit presents evidence in the lives of believers that we have missed the mark. That evidence often can be the ability to see the pain we have caused in the lives of those we have wronged. Many times, the Holy Spirit will remind us of past sin when we are reading the Bible, as certain passages can bring to remembrance sinful actions in our lives. Yet if we have soft and pliable hearts, the Holy Spirit does His convicting in a soft and encouraging way. Often, we lose sight of the depth of depravity in our own lives, seeing the sin of others as being much worse than our own.

Yet Paul best understood the heart of a believer, judging himself to be the chief of sinners (1 Timothy 1:15). What is the greatest sin? All of us seem to put our own spin on that question. To King David, it might be committing adultery with the wife of a friend before arranging his death to cover the crime (2 Samuel 11). To Moses, it might be murdering an Egyptian who was beating a Jew (Exodus 2). To any of us, that greatest of sins might be construed as the one that caused the most damage in our lives. Yet the greatest sin is unbelief! Without trusting Jesus

Christ as Lord and Savior, we are destined for hell, regardless of the quantity or quality of sins in our lives.

The Holy Spirit also convicts us of righteousness, through the death and resurrection of Jesus. When Jesus died, He was punished for our sins, taking the judgment we earned and deserved. When Jesus rose from the dead, He imparted righteousness to the lives of believers. Instead of standing in front of God as pardoned criminals, because of the resurrection of Jesus, God sees righteousness in us! Think of Barabbas, the murderer set free on Passover when the innocent Jesus was crucified (Mark 15:6). Did anyone look at Barabbas and see a good man? Certainly, all continued to avoid him after his release from prison! Though Barabbas had been pardoned, everyone knew his guilt and did not expect the leopard to change its spots! Because of the conviction of the Holy Spirit, God sees us as unblemished, not pardoned! We gain God's righteousness!

[8] Yet indeed I also count all things loss for the excellence of the knowledge of Christ Jesus my Lord, for whom I have suffered the loss of all things, and count them as rubbish, that I may gain Christ [9] and be found in Him, not having my own righteousness, which *is* from the law, but that which *is* through faith in Christ, the righteousness which is from God by faith; Philippians 3:8-9 (NKJV)

Thirdly, the Holy Spirit convicts us of judgment. Though Judgment Day is a future event, judgment already has occurred. When sin entered the world, all of creation changed according to Paul. We live on a judged world, and he who has dominion over this world, Satan, already has been judged as destined for hell. Nothing will change that. In the same manner, God already knows each of us who will be seated in the heavens as His judgment already has designated that we are all sinners. Without Christ Jesus in our lives, we are destined for hell. This world has been declared lost, and individually, all we can do to change that is to feel the conviction of the Holy Spirit, admit our guilt, and come to a saving knowledge of Jesus!

Instead of walking in the pride of spiritual superiority, each of us needs to walk in humbleness, knowing that without God's forgiveness, we are lost. There is nothing we ever could do to earn His forgiveness, yet to receive that gift, we need to open our hearts. If the Holy Spirit has not convicted us, we are in no better place than a jailhouse lawyer. Guilty, as charged, and humbled by God's Gift!

[36] "Therefore let all the house of Israel know assuredly that God has made this Jesus, whom you crucified, both Lord and Christ."
[37] Now when they heard *this,* they were cut to the heart, and said to Peter and the rest of the apostles, "Men *and* brethren, what shall we do?"
[38] Then Peter said to them, "Repent, and let every one of you be baptized in the name of Jesus Christ for the remission of sins; and you shall receive the gift of the Holy Spirit. [39] For the promise is to you and to your children, and to all who are afar off, as many as the Lord our God will call."
Acts 2:36-39 (NKJV)

December 12: No obstacles!

There are times when obstacles change our paths and other times when those obstacles can change the destination. In the winter, the east entrance to Yosemite National Park closes after the first snow, and does not reopen until the winter's snow has melted. During the summer, a drive to the Yosemite Valley floor from that east entrance takes two hours, but in the winter, it is a day's journey to go around the Sierra Nevada Mountains. Without enough time or gas to make the change in plans, travelers might finish that journey much differently when faced with the obstacle of snow.

As Christians, we often find obstacles in our lives, yet the path to Jesus always remains clear. Because all things are possible through Christ who strengthens us (Philippians 4:13), there is no such thing as an insurmountable problem or concern. When

Jesus was in the midst of His ministry, He gave us many examples of the paths and destinations He changed.

[17] Now it happened on a certain day, as He was teaching, that there were Pharisees and teachers of the law sitting by, who had come out of every town of Galilee, Judea, and Jerusalem. And the power of the Lord was *present* to heal them. [18] Then behold, men brought on a bed a man who was paralyzed, whom they sought to bring in and lay before Him. [19] And when they could not find how they might bring him in, because of the crowd, they went up on the housetop and let him down with *his* bed through the tiling into the midst before Jesus.
[20] When He saw their faith, He said to him, "Man, your sins are forgiven you."
Luke 5:17-20 (NKJV)

What do we do when confronted with a closed door? For the faint of heart, that blocked entryway ends the journey, yet to those with faith, it only challenges them to find another way to complete the journey. Though confronted with a doorway blocked by the crowd, the men described by Luke carried their friend to the rooftop and found a different entrance! Jesus accomplished a healing of pure grace, as the paralyzed man did not ask to be healed. Additionally, that man's healing gave him spiritual life, as Jesus forgave his sins!

In this physical realm, we often lose sight of the spiritual significance. When praying for the Lord's healing, we seem to spend far too much time worried about our physical infirmities, when spiritual cleansing is the greatest possible gift. If the hurdle facing us is too high to jump, we can run under the hurdle or around it. It might add a few steps to the journey, but even with a change of scenery, God can accomplish the same results. Instead of praying for specific results, we should ask for God's hand to place us on the paths that He wills for our benefits and for His glory!

Jesus opens doors and shuts them, yet He never closes a door without opening a window, unless He has a roof-raising experience in mind! But before He opens the doors for us, we need to open the doors of our heart to Him. Never lose faith, even when faced with the highest hurdle!

⁷ "Ask, and it will be given to you; seek, and you will find; knock, and it will be opened to you. ⁸ For everyone who asks receives, and he who seeks finds, and to him who knocks it will be opened.
Matthew 7:7-8 (NKJV)

December 13: Forty!

In the Bible, numbers are significant. This should not be surprising as with all the advancements that have occurred in the field of mathematics, God invented math! Additionally, every word, space and stroke of the pen is significant in the Bible:

For assuredly, I say to you, till heaven and earth pass away, one jot or one tittle will by no means pass from the law till all is fulfilled.
Matthew 5:18 (NKJV)

Jot, or "*jod*," is the smallest letter of the Hebrew alphabet. In the name of God, יהוה, it is the first letter, which is the letter to the farthest right in Hebrew. That same letter is *iota* in Greek, while the "tittle" is the diacritic. In the English language, that would be the dot on the "i" or "j." God tells us the importance of even the smallest part of the Bible through the above verse. In regard to numbers, "40" occurs frequently in the Bible. Scholars believe that "40" stands for a test, trial, period of probation or period of chastisement. That all began in Genesis 7:4 when God caused it to rain for 40 days and 40 nights. Interestingly, "40" is the product of 5 and 8, with 5 reflective of grace and 8 standing for new beginnings or renewal. Numerologists often can belabor the point when dealing with numbers. But God certainly demonstrated to the eight people not destroyed in the Great

Flood that they had endured a test, when given the new beginning of the world at the peak of Mount Ararat!

Moses lived to be 120 years old, and his life reflected three distinctly-different, 40-year periods. He lived in Pharaoh's court for the first 40 years of his life, then after murdering an Egyptian who was beating a Hebrew slave, fled to Midian for the next 40 years. (Acts 7) At the age of 80, God called Moses to lead the Hebrew nation, and continued on a 40-year trial in the wilderness, a journey that would have taken 11 days if they traveled in a straight line! Additionally, when Moses went to the top of Mount Sinai to receive the Law, he remained there with the Lord fasting for 40 days. After coming down the mountain and finding the Jewish people worshipping a golden calf, Moses broke the two tablets of commandments, and then went back up Mount Sinai again. This time, Moses fasted and prayed for the lives of his friends and brother for another 40 days. Through this trial, Moses revealed his love for God's people!

When the Lord sent Jonah to preach to the people of Nineveh, Jonah disobeyed God and went in the opposite direction. Yet God caused the people aboard Jonah's ship to toss him into the waves, in an attempt to stop the storm. A big fish swallowed Jonah and he remained in the belly of the fish for three days and three nights. After being spit onto the shores, Jonah decided to heed the words of God, and went to Nineveh, though he did not want God to save the Ninevites.

[3] So Jonah arose and went to Nineveh, according to the word of the LORD. Now Nineveh was an exceedingly great city, a three-day journey *in extent*. [4] And Jonah began to enter the city on the first day's walk. Then he cried out and said, "Yet forty days, and Nineveh shall be overthrown!"
Jonah 3:3-4 (NKJV)

God gave the people of Nineveh 40 days to change their ways, and amazingly, every single person in Nineveh began to believe and follow the Lord, beginning with fasting and mourning! In this 40-day test, Jonah demonstrated disdain for the people, as they were his enemies. Jonah did not want to share his God with those he hated. In some ways, Jonah passed his test, as he heeded the words of the Lord, yet in other ways, his actions did not reveal the love of the Lord.

There are many other 40-day or 40-year periods described in the Bible, including 40 years of rest when Othniel was judge (Judges 3:9), another 40-year rest of the land under Barak (Judges 5:31), and yet another quiet period for the country under Gideon (Judges 8:28). But the most significant was a 40-day period when Jesus was tempted by Satan in the wilderness, beginning our Lord's ministry. Immediately after John baptized Jesus in the Jordan River, an event well-attended by Father, Son and Holy Spirit, the Messiah endured a 40-day fast. Satan came at Jesus with guns blazing, attempting to lure Jesus away from the Father through the lust of the flesh, the lust of the eyes and the pride of life. It is impossible for us to grasp that Jesus was 100% man at the same time He was 100% God, yet Satan pulled out the stoppers to get Jesus to sin. If Jesus had fallen, even once, He would have lost the ability to be the sacrifice for our sins and all would have perished. When we feed the flesh, the flesh increases and when we feed the Spirit, the Spirit increases, so it is not coincidence that Jesus entered this battle without food or water.

[1] **Then Jesus, being filled with the Holy Spirit, returned from the Jordan and was led by the Spirit into the wilderness,** [2] **being tempted for forty days by the devil. And in those days He ate nothing, and afterward, when they had ended, He was hungry.**
[3] **And the devil said to Him, "If You are the Son of God, command this stone to become bread."**
[4] **But Jesus answered him, saying, "It is written, *'Man shall not live by bread alone,* but by every word of God.' "**
[5] **Then the devil, taking Him up on a high mountain, showed Him all the kingdoms of the world in a moment of time.** [6] **And the devil said to Him, "All this authority I will give You, and their glory; for *this* has been delivered to me, and I give**

it to whomever I wish. ⁷ Therefore, if You will worship before me, all will be Yours."
⁸ And Jesus answered and said to him, "Get behind Me, Satan! For it is written, *'You shall worship the LORD your God, and Him only you shall serve.'* " ⁹ Then he brought Him to Jerusalem, set Him on the pinnacle of the temple, and said to Him, "If You are the Son of God, throw Yourself down from here. ¹⁰ For it is written:
'He shall give His angels charge over you,
To keep you,'
¹¹ and,
'In their *hands they shall bear you up,*
Lest you dash your foot against a stone.' "
¹² And Jesus answered and said to him, "It has been said, *'You shall not* tempt the LORD your God.' "
¹³ Now when the devil had ended every temptation, he departed from Him until an opportune time.
Luke 4:1-13 (NKJV)

Certainly, all of us will endure 40-day tests, too. Yet God has revealed His hand in each of our lives, reminding us that we can stand on the promises of His Word. A wise man once said that if we are not being attacked by Satan and his demons, we are not accomplishing anything for the Lord. Satan hates those who do the Lord's bidding. If the attacks are coming, know that we must be doing something right!

¹² Beloved, do not think it strange concerning the fiery trial which is to try you, as though some strange thing happened to you; ¹³ but rejoice to the extent that you partake of Christ's sufferings, that when His glory is revealed, you may also be glad with exceeding joy.
1 Peter 4:12-13 (NKJV)

December 14: Can the past ruin the present!

With an emphasis on profit-loss statements, Individual Retirements Accounts (IRAs) and healthy bank accounts, especially in an economy that is spiraling downward, where will people turn when savings have been depleted? In December of 2010, the national unemployment rate reached 9.8%, and while the other 90.2% may be employed, salaries and wages earned have dropped drastically for the vast majority of all in the workplace. It is easy to rely on self when all is going well, but when real trouble begins, where is there to turn? Sadly, tough economic times see a stark increase in suicide rates, along with drug abuse and alcoholism.

Though we have the tendency to rely on self and our financial well-being, God desires for us to rely on Him, and instead, gain spiritual well-being. One of the best biblical examples of that occurs when the rich, young ruler approached Jesus, and asked what was necessary to follow Him:

[22] So when Jesus heard these things, He said to him, "You still lack one thing. Sell all that you have and distribute to the poor, and you will have treasure in heaven; and come, follow Me."
[23] But when he heard this, he became very sorrowful, for he was very rich.
[24] And when Jesus saw that he became very sorrowful, He said, "How hard it is for those who have riches to enter the kingdom of God! [25] For it is easier for a camel to go through the eye of a needle than for a rich man to enter the kingdom of God."
Luke 18:22-25 (NKJV)

Many people reading this passage misinterpret the message, thinking that we are called to take vows of poverty in order to follow our Savior. Yet God blessed King Solomon with more wealth than anyone else in the world. For the rich, young ruler, wealth was an idol, and if we are willing to worship the Lord, it must be in spirit and in truth. When something else gets in the way, and is more important to us than God, we cannot follow Him! Because God desires a relationship with us, He frequently places us in situations where we will look to Him as our provider, rather than relying on self. Paul summed it up:

[7] But what things were gain to me, these I have counted loss for Christ. [8] Yet indeed I also count all things loss for the excellence of the knowledge of Christ Jesus my Lord, for whom I have suffered the loss of all things, and count them as rubbish, that I may gain Christ [9] and be found in Him, not having my own righteousness, which *is* from the law, but that which *is* through faith in Christ, the righteousness which is from God by faith; [10] that I may know Him and the power of His resurrection, and the fellowship of His sufferings, being conformed to His death, [11] if, by any means, I may attain to the resurrection from the dead.
Philippians 3:7-11 (NKJV)

We need to pile our pasts on the rubbish heap when we come to the Lord. Our pasts include our accomplishments, egos and treasures, all stored up to make us feel better, stronger and more competent. But the good news is that the rubbish heap also includes our sins, taken away by a Savior who loves us. Those sins are heavy burdens to carry, but He enables us to cast that weight aside! If enduring a difficult time, Paul reminds us that when we suffer, we are baptized into our Lord's suffering, that we may know an inkling of what our Savior endured for us to be saved. It is easy to become overwhelmed with what seem to be insurmountable difficulties, but we know that our God loves us and does not seek to destroy us. It certainly is a test. Will we continue to rely on self or begin to rely on Him?

God goes to incredible lengths to provide for His people. Recounted in Genesis 37-44, God allowed Joseph's brothers to cast him into a pit that others would find him. Joseph was taken into slavery and imprisoned before sharing God's interpretation of a dream. That event caused a change in Joseph's life. No longer a slave, Joseph became the second most powerful man in Egypt behind only Pharaoh. With God's foreknowledge of an approaching famine, Joseph saved enough grain to sustain all of Egypt. His brothers came to Egypt to acquire enough grain to sustain their families, as well, and were unknowingly confronted by the brother they had sought to kill. Instead of feeling any bitterness to those brothers, Joseph wept and provided in abundance. God's miraculous hand prepared a path for His people, in the midst of famine. That plan involved what many would term insurmountable difficulties, like famine, slavery and imprisonment, but those were temporary obstacles to reach the goal of trusting in God.

It all comes down to trust. If we as Christians truly believe what we claim to believe, we need to exhibit that faith in the best of times and also in the worst of times! By living with joy in the midst of turmoil, our lives can speak volumes to a hard-of-hearing world that desperately needs to hear about a God who loves, provides and saves.

Some *trust* in chariots, and some in horses;
But we will remember the name of the LORD our God.
Psalm 20:7

"But woe to you who are rich,
For you have received your consolation.
  Luke 6:24 (NKJV)

December 15: Whose battle is it?

Most of us have known a business associate or competitor who seemed to thrive while exhibiting pride and a complete lack of integrity. It can be a huge challenge to not get caught up in the desire to sink to their level. If they spread vicious lies about us, do we decide that *"quid pro quo"* is the way to go, exposing them? Jesus handled it in a different way when the false accusations came upon Him.

He was oppressed and He was afflicted,
Yet He opened not His mouth;
He was led as a lamb to the slaughter,
And as a sheep before its shearers is silent,
So He opened not His mouth.
Isaiah 53:7 (NKJV)

When we are walking with the Lord, anything that happens in our lives He has allowed for a purpose. Rather than moaning or complaining, God wants us to bring every issue to Him. We love to question God, but those answers are not the important part of the puzzle as He already has told us that we shall walk by faith, not by sight (2 Corinthians 5:7). "Why, God?" Alfred Lord Tennyson said, "Ours is not to reason why; ours is just to do and die." Tennyson had it mostly right. With God, we do not have to reason why, but ours is to do and to live! We do not have to defend ourselves because God will defend us. He is the Way, the Truth and the Life (John 14:6)! There is no path any of us should prefer to be on than His. When lies darken our days, His Truth will endure forever, and God always has the last word! In Him, we have abundant life, and it cannot be more abundant than what He already has planned for us. It ends with a gift greater than winning the largest lottery in the history of the world, our eternal salvation!

When the giant Goliath seemed to be a huge thorn in the flesh of Israel, God handled the situation in His perfect timing (1 Samuel 17). Goliath was filled with pride. At his size, he never had been defeated. He laughed at the boy who came to confront him and laughed at the handful of five pebbles in the hand of David. He laughed at the sling in David's hand, taunting all the way. David righteously believed in the power of God, rather than in the power of man, and knew that without the Lord's hand, he, too, was destined for failure. Goliath's prideful taunting ended immediately when the first of David's small rocks made a deep impression upon the giant's skull, instantly killing him. Rather than sink to Goliath's level, bragging of his own accomplishments and power, David relied on the Lord. When God wants to make an impression, He does it with ease and perfection!

[1] I, therefore, the prisoner of the Lord, beseech you to walk worthy of the calling with which you were called, [2] with all lowliness and gentleness, with longsuffering, bearing with one another in love, [3] endeavoring to keep the unity of the Spirit in the bond of peace.

Ephesians 1:1-3 (NKJV)

Paul reminds us in the verse above to walk worthy of God's calling. "Worthy" is the Greek word *axios*, which referred to the scales used in the Greek marketplace. In that economy based on weight, a vendor would place the item for sale on one side of the scale and the currency on the other side of the scale. When in balance, the trade was a good one. God desires for us to be in balance, as well. Our walk with Him should be the same on a Sunday at church and in our business dealings during the week. Instead of lying, cheating and stealing to get ahead, God desires for us to act with His moral standards in all situations. If an enemy spreads vicious lies that cause pain, God will defend His honor, for when we have been purchased with His blood, that honor is no longer ours!

"Character" has been described as who we are when no one is looking. We either have character or we are one! As Christians, we have a higher calling to serve a God who loves us. Do not get caught up in the ways of the world, battling for more possessions, accomplishments and trophies. God will bring all of our successes and all or our failures, both for His purposes! Never lose sight of the fact that God can change the most hateful people with His salvation, just as He changed each of us!

[19] **Beloved, do not avenge yourselves, but** *rather* **give place to wrath; for it is written,** *"Vengeance is Mine, I will repay,"* **says the Lord.** [20] **Therefore**
"If your enemy is hungry, feed him;
If he is thirsty, give him a drink;
For in so doing you will heap coals of fire on his head."
[21] **Do not be overcome by evil, but overcome evil with good. Romans 12:19-21 (NKJV)**

December 16: Look introspectively!

When the queen in "Snow White and the Seven Dwarves" looked into a mirror and asked, "Who is the fairest of them all," she was not happy when the honest answer applied to Snow

White, not herself. A problematic area for all possessed with pride arises when we do not see what others see, when judgment becomes clouded by ego. While this attribute may be more prevalent in those not filled by the Holy Spirit, God warns Christians of the harm we can cause with the same action.

[39] And He spoke a parable to them: "Can the blind lead the blind? Will they not both fall into the ditch? [40] A disciple is not above his teacher, but everyone who is perfectly trained will be like his teacher. [41] And why do you look at the speck in your brother's eye, but do not perceive the plank in your own eye? [42] Or how can you say to your brother, 'Brother, let me remove the speck that *is* in your eye,' when you yourself do not see the plank that *is* in your own eye? Hypocrite! First remove the plank from your own eye, and then you will see clearly to remove the speck that is in your brother's eye.
[43] "For a good tree does not bear bad fruit, nor does a bad tree bear good fruit. [44] For every tree is known by its own fruit. For *men* do not gather figs from thorns, nor do they gather grapes from a bramble bush. [45] A good man out of the good treasure of his heart brings forth good; and an evil man out of the evil treasure of his heart brings forth evil. For out of the abundance of the heart his mouth speaks.
Luke 6:39-45 (NKJV)

What do we see when we look into a mirror? We should see a sinner saved by grace staring back into our own eyes, a veritable "Plankenstein!" New believers typically walk in a freedom that sometimes can seem like ancient history to more mature believers. Having a great burden lifted from their shoulders in the Lord's forgiveness of sins brings exultant joy.
Unfortunately, the next stage after that joy typically is legalism. When God removes sinful areas from our own lives, we often see that same sin in the lives of others and come down hard on them. Yet God is the one who cleans our lives. His process may operate in a different order for different people. Rather than judging and condemning our Christian brothers and sisters, we should encourage them in their walks with the Lord. An old

saying reminds us that we can attract more flies with honey than with vinegar, and in the same manner, people respond to love.

When Paul looked into the mirror, he saw the chief of sinners, not an eloquent, educated preacher, teacher and author:

**[14] And the grace of our Lord was exceedingly abundant, with faith and love which are in Christ Jesus. [15] This *is* a faithful saying and worthy of all acceptance, that Christ Jesus came into the world to save sinners, of whom I am chief. [16] However, for this reason I obtained mercy, that in me first Jesus Christ might show all longsuffering, as a pattern to those who are going to believe on Him for everlasting life. [17] Now to the King eternal, immortal, invisible, to God who alone is wise, *be* honor and glory forever and ever. Amen.
1 Timothy 1:14-17 (NKJV)**

God chose to use Paul to write a majority of the New Testament. If anyone could have been blindsided by spiritual pride, Paul would have been in front of the line with the might of his ministry for the Lord. Yet Paul never lost sight of the man who violently had persecuted the Church of Jesus Christ. When God removes our sins, He places them behind His back (Isaiah 38:17), casts them into the depth of the ocean (Micah 7:19) and removes them as far as the east is from the west (Psalm 103:12). Though we no longer should allow those sins to weigh us down, it is healthy to remember the brokenness that we both felt and caused by our sins. That healthy reminder is a wonderful gift when faced with a fellow believer struggling in a sin God has swept out of our lives. Without Him, we are nothing! Without His forgiveness, we are dead in our trespasses. Without His grace, we are unsaved sinners. Rejoice in the gifts He has given and share that joy with Christian brethren, without judgment or condemnation!

**and are confident that you yourself are a guide to the blind, a light to those who are in darkness,
Romans 2:19 (NKJV)**

December 17: Abandoned!

In law, abandonment means to relinquish or renounce an interest, claim, privilege, right or possession with the intent of never resuming any of those again. When it comes to inanimate objects like land, only the owner can abandon the property. Yet in regard to people, both parties can abandon or be abandoned. All of us have at times felt abandoned by those we love, left alone to fend for ourselves on the seas of distress. Certainly, that is a common feeling with anyone who has either thought about or acted on the desire to commit suicide. Where do we turn when there is nowhere else to turn?

In the Bible, a frequent term for abandon is forsake, which appears 143 times in the Old Testament and eight times in the New Testament, in the King James Version. Jesus spoke the word from the cross in reference to the Father and the Holy Spirit, a repeat of the prophetic utterance of King David in Psalm 22.

[45] Now from the sixth hour until the ninth hour there was darkness over all the land. [46] And about the ninth hour Jesus cried out with a loud voice, saying, "Eli, Eli, lama sabachthani?" that is, *"My God, My God, why have You forsaken Me?"*
Matthew 27:45-46 (NKJV)

Unlike our legal interpretation of abandonment, or being forsaken, God did not turn His back on Jesus with the intent of not resuming that relationship again. Instead, when the sins of the world were placed upon the shoulders of Jesus, God had to look away. A righteous God cannot be a part of unrighteousness, and for that reason, sin created separation, just as it does when we sin. That separation was wider than the Grand Canyon! We can see that separation in the words of our Savior, as He no longer used His typical term of relationship, "My Father." Instead, Jesus spoke the words, "My God, My God," the first referring to the Father and the second referring to the Holy Spirit. The separation from His Father and the Holy Spirit that Jesus felt was the only time in all of eternity that He would experience such utter pain and hopelessness. To Jesus, the separation was devastating. That is the same feeling those in hell will experience, yet the duration will be for eternity, rather than for a moment!

We can lose sight of the fact that **we caused** that sadness in our Savior. Jesus did not commit any sin to cause separation from God. Instead, that separation occurred when our sin was placed upon His shoulders. We can rejoice that as believers, our sin certainly causes brokenness, but it already has been paid for! God told us in Genesis 28:15, Deuteronomy 31:6, Deuteronomy 31:8, Joshua 1:5 and Hebrews 13:5 that He never will leave us or forsake us! No matter what depth of duress we find ourselves in, God never will turn His back on us!

Why does it feel like there are times when we are fighting the battles alone? If it is not because God has forsaken us, it is because we have forsaken God! This happens for a variety of reasons, though pride seems to be at the forefront. Often, we forget who is fighting the battles for us, and we let our own arrogance take credit for success. That is the first step of approaching failure, for God deserves all honor. Secondly, that seeming aloneness occurs when we grow complacent in our walks with the Lord, by failing to exhibit faithfulness. Sometimes, one bad decision can start us on a journey that leads far away from the Lord!

[1] **"Now it shall come to pass, if you diligently obey the voice of the LORD your God, to observe carefully all His commandments which I command you today, that the LORD your God will set you high above all nations of the earth.** [2] **And all these blessings shall come upon you and overtake you, because you obey the voice of the LORD your God: Deuteronomy 28:1-2 (NKJV)**

In the passage quoted above, the word for "diligence" does not refer to a momentary occurrence. We can be diligent one day and not be diligent the next. Instead, this passage describes faithfulness, daily diligence, in hearing the voice of God. Obviously, we cannot hear without listening! The voice of God is most apparent and available in the Bible, so we are to remain faithfully in His Word. Additionally, to obey His voice, we need to be doers of the Word, not just hearers of the Word. When we choose to disobey the Lord, He does not leave us, yet we turn away from Him. When facing darkness, we feel alone in the battle, yet God remains there with us, right behind us, waiting for us to turn around and run into His arms again!

If we have Jesus as our Savior, we never will be forsaken, but in our walk, we must not forsake Him! There is not a more painful or lonely place. If feeling that loss, turn around and run back into His arms. God will respond just like the father when the prodigal son returned, having wasted his inheritance. God clothes us, gives us His name and kills the fatted calf to feed us in celebration of the one who was lost, but now is found! Turn, turn, turn!

[19] **But Joshua said to the people, "You cannot serve the LORD, for He *is* a holy God. He *is* a jealous God; He will not forgive your transgressions nor your sins.** [20] **If you forsake the LORD and serve foreign gods, then He will turn and do you harm and consume you, after He has done you good." Joshua 24:19-20 (NKJV)**

December 18: Choices

Each choice in life is pivotal as even what seems to be the simplest decision can lead to unforeseen, far-reaching consequences. While there are few unchangeable decisions, it often is difficult to turn around and head in the direction from whence we came. It seems like a waste of both time and energy to walk up the same hill again, yet if lessons have been learned on the erroneous path, waste does not occur.

As Christians, the ultimate decision typically involves brokenness. When life is not working out the way we planned, desired or hoped, we often try harder. Each person has an individual breaking point, when they finally grasp it is not going to change. That brokenness can come from drug abuse, sickness, loss of relationship, loss of career or any number of other possibilities. Yet when we try to fill the emptiness in our souls, only Jesus can fill that void. The ultimate decision is when we decide to follow Him.

What seems to be a forward path rarely proceeds directly. Instead, there are mountains and valleys; right turns and left turns; and tumbles and falls, with bumps and bruises along the way. Sometimes, the new path intersects the old path again. When our eyes are focused on Jesus, we ignore that intersection and proceed on the path toward the Lord. Yet our former master, the devil, reminds us of the pleasure associated with our old sin. If we are listening to the Holy Spirit, we realize that Satan reveals only a modicum of truth, as pleasure was only a small portion of the past. Instead, God reminds us of the permeating brokenness involved in our sinful choices. Many Christians still choose that old sinful path, and once again, find themselves moving in the wrong direction.

In Matthew 18, Jesus teaches us how to handle a brother who has sinned against us. First, we are to go to the brother. This does not say anything about a phone call, a letter or an email, but instead, a journey. Going to the brother rather than requiring the brother to come to us demonstrates humility. Yet if that does not bring restitution, our next step according to Jesus is to take others with us on another journey to the brother. Humility continues and with witnesses involved, a difference of opinion can be overruled by logic. Yet if that step also fails, Jesus gives us a third part of the process, to take the matter before the church. If there is still not repentance, the church is to accomplish the most difficult of tasks, according to the writings of Paul:

[1] It is actually reported *that there is* sexual immorality among you, and such sexual immorality as is not even named among the Gentiles—that a man has his father's wife! [2] And you are

puffed up, and have not rather mourned, that he who has done this deed might be taken away from among you. ³ For I indeed, as absent in body but present in spirit, have already judged (as though I were present) him who has so done this deed. ⁴ In the name of our Lord Jesus Christ, when you are gathered together, along with my spirit, with the power of our Lord Jesus Christ, ⁵ deliver such a one to Satan for the destruction of the flesh, that his spirit may be saved in the day of the Lord Jesus.
1 Corinthians 5:1-5 (NKJV)

What seems to us like harsh judgment actually involves the most loving decision. Delivering a fellow believer to Satan, according to the verse above, is to destroy the flesh, not the Spirit! The situation at the Church of Corinth had to do with sexual immorality, but any ostentatious venture into sin without repentance earns the same procedures and treatment. Once the Holy Spirit takes up residence in the life of a believer, He is there to stay. The Holy Spirit is not looking to move to a better place, like "The Jefferson's." Neither are there foreclosures on His present home. He continues to reside in the believer even with the choice to walk with Satan on that sinful path again. There is no more painful or desolate life than that of a believer who has walked away from God. For the Lord will allow Satan to bring abject poverty into that life. Brokenness will occur again, as Satan will destroy the flesh, which is the pride that has crept back into the life of the wayward believer. When that brokenness occurs, it is time for another "about-face."

God's love is amazing! Any time we are willing to turn around and face Him again, He is willing to take us back into His arms! That kind of unconditional love is not what we are accustomed to in our interpersonal relationships, but God's love is unlike anything we ever have experienced. Are there still ramifications of our sinful choices? Yes, but those consequences are limited to this world. For example, if a believer falls away from the Lord and is arrested for committing murder, the Lord's forgiveness still exists, but the believer likely will serve a prison sentence. While the time in prison may be difficult, God will continue to hold the hand of the one convicted. He never will leave us or forsake us! Paul found a captive audience in the times he spent in prison. God can continue to use us no matter where we are, as long as our vessel is clean. That cleanliness involves repentance and the forgiveness of our sins.

For those who have walked away from the Lord, He desires to fellowship closely with us again! Just as God gently called out to Adam after the initial sin, He calls out to us in our sin. We break God's heart when we sever that relationship, but it does not surprise Him. Because He never will let go of us, He knows that we will come back to Him, and exactly when that will happen. When we come back, the Lord restores the years that the swarming locust has eaten (Joel 2:25). That means that God will bring us to the place He desires us to be; He completes the work is us. All we need to do is decide to follow Him. If on the wrong path, turn around. Recommit that life to Jesus. He will welcome any of us back into His arms!

"No one can serve two masters; for either he will hate the one and love the other, or else he will be loyal to the one and despise the other. You cannot serve God and mammon. Matthew 6:24 (NKJV)

December 19: Seeds that grow

In the last 100 years, the world has seen many developments in farming. Yet without the cooperation of sun and rain, scientific improvements are no help. Farmers can work from dawn to dusk, but drought or flood can erase all of that effort. In the same manner, the sun begins the process of photosynthesis to feed the plant, but too much sun can burn up the plant. Though man's hard work and knowledge certainly increase the opportunities for a bountiful harvest, without the extraneous hand of God supplying optimal conditions, it is all for nothing.

In 2007, one-third of all of the workers in the world were involved in the field of agriculture. As Christians, 100% of us should be involved in God's harvest. We can see in the first chapter of the Bible that God designed seed to yield food for us, in a physical sense:

²⁹ And God said, "See, I have given you every herb *that* yields seed which *is* on the face of all the earth, and every tree whose fruit yields seed; to you it shall be for food. ³⁰ Also, to every beast of the earth, to every bird of the air, and to everything that creeps on the earth, in which *there is* life, *I have given* every green herb for food"; and it was so. ³¹ Then God saw everything that He had made, and indeed *it was* very good. So the evening and the morning were the sixth day.
Genesis 1:29-31 (NKJV)

While the seed of the ground feeds us physically, God also designed seed to feed us in a spiritual sense. According to Luke 6:11, the seed is the Word of God. In Matthew 13:3-9, Jesus teaches us about the sower and the four, different soils. Some seed fell by the wayside, some in stony places, some among thorns and some in good earth. Additionally, Jesus explained this parable, telling His disciples that the seed sown by the wayside exemplified those who do not understand God's Word, as Satan snatches away what was sown in that person's heart. At the same time, seed sown in stony places had no roots. Though it grew fast, when difficulties arose, the plant died. This soil was emblematic of the people who do not deeply believe in God or His Laws. When troubles arise, and the fight-or-flight instinct takes over, they flee. Thirdly, Jesus described seed sown among thorns. According to our Lord, that points to people who allow the cares of the world to get in the way, choking out any growth. That soil, or type of person, becomes unfruitful. Lastly, there was seed sown on rich soil. That believer is the one who hears and understands the Word, thanks to the Holy Spirit, who sows the seed.

Through the gifts of the Holy Spirit, believers get to be a part of that soul-farming process! God uses us, but that does not mean that God needs us. Any part of the process is a blessing, and is all about God, not about us, so make sure that pride does not enter the picture:

⁵ **Who then is Paul, and who *is* Apollos, but ministers through whom you believed, as the Lord gave to each one?** ⁶ **I planted, Apollos watered, but God gave the increase.** ⁷ **So then neither he who plants is anything, nor he who waters, but God who gives the increase.** ⁸ **Now he who plants and he who waters are one, and each one will receive his own reward according to his own labor.**
1 Corinthians 3:5-8 (NKJV)

Each of us as believers should be able to reflect upon our lives and see the people God used to plant the seed, to water the seed or even to harvest the seed. At the same time, God uses us in the lives of others. There is nothing as humbling as when God allows us to see a changed or changing life in front of our eyes. If He uses us in the process, that involvement increases our faith, as we get to see His continued love affecting others in the same way that it affected and continues to affect us.

Want to be used by God? Remember that God uses clean vessels. That does not mean that we are no longer sinners, but if we are walking in unrepentant sin, pointing to pride, God desires for us to become clean again. Unfortunately, many Christians seem to struggle with pride by desiring large or powerful ministries. Yet the one-on-one interactions of our lives seem to make larger impacts. That interaction takes time and heart, but if we are willing, God is able! But remember, the Holy Spirit prepares the hearts of those receiving the seed. We might plant or water, but without the Son, that seed cannot grow!

³⁵ **But someone will say, "How are the dead raised up? And with what body do they come?"** ³⁶ **Foolish one, what you sow is not made alive unless it dies.** ³⁷ **And what you sow, you do not sow that body that shall be, but mere grain—perhaps wheat or some other *grain*.** ³⁸ **But God gives it a body as He pleases, and to each seed its own body.**

1 Corinthians 15:35-38 (NKJV)
December 20: Immanuel

Even in a struggling economy, malls and stores remain crowded with shoppers as Christmas approaches. In every toy store, children can be heard uttering their mantra of "I want," regardless of cost, need or logic. Though significantly a Christian holy day, Christmas is celebrated by many non-Christians, as well, and it has become the most lucrative time in retail regardless of religious belief. With the tradition of gift giving, the commercialism of Christmas has saddened some while lining the pockets of many others.

During the reign of Constantine from 306-337, the Roman emperor became a Christian and wanted to bring others to that belief. Rather than allowing them to come on their own terms, he paid pagans to adopt Christianity. Instead of coming with hearts to know the Lord, they brought their own polytheistic beliefs and intertwined them with Christianity. For the pagans, winter solstice was one of the most important days of the year, commemorating rebirth. Upon establishment of the Julian calendar, December 25 was set aside for winter solstice.

In the days of Constantine, the same date was set aside to commemorate the birth of Jesus, but Bible scholars believe the actual birth of the Messiah occurred sometime in the autumn, potentially on one of the Jewish feast days. Some scholars believe that Rosh Hashanah, the Feast of Trumpets, is the most likely day. Of the seven feasts of Moses discussed in Leviticus 23, there are three spring feasts, one summer feast and three fall feasts. All of the spring feasts were fulfilled in the death of Jesus. Others believe that John pointed the birth of Jesus to the Feast of Tabernacles when he called Jesus the "Word of God," and wrote,

[1] **In the beginning was the Word, and the Word was with God, and the Word was God.** [2] **He was in the beginning with God.**

John 1:1-2 (NKJV)

In verse 14 of the same chapter, John wrote, "And the Word became flesh and dwelt among us," using the Greek word "*skenoo*" for dwelt. That word also is translated "tabernacle," so we understand that "the Word became flesh and was 'tabernacled' among us." In the Old Testament, the tabernacle was a building, a copy of one in heaven according to Paul in Hebrews 8:5. But Jesus departed heaven and came to dwell with us, as God walked on the earth. After Jesus returned to heaven, the tabernacle in Jerusalem was destroyed in A.D. 70. When Jesus departed earth, He left His Holy Spirit to dwell within each believer.

As this Christmas week begins, regardless of the actual day that saw the birth of Jesus, we have much to celebrate. God willingly departed the perfection of heaven for a broken world filled with broken people. Jesus came to share our lives. He was faced with the same temptations, the same sorrows and the same pains as all of us. Yet Jesus lived a perfect life, and in His death, received the punishment earned by each of us through our sins. From the beginning, this was the Father's plan! He told us about it many years before the event occurred. When reaching out to Ahaz, the 11th king of Judah, God encouraged Isaiah to offer King Ahaz a sign, to prove the power of God. In a feigned act of piety, Ahaz refused, but God named that miraculous sign through Isaiah:

[10] Moreover the LORD spoke again to Ahaz, saying, [11] "Ask a sign for yourself from the LORD your God; ask it either in the depth or in the height above."
[12] But Ahaz said, "I will not ask, nor will I test the LORD!"
[13] Then he said, "Hear now, O house of David! *Is it* a small thing for you to weary men, but will you weary my God also?
[14] Therefore the Lord Himself will give you a sign: Behold, the virgin shall conceive and bear a Son, and shall call His name Immanuel. [15] Curds and honey He shall eat, that He may know to refuse the evil and choose the good. [16] For before the Child shall know to refuse the evil and choose the

good, the land that you dread will be forsaken by both her kings. ¹⁷ The LORD will bring the king of Assyria upon you and your people and your father's house—days that have not come since the day that Ephraim departed from Judah." Isaiah 7:10-17 (NKJV)

The virgin birth has been one of the most contentious aspects of Christianity, as many have difficulty believing in miracles. The writers of the Revised Standard Version of the Bible fell into this trap, translating the Hebrew word for virgin, *alma*, to instead mean "young woman." What would be the miracle of a sign to King Ahab when a young woman had a baby? That is ordinary, but a virgin giving birth would be outrageous, pointing to God's power. There were four other parts of the prophecy, as well. His name would be Immanuel, which means "God with us." He would eat curds and honey, testifying of the modest means of His birth and life. Those who think that the gold, frankincense and myrrh brought by the magi at the birth of Jesus made Him rich are misunderstanding this passage. God is our provider, who gives what we need. Certainly, He provided for Joseph, Mary and Joseph to make their way to Egypt, but God did not put them up in the Ritz-Carlton! Additionally, the prophecy mentions the destruction of the northern tribes by the Assyrians, and before the Child is born, both the northern and southern kings would be gone.

As we begin to celebrate Christmas, focus on the Greatest Gift. A huge, wrapped box underneath the Christmas tree does us no good until we open that gift, and in the same manner, without opening our hearts to Jesus, His life, death and resurrection cannot do us any good. For those who do not know Him, now is the perfect time for a life-changing experience. For those who know Him already, are we giving Him our focus? Draw closer to God and He will draw closer to us! By reflecting upon what He did for us, we can better understand how much God loves us. Jesus endured so much for us, and that began when God became man almost 2,000 years ago!

⁸ He will pass through Judah,

He will overflow and pass over,
He will reach up to the neck;
And the stretching out of his wings
Will fill the breadth of Your land, O Immanuel.
⁹ "Be shattered, O you peoples, and be broken in pieces!
Give ear, all you from far countries.
Gird yourselves, but be broken in pieces;
Gird yourselves, but be broken in pieces.
¹⁰ Take counsel together, but it will come to nothing;
Speak the word, but it will not stand,
For God *is* with us."
Isaiah 8:8-10 (NKJV)

December 21: Star of wonder, star of night!

When Isaiah offered King Ahaz a sign of God's power and existence, he told Ahaz to **"ask it either in the depth or in the height above,"** according to Isaiah 7:11. Should it surprise us that God gives us signs in the heavens and the earth? As Christmas approaches, we can look back to the events that occurred almost 2,000 years ago and see God's signs and wonders. Yet because God never changes, we should understand that He continues to operate in the same manner today.

"But you, Bethlehem Ephrathah,
Though you are little among the thousands of Judah,
Yet out of you shall come forth to Me
The One to be Ruler in Israel,
Whose goings forth *are* from of old,
From everlasting."
Micah 5:2 (NKJV)

Years before the birth of Jesus, Micah penned this prophecy of the place of our Lord's birth, the little town of Bethlehem, which means "house of bread" in Hebrew. With it all being a part of God's plan, the "Bread of life" of John 6:48 was born in the same village that witnessed the birth of King David. This was not where Mary and Joseph lived, but because of an edict from

Caesar, they made the 80-mile, difficult journey, even though Mary was about to give birth.

¹ And it came to pass in those days *that* a decree went out from Caesar Augustus that all the world should be registered. ² This census first took place while Quirinius was governing Syria. ³ So all went to be registered, everyone to his own city.
⁴ Joseph also went up from Galilee, out of the city of Nazareth, into Judea, to the city of David, which is called Bethlehem, because he was of the house and lineage of David, ⁵ to be registered with Mary, his betrothed wife, who was with child. ⁶ So it was, that while they were there, the days were completed for her to be delivered. ⁷ And she brought forth her firstborn Son, and wrapped Him in swaddling cloths, and laid Him in a manger, because there was no room for them in the inn.
Luke 2:1-7 (NKJV)

Though most modern interpretations of the birth of Jesus seem to present a large congregation at the manger, the Bible reveals that the "Star of Bethlehem" began on the night of Christ's birth and drew the magi, the kings of the east, to begin over a 500-mile journey to find Him. Though the journey of Mary and Joseph certainly was not an easy one, especially in regard to the difficult terrain and the condition of Mary, the journey of the magi was much farther. Daniel gives us insight into these men, for in the court of King Nebuchadnezzar during the Jewish captivity in Babylon, Daniel was in charge of these astronomers. A recent article reveals that the mathematicians of ancient Babylon were using the Pythagorean Theorem 1,000 years before the ancient Greek mathematician Pythagoras postulated it. These were wise men, and under the tutelage of Daniel, also were well-informed in the Old Testament prophecies.

¹ Now after Jesus was born in Bethlehem of Judea in the days of Herod the king, behold, wise men from the East came to Jerusalem, ² saying, "Where is He who has been born King of

the Jews? For we have seen His star in the East and have come to worship Him."
Matthew 2:1-2 (NKJV)

This star was not just any star; it was "His star!" Modern science tells us that because most stars are many light years away, that if we see that star turn into a nova, becoming much brighter before returning to its original brightness, that the actual event occurred up to a thousand years in the past. Because our sun is closer, through telescopes, we presently can see events that took place three to five days in the past. Yet in regard to the Star of Bethlehem, if this earthly, scientific knowledge is accurate, Jesus created the star and set it to become a nova on His alarm clock, for the time when He departed heaven for earth. The star was a welcoming committee announcing His arrival. For the magi, who certainly knew of the coming Messiah, it was a timer as much as it was a guiding light.

[3] When Herod the king heard *this,* he was troubled, and all Jerusalem with him. [4] And when he had gathered all the chief priests and scribes of the people together, he inquired of them where the Christ was to be born.
[5] So they said to him, "In Bethlehem of Judea, for thus it is written by the prophet:
Matthew 2:3-5 (NKJV)

Why was Herod troubled? It had to do with his own pride, for as king, he did not want to be supplanted by a greater king. Yet this fear affected all of Jerusalem, which points directly to the contingent of foreigners making this journey. Though tradition tells us of Caspar, Melchior and Balthazar as the three wise men, the Bible does not ever mention their names or numbers. As travel in that time into foreign territory carried with it a high-degree of risk, chances are that this was not a small band of magi. Instead, with a background of Daniel's teaching, the magi anxiously had been awaiting the appearance of God on earth. This likely could have been a large caravan, consisting of the magi, servants and soldiers. That presence certainly would have troubled Herod and all of Jerusalem.

⁷ Then Herod, when he had secretly called the wise men, determined from them what time the star appeared. ⁸ And he sent them to Bethlehem and said, "Go and search carefully for the young Child, and when you have found *Him,* bring back word to me, that I may come and worship Him also."
⁹ When they heard the king, they departed; and behold, the star which they had seen in the East went before them, till it came and stood over where the young Child was. ¹⁰ When they saw the star, they rejoiced with exceedingly great joy. ¹¹ And when they had come into the house, they saw the young Child with Mary His mother, and fell down and worshiped Him. And when they had opened their treasures, they presented gifts to Him: gold, frankincense, and myrrh.
¹² Then, being divinely warned in a dream that they should not return to Herod, they departed for their own country another way.
Matthew 2:7-12 (NKJV)

Herod directed the magi to Bethlehem, having asked the rabbis about prophetic writings of the Messiah's birth. The magi knew of Herod's evil intentions, as God had warned them in a dream. Upon beginning their journey again, the magi saw the star and rejoiced with exceedingly great joy. Imagine the joy when they saw the Child! Certainly, this was not a newborn baby, as He had been when the magi first saw the star, and they spoke to Herod of a child who already had been born. The gifts given to Jesus helped support a poor young couple that immediately fled to Egypt, based on the desires of Herod to kill Him. God always provides!

Just as God gave a sign in the heavens to those interested on the night of our Lord's birth, He continues to speak to us. In 2010, a total lunar eclipse occurred on the winter solstice. Those two events have not coincided since 1554. Is it a sign? Well, it certainly is not a coincidence, as God always has a purpose and a plan. We do not know what that sign points to, yet Jesus told us that in the end days, He would give us signs in the heavens. Just as in the days of the magi, those signs are for timing. Are we in those days?

²⁵ **And there will be signs in the sun, in the moon, and in the stars; and on the earth distress of nations, with perplexity, the sea and the waves roaring;** ²⁶ **men's hearts failing them from fear and the expectation of those things which are coming on the earth, for the powers of the heavens will be shaken.**
Luke 21:25-26 (NKJV)

December 22: Mary, Mary, Babe to carry!

God chose a young virgin to carry the Messiah to a broken world. Jesus could have come to earth the same way He departed, in a cloud. But God chose this vessel and this way. Did Mary earn this gift by her sinlessness? Certainly not, and neither did she become the queen of heaven. Mary was born, lived and died, just as other women. God has granted Mary a place in heaven, just like other godly women. She was an ordinary woman who completed an extraordinary task that never will be forgotten. Mary willingly endured a difficult journey, which began with the unmarried, young woman becoming impregnated by the Holy Spirit. According to Old Testament law, a pregnant, unmarried woman should be stoned to death, yet this young woman bravely believed in God's power to sustain her.

²⁶ **Now in the sixth month the angel Gabriel was sent by God to a city of Galilee named Nazareth,** ²⁷ **to a virgin betrothed to a man whose name was Joseph, of the house of David. The virgin's name** *was* **Mary.** ²⁸ **And having come in, the angel said to her, "Rejoice, highly favored** *one,* **the Lord** *is* **with you; blessed** *are* **you among women!"**
Luke 1:26-28 (NKJV)

The story begins in the sixth month of Elizabeth's pregnancy, three months before she was to give birth to John the Baptist. Elizabeth and Mary were relatives (Luke 1:36), though we do not know how closely related those two women were. Mary's father was from the tribe of Judah, while Elizabeth's came from the tribe of Levi (Luke 1:5). While many believe that made the two distant relatives, because tribal allegiance had to do with the father instead of the mother, these two may have been first cousins, or more distant cousins. It is important that John entered the world before Jesus, as John was to "prepare the way of the Lord."

Gabriel, an angel of the Lord who already had brought messages to Daniel and Zechariah, came to visit Mary. She was a young virgin, betrothed to Joseph. While betrothed is similar to our term for engaged, there was a major difference in the Hebrew tradition. A betrothal was as significant as a marriage, binding the two together. To end a betrothal, a divorce must occur. Instead of just setting a date for a wedding, the husband-to-be would go to prepare a place for his new family, just as Jesus departed this earth to prepare a place for the brides of Christ, His followers (John 14:2-3). Gabriel has a specific message for Mary, that she is "highly favored" and blessed among women. Yet her name means "bitterness" in Hebrew, possibly pointing to the pain and agony of watching her son die on the cross.

Are there times when we are highly favored in the eyes of God, but feel like we do not matter at all? Certainly, Mary understood the honor God was granting her to carry the Messiah. Yet it must have been difficult to raise a perfect child! Knowing He was the Son of God, how did she ever correct Him? Maybe He never needed correcting, which would be another difficulty as His mother. How did Mary feel when she sinned in front of the young Jesus? It is difficult enough to deal with our children when they have become more intelligent than us, but for imperfection to raise perfection had to be a burden. It all culminated on the day of our Lord's crucifixion, as watching her son tortured, beaten and crucified had to grieve Mary's heart. Did she still feel highly favored?

God has promised only good for His followers, yet when in the midst of trial, we can lose sight of His great work, His purpose and His plan. Each of us has the tendency to create our own difficulties with our bad choices, yet even without those bad choices, our paths would be bumpy. We are baptized into the suffering of Jesus when we suffer, yet our "light affliction" is not burdensome in relation to what our Savior endured for us. Still, it gives us an inkling of His pain. If we feel alone, Jesus knows that feeling. That is not head knowledge, but heart knowledge, as Jesus experienced that loneliness when He cried, "My God, My God, why have You forsaken Me?" If we feel stressed, Jesus knows our pain. He sweated blood on the night of His crucifixion! Are we in physical pain? Nothing can be as painful as death by crucifixion. Is it emotional pain we are enduring? What would it feel like to be willing to give our life for the world, but no one cared?

As Christians, we are "highly favored," as God chose us! Our Savior came to this world almost 2,000 years ago and endured it all. Amazingly, it was worth it for Him and worth it for His Father, as we obtained relationship with both of them because of His works. Every day should be Christmas in our hearts, so rejoice in God, who became man for us! "O, come let us adore Him, Christ, the Lord!"

Now the birth of Jesus Christ was as follows: After His mother Mary was betrothed to Joseph, before they came together, she was found with child of the Holy Spirit. Matthew 1:18 (NKJV)

December 23: God gives the increase!

While many Protestant churches have strong tendencies of de-emphasizing the role that Mary played in the birth of the Messiah, many Catholic churches seem to overemphasize her role. A healthy perspective is that Jesus chose to endure all of the same difficulties in our paths, including birth, childhood, adolescence, adulthood, disease, temptation and death. Additionally, He chose the vessel of Mary. Somehow, Joseph gets lost in the mix, due in part to the fact that Joseph was not part of the conception of the Savior. Yet Joseph played a godly role in the life of Jesus, protected his family and also was chosen by God. Joseph's name in Hebrew means "God increases," and Joseph's life reveals that increase.

[18] Now the birth of Jesus Christ was as follows: After His mother Mary was betrothed to Joseph, before they came together, she was found with child of the Holy Spirit. [19] Then Joseph her husband, being a just *man*, and not wanting to make her a public example, was minded to put her away secretly. [20] But while he thought about these things, behold, an angel of the Lord appeared to him in a dream, saying, "Joseph, son of David, do not be afraid to take to you Mary your wife, for that which is conceived in her is of the Holy Spirit. [21] And she will bring forth a Son, and you shall call His name JESUS, for He will save His people from their sins." Matthew 1:18-21 (NKJV)

We all have dreams, but how many of us act on those dreams? In the eyes of most men, if we never have had relations with our fiancé, and she turns up pregnant, it is time to find a new sweetheart. Amazingly, Joseph believed Mary's extraordinary explanation, and immediately acted upon the instructions given by the angel in a dream. Joseph did not hesitate, but acted in protection of his betrothed, who rightfully, could have been put to death by Old Testament law. Joseph exhibited much kindness and love throughout an ordeal that was anything but normal. God chose Joseph for the attributes exhibited in the midst of severe trials. We know from Matthew 1:25 that Joseph did not know his wife in a sexual way until after the birth of Jesus.

The next mention of Joseph in the Bible occurs when an angel once again appears in one of his dreams, warning Joseph of Herod's evil intentions. Once again, rather than stewing over what to do, or even praying and waiting upon the Lord for an answer, Joseph demonstrated that he was a man of action, and protection. He immediately packed up his wife, child and belongings and headed for Egypt. In an act of self-preservation, Herod mandated that all boys aged three and under should be put to death in the region! Yet with the words of the Holy Spirit and the quick decision to follow by Joseph, young Jesus arrived safely in Egypt. While in Egypt, a third dream occurred, with God once again speaking to Joseph through an angel, and then a fourth dream occurred while on the journey:

[19] **Now when Herod was dead, behold, an angel of the Lord appeared in a dream to Joseph in Egypt,** [20] **saying, "Arise, take the young Child and His mother, and go to the land of Israel, for those who sought the young Child's life are dead."** [21] **Then he arose, took the young Child and His mother, and came into the land of Israel.**
[22] **But when he heard that Archelaus was reigning over Judea instead of his father Herod, he was afraid to go there. And being warned by God in a dream, he turned aside into the region of Galilee.** [23] **And he came and dwelt in a city called Nazareth, that it might be fulfilled which was spoken by the prophets, "He shall be called a Nazarene."**
Matthew 2:19-23 (NKJV)

Our faith grows when God carries us through trials. Having correctly acted on two previous dreams, Joseph easily accepted that the third dream involving the angel was also correct, and brought Jesus back to Israel. A fourth dream advised Joseph to avoid Judea, so the husband and father followed God and His advice back to Nazareth. The carpenter protected his family, and most importantly, our Savior. Stepping out in faith requires complete trust in God. Did Joseph ever doubt that he was acting righteously? As a man, he certainly had much time to reflect upon each decision on the journeys from Nazareth to Bethlehem, from Bethlehem to Egypt and from Egypt to Nazareth. Certainly, Satan tried to get Joseph to doubt and question his decisions, and also his faith, yet Joseph righteously performed the duties ordained by God. The next and final time we see Joseph, he is searching for the 12-year-old Jesus:

[41] **His parents went to Jerusalem every year at the Feast of the Passover.** [42] **And when He was twelve years old, they went up to Jerusalem according to the custom of the feast.** [43] **When they had finished the days, as they returned, the Boy Jesus**

lingered behind in Jerusalem. And Joseph and His mother did not know *it;* [44] but supposing Him to have been in the company, they went a day's journey, and sought Him among *their* relatives and acquaintances. [45] So when they did not find Him, they returned to Jerusalem, seeking Him. [46] Now so it was *that* after three days they found Him in the temple, sitting in the midst of the teachers, both listening to them and asking them questions. [47] And all who heard Him were astonished at His understanding and answers. [48] So when they saw Him, they were amazed; and His mother said to Him, "Son, why have You done this to us? Look, Your father and I have sought You anxiously."
Luke 2:41-48 (NKJV)

Luke aptly describes the role Joseph played in the life of Jesus. While God would remain the Father of our Lord, Joseph was the earthly father of Jesus. Joseph knew that they were not related by blood, but Joseph's love for Jesus was every bit as strong as that of any earthly father. Anxiously looking for his son, Joseph was relieved to see Jesus teaching at the temple. The Bible never mentions Joseph again. Whether or not Joseph died sooner or later, he influenced Jesus at least up until the age when a young Jew becomes a man, at his bar-mitzvah.

Appointed by God, Jesus was the well-loved, adopted son of Joseph. Adoption is an interesting subject in the Bible. According to Roman law, adoption involved all of the same rights as a child with a legal bloodline, including the rights of inheritance. Though many adopted children in our culture feel unloved, there is a special quality of a parent who chooses to raise a child that someone else has brought into the world. As Christians, we are adopted children of God. Joseph's love for Jesus is an example of that as God's love for us involves care, protection and inheritance! On this Christmas, remember that God places us into families for His reasons, but He chose us as His adopted children! We will share in the inheritance of His Son. God spoke to Joseph just as He speaks to us, and increased the love in Joseph, to care for his wife, son and all of us in the process!

So then neither he who plants is anything, nor he who waters, but God who gives the increase.
1 Corinthians 3:7

Therefore I will divide Him a portion with the great,
And He shall divide the spoil with the strong,
Because He poured out His soul unto death,
And He was numbered with the transgressors,
And He bore the sin of many,
And made intercession for the transgressors.
Isaiah 53:12 (NKJV)

December 24: Tidings of comfort and joy!

After an 80-mile journey from Nazareth to Bethlehem, Mary and Joseph arrived. Tradition tells us that everywhere they looked to stay, they were turned down, but that account does not exist in the Bible. We do know that they laid Jesus in a manger, because there was no room for him in the "*kataluma*," a Greek word meaning guest chamber, guest room or inn. Most movies or plays depict Mary arriving on the night of the birth of Jesus, but Luke 2:6 states that while they were in Bethlehem, Mary gave birth. Bethlehem was the city of Joseph's ancestors, so they might not have been absolutely alone, and may have arrived a month before the birth. Origen, an early church father, wrote that Jesus was born in a cave, which could have been the case. We do know that Mary did not check in to St. Joseph's Hospital. There is no account of a doctor or a mid-wife, and likely, Joseph delivered baby Jesus. In the agrarian economy of those days, most men typically had helped in the delivery of animals, so this probably was not as far of a stretch for Joseph as it would be for men today. Yet, Mary had no epidural anesthesia to ease the pain.

Tradition also tells us that the kings of the east, the magi, were present that night, having been led by a star. Yet that also is an untruth, as the magi began their journey from Babylon having seen the star that night, signifying the birth of Jesus. Certainly, they had been waiting for this event, but it is doubtful that the magi departed immediately. Instead, there was packing to do, and likely, they asked soldiers and servants to prepare for the 500-600 mile journey. So who was there?

[8] Now there were in the same country shepherds living out in the fields, keeping watch over their flock by night. [9] And behold, an angel of the Lord stood before them, and the glory of the Lord shone around them, and they were greatly afraid. [10] Then the angel said to them, "Do not be afraid, for behold, I bring you good tidings of great joy which will be to all people. [11] For there is born to you this day in the city of David a Savior, who is Christ the Lord. [12] And this *will be* the sign to you: You will find a Babe wrapped in swaddling cloths, lying in a manger."
[13] And suddenly there was with the angel a multitude of the heavenly host praising God and saying:
[14]"Glory to God in the highest,
And on earth peace, goodwill toward men!"
Luke 2:8-14 (NKJV)

Most of us can close our eyes and hear Linus quoting these verses from memory in his speech to Charlie Brown when asked what Christmas is all about. We see shepherds and angels present. In the Bible, almost every time an angel appears, he does so with the words, "Fear not." What is it about angels that scare people? It could be that they are very large, as we know that a race of giants was the offspring of the demonic angels that took earthly wives in Genesis 6:2. We also know that our depiction of angels is often contrary to the biblical one. They are not fat little children, nor are they women. The Hebrew words *seraphim* and *cherubim* both contain the suffix "im," which means male and plural. One angel spoke but that was followed by a multitude of the heavenly host singing praises to the Lord. Angels are eternal beings, and are as great in multitude as the sands of the seas. Daniel speaks of 10,000 times 10,000 angels surrounding the throne of God, 100 million! (Daniel 7:10) Imagine the gift to those shepherds that night, to hear the heavenly host singing praises to God! The shepherds heard the angel's words, and then went into Bethlehem to seek the Child. How interesting that our Lord, the Good Shepherd, announced His arrival to those shepherds first. The kings of the east did not come until later. In the first coming of Jesus, He came as a shepherd, but in the second coming of Jesus, He will come as a conquering King!

After Mary's Levitical cleansing time (Leviticus 12:2-8), the couple carried the infant into Jerusalem to offer a sacrifice of two turtledoves or pigeons, the sacrifice of a poor family, for a male that has opened the womb, and additionally, for Jesus to be circumcised at the temple. Two other "passers-by" demonstrated divine appointments. First, a Spirit-filled man named Simeon had his life's ambition fulfilled, as he had been told by God that he would not die until the Messiah came:

[27] So he came by the Spirit into the temple. And when the parents brought in the Child Jesus, to do for Him according to the custom of the law, [28] he took Him up in his arms and blessed God and said:
[29]"Lord, now You are letting Your servant depart in peace, According to Your word;
[30]For my eyes have seen Your salvation
[31]Which You have prepared before the face of all peoples,
[32]A light to *bring* revelation to the Gentiles,
And the glory of Your people Israel."
[33] And Joseph and His mother marveled at those things which were spoken of Him. [34] Then Simeon blessed them, and said to Mary His mother, "Behold, this *Child* is destined for the fall and rising of many in Israel, and for a sign which will be spoken against [35] (yes, a sword will pierce through your own soul also), that the thoughts of many hearts may be revealed."
Luke 2:27-35 (NKJV)

Simeon's prophecy pointed to the severe pain that Mary would feel at her Son's crucifixion, as Jesus was pierced in the side, Mary was pierced in her soul. Then in Luke 2:36-38, we read of the prophetess Anna, who had served the Lord as a widow for over half a century. God also gave Anna spiritual insight into the infant Jesus, as she spoke to everyone of the redemption He was bringing.

On that night almost 2,000 years ago, Jesus entered this broken world and was greeted by His mother, His earthly father, a heavenly host of angels and a band of lowly shepherds. Days later, His coming fulfilled the lives of Simeon and Anna. Yet, each Christmas that we celebrate should take us back to that time, to that moment. Were we there when the Savior came to save us? He came for Jews and Gentiles; He came to save the world. At Christmas, we offer gifts to one another to celebrate our love, yet on that night, the Father gave the Greatest Gift to each of us. Someday, we will hear the heavenly host singing praises to our Lord, and we will join in the Hallelujah chorus, King of kings and Lord of lords, and He shall reign forever and ever!

She said to Him, "Yes, Lord, I believe that You are the Christ, the Son of God, who is to come into the world." John 11:27 (NKJV)

December 25: Merry Christmas!

In celebration of the birth of our Savior, let's sing:

Hark the herald angels sing, "Glory to the newborn King.
Peace on earth and mercy mild, God and sinners reconciled."
Joyful all ye nations rise, join the triumph of the skies
With angelic host proclaim, Christ is born in Bethlehem
Hark the herald angels sing, "Glory to the newborn King."

Isaiah foretold of this blessed event many years before:

[1] **Nevertheless the gloom *will* not *be* upon her who *is* distressed,
As when at first He lightly esteemed
The land of Zebulun and the land of Naphtali,
And afterward more heavily oppressed *her*,**

By the way of the sea, beyond the Jordan,
In Galilee of the Gentiles.
² The people who walked in darkness
Have seen a great light;
Those who dwelt in the land of the shadow of death,
Upon them a light has shined.
³ You have multiplied the nation
And increased its joy;
They rejoice before You
According to the joy of harvest,
As *men* rejoice when they divide the spoil.
⁴ For You have broken the yoke of his burden
And the staff of his shoulder,
The rod of his oppressor,
As in the day of Midian.
⁵ For every warrior's sandal from the noisy battle,
And garments rolled in blood,
Will be used for burning *and* fuel of fire.
Isaiah 9:1-5 (NKJV)

As in all areas of Scripture, context is very important in these verses, as some apply to historical times, when Jesus Christ walked as a Man upon this earth, while others apply to events yet to happen. God "lightly esteemed" Zebulun and Napthali through the life of Jesus. The childhood home of Jesus, Nazareth, is in Zebulun, while Capernaum, a prominent town in the ministry of Jesus, is in Naphtali. Additionally, those areas have been "heavily oppressed" by God today, as Capernaum, which was thriving in the time of Jesus, is now uninhabited, while Bethlehem is an Arab capital, unfriendly to Jews and Christians.

Georg Friedrich Händel made many of the words of this chapter resonate through his oratorio "Messiah," which begins with the second verse. That darkness described by Isaiah directly applied to the Jews in the Babylonian captivity, but just as strongly describes each Christian who has come to know Jesus as Lord and Savior. He is the greatest light at the end of the tunnel! When adopted into the family of God, we are granted the same rights of inheritance as Jesus. He earned the inheritance with His life, but we are joint heirs because of His love. Isaiah 53 tells us that, "He will divide the spoil with the strong." The spoil that each of us receives for accomplishing one task will be sufficient to last us for eternity. What is that one task? Asking Jesus into our hearts as Messiah! When that is accomplished, Jesus takes away our bondage to sin! Then Isaiah points us to the greatest event in man's history:

**⁶ For unto us a Child is born,
Unto us a Son is given;
And the government will be upon His shoulder.
And His name will be called
Wonderful, Counselor, Mighty God,
Everlasting Father, Prince of Peace.
⁷ Of the increase of *His* government and peace
There will be no end,
Upon the throne of David and over His kingdom,
To order it and establish it with judgment and justice
From that time forward, even forever.
The zeal of the Lord of hosts will perform this.
Isaiah 9:6-7 (NKJV)**

These verses are familiar to most of us, and sometimes with that familiarity, we seem to miss the depth and juxtaposition of the opening phrases. Though to us, a child and a son may be the same, that is not the point of this passage. **"Unto us a Child is born"** refers to the humanity of Christ, who chose to leave the perfection of heaven and enter into a frail, human body, to share His amazing love with us all. **"Unto us a Son is given"** refers to His deity. John told us that God gave His only Son, so that all might know Him and have eternal life. It is so hard for our human minds to comprehend that Jesus is fully God and fully Man, but when we get to heaven, there will be a Man on the throne of God.

Then, Isaiah gives us different names of Jesus. Though He is a wonderful counselor, there is a comma between those two names. First, He is Wonderful, which is the Hebrew word *pele*.

While the English word, wonderful, does describe Jesus, this Hebrew word is better translated "incomprehensible," or too difficult to know. It is a noun, not an adjective. His name is Wonderful! He also is our Counselor. He represents each of us as the Greatest Counselor in the high court of His Father, and this Counselor will win every case! He is Mighty God, with the Hebrew word EL meaning "God," like Immanu-EL! He is not just mighty but all powerful!

He is the everlasting Father, more specifically, "the Father of eternity." A father is responsible for creating birth, and He is the Seed of the birth of all creation. This points to the triune nature of God, as does the final name listed here, the Prince of Peace, with a dove being emblematic of both peace and the Holy Spirit. When Jesus rules on the throne of David for 1,000 years, there will be no more war. There never has been a time without war on this planet. The verses culminate with a description of the future presence of Jesus upon the earth.

What a glorious day, a Savior is born in Bethlehem! "Glory to the newborn King." Glory to Jesus, who saves us from our sins! God with us, Immanuel, was born!

Therefore the Lord Himself will give you a sign: Behold, the virgin shall conceive and bear a Son, and shall call His name Immanuel.
Isaiah 7:14 (NKJV)

December 26: Happiness and joy

What would we rather have, happiness or joy? Some people equate the two, but there are distinctive differences. Happiness is fleeting, based on different situations, events and states of mind. But joy has nothing to do with the situation. Instead, joy is reflective of whether or not the person in the midst of the situation is relying on his own power or the power of the Holy Spirit. Joy is one of the fruits of the Spirit mentioned in Galatians 5, and as believers we will exhibit all of the fruits of the Spirit at least part of the time. Joy is most apparent in people who are in the midst of trial, and points directly to the glory of God, for without Him, we would show discouragement rather than His strength in those difficult times. Some people pray for trials to end, but godly people pray for strength to endure the trials.

that in a great trial of affliction the abundance of their joy and their deep poverty abounded in the riches of their liberality.
2 Corinthians 8:2 (NKJV)

Maturity of the believer can add to that joy, for with maturity comes the experience of learning to rely on the Lord's power in the midst of hardship. Job certainly endured more than anyone in the Old Testament, including the death of all 10 of his children in one day! His faith in the Lord never wavered, and God's strength allowed Job to endure. After that time, Job was able to reflect upon what God had done in his darkest hour. It was faith-building, for Job understood that if God helped him through the most difficult time in his life that He also was willing and able to help him in less difficult times. In the New Testament, Jesus suffered most of all, and retained His joy throughout. Most people respond with something along the lines of, "Yeah, but I am not Jesus!" Truly, we are not Jesus, but He dwells inside of us. Paul suffered greatly, and his joy remained steadfast, due to the presence of God within him!

[6] Be anxious for nothing, but in everything by prayer and supplication, with thanksgiving, let your requests be made known to God; [7] and the peace of God, which surpasses all understanding, will guard your hearts and minds through Christ Jesus.
Philippians 4:6-7 (NKJV)

Peace in the midst of success is easy to attain, yet peace in the midst of trial is impossible, without God's hand. That is why it surpasses understanding. We are called to stand on God's promises and to endure whatever He places in our paths. If our lives are a sweet-smelling aroma to the Lord, and to the broken and dying world around us, God can use our lives to reach others. If the world crushes the rose petals of our lives, we should let the fragrance reach many! When Jesus came into this world, He brought us joy in abundance, as no matter what happens here, His children will be with Him for all eternity!

[10] Then the angel said to them, "Do not be afraid, for behold, I bring you good tidings of great joy which will be to all people. [11] For there is born to you this day in the city of David a Savior, who is Christ the Lord.
Luke 2:10-11 (NKJV)

The joy we have been given is great joy, abundant, powerful and enduring. Birds sing their joyful song each day, as God's mercies are new each morning. We should not be sidetracked by the perceived difficulties. When we look back, it rarely is as difficult as we thought it was at the time. An old adage says, "What does not kill you makes you stronger." If our confidence is in God any trial can be handled with joy, for He is our strength!

Then he said to them, "Go your way, eat the fat, drink the sweet, and send portions to those for whom nothing is prepared; for *this* day *is* holy to our Lord. Do not sorrow, for the joy of the LORD is your strength."
Nehemiah 8:10 (NKJV)

Now may the God of hope fill you with all joy and peace in believing, that you may abound in hope by the power of the Holy Spirit.
Romans 15:13 (NKJV)

December 27: Cover me...I'm going in!

When eating a peanut, we discard the shell, but that shell is not less important than what lies on the inside. An egg operates in the same manner, as without the shell, it would be incredibly difficult to preserve the egg white and egg yolk on the inside. Additionally, it would be incredibly difficult to transport! Our human bodies exist similarly, both in a spiritual and a physical sense. The epidermis, or outside covering of the body, helps to protect the inner organs, muscles and blood vessels. Yet if someone gets skin cancer, we cannot survive simply by peeling all of the skin away. Our outer shell gives us shape!

Yet the inside is significant, especially in a spiritual sense. No matter how many layers that we build up on the outside, that does not change who we are on the inside.

> "A human being has so many skins inside, covering the depths of the heart. We know so many things, but we don't know ourselves! Why, thirty or forty skins or hides, as thick and hard as an ox's or bear's, cover the soul. Go into your own ground and learn to know yourself there."
> --Meister Eckhart, German theologian (1260-1328)

As Christians, we should be cautious not to let the dirt of the world build up so thickly on our exteriors that we resemble the world more than we resemble our Lord. That exterior shell needs to change as completely as the heart on the interior when we give our lives to the Lord, though it is not an overnight process. What should others see when they look on the outside of a Christian?

[12] Therefore, as *the* elect of God, holy and beloved, put on tender mercies, kindness, humility, meekness, longsuffering; [13] bearing with one another, and forgiving one another, if anyone has a complaint against another; even as Christ forgave you, so you also *must do*. [14] But above all these things put on love, which is the bond of perfection. [15] And let the peace of God rule in your hearts, to which also you were called in one body; and be thankful. [16] Let the word of Christ dwell in you richly in all wisdom, teaching and admonishing one another in psalms and hymns and spiritual songs, singing with grace in your hearts to the Lord. [17] And *whatever* you do in word or deed, *do* all in the name of the Lord Jesus, giving thanks to God the Father through Him.

Colossians 3:12-17 (NKJV)

Because only God can see the motives behind our actions and see inside the heart, we are to "put on" tender mercies, humility, meekness, longsuffering, bearing with one another, forgiving one another, and most importantly, love. Those attributes can soften the hard heart of another, just as God's love softened our hearts as believers. David's prayer was the same as all of us when we came to the Lord:

**Create in me a clean heart, O God,
And renew a steadfast spirit within me.
Psalm 51:10 (NKJV)**

The inward change that God gives us instantly is a clean heart, yet the dirty mind needs to go, too. Otherwise, we are throwing out the baby with the bath water! Renewal is that process of being born again. Walking daily with the Lord helps us to peel off those exterior coats that disguise the heart within.

**[1] I beseech you therefore, brethren, by the mercies of God, that you present your bodies a living sacrifice, holy, acceptable to God, *which is* your reasonable service. [2] And do not be conformed to this world, but be transformed by the renewing of your mind, that you may prove what *is* that good and acceptable and perfect will of God.
Romans 12:1-2 (NKJV)**

When renewal transcends the heart and journeys to the mind, then we begin to walk with the Lord in a manner that reflects His attributes, rather than our own attributes. Once again, this is a process that involves daily prayer, daily Bible study and daily fellowship with the Lord and His people. Without that trio, we all tend to fall back to the ways of the world. Instead of having tender mercies we are judgmental and harsh in our punishment. Instead of being kind, we are cruel. Instead of being humble, we are filled with pride and ego. Instead of being meek, we are out of control with rage. Instead of exhibiting longsuffering, we are quick to anger. Instead of bearing with one another, we turn our backs on anyone who requires work or extra effort. Instead of forgiving others, we carry the residual of pain of how they hurt us. Instead of love, we hate.

Satan attempts to copy God, yet his attributes reveal his nature as the anti-Christ. Without the presence of God dwelling within us, we cannot exhibit the Lord's attributes. First, we need to get through that hard exterior and see who God wants us to be on the inside. Then, we need to let that exterior become more than protection and transportation for our hearts. Let our actions reflect the heart change that God already has accomplished!

[18] My little children, let us not love in word or in tongue, but in deed and in truth. [19] And by this we know that we are of the truth, and shall assure our hearts before Him.
1 John 3:18-19 (NKJV)

December 28: No middle ground!

In each continent is a drainage basin called the Continental Divide. On one side of that drainage basin, all rainfall and snowmelt eventually find a way to the ocean to the east, while on the other side of that basin the water moves to the ocean on the west. Interestingly, this does not exist in the geographic center of the continent, but has more to do with altitudes, topography of the continent and the layout of the bodies of water. For example, in the United States, the Continental Divide runs through the Rocky Mountains, much closer to the Pacific Ocean than the Atlantic Ocean. When rain falls in the same location within the United States, it is either of the Pacific or the Atlantic.

As Christians, we also are one-sided, though we often forget that we are facing spiritual battles continuously. Paul reminds us in Ephesians 6 of the strength and need for the whole armor of God in the lives of His followers, as believers are all members of God's army. Thirty years ago, congregations around this nation sang, "Onward Christian Soldier" often, but while spiritual warfare has intensified since that time, we seem to have forgotten our parts in God's war.

Satan and his demons certainly besiege believers in Jesus Christ, but Christians cannot be demon possessed. Because Jesus dwells in the hearts of His followers, He will not share that residence with Satan. Possession points to ownership, and because we have been purchased by the blood of Jesus, He owns us! Jesus has promised that He will not sell us to someone or give us away. He never will leave us or forsake us! Yet demon oppression is another story entirely. When believers choose to walk with Satan, they give him an opening into their lives. Those erroneous choices include using drugs, dabbling in the occult with fortune-telling, or any number of inopportune choices that conflict God's Word. Demon oppression can have severe affects on the lives of Christians, but Satan is limited by God's power, which will bind the enemy. Our part in that process is to repent of our sins and seek the Lord fully. Bible study, prayer, fasting and Christian fellowship will strengthen us, making us stronger soldiers when the battles arise.

He who is not with Me is against Me, and he who does not gather with Me scatters abroad.
Matthew 12:30 (NKJV)

There are far more people who are against Jesus than with Him, yet this battle is not decided by the size of the army. Instead, it is decided by the power of God! In this world, we have double agents in almost every war, trying to play both sides for financial gain, or to ensure that whichever side proves victorious, they also will win. Yet in God's battle, there are no double agents. We each get to make the choice of which side we are willing to fight for. It is a matter of fact that not making a choice is a choice! Once we make that choice to follow Jesus, the Holy Spirit takes up residence in our hearts, and at that time, we are in His ownership and possession!

But you are not in the flesh but in the Spirit, if indeed the Spirit of God dwells in you. Now if anyone does not have the Spirit of Christ, he is not His.
Romans 8:9 (NKJV)

God does not need us to fight His battles, but He uses us in that process to build our faith. How do we handle those attacks when the Lord places us in the midst of battle? Understand that He has promised His followers that He never will give us more temptation than we can handle (1 Corinthians 10:13). If that temptation is intense, God is complimenting us that He has made us very strong in Him. Additionally, God places many of His soldiers on the front lines in the battle against demons. Satan always fights back, so if we are being attacked strongly, it is because Satan hates us intensely! That is a back-handed compliment as Satan does not hate his own supporters, but instead, hates the ones who love the Lord. The more we love Jesus, the more the devil will hate us!

Never forget that the battle belongs to the Lord. We are foot soldiers at His beck and call. In the same manner that soldiers go through intense training to prepare for war, our intense training should come from God's Word. That training ensures that when faced with extreme adversity, we will continue to act in the manner we have been trained, to lean on God instead of self. Additionally, each situation God places us in prepares us for another difficult battle. Trust in God as He will win the war!

[13] In Him you also *trusted*, after you heard the word of truth, the gospel of your salvation; in whom also, having believed, you were sealed with the Holy Spirit of promise, [14] who is the guarantee of our inheritance until the redemption of the purchased possession, to the praise of His glory.
Ephesians 1:13-14 (NKJV)

December 29: The secret to our success...

Rodan of Alexandria said, "It isn't the mountain ahead that wears you out; it's the grain of sand in your shoe." We should not be exhausted by the situations ahead of us, though the journeys behind us can wear us down. Another adage tells us that we cannot know a man without walking in his shoes. The human tendency is to look at others and see the comparative ease in their lives, but all of us have our own burdens to carry. Most of the time, we unknowingly choose those burdens with our own erroneous decisions. Additionally, God allows those burdens to fit His plan and His purposes.

As Christians, the secret to our success is two-fold, contentment and trust in God. With the human condition, that contentment can be difficult to find. In the Garden of Eden, Adam and Eve demonstrated a lack of contentment. God perfectly prepared the place before the creation of man, as Adam stepped into a paradise. That paradise included abundant food, with one stipulation from God.

[15] Then the LORD God took the man and put him in the garden of Eden to tend and keep it. [16] And the LORD God commanded the man, saying, "Of every tree of the garden you may freely eat; [17] but of the tree of the knowledge of good and evil you shall not eat, for in the day that you eat of it you shall surely die."
Genesis 2:15-17 (NKJV)

Is it ever enough for us? We always seem to desire more than abundance! In the same manner that Adam and Eve yearned for what they did not have, all of us have the tendency of looking at the lives around us with yearning. "I wish I had that car," we might say, unsatisfied with the transportation the Lord has provided. "I wish I was married instead of single," we might say, unaware of the difficulties our married friends might be experiencing. "I wish I had a higher paying job," we might say, not considering that more money in our pockets might cause us to turn our backs on the Lord! The tenth commandment reminds us what God says about that behavior:

"You shall not covet your neighbor's house; you shall not covet your neighbor's wife, nor his male servant, nor his female servant, nor his ox, nor his donkey, nor anything that *is* your neighbor's."
Exodus 20:17 (NKJV)

The opposite of covetousness is contentment. Contentment is the peace and acceptance in the present, no matter what trial or condition is facing us. When we are discontent, we desire a different path for ourselves than God desires for us! He is omniscient, and sees the end of each situation. Additionally, because He is incapable of giving bad gifts to His children, we should be able to accept whatever He places in our paths with gladness!

**Let your conduct *be* without covetousness; *be* content with such things as you have. For He Himself has said, *"I will never leave you nor forsake you."*
Hebrews 13:5 (NKJV)**

If we have an obstacle in our path that seems to be insurmountable then God must want us to be right where we are, as He desires to draw us closer to Him. Does it seem like others have an easier road, filled with more blessings? God has a plan in each of our lives. As He formed us to be His unique creations, He also planned a path knowing our strengths, weaknesses, likes and dislikes. Trusting in Him involves that walk by faith, not by sight, but God does not expect us to walk blindly. In our lives, He demonstrates His love for us by His continued provision. By looking back, we can remember miracles He has performed, to bless us personally. Those events make it easier to see His love in the present and trust Him for the future! Worry points to lack of trust in the same way that covetousness points to lack of contentment. When we worry, we accuse God of lying, for He has promised that He will provide all of our needs. Without faith applying to our lives, our beliefs are only words! We should be content wherever He has us and trust Him, for He cares for us!

[11] Not that I speak in regard to need, for I have learned in whatever state I am, to be content: [12] I know how to be abased, and I know how to abound. Everywhere and in all things I have learned both to be full and to be hungry, both to abound and to suffer need. [13] I can do all things through Christ who strengthens me.

Philippians 4:11-13 (NKJV)

December 30: Memories

Someone once said that memory is a way of holding onto the things we love, the things we are and the things we never want to lose. Memories have more to do with moments than with days or years, and consequently, rarely give us a realistic perspective. For example, by only remembering the pleasures associated with sin, rather than the brokenness that accompanied that pleasure, we cloud the rose-colored glasses with the pinkest possible hue. Memories can be bad or good. As Christians, we often carry too many memories of our sinful pasts. When God gives us new lives in Him, we should forget the actions of the old man who has been left dead in his sins and focus on the new man. Del Tackett, the creator of "The Truth Project," shared this statement in one of the lessons:

> "We often forget what we should remember, and remember what we should forget."

History tells us to "Remember the Alamo" and "Remember the Maine," but after many generations have passed, we have forgotten those events. Certainly, most alive today remember 9/11, but someday, that will be forgotten, as well. As history repeats itself, by focusing upon the past, we can learn lessons. Unfortunately, most of us have great difficulty in learning lessons from the experiences of others and must learn lessons the hard way, through the "school of hard knocks." The Greek word "*ginosko*" points to that experiential knowledge. As Christians, we first should remember that God remembers His promises! Consequently, we should remember those promises and stand firmly upon them. We also should remember God's faithfulness, His goodness, His blessings, and the miracles He has worked in our lives. Additionally, we should remember who we are in Jesus Christ, and especially, we should remember the cross, the person, place and moment that gave us life and made our lives worth living. Especially in the midst of battle, we should remember God's promise of Satan's future! God tells His people to remember.

Just as God parted the waters of the Red Sea during the exodus of the Jews to the Promised Land, He also parted the waters of the Jordan River to ease their passage. God gave the Jews specific instructions concerning that event:

[4] Then Joshua called the twelve men whom he had appointed from the children of Israel, one man from every tribe; [5] and Joshua said to them: "Cross over before the ark of the LORD your God into the midst of the Jordan, and each one of you take up a stone on his shoulder, according to the number of the tribes of the children of Israel, [6] that this may be a sign among you when your children ask in time to come, saying, 'What do these stones *mean* to you?' [7] Then you shall answer them that the waters of the Jordan were cut off before the ark of the covenant of the LORD; when it crossed over the Jordan, the waters of the Jordan were cut off. And these stones shall be for a memorial to the children of Israel forever."
Joshua 4:4-7 (NKJV)

Those stones today are forgotten, and needless to say, most Jews have forgotten the miracle God performed in their lives that day. In the same manner, after giving them the Law, He commanded them to pass down those Laws and stories to the next generations. At Passover, that is the point of the Seder, to remind those who did not directly experience His hand of salvation what God did to save them, as well. For if God had allowed the Jews to be destroyed that day, they still would be gone! Psalm 78 emphasizes what occurs when we forget God's personal and miraculous accomplishments in our lives.

What should we forget? Certainly, our sins are at the top of that list. If God can forget those sins, why do we keep dredging them up? There is a benefit in the healthy reminder of who we used to be before that knowledge of Jesus Christ changed us in the twinkling of an eye. Yet the memory of that sin should not be a burden to weigh us down. Let go and let God! In the same manner, we should forget the sins of others.

"Judge not, and you shall not be judged. Condemn not, and you shall not be condemned. Forgive, and you will be forgiven.
Luke 6:37 (NKJV)

We need to let past mistakes go! One of the titles of Satan is the "accuser of the brethren." (Revelation 12:10) Because that title describes his actions, we should not mimic Satan when dealing with self or others. Jesus has forgiven us, and also forgiven our Christian brothers and sisters.

If we confess our sins, He is faithful and just to forgive us *our* sins and to cleanse us from all unrighteousness.
1 John 1:9 (NKJV)

If our past is weighing us down, God is not the one placing that burden on our shoulders. When Satan reminds us of our past, remind him of his future! Remember what we are to remember and forget what we are to forget!

And be kind to one another, tenderhearted, forgiving one another, even as God in Christ forgave you.
Ephesians 4:32 (NKJV)

December 31: You'll never walk alone again!

Unlike Three Dog Night's interpretation that "one is the loneliest number," one represents unity. There is one God in three, unified persons, the Father, the Son and the Holy Spirit. Many weak analogies attempt to give our limited, human brains an inkling into the triune nature of God. One of those tells us that there are three parts of an egg: the shell, the egg white and the egg yolk. Yet that analogy is very limited as we cannot separate God like an egg. The best interpretation seems to be mathematical. While $1 + 1 + 1 = 3$, we also know that $1 \times 1 \times 1 = 1$! When God gave the commandments to Moses, the first was "you shall have no other gods before Me!" (Exodus 20:3). There is only one God, yet we know from the first verse of the Bible that God is more complicated than that. *Elohim*, the Hebrew word for God, refers to plurality.

Lucifer was at one time God's most powerful angel, yet his pride pushed him to lead a mutiny against the Lord, including one-third of the heavenly host. Isaiah writes about that event:

[13] **For you have said in your heart:**
I will ascend into heaven,
I will exalt my throne above the stars of God;
I will also sit on the mount of the congregation
On the farthest sides of the north;
[14] **I will ascend above the heights of the clouds,**
I will be like the Most High.'
[15] **Yet you shall be brought down to Sheol,**
To the lowest depths of the Pit.
Isaiah 14:13-15 (NKJV)

Satan's pride is exemplified in the fact that his goal was to exalt his throne above the stars of God, yet he also said, "I will be like the Most High," demonstrating that even in his most prideful boast, Satan realized that it was impossible to be greater than God! While there are many religions, there is only one God. That is not to say that the God of Judaism and Christianity is also the God of Islam, Hinduism or Buddhism. Sadly, without even knowing it, those people worship Satan, as he attempts to copy God in that desire to "be like the Most High." God is incapable of changing and the god of those other religions is capricious. With seven significant as the number of spiritual perfection, we can see unity through God and all He touches:

[4] ***There is*** **one body and one Spirit, just as you were called in one hope of your calling;** [5] **one Lord, one faith, one baptism;** [6] **one God and Father of all, who** ***is*** **above all, and through all, and in you all.**
Ephesians 4:4-6 (NKJV)

The church, the body of Christ, has been united by God for His purposes. Heaven will not be segregated with Baptists on one street, Presbyterians on another and Episcopalians on a different street. Our God of unity desires for all of us to walk in that unity.

Jesus said to him, "I am the way, the truth, and the life. No one comes to the Father except through Me.
John 14:6 (NKJV)

There are not multiple paths to God, as Jesus reminded us that He is the one way. Additionally, Jesus is the only truth and the only life. Yet as Christians, we are united by Him. The walk of a Christian is not on a lonely road. Though there are times when God may call us to walk in desolate areas, because we are united in Him, He always will walk with us. Writing these devotionals has been a challenging road, but there have been far more blessings than hardships. With the one-year goal having been satisfied, the more important goal remains – to draw closer to the Lord on a daily basis. That race continues until the Lord calls us home to be with Him.

^{24} Do you not know that those who run in a race all run, but one receives the prize? Run in such a way that you may obtain *it*. ^{25} And everyone who competes *for the prize* is temperate in all things. Now they *do it* to obtain a perishable crown, but we *for* an imperishable *crown*. ^{26} Therefore I run thus: not with uncertainty. Thus I fight: not as *one who* beats the air. ^{27} But I discipline my body and bring *it* into subjection, lest, when I have preached to others, I myself should become disqualified.
1 Corinthians 9:24-27 (NKJV)

In the Broadway musical Carousel, one of the most poignant moments occurs at the singing of the song, "You'll Never Walk Alone, Again." That is the promise God makes to each of us as Christians. No matter how difficult the road we are on, He is there with us. When we need direction, He leads us, on the paths of righteousness for His name's sake. When we choose to walk in sin, He walks closely behind us, waiting for us to turn around and run into His loving arms again. But most of the time, He walks beside us as our best friend. What a miracle that the Creator of all calls us His friends! Walk with Him to the end of the race!

**I have fought the good fight,
I have finished the race, I
have kept the faith.
2 Timothy 4:7 (NKJV)**

Acknowledgements

In closing this 365th devotional, I wanted to personally thank each and every one who has shared in the journey. With the amount of study time applied to completing this task, certainly, my biblical knowledge has increased. Yet without allowing that knowledge to impart wisdom to my heart, the journey was a waste of time. That has not been the case. It has been an enormous blessing to accomplish the goal of drawing closer to God, but that is a lifelong journey that only has begun! God has told us that if we seek Him, we will find Him, and if we draw near to Him, He will draw near to us. Those promises are ones He fills in an ongoing way. While I did draw closer to the Lord through this process, I still have many more areas of my life that I can lay down at the foot of the cross. I desire this for myself, and for each of you.

Though our walks with the Lord are unique and personal, our paths intersect often with fellow believers. We can encourage others when those journeys appear too difficult to manage. Once again, thanks for reading the devotionals and sharing in the love of Jesus Christ, who deserves all praise and adoration. To God be the glory!

Special thanks to Mitch Gonzales, Todd Williams and Dave Rann, who helped to get this published with amazing generosity and encouragement. Shari Cheves, who designed the cover, also has been instrumental in getting me to the finish line. Though Jeff Kirst preferred a shorter devotional, our discussions of biblical principles helped to add fresh perspective. I also would like to thank Anthony Herron, who started me on a new journey by teaching me the Hebrew alphabet! My sister, Julee Weems, kept pushing me forward with baby Declan on her knees! Andy Kliss has been a godly friend since the day I gave my life to the Lord and continues to walk beside me! My relationship with my Dad never has been closer thanks to the miracles God has performed in both of our lives. He and his sweet wife, Mary Glaub, read the devotionals daily when in the blog format, and also inspired me. Thanks to two godly teenagers: Josh Fuller, who worked in my summer camps, and Jessica Kenaston, who shines with the love of Jesus every time she comes to the tennis court! I also would like to thank the Harms family: Aaron, David and Nieka; the Morgan family: Matthew, Doug and Teresa; and the Ostenson family: Tommy, Tom and Ginger. I will continue to be amazed at the miracles God performs when other believers intersect our lives. Some of those He places on the same paths, so we can continue the journey together. My favorite part is that our journeys will culminate in the same place!

Blessings, in the name of our Savior, Jesus,
Garry Glaub

To God Be the Glory Daily Devotional Newsletter

My next project is to create much shorter books for small group studies. Some of these will be subject-based, such as grace, trust or purity. Others will be based on books of the Bible, such as the Book of Ruth. Additionally, I will be writing a monthly newsletter. If you would like to be included on the mailing list for this newsletter, please contact me at gg4jesus@gmail.com. To purchase more copies of this devotional, please use the same address, or go directly to www.garryglaub.com.

Blessings in Jesus!

Garry Glaub

www.garryglaub.com
gg4jesus@gmail.com